DATE DUE

DEMCO 38-296

FAR-FETCHED FACTS

Far-Fetched Facts

*The Literature of
Travel and the Idea
of the South Seas*

NEIL RENNIE

CLARENDON PRESS · OXFORD

1995

ss, Walton Street, Oxford OX2 6DP

ford New York
kland Bangkok Bombay
Town Dar es Salaam Delhi
g Kong Istanbul Karachi
Kuala Lumpur Madras Madrid Melbourne
Mexico City Nairobi Paris Singapore
Taipei Tokyo Toronto
and associated companies in
Berlin Ibadan

Oxford is a trade mark of Oxford University Press

Published in the United States
by Oxford University Press Inc., New York

© Neil Rennie 1995

British Library Cataloguing in Publication Data
Data available

Library of Congress Cataloging in Publication Data
Rennie, Neil.
Far-fetched facts : the literature of travel and the idea of the
South Seas / Neil Rennie.
Includes bibliographical references and index.
1. Travel in literature. 2. Oceania in literature. 3. Oceania—
Description and travel. I. Title.
PN56.T7R46 1995
809'.93355—dc20 94-49531
ISBN 0-19-811975-5

1 3 5 7 9 10 8 6 4 2

Typeset by Graphicraft Typesetters Ltd., Hong Kong
Printed in Great Britain
on acid-free paper by
Biddles Ltd., Guildford and King's Lynn

Preface

Implicit in this book is an argument that factual and fictional accounts of distant travel to different places located at different times on the expanding frontier of the 'known' world can be seen as engaged in a historical process in which literary commonplaces were repeatedly displaced and relocated in geographical space, repeatedly exposed as literary fiction and discovered as geographical fact. The commonplaces of South Sea travel literature were present in the literature of real and imaginary travel long before the Western discovery of the South Seas, and can be traced from classical times through the early accounts of the new world of America to the accounts of the South Sea islands that lay beyond.

I would like to thank Harry Maude of the Research School of Pacific Studies at the Australian National University, Canberra, for giving me—here in the Antipodes—some directions on my setting out, and I must exonerate as well as thank those who made many helpful suggestions along the way: John and Winifred Rennie, Hugo Williams, Karl Miller, and Philip Horne.

While it has been my concern in this work to treat the works of travellers, I have not forgotten the treatment those travellers gave to their own subjects: the savages. The literature of travel to distant, illiterate peoples comes, by definition, from only one side of the world. Savages speak to us, if at all, ventriloquially—in our own words. As they will have so little to say in this work, then, which is concerned with those who spoke about them, for them, or against them, I shall give the last word in this preface to King Finow of Tonga, quoted in a passage from John Martin and William Mariner's *Account of the Natives of the Tonga Islands* (1817):

This mode of communicating sentiment was an inexplicable puzzle to Finow . . . He thought a little within himself; but his thoughts reflected no light upon the subject. At length he sent for Mr. Mariner, and desired him to write down something: the latter asked what he would choose to have written; he replied, put down me: he accordingly wrote, '*Feenow*' (spelling it according to the strict English orthography); the chief then sent for another Englishman who had not been present, and commanding Mr. Mariner to turn his back, and look another way, he gave the man the paper, and desired him to tell what that it was: he accordingly pronounced aloud the name of the king, upon which Finow snatched the paper from his hand, and, with astonishment, looked at it, turned it round, and examined it in all directions: at length he exclaimed, 'This is neither like myself nor any body else! Where are my eyes, where is my head?—where are my legs?—How can you possibly know it to be I?"

Contents

List of Plates

(between pp. 152–153)

I

The Distant Past

C'est quasi le même de converser avec ceux des autres siècles que de voyager.

(Descartes, *Discours de la méthode*)[1]

To discover a place remote in space—remote, that is, from civilized culture—was to discover a place apparently remote in time, a place with a 'primitive' culture, primal, original, like the beginning of the world. Thus men turned from what was new, an unknown culture, to what was old, but known in their own culture: the beginning of the world. Like the Aborigine woman that Joseph Banks watched on the shore from the newly anchored *Endeavour*, who 'often lookd at the ship but expressd neither suprize nor concern', gathering her fuel and lighting her fire, men turned from what was new to what they knew, but what they 'knew' about the beginning of the world was textual, not empirical, was only what they had read and believed.[2] So travel from civilization tended to be regressive, the traveller discovering not a new land so much as a new location for old, nostalgic fictions about places lost in the distant past, now found in the distant present, found and confirmed, it seemed, in the form of exotic facts. This chapter will provide a historical background to the literature of travel, therefore, as a demonstration of the confusion of fact and fiction as well as new and old in the literature of travel, and as an introduction to the European discovery of the South Seas, which was in many ways a rediscovery of this historical background in a new geographical location. The reader will thus be prepared, as the traveller was prepared, by a long history, before seeing the South Seas.

Among the early—though not the earliest—records of travel is the Old Testament account of the expedition (*c.*945 BC) of Solomon's ships to Ophir: 'And they came to Ophir, and fet from thence gold foure hundred and twentie talents, and brought it to king Solomon.'[3] The redactors of the book of Kings do not tell us the location of Ophir. There was nothing, therefore, to prevent Columbus from claiming he had found it in Hispaniola, or Mendaña from supposedly discovering it in the South Seas, where the Solomon Islands now are.[4] 'This Golden Countrey is like Gold, hard to find and much quarrelled', observed Samuel Purchas, and the interesting question of the exact location of Solomon's source of gold exercised the various minds of Raleigh, Cowley, Sir Thomas Browne, and Kant, among others.[5] Sir Epicure Mammon was tempted by a short cut in *The Alchemist*:

> Come on, sir. Now, set your foot on shore
> In *novo orbe*; Here's the rich Peru:

And there within, sir, are the golden mines,
Great *Salomon's Ophir*! He was sayling to't,
Three yeeres, but we have reach't it in ten months.[6]

Another early voyage which has afforded ample scope for speculation through the ages is that of Hanno the Carthaginian, who commanded an expedition which sailed, probably in the early fifth century BC, round the west coast of Africa, perhaps as far as Mount Cameroon. We have what seems to be Hanno's own account of his voyage in a Greek translation made, presumably from a Punic original, probably in the third century BC.[7] At the furthest extent of his voyage, either Sierra Leone (according to some modern estimates) or Cameroon (according to others), Hanno came to a bay containing an island, 'having a lake, and in this lake another island, full of savage people, the greater part of whom were women, whose bodies were hairy, and whom our interpreters called Gorillae [Γορίλλας]'.[8]

Over the years Hanno's voyage has been the subject of much controversy—about its veracity, its geography, and its γορίλλας. These questions seemed to be settled in the mid-nineteenth century when the hairy Gaboon gorillas were named, or renamed, by an American named Savage.[9] If Hanno's γορίλλας were indeed gorillas, his concept of humanity would seem commendably broad, or impossibly vague, but only when judged by the light of modern knowledge. Rousseau argued that the West African creatures called 'Pongos' with bodies 'full of haire', described by Andrew Battell in *Purchas His Pilgrimes*, were probably 'en effet de véritables hommes Sauvages', victims of Battell's ethnocentricity and prejudice.[10] Rousseau's Scots admirer, Lord Monboddo, famous for his all-too-human orang-utans, who 'carry off negroe girls, whom they . . . use both for work and pleasure', cited an eighteenth-century eyewitness account of 'two girls' from 'the inland country, above the mouth of the river Gaboon', who were mistakenly classified by the natives as 'monkies'.[11] The 'Pongos' were probably gorillas but the 'two girls' may have been either gorillas or girls.[12] The fine lines of the distinctions between men and apes have only been drawn by physical anthropologists in relatively recent times.

Some developments in the early history of geography should be mentioned. The philosopher Anaximander (c.611–546 BC), according to the geographer Eratosthenes (c.276–194 BC), 'was the first to publish a geographical map', reputed to be the map of the world mentioned by Herodotus, which showed 'the circuit of the whole earth, every sea, and all rivers'.[13] Pythagoras (born c.582 BC) or, more probably, the Pythagoreans, made the decision, on philosophical principle, that the earth was 'spherical and inhabited round about', a doctrine supported by Plato and Aristotle.[14] Herodotus himself (c.484–425 BC)—who deserves to be considered as a geographer, though he was more of a traveller than a scholar—acquired personal experience of much of the then known world. His *Histories* have been praised in modern times for their scientific method, but some of his reports—of an ant, for example, 'bigger than a fox, though not so big as a dog'—were marvellous enough to be copied in *Mandeville's Travels* and mocked by Lucian and Rabelais.[15]

Homer, according to the geographer Strabo (*c*.64 BC–AD 20), was 'the founder of the science of geography', but he was not the founder of the traveller's tale, which seems to be as old as fiction itself.[16] One of the earliest of extant stories, composed in the Twelfth Dynasty of Egypt, a thousand years before the *Odyssey*, is 'The Shipwrecked Sailor', a tale of a lone survivor on a marvellous island.[17]

Strabo goes to some lengths to rationalize the geography of the *Odyssey* and to defend the founder of his science from the criticisms of Eratosthenes, who saw Homer as an entertainer rather than a geographer, and expressed his professional opinion of the scientific value of Homer's work by remarking: 'You will find the scene of Odysseus's wanderings when you find the cobbler who sewed up the bag of winds.'[18] The sarcasm of Eratosthenes would seem to be justified. But Strabo, less sceptical, argued that 'to hang an empty story of marvels on something wholly untrue is not Homer's way of doing things' and the reality of Homer's geography was frequently attested.[19] In the fifth century BC Thucydides recorded reports that the Cyclopes had lived in Sicily.[20] In the third century BC Theocritus, Sicilian born, spoke of 'my countryman the Cyclops'.[21] Baedeker, more recently, recommends a view to the modern traveller in Sicily, as 'the train approaches the sea', of 'the rocks which the blinded Polyphemus hurled after the crafty Ulysses'.[22] Calypso has been more variously located, in Malta, in Madeira, in Iceland.[23] Many, from ancient times to modern, in the Mediterranean as well as in a library, by air as well as by sea, in the Adriatic as well as in the Mediterranean, have tried to chart Odysseus' course.[24]

If we turn, however, from the geography of the Mediterranean to the text of the *Odyssey*, we find that Homer makes Odysseus narrate the most incredible episodes of the *Odyssey*, such as the stories of the Cyclops and of Circe, which Odysseus tells to King Alcinous and his court. The King's critical commentary opens the question about traveller's 'lying yarns which nobody can test' only to close it, diplomatically turning a consideration of the empirical value of Odysseus' yarn into an appreciation of its aesthetic value. Odysseus' truth cannot be proved but his artistry can be approved. Like Homer, Odysseus gives pleasure:

'Odysseus', said Alcinous, 'we are far from regarding you as one of those imposters and humbugs whom this dark world brings forth in such profusion to spin their lying yarns which nobody can test. On the contrary, not only is your speech a delight but you have sound judgement too, and you have told us the stories of your compatriots and your own grievous misadventures with all the artistry that a ballad-singer might display.'[25]

Odysseus tells his tale to Alcinous after hearing the court bard sing of 'the renowned Odysseus' and in response to Alcinous' request that he reveal his name.[26] As travellers, both Telemachus, in search of his father, and Odysseus, in search of his home, are unknown men, men whose identity is in question. Odysseus, particularly, is obliged continually to conceal, and ultimately to reveal and then have tested, his true identity.[27] As a traveller he is 'Nobody', the name by which he identifies himself to the Cyclops.[28] The characterization of Odysseus, as a lover of deceit, of disguise, and above all of lying tales, suits his role as traveller rather than as King of Ithaca. Indeed it seems that Odysseus is most himself, and most at home, as a traveller. Even on his return to Ithaca he conceals his identity, telling Athene, herself in disguise, a lying tale and giving himself a false identity, as a Cretan. She is amused: 'And so my stubborn friend, Odysseus the arch-deceiver, with his craving for intrigue, does not propose even in his own country to drop his sharp practice and the lying tales that he loves from the bottom of his heart.'[29]

Several times again on Ithaca Odysseus tells a lying tale about himself. To Eumaeus, the herdsman, he furnishes at great and unnecessary length a fictitious autobiography, in which he even describes a meeting with Odysseus. Again to the suitors he tells a false tale and again to Penelope: 'He made all these lying yarns of his so convincing that, as she listened, the tears poured from Penelope's eyes and bedewed her cheeks.'[30] And, yet again, when there can no longer be any excuse for subterfuge, Odysseus cannot resist telling his own father another false tale.

Thus, by placing the fantastic voyages of the *Odyssey* in their context, amongst the 'lying tales' Odysseus tells, we see their literary significance, inextricable as it is from the theme of the hero's rediscovery of his true identity and social role (as father of Telemachus, husband of Penelope, and King of Ithaca), and from the character of Odysseus himself, the 'arch-deceiver', who tells stories with 'all the artistry that a ballad-singer might display', and lies like 'some bard inspired to melt one's heart with song'.[31] Travellers, like authors, have always had a reputation for making things up. Nevertheless, the desire to verify the *Odyssey*, particularly acute in modern times, has sent scholars sailing—and flying—with the bard Homer as navigator. It was in this spirit that Schliemann, after a few days' digging on Ithaca, discovered Laertes' farm and ten of Eumaeus' pigsties.[32]

If the *Odyssey* is about the nature of a man, a nature to be defined by his travels and his return to his own land and his own role, as King, it is also, as the story of a traveller, about the nature of mankind, each new encounter with strangers raising the repeated question 'whether they are brutal and lawless savages or hospitable and god-fearing people'.[33] The former are typically cannibal men, the Cyclops, the Laestrygonians, the latter typically sensual women, enforcers not breakers of the laws of hospitality, whose threat to the traveller comes in the form of a temptation—to be a traveller no longer, to remain on Calypso's island, Circe's island, the Sirens' island, and never to reach that final destination, Penelope's island. While the traveller discovers an answer to his question in the forms of cannibal man or sensual woman, the alternatives—male or female, oral or vaginal—can also be seen as cultural alternatives—primitive or civilized. This is not to say that the *Odyssey* is a work of anthropology or comparative sociology any more than a textbook of geography, but simply that it is, after all, the tale of one who 'saw the cities of many peoples . . . and learnt their ways'.[34] There is an obvious contrast between the crude and primitive nature of the Cyclopes, 'who never lift a hand to plant or plough', and the refined and civilized culture of the Phaecians, exemplified in the cultivated beauty of King Alcinous' garden.[35]

Although the *Odyssey* does not idealize the primitive condition, there was in classical Greek literature a long tradition of primitivism of the kind which idealizes primitive man in the primarily chronological rather than in the primarily cultural sense of primitive, meaning primal, original, and located in the past.[36] In his *Works and Days*, Hesiod (Homer's approximate contemporary) described a 'golden race' (χρύσεον γένος) of mortal men:

> These lived in the reign of Kronos, king of heaven,
> And like the gods they lived with happy hearts
> Untouched by work or sorrow. Vile old age
> Never appeared, but always lively-limbed,
> Far from all ills, they feasted happily.
> Death came to them as sleep, and all good things
> Were theirs; ungrudgingly, the fertile land
> Gave up her fruits unaided. Happy to be
> At peace, they lived with every want supplied,
> Rich in their flocks, dear to the blessed gods.[37]

That is the *locus classicus* of a myth that would be adapted again and again in Western history—notably, in classical times, by Ovid, who emphasized the cultural differences of the 'Golden Age' by cataloguing the absent features of civilization: no laws, no wars, no agriculture, no private ownership of land, no knowledge of iron or gold.[38] The myth of the Golden Age was also blended with other myths, as we shall see, myths which sought to locate in a geographical present what was lost in a historical past, and it would become the classical counterpart of the biblical myth of Paradise, with which it was also blended, and which likewise took a geographical as well as a historical form, in the belief in the continued existence of the terrestrial Paradise.

After Hesiod's golden race came, in his version of the myth, a silver, a bronze, and then a fourth race:

> A godlike race of heroes, who are called
> The demi-gods—the race of men before our own.[39]

Some of these heroes—only those who had survived their heroic deeds, according to Hesiod—were preserved by Zeus:

> The son of Kronos gave [them] life
> And homes apart from mortals, at Earth's edge.
> And there they live a carefree life, beside
> The whirling Ocean, on the Blessed Isles.
> Three times a year the blooming fertile earth
> Bears honeyed fruits for them, the happy ones.
> And Kronos is their king, far from the gods,
> For Zeus released him from his bonds, and these,
> The race of heroes, well deserve their fame.[40]

The idyllic condition of the Blessed Isles, and the continued rule of the otherwise deposed Kronos, suggest that they are a geographical relocation, 'at Earth's edge', of the remote age of the golden race.[41] Thus the myth of the Blessed Isles encouraged the hope that the Golden Age still continued to exist, at least somewhere in the world.

The Blessed Isles were themselves identified, or conflated, with Elysium, another exclusive home for retired heroes at the furthest limits of the world. Elysium makes its first recorded appearance in the *Odyssey*, when Menelaus is assured by Proteus that:

the immortals will send you to the Elysian plain ['Ηλύσιον πεδίον] at the world's end, to join red-haired Rhadamanthus in the land where living is easiest for mankind, where no snow falls, no strong wind blows and there is never any rain, but day after day the West Wind's tuneful breeze comes in from Ocean to refresh its folk.[42]

The scholar Servius, commenting in the fourth century AD on the *Aeneid*, writes that, in the opinion of the philosophers, Elysium is the Blessed Isles.[43] Horace, who says wisely in his *Odes* that travellers never escape themselves, writes nevertheless in his sixteenth 'Epode':

Let us seek the Fields, the Happy Fields, Islands of the Blest, where every year the land, unploughed, yields corn, and ever blooms the vine unpruned . . . Jupiter set apart those shores for a righteous folk, ever since with bronze he dimmed the lustre of the Golden Age. With bronze and then with iron did he harden the ages, from which a happy escape is offered to the righteous.[44]

Here, then, we seem to have a whole complex, the Elysian Fields, the Blessed Isles, and the Golden Age, all reduced to one, and all located somewhere in space, on 'illa . . . litora', 'those shores'.

Strabo in his *Geography* was rather more precise, affirming that 'the islands of the Blest lie to the westward of most western Marusia [i.e. Morocco, approximately]'.[45] He was probably thinking of the modern Canary Islands, and so was Pliny when he placed the Blessed Isles 'to the left hand of Mauretania'. The islands have become so realistic they are no longer poetic, one 'Ninguaria, so named from its perpetual snow, and wrapped in cloud; and next to it one named Canaria, from its multitude of dogs of a huge size.' They are 'plagued with the rotting carcases of monstrous creatures that are constantly being cast ashore by the sea'.[46]

The development of these myths shows the desire of men to locate the imaginary historical past in the real geographical present. Sailors of the late Middle Ages and the Renaissance sailed in hope of reaching such islands, celebrated still in literature and legend, and when they did not find them they did not forget them, or return them to their historical and legendary context, but relocated them, somewhere just beyond the current limits of their explorations.[47] On the basis of his interpretation of Homer's text Plutarch transferred elusive Elysium to the moon—beyond the reach of sailors but not of writers, who for a long time placed their utopias there, until modern times, when, as F. E. and F. P. Manuel say in their history of *Utopian Thought*, 'the moon has suffered the fate of Tahiti'.[48]

Men in classical times were willing to admire the virtuous bliss of contemporary primitives as well as historical ones. Lovejoy and Boas, in their history of primitivism in antiquity, distinguish between the real contemporary primitive peoples and the imaginary.[49] In the latter category they place the Hyperboreans, who, according to Pindar, spend their time feasting, playing the lyre, and dancing, untroubled by illness or old age, and are located in the far north, from whence the north wind (βορέας) blows.[50] In the former category, of 'real savage peoples', they place the Scythians, Homer's 'Abii, the most righteous of men'.[51] Real they may have been, but accounts of them are not based on much greater knowledge than are accounts of the Hyperboreans (who may have lived in Britain) Strabo, quoting Homer and Aeschylus on the Scythians, praises their simple and righteous life, but regrets that 'our mode of life has spread its change for the worse to almost all peoples, introducing among them luxury'.[52] Thus he deplores the effects of civilization on the Scythians, as Ronsard and Montaigne would deplore its effects on the American Indians and, as Lovejoy and Boas comment, 'much in the manner of writers of today [1935] upon the Polynesians'.[53]

Many classical writers developed this Scythian theme, with its implicit contrasts between nature and culture, virtue and vice.[54] Among the numerous and various men who were known as the Seven Wise Men was the legendary (or semi-legendary) Anacharsis, a Scythian.[55] Some anonymous writer, probably of the first century BC, and possibly a Cynic, produced the so-called *Letters* of Anacharsis, which made use of the Scythian sage as a critic of civilization in much the same way that French writers of the Renaissance would use their red Indian 'philosophe nu', and Diderot his Tahitian.[56] Other authors, however, portrayed the Scythians as types, not of primitive nobility, but of primitive savagery. The Christian Tertullian was zealously disgusted:

They have no fixed abode; their life has no germ of civilization; they indulge their libidinous desires without restraint, and for the most part naked . . . The dead bodies of their parents they cut up with their sheep, and devour at their feasts . . . In their climate, too, there is the same rude nature . . . All things are torpid, all stiff with cold. Nothing there has the glow of life, but that ferocity which has given to scenic plays their stories of the sacrifices of the Tauri, and the loves of the Colchi, and the crosses of the Caucasi.[57]

Cultural primitivism, the cult of the savage, which Lovejoy and Boas defined as 'the discontent of the civilized with civilization', is based on certain underlying associations, of virtue with nature and of nature with savages—peoples supposedly without a culture, living in a pure and exemplary state of nature.[58] That primitivism is the product of civilization is obvious, but none the less paradoxical, and some understanding of how logic might lead to this paradox may be gained from a distinction between two key words in the philosophical vocabulary of fifth-century Athens.

In fifth-century Greek usage the word νόμος, law, was opposed to the word φύσις, nature. And, partly as a result of the recent awakening of political and cultural consciousness, which revealed νόμος to be arbitrary, varying from one political regime to another and, most dramatically, from one culture to another, the opposition between νόμος and φύσις, which already implied a contradiction between culture and nature, came to have a new philosophical (and ethical) significance, as φύσις was used to mean 'true' and νόμος to mean 'false'. This semantic change, partly caused by Greek awareness of other cultures, was to have its effect on Greek perception of other cultures, particularly those of peoples who seemed to live, not according to the arbitrary and false dictates of νόμος, but according to those of φύσις, nature and truth.[59]

The Sophists were to a great extent responsible for the opposition between νόμος and φύσις, but, although they made use of cultural relativism as a philosophical tactic and of φύσις as a standard of truth, there are few signs that they took their approval of φύσις to the full extent of primitivist admiration for the savage condition. Cynic philosophy, however, was primitivist in many respects. The philosopher Diogenes, ridiculing Plato's theory of ideas, requesting Alexander to step out of the light, sleeping and eating anywhere, masturbating in the market place, demonstrated in the very midst of the city the philosophical merits of a life lived according to nature. The appeal to nature, in the form of an uncivilized culture, as an ethical and philosophical standard, can be seen in some of the opinions attributed by history to Diogenes, for example that there is nothing wrong with eating human flesh, 'this, he said, being clear from the custom of some foreign nations'.[60]

Plato had no admiration for the savage way of life. His ideal republic was a city. It is true that Socrates begins by describing its inhabitants as leading a simple life, reclining on 'rustic beds strewed with bryony and myrtle', clothed only according to the dictates of summer and winter, and feeding on plain and wholesome food, but all this meets with the objection of Glaucon that Socrates is 'founding a city for pigs' and Socrates drops this urban pastoral idyll and turns instead to the description of a 'luxurious city' where 'the requirements . . . will no longer be confined to necessities'.[61] The city of the *Republic* is not, moreover, the supposedly real city of a traveller's tale, a city located somewhere 'at the ends of the Earth', or on the moon, but 'a city whose home is in the ideal'.[62]

In the *Timaeus*, however, in response to Socrates' desire to see the city of the *Republic* 'in motion', Critias proposes that: 'The city and citizens which you yesterday described to us in fiction, we will now transfer into the world of reality.'[63] Critias begins this process with a traveller's tale, but this is only a device for introducing and authenticating the promised account of the real ideal city, which the traveller has heard in Egypt, and is 'certainly true', a historical record preserved by learned and venerable Egyptian priests—a record not of a foreign, exotic city, but of Athens itself, primeval, antediluvian Athens.[64] The visit to Egypt, then, is merely a useful geographical detour, and it is plain that by 'the world of reality' Critias means the world of ancient history, of 'nine thousand years' before.[65]

Critias' recitation of this mythical history is postponed to the *Critias*, where we hear of the primevally ancient Athenians, widely renowned for their beauty and virtue, who lived, somewhat in Golden Age style, simply, with all things in common and without gold and silver, in an Athens then surrounded by rich soil, plentiful timber and 'lavishly provided with springs and rivers'.[66] But most of that unfinished dialogue is taken up with the contrasting and somewhat more impressive description of the luxurious and powerful civilization of Atlantis, against which the primeval Athens was to wage a successful war and thus demonstrate 'in motion' its claim to be the ideal city of the *Republic* transferred to the world of reality. It was not this virtuous primeval Athens that took hold of readers' imaginations, however, but its opponent, the island-continent of Atlantis, and the fact, according to the *Critias*, that it was lost beneath the sea as a result of earthquakes did not prevent its resurfacing in the Renaissance, whether in real form, as America, perhaps, or in fictional form, as Bacon's *New Atlantis*.[67]

In the Hellenistic age many elements from the accumulating tradition—of primitivism, mythical islands, and ideal societies—were given the form of imaginary voyages to fabulous lands, sometimes influenced by tales of the East. Of what was undoubtedly a large number of these Hellenistic imaginary voyages only fragments from a few authors have survived. The work of Iambulus, for example, survives thanks to the first-century BC historian, Diodorus Siculus, who provided a summary which found its way into at least two sixteenth-century collections of voyages.[68] According to his tale, which is narrated in the first person, Iambulus, after sailing south from Ethiopia for some months, came upon a group of islands, the Islands of the Sun, located near the Equator, where the climate was (however) 'most temperate', and the long-lived and learned inhabitants, who have tall, beautiful, extraordinarily rubbery bodies, enjoy fruits which ripen throughout the whole year—in a fashion so much like those in King Alcinous' garden that Iambulus (or perhaps Diodorus) quotes the passage from the *Odyssey*. These happy and marvellous people take turns doing the various chores and hold their wives, children, and, apparently, their other property in common. Iambulus was not up to their standards, however, and he and his companions were expelled as 'malefactors' who had been 'educated to evil habits'. Iambulus was able to find his way home again to Greece and to tell his tale, which he said 'deserved to be written down'.[69] The philosophical opinions of these Hellenistic writers (like the details of their lives and the dates of their works) are not easy to determine. Erwin Rohde, in his study *Der Griechische Roman und Seine Vorläufer*, sees Iambulus as a Stoic who had used his tale to represent as fact what the Stoic teachers advocated in theory, but some aspects of his utopia are closer to the doctrines of the Cynics than the Stoics, and some aspects—the rubbery bodies, for instance—are more fantastical than philosophical.[70]

Such imaginary voyages must have been well known in the second century AD because Lucian (*c*.AD 120–90) wrote a parody which depends upon his reader's knowledge of them. But Lucian does not parody only the likes of Iambulus (whom he names). He also parodies real travellers like Herodotus, philosophers like Plato, and authors like Homer and all the others who had written of fantastic and legendary islands. We may presume, therefore, that he perceived all these writers to be connected by a common tradition, and we can deduce what he thought characterized and unified this tradition from his own description of his work, which he recommends to his readers

not only for the novelty of its subject, for the humour of its plan and because I tell all kinds of lies in a plausible and specious way, but also because everything in my story is a more or less comical parody of one or another of the poets, historians and philosophers of old, who have written much that smacks of miracles and fables.[71]

So the butt of Lucian's *True Story*, as his title implies, is travel as fiction, as realistic but fantastic fiction, as plausible lies. His own *True Story* is of a long, wandering sea voyage which includes, among its fantastic ports of call (e.g. the moon), a visit to an island where, in a perpetual springtime, fruit and flowers grow in abundance, songbirds and breezes make music in the trees, and where, for good measure, bread grows ready-baked and springs run with honey, milk, and wine. This, it transpires, is the Isle of the Blessed, inhabited by all the heroes, the poets, and the philosophers—except Plato ('it was said that he was living in his imaginary city under the constitution and the laws that he himself wrote').[72] The members of this select community, when they are not enjoying the luxuries of their bejewelled city, or taking advantage of the communality of wives, relax in the Elysian Fields, drinking the wine that automatically fills the cups that grow on the glass trees, and listening—in the company of Homer and Odysseus, of course—to recitations of the Homeric epics.

Leaving the Isle of the Blessed reluctantly, Lucian and his crew visit the very unpleasant Isles of the Wicked, where the inhabitants are being punished—most severely of all, those who told lies, amongst whom are Ctesias (whose marvellous account of India has largely been lost) and Herodotus. 'On seeing them', says Lucian, 'I had good hopes for the future, for I have never told a lie that I know of.'[73] His *True Story*, after many other incredible adventures, ends in the Antipodes, where the voyagers are shipwrecked and the readers are left with the promise of a sequel, which promise, as a Greek scribe wrote in the margin of Lucian's text, is 'the biggest lie of all'.[74]

Lucian's *True Story* shows that fantastic tales of travel were familiar to Lucian's public and that this public could see that such tales had gone too far. Lucian knew why travel and lies keep company. As he remarks of one of his own incredible discoveries: 'Anyone who does not believe this is so will find, if ever he gets there himself, that I am telling the truth.'[75] He will not name all the authors of the kind he is parodying, he says, 'as you yourself will recognize them from your reading'. But he names the father of them all: 'Their guide and instructor in this sort of charlatanry is Homer's Odysseus, who tells Alcinous and his court about winds in bondage, one-eyed men, cannibals and savages; also about animals with many heads, and transformations of his comrades wrought with drugs.'[76] And, to the whole literary tradition Lucian is parodying, made up of philosophy, geography, epic, and romance, he adds another genre: parody. He is not like his precursors, he protests, while mocking their protestations of truth, because 'I shall at least be truthful in saying that I am a liar'.[77]

Lucian was a contemporary of Ptolemy, whose *Geography* (*c*.AD 150) was the culmination of that classical science, a treatise on mapping the globe. Like his predecessors, though with better reason, Ptolemy believed in the doctrine of the Pythagoreans, that the world was 'spherical and inhabited round about'.[78] His work would interest Columbus, but it did not suit the new doctrines of Christianity.[79] Some Christians ignored classical geography, recognizing like St Ambrose (AD 340–97) that 'to consider the nature and position of the earth does not help us in our hope of a life to come', and some attacked it.[80] Cosmas, a sixth-century Alexandrian who had been a merchant and had travelled widely, made it the object of his *Topographia Christiana* to refute pagan geography, which he did from the evidence of the Bible. The Bible tells us that man lives on the 'face of the earth'. Therefore there can be no Antipodes. Therefore the world is flat. The Antipodes were, moreover, patently ridiculous: 'For to think that there are Antipodes compels us to to think also that rain falls on them from an opposite direction to ours; and any one will, with good reason, deride these ludicrous theories, which set forth principles incongruous, ill-adjusted, and contrary to nature.'[81] Cosmas, however, was an extreme case, and by no means all geographers of the Middle Ages thought of the world as flat. Many continued to believe in the sphericity of the earth and in the Antipodes, 'terra australis nondum cognita', separated from 'terra firma', the habitable world, by a great sea and the burning heat of the sun.[82]

Given the Christian world-view of the Middle Ages it was natural that the location of Paradise should be of geographical importance. In Christian belief the word 'Paradise' referred both to a lost Garden of Eden and to a future otherworld. But there was another possibility also, that the earthly Paradise still existed, that Paradise was not located only in the distant past or the otherworldly future but in the distant present, somewhere in this world. The Bible was vague about the location of the 'garden eastward in Eden', but it gave hope that Paradise still existed, for God had placed cherubim to guard it after the fall.[83] The continued existence of the earthly Paradise was, in fact, a matter of orthodox Christian belief. It was shown on many medieval maps. In the Mappa Mundi of Hereford (*c*.1300), which has Jerusalem in the centre, Paradise appears as a circular island at the eastern end of the world, beyond India (see Plate 1).[84] Until late in the seventeenth century, long after the great age of discovery, scholars continued to discuss the whereabouts of the terrestrial Paradise.[85]

At the beginning of the fourteenth century, Dante portrayed the earth as spherical, as historians of geography remark, and at the end of the *Inferno* Virgil escorts the poet, via Satan's anus at the centre of the earth, to the Antipodes, where, on an island, at the top of Mount Purgatory, is the earthly Paradise.[86] Vespucci,

sailing to America, recalled Dante's visit to the Antipodes in the *Purgatorio*, which
he quotes in his letter describing his voyage.[87] When Dante and his fellow pilgrims
finally complete their ascent of Mount Purgatory they reach the terrestrial Paradise
and encounter the mysterious Lady Matilda, who informs them:

> Quelli ch'anticamente poetaro
> l'età dell'oro e suo stato felice,
> forse in Parnaso esto loco sognaro.

Dante turns to Virgil and Statius:

> e vidi che con riso
> udito avean l'ultimo costrutto.[88]

Thus, in the early Renaissance, the pagan and the Christian interpenetrated. Just
as Tertullian in the second century had likened Paradise to the Elysian Fields, so
in the fourteenth century the moralists at work translating and interpreting Ovid
likened the Golden Age to the earthly Paradise.[89]

The Christians of the Middle Ages, however, had no need to make such explanations of classical myth, and they had no need of the Golden Age either, for they
had their own equivalent. As early as the mid-sixth century St Brendan was said
to have reached the earthly Paradise, located very vaguely on an island somewhere
west of Ireland (not to the east). St Brendan's Isle, sometimes confused with the
Blessed Isles, was often marked on maps (e.g. the Hereford Mappa Mundi),
retreating westward from advancing geographical knowledge.[90] The tale of its
discovery survives in a Latin version of the ninth or tenth century and tells of a
voyage to an island, where, on top of a mountain and enclosed by a jewelled wall,
Brendan found the earthly Paradise, as good as new: 'a land fertile in watered
groves, with orchards and meadows unceasingly in bloom . . . The rivers there
flowed with milk, and the dew lightly dropping from heaven was the sweetest
honey. The mountains were purest gold, and the sand the most precious gems.'[91]
St Brendan's Isle was searched for but never found again, and therefore became
known as Perdita, though it appeared on maps as late as 1755.[92]

Another medieval legend would add to the rich confusion, the legend of Prester
John, the priestly Christian king. About 1165 there appeared a fictitious letter,
which was widely circulated and translated, from Prester John to the Emperor of
Byzantium, extolling the wealth and wonders of Prester John's land and the prodigious virtues of his people, and mentioning that Paradise was in the region of his
kingdom, itself reputedly somewhere in India or, alternatively, in Ethiopia.[93] In
1177 Pope Alexander III sent off a letter to Prester John, carried by an envoy of
whose fate nothing is known, and in the following years other travellers endeavoured to contact him.[94] Still, in 1460, Prince Henry the Navigator hoped to meet
him, and Vasco da Gama carried letters to him round the Cape.[95]

The rapid expansion of the Mongol Empire in the thirteenth century brought
Europe and the Far East into direct contact for the first time.[96] As one historian

says, it was an event as important for the commerce of the Middle Ages as the discovery of America was for the Renaissance. It was 'la découverte de l'Asie'.[97] Among the first to take advantage of the access to the East now opened was Marco Polo, who set out with his father and uncle in 1271 from Acre in Palestine and returned to Venice in 1295.

One medievalist considers Polo 'incomparably the greatest traveller and the most magnificent observer of the whole Middle Ages'.[98] The greatest traveller he certainly was, as far as we know—for not all travellers leave a literary trail—but there is much of note in China that Polo failed to observe (the Great Wall, tea drinking, footbinding, and printing, for example) and, although he observed only a few incredible marvels (such as 'men with tails' and 'heads like dogs'), what he did observe of the magnificent East he tended to magnify.[99] He was nevertheless a genuine traveller and observer, but he might merely have produced a merchant's guidebook to the East, as others did, or, more likely, nothing at all, and certainly nothing like the popular work which has brought his fame and reputation, had it not been for a chance encounter, in circumstances far removed from the magnificent scenes of his travels and observations, as recorded in the Prologue to his *Travels*:

Afterwards, in the year of the Nativity of Our Lord Jesus Christ 1298, while he was in prison in Genoa, wishing to occupy his leisure as well as to afford entertainment to readers, he caused all these things to be recorded by Messer Rustichello of Pisa, who was in the same prison.[100]

Messer Rustichello, no mere amanuensis, was identified in 1833 as a professional writer of romances, once employed by Prince Edward of England (later to become Edward I), but the full significance of this statement in the Prologue to the *Travels* was not recognized until 1928, when the first and fullest assessment of Rustichello's contribution to Marco Polo's *Travels* was made by L. F. Benedetto in his introduction to his edition of the early fourteenth-century French manuscript which is now believed to be closest to Rustichello's original, written in Italianate French.[101] Benedetto compared the *Travels* with Rustichello's other work and found in the *Travels* many of the romance writer's characteristic phrases and narrative patterns. He demonstrated, in particular, that the invocation which opens the *Travels*, to its audience, 'Seignors, enperaor et rois', etc., occurs practically verbatim in an Arthurian romance by Rustichello, and that whole sections of the *Travels* have been adapted, with little revision, from the same source.[102] The dramatic presentation of Marco Polo's reception at the court of Kubilai Khan at Shang-tu, for example, is closely modelled on Rustichello's own rendering of the reception of Tristan at King Arthur's court at Camelot. Indeed, as Benedetto says: 'L'arrivo dei Polo alla corte di Kubilai, il loro soggiorno, il loro ritorno a Venezia diventano un'avventura di cavaliere errante, ospitato per qualche tempo in qualche castello e poi rilasciato al proprio destino.'[103] If Polo travelled in the medium of romance, it was because Rustichello knew the way. There can be little doubt that

Rustichello is, as Benedetto says, responsible for the narrative method of the *Travels*, in which 'gli elementi storici e novellistici alternano convenientemente colle aride nomenclature geografiche'.[104] His most important contributions, however, are the characterization of Polo as a knight adventurer, of the Great Khan as a kind of King Arthur, and the portrayal of Polo's Orient as an exotic 'reame di Logres o di Cornovaglia'.[105]

It is worth asking how a romance writer could have exerted such an influence over the description of an Orient he had never witnessed, or, rather, how the medieval romance could have been so easily adapted to become the medium for Polo's *Travels*. Gillian Beer, in her study of the romance genre, writes that 'from the time of the crusades its achievement has been affected by the culture of the East'.[106] She observes also the importance in romance of magnificent marvels and, most significantly, she stresses that 'romance depends considerably upon a certain set *distance* in the relationship between its audience and its subject-matter'.[107] This distance, which could take a number of forms, was usually one of time, but in Marco Polo's *Travels* we can see a different kind of romance, based, not on fabulous history, but on fabulous but real geography, on distance—literally—in space.

The replacement of the Mongols by the Ming dynasty, hostile to foreigners, in 1368, closed off access to the Far East for centuries to come, but not the appetite for news. *Mandeville's Travels* was originally written in French by an author who had probably never travelled very far from a library.[108] The work, composed about 1357, is in fact a compilation, compiled from other compilations, notably the *Speculum Mundi* of Vincent de Beauvais, and from the works of real travellers to the East and the Far East, such as the Franciscans Odoric and Carpini (an envoy from the Pope to the Great Khan) and Marco Polo.[109] The author, whom for want of another name we shall call 'Mandeville', recognized that 'many men have great liking to hear speak of strange things of diverse countries', and produced a work which combined the wide-ranging reference of an encyclopedia with the eyewitness authority and romantic appeal of a work by a (supposedly) real traveller.[110] 'Mandeville' selected and developed material from a wide range of sources and added to his collection of 'strange things' some extra wonders and marvels—for he knew too that 'men say always that new things and new tidings be pleasant to hear'.[111] He gave both verisimilitude and romantic glamour to this structure of fabulous 'facts' by enclosing it in an entirely fictitious but realistic framework of the travels of an imaginary man, employed as what an American Chaucerian calls a 'fictive narrator'.[112] This hero, who 'rivalled', as 'Mandeville's' modern editor says, 'the popularity of the traditional heroes of romance', was the purportedly real knight adventurer, Sir John Mandeville, 'born in England in the town of St Albans', according to the *Travels*, who tells us at the end of the book that after thirty-four years of travel he has 'come home maugree myself to rest for gouts arthritic that me distrain'.[113] *Mandeville's Travels* had great success, was copied, translated and printed all over Europe, and outdid in popularity, as it did in marvels, the less extravagant *Travels* of Marco Polo.[114]

The work itself is divided into two parts, the first being devoted to the Near East and the Holy Land, and the second and much larger part transporting the narrator to the Far East, from the miracles of God to those of nature, or, rather, from the land of scripture to the land of romance—where the author, as Steele remarked in the *Tatler*, could have 'an Opportunity of showing his Parts without incurring any Danger of being examined or contradicted'.[115] While Asia was in medieval times a land of fabulous wealth and wonders, India, by a classical tradition that dates back to the lost work of Ctesias, punished by Lucian in his Isles of the Wicked, supplied the needs of men for monsters.[116] Thus, after 'Mandeville's' reader's faith has been tested by the Christian marvels of the Holy Land, he is taken, via the Ethiopians, with their single foot 'so large that it shadoweth all the body against the sun', to all the possibilities afforded by the islands of Ind, where he meets Polo's meagre collection of monsters, supplemented by Odoric's, and further supplemented by the classical collections in Pliny's *Natural History* and Solinus' third-century AD *Polyhistor*, furnished to 'Mandeville' at second or third hand by contemporary encyclopedias like that of Vincent de Beauvais.[117] Here are Polo's men with 'hound's heads', then headless men whose 'eyes be in their shoulders, and their mouth . . . in the midst of their breast' and 'folk that have great ears and long that hang down to their knees' and cyclopes and pygmies and hermaphrodites and a whole troupe of other 'folk of diverse shape and marvellously disfigured'.[118] Sir Thomas Browne pronounced: 'We relinquish as fabulous what is delivered of Sternopthalmi, or men with eyes in their breast'.[119] But Raleigh heard tales of them in Guiana and wrote: 'Such a nation was written of by Mandevile, whose reports were holden for fables many yeeres, and yet since the East Indies were discovered, we find his relations true of such things as heretofore were held incredible.'[120] True or false, such monsters were favourites with the Elizabethan and Jacobean writers. Shakespeare's references in *The Tempest* (where Caliban himself is 'deformed') and in *Othello* to 'men whose heads do grow beneath their shoulders' are only two of many.[121] One of Spenser's 'salvage' men in *The Faerie Queene* wears the ears of another of 'Mandeville's' monsters, although a little shorter:

> And downe both sides two wide long eares did glow,
> And raught downe to his waste, when up he stood.[122]

After the monsters of Ind we pass on to the other two most popular features of *Mandeville's Travels*, the descriptions of the kingdoms of the Great Khan and Prester John. 'Mandeville's' account of the Khan and the marvels of his court is based, with added embellishments, on the accounts of real travellers like Odoric and Polo and, in case we have any doubts about such reports, 'Mandeville' says that he and his companions

served this emperor and were his soldiers fifteen months . . . And the cause was for we had great lust to see his noblesse and the estate of his court and all his governance, to wit if it were such as we heard say that it was. And truly we found it more noble and more excellent and richer and more marvellous than ever we heard speak of, in so much that we would never have lieved it, had we not seen it.[123]

For his account of the land of Prester John, which he describes as an island, 'Mandeville' made use of the forged letter from Prester John, which had acquired over the years a great many fictitious interpolations, to which 'Mandeville' adds some inventions of his own.[124] Of the terrestrial Paradise, supposedly somewhere in the vicinity of Prester John's kingdom, 'Mandeville' provides an account partly derived from the book of Genesis and partly original, all of which information he claims to have heard from 'wise men beyond'.[125] He cannot provide an eyewitness account, he says, for the very good reason that he has not been there: 'Of Paradise ne can I not speak properly, for I was not there. It is far beyond, and that forethinketh me, and also I was not worthy.'[126] With Prester John and Paradise the limits of the medieval world are reached. 'Mandeville' is sure that there are 'many other marvels beyond that I have not seen', but of course, as he has not seen them, 'I cannot speak properly to tell you the manner of them.'[127]

Mandeville's Travels has a place in the history of travel as well as of literature. Hakluyt included 'Mandeville' in the first edition of his *Principall Navigations* but dropped him from his second edition, substituting genuine travellers to the East, Odoric and Carpini.[128] Purchas published some extracts of 'Mandeville' 'for his merit', but suspected that 'some later Fabler . . . hath stuffed this storie'.[129] Real travellers, like Frobisher, took copies of *Mandeville's Travels* with them on their voyages.[130] But Robert Burton in his *Anatomy*, on an imaginary voyage round the world to check the reports of travellers, 'would examine the true seat of that terrestriall Paradise, and where *Ophir* was . . . [and] censure all Plinies, Solinus, Strabo's, Sr. John Mandeviles [and] Marcus Polus lyes'.[131] True or not, the popularity of the *Travels* continued through the great age of discovery, though it was recognized that 'Mandeville' went rather further than real travellers:

> Drake was a didapper [i.e. a duckling] to Mandeville.
> Candish, and Hawkyns, Furbisher, all our voyagers
> Went short of Mandeville.[132]

In the eighteenth century 'Mandeville' became known as 'the father of lies', but also as 'the father of English prose', a title he lost in the nineteenth century when it was demonstrated that *Mandeville's Travels* was originally written in French and not by Sir John Mandeville, and that 'the father of English prose' was therefore some anonymous translator.[133] 'Mandeville's' reputation has more recently revived, ambiguously, both as a collator of contemporary 'facts', who 'accurately incorporates much, indeed most, of medieval knowledge of the world', and as an early master of the technique of realistic fiction, who 'knew how to secure that "willing suspension of disbelief" which is the foundation of all great fiction'.[134] Whatever 'Mandeville's' literary reputation, his place in the history of travel is secure. J. H.

Parry, in his history of European exploration in the Renaissance, writes of *Mandeville's Travels*: 'probably no book did more to arouse interest in travel and discovery, and to popularize the idea of a possible circumnavigation of the globe'.[135] The world, according to 'Mandeville', was 'of round shape and form', and so 'men may environ all the earth of all the world as well under as above and turn again to his country'.[136] Andrés Bernáldez, who knew Columbus well, stated that the great discoverer was very skilled in the art of cosmography, having read Ptolemy and other books, and John Mandeville.[137]

Although Columbus and Vespucci were Italians, they were employed by Spain and Portugal, the nations which initiated the great discoveries of the Renaissance. These nations led the way, A. P. Newton suggests in his introduction to *The Great Age of Discovery*, 'not because they were the first . . . to be imbued with the modern spirit of enquiry, but paradoxically [because] they were the last to retain the medieval inspiration of the crusaders, the paladins and the knight errants'.[138] As another historian, Antonio Pastor, has demonstrated, 'the first all-important impetus was steeped in the spirit of romance'.[139] If romance was not compatible with European reality, as we know from Cervantes, might it not regain its credibility in a new and different world? As Pastor writes: 'the flight from reality in Europe not only induced people to buy romances of chivalry . . . but also to take ship and revive the life of fantastic freedom of knight-errantry, conquering in reality the islands which Don Quixote conquered in imagination for his faithful squire.'[140]

Diaz, on the road to Mexico with Cortez, could only describe what he saw as a scene from a romance: 'we were amazed and said that it was like the enchantments they tell of in the legend of Amadís'.[141] When the Spaniards named California, which they thought was an island, they took its name from another romance by the author of *Amadís*, and called it after his imaginary Indian island, 'near the earthly Paradise, very rich in gold and jewels'.[142] The aura of romance lingered long over the New World, as seen in the literature of its discovery, exploration, and conquest, in which, as the historian J. R. Hale says, the voyagers 'could see themselves as the protagonists of a new cycle of romances'.[143] And if romance was real in America, that proved that romance was real, and that literary fiction could be fact. If the New World was fact, then its geographical reality was evidence of the reality—even of the historical reality—of the lost world of romance. So Spenser argued in *The Faerie Queene*:

> Right well I wote most mighty Soueraine,
> That all this famous antique history,
> Of some th'aboundance of an idle braine
> Will iudged be, and painted forgery,
> Rather then matter of iust memory,
> Sith none, that breatheth liuing aire, does know,
> Where is that happy land of Faery,
> Which I so much do vaunt, yet no where show,
> But vouch antiquities, which no body can know.

> But let that man with better sence aduize [consider],
> That of the world least part to us is red [known]:
> And dayly how through hardy enterprize,
> Many great Regions are discouered,
> Which to late age were neuer mentioned.
> Who euer heard of th'Indian *Peru*?
> Or who in venturous vessell measured
> The *Amazons* huge riuer now found trew?
> Or fruitfullest *Virginia* who did euer vew?[144]

But what did Columbus discover in the New World which, as far as he was concerned, was no such thing? We must first consider where he thought he was going when he set out from Spain. It is clear from the digest of Columbus's lost journal made by the historian Las Casas, who frequently quotes Columbus's own words, that he thought he was going to the East, to the 'lands of India' and 'a prince who is called "Grand Khan"'.[145] Columbus had read Polo's *Travels* as well as *Mandeville's Travels*. In his biography of Columbus, his son, Fernando, names the works of 'Marco Polo, a Venetian, and John Mandeville' in his account of the reasons for his father's voyage.[146] Columbus's copy of Polo's *Travels*, a Latin translation of 1485, survives with his annotations.[147] In the opinion of Columbus's modern biographer, S. E. Morison, 'Marco Polo contributed more than any other author to his geographical ideas'.[148] In his copy of *Mandeville's Travels*, which has not survived, Columbus might have marked, among the marvels of the East, the story of a man who 'had environed all the earth'.[149] As Bernáldez informs us, Columbus 'had the opinion that . . . this world and the firmament of land and water can be transversed round about by land and water, as John Mandeville relates'.[150] Yes, Columbus was going to the East, like Marco Polo and 'Mandeville', except that, unlike them, he was going west: 'not . . . to the East by land, by which way it is customary to go, but by the route to the West, by which route we do not know for certain that anyone previously has passed.'[151]

On 21 October 1492, nine days after his landfall in the Bahamas, which bore little resemblance to the marvellous lands described by Polo and 'Mandeville', Columbus, ever hopeful, wrote in his journal:

I will leave for another very large island that I believe must be Cipangu according to the indications that these Indians that I have [i.e. that he had abducted] give me, and which they call Colba . . . But anyway I am still determined to go to the mainland and to the city of Quinsay and to give Your Highnesses' [Ferdinand and Isabella's] letters to the Grand Khan and to ask for, and to return with, a reply.[152]

'Cipangu' is Marco Polo's name for Japan, where 'they have gold in the greatest abundance' and 'pearls in the greatest abundance, round and large and red'.[153] 'Gold in the greatest abundance', wrote Columbus in the margin of his copy of Polo's *Travels*, and 'red pearls'.[154] The 'Indians', however, seem to know Cipangu by the name of 'Colba' (Cuba). The 'city of Quinsay' (Kinsai, or Hangchow) on 'the mainland' (of China) was 'the greatest city in the world', Polo stated and Columbus noted.[155] Just as Vasco da Gama had carried letters for Prester John, so Columbus carried letters for the 'Grand Khan'. Because his information came from travellers like Polo, he was not to know that, since the fall of the Mongol dynasty in 1368, more than a century before he set out, there was no longer any 'Grand Khan' for him to meet. Neither was he to know that, between him and 'Quinsay', there lay a new continent: the 'new world' described in Vespucci's *Mundus Novus* (1504), which Waldseemüller in his *Cosmographiae Introductio* (1507) called '"America", after its sagacious discoverer', Amerigo Vespucci.[156] Thus, a year after Columbus's death, the credit for his discovery was given to another, more sagacious, who had realized what Columbus had discovered. Columbus himself was in the wrong place at the wrong time.

So Columbus sailed around the West Indies, searching for signs of the East, describing each island as a *locus amoenus*—like the garden in the thirteenth-century *Roman de la Rose*, for example, with green trees, singing birds, and sweet breezes—and repeating again and again the formula 'como en el abril en el andaluzia' ('as in April in Andalusia'), until at Cuba he added to his exhausted catalogue of delights the rhetorical trope the literary historian Ernst Curtius calls the 'inexpressibilty topos': 'my tongue could not tell the whole truth nor my hand write it. Truly, I was so astonished at the sight of so much beauty, that I do not know how to express it.'[157] The West Indies, however, for all their literary beauties, were not the marvellous Orient of Polo and 'Mandeville'. The native 'Indians', 'naked as their mothers bore them', with 'handsome bodies and good faces', would make 'good and intelligent servants . . . and . . . would easily be made Christians', but they were not the splendid, opulent denizens of Cipangu, or even the monsters of Ind.[158]

Nevertheless, in his 'Letter' written on his return journey, which had, after all, to report a great success, Columbus vaguely identifies Cuba with 'the mainland, the province of Cathay' (although he describes it as an 'island') and Hispaniola, by implication, is Cipangu.[159] In the latter island he has, so he says, taken possession of a large town 'in the best position for the mines of gold and for all intercourse . . . with the mainland . . . belonging to the Grand Khan, where will be great trade and gain'.[160] The 'Indians' are more realistically described, though not disinterestedly, as 'incurably timid' and 'generous with all they possess'.[161] He mentions some 'people . . . born with tails' who were probably 'Mandeville's' or Polo's, and some 'who eat human flesh', the people called 'Caribs' or 'Canibales' (identified by Columbus in his journal as Khanibals, 'people of the Grand Khan'—'gente del Gran Can'), and also some Amazons, perhaps from *Mandeville's Travels*.[162] But he writes: 'I have not found the human monsters which many people expected'.[163]

An Italian named Giuliano Dati immediately translated Columbus's 'Letter' into *ottava rima* and thus his discoveries into the poetic medium of romance.[164] But Columbus's death in Valladolid in 1506 went unrecorded by the city chronicle.[165] His elevation to literary fame and heroic status was slow. Although he appeared in

Fracastoro's poem *Syphilis* in 1530, the poem that gave its name to the new disease Columbus had brought from the New World, it was not until 1581 that he became the hero of a major—meaning large—poetic work, Lorenzo Gambara's *De navigatione*.[166] He went on, however, to become the hero of a number of late sixteenth-century Italian epics and to appear on stage in 1614 as the protagonist of Lope de Vega's *El Nuevo Mondo*, in which can be discerned the beginnings of his later popular portrayal as a thoroughly romantic hero, the poetic dreamer mocked and persecuted by an incredulous and cruel world.[167] Thus did literature claim Columbus as its own.

He would be portrayed as a man of prophetic vision who had imagined a New World and then proved it true. But Columbus did not travel to find what he had imagined; he travelled to find what he had read about and had better reason to believe. And if he had reason to believe what he read about in Polo and 'Mandeville', he had even more reason to believe what he read about in the Bible, and discovered on his third voyage (1498–1500). In the letter he wrote to Ferdinand and Isabella from Hispaniola in which he tells of this third voyage, Columbus gives us an account of his geographical ideas, which he does at the point in his narrative where he is describing the American mainland, or 'the land of Gracia' as he calls it, as seen from the Gulf of Paria, near the mouths of the Orinoco River:

I have been led to hold this [opinion] concerning the world, and I find that it is not round as they describe it, but that it is the shape of a pear which is everywhere very round except where the stalk is, for there it is very prominent, or that it is like a very round ball, and on one part of it is placed something like a woman's nipple [una teta de muger].[168]

He has located this protuberance in the 'land of Gracia', he writes, and upon it, he is 'convinced' and 'assured in my heart', is the site of the terrestrial Paradise:

I do not hold that the earthly Paradise is in the form of a rugged mountain, as its description declares to us, but that it is at the summit, there where I have said that the shape of the stalk of the pear is, . . . and I believe that this water [the water of the Orinoco] may originate from there . . . These are great indications of the earthly Paradise, for the situation agrees with the opinion of those holy and wise theologians, and also the signs are very much in accord with this idea.[169]

If you can sail west to the East, you can sail west to Eden. In his journal of his first voyage Columbus hinted at the proximity of 'the terrestrial Paradise' to his new discoveries, which were also located, he pointed out, 'at the end of the Orient'.[170] Vespucci made similar hints, but more ambiguously, in words which could be read as an affirmation of Paradisal reality, or as a merely fanciful analogy. In his letter of 1500 he reported that the American trees were 'so beautiful and fragrant that we thought we were in a terrestrial paradise'.[171] In his letter of 1502, reporting another voyage, he wrote again: 'I fancied myself near the terrestrial Paradise'.[172]

The myth of the Golden Age, which the Middle Ages had replaced with that of the terrestrial Paradise, was revived by the Renaissance, and the two conceptions run jointly through the literature of America, passing, however, from the status of American reality to the status of American analogy, and, finally, of American mythology. The scholar Pietro Martire d'Anghiera, an Italian at the court of Ferdinand and Isabella, was responsible more than any other man, and certainly more than Columbus, for discovering Columbus's discoveries to Europe.[173] In his *Decades de Orbe Novo* (of which the first part was printed in a pirated edition of 1504, before its authorized publication in 1511) he portrayed Columbus's discoveries in the terms of humanist scholarship, the empirical discovery of the New World appearing, therefore, in the light of the textual discovery of the ancient world. Among the inhabitants of Hispaniola, according to Pietro Martire (in Richard Eden's translation):

fewe clothes serve the naked: weightes and measures are not needefull to such as can not skyll of crafte and deceyte and have not the use of pestiferous monye, the seede of innumerable myscheves. So that if we shall not be ashamed to confesse the truthe, they seeme to lyve in that goulden worlde of the whiche owlde wryters speake so much.[174]

While in Cuba:

it is certeyne, that amonge them, the lande is as common as the sonne and water: And that Myne and Thyne (the seedes of all myscheefe) have no place with them. They are contente with soo lyttle, that in soo large a countrey, they have rather superfluitie than scarsenes. Soo that (as wee have sayde before) they seeme to lyve in the goulden worlde, without toyle, lyving in open gardens, not intrenched with dykes, dyvyded with hedges, or defended with waules. They deale trewely one with an other, without lawes, without bookes, and without Judges.[175]

Vespucci's Venezuelans could easily be given the same interpretation as Columbus's West Indians. According to Vespucci's account (and negatives were characteristic of accounts of the Golden Age) the Indians had no clothes, no kings, no laws, no religion, and no private property.[176] Inspired by such accounts as these, and Ovid's of the Golden Age, Ronsard in his 'Complainte contre Fortune' (1559) wrote of an America:

> où le peuple incognu
> Erre innocentement tout farouche & tout nu,
> D'habis tout aussi nu, qu'il est nu de malice,
> Qui ne cognoist les noms de vertu, ny de vice,
> De Senat, ny de Roy, qui vit à son plaisir
> Porté de l'apetit de son premier desir,
> Et qui n'a dedans l'ame, ainsi que nous, emprainte
> La frayeur de la loy, qui nous fait vivre en crainte:
> Mais suivant sa nature est seule maistre de soy:
> Soymesmes est sa loy, son Senat, & son Roy:
> Qui à grands coups de soc la terre n'importune,
> Laquelle comme l'air à chacun est commune,

> Et comme l'eau d'un fleuve, est commun tout leur bien,
> Sans procez engendrer de ce mot Tien, & Mien.

In short:

> Ils vivent maintenant en leur age doré.[177]

Drayton's well-known ode 'To the Virginian Voyage' (1606) combines both the analogies, the medieval and the Renaissance, the biblical and the classical, addressing the 'brave Heroique' voyagers who will travel to 'Earth's onely Paradise', where 'the golden Age still Nature's lawes doth give'.[178]

None of this is odd. If the New World was to be described—and not merely in terms of the monstrous and the marvellous—it was natural and inevitable that it should be described in terms with which European culture was already familiar. If the biblical and classical texts provided the obvious sources of analogy for the New World and its inhabitants, that was not only because these texts, ancient in themselves, provided nostalgic accounts of man's earliest, most primitive condition, but also, perhaps, because these texts were themselves foreign in origin, were to that extent exotic as well as nostalgic.

To admire a bygone age, a mythical age, is one thing; to redirect that admiration to a contemporary culture, supposedly real, is another. Drayton's Virginia voyagers are 'brave Heroique' colonists, epic adventurers, to whom a Golden Age destination, described without mention of its Indian inhabitants, seems justly appropriate. But Ronsard's French voyagers, Villegagnon's colonizing expedition to Brazil, are recognized as enemies, not heroes, of the Golden Age they sail to colonize, and Ronsard appeals to Villegagnon to abandon his colonizing enterprise, which will bring to an end the Indians' 'age doré' by introducing the corruptions of civilization:

> Pource laisse les là, ne romps plus (je te prie)
> La tranquille repos de leur premiere vie:
> Laisse les, je te pry, si pitié te remord,
> Ne les tourmente plus, & t'en fuy de leur bord.
> Las! si tu leur aprens à limiter la terre,
> Pour agrandir leurs champs, ils se feront la guerre,
> Les proces auront lieu, l'amitié defaudra,
> Et l'aspre ambition tourmenter les viendra,
> Comme elle fait icy nous autres pauvres hommes,
> Qui par trop de raison trop miserables sommes.[179]

Ronsard's 'Complainte' was published in 1559 and, 'dès cette date', writes Gilbert Chinard in his literary history *L'Exotisme américain*, 'l'Amérique commence à devenir la terre d'élection de l'utopiste et du philosophe.'[180] To praise a contemporary yet very different culture, particularly (and perhaps inevitably) in terms that catalogue its freedom from nearly every aspect of one's own, is implicitly, if not explicitly, to question or to criticize, not only one's own culture, but even culture itself. But

Thomas More had already demonstrated in 1516 that distant discovery could be used to raise questions about European society.

More's *Utopia* is set within a realistic narrative frame. His imaginary voyager, Raphael Hythlodaye, is introduced into the context of More's account of his own real embassy in 1515 to the Netherlands, where the imaginary Raphael tells his tale to two real people, More and Peter Giles. This tale is itself introduced into the context of the real voyages of Amerigo Vespucci (neither More nor his reader was to know that some twentieth-century scholars would decide that Vespucci's *Four Voyages*, to which More refers, was a forgery):

> for the desyre that he [Raphael] hadde to see and knowe the farre contreys of the worlde, he joyned him selfe in companye wyth Amerike vespuce, and in the iii. laste voyages of thoes iiii., that be nowe in prynte and abrode in everye mans handes, he contynued styll in hys companye; savynge that in te [the] laste voyage he came not home again wyth hym.[181]

So Raphael's travels and his discovery of Utopia are grafted onto the genuine travels of More and onto the (supposedly) genuine travels of Vespucci. Utopia, however, despite the absence of kings and private property, bears little relation to Vespucci's America. Utopia is an urban civilization, not a Golden Age society or a terrestrial Paradise (though More did believe in the continued existence of Paradise on earth).[182] Utopia was more influenced by the literary discoveries of the Renaissance than by the geographical discoveries. More knew Iambulus' fictional voyage (via Diodorus Siculus) as well as the work of Plato and of Lucian (which Raphael introduces to the 'delyted' Utopians).[183] But to the Renaissance voyages More was indebted for providing a method for presenting a contemporary society in contrast with his own. When More and Giles question Raphael about his travels, they want to hear about 'actes and constytutyons wherby thies our cytyes, nations, contreys, and Kyngdomes maye take ensample, to amende theyre faultes, enormytyes and errors'.[184] More is not interested in exotic cultures, 'devowerers of people, and suche lyke', but in civilized political systems: 'of such thynges dyd we busilie enquyre and demaunde of hym, and he lyke wise verye wyllynglye tolde us of the same. But as for monsters, because they be no newes, of them we were nothynge inquysitive.'[185]

Travel and social reform go hand in hand. The Utopians, who 'have delyte to hear what ys done in everye lande', eagerly travel abroad 'to thentente they maye the better known the owte landes of everye syde', and, on meeting and learning from Raphael, 'they quickelye ... made their owne, what so ever is among us wealthely [i.e. well] devysed'.[186] Only travel can cross the no man's land of the ocean which separates and seals off one culture from another, and only travel can bring those cultures together with the striking effect of a juxtaposition. It is to travel as an education in comparative sociology that More owes the idea of his two books of the *Utopia*, the first presenting England (or Europe), and the second 'that newefonnde parte of the worlde, which is scasely so farre from us beyonde the lyne equinoctiall, as owre lyfe and manners be dissidente from theirs'.[187] And, by way of travel, More was able to locate an ideal society, not in ancient history, as Plato did, but in contemporary geography. As for the classical writers' ignorance of Utopia, well, that is only to be expected, because 'in our time divers landes be found, which to the olde Geographers were unknowen.'[188]

Thomas More contrasted European culture with a civilized culture that was located in contemporary geography, but located nowhere (οὐ τόπος, not place). Montaigne, however, like Ronsard, contrasted European culture with a primitive state of nature, a state of nature in America. Dismissing the charges of barbarity and savagery against the Indians, in his ironically named essay 'Des cannibales', first published in 1580, Montaigne argues by analogy:

Ils sont sauvages, de mesme que nous appellons sauvages les fruicts que nature, de soy et de son progrez ordinaire, a produicts: là où, à la verité, ce sont ceux que nous avons alterez par nostre artifice et detournez de l'ordre commun, que nous devrions appeller plustost sauvages.[189]

Montaigne goes on to point out the significance of America, which is real and no mere literary fiction, for political philosophy. Knowledge of America is knowledge worth having, he argues (in the English of John Florio's translation of 1603):

I am sorie, Licurgus and Plato had it not: for what in those nations wee see by experience, doth not onelie exceed all the pictures wherewith licentious Poesie hath prowdly imbellished the golden age, & al hir quaint inventions to faine a happy condition of man, but also the conception & desire of Philosophie. They could not imagine a genuitie so pure and simple, as we see it by experience; nor ever beleeve our societie might be maintained with so little arte and human combination. It is a nation, would I answere Plato, that hath no kinde of traffike, no knowledge of Letters, no intelligence of numbers, no name of magistrate, nor of politike superioritie; no use of service, of riches, or of poverty; no contracts, no successions, no dividences, no occupation but idle; no respect of kindred but common, no apparrell but naturall, no manuring of lands, no use of wine, corne, or mettle. The very words that import lying, falshood, treason, dissimulation, covetousnes, envie, detraction, and pardon, were never heard of amongst them. How dissonant would hee finde his imaginary common-wealth from this perfection?[190]

That Montaigne's words—in Florio's translation—are used by Gonzalo in Shakespeare's *The Tempest* (1611) was recognized long ago, in the eighteenth century.[191] Like many others in the play, Gonzalo imagines himself in charge of Prospero's— or Caliban's—island:

> I' the commonwealth I would by contraries
> Execute all things; for no kind of traffic
> Would I admit; no name of magistrate;
> Letters should not be known; riches, poverty,
> And use of service, none; contract, succession,
> Bourn, bound of land, tilth, vineyard, none;
> No use of metal, corn, or wine, or oil;
> No occupation; all men idle, all;

> And women too, but innocent and pure:
> No sovereignty . . .

Continuing his speech, despite the jeering interruptions of Antonio and Sebastian (who have their own schemes), Gonzalo stresses that Nature, not Art, will produce all, 'all abundance, To feed my innocent people', and concludes:

> I would with such perfection govern, sir
> T'excel the Golden Age.[192]

In his late plays Shakespeare was much concerned with the relation between Nature and Art, which is a major theme of *The Tempest*. Montaigne, in the passage quoted above from Florio's translation of 'Des cannibales', defined American Indian culture as European culture minus the culture—as Nature, in fact—and in *The Tempest* Caliban, 'a born devil, on whose nature Nurture can never stick', is used, as Montaigne's Indians were, to represent natural man.[193] But Caliban, whose inferior, primitive Nature contrasts with the superior, civilized Art of Prospero, is shown to be far from the innocent 'perfection' of the peoples of Montaigne's America and Gonzalo's imaginary commonwealth.

So Caliban, the anagram, is Shakespeare's answer to Montaigne's 'cannibales'. He is presented in the tradition of the long-eared, lascivious 'salvage' man in Spenser's *The Faerie Queene*, who 'liu'd all on rauin and on rape', not in the tradition of Spenser's other 'salvage' man, who is virtuous and chivalrous and 'borne of noble blood', a relation of Montaigne's 'cannibales' and of the noble savage.[194] The two types have a long history and represent two fundamentally opposed attitudes of civilized man to primitive man. Columbus on his first voyage had found the Arawak Indians good, generous, timid, 'gentle and . . . always laughing', but he had heard also of the Caribs, or 'Canibales', a people who are 'very fierce and who eat human flesh'.[195] In the Arawaks and the Caribs we can see the beginnings of the American history of the 'good Indian' and the 'bad Indian', who were often the same Indian, just as the good Scythian and the bad Scythian had been the same Scythian, differently viewed.[196]

On 2 July 1584, Captain Arthur Barlowe, approaching the North Carolina coast, 'found shole water, which smelt so sweetely, and was so strong a smell, as if we had bene in the midst of some delicate garden, abounding with all kind of odoriferous flowers, by which we were assured, that the land could not be far distant'. To describe Roanoke Island and its Algonquian inhabitants, he produced the appropriate literary analogies as readily as Drayton or Ronsard: 'wee found the people most gentle, loving and faithfull, void of all guile, and treason, and such as lived after the manner of the golden age. The earth bringeth foorth all things in aboundance, as in the first creation, without toile or labour.'[197] Published in Hakluyt's *Principal Navigations*, this was colonial propaganda such as even Drayton, the professional, could not improve—except by emptying his Virginian ode of Indians, and reassigning their Paradise and Golden Age to the 'brave Heroique' colonists.[198]

But to colonize the paradisal Virginia Drayton had advertised was to find oneself in Jamestown, a town in name only, subjected to 'the assaults, and ambuscadoes of the Salvages', or in Indian captivity like John Smith, surrounded by dancing savages 'yelling out such hellish notes and screeches',

> As if neare led to hell,
> Amongst the Devils to dwell.[199]

Looking at Cape Cod from the *Mayflower* in 1620, William Bradford considered where the Pilgrims were:

Being thus passed ye vast ocean . . . they had now no freinds to welcome them, nor inns to entertaine, or refresh their weatherbeaten bodys, no houses, or much less townes to repaire too, to seeke for succoure . . . Besides what could they see, But a hidious & desolate wildernes, full of wild beasts, & willd men . . . nether could they (as it were) goe up to ye tope of pisga, to vew from this willdernes, a more goodly cuntrie to feed their hops; for which way so ever they turnd ther eys (save upward to ye heavens) they could have little solace or content, in respecte of any outward objects.[200]

'In respecte of any outward objects', then, there were no friends, no inns, no houses, no towns—a catalogue of the absent items of culture resulting, not in a Golden Age or a natural Paradise, but in a wilderness, a wilderness with none of the benefits of culture and with no Mount Pisgah, either, from which to see the biblical Promised Land. But this was only 'in respecte of any outward objects' and, as Bradford proudly stated, the Pilgrims 'looked not much on those things'.[201] They looked to the Bible, instead, and read America there, interpreting the New World as they did the Old Testament, typologically. What they saw in the New World varied, but not how they saw it, for, like the poet Edward Taylor, they saw 'the world slickt up in types'.[202] Thus America was the Promised Land, but also, according to the Puritan historian Cotton Mather, 'the Wilderness thro' which we are passing to the Promised Land'.[203]

The Puritan narratives of Indian captivity, like Mary Rowlandson's *Narrative* of 1682, repeat the experience of immigration, of leaving England and arriving in America. The captive is bereft of home and family, bereft of all that is culturally familiar, except faith, and confronted by a 'vast and howling *Wilderness*' of wild beasts and wild men: 'Oh, the roaring, and singing, and dancing, and yelling of those black creatures in the night, which made the place a lively resemblance of hell.'[204] The anonymous preface to Mary Rowlandson's *Narrative* makes sure that the reader recognizes her Indian captors for what they are: 'such atheisticall proud, wild, cruel, barbarous, bruitish (in one word) diabolicall creatures'.[205] In his *Magnalia Christi Americana* (1702) Cotton Mather took the same view, that the Indian is 'Diabolical', a type of Satan, the snake, a view which persisted until in time it was recognized that these types depended on Puritan theology, not American reality, and Fenimore Cooper, turning the Puritan captivity narrative into the American novel, ironically named his noble savage Indian 'Chingachgook, which signifies big sarpent'.[206] Cooper's Indian, however, in *The Last of the Mohicans; A Narrative of 1757* (1826), is a historical fiction; the noble savage no longer inhabits the factual present, but has returned to the fictional past, and perished, 'gone to the happy hunting grounds', the 'last' of his tribe.[207]

As the Indians were discovered apparently living in the past, so the past was where they apparently belonged, and would soon really belong, no longer living. This seemed as obvious to Montaigne in the sixteenth century as it did to Cooper in the nineteenth. While 'Des cannibales' portrays the Indians in their natural state, Montaigne's later essay 'Des coches' presents their conquest by the vainglorious, savage Spaniards, a fate anticipated in 'Des cannibales' by the description of Indians 'ignorans combien coutera un jour à leur repos et à leur bon heur la connoissance de corruptions de deçà, et que de ce commerce naistra leur ruyne'.[208]

Montaigne's account of the fate of the newly discovered world is not unlike Milton's account of the fate of the newly created world. In Hell Milton's Beelzebub outlines Satan's plan for Paradise:

> here perhaps [in the 'new world']
> Some advantageous act may be achieved
> By sudden onset, either with hell fire
> To waste his whole creation, or possess
> All as our own, and drive as we were driven
> The puny habitants, or if not drive,
> Seduce them to our party . . .[209]

Satan on his exploratory voyage to Paradise, 'harder beset And more endangered, than . . . Ulysses', is portrayed as the hero of an epic voyage of classical literature, and also as a modern voyager who glorifies his purpose with talk of 'Honour and empire' to be gained 'by conquering this new world'.[210]

As Satan travels though space across Chaos, that 'dark Illimitable ocean', and is likened in the epic similes to an explorer in the fallen world of contemporary geography, the reader feels the temptation to believe that Paradise can still be found in the modern world, like some Eldorado in an undiscovered land, perhaps somewhere in the New World.[211] Thus Satan first glimpses the 'new world':

> As when a scout
> Through dark and desert ways with peril gone
> All night; at last by break of cheerful dawn
> Obtains the brow of some high-climbing hill,
> Which to his eye discovers unaware
> The goodly prospect of some foreign land
> First-seen, or some renowned metropolis
> With glistering spires and pinnacles adorned
> Which now the rising sun gilds with his beams.[212]

As Satan approaches Eden, however, Milton multiplies the exotic references so that Paradise seems to become lost, not lost forever in the distant past, but lost, nevertheless, in a confusion of distant names and places, appearing, for example, with its sweet smells wafted to Satan on the breeze:

> As when to them who sail
> Beyond the Cape of Hope, and now are past
> Mozambic, off at sea north-east winds blow
> Sabean odours from the spicy shore
> Of Arabie the blest . . .[213]

Milton deliberately exploits the possibilities offered at a distance—in traversible miles not irreversible years—by such frustrating but tempting geographical details, inviting the reader to engage in the fruitless speculation about the location of the terrestrial Paradise that continued in the seventeenth century long after Purchas had written that 'the place cannot be found in earth, but is become a commonplace in mens braines, to macerate and vexe them in the curious search hereof'.[214] But Milton is careful, later, to disabuse us. When the fall came, it came to the whole world. There was only one fall in a new world, the original in Eden, when Adam and Eve first covered their nakedness, for:

> Such of late
> Columbus found the American so girt
> With feathered cincture . . .[215]

And after his description of the fall Milton replaces Paradise irrevocably in the past, sternly telling us the modern condition of Eden: 'an island salt and bare'.[216]

Long before *Paradise Lost*, however, a journey through a steaming jungle to cross that obstacle, America, resulted in a discovery from a hilltop:

On Tuesday the twenty-fifth of September of the year 1513, at ten o'clock in the morning, Captain Vasco Núñez [de Balboa], having gone ahead of his company, climbed a hill with a bare summit, and from the top of this hill saw the South Sea. Of all the Christians in his company, he was the first to see it. He turned back toward his people, full of joy, lifting his hands and his eyes to Heaven, praising Jesus Christ and his glorious Mother the Virgin, Our Lady. Then he fell upon his knees on the ground and gave great thanks to God for the mercy he had shown him, in allowing him to discover that sea.[217]

The South Seas, where voyagers were to rediscover the lost Paradise, and also a Paradise lost, have always depended on the observer's point of view. Standing upon a peak in Darien, which runs from east to west, Balboa looked south at the ocean which Magellan, from a different point of view, would call, in hope, 'Pacific'.[218]

'Quelle verité [est-ce] que ces montaignes bornent', asked Montaigne, 'qui est mensonge au monde qui se tient au delà?'[219] That was the new world seen by Montaigne, like a vision from a mountain, a world of truth that was merely relative, that changed as you travelled, that was a lie on the other side of the mountain. But for the philosopher Francis Bacon the travellers of the Renaissance had discovered a 'New Continent' of truth, of truth not based on the authority of ancient texts, but on experience of the real world, a world of truth that was not relative, but absolute. Thus, as Cowley wrote:

> Bacon, like Moses, led us forth at last,
> The barren Wilderness he past,
> Did on the very Border stand
> Of the blest promis'd Land,
> And from the Mountains Top of his Exalted Wit,
> Saw it himself, and shew'd us it.[220]

It is to these two points of view—Montaigne's and Bacon's—that we must turn in the next chapter.

2

Far-Fetched Facts

Il me semble que ce que nous voyons par experience en ces nations là, surpasse
non seulement toutes les peintures dequoy la poësie a embelly l'age doré et
toutes ses inventions à feindre une heureuse condition d'hommes, mais encore
la conception et le desir mesme de la philosophie.

(Montaigne, 'Des cannibales')[1]

In Rabelais's account of the voyage of Pantagruel, grandson of the King of Utopia,
to consult the oracle of the Holy Bottle, 'pres le Catay en Indie superieure', the
voyagers encounter in imaginary Satinland a monstrous old man named Ouy-dire,
Hearsay, an authority on all the exotic nations and peoples of the world.[2] He is
blind and crippled, but his body is covered with ears and he is talking with seven
tongues, each divided into seven parts, to an audience which includes Herodotus,
Pliny, Strabo, Marco Polo, Pietro Martire, and many others 'cachez derriere une
piece de tapisserie en Tapinois escrivans de belles besongnes [stealthily writing the
grandest works], & tout par Ouy dire.'[3] One of those named amongst this crowd
of ancient and modern authors of travel literature is the French explorer Jacques
Cartier (1491–1557), thought by some twentieth-century scholars to be the original
for Pantagruel's pilot on his voyage, called Jamet Brayer.[4] But the real Jacques Cartier,
like many other Renaissance voyagers, learned to distrust Rabelais's Ouy-dire. If
the world was now better known, he claimed, it was not because of the theories of
the 'saiges philosophes du temps passé', but because 'les simples mariniers de present
. . . ont congneu le contraire d'icelle opinion des philosophes par vraye experience.'[5]

'Let it be said in a whisper', wrote Vespucci, 'experience is certainly worth more
than theory.'[6] The whisper grew louder. 'Experience runs counter to philosophy',
announced Gómara in his *Historia General de las Indias*, and Oviedo, in his *Historia*,
reminded his readers that: 'What I have said cannot be learned in Salamanca,
Bologna or Paris'.[7] The age of discovery was an age that witnessed the beginnings
of the triumph of experience over authority. The voyagers were not the only ones
to make new discoveries, but geographical exploration, which J. H. Parry calls the
'most empirical of all forms of enquiry, and most destructive of purely *a priori*
reasoning', could serve as a model of empirical method.[8] What Columbus discovered in the New World was not new, but very old indeed, as we know: the
terrestrial Paradise described in the book of Genesis, and, according to Pietro
Martire, 'that goulden worlde of the whiche owlde wryters speake so much'. But
if the New World were truly 'new', as Vespucci claimed, not merely a rediscovery

of the truth of those ancient texts describing man's earliest beginnings, but truly 'new', then it necessitated a new world-view, one based—not on the authority of the Bible and the classics—but on experience of the world, the New World. The experience of the simple sailors of the present began slowly to wear away the foundations of the authority of the past.

The Renaissance discovered man and the world, according to Michelet's famous formula, to which we might add that man in the newly discovered world was discovered naked, his 'shameful part uncovered'.[9] To discover man in this new world was also to discover, by contrast, civilized man. 'Pour étudier l'homme', as Rousseau said, 'il faut apprendre à porter sa vüe au loin'.[10] The 'brave new world' Miranda discovers when she sees Ferdinand in *The Tempest* is the old world. Civilized man, compared to Caliban, is a wonder; the old world, too, a new world:

> How beauteous mankind is! O brave new world,
> That has such people in't![11]

To discover men who lived, as Vespucci reported, without property, gods, kings, or clothes, was to discover the 'brave new world' of civilization. It was to discover that civilization, the traditional world of European culture, was something strange and wonderful by contrast with a world where men lived, it seemed, according to the laws of nature. It was to discover that the world of civilization was a work of art, but also, by the same token, an artificial world.

The most comprehensive survey of the literature of the Renaissance voyages has been made by Geoffroy Atkinson in *Les Nouveaux Horizons* (1935), a study of more than 550 texts printed in French between 1480 and 1609 on the subject of Asia, Africa, or America. He writes:

S'il y a, chez les voyageurs, chez les auteurs d'*Histoires* et chez les cosmographes de la Renaissance française, une constatation qui devient banale, pour nous, à force de répétition, c'est à coup sur la constatation qu'il y a des peuples nus. Pour ces auteurs, cependant, cette constatation n'était pas du tout une banalité. C'était, au contraire, l'un des *faits* les plus étonnants de leur époque.[12]

'All of them go around as naked as their mothers bore them', observed Columbus on the day he discovered the New World, a fact covered with a fig-leaf in *Paradise Lost*, where 'Columbus found the American so girt'.[13] Such a discovery presented a challenge not only to the text of the Bible but also to a fact of nature—for such, in Europe, did shame appear to be. So many facts which had seemed to be facts of nature were discovered to be facts only of civilized culture: costume—or no costume—was just custom.

Such facts found their way into literature. Ronsard's friend, Jodelle, wrote of the Brazilian Indians:

> Ces barbares marchent tous nuds,
> Et nous nous marchons incognus,
> Fardez, masquez.[14]

And Montaigne, inspired by the 'cannibales', wrote 'To the Reader' of his *Essais* that he had wished to reveal himself as frankly and truthfully as 'la reverence publique' permitted: 'Que si j'eusse esté entre ces nations qu'on dict vivre encore sous la douce liberté des premieres loix de nature, je t'asseure que je m'y fusse très-volontiers peint tout entier, et tout nud.' Because, he said, 'c'est moy que je peins.'[15] All Montaigne's *Essais* are summed up in this image, an image of truth discovered, the naked truth. The Indians were naked, but civilized men, as Jodelle said, were 'incognus'. So Montaigne would discover himself, a man, to the extent that his respect for the customs of his own culture permitted. This respect for 'la reverence publique' of civilized culture diminished as Montaigne's respect for the truth increased 'et je l'ose dire . . . un peu plus', as he dared to stand 'entier et descouvert sans consideration d'autruy', and to expose himself completely, declaring: 'Chacune de mes pieces me faict esgalement moy que toute autre. Et nulle autre ne me faict plus proprement homme que cette-cy. Je dois au publiq universellement mon pourtrait.'[16]

Many of Montaigne's meditations on the nature of man begin by considering 'ce monde des Indes nouvelles' ('De la coustume') or 'la façon d'aller tout nud de ces nations dernierement trouvées' ('De l'usage de se vestir').[17] For to see human nature laid bare, stripped of the disguise of culture, where better to look than at the inhabitants of the New World, naked of European custom, as of costume? When he read Jean de Léry's account of the Brazilian Indians, for example, Montaigne would have observed, not only that the Indians were naked and unashamed, in contradiction to 'ce qu'enseigne la sainte Escriture d'Ada[m] & Eve', as Léry reported, 'chose non moins estra[n]ge que difficille a croire, à ceux qui ne l'ont veu, tant hommes, femmes, qu'enfans, no[n] seulement sans cacher aucunes parties de leurs corps, mais aussi sans en avoir nulle honte ni vergongne', but also that 'les attifez, fards, fausses peruques, cheveux tortillez, grands collets fresez, vertugales, robes sur robes & autres infinies bagatelles dont les femmes de pardeçà se contrefont & n'ont jamais assez, sont sans comparaison cause de plus de maux que la nudité ordinaire des femmes Sauvages'.[18] Burton quotes this passage from Léry in his *Anatomy* and notes justly: 'His country-man *Montagne* in his *Essayes*, is of the same opinion'.[19] It was no wonder that, as Léry said, the 'Sauvages . . . furent . . . estonnez de voir des femmes vestues'.[20] As Montaigne pointed out, after citing some of the strange customs 'en ce monde des Indes nouvelles': 'Ces exemples estrangers ne sont pas estrange' (these foreign/strange examples are not strange/foreign). Because: 'Les barbares ne sont de rien plus merveilleux, que nous sommes à eux, ny avec plus d'occasion; comme chacun advoüeroit, si chacun sçavoit, après s'estre promené par ces nouveaux exemples, se coucher sur les propres et les conferer sainement.'[21]

'Que sais-je' was Montaigne's motto and ἐπέχω, 'I suspend [judgement]', was one of several quotations from the Sceptic, Sextus Empiricus, that were—and still are—inscribed on the beams of his study.[22] Sextus (*c*.AD 160–210), whose *Outlines of Pyrrhonism* emerged from the obscurity of Greek manuscripts into a Latin translation published in 1562, had formed the doctrines of earlier Sceptics into a kind of Sceptics' handbook, with chapters about such things, for instance, as the properly equivocal use 'Of the Expressions "Perhaps", "Possibly" and "Maybe" '.[23] In this work he described the ten ' "modes" by which suspension [of judgement] is supposed to be brought about'.[24] The tenth of these 'modes' was based 'on the disciplines and customs and laws' and the procedure was as follows:

we say that amongst the Persians it is the habit to indulge in intercourse with males, but amongst the Romans it is forbidden by law to do so; and that, whereas with us adultery is forbidden, amongst the Massagetae it is traditionally regarded as an indifferent custom, as Eudoxus of Cnidos relates in the first book of his *Travels*; [etc.] [Thus] so much divergency is shown to exist in objects, we shall not be able to state what character belongs to the object in respect of its real essence, but only what belongs to it in respect of this particular rule of conduct, or law or habit . . . [Thus] we are compelled to suspend judgement.[25]

Clearly Sextus was not sceptical about the *Travels* of Eudoxus, and clearly he did not compare contradictory customs in order to arrive at the truth or the real essence of the object, but in order to demonstrate the impossibility of determining the truth. Montaigne was less dogmatic a Sceptic and less systematic a philosopher, and he used Sextus' method to both of these different effects, sometimes to discover a truth or 'loix naturelle' hidden by culture, sometimes, more radically, to discover no law of nature at all but only customs, culturally relative. In 'De la coustume' he wrote: 'Qui voudra se desfaire de ce violent prejudice de la coustume . . . rapportant les choses à la verité et à la raison, il sentira son judgement comme tout bouleversé, et remis pourtant en bien plus seur estat.'[26] While in 'Des cannibales' he wrote: 'comme de vray, il semble que nous n'avons autre mire de la verité et de la raison que l'exemple et idée des opinions et usances du païs où nous sommes.'[27]

Sometimes, then, Montaigne is a thorough Sceptic and uses customs as evidence to overturn truth and reason; sometimes he uses the same method to establish truth and reason. But, as he approved of the Sceptics' practice of observing the local customs and beliefs, whatever they might be and however absurd, we can never tell whether Montaigne really believed in the truth and reason of his own culture or not.[28] We must suspend judgement.

What is certain, however, is that Montaigne was interested in the customs of the New World. He could have confined himself to classical evidence; there was an ample supply of strange customs in the works of the many classical authors with which he was familiar. Yet again and again in his *Essais* he uses the 'nouveaux exemples' from the modern voyagers. What is also certain is that these 'nouveaux exemples', whether they were to be used to discover truth or deny its very basis, had themselves to be presented as truth, as facts. In this respect, although, like Sextus, Montaigne was inconsistent, he was rather more careful and particular than Sextus had been.

Let us follow Montaigne's procedure in his famous essay 'Des cannibales', which, on the basis of such supposed facts about 'cannibals', was to build conclusions that were radical for Europeans, as well as to set the pattern, for modern times, of the good savage. He begins by consulting the ancients on the subject of America. First he tells us Plato's story of Atlantis (which he lifts from Chauveton's French version of Benzoni's *Historia del Mondo Nuovo*) but, he concludes, 'il n'y a pas grande apparence que cette Isle soit ce monde nouveau que nous venons de descouvrir'.[29] Then (still following Chauveton) he turns to Aristotle and his story of an island in the Atlantic, colonized and then abandoned by the Carthaginians: 'L'autre tesmoignage de l'antiquité, auquel on veut rapporter cette descouverte, est dans Aristote.'[30] But again: 'Cette narration d'Aristote n'a non plus d'accord avec nos terres neufves.'[31] At this point he turns, immediately and abruptly, from the 'tesmoignage[s] de l'antiquité', from Plato and Aristotle, to his own servant, a man who had spent some ten or twelve years in America:

Cet homme que j'avoy, estoit homme simple et grossier, qui est une condition propre à rendre veritable tesmoignage; car les fines gens remarquent bien plus curieusement [carefully] et plus de choses, mais ils les glosent; et, pour faire valoir leur interpretation et la persuader, ils ne se peuvent garder d'alterer un peu l'Histoire; ils ne vous representent jamais les choses pures, ils les inclinent et masquent selon le visage qu'ils leur ont veu; et, pour donner credit à leur jugement et vous y attirer, prestent volontiers de ce costé là à la matiere, l'alongent et l'amplifient. Ou il faut un homme très-fidelle, ou si simple qu'il n'ait pas dequoy bastir et donner de la vray-semblance à des inventions fauces, et qui n'ait rien espousé. Le mien estoit tel; et, outre cela, il m'a faict voir à diverses fois plusieurs matelots et marchans qu'il avoit cogneuz en ce voyage. Ainsi je me contente de cette information, sans m'enquerir de ce que les cosmographes en disent.[32]

Here, then, we have—by way of an apparently casual transition from 'Aristote' to 'cet homme que j'avoy'—a carefully contrived juxtaposition which is a dramatic demonstration of the transition from authority to experience by way of the New World. Not only does Montaigne turn from the the authority of Plato and Aristotle to the experience of modern times, but he turns also from the authorities of modern times, the 'cosmographes' (who, he complains, because they have seen Palestine will give us news of all the world), to the experience of his servant, 'simple et grossier', and of the simple sailors and merchants.[33] It is, as Cartier claimed, 'les simples mariniers de present' who have become the new authorities 'par vraye experience'.

Yet Montaigne returns to classical culture for analogies for the cannibals' state of nature. He is sorry, he says, that the ancient world had no knowledge of the New World:

Il me desplait que Licurgus et Platon ne l'ayent eüe; car il me semble que ce que nous voyons par experience en ces nations là, surpasse non seulement toutes les peintures dequoy la poësie a embelly l'age doré et toutes ses inventions à feindre une heureuse condition d'hommes, mais encore la conception et le desir mesme de la philosophie. Ils n'ont peu imaginer une nayfveté si pure et simple, comme nous la voyons par experience; ny n'ont peu croire que nostre societé se peut maintenir avec si peut d'artifice et de soudeure humaine.[34]

When Montaigne invokes the classical Golden Age and utopia, however, it is to point out that the New World not only surpasses these conceptions of the ancient world but is itself no mere conception. Unlike its classical precedents, the New World is not a poetical invention or a philosophical dream. Unlike such products of the imagination, the New World is real: 'nous [le] voyons par experience.'

Montaigne makes a number of radical remarks in his essay: that 'barbarity' is a relative term, 'chacun appelle barbarie ce qui n'est pas de son usage'; that it is the Europeans who have been corrupted by art who should be called 'sauvages', not the cannibals who are like 'fruicts que nature . . . a produicts'.[35] This is, as A. O. Lovejoy says, 'the *locus classicus* of primitivism in modern literature'.[36] But we should notice here that Montaigne always refers us, as much as he can, to first-hand evidence, to his own experience. He has tasted some of the cannibals' food (not cannibal) himself; he has a collection of their artefacts in his own home; he has in his possession some of their songs, which he quotes; and, finally, he has seen three cannibals at Rouen and even interviewed one of them himself.

It is into the mouths of these three cannibals that Montaigne places his most direct and telling criticisms of his own culture, thus making them the descendants of the classical noble primitives (he refers twice to the Scythians) and the ancestors of those in times to come who would comment critically on civilized culture from the savage point of view. There were precedents also in the modern literature of travel for the type of the 'philosophe nu'. Such a one appears, for example, in Léry's *Voyage*, and the marginal gloss to his speech to the French colonists, who are 'de grands fols', reads: 'Sentence notable & plusque Philosophale d'un Sauvage Amériquain.'[37] Montaigne's Indians, he tells us, were shown 'nostre façon, nostre pompe, la forme d'une belle ville' and asked what had most impressed them. They replied that they found it very strange ('fort estrange') that a child (the 12-year-old King Charles IX) should be in charge, and strange ('estrange') also that all the men they saw emaciated with hunger and poverty did not take by the throat all the other men they saw stuffed and gorged with all sorts of things, or set fire to their houses instead of begging at their doors.[38]

The way to these revolutionary perceptions of the European distribution of status and wealth—so familiar as to have seemed inevitable and natural—has been prepared by Montaigne's transfer of the credit for knowledge from the authority of the 'fines gens' who 'ne vous representent jamais les choses pures' to the simple but pure experience of a mere servant and, thence, to the even simpler, purer experience of savages. But those, like Margaret Hodgen in her history of *Early Anthropology*, who praise Montaigne's 'ethnological sophistication', and admire his preference for oral testimony rather than that of the authors of books on the New World, ignore the findings of the literary historians who have established Montaigne's wide reading of the contemporary literature on the New World and disproved his claim that he followed only the testimony of his servant, and of simple sailors and merchants, and was 'contente de cette information'.[39] Doubt has even been cast, which need not surprise us, on the precise truth of Montaigne's encounter with the cannibals at Rouen. Montaigne, after all, was not himself 'simple et grossier'. But even if he did give, to use his own words about the 'fines gens', 'de la vray-semblance à des inventions fauces', he recognized the importance, in presenting the case of the cannibals of the New World, of basing that case upon experience, which, supremely, could give it 'vray-semblance'.

On the basis of experience even the cannibals at Rouen, coming from a utopian Golden Age 'que nous voyons par experience', can speak with an authority that the ancients lack, and Montaigne ends his essay, which began with the worthless testimony of Plato and Aristotle on a New World of which they knew nothing, with the pregnant testimony of the cannibals on the Old World, seen anew. Well, the cannibals do not seem so very terrible, concludes Montaigne, 'mais quoy', but then, 'ils ne portent point de haut de chausses!' They do not wear breeches.[40]

Montaigne had followers in the first part of the seventeenth century, 'libertins' like La Mothe Le Vayer (1588–1672), a Sceptic whose favourite device was the tenth 'mode' of 'le divin Sexte', and who was, therefore, well read in the literature of travel.[41] In the latter part of the seventeenth century, however, Montaigne fell into disfavour, although Pierre Bayle (1647–1706), who believed that modern philosophy began with the rediscovery of Sextus, carried on the tradition of Scep-tical arguments drawn from the evidence of travellers, a practice which would be revived, for their own purposes, by the 'philosophes' of the Enlightenment.[42] There is thus a literary and philosophical tradition, built upon the experience of the voyagers, which connects the work of Montaigne with that of Rousseau, Diderot, and Voltaire.[43]

An important factor contributing to the (temporary) decline of Montaigne's influence was the success of Descartes.[44] Descartes began, as he tells us in his *Discours de la méthode*, by reading the ancients and by travelling, which is 'quasi le même', he says, and taught him 'à ne rien croire trop fermement de ce qui m'avait été persuadé que par l'exemple et par la coutume'.[45] He rejected both of these procedures, however, in which he found 'guère de quoi m'assurer' and, again like Montaigne, proceeded to doubt, but less successfully, as is well known, with the result that he convinced himself and many others, not only that he was doubting, but that therefore he himself and God, 'innate ideas' and a good many other things, were indubitable.[46]

Scepticism did much to raise Renaissance thought above the clouds of medieval scholasticism, but there were those, like Francis Bacon, who did not 'delight in Giddiness' and wished, like Descartes, to find 'de quoi s'assurer'.[47] Bacon certainly knew Montaigne's *Essais*, after which he is believed to have named his own *Essayes*. His own philosophy began, he said, from a Sceptical position:

The doctrine of those who have denied that certainty could be attained at all, has some agreement with my way of proceeding at the first setting out; but they end in being infinitely separated and opposed. For the holders of that doctrine assert simply that nothing can be known; I also assert that not much can be known in nature by the way which is now in use. But then they go on to destroy the authority of the senses and understanding; whereas I proceed to devise and supply helps for the same.[48]

For Bacon the senses, aided by his experimental method, would attain certain knowledge of nature.

He was neither Sceptic nor primitivist:

let a man only consider what a difference there is between the life of men in the most civilised province of Europe, and in the most barbarous districts of New India; he will feel it to be great enough to justify the saying that 'man is a god to man', not only in regard of aid and benefit, but also by a comparison of condition. And this difference comes not from the soil, not from climate, not from race, but from the arts.[49]

There is no question, here, of 'barbarity' being a relative matter. The American Indians proved, like Caliban, the superiority of art to nature, and also the possibility of progress, which Montaigne doubted.[50] Bacon argued that 'their nakedness', which was 'a great defacement (for in the acknowledgement of nakedness was the first sense of sin)', and 'their idiocy, in thinking that horses did eat their bits, and letters speak, and the like', and, above all, 'their eating of men', which was 'an abomination', justified the Indians' invasion and conquest by the Spaniards, whose own barbarity Montaigne had demonstrated in his essay 'Des coches' (which is not about coaches).[51] Bacon approved of colonization, and recommended that the colonizers should, if they 'plant [colonize] where savages are, . . . send oft of them, over to the Country, that Plants, that they may see a better Condition then their owne, and commend it'.[52] So much for the cannibals' experience of France.

Yet, like Montaigne, Bacon read the accounts of the voyagers, whose routes can even be traced in his work as he followed them from place to place, collecting the facts to be found in the wake of their experience, facts not to induce Scepticism, but to lay the foundations of a new method, a scientific method, for determining, with certainty, the truth.[53] As he said: 'Distant voyages and travels have brought to light many things in nature, which may throw fresh light on human philosophy and science and correct by experience the opinions and conjectures of the ancients.'[54] He notes the use of 'characters real' (pictograms) in China; the coincidence of tides in America and in Spain and Africa, 'as has been observed by Acosta and others, after careful research'; that perfumes 'act at remarkable distances, as those find who sail along the coasts of Florida'.[55] He connects Gilbert's theory of magnetism and 'the water-spouts, often seen in the voyage over the Atlantic Ocean'; connects cannibalism and syphilis 'for that it is certain that the cannibals in the West Indies eat man's flesh, and the West Indies were full of the pocks when they were first discovered'.[56]

But the new discoveries were significant for Bacon not just because they increased 'our stock of experience' but also because they were new. As for the ancient Greeks:

of the regions and districts of the world they knew but a small portion; . . . much less were they acquainted with the provinces of the New World . . . In our times on the other hand both many parts of the New World and the limits on every side of the Old World are known, and our stock of experience has increased to an infinite amount.[57]

In 1522 the ship *Vittoria*, commanded by Juan Sebastian del Cano, returned to Seville, from whence three years before, in 1519, with four other ships commanded by Magellan, it had sailed. On the coast of South America Magellan's expedition had encountered the Patagonian giants, 'calling loudly for "Setebos" ' (Caliban's 'dam's God' in *The Tempest*), and sailed on through the Straits, into the ocean that 'is very pacific, for . . . we did not suffer any storm', past 'Cipangu' (so they believed) to the 'islands of Ladroni [i.e. of Thieves]' (Guam and Rota in the Marianas), where the first Pacific islanders to encounter Europeans were 'very thievish', and 'thought, according to the signs which they made, that there were no other people in the world but themselves'.[58] Killing seven of these 'thieves', now better informed, they had sailed on to the Philippines (not yet so named) where they met some men in a boat, who, when addressed in Malayan by Magellan's Sumatran slave, 'immediately understood him'.[59] They had crossed the ocean Balboa had sighted from Darien and succeeded, where Columbus had failed, in reaching the East by sailing west. Although only one ship, the *Vittoria*, completed the circumnavigation, Magellan's expedition, which he did not survive, had proved by experience what had hitherto been learned surmise, that the world was really round.[60]

Bacon drew the conclusions, in *The Advancement of Learning*:

For it may be truly affirmed to the honour of these times, and in virtuous emulation with antiquity, that this great building of the world had never through-lights made in it, till the age of us and our fathers. For although they had knowledge of the antipodes . . . yet that mought be by demonstration and not in fact; and if by travel, it requireth the voyage but of half the globe. But to circle the earth, as the heavenly bodies do, was not done or enterprised till these later times: and therefore these times may justly bear the word . . . *plus ultra*, in precedence of the ancient *non ultra*.[61]

So the voyagers had proved as a fact, not only that the earth could be circled, but also that the ancients could be surpassed. And, in an age of discovery, advancing beyond the limits of the ancients, might there not be more new facts to be discovered by the heroic empirical method of the voyagers? Bacon continued:

And this proficience in navigation and discoveries may plant also an expectation of the further proficience and augmentation of all sciences; because it may seem they are ordained by God to be coevals, that is, to meet in one age. For so the prophet Daniel speaking of the latter times foretelleth, *Plurimi pertransibunt, et multiplex erit scientia*: as if the openness and through-passage of the world and the increase of knowledge were appointed to be in the same ages; as we see it is already performed in great part: the learning of these later times not much giving place to the former two periods or returns of learning, the one of the Grecians, the other of the Romans.[62]

The analogy between the new world of the voyagers and the new world of learning to be discovered and explored was Bacon's recurrent theme.[63] Advancing the example of the voyagers again in 'The Refutation of Philosophies', he wrote:

It would disgrace us, now that the wide spaces of the material globe, the lands and seas, have been broached and explored, if the limits of the intellectual globe should be set by the narrow discoveries of the ancients. Nor are those two enterprises, the opening up of the earth and the opening up of the sciences, linked and yoked together in any trivial way.[64]

Yet, although Bacon denied that he 'linked and yoked' voyagers and science 'in any trivial way', it was, despite his ample use of the voyagers in his scientific writings, and the support he derived from the prophecy of Daniel, at least partly as a persuasive analogy, and even as decorative imagery, that he invoked the heroic example of the modern voyagers. The frontispiece of the *Instauratio Magna* shows a ship sailing forth between two pillars, the Pillars of Hercules, representing the geographical and intellectual limits of the ancients, to discover, presumably, the 'intellectual globe', while underneath appears, of course, Bacon's favourite text from the prophet Daniel: *multi pertransibunt & augebitur scientia.*[65] 'For how long', he asked in the *De Augmentis*, 'shall we let a few received authors stand up like Hercules' Columns, beyond which there shall be no sailing or discovery in science?'[66]

It was because Bacon imagined science as a ship on a voyage to a new world of fact based on experience that he presented his *New Atlantis* as the narrative of a discovery in the South Seas. He surmised, with many others (though not Montaigne), that America was to be identified with Plato's island of Atlantis, destroyed 'not by Earth-quakes, (as the Egyptian Priest told Solon, . . . that it was swallowed by an Earth-quake;) but . . . by a Particular Deluge. For Earth-quakes are seldome in those Parts.'[67] So, preferring new to old, Bacon invented a 'new Atlantis', placing it well beyond the limits of ancient geography in 'that part of the South Seas [which] was utterly unknown; and might have islands or continents, that hitherto were not come to light.'[68]

We should now trace the history of such South Sea 'islands and continents, that hitherto were not come to light'. In 'that part of the South Seas [which] was utterly unknown' cosmographers and pilots in the sixteenth century located Solomon's Ophir, which had not been credibly rediscovered anywhere else, and there, also, they imagined a large antipodean continent, ultimately of Pythagorean origin, which came to be known as Terra Australis. These two conceptions were easily confused and it was rumoured in sixteenth-century colonial Peru, a rumour encouraged by Inca legends of gold in the islands of the Pacific, that Ophir might be near or even part of the great austral continent.[69] It was this mixture of Indian, biblical, and classical lore that inspired the Spanish explorations in the Pacific, explorations that had a way of turning rumours into what seemed to be realities.

Authors too were inspired by geographical myth. The future bishop Joseph Hall chose Terra Australis for the location of his *Mundus Alter et Idem, sive Terra Australis ante hac semper incognita longis itineribus peregrini academici nuperrime lustrata,* supposedly written by Mercurio Britannico, published *c.*1605, and in translation *c.*1608 as *The Discovery of a New World or A Description of the South Indies Hetherto Unknowne By an English Mercury.* This work, which burlesques the contemporary narratives of voyagers (Hakluyt's *Principal Navigations* had recently been published), is mainly a satire of those aspects of European culture to which Hall took exception, making use, for this purpose, of the device also employed in Richard Brome's play *The Antipodes* (1640), of turning the norms of the world upside down.[70] Although the maps provided are realistic and accord in outline with representations of Terra Australis by Mercator, Ortelius, and others, the new *Mundus* is more *idem* than *alter* and the countries around which the narrator, Mercurius, is artlessly trundled—Tenter-belly, with its two provinces of Eat-allia and Drink-allia, Shee-landt (a kind of shrewish Amazonia), Foolania and Theeve-ingen—do not reveal anything hitherto unknown to Europeans or, for that matter, to readers of Rabelais.[71]

The work is, however, worthy of notice as an imaginary voyage in the manner of Lucian and Rabelais, and also for its primacy in discovering, for fiction, the territory of Terra Australis. Milton connected Hall's work with the utopian tradition, and took a dim view of it which is not altogether unjust:

That grave and noble invention which the greatest and sublimest wits in sundry ages, *Plato in Critias*, and our two famous countreymen, the one in his *Utopia*, the other in his new *Atlantis* chose, I may not say as a feild, but as a mighty Continent wherein to display the largenesse of their spirits by teaching this our world better and exacter things, then were yet known, or us'd, this petty prevaricator of *America*, the zanie of *Columbus*, (for so he must be till his worlds end) having rambl'd over the huge topography of his own vain thoughts, no marvell, if he brought us home nothing but a meer tankard drollery, a venereous parjetory for a stewes [i.e. a libidinous decoration for a brothel].[72]

In the introductory chapter of Hall's *Discovery of a New World*, Beroaldus, a Frenchman, says he is 'fully perswaded that some part of these West *Indies* was that Ophir' of Solomon, though he cites 'five severall opinionists touching this'.[73] Terra Australis, however, remains to be discovered:

It hath ever offended mee to looke upon the Geographicall mapps, and finde this: *Terra Australis, nondum Cognita*. The unknowne Southerne Continent. What good spirit but would greeve at this? If they know it for a Continent, and for a Southerne Continent, why then doe they call it unknowne? But if it bee unknowne; why doe all the Geographers describe it after one forme and site? Idle men that they are, that can say, this it is, and yet wee know it not: How long shall wee continue to bee ignorant in that which wee professe to have knowledge of?[74]

It is to meet this challenge and determine the facts that Mercurius sets off to Terra Australis in his aptly named ship 'The Fancie'.[75]

Burton, later in the century, was also interested in this question, as well as in 'where *Ophir* was, whence *Solomon* did fetch his gold', questions to which a possible answer was somewhere in 'that part of the South Seas [which] was utterly unknown'.[76] In November 1567 a young Spaniard named Alvaro de Mendaña left Callao, Peru, in charge of an expedition to discover a rich 'continent' and 'convert to Christianity all infidels'.[77] Eighty days later, on 7 February 1568, thanks to 'the Glorious Mother of God, . . . to whom we all prayed, singing the *Te Deum laudamus*', they sighted Ysabel Island (as they called it, after Santa Ysabel), which proved to be merely one of a group of islands and not a continent.[78] Nor, as they proceeded to explore the islands, did they discover any convincing signs of gold—only infidels, who quickly learnt to say 'Fuera! Fuera!' ('Away!') to the strangers who had come so far to kill them and to kidnap their children.[79] Faced with the hostility of the islanders and the absence of gold, Mendaña and his men returned, not without difficulty, suffering, and great loss of life, to Peru, inspiring there wild rumours of gold in the islands they had discovered, which were soon known as 'The Isles of Solomon'.[80]

It was now Mendaña's mission to return and colonize the Solomon Islands, which were, however, destined to remain for two centuries, as a modern historian says, unthinkingly, 'lost to the sight of men' (white men).[81] It was not until 9 April 1595 that he was able to embark again from Callao with a second expedition, this time with Pedro Fernández de Quirós as his chief pilot. On 21 July an island was sighted, which Mendaña 'thought was the land he sought', ordering the singing of the 'Te Deum'.[82] This island was not one of the Solomons, however, but one of the group Mendaña named, realizing he had made a new discovery, 'Las Marquesas', in honour of his patron, the Marquis of Cañete.[83] The Marquesan natives were 'almost white and of very graceful shape, well-formed, robust' and 'naked, without any part covered', and the women were both 'prettier than the ladies of Lima, who are famed for their beauty', and 'ready to come near in friendly intercourse'.[84] Quirós saw a boy with a face 'like that of an angel' and 'never in my life felt such pain as when I thought that so fair a creature should be left to go to perdition'.[85] Trouble started almost immediately, however, for, as Quirós realized, 'we did not understand them', and soon the Marquesans were asking, 'by signs, when the Spaniards would go'.[86] They stayed for a fortnight, teaching the Marquesans 'to make the sign of the cross' and shooting them.[87] One Spaniard killed 'lest he should lose his reputation as a good marksman', another simply 'because he liked to kill'.[88] When the Spaniards did leave, to continue their search for the Solomon Islands, Quirós took the score: 'It may be held as certain that two hundred natives were killed in these islands'.[89] Such was the result of the first substantial contact between Europeans and Polynesians.[90]

The expedition sailed on to the island of Ndemi, which Mendaña called Santa Cruz, and which forms part of the group now known collectively by that name. The people were 'of a black colour; some of them tawny, with frizzled hair' and Mendaña assumed again that he had reached the Solomons, but was soon undeceived.[91] It was decided, nevertheless, to establish a colony, and so began what Quirós wittily called 'the tragedy of the islands where Solomon was wanting'.[92] The unwise colonists grumbled, killed natives, and, finally, each other. Then sickness came to them as a punishment from God and Mendaña himself died, nominating his wife Governess of the colony. The survivors returned to their ships, now scarcely seaworthy, and, a little over two months after they had discovered the island, abandoned the colony. After a further futile attempt to find the illusive Solomons, the dilapidated ships were turned to head for Manila, with sickness and deaths on board and a great lack of food and water, which 'the Governess used . . . very largely, requiring it to wash her clothes'.[93] Two ships of the four that left Callao survived, one reaching Mindanao and the other, thanks to Quirós, reaching Manila in February 1596, with fifty of her starving company dead and two of the Governess's pigs alive.

Quirós was from this time forth obsessed with the idea of discovering the great southern continent, which he believed must be near the Marquesas, and with saving the souls of so many who, without his help, would, like the Marquesan boy with the angelic face, 'be left to go to perdition'. So he argued, to the Pope at Rome, the King of Spain, and others, and by his sustained and determined efforts was able to sail from Callao in charge of another expedition on 21 December 1605. On 1 March 1606, after discovering several of the Tuamotus islands, the Spaniards sighted an island now generally identified as Rakahanga in the Northern Cooks, where they encountered 'beautiful, white, and elegant people' and 'women, who, if properly dressed, would have advantages over our Spanish women', and Quirós saw a boy so beautiful 'that to see him was the same as to see a painted angel'.[94] Sailing on, they found Taumako, one of the Duff islands, where a native told of 'a very large land' and 'opened both his arms and hands without making them meet'.[95] To this 'muy grande terra' they sailed, Quirós saying 'Put the ships' heads where they like, for God will guide them as may be right', and discovered the largest island of the group Cook would later name the New Hebrides.[96]

Quirós kissed the ground, crying 'O Land! sought for so long, intended to be found by so many, and so desired by me!'[97] With much ceremony his generous deed of possession was read out:

I take possession of this bay, named the Bay of St Philip and St James, and of its port named Santa Cruz, and of the site on which is to be founded the city of New Jerusalem . . . and of all this region of the south as far as the Pole, which from this time shall be called Australia del Espiritu Santo, with all its dependencies and belongings.[98]

Against the usual background of trouble with the natives, who were kidnapped, robbed, and killed, Quirós elected a municipality and administrative officers 'as is usual in a city that was the capital of a province', planted gardens, named the river the 'Jordan', and instituted the 'order of the Holy Ghost', of which every man was made a member, so that there were 'sailor-knights, . . . mulatto knights and negro-knights and Indian-knights and knights who were knight-knights'.[99] 'Triumphal arches' were built and the festival of Corpus Christi celebrated with a procession, dancing, masses, and hymns, while the birds, too, 'sang and chaunted', and a poem was composed, concluding 'God His secrets now lays bare'.[100] Then:

The Captain [Quirós] sent some of the people on board again, and marched inland with the rest to the sound of drums. He saw what he had sown already sprouting, the farms, houses, fruit orchards; and having walked for a league, he returned as it was getting late. When he came on board, he said that as these natives were at war with us, and there was not a chance on our side, we would leave port next day.[101]

So ended the second European colony in the South Seas, after only a month, but not Quirós's dream, for he returned to America and to Spain and wrote 'memoriale' after 'memoriale', of which one in particular, his eighth, was subsequently published, by Purchas among others (in his *Pilgrimes*), and widely distributed in Europe. In this Quirós extolled the 'excellencies' of his discovery of 'one fourth of the world', its lands 'better than Spain' and others beyond that 'should be an earthly paradise', its 'silver and pearls, which I saw, and gold', its 'decent people, clean cheerful and reasonable'.[102] There 'we found great harmony, caused by millions of different sorts of little birds like nightingales, thrushes', etc., and 'smelt many odours of flowers'.[103] He ended this poetical catalogue of sensory experiences by comparing himself to Columbus: 'If his conjectures made Christobal Colon pertinacious, they make me as importunate respecting what I saw and felt.'[104] Burton wondered whether 'that hungry Spaniards discovery of *Terra Australis Incognita* . . . be as true as that of *Mercurius Britannicus*, or his of *Utopia*'.[105] And indeed what Quirós 'saw and felt' in his Terra Australis was, like Terra Australis itself, fictitious. As a member of Cook's expedition remarked, when Cook rediscovered the island of Espiritu Santo in 1774: 'Mr Quiros's Zeal and warmth for his own favourite projects has carried him too far in the qualities he has attributed to this Country'.[106]

R. R. Cawley, in *Unpathed Waters: Studies in the Influence of the Voyagers on Elizabethan Literature*, has already suggested a connection between Quirós's last voyage (1605–6) and Bacon's *New Atlantis*. Certainly Bacon was interested in the question 'whether there is any Southern Continent, or only islands'; accounts of Quirós's discovery were circulating before 1624, the conjectured date of the composition of the *New Atlantis*, and, as Cawley points out, the voyagers in the *New Atlantis* communicate with the New Atlanteans in Spanish, and sail, like Quirós, from Peru.[107] It is also possible that Bacon could have heard of the previous voyage of Quirós, in company with Mendaña (1595–6), and of Mendaña's own previous voyage (1567–9), which discovered the Solomon Islands. News of Mendaña's return from his first voyage 'to seeke Salomon's Islands' reached England in 1572 and was reported by Hakluyt in his enlarged second edition (1598–1600).[108] It could not have failed to interest Bacon, who called the ancient lawgiver and King of the *New Atlantis* 'Solamona', and named its main institution Salomon's House after 'the King of the Hebrews'.[109]

In any case 'that part of the South Seas [which] was utterly unknown; and might have islands or continents, that hitherto were not come to light' was now becoming the last remaining place on earth where a voyager, or an author, could discover 'one fourth of the world', like Quirós, or 'the huge topography of his own vain thoughts', as Hall did, or 'a mighty Continent wherein to display the largenesse of [his] spirits', like Bacon; where a discoverer could, as Steele said of 'Mandeville's' fourteenth-century East, have 'an Opportunity of showing his Parts without incurring any Danger of being examined or contradicted'; where, in short, a fiction could be fact.[110] When Burton invented 'an *Utopia* of mine own, a new *Atlantis*, a poetical Common-wealth of mine own', he proposed that 'it may be in *Terra Australi[s] Incognita*, there is room enough (for of my knowledge neither that hungry *Spaniard*, nor *Mercurius Britannicus*, have yet discovered half of it)'.[111]

Although 'Truth, is a Naked, and Open day light', Bacon knew that a 'mixture of a Lie doth ever adde Pleasure.'[112] Also, as he argued in his Preface to *The Wisdom of the Ancients*, the use of fiction, in the form of fables or parables, was 'of prime use to the sciences, and sometimes indispensable: I mean the employment of parables as a method of teaching, whereby inventions that are new and abstruse and remote from vulgar opinions may find an easier passage to the understanding'.[113]

About to make new discoveries, remote from vulgar opinions, Bacon's fictional voyagers in the South Seas, 'finding ourselves in the midst of the greatest wilderness of waters in the world, without victual, . . . gave ourselves for lost men, and prepared for death'.[114] Yet they prayed to God, that 'he would now discover land to us that we might not perish. And it came to pass' that he did.[115] It is God, then, not human science, that discovers the island of New Atlantis, or Bensalem, as the natives call it, which seems to the voyagers 'a picture of our salvation in heaven', 'a land of angels', a 'happy land'.[116]

Once accommodated in the House of Strangers, to which they are initially restricted, the voyagers learn at length from its Governor, a flat character in an azure gown and white turban, how Bacon's account of the *New Atlantis* supersedes that 'which is made by a great man with you' of the old 'Atlantis (that you call America)'.[117] Although Plato's tale is mostly 'poetical and fabulous', yet it is true that 'about three thousand years ago . . . and an age after, or more', old Atlantis flourished and made great expeditions to the Mediterranean and the South Seas, and, whether or not it was defeated by Athens ('I can say nothing'), it certainly was defeated by the New Atlantis, which overcame the old 'without striking stroke'.[118] Then, less than a hundred years later, the old Atlantis was destroyed, not by an earthquake, 'as your man saith', 'but by a particular deluge'.[119] Hence the 'rudeness and ignorance' of the present inhabitants of America.[120] Hence, too, the superiority of the New Atlantis to the old, and of Bacon's myth to Plato's.

In those days—the Governor's lecture continues—'the navigation of the world, (specially for remote voyages,) was greater than at this day.'[121] Not only the Americans (of old Atlantis), but the Phoenicians, the Carthaginians, the Chinese, and others, and of course the people of Bensalem (the New Atlantis), had great fleets and sailed around the world. But the Americans were deluged and, with the singular exception of Bensalem, 'navigation did everywhere greatly decay', although, as the Governor notes, 'it is increased with you within these six-score years' and has, therefore, we should note, allowed Europe, once again, with God's helping hand, access to the 'happy land' of Bensalem.[122] As for distant voyaging from Bensalem itself, where navigation did not decay, the King and lawgiver, Solamona, who reigned 'about nineteen hundred years ago', 'thought fit altogether to restrain it'.[123] But 'he made nevertheless this ordinance':

That every twelve years there should be set forth out of this kingdom two ships, appointed to several voyages; That in either of these ships there should be a mission of three of the Fellows or Brethren of Salomon's House; whose errand was only to give us knowledge of the affairs and state of those countries to which they were designed, and especially of the sciences, arts, manufactures, and inventions of all the world; and withal to bring unto us books, instruments, and patterns in every kind; . . . thus you see we maintain a trade, not for gold, silver, or jewels; nor for silks; nor for spices; nor any other commodity of matter; but only for God's first creature, which was *Light*: to have *light* (I say) of the growth of all parts of the world.[124]

This, then, was the proper function of voyages: to discover knowledge. Bacon's European voyagers may have depended on God for their discovery of Bensalem, but in that 'happy land' such discoveries are organized by men. Plato in the *Laws* combines severe restrictions on travel for his citizens with a plan for an incorruptible observer, who travels to compare his society with others and to recommend improvements of his own if necessary.[125] The inhabitants of another 'Feigned Commonwealth'—as an inhabitant of Bensalem calls More's *Utopia*—eagerly travel so that 'they maye the better knowe the owte landes', as we have noticed, but they do not do so in the methodical fashion prescribed by Plato and Bacon, and also by Burton, who, in his own 'new Atlantis', would 'have certain ships sent out for new discoveries every year, & some discreet men appointed to travel into all neighbour kingdoms by land, which shall observe what artificial inventions, and good laws are in other Countries'.[126] Bacon's voyagers, when they return to Europe, will be able to report all the inventions of Bensalem, including, of course, systematic voyages for the discovery of inventions.

These explanations have involved the Governor in a digression, for which he apologizes. In order to make plain to the European voyagers the importance of voyages from Bensalem, and indirectly to imply the potential significance of their own voyage, he has had to tell them of King Solamona and of his foundation of Salomon's House, which, however, is hardly a digression in his account of Bensalem, for this institution is 'the lanthorn of this kingdom'.[127] Named after the biblical King Solomon, to whom King Solamona of Bensalem believed himself symbolically related ('finding himself to symbolize in many things with that king of the Hebrews'), and 'dedicated to the study of the Works and Creatures of God', Salomon's House is indeed the most important feature of Bensalem, as it is of Bacon's *New Atlantis*.[128]

We also learn about Bensalem that it is a Christian society, having received its own revelation, twenty years after Christ's ascension, by way of a miraculous apparition, which was verified at the time as 'a true miracle' by a member of Salomon's House.[129] The society of Bensalem is now devoutly Christian (the Governor's white turban has 'a small red cross on top') and it also respects the institutions of marriage and the family (as Bacon's narrator is able to observe for himself, when the visitors are eventually allowed out of the House of Strangers and

he is relieved for a while from the job of narrating the narrations of others).[130] All
this Bacon was anxious to emphasize in order to demonstrate that a kingdom with
a scientific institution as its 'lanthorn' need not be atheistic or revolutionary in
other respects.

There is, however, little social contact between the kingdom and its 'lanthorn'.
The society of Bensalem receives the selected benefits of Salomon's House, which
passes on 'such new profitable inventions as [they, the Fellows of Salomon's
House] think good', but when a Father of Salomon's House comes to the capital
it is a great event, for 'we have seen none of them this dozen years'.[131] This august
visitor, a flat character in 'shoes of peach-coloured velvet', offers a 'private conference' to one of the European voyagers and Bacon's narrator is the lucky man
chosen by his companions.[132] It is from the account given by the Father of Salomon's
House, which Bacon's narrator is granted permission to publish 'for the good of
other nations', that the latter learns all he knows, and all we know, of the marvels
of Salomon's House.[133]

We need not hear in its entirety the complete 'relation of the true state of
Salomon's House', another, rather boastful lecture.[134] The goal of Salomon's House,
its Father says, 'is the knowledge of Causes, and secret motions of things; and the
enlarging of Human Empire, to the effecting of all things possible'.[135] To these ends
the Fellows have, among other facilities for observation and experiment: 'perspective-
houses' with telescopes and microscopes and means to make 'all delusions and
deceits of the sight'; 'sound-houses', where they 'represent and imitate all articu-
late sounds and letters, and the voices and notes of beasts and birds' and 'convey
sounds in trunks and pipes, in strange lines and distances'; 'perfume-houses',
where they 'imitate smells' and 'make divers imitations of taste'; 'engine-houses',
where they make weapons 'more violent than yours are', 'imitate also flights of
birds', 'have ships and boats for going under-water', and 'imitate also motions of
living creatures, by images'; and 'houses of deceits of the senses', where they
'represent all manner of feats of juggling, false apparitions, impostures and illusions', although 'we do hate all impostures and lies'.[136]

It is in their gardens and parks, however, that the Fellows' most questionable
activities take place. There they make plants 'by art greater much than their
nature; and their fruit greater and sweeter and of differing taste, smell, colour, and
figure, from their nature'.[137] As for the birds and beasts: 'By art likewise, we make
them greater or taller than their kind is' and 'have produced many new kinds' by
interbreeding and also completely artificially, 'whereof some are advanced (in
effect) to be perfect creatures'.[138] These, of course, are creatures of man, not God,
and the works of Salomon's House cannot be said to be confined to the definition
given them by the Governor of the House of Strangers: 'the study of the Works
and Creatures of God'. The Fellows do not neglect 'hymns and services, which we
say daily of laud and thanks to God for his marvellous works', but some of the
marvellous works of Salomon's House are clearly not God's.[139]

On Bensalem as on Prospero's island, which was once Caliban's, art is superior to nature. But these islands were themselves works of art, of fiction. Montaigne believed that the state of nature inhabited by the 'cannibales' in America demonstrated 'par experience' 'une heureuse condition' that Plato and the poets could not even have imagined in their fictions, while for Bacon America demonstrated in fact, as Bensalem did in fiction, that man could attain a happy condition and become 'a god to man' by art. If 'Des cannibales' showed the happy condition of America, Montaigne's later essay, 'Des coches', showed the full extent of the fall from that condition brought about by the Spanish invasion, a fall hinted at in 'Des cannibales' by Montaigne's passing comment that the Indians at Rouen little knew 'combien coutera un jour à leur repos et à leur bon heur la connoissance des corruptions' of Europe.[140] Bacon, who thought the Spanish invasion justified by the ignorance, nakedness, and barbarity of the Indians, maintained in *The Advancement of Learning* 'that it was not the pure knowledge of nature and universality, a knowledge by the light whereof man did give names unto other creatures in Paradise, . . . which gave occasion to the fall; but it was the proud knowledge of good and evil'.[141] It might be argued that the knowledge to name God's creatures is one thing and the knowledge to make your own 'perfect creatures' is another, but Bacon believed that postlapsarian man could improve his condition by knowledge and art and still believe in God and heaven, as do the inhabitants of the 'happy land' of Bensalem, which is a kind of paradise on earth. After all it is God who discovers Bensalem to the voyagers, Bensalem which appears to them as 'a picture of our salvation in heaven'.

To that extent Bacon's Bensalem belongs to the tradition of island paradises discovered in fiction by voyagers. But this, the first of many purely fictional islands in the South Seas, is not a natural paradise, but an artificial paradise. The sensory experiences are provided, not by odoriferous flowers, harmonious birds, and unashamedly naked island girls, like those encountered on the voyages of Mendaña and Quirós, but by the 'sound-houses' with their artificial birdsong, the 'perfume-houses' with their artificial smells, and by the 'houses of deceits of the senses', with their 'false apparitions, impostures and illusions'. It is remarkable that on this first South Sea island of fiction, the voyagers should discover, of all things, a 'happy land' of art, not nature, of synthesizers, telephones, aeroplanes, submarines, and the like. Yet, as we have been told, Bensalem is nonetheless a kind of promised land. The voyagers say that their 'tongues should first cleave to the roofs of [their] mouths' before they should forget Bensalem, echoing the words spoken by the Jews, weeping by the rivers of Babylon, and remembering Jerusalem.[142]

Amongst the statues of 'all principal inventors' in Salomon's House, there is 'the statua of your Columbus that discovered the West Indies'.[143] The importance of the art of navigation in Bensalem, which art 'is increased with you within these six-score years', has already been stressed by the Governor of the House of Strangers. From the Father of Salomon's House we learn further that, of the thirty-six Fellows, there are 'twelve that sail into foreign countries'.[144] If the voyagers of the Renaissance who sailed by art could discover a state of nature, they could also discover, by contrast, the state of art in Europe and the possibility of progress. They could discover a new world in Europe, as Bacon's voyagers discovered Bensalem, as Miranda on Prospero's island discovered a 'brave new world'. That is the meaning of Bacon's *New Atlantis*.

Burton considered utopias 'to be wished for, rather then effected'. Works like 'that new *Atlantis*' were 'witty fictions, but meer *Chimeras*', mere works of art.[145] But the example of Columbus gave Bacon hope that a new world of science could be discovered in fact as Bensalem was in fiction. As he wrote in the *Novum Organum*:

it is fit that I publish and set forth these conjectures of mine which make hope in this matter reasonable; just as Columbus did, before that wonderful voyage of his across the Atlantic, when he gave the reasons for his conviction that new lands and continents might be discovered besides those which were known before; which reasons, though rejected at first, were afterwards made good by experience, and were the causes and beginnings of great events.[146]

Columbus's reasons and convictions, of course, as we know, were nothing of the kind, and were afterwards disproved. But for Bacon, as for Quirós, he was the man whose vision of a New World, 'though rejected at first', was 'afterwards made good by experience'. Bacon's brave new world of scientific knowledge 'made good by experience' was itself only a hypothesis, not yet 'made good'. But he was convinced that a voyage in the course of progress would prove it true 'by experience', would discover that 'New Continent'. And 'even if the breath of hope which blows on us from that New Continent were fainter than it is and harder to perceive; yet the trial . . . must by all means be made'.[147]

In a preface to the posthumously published *New Atlantis: A Worke unfinished* (1627), Bacon's secretary, William Rawley, wrote:

This fable my Lord devised, to the end that he might exhibit therein a model or description of a college instituted for the interpreting of nature and the producing of great and marvellous works for the benefit of men, under the name of Salomon's House, or the College of the Six Days' Works. And even so far his Lordship hath proceeded, as to finish that part. Certainly the model is more vast and high than can possibly be imitated in all things; notwithstanding most things therein are within men's power to effect.[148]

Like his heroic, scientific Columbus, Bacon could give his reasons for his belief in a new world but, unlike this Columbus, he could make the voyage only in fiction. At the end of the unfinished *New Atlantis* appear the words 'The rest was not Perfected'.[149] Yet, as Cowley wrote in his ode 'To the Royal Society', employing the figure of the discoverer's vision from a mountain, Bacon, although he could not enter in himself, had led the way from 'Errors' and pointed out the promised land:

> Bacon, like Moses, led us forth at last,
> The barren Wilderness he past,
> Did on the very Border stand
> Of the blest promis'd Land,

And from the Mountains Top of his Exalted Wit,
Saw it himself, and shew'd us it.[150]

Sprat, too, in his *History of the Royal Society* (1667) to which Cowley's ode was prefixed, acknowledged the part played by the 'Mountains Top' of Bacon's wit, by his 'Imagination', as the basis for the Royal Society: Bacon 'had the true Imagination of the whole extent of this Enterprize, as it is now set on foot'.[151]

The model may have been 'vast and high' but it was not altogether beyond the power of men to effect. Nevertheless we should not forget the nature of the model, to which a brand new adjective was applied.[152] In the words of another of Bacon's many admirers, Joseph Glanvill, the '*Great* Man' had 'form'd a *Society* of *Experimenters* in a *Romantick Model*'.[153] The Royal Society, dedicated to the discovery of facts, was itself discovered in fiction. Burton had thought the *New Atlantis* a 'witty fiction' not to be 'effected' but others later in the century considered it, although 'Romantic', not incapable of being translated from South Sea fiction into English fact. John Evelyn, himself a traveller with scientific interests, wrote in 1661 that Bacon's 'stupendious *Idea*' of Salomon's House, 'however lofty, and to appearance *Romantic*, has yet in it nothing of Impossible to be effected'.[154]

Evelyn himself outlined a scheme for a college of experimental philosophy in a letter to Boyle, and notably, if unsuccessfully, so did Samuel Hartlib, another admirer of Salomon's House, whose *A Description of the Famous Kingdome of Macaria* (1641) was one of the earliest of such schemes.[155] Hartlib's kingdom never had the 'visible being' he hoped, but, by 1660, when he was advocating yet another exotic society, Antilia, such schemes were the order of the day.[156] Of these the one with the most immediate practical effect was Cowley's *A Proposition for the Advancement of Experimental Philosophy* (1661). Cowley's proposed 'Philosophical Colledge' was more modest than Salomon's House, which he described as 'a Project for Experiments that can never [itself] be Experimented', but nevertheless he stipulated that 'of the twenty Professors four be always travelling beyond Seas' in Europe, Asia, Africa, and America.[157] These 'four Professors Itinerant', 'at their going abroad', were to 'take a solemn Oath never to write any thing to the Colledge, but what . . . they shall fully believe to be true'.[158]

The Royal Society itself, which can be said to date at least from 1660 (Cowley being a member of the group from 1661), received its Charter, and became properly Royal, in 1662. One of its earliest publications in its *Philosophical Transactions* was a paper entitled 'Directions for Sea-men, bound for far Voyages', which directed the far-voyagers 'to study *Nature* rather than *Books*, and from the Observations, made of the *Phaenomena* and Effects she presents, to compose such a History of Her, as may hereafter serve to build a Solid and Useful Philosophy upon'.[159]

The collection of the vast amount of empirical data for a 'Natural and Experimental History' such as Bacon had envisaged inevitably necessitated a co-operative effort, 'requiring as it does many people to help', and these helpers, by the nature of the work and of Bacon's method, which 'leaves but little to the acuteness of wits, but places nearly all wits and understandings nearly on a level', did not have to be learned men.[160] Indeed the seventeenth-century practitioners of the experimental philosophy, the '*Baconical* philosophers' (as a conservative opponent referred to them), tended to favour those whose natural senses were not blunted and befuddled by too much contact with books or culture.[161] Anticipating them, Purchas had pointed out the merits of travellers 'of meane qualitie': 'I mention Authors sometimes, of meane qualitie, for the meanest have sense to observe that which themselves see, more certainly then the contemplations and *Theorie* of the more learned.'[162] The Royal Society's preference for the less learned is evident from its views on prose, which Sprat said the Society wished to see returned to 'the primitive purity': 'They have exacted from all their members, a close, naked, natural way of speaking; . . . preferring the language of Artizans, Countrymen, and Merchants, before that, of Wits, or Scholars.'[163] We should notice the metaphor applied to language by those who wished to strip it, as Sprat did, of 'these specious *Tropes* and *Figures*'.[164] The 'naked truth' was the catch-phrase of an age which aimed to discover Nature in a 'naked, natural' prose.[165] We may recall here Montaigne's preference for the testimony of his servant, 'simple et grossier', as well as his views on prose style, which he thought ought to imitate 'cette desbauche qui se voit en nostre jeunesse, au port de leurs vestemens'.[166] It was also Bacon's aim, if not his invariable practice, 'to set everything forth, as far as may be, plainly and perspicuously (for nakedness of the mind is still, as nakedness of the body once was, the companion of innocence and simplicity)'.[167] In his enthusiasm to discover Nature Sprat was uninhibited by thoughts of shame, or its cause, as his own 'specious *Tropes*' reveal: 'The Beautiful Bosom of *Nature* will be Expos'd to our view: we shall enter into its Garden, and taste of its *Fruits*.'[168]

And where better to discover Nature than in a state of nature? The philosophers of the Royal Society, of course, had admonished the voyagers 'to study *Nature*, rather than *Books*'. But, as philosophers themselves do not inhabit a state of nature, and as Cowley's project for 'Professors Itinerant' proved itself to be a project that could not be experimented, it was necessarily in books that the philosophers looked to discover Nature, in travel books. And so it was that the accounts of the voyagers, those travellers' tales traditionally associated with lying fictions, did indeed form the basis, as the Royal Society's *Transactions* put it, for 'a Solid and Useful Philosophy'.

At the very outset of the discovery of the New World, Vespucci had reported 'people entirely naked' who 'live according to nature', not only with no clothes, but also with 'no religious faith' and 'no king'.[169] The impact of such revelations was slow, but, as Purchas said, travellers provided 'sensible materials (as it were with Stones, Brickes and Mortar) to those universall Speculators for their Theoricall structures' and, as the experimental philosophers turned to travel literature, the 'naked truth' they discovered had consequences for religion and politics as well as philosophy.[170] Montaigne, we know, had already recognized some of the philosophical consequences and had also, through the mouths of the 'cannibales' at

Rouen, clearly expressed the political consequences. But, as Geoffroy Atkinson and R. W. Frantz have shown, many seventeenth- and eighteenth-century theorists of religion and government, as well as philosophers, both in France and England, made use of the exotic new facts as 'Stones, Brickes and Mortar' to construct their arguments.[171]

The English Deists, for example, derived support for their belief in a 'natural religion' from the voyagers, in particular, Frantz says, from observations such as those of the exemplary religious practices of the natives of Madagascar contained in a work entitled *Madagascar: or, Robert Drury's Journal, during Fifteen Years Captivity on that Island* (1729).[172] Political liberals, too, would have been pleased to read in that work that the natives of Madagascar observed 'no Distinction or Property of Lands' and made 'no religious Scruples of their Kings being their Master by divine Authority'.[173]

The various, and variously reported, exotic social systems of peoples supposedly living in a state of nature could provide evidence for proponents of various political theories, who, for all their differences, shared these two assumptions: that a political theory required a historical basis in man's original, natural condition, and that distant savages provided contemporary evidence of such a condition. Such evidence, of course, was open to interpretation. For Hobbes, who sought to justify absolutism, the conditions in a state of nature, so praised by Montaigne, were decidedly nasty. In a well-known passage in *Leviathan* (1651) the Golden Age topos is adapted to list the absence, not of the defects of civilized culture, but of its benefits. Without all these, the life of man was 'solitary, poore, nasty, brutish, and short'. The 'savage people in many places of *America*', he added, '. . . live at this day in that brutish manner'.[174] For Locke, on the other hand, in the second of his *Two Treatises of Government* (1690), the 'State of Nature' was 'a State of perfect Freedom . . . [and] also of Equality'.[175] Locke did not place his 'State of Nature' in America, but the frequent references in the second of his *Treatises* to 'an Indian, in the Woods of America' and to 'the People of America who . . . enjoy'd their own natural freedom' are indications of the model he had in mind. As he said: 'in the beginning all the world was America'.[176]

The various areas of controversy touched by the voyagers' new facts were themselves interconnected. Just as political discussion raised religious issues, so too did philosophical discussion, and so it was that God, and the savages who did not believe in him, had inevitably to appear and play their parts in the empirical philosophy of knowledge. When Locke wished to prove that all knowledge is founded on experience he had to dispose of the doctrine of innate ideas, which he did by showing that such ideas were not universal. With this aim in *An Essay Concerning Humane Understanding* (1690) he turned to the works of the voyagers for evidence. Dismissing one innate idea after another, he came to the most important of all, for 'If any Idea can be imagin'd innate, the Idea of God may, of all others'. And yet:

Besides the Atheists, taken notice of amongst the Ancients, and left branded upon the Records of History, hath not Navigation discovered, in these latter Ages, whole Nations, at the Bay of Soldania, in Brazil, and the Caribee Islands, &c. amongst whom there was to be found no Notion of a God.[177]

In this fashion Locke goes on, adding the civilized Siamites and Chinese to the catalogue of savages who do not believe in a God and will serve to refute philosophers who believe in Descartes. And, at the bottom of the page, supporting his 'Solid and Useful Philosophy' from the footnotes, are the voyagers, the new authorities. Locke's philosophy was based on experience, not authority, but even Locke had no experience of savages. Of the books he cites many are in French (he even cites a French translation of an English traveller's account) and amongst them is Montaigne's unacknowledged source, Jean de Léry, who had reported of the Brazilian 'Sauvages nommez Tououpinambaoults' that: 'ils ne co[n]fessent, ni adoret, aucuns dieux celestes ni terrestres.'[178]

And indeed Montaigne had anticipated Locke, who demonstrated in his *Essay*—with the support of the voyagers, of course—that the workings of the human conscience, like belief in a God, were not universal and were therefore not 'Proof of innate Priniciples'.[179] In his essay 'De la coustume' Montaigne had cited custom after custom, not neglecting those of the New World, to prove that: 'Les loix de la conscience, que nous disons naistre de nature, naissent de la coustume.'[180] In the 'Apologie de Raimond Sebond' Montaigne had reached the same conclusion for which Locke was aiming, and reached it by means of the same method of argument. There were no laws, he said, 'empreintes en l'humain genre par la condition de leur propre essence'. The only possible proof of such innate principles could be 'l'université de l'approbation', and yet they would be contradicted 'non par une nation, mais par plusieurs'.[181] But Montaigne had gone rather further than Locke (who was no follower of Sextus). Where Locke had used the savages and the same argument to prove, ultimately, that the only solid basis for truth was experience, Montaigne had used the same means, more than once in his *Essais*, to prove that there could be no solid basis for truth, that 'nous n'avons autre mire de la verité et de la raison que l'exemple et idée des opinions et usances du païs où nous sommes', as he wrote in 'Des cannibales'.[182] In the 'Apologie' Montaigne applied Locke's argument to truth itself, which, if it had a real essence, 'doit avoir un visage pareil et universel', and asked, rhetorically: 'Quelle verité [est-ce] que ces montaignes bornent, qui est mensonge au monde qui se tient au delà?'[183]

Montaigne's scepticism, of course, like Locke's empiricism, depended on belief in travellers' accounts of the new world 'que nous voyons'—vicariously—'par experience'. This faith was shared also, to a considerable extent, by Locke's critics. Edward Stillingfleet, Bishop of Worcester, did not argue with Locke's use of the testimony of travellers to prove that ideas of a God are not innate; he argued instead that Locke's travelling authorities were 'very ill chosen' and that 'their Testimony is contradicted' by that of other, better chosen, travellers.[184] To which Locke replied, in defence of 'the credibility of those Authors I have quoted', that they were respectable and reliable men: Sir Thomas Roe was 'an Ambassador from the King of *England*'; John Ovington (author of *A Voyage to Suratt*) was 'a Divine of the Church of *England*'.[185] Stillingfleet was adamantly unsatisfied and in a work published posthumously in 1701 continued to dispute Locke's choice of travellers, citing at length the testimony of several other travellers, 'the most free and disinteress'd Persons', on the religious beliefs of the American Indians and the Hottentots.[186]

Charles Gildon, likewise, disagreed with Locke's choice of 'Authorities', not his philosophical method. It was the former, not the latter, 'which the last account of [the Cape of Good Hope] proves to be false'.[187] And in Scotland Sir William Anstruther argued along similar lines, that Locke's conclusion was based 'on too slender Grounds', not because it was based on travellers' accounts, but because 'the contrary is discovered by a more accurate Enquiry of those who travelled'.[188] None of these gentlemen doubted Locke's method of building philosophical conclusions on the basis of travellers' reports; it was for them only a question of which travellers should be believed—theirs not Locke's.

Shaftesbury, however, raised an old-fashioned doubt about Locke's authorities, mocking a philosopher who drew conclusions about the idea of God from the evidence about barbarian savages in barbarian travellers' tales. Thus he protested against the revolution we first noticed in Montaigne's 'Des cannibales', where philosophical authority passes from Plato and Aristotle to a servant, and finally to savages:

the credulous Mr Locke, with his *Indian*, Barbarian Stories of wild Nations, that have no such Idea, (as Travellers, learned Authors! and Men of Truth! and great Philosophers! have informed him;) . . . had more Faith, and was more learn'd in Modern *Wonder-Writers*, than in Antient Philosophy.[189]

In *Advice to an Author* (1710) Shaftesbury criticized more generally the new philosophical faith in those old mongers of wonders and monsters, the travellers: 'Monsters and Monster Lands were never more in request: And we may often see a Philosopher, or a Wit, run a Tale-gathering in those *idle Desarts*, as familiarly as the Silliest Woman, or merest Boy.'[190] He scoffed at the new method of such philosophers, who placed their faith in travellers rather than in 'Antient Philosophers', and studied the 'monstrous Accounts of monstrous Men' rather than the civilized accounts of civilized men. These supposedly sceptical philosophers were not very sceptical—were indeed very credulous—in their faith in travellers' tales:

It must certainly be something else than *Incredulity*, which fashions the Taste and Judgment of many of these Gentlemen, whom we hear censur'd as Atheists, for attempting to philosophize after a newer manner than has been known of late . . . Historys of *Incas* or *Iroquois*, written by Fryars and Missionarys, Pirates and Renegades, Sea-Captains and trusty Travellers, pass for authentick Records, and are *canonical*, with the Virtuoso's of this sort . . . They have far more Pleasure in hearing the monstrous Accounts of monstrous

Men, and Manners; than the politest and best Narrations of the Affairs, the Governments, and Lives of the wisest and most polish'd People.[191]

Shaftesbury's protest brings home to us the changed fashion with regard to travellers' tales, basic texts for builders of the new empirical philosophy, and crucial evidence for or against a universal belief in a God. Shaftesbury also doubted, with good reason, the 'Veracity or Judgment of the Relater; who cannot be supposed to know sufficiently the Mysteries and Secrets of those Barbarians; whose Language they but imperfectly know'.[192] Certainly there were grounds to doubt the veracity of pirates, sea-captains, missionaries, and even royal ambassadors, and to doubt their capacity as social anthropologists, but while Shaftesbury doubted their veracity he did not doubt their reality. While he suspected that the authors of travel books might be liars, he did not suspect that they might not be travellers. But that work, *Madagascar: or, Robert Drury's Journal*, for example, with its thought-provoking accounts of the politics and religion of the natives, has, as we shall see, been pronounced 'clearly a work of fiction'.[193] Its author, according to the scholar J. R. Moore, was no pirate, sea-captain, or missionary, but Daniel Defoe, the same who wrote *Robinson Crusoe* and its Preface: 'The Editor believes the thing to be a just History of Fact; neither is there any Appearance of Fiction in it.'[194]

It is to such fictitious travels, without 'any Appearance of Fiction', that we must turn in the next chapter, where we shall discover also another philosophical college in the unknown South Seas, the Academy of Balnibarbi. If the travellers could provide 'facts' for philosophers, so too could the authors of fictions.

3

Far-Fetched Facts and Fiction

The Editor believes the thing to be a just History of Fact; neither is there any Appearance of Fiction in it.

(Defoe, Preface to *Robinson Crusoe*)[1]

Madagascar: or, Robert Drury's Journal, during Fifteen Years Captivity on that Island was published in London in 1729. The title page claimed that 'The Whole is a Faithful Narrative of *Matters of Fact*, interspers'd with Variety of surprising Incidents', 'Written by Himself', and at the beginning of the book appeared a testimonial by a Captain William Mackett:

This is to Certify, That Robert Drury, Fifteen Years a Slave in Madagascar, now living in London, was redeem'd from thence and brought into England, his Native Country, by Myself. I esteem him an honest, industrious Man, of good Reputation, and do firmly believe that the Account he gives of his Strange and Surprising Adventures is Genuine and Authentick.[2]

There followed an anonymous Preface, with this opening sentence:

At the first Appearance of this Treatise, I make no Doubt of its being taken for such another Romance as *Robinson Cruso*; but whoever expects to find here the fine Inventions of a prolifick Brain will be deceiv'd; for so far as every Body concern'd in the Publication knows, it is nothing else but a plain, honest Narrative of Matter of Fact.[3]

The author of the Preface went on to explain that, although the 'Original was wrote by Robert Drury', the 'Transcriber' (presumably the author of the Preface) had 'put it in a more agreeable Method'.[4] He also vouched for the authority of Captain Mackett, 'a Person of the highest Reputation for Integrity and Honour', and insisted in particular that those parts of Drury's account which were about 'Natural Religion' or the 'Original of Government' were 'Facts' and that, on those subjects, 'the Transcriber is only answerable for putting some Reflections in the Author's Mouth'.[5] Some such reflections follow in the Preface, including a critique of Hobbes based on the Madagascar evidence, which shows 'the true State of Nature: From hence arise benign Dispositions, Softness of Temper' and 'the Devotion of these People, who seek God on every Occasion'.[6]

The account itself, *Madagascar: or, Robert Drury's Journal*, tells the story of a boy who went to sea against his parents' advice aboard a ship called the *Degrave* and—'Providence herein justly punish'd my Disobedience'—was shipwrecked at

Madagascar, where he lived among the natives for many years before being rescued by the reputable Captain Mackett, who found a 'wild Englishman', 'naked
except the Lamber' (i.e. the 'lamba', the native dress), who 'could speak but little
English', but whom he 'soon restor'd . . . to an European Form'.[7] The work contains, in addition to the kind of 'Facts' about the 'state of Nature' referred to in the
Preface, a generous quantity of botanical, zoological, and ethnographical information, including a useful 'Vocabulary of the *Madagascar* Language'.[8]

'At the first Appearance of this Treatise', and for many years after, it seems to
have been accepted as a true story. A reviewer in the *Critical Review* of a new
edition published in 1807 considered *Madagascar: or, Robert Drury's Journal* 'in
the main founded on fact', and in the *Monthly Review* the reviewer declared that
'the genuineness of Drury's Adventures does not admit of question'.[9] Later in the
nineteenth century, missionaries, geographers, the compiler of a *Malagasy–English
Dictionary*, and historians with firsthand knowledge of Madagascar and the Malagasy
people had no doubt of the work's status as fact, apart from some inaccuracies in
the Malagasy 'state of Nature' which could be attributed to the sentiments of the
'Transcriber'.[10] 'Des malgaches qui ont des larmes aux yeux, ce n'est pas commun!'
scoffed one hard-bitten old hand.[11] In 1911, *Madagascar: or, Robert Drury's Journal*
was cited by the *Encyclopaedia Britannica* as an authoritative work on Madagascar.[12]

In 1890, however, Captain Pasfield Oliver, himself an authority on Madagascar,
argued in his introduction to a new edition of *Madagascar: or, Robert Drury's
Journal* that the work was indebted to Étienne de Flacourt's *Histoire de Madagascar*
(1658) and, comparing passages with *Captain Singleton* and other works by Defoe,
suggested that 'the editing of Drury was done by Defoe, or at all events by one
who aped Defoe's methods closely'.[13] Since then the issue has been whether Defoe
merely edited the work or completely fabricated it. In 1939 J. R. Moore, an
authority on Defoe rather than Madagascar, produced a study of *Madagascar: or,
Robert Drury's Journal* which dismissed Robert Drury as nothing more than 'a
convenient name to give a semblance of truth to the story' and concluded that: 'In
style, in method, and in ideas it is a characteristic romance by the author of
Robinson Crusoe'.[14]

In 1943 Moore published a further study, to reinforce the conclusion of his
previous work and to explain the apparent paradox that, although 'the *Journal* is
clearly a work of fiction, expressing many of Defoe's own interests and observations and written throughout in his own style', nevertheless 'it gives one of the
most realistic accounts of Madagascar in existence'.[15] Again dismissing 'any notion
of an actual journal', and doubtful of the influence of Flacourt's *Histoire*, Moore
suggested other sources for Defoe, chiefly: Robert Knox's *An Historical Relation of
the Island of Ceylon* (1681), which affords some parallels to Drury's story but little
information about Madagascar, and 'A Relation of Three Years Sufferings of
Robert Everard, upon the Coast of Assada near Madagascar' (first published in the
1732 edition of Churchill's *Voyages*).[16] As Assada is an island only a few miles from
Madagascar, Everard's 'Relation' might have been more promising than Knox's

Ceylon as a potential source for Defoe, but—inconveniently—Everard's 'Relation' was published three years after *Madagascar: or, Robert Drury's Journal*, and one year after Defoe's death. Moore's attempts to circumvent this difficulty involved him in 'fascinating speculations', and in a 'tempting supposition' which is not hard to resist.[17]

In addition Moore provided a number of textual parallels in which, he claimed, 'we recognise the author's style'.[18] Crusoe's description of 'my dog', for example, 'which was now grown very old and crazy [infirm]', is echoed in *Drury's Journal* by the description of a 'pirate ship growing old and crazy', and the words 'a miserable slave' in *Robinson Crusoe* are matched in *Drury's Journal* by the words 'my miserable slavery'.[19] The words 'heartily' and 'in general' are also, Moore noted, to be found in both works.[20] It was Moore's concluding chapter, however, on the 'Underlying Sense of Fact' in *Madagascar: or, Robert Drury's Journal*, that seemed to him to clinch his argument that the work is a fiction by Defoe, for this above all is 'characteristic of Defoe—the underlying sense of fact'.[21]

In 1961 *Drury's Journal* was the subject of another book-length study, by A. W. Secord, a less prejudiced student of Defoe's sources, who was able to prove that Robert Drury was a real person, that he was aboard the *Degrave*, which was shipwrecked at Madagascar, and that (less certainly, but very probably) he was rescued by Captain Mackett, having spent almost fourteen years on Madagascar. For the outer framework of *Madagascar: or, Robert Drury's Journal*, therefore, Secord was able to provide convincing corroboration. The core and major part of the story, however, which tells of Drury's life among the natives of Madagascar between 1703 and 1716, 'cannot, except here and there, be authenticated with documentary evidence', as Secord admitted, giving the very good reason that 'there was at that time no written language among the natives'.[22] Having come to this full stop only after a good deal of rewarding reading in archives and maritime records, Secord justifiably felt that he had found enough evidence to decide that Robert Drury was probably the 'principal source' for the whole of *Drury's Journal*, but he went no further, adding that 'this conclusion agrees . . . with the assumption that Defoe was the "transcriber" who put Drury's manuscript into "a more agreeable Method"'.[23]

Secord's conclusion about Drury is well founded, but not the 'assumption' about Defoe, which survives from Secord's assertion in an article in 1951 that 'Defoe must have been that transcriber'.[24] The external evidence supposedly connecting Defoe with *Drury's Journal* is evidence of no such thing. That the brother of Mrs Veal (of Defoe's *True Relation*) married the daughter of the *Degrave*'s dead captain does not imply that Defoe transcribed *Drury's Journal*, and that Drury lived at Stoke Newington on his return, near Defoe, is a supposition without foundation.[25] According to eighteenth-century testimony, Drury lived 'at his house in Lincoln's Inn Fields', where he was often seen to throw a javelin with Malagasy accuracy, 'and strike a small mark at a surprizing distance'.[26] His bones are in the Strand under King's College, Defoe's in Bunhill Fields, Finsbury, and any meeting between them is, like the legendary meeting between Defoe and Selkirk, a matter of mere supposition, not to say fiction.[27]

The case for connecting Defoe with *Drury's Journal* rests, therefore, on internal evidence—on verbal and narrative parallels of no significance in eighteenth-century accounts of travel, where 'old and crazy' ships or dogs and 'miserable' slaveries, for example, are surely not distinctive signs of Defoe's diction or imagination. Such evidence would not seem to constitute proof, but the connection between Defoe and *Madagascar: or, Robert Drury's Journal*, supposedly established by Moore, is generally accepted as satisfactorily proven, despite some recent scepticism about the whole grossly swollen canon of Defoe's writings.[28] The book is routinely ascribed to Defoe by his critics and is listed as his work in the British Library catalogue, revised on the advice of J. R. Moore, as it is in the standard bibliography of Defoe's writings, compiled by J. R. Moore.[29]

Why should a reputable authority on Defoe devote so much labour to the composition of a testimonial to prove that this popular English novelist must be the author of an accurate, unprecedented, full-page description of the *Centetes ecaudatus* (an animal found only in Madagascar)? 'It is about the Bigness of a Cat, but its Nose, Eyes, and Ears are like a Hog; it has Bristles also on its Back, and no Tail; the Feet are like a Rabbit's. Their chief Food is Beetles and young Snails, which they rout up with their Noses [etc.].'[30] Why attempt to prove that Defoe was the author of long accounts of the '*Vounturk . . . a* Tree, or Plant', of the Malagasy burial rites, and of the ceremony of circumcision, complete with blessing on the initiated boy? 'Tyhew Deaan Unghorray, Deaan Antemoor, Deaan Anebeleshy, Deaan Androfertraer, Deaan Meguddumdummateun, an Ruey Owley, Heer-razehu, ittoey Zorjer, ittoey acquo toey Anomebay loyhe ittoey handrabeck enney Raffa loyhe.'[31] Why should Defoe have been the author, or even the 'Transcriber' of all this, labouring away at Stoke Newington on a 'Vocabulary of the *Madagascar* Language' containing the handy Malagasy words 'wooley', 'munghatchs', 'mermauny', and 'mungary', for 'arse', 'fart', 'piss', and 'shit'?[32] The question worth pursuing here is not whether Defoe wrote *Drury's Journal*, but why the difference between a narrative of travel and a novel should be so hard to tell.

During the Restoration period and the early eighteenth century the publication in England of accounts of voyages and foreign lands, which had lapsed since the times of Hakluyt and Purchas, was revived. With the beginning of the eighteenth century the fashion for travel literature, second in popularity only to theology, became established.[33] 'There are no books which I more delight in than in travels', enthused Steele in the *Tatler* in 1710, but Shaftesbury was a more critical observer of the new vogue, remarking in the same year that: '*Barbarian* Customs, Savage Manners, *Indian* Wars, and Wonders of the *Terra incognita*, employ our leisure Hours, and are the chief materials to furnish out a Library. These are in our present Days what *Books of Chivalry* were, in our Forefathers.'[34] So the wonders of savage manners and distant lands, the exotic facts of ethnography and geography, replaced the wonders of courtly rituals and the enchanted past, the nostalgic

fictions of chivalry and history. The relation between travel and romance is as old
as Polo and 'Mandeville', we know, and prefigures the confusion we are now
witnessing between travel and the novel. As the fresh wonders of travel opened a
more credible escape than the faded wonders of romance, the way was paved with
factual exactitude. Exit the fabulous dragon and enter the *Centetes ecaudatus*, cat-
sized, hog-faced, and rabbit-footed, monstrous but down to earth, breathing no
fire but rooting up beetles, not to mention young snails, with its nose. Far-fetched
facts provided entertainment as well as edification, filling the casual reader's
'leisure Hours' as well as the philosopher's working day, and were imported,
therefore, or manufactured, at a profit. Swift's 'project which will tend to the great
benefit of all mankind, & produce a handsom Revenue to the Author', satirizes the
lucrative fashion for exotic information: 'He intends to print by Subscription in 96.
large volumes in *folio*, an exact Description of *Terra Australis incognita*, collected
with great care & pains from 999. learned & pious Authors of undoubted veracity.'[35]

The renewed popularity of travel literature reflects increased maritime as well as
literary activity, and the most important figure here, in both spheres, is the buccaneering writer William Dampier, whose voyages and accounts of voyages inspired a number of other travels and texts: the voyages, for example, of Edward
Cooke, Woodes Rogers, and George Shelvocke, who went around the world and
furnished the libraries with Cooke's *A Voyage to the South Sea, and Round the
World* (1712), Rogers's *A Cruising Voyage Round the World* (1712), and Shelvocke's
A Voyage Round the World by Way of the Great South Sea (1726).

The publication in 1697 of Dampier's first book, *A New Voyage Round the
World*, is usually cited as the initial cause of these far-reaching effects.[36] The book
went through two editions in the year of its publication, a third in 1698, and made
a literary lion of an old sea-dog.[37] Dampier, plundering the Spanish Main and
dining with Pepys and Evelyn, revived interest not only in voyages and accounts
of voyages generally, but specifically in the South Seas, where Selkirk danced with
his goats and Gulliver travelled.[38] Dampier the sailor discovered little of the South
Seas, but Dampier the author discovered much. 'To his countrymen he discovered', as one historian says, 'the whole South Seas.'[39]

Pre-eminent among the sailors of his time as a far-traveller and an author,
Dampier was also an amateur scientist, his books discovering to botanists and
zoologists the distant plants and fishes to which they gave his name—*Dampiera
incana*, *Dampiera cyclopthalmus*, *Dampiera spilopterus*, etc.—while geographers and
sailors were also indebted to his prose for its clear observations of mysterious
winds and tides.[40] He was, in short, exactly the kind of traveller to whom the Royal
Society had addressed its 'Directions for Sea-men, bound for far Voyages', and in
return he addressed his travels to the Royal Society. In the dedication of his first
book, *A New Voyage*, 'To the Right Honourable Charles Mountague, Esq; President of the Royal Society', Dampier avowed 'a hearty Zeal for the promoting of
useful knowledge' and a desire 'to bring in my Gleanings here and there in Remote
Regions, to that general Magazine, of the knowledge of Foreign Parts'.[41]

The Royal Society's 'Directions' to 'study *Nature*' are again reflected in Dampier's Preface to his *A Voyage to New Holland* (1703), which also expresses his preference for the 'naked, natural' prose of 'Mathematical plainness' that Sprat had recommended when declaring the Royal Society's 'constant Resolution . . . to return back to the primitive purity, and shortness, when men delivered so many *things*, almost in an equal number of *words*'. Proudly, Dampier remarked that:

It has been Objected against me by some, that my Accounts and Descriptions of Things are dry and jejune, not filled with variety of pleasant Matter, to divert and gratify the Curious Reader. How far this is true, I must leave to the World to judge. But if I have been exactly and strictly careful to give only *True* Relations and Descriptions of Things (as I am sure I have;) and if my Descriptions be such as may be of use not only to my self (which I have already in good measure experienced) but also to others in future Voyages; and likewise to such Readers at home as are more desirous of a Plain and Just Account of the true Nature and State of the Things described, than of a Polite and Rhetorical Narrative: I hope all the Defects in my Stile, will meet with an easy and ready Pardon.[42]

It would be too simple to attribute Dampier's zeal for 'a Plain and Just Account of the true Nature and State of the Things described' directly to the Royal Society's 'Directions' and to its preference, to quote Sprat again, for 'the language of Artizans, Countrymen, and Merchants, before that, of Wits, or Scholars'. Dampier was a tenant farmer's son from East Coker, Somerset, and his protestations have their precedent in the Renaissance voyagers' plain and simple experience of the New World, as his response to the Royal Society has its complement in Bacon's response to the voyagers. Far-voyagers have a particular relation to the state of 'true Nature', to which it was supposed they travelled, and a particular relation also to a 'Plain' language, which must reveal that 'true Nature' to the readers of a civilized culture, in a 'naked, natural' way. Distant travellers like Dampier, their language naturally more like that of Merchants than Wits, travel naturally in the direction advocated by the Royal Society for language. They 'return back to the primitive purity'. The paradox Sprat's metaphors reveal, scientific progress as regress, is the paradox of the voyagers, sailing by art to nature.

Dampier's protestations of truth, like his plain language resembling Sprat's 'Mathematical plainness', are signs not only of the traveller's new tendency to science, but also of his old tendency to lie. Plain language reveals the 'true Nature' of things and also the traveller's need to convince the reader of the 'true Nature' of the traveller. An eighteenth-century sailor turned South Sea historian, James Burney (brother of Fanny), paid a typical tribute to Dampier's 'useful information' and also to the manner in which he 'communicated his information'—'in a style perfectly unassuming, equally free from affectation and from the most distant appearance of invention'.[43] Such is the style of Dampier—and also of Defoe. Off the west coast of Australia Dampier caught an admirably mathematical shark in his 'naked, natural' prose:

Among them we caught one which was 11 Foot long. The space between its 2 Eyes was 20 Inches, and 18 Inches from one Corner of his Mouth to the other. Its Maw was like a Leather Sack, very thick, and so tough that a sharp Knife could scarce cut it: In which we found the Head and Boans of a *Hippopotomus*; the hairy Lips of which were still sound and not putrified, and the Jaw was also firm, out of which we pluckt a great many Teeth, 2 of them 8 Inches long, and as big as a Mans Thumb, small at one end, and a little crooked; the rest not above half so long.[44]

The whole passage is mathematical, but the shark was real and the hippopotamus was not. The seas around Australia have been searched for Dampier's 'Hippopotomus', but none has ever been found, because none exists.[45] Language of perfect 'Mathematical plainness' can describe a fiction as accurately as a fact, intentionally as well as unintentionally.

Between 1675 and 1678 Dampier spent about two years mostly cutting and loading logwood at the Bay of Campeachy (Campeche) in Mexico, like the captain of the ship encountered by Gulliver on his fourth voyage, 'who was going to the Bay of Campechy to cut Logwood'.[46] Dampier's experiences with the logwood cutters and the bands of buccaneers in the Bay of Campeachy and the Caribbean (which precede the events described in his first publication, *A New Voyage*) were published in his second book, *Voyages and Descriptions* (1699), and two of these experiences have attracted the attention of historians of literature. Landing on the beach of 'a sandy Bay' on an island near Cuba, Dampier and some companions in search of 'Beef and Hog' noticed the prints made by 'much footing of Men and Boys; the Impressions seemed to be about 8 or 10 days old, we supposed them to be the track of Spanish Hunters. This troubled us a little.'[47] This passage, combining the discovery of footprints with fear of a potential enemy, has been proposed as Defoe's inspiration for the famous footprint in *Robinson Crusoe*, but the suggestion seems rather unnecessary.[48] Footprints, even on sandy beaches, are surely not beyond the reach of Defoe's own experience or imagination.

Dampier's description of the spider monkeys of Campeachy is more unusual, and makes a more vivid impression:

The Monkies that are in these Parts are the ugliest I ever saw. They are much bigger than a Hare, and have great Tails about two foot and half long. The under-side of their Tails is all bare, with a black hard skin; but the upper side, and all the Body is covered with course, long, black, staring Hair . . . They were a great Company dancing from Tree to Tree, over my Head; chattering and making a terrible Noise, and a great many grim Faces, and shewing Antick Gestures. Some broke down dry Sticks and threw at me; others scattered their Urine and Dung about my Ears.[49]

Dampier's experience was not unique in the literature of Restoration and early eighteenth-century travel, and there is no firm evidence that Swift read Dampier's *Voyages and Descriptions*.[50] It is no insult to Swift's famously excremental imagination, however, if we compare Gulliver's experience with that of his 'Cousin *Dampier*', as Swift called him.[51] Abandoned in Houyhnhnmland by a mutinous crew, Gulliver encounters some strange creatures:

Their Heads and Breasts were covered with a thick Hair, some frizled and others lank, they had Beards like Goats, and a long ridge of Hair down their Backs, and the fore-parts of their Legs and Feet, but the rest of their Bodies were bare, so that I might see their Skins, which were of a brown buff Colour. They had no Tails, nor any Hair at all on their Buttocks, except about the *Anus* . . . Upon the whole, I never beheld in all my Travels so disagreeable an Animal . . . [A] Herd of at least forty came flocking about me from the next Field, houling and making odious Faces . . . Several of this cursed Brood getting hold of the Branches behind leaped up in the Tree, from whence they began to discharge their Excrements on my Head . . .[52]

In a way, of course, Yahoos are no more exotic than footprints, but not Yahoos like those of Houyhnhnmland, who 'climbed high Trees, as nimbly as a Squirrel', and 'would often spring, and bound, and leap with prodigious Agility'.[53]

Dampier's *A New Voyage Round the World* does not describe a single voyage, but many, back and forth and from place to place, which eventually took him round the world and returned him to England, after about twelve and a half years. His adventures on these voyages are, as he says in his Preface, a 'Thread', and on this 'Thread' he connects descriptions of 'such Observables as I met with', which he recorded in his journal.[54] Having tramped across America, from the Pacific to the Caribbean via the Isthmus of Darien, with his journal enclosed in a 'large Joint of Bambo', Dampier found himself in the Pacific again in 1684, when his ship called at the island of Juan Fernandez for refreshment.[55] On this island, where Selkirk would be marooned in 1704, Dampier met Selkirk's precursor, 'a *Moskito Indian*, whom we left here when we were chaced hence by three *Spanish* Ships in the year 1681'.[56] This Indian, 'named *Will*', has not gone unnoticed by those in search of Defoe's sources and, more to the point, was not missed by Selkirk's discoverer, Woodes Rogers, who remarked in his account of Selkirk in *A Cruising Voyage* that '*Dampier* talks of a *Moskito Indian* . . . who . . . liv'd here three years alone, and shifted much in the same manner as Mr. *Selkirk* did'.[57] The passage in Dampier's *A New Voyage* is worth quoting at length, not only because Will may be a model for Robinson Crusoe, but as an illustration of Dampier's plain and precise ethnography. Such laborious descriptions of primitive tools, artefacts, and techniques were unusual, before *Robinson Crusoe*, in fiction, but are turned by Defoe to the purpose of depicting the particular culture of Crusoe—his tools, artefacts, and techniques, his house-building, planting, and construction of a canoe 'such as the Natives of those Climates make'.[58]

This *Indian* lived here alone above 3 years, and altho he was several times sought after by the *Spaniards*, who knew he was left on the Island, yet they could never find him. He was in the Woods hunting for Goats, when Captain *Watlin* drew off his men, and the Ship was under sail before he came back to shore. He had with him his Gun and a Knife, with a small Horn of Powder, and a few Shot; which being spent, he contrived a way by notching his

Knife, to saw the barrel of his Gun into small pieces, wherewith he made Harpoons, Lances, Hooks and a long Knife; heating the pieces first in the fire, which he struck with his Gun-flint, and a piece of the barrel of his Gun, which he hardened; having learnt to do that among the *English*. The hot pieces of Iron he would hammer out and bend as he pleased with Stones, and saw them with his jagged Knife, or grind them to an edge by long labour, and harden them to a good temper, as there was occasion. All this may seem strange to those that are not acquainted with the Sagacity of the *Indians*; but it is no more than these *Moskito* men are accustomed to in their own Country, where they make their own Fishing and Striking Instruments, without either Forge or Anvil; tho they spend a great deal of time about them.

Other Wild *Indians* who have not the use of Iron, which the *Moskito* men have from the *English*, make Hatchets of a very hard stone, with which they will cut down Trees, (the Cotton Tree especially, which is a soft tender Wood) to build their Houses or make Canoas; and though in working their Canoas hollow, they cannot dig them so neat and thin, yet they will make them fit for their service. This their digging or hatchet-work they help out by fire; whether for the felling of the Trees, or for the making the inside of their Canoa hollow . . . But to return to our *Moskito* man on the Isle of *John Fernando*. With such Instruments as he made in that manner, he got such Provision as the Island afforded; either Goats or Fish. He told us that at first he was forced to eat Seal, which is very ordinary Meat, before he had made Hooks: but afterwards he never kill'd any Seals but to make lines, cutting their skins into thongs. He had a little House or Hut half a Mile from the Sea, which was lined with Goats skin; his Couch or Barbecu of sticks lying along about 2 foot distant from the ground, was spread with the same, and was all his Bedding. He had no Cloaths left, having worn out those he brought from *Watlin*'s Ship, but only a Skin about his Waste.[59]

Some years and many miles later, on 4 January 1688, Dampier, aboard another ship, 'fell in with the Land of *New Holland*', as he casually says.[60] He was thus among the first Englishman to set foot on Australia, and the very first to describe its Aborigines in print. These people, who 'grinn'd like so many Monkeys', together with the monkeys of Campeachy and the Hottentots of South Africa, with whom Dampier compares them, have been proposed as possible sources for the Yahoos, a possibility to be judged in the knowledge that Swift owned a copy of Dampier's *A New Voyage*.[61] According to Dampier, the Aborigines

are the miserablest People in the world. The *Hodmadods* of *Monomatapa*, though a nasty People, yet for Wealth are Gentlemen to these; who have no Houses, and Skin Garments, Sheep, Poultry, and Fruits of the Earth, Ostrich Eggs, &c. as the *Hodmadods* have: and setting aside their humane shape, they differ but little from Brutes.[62]

This comment can be compared with Gulliver's on the Yahoos, whose human shape he did not at first recognize: 'I never beheld in all my Travels so disagreeable an Animal.'[63]

Although Dampier himself is not prominent among the 'Observables' in his book, and does not give us 'a Scetch of my Figure', as Crusoe does, he is not invisible, and presents his serious reflections as well as his surprising adventures.[64] Travelling by canoe from the Nicobar Islands to Sumatra, later in 1688, he experienced a terrible storm and had to face the prospect of a voyage to 'another World':

I made very sad reflections on my former Life, and lookt back with horrour and detestation, on actions which before I disliked, but now I trembled at the remembrance of. I had long before this repented me of that roving course of life, but never with such concern as now. I did also call to mind the many miraculous acts of Gods Providence towards me, in the whole course of my life, of which kind, I believe few men have met with the like.[65]

Having survived the storm, Dampier acquired in the East Indies the rights to a 'Painted Prince, whose Name was *Jeoly*' (a tattooed man from Miangas, near Mindanao) and, considering 'what might be gain'd by shewing him in *England*', he escaped from the clutches of the Governor of Sumatra, taking only his Jeoly and his journal, and returned home, reaching England in September 1691, with only these two assets after twelve and a half years of buccaneering and roving.[66] He soon sold his painted Prince, who was advertised by his new owners as 'exposed to publick view every day' and privately by appointment to 'Persons of Quality', much as Gulliver was exhibited in Brobdingnag, or as Trinculo hoped to exhibit Caliban.[67] His journal—revised it seems, though the original is lost—was published some years later as *A New Voyage Round the World*, in 1697, when its success brought Dampier to the attention of the virtuosi, the literati, and also the government, who accepted his proposal for a voyage of exploration to New Holland (Australia) and sent him off on his travels again in 1699 as Captain of the rotting *Roebuck*.[68]

The voyage, as a voyage of exploration and in other respects, was not the success it might have been. In a less unseaworthy ship and with a less unruly crew, Dampier might have outdone the Dutch explorers and anticipated Cook's discovery of the fertile east coast of Australia, but instead he touched at a barren part of the west coast, and again further north, on equally unpromising land.[69] On its return journey the *Roebuck* came to pieces and foundered at Ascension Island in the Atlantic, where Dampier and his crew, thanks to 'God's Providence', survived by eating turtles and goats until they were rescued by an English man-of-war and returned to England, where Dampier was convicted by a court martial of 'very hard and cruel usage' of his recalcitrant Lieutenant, whom he had placed in irons and unloaded at Bahia.[70]

Dampier did, however, explore the coast of New Guinea and discover a strait which is now named after him, the Dampier Strait between New Guinea and New Britain (named by Dampier 'Nova Britannia').[71] His contributions to fiction are less certain, but it has been argued that his descriptions of natives in *A Voyage to New Holland* supplied material for the imaginary South Sea discoveries reported in Defoe's own *A New Voyage* (1724) and also for the lands encountered by the hero of Defoe's *Captain Singleton* (1720) on his fictitious voyage, more adventurous than Dampier's, around the south of Australia.[72]

After publishing his account of his Australian voyage, as *A Voyage to New Holland*, Part I (1703) and Part II (1709), Dampier wrote no more books, although he did make more voyages, and commanded the ship that accompanied the one that marooned a cantankerous Scotsman, Alexander Selkirk, on Juan Fernandez. To

Selkirk's initial dismay, apparently, Dampier was also aboard the vessel captained by Woodes Rogers which sent a boat into the shore of Juan Fernandez four years later in 1709, a boat which returned, as Rogers tells us, 'and brought abundance of Craw-fish, with a Man cloth'd in Goat-Skins, who look'd wilder than the first Owners of them'.[73]

Selkirk must be the most famous 'source' in English literature.[74] That Defoe read accounts of his life on Juan Fernandez there can be little doubt, and Crusoe, although inhabiting a tropical island in the Orinoco archipelago, where 'the Weather was so violent hot, that there was no need of Cloaths', nevertheless wears Selkirk's Juan Fernandez goatskins.[75] As Steele said in his article on Selkirk, his 'name is familiar to Men of Curiosity', and of Defoe's curiosity and knowledge, about geography and travel in particular, there is good evidence.[76] Like the man of learning he describes in his essay 'On Learning', Defoe

had all the World at his Fingers' ends. He talked of the most distant Countries with an inimitable Exactness; and, changing from one Place to another, the Company thought, of every Place or Country he named, that certainly he must have been born there. He knew not only where every Thing was, but what every Body did in every Part of the World.[77]

Now Defoe, who was born in Cripplegate, London, did not acquire his exact knowledge of 'the most distant Countries' by sailing around the world with a journal in a tube of bamboo. Nor did he acquire it by spontaneous inspiration, or by exercising his powerful imagination. For the information 'at his Fingers' ends' he had other sources. As he pointed out in *The Compleat English Gentleman*, such a gentleman could make up for his lack of buccaneering background and exotic birthright, because 'he may make the tour of the world in books . . . He may go round the globe with Dampier and Rogers, and kno' a thousand times more in doing it than all those illiterate sailors.'[78] As it happens—fortunately for the English Gentleman in need of completion—Dampier and Rogers were not illiterate. Rogers's own *A Cruising Voyage* and his subordinate officer Edward Cooke's *A Voyage to the South Sea* provided accounts of Selkirk's experience on distant Juan Fernandez, and gave those accounts, as Steele's paper did not, in the context of a narrative of travel, the kind of work that *Robinson Crusoe* purported to be—a work not of fiction but of fact, not written by Defoe, but 'Written by Himself'.[79]

In a letter to the *Weekly Journal* one of Defoe's contemporaries and enemies remarked that his work was characterized by 'the little Art he is truly master of, of forging a Story and imposing it on the World for Truth'.[80] Whether we think this was a little art or a great art, we should remember that it was not an art of which its master was proud, unless in secret. The opinion that *Robinson Crusoe* was a clever fiction, 'all form'd and embellish'd by Invention', was an accusation from which Defoe defended himself as well as he could, insisting—or rather making Crusoe insist, in his *Serious Relections* (1720)—that the events in his story 'are all historical and true in Fact'.[81] Defoe's realism is not the conventional realism of the novel. He did not aim to suspend disbelief, but to do away with it completely. His

critic in the *Weekly Journal* spoke not of verisimilitude, but of 'forging a Story'.
It may be that the 'Seals' Crusoe sees are astray on an island in the Orinoco
archipelago, like the 'Tygers' in *Captain Singleton*'s Africa—or the 'Hippopotomus'
in Dampier's Australia.[82] It may be that the 'Seals' properly belonged on Juan
Fernandez, but how many of Defoe's readers knew that, or know it now?[83] According to a critic writing in 1753, *Robinson Crusoe* 'was written in so natural a manner,
and with so many probable incidents, that, for some time after its publication, it
was judged by most people to be a true story. It was indeed written upon a model
entirely new.'[84]

There is a passage in Edward Cooke's *A Voyage to the South Sea* which shows
the travel writer's concern, as a traveller, with fact, and also his concern, as a
writer, with convincing the reader of this concern with fact. Because, of course, a
traveller may be a liar as well as a traveller, or not a traveller at all. He may be,
Defoe may have thought, Defoe. I quote from Cooke's Introduction to the second
volume of his *Voyage* (1712):

In the first Volume there is Mention made of one Alexander Selkirk, (so commonly call'd,
but his right Name is *Selcrag*) who being left on the Island *John Fernandes*, continu'd there
four Years and four Months, without any human Society. That short Hint rais'd the
Curiosity of some Persons to expect a more particular Relation of his Manner of living in
that tedious Solitude . . . It would be no difficult Matter to embellish a Narrative with many
Romantick Incidents, to please the unthinking Part of Mankind, who swallow every Thing
an artful Writer thinks fit to impose upon their Credulity, without any Regard to Truth or
Probability. The judicious are not taken with such Trifles; their End in Reading, is Information; and they easily distinguish between Reality and Fiction. We shall therefore give
the Reader as much as may satisfy a reasonable Curiosity, concerning this Man, without
deviating into Invention.[85]

In the realistic imitation of real travel books, Defoe had precursors. Most of
their works are imaginary voyages to utopias, but their use of realistic effects—
names, dates, incidental details—makes their social fantasies more believable than
the utopias of More and Bacon, which were not designed to deceive. A short work
published in London in 1668, entitled *The Isle of Pines, or, A late Discovery of a
fourth Island in Terra Australis, Incognita*, introduced itself on the title-page as the
'True Relation' of an Englishman, George Pine, who had been shipwrecked with
four women on an island near Terra Australis 'in the dayes of Queen *Elizabeth*',
his 'True Relation' having been given by his grandson to a Dutch ship which had
rediscovered the island, the Isle of Pines, in 1667, inhabited by George Pine's 'ten
or twelve thousand' descendants.[86]

The 'True Relation' describes the shipwreck of the *India Merchant*, caught in a
storm off Madagascar, and the survival of Pine himself, a bookkeeper by profes-
sion, and his master's daughter and three female servants, on an uninhabited island
'so very pleasant', with its variety of fruits and birds and its warm climate, 'that
this place (had it the culture that skilful people might bestow on it) would prove
a Paradise'.[87] In practical and credible fashion, they build a shelter from debris

salvaged from the wreck, and then live polygamously, Pine characteristically keeping a careful account of his multiplying family of Pines. The second generation, of necessity, breed incestuously, but Pine prevents marriages between siblings of the third generation and, as a further sign of returning propriety, enjoins regular readings of the Bible.

This brief account, licensed in June 1668, was quickly followed by a sequel and by a complete version combining the original story with the sequel and adding two prefatorial letters 'to a Credible person in *Covent Garden*' which give supporting evidence of the true existence of the Isle of Pines.[88] The sequel also contributed to verisimilitude, taking the form of a 'Letter to a friend in *London*, declaring the truth of his Voyage', by Henry Cornelius Van Sloetten, the Dutch rediscoverer of the Isle of Pines.[89] Apologizing for 'my blunt Phrases, as being more a Seaman than a Scholler', Van Sloetten describes receiving from George Pine's grandson, William Pine, the 'Prince or chief Ruler', 'two sheets of paper fairly written in *English*, (being the same Relation which you had printed with you at *London*)'.[90] He also receives and narrates the subsequent history of the Isle of Pines, featuring an outbreak of 'wantonness' caused by not 'hearing the Bible read', an outbreak righteously quashed by George's son, William's father, who enforces with laws the resumption of Bible reading and propriety.[91] Van Sloetten concludes his letter by admitting that the Isle of Pines 'is a thing so strange' that he fully expects those 'as will believe nothing but what they see, applying that Proverb unto us, *That Travelors may lye by authority*'.[92]

The most plausible view of *The Isle of Pines*—a view which is not contradicted by the immediate discovery of a German interpreter in 1668 that 'PINES mit versetzten Buchstaben PENIS bedeute'—is that indicated by a contemporary, the historian Anthony à Wood, who identified its author as Henry Neville and stated that when first published it 'was look'd upon as a meer sham or piece of drollery'.[93] As drollery it served to provide Dryden's play *The Kind Keeper; or, Mr. Limberham* with a joke about 'a likely proper Fellow' who 'looks as he cou'd People a new Isle of *Pines*', and as a sham it was particularly successful on the continent, where it was published in Dutch, French, Italian, and German editions.[94] In Germany it was included in a respectable collection of voyages to Africa, and in Spain the eighteenth-century philosopher Benito Gerónimo Feijoo used its story of 'multiplicacion' as evidence against the theory that the world's population was shrinking.[95] More recently, Neville's realistic reference to 'a sort of fowl about the bignesse of a Swan, very heavy and fat, that by reason of their weight could not fly', has been taken as 'historical evidence'.[96] 'The "fowl" aforementioned is undoubtedly a Dodo', writes Masauji Hachisuka in *The Dodo and Kindred Birds* (1953), referring to 'Pine, George, *The Isle of Pines*', a work 'written about 1648 in Mauritius', which 'leaves a brief but extremely valuable account of the natural products including the Dodo, and of the growth of the island's population'.[97] George Pine's mention of 'a sort of fowl much like our Ducks' is the 'sole observation', according to Hachisuka, of the *Anas theodori*, or Mauritian Duck, otherwise known only from a few fragmentary 'osseus remains' excavated in the nineteenth century by Théodore Sauzier, in whose honour the Duck was named by Professors Newton and Gadow of Cambridge.[98]

Such imaginary voyages depended on the popularity of real accounts of travel, which, in France as in England, replaced romances in the popular taste, as a remark by Chapelain, the seventeenth-century poet and critic, in a letter dated 1663, suggests: 'Nostre nation a changé de goust pour les lectures et, au lieu des romans . . . les voyages sont venus en crédit et tiennent le haut bout dans la Cour et dans la Ville.'[99] In order to locate their ideal societies in the real world and still retain the reader's belief, the authors turned from increasingly familiar America to the possiblities afforded by the great, vague Austral continent.[100]

Quirós's description of his Terra Australis helped to inspire *La Terre Australe connue* (1676), otherwise known as *Les Avantures de Jacques Sadeur*, purportedly 'par Mr Sadeur', but really the work of a dissipated and discontented Protestant named Gabriel Foigny, whose preface declared it to be the memoirs of Sadeur, a deceased traveller from Madagascar, found among his belongings: 'une espece de livre fait de feuilles, long de demi pied, large de six doits, & épais de deux.'[101] The 'avantures' of Jacques Sadeur in the 'Terre Australe' are not so precisely realistic as this description of the manuscript which contained them, but they are intended to deceive, there being, according to the preface, 'rien d'impossible' about them.[102] The account of the utopian society of the naturally naked 'Australiens', of whom 'on diroit facilement qu'Adam n'a pas peché en eux', and who 'ne savent ce que veut dire le mien & le tien', is provided as purportedly factual evidence of a superior alternative to European society (and shows the continuity in voyage literature between the themes of the Golden Age, or Eden, and the social and political ideals of the eighteenth-century radicals).[103] Even Foigny's fabulous Urgs, which transport him by air to his ideal Austral land from the debris of his shipwreck in the real world, are as accurately measured as Dampier's shark, being

de la grosseur de nos bœufs, d'une tête longue qui finit en pointe, avec un bec d'un grand pied, plus dur & plus affilé que l'acier aiguisé. Ils ont de vrais yeux de bœuf, qui sortent de leur tête, deux grandes oreilles . . . un corps long de 12. pieds & large de quatre [etc.].[104]

Sadeur's Austral adventures, which were published in an English translation in 1693, were followed by the *Histoire des Sevarambes*, the work of Denis Vairasse d'Alais, another Protestant.[105] Published in two parts in Paris in 1677 and 1678–9 and in English in London in 1675 and 1679 (where the English edition of the first part preceded the French), the *Histoire des Sevarambes* pretended to be an account of the personal experience of a certain Captain Siden in Austral lands, supposedly written by Siden (an anagram of Denis) himself. Denis Vairasse, the real author, in his role as the editor of Siden's account, makes an elaborate case for its authenticity in the preface 'Au Lecteur', in which he produces various kinds of corroborating evidence (including an imaginary letter by an imaginary witness, Thomas Skinner) and points out about his own story, allegedly Siden's, that: 'Elle est écrite d'une maniere si simple, que personne, à ce que j'espere, ne doutera de la verité de ce qu'elle contient, le Lecteur pouvant remarquer aisément qu'elle a tous les caracteres d'une Histoire veritable.'[106] Siden's Austral discovery (again a utopian society in obvious contrast with Europe, and probably indebted to 'la nouvelle Atlantis du Chancelier Bacon'—which Siden calls a work of 'imagination'—as well as to an authentic account of Australian shipwreck) was indeed, just as Vairasse hoped, very credible.[107] According to a contemporary reviewer in the *Journal des Sçavans*, who did not give his own opinion: 'Les uns l'ont regardé comme une belle idée, & les autres ont crû de bonne foy tout ce qui y est rapporté sur la découverte'.[108]

In the wake of the voyages of Sadeur and Siden, came the *Voyages et avantures de Jaques Massé* (1710) (also published in English in 1733), supposedly written by Massé himself, but actually the work of Simon Tyssot de Patot, a fierce free-thinker, who adds to the verisimilitude of Massé's voyage by adding a prefatorial 'Lettre de L'editeur', who confesses that on a first reading 'je soupçonnois que l'Auteur s'étoit servi du privilége des Voyageurs, en mêlant à sa Relation un peu de Romanesque: mais après une seconde lecture, & un examen plus particulier, je n'y ai rien trouvé que de fort naturel & de très-vraisemblable'.[109] Beached on the Austral continent by a storm, Massé and a companion explore the interior, build a credible raft with which to cross a large lake, and then discover the Austral society, where they visit the court of King Bustrol, to whom Massé delivers a long account of Europe, not forgetting to mention wars, unjust and unpleasant social and political conditions, and the like. The King makes Tyssot's point: 'Je plains votre Sort, dit le Roi: à ce compte vous n'êtes proprement que la Proye des méchans, des esclaves, & de miserables Victimes de l'Ambition & de l'Intérêt de vos Souverains: les Chiens sont plus heureux chez moi, que les Hommes ne le sont en vos Quartiers.'[110] Massé's stay in the Austral society is kept amusing by various 'avantures' and rendered more credible by the addition of various supplementary 'voyages', to Goa and to Algeria, where Massé spends time, like Crusoe, in miserable slavery, before reaching liberal London, supposedly, and a writing desk.

Massé's conversation with King Bustrol is rather like Gulliver's with the King of Brobdingnag, and a case has been made that Tyssot's book is 'A New Source for *Gulliver's Travels*', though the argument is not conclusive, or even convincing.[111] The realistic detail of Tyssot, notably in his description of the construction of the raft—'Nous coupâmes premiérement dix arbres de sept à huit pouces de diamettre, dont nous ôtâmes les branches [etc.]'—is comparable with Defoe's in *Robinson Crusoe* and some incidents in the two novels have been compared, though not with the result of establishing Tyssot's influence on Defoe.[112] The works of Foigny and Vairasse have also been suggested as sources for Swift and Defoe, but again the evidence is not compelling, although the *Histoire des Sevarambes*, in its English form as *The History of the Sevarites*, did form the basis for a bogus third volume of *Gulliver's Travels* that appeared in 1727.[113]

These pioneering precursors of Crusoe and Gulliver voyage realistically to a purpose, which is to locate their utopian discoveries among the other, real discoveries of alternative cultures, in the real world. To the experience of the real voyagers, the authors Foigny, Vairasse, and Tyssot wished to add some more proofs, some fictional empirical evidence. As Jacques Sadeur said, speaking for Foigny: If Europe 'pouvoit communiquer avec les Australiens, elle ne fût tout autre qu'elle n'est maintenant'.[114] Foigny and his successors put Europe in touch. Their works, wrote Hazard in *La Crise de la conscience européenne* (1935), 'présagent non seulement Swift, Voltaire, Rousseau: mais l'esprit jacobin; mais Robespierre'.[115]

A voyage which is usually grouped by literary historians with these French imaginary voyages, although it does not contain a message from the 'Australiens', is the *Voyage et avantures de François Leguat et de ses compagnons, en deux isles desertes des Indes Orientales*, published in London in French in 1707, and in English in 1708.[116] According to the very circumstantial account in the *Voyage*, Leguat was a French Protestant who went to Holland in 1689 as a consequence of the revocation of the Edict of Nantes in 1685, and engaged there in a scheme proposed and publicized by a French Protestant exile, the Marquis Henri Du Quesne, to form a colony on the island of Réunion (which Du Quesne attractively named 'Eden') in the Indian Ocean. The prospective colonists, all male and about ten in number, sailed aboard the *Hirondelle* in September 1690, and, as Réunion was found to be in French possession, were deposited instead on the uninhabited island of Rodrigues, in May 1691.

The *Voyage de Leguat* provides long, detailed descriptions of the flora and fauna observed on Rodrigues. Some birds called 'Gelinotes' are as mathematical as Foigny's fabulous Urgs and as flightless as Neville's supposed Dodo: 'Elles ont un ourlet rouge autour de l'œil. Et leur bec qui est droit & pointu, est rouge aussi; long d'environ deux pouces. Elles ne sauroient guéres voler, la graisse les rendant trop pesantes.'[117] Several pages are devoted to a minute description of some other birds, the 'Solitaires', who have, like the 'Australiens', a message:

J'envoyois l'homme à l'école des Bêtes. Je loüois mes Solitaires de ce qu'ils marioient jeunes; (ce qui est une sagesse de nos Juifs) de ce qu'ils satisfaisoient à la Nature, dans le temps propre, & dès que la Nature a besoin d'être satisfaite; selon l'état de cette même Nature, & conformément à l'intention du Créateur.[118]

Leguat considered Rodrigues 'un Paradis terrestre' but, after two years without natural satisfaction, his companions argued that the Creator had said himself of the original Paradise 'qu'il n'étoit pas bon que l'homme fut seul', and the colonists laboriously constructed a boat and sailed hazardously but hopefully to the Dutch colony of Mauritius, where an argument with the authorities about some valuable ambergris resulted in their confinement on a small islet off the coast, the second of the 'deux isles desertes' mentioned in the book's title.[119] Leguat and some survivors of this second desert island were eventually shipped to Batavia, where they were in time released and allowed to return to Holland. Leguat himself seems thereafter to have migrated to England, where the *Voyage de Leguat* was published with a Preface containing his 'serious reflections' on his desert island experience on Rodrigues:

Recueilli très-profondément en moi-même, mes serieuses réflexions m'ont fait voir là, comme au doit & à l'œil, le néant d'une infinité de choses qui sont en grand' vogue parmi les habitans de cette malheureuse Terre; de cette Terre, où l'Art detruit presque toûjours la Nature, sous prétexte de l'embellir.[120]

An account in the *Journal des Sçavans* did not question the authenticity of the *Voyage de Leguat*, but a contemporary travel writer, Casimir Freschot, who had been gratuitously attacked in its Preface, responded by pronouncing in his *Nouvelle relation de la ville & republique de Venise* (1709) that the Preface to the *Voyage de Leguat*, and the editing of the 'veritables *riens*' of the *Voyage* itself, were the work of François Maximilien Misson, a French Protestant living in England, the author of a successful—and rival—guide to Italian tourism, the *Nouveau voyage d'Italie*.[121] Misson replied to this assertion in the Preface to the fourth English edition of his *A New Voyage to Italy* (1714), not by denying his authorship of the Preface to the *Voyage de Leguat*, but by declaring, 'in favour of Mr. *Leguat*, that the Relation he has published, is *faithful* and *true*', a declaration that did little to settle the question and nothing to prevent A. A. Bruzen de la Martinière, in his *Dictionnaire géographique* (1768), from placing the *Voyage de Leguat*, without explanation or justification, in the category of 'voyages fabuleux . . . qui n'ont pas plus de réalité que les songes d'un fébricant'.[122]

In 1887, however, Théodore Sauzier—of the supposed *Anas theodori* observed in Neville's *Isle of Pines*—republished the Marquis Du Quesne's lost *Recueil de quelques mémoires servans d'instruction pour l'établissement de l'isle d'Eden* (which he had found at a sale) and, quoting a notice printed in 1735 of the death in London, 'âgé de nonante-six ans', of François Leguat, 'le même qui publia . . . *Voyages et aventures de François Leguat*', argued in an introduction to his new edition of Du Quesne's *Recueil* that these discoveries were convincing evidence of the authenticity of the *Voyage de Leguat*, not to mention its interesting birds.[123] The attention of naturalists had already been attracted, earlier in the nineteenth century, to the extinct fauna of Mauritius and the adjacent islands, notably the wonderful Dodo. Some bones of a large bird were found on Rodrigues and, on comparison with the Dodo's remains at Oxford, were declared to be those of a closely related and similarly extinct bird, which was thought to be the 'Solitaire' described in the *Voyage de Leguat*.[124] In the 1860s more bones were sought and found on Rodrigues and were skilfully assembled into the skeleton of the extinct 'Solitaire' by Alfred Newton, Professor of Zoology at Cambridge, the same who had named the *Anas theodori* in honour of Théodore Sauzier.[125] In 1874 the British Government sent an expedition to Rodrigues with the primary aim of observing the transit of the planet Venus across the sun from a vantage point in the Indian Ocean, and naturalists were despatched to accompany the astronomers. The subsequent reports on the flora and fauna of Rodrigues, by Dr Balfour, Mr Slater, Mr Gulliver, and others, were published in the *Philosophical Transactions of the Royal Society* in 1879.[126] The flightless 'Gelinote' described in the *Voyage de Leguat* was deemed to be another extinct bird, unique to Rodrigues, and Professor Alphonse Milne-Edwards of the

Paris Museum of Natural History proposed the name *Erythromachus leguati* for it, though Dr Günther of the British Museum and Professor Newton of Cambridge thought *Aphanapteryx leguati* more apt.[127]

With the *Voyage de Leguat* in credit with the scientific community, Captain Pasfield Oliver, who had just edited *Madagascar: or, Robert Drury's Journal*, produced a scholarly edition of the English version of the *Voyage de Leguat* for the Hakluyt Society in 1891, comprehensively annotated by scientific experts, and with a photograph of the reconstructed skeleton of Leguat's 'Solitaire' as a frontispiece. In a series of appendices on the extinct birds of Rodrigues, the leading dodologists agreed that their examinations of old bones had confirmed the 'extraordinary fidelity' of the *Voyage de Leguat* and 'the exactitude of his observations', with the sole exception of his account of the admirable monogamy of the 'Solitaire', a 'particular in which Leguat may have erred' because of 'his anxiety to point a moral'.[128]

Some thirty years later, with the *Voyage de Leguat* and its birds recognized in the *Encyclopaedia Britannica* and Larousse's *Grand Dictionnaire*, the literary historian Geoffroy Atkinson included the *Voyage de Leguat* in the second of his two studies of French imaginary voyages, *The Extraordinary Voyage in French Literature from 1700 to 1720* (1922), arguing that the *Voyage* 'is a novel' and 'a fiction'.[129] Sauzier's discovery of Du Quesne's *Recueil* proved a 'historical' background for the 'novel', Atkinson conceded, but 'what follows in the *Voyage de François Leguat* is not corroborated by documentary evidence, and would appear to be quite without foundation in fact'.[130] Taking the observations of birds on Rodrigues as the basis of the case for the authenticity of the *Voyage de Leguat*, Atkinson compared the descriptions of the 'Gelinote' and 'Solitaire' in the *Voyage* with descriptions of birds in Madagascar, Mauritius, and Réunion by previous travellers, and concluded, not merely that the birds in the *Voyage de Leguat* could have been plagiarized and, in part, invented, but that they actually were plagiarized and invented. For the many details in the description of the 'Solitaire' that were without parallel in any of the previous voyages that he had laboriously explored, Atkinson accounted by suggesting that they 'could have been observations on European bird skeletons, or could have been invented to add realism' after the manner of Gabriel Foigny.[131] In any case, the names of Leguat's companions could not be taken seriously as those of real people by anyone acquainted with Vairasse's 'Thomas Skinner', Atkinson argued, and the stories in the *Voyage* about ambergris and imprisonment in Mauritius could have been taken from stories about ambergris in Mauritius and imprisonment on an island off Capetown which had appeared in earlier accounts of voyages, published in 1680 and 1677.[132] As so much of the *Voyage de Leguat* was 'evidently borrowed from . . . earlier writers', Atkinson concluded that 'not even the shell of the story is left' and that therefore the *Voyage de Leguat* was certainly 'a desert island novel', probably written by François Maximilien Misson.[133]

Atkinson's findings were accepted by literary historians of the 1920s, such as E. A. Baker and A. W. Secord, who passed them into the mainstream of Defoe studies, where reference persists in informed discussion of *Robinson Crusoe* to Misson's 'imaginary voyage', and they were repeated in detail in 1962 in P. G. Adams's *Travelers and Travel Liars 1660–1800*, which added that 'as late as 1939 the *Encyclopaedia Britannica* . . . was still listing [Leguat] as the most important source for the early history of Rodrigues'.[134] As late as 1983, in Adams's *Travel Literature and the Evolution of the Novel*, we are told again of Misson's 'amazing invention'.[135]

But in the archives of the Dutch authorities at the Cape of Good Hope, published in English translation in 1896, there is a letter of 2 July 1694, signed by the Dutch commander of Mauritius, reporting his discovery, on a journey round the island, of 'a sloop of the men left by the Marquis du Quesne of the frigate *Hirondel* on the island of Diego Rodriguez, [who,] after having been there two years, and hearing nothing of the Marquis, had (seven of them) decided to . . . proceed hither'.[136] Other letters from Mauritius in the Dutch archives specify that the Frenchmen from Rodrigues 'arrived here in 1693, with a boat made there by themselves', list the names of the men as given in the *Voyage*, not forgetting one 'Le Guage', and describe, from the Dutch point of view, the imprisonment of the Frenchmen 'on an islet' and the dispute over 'a piece of ambergris'.[137] There can be no doubt that the *Voyage de Leguat* is fact, not fiction, and that real and imaginary voyages can be hard to tell apart.

Whether Defoe believed in the *Voyage de Leguat* or not we cannot know, but it does seem possible, if not probable, that he read it. The influence of this 'desert island novel' on *Robinson Crusoe* has been described as 'minor' but 'certain'.[138] Similarities between the two works, however—the growing of grain, the stock of civilized provisions, the religious devotions, and the construction of a boat, as well as the implicit themes of the virtue of necessity and the benevolence of Providence— could, given the conditions of desert islands, be ascribed to coincidence rather than influence. The case for Leguat's influence on Defoe's *Captain Singleton* is rather more convincing, and goes beyond coincidences to similarities of detail and even diction in the construction of Leguat's boat on Rodrigues and Singleton's on Madagascar.[139]

The border between factual and fictional voyages can easily be crossed and can even move. It has been argued, however, that *Robinson Crusoe* does not derive from the facts of the Selkirk story, and is not the 'fictitious book of travel' literary historians take it to be—not because it is, on the contrary, a factual book of travel, but because the thematic concerns critics have discovered in it, particularly with the idea of Providence, clearly distinguish it from authentic travel books, which 'seem to lack ideological content', according to J. Paul Hunter.[140] But the economic and religious ideologies which have been found in *Robinson Crusoe* are quite at home in the literature of authentic travel. Selkirk's own comment, recorded by Woodes Rogers, that 'he was a better Christian while in this Solitude than ever he was before', would not go amiss in an essay on *Robinson Crusoe*.[141] Rogers himself did not fail to notice the ideological contents of his narrative of Selkirk's experience, remarking that 'we may perceive by this Story the Truth of the Maxim, That Necessity is the Mother of Invention', and that, in Selkirk's circumstances, 'nothing but the Divine Providence could have supported any Man'.[142] Rogers's account of Selkirk was indeed so ideological that a catchpenny pamphlet published in 1712 entitled *Providence Display'd, Or a very Surprizing Account of one Mr. Alexander Selkirk*, supposedly 'Written by his own Hand', was simply a plagiarized version of Rogers's own account in *A Cruising Voyage*.[143] Even scientific Dampier remarked upon 'the many miraculous acts of Gods Providence towards me, in the whole course of my life' and, like Dampier and, of course, Crusoe, Robert Drury discerned the theme of God's Providence beneath the surface narrative of his travels, seeing his shipwreck on Madagascar as evidence that 'Providence herein justly punish'd my Disobedience'.[144] Leguat's *Voyage* has a similar 'ideological content'. As Oliver remarked in his edition, 'we find the word "Providence" on the first and last pages of his book'.[145] And if Drury's and Leguat's books are not 'fictitious books of travel' there is only one alternative: that they are—what they really are—authentic books of travel.

The economic and religious ideas critics find in *Robinson Crusoe* are often combined—and confused—in the accounts of genuine travellers. Columbus sailed for souls and gold: for 'the turning of so many peoples to our holy faith, and afterwards for temporal benefits', as he put it.[146] These mixed motives were common to the Renaissance voyagers and Bernal Díaz expressed the muddled greed and zeal of many others when he wrote that he went to the Indies 'to give light to those who were in darkness, and also to acquire riches'.[147] The Indians could be enlightened and also enslaved, as Columbus remarked immediately on landing in the West Indies, an idea Crusoe put into imaginary practice with Friday. In *Gulliver's Travels* Swift satirized the greed that travelled under the colours of civilization and piety:

A Crew of Pyrates are driven by a Storm they know not whither, at length a Boy discovers Land from the Top-mast, they go on Shore to Rob and Plunder; they see an harmless People, are entertained with Kindness, they give the Country a new Name, they take formal Possession of it for their King, they set up a rotten Plank or a Stone for a Memorial, they murder two or three Dozen of the Natives, bring away a Couple more by Force for a Sample, return home, and get their Pardon. Here commences a new Dominion acquired with a Title by *Divine Right*. Ships are sent with the first Opportunity, the Natives driven out or destroyed, their Princes tortured to discover their Gold; a free Licence given to all Acts of Inhumanity and Lust, the Earth reeking with the Blood of its Inhabitants: And this execrable Crew of Butchers employed in so pious an Expedition, is a *modern Colony* sent to convert and civilize an idolatrous and barbarous People.[148]

The plot of *Robinson Crusoe* is, in outline, rather like that of *The Tempest*, with Friday playing the part of Caliban, and, like Prospero, Crusoe has frequently been seen as a 'prototype' (as James Joyce told the Italians) of the British colonist, while his story has even been described as a 'by-product' of Defoe's project, promulgated in *An Historical Account of the Voyages and Adventures of Sir Walter Raleigh*

(1719), to colonize Guiana, to the south-east of Crusoe's island.[149] Indeed the arguments for colonizing Chile in Rogers's *A Cruising Voyage* seem so like those in Defoe's *An Essay on the South-Sea Trade* (1712) that Rogers's modern biographer speculates that Defoe must have co-authored Rogers's travel book (though *A Cruising Voyage* is not included in Moore's comprehensive bibliography of Defoe's works).[150]

Defoe's fictitious *A New Voyage Round the World* (1724), for all its criticisms of other (genuine) accounts of voyages, which have not 'diverted us' and 'have little or nothing of story in them', has most of its own 'story' devoted to the undiverting purpose of demonstrating by fictitious example the practicability and profitability of the theoretical Chilean colony advocated in *An Essay on the South-Sea Trade*.[151] Profit, not Providence (which is never mentioned), is also the theme of the large part of *A New Voyage* which precedes Defoe's Chilean colonizing propaganda. This describes the fictitious voyagers' discoveries of South Sea islands, including some which are not the expected Austral continent, but which Defoe's anonymous narrator is convinced 'are the same which the ancient Geographers have call'd *Solomon*'s Islands', of which previous South Sea explorers have given no accounts, 'except such as are Romantick, and not to be depended upon'.[152] What is to be depended upon, instead, is that Defoe's voyagers discover oysters brimming with pearls and aptly name the exciting islands 'the *Pearl-Islands*'.[153] The South Sea islands in *A New Voyage* are utopias of trade and empire, as the 'story' all too clearly demonstrates with its accounts of pearls, gold, and sailors who jumped ship in their eagerness 'to plant there'.[154] The narrator shows Defoe's characteristic practicality by remarking that 'the Natives will bestow Wives upon them' and, naked and semi-naked, would 'take off a very great Quantity of *English* Woollen-Manufactures'.[155]

The colonial motif is obviously allied to the economic motive, which is for Crusoe, as for his real-life counterparts, a powerful force, sending him and them away from family and home. By Defoe's time the crusading fervour of the days of the Conquistadors had waned, and of all the motives for exploration and colonization the most propulsive was the economic one.[156] The voyage which takes Crusoe to his island was intended as a slaving voyage to Africa, 'to purchase upon the Coast, for Trifles, . . . *Negroes*, for the Service of the *Brasils*, in great Numbers'.[157] Europe consumed coffee, sugar, and tobacco; and coffee, sugar, and tobacco consumed slaves. As Voltaire noticed,

> Le superflu, chose très nécessaire,
> A réuni l'un et l'autre hémisphère.[158]

Slaves were what the reputable Captain Mackett was after, when he found Drury on Madagascar.[159]

While Defoe's utopias of trade and empire are very like those of real travellers, they would seem to be very different from the primitivist utopias of the French imaginary voyages, for instance, or even the 'Paradis terrestre' of Leguat's real

Rodrigues, subject of his 'serieuses réflexions' about 'la Nature'. 'Crusoe's utopia', as M. E. Novak says, 'emerges as almost the exact opposite' of Gonzalo's utopia in *The Tempest* (which, as we know, was also Montaigne's in 'Des cannibales').[160] This is so, but Crusoe's utopia is not quite the same as Defoe's. *Robinson Crusoe* 'is fundamentally anti-primitivist', declares Ian Watt, and Novak remarks that 'instead of sending his civilized man back to nature for reformation . . . Defoe almost reverses the process'.[161] But these critics confuse Defoe with Crusoe. Defoe imposes the process of the return to nature before Crusoe reverses it. Crusoe was, as he complains, 'reduced to a meer State of Nature' by his shipwreck.[162] Defoe does not send Crusoe to the island of Bacon's *New Atlantis*, which is a proper example of a 'fundamentally anti-primitivist' work. Crusoe is indeed sent back to nature for reformation. Of course the direction that reformation then takes is away from a primitive state of nature to a state of culture, but that culture is not civilized culture. For all the civilized equipment salvaged from the wreck and for all Crusoe's own civilized Englishness, his island culture is more like that of Dampier's Moskito Indians, who have learnt 'from the *English*', than it is like the culture of civiliza-tion. As his goatskin clothing indicates, by contrast with Friday's initial nakedness and also with the civilized costume Crusoe puts on to leave his island, his culture is carefully balanced at a point between nature and civilization. The shipwreck which reduces Crusoe to a state of nature is therefore as important as—is indeed the basis for—his achievement of a kind of culture which is as anti-primitivist as Crusoe can manage under the primitivist conditions imposed upon him by Defoe. The obvious differences between *Robinson Crusoe* and the primitivist tradition in travel literature should not obscure the similarities.

Swift's work seems as far as Defoe's from this tradition, or further, and a critic has stated firmly that 'in *Gulliver's Travels* there is no primitivism'.[163] Of course natural man in the land of the Houyhnhnms is the unattractive Yahoo, not the Houyhnhnms Gulliver finds so very attractive, who—or which—are horses. Clearly Swift's primary aim is not to idealize natural man and contrast him with civilized man, but the very opposite, to portray natural man as vile and bestial and to suggest his resemblance to civilized man by contrast with an ideal type, not of men, but of horses. The Yahoos are, therefore, a satirical portrait of the inhabitants of the 'state of nature' idealized by philosophers like Montaigne. The Yahoos' state of nature is much closer to the brutish condition described by Hobbes than to the reasonable freedom and equality described by Locke. But we should also recognize that Swift's satire has more than a single aim, and can reverse its direction com-pletely. The Houyhnhnms are 'horses', it is true, but then the Houyhnhnms are no ordinary horses. Indeed, just as the Yahoos are more like monkeys than men, so the Houyhnhnms are more like men than horses. To a considerable extent, then, they do indeed represent natural man in an ideal society which is contrasted with European civilization. To that extent the Yahoos represent the ignoble savage, and the 'Noble *Houyhnhnms*' the noble savage.[164]

The Houyhnhnms are blissfully ignorant of the uses of money and iron, their virtue is 'endowed by Nature', and they are shamelessly naked and 'could not understand why Nature should teach us to conceal what Nature had given'.[165] The dialogue between Gulliver and his Houyhnhnm master follows the conventions of that between civilized man and 'philosophe nu', and the typical catalogue of absent civilized vices is duly presented by Swift: 'Here were no Gibers, Censurers, Back-biters, Pick-pockets, Highwaymen, Housebreakers, Attorneys, Bawds, Buffoons, Gamesters, Politicians, Wits . . . [etc.].'[166] The conclusion that the Houyhnhnms are noble savages is inevitable and quite correct, provided that we remember that in so far as the Houyhnhnms are ideal and noble they are also 'horses', while the Yahoos are 'men', and that in so far as the Houyhnhnms are human they are also subject to human faults. Such, for example, is their smug and parochial pride in their own superiority, implied by the etymology of their own name in their own language: *'the Perfection of Nature'*.[167] Swift's satire can reverse its direction completely.

Of course *Gulliver's Travels* descends from a long line of fantastic voyages that reaches back beyond the realistic voyages of Dampier and Defoe. Lucian's *True Story*, long recognized as an influence, may have offered various possible sugges-tions to Swift—for giants, for instance, which Lucian encountered on the moon—and Lucian's description of the moon itself, as 'a great country [in the air], resembling an island' with 'another country [the earth] below', is paralleled by Swift's flying island of Laputa, also with another country (Balnibarbi) below.[168] Swift's debt to Rabelais (himself indebted to Lucian) was noticed by Pope in *The Dunciad* and discussed by Voltaire, but does not amount to very much when measured in terms of specific details, such as the excremental exploits of giants, or the probable contributions of Rabelais's experimenters—'avec force merde Chrestienne'—to the experiments of Swift's Academy of Lagado.[169] A more spe-cific debt, perhaps, is owed by Swift to the two extra-terrestrial voyages of Cyrano de Bergerac, admirer of Montaigne and author of the posthumously published *Estats et empires de la lune* (1657) and *Estats et empires du soleil* (1662).[170] On the moon, for example, among other Gulliverian experiences, Cyrano (who travels *in propria persona*) encounters giants with 'la figure et le visage comme nous', but who walk on all fours, 'à quatre pattes', and consider Cyrano to be a 'beste monstrueuse'.[171]

Of the family resemblance between *Gulliver's Travels* and these works of Lucian, Rabelais, and Cyrano de Bergerac there can be little doubt, but *Gulliver's Travels* is not without some relation, also, to real and realistic voyages. Such voyages provoked doubts about the reality or universality of European nature and culture and these doubts could in turn provoke relativistic thinking of the kind to be found in Montaigne's *Essais* or, for example, in the description of pygmies in *Mandeville's Travels*: 'And of those men of our stature have they as great scorn as we would have among us of giants if they were among us'.[172]

Pygmies were also to be found in the accounts of real voyages of the sixteenth and seventeenth centuries, and giants were reported in Patagonia, not only by Pigafetta on Magellan's voyage, but by later voyagers, and were famous in the

eighteenth century even after the publication of *Gulliver's Travels*. Horace Walpole
was amused, informing a correspondent that 'Captain Byron has found a nation of
Brobdinags on the coast of Patagonia', and publishing a Swiftian satire, *An Account
of the Giants Lately Discovered* (1766): 'The first Thought that will occur to every
good Christian, is, that this Race of Giants ought to be exterminated, and their
Country colonized.'[173] But an anonymous account of Byron's voyage, which spoke
moderately of men averaging 'about eight feet' (who had grown considerably in the
illustrations—see Plate 2), was 'undoubtedly genuine', the *Gentleman's Magazine*
decided, and the Royal Society published 'An Account of the very tall Men, seen
near the Streights of Magellan' in the *Philosophical Transactions*.[174] Such beings
were still credited, so long as they kept their distance. As Gulliver says:

It might have pleased Fortune to let the *Lilliputians* find some Nation, where the People
were as diminutive with respect to them, as they were to me. And who knows but that even
this prodigious Race of Mortals [the Brobdingnagians] might be equally overmatched in
some distant part of the World, whereof we have yet no Discovery?[175]

Gulliver had room enough to make all his discoveries on earth and no need to
follow Cyrano to the sun and moon. Arbuthnot's story about *Gulliver's Travels* is
well known: 'I lent the Book to an old Gentleman, who went immediately to his
Map to search for Lilly putt'.[176] The geography of *Gulliver's Travels* is fantastic, of
course, but it is nevertheless realistic. Lilliput, naturally, would have been too
small to appear on the old gentleman's map, but it might have existed all the same.
Swift took care to place Gulliver's discoveries in parts of the world 'whereof we
have yet no Discovery', and did so without resorting to the fabulous Austral
continent which he had once thought of using for 'A Voyage into *England*, by a
Person of Quality in *Terra Australis incognita*'.[177] As distant, unknown parts of the
world where new discoveries could plausibly be located, the Pacific and the seas
around Australia provided Swift's best opportunities. Lilliput is in the Indian
Ocean, although 'Northwest of *Van Diemen's land*' (Tasmania), and the land of the
Houyhnhnms is south of New Holland (Australia), to which Gulliver paddles in
his canoe of Yahoo skins.[178] Brobdingnag is a peninsula (an enormous peninsula)
jutting into the Pacific from North America, and Laputa, Balnibarbi, Glubbdubdrib,
and Luggnagg are also in the conveniently distant Pacific, east of real Japan.

Gulliver's remote discoveries were documented, like genuine discoveries, with
maps and longitudes and latitudes, and were combined with other realistic effects,
like the prefatorial letters from the 'Publisher' to the reader and from Gulliver to
his Cousin Sympson, which have their precedent in the letter from Thomas
Skinner prefacing Vairasse's *Histoire de Sevarambes*. As *Gulliver's Travels* was read
by everyone 'from the highest to the lowest', according to Gay, the authenticating
devices employed by Swift may have served equally to amuse 'the highest', as
parody, and to deceive 'the lowest'.[179] They may have served, that is, to induce
belief, in the same way as realistic voyages like *Robinson Crusoe* induced belief, or
the works of real voyagers, like Gulliver's 'Cousin *Dampier*', referred to in Swift's

prefatory letter.[180] The success of Swift's realistic effects cannot, perhaps, be very accurately gauged by the gleeful accounts given by Swift and his circle about those gulled by *Gulliver's Travels*. Arbuthnot tells not only of the 'old Gentleman' with an interest in discovering Lilliput on his map, but also of 'a Master of a ship, who [claimed], that he was very well acquainted with Gulliver'.[181] Swift had his own story about an Irish Bishop, who 'said, that Book was full of improbable lies, and for his part, he hardly believed a word of it'.[182] Although we may not find these stories in themselves very credible or realistic, they do nevertheless suggest that for Swift and his intimates the realism of *Gulliver's Travels* was something more than mere parody.

The realism of *Gulliver's Travels* has even been attributed to the influence of Defoe, but an answer to the question of Defoe's influence on the circumstantial realism of *Gulliver's Travels* is of less importance than a recognition that the methods of Swift and Defoe are comparable, even similar, and that Swift's realism is also a parody of realism—a parody that is, at times, satirical.[183]

Like Defoe and Defoe's French precursors, Vairasse and others, Swift knew how to place fiction in a context of fact. Just as Tyssot's narrator Jaques Massé moves from Austral utopia to 'real' Goa in the *Voyages et avantures de Jaques Massé*, or as Defoe's Singleton travels from 'real' Africa across imaginary Africa and into 'real' Africa again, so does Gulliver travel from the land of the Houyhnhnms to New Holland and from Luggnagg to Japan. Swift satirically parodies the realistic transition between real and imaginary geography in a passage of elaborate nautical detail which accomplishes Gulliver's removal from 'a little to the East of the *Molucca* Islands' to Brobdingnag:

Finding it was like to overblow, we took in our Sprit-sail, and stood by to hand the Fore-sail; but making foul Weather, we look'd the Guns were all fast, and handed the Missen. The Ship lay very broad off, so we thought it better spooning before the Sea, than trying or hulling. We reeft the Fore-sail and set him, we hawl'd aft the Fore-sheet; the Helm was hard a Weather. The Ship wore bravely. We belay'd the Fore-down-hall; but the Sail was split, and we hawl'd down the Yard, and got the Sail into the Ship, and unbound all the things clear of it.[184]

The passage (which continues at length) is at once a satirical demonstration of the futility of human endeavour to control the elements by skill and technical expertise (for all their efforts the sailors end up 'about five hundred Leagues' off course) and of the ability of ships and nautical realism, when under the control of an author, to transport a reader from the real world to a world of the author's invention.[185] It was pointed out long ago that Swift copied the passage almost verbatim from the frenetic instructions on the 'Working of a Ship in all Weathers' given in Captain Samuel Sturmy's *Mariner's Magazine* (1669), which is the only absolutely indisputable 'source' for *Gulliver's Travels*:

It is like to over-blow; Take in your Sprit-sail, stand by to hand the Fore-sail . . . We make foul weather, look the Guns be all fast, come hand the Mizen. The Ship lies very broad off;

it is better spooning before the Sea, than trying or hulling; go reefe the Fore-sail, and set him; hawl aft the Fore-sheet; the Helmne is hard a weather . . . The Ship wears bravely . . . belay the fore doon hall . . . The sail is split; go hawl down the Yeard, and get the Sail into the Ship, and unbind all things clear of it . . . [etc.].[186]

Another example of Swift's mixture of maritime fact with fiction is provided by A. W. Secord's discovery that the *Antelope*, the ship in which Gulliver sails from Bristol for the South Seas (and Lilliput) on 4 May 1699, is the very same *Antelope* with which Dampier's ship 'jog'd on in company' when approaching the Cape of Good Hope on the way to New Holland on 3 June 1699.[187] Another such instance, of course, is Gulliver's reference to his relation, 'my Cousin *Dampier*', and 'his Book called, *A Voyage round the World*', a book we know was in Swift's possession.[188] Yet another instance, which would give a further twist to the complication of fact and fiction, is the probable dependence of Swift's account of the Lilliputian way of writing—in comparison with the European, Arab, and Chinese ways—on a similar comparative account supplied in Captain William Symson's *A New Voyage to the East-Indies* (1715), a work which is itself a fabrication with a fictitious author (although cited as genuine in the notes to Oliver's edition of *The Voyage of François Leguat*).[189]

Gulliver's Travels is not without some relation to the real and realistic voyages and their needs to carry conviction to their readers. The subjects of 'The Author's Veracity' and 'His Censure of those Travellers who swerve from the Truth' are major concerns in Swift's final chapter, which begins with Gulliver's address to his 'Gentle Reader':

Thus, Gentle Reader, I have given thee a faithful History of my Travels for Sixteen Years, and above Seven Months, wherein I have not been so studious of Ornament as Truth. I could perhaps like others have astonished thee with strange improbable Tales; but I rather chose to relate plain Matter of Fact in the simplest Manner and Style, because my principal Design was to inform, and not to amuse thee.[190]

These remarks, of course, are just like those of Dampier in his prefaces, stressing his commitment to facts, to a plain style, and to informing the reader. Gulliver goes on to express his opinion that authors of books of voyages should be put on oath to write only the truth: 'for, then the World would no longer be deceived as it usually is, while some Writers, to make their Works pass the better upon the Publick, impose the grossest Falsities on the unwary Reader'.[191] For his own part, he has 'imposed on myself as a Maxim, never to be swerved from, that I would *strictly adhere to Truth*'.[192]

All this is corroborated by 'The Publisher', who assures us that Mr Gulliver is 'distinguished for his Veracity', and notes 'an Air of Truth apparent through the Whole'.[193] The book is, however, subject to a fault characteristic of travel books: 'The Style is very plain and simple; and the only Fault I find is, that the Author, after the Manner of Travellers, is a little too Circumstantial.'[194] Travellers, of course, were circumstantial for a reason: to make a strange and distant world appear substantial and real to the reader, as Defoe did, and Swift too. In his edition of Swift's *Works*, Scott noticed that: 'Even Robinson Crusoe (though detailing events so much more probable,) hardly excels Gulliver in gravity and verisimilitude of narrative. The character of the imaginary traveller is exactly that of Dampier, or any other sturdy nautical wanderer of the period.'[195] We may recall James Burney's description of Dampier's style as 'equally free from affectation and from the most distant appearance of invention'.[196] It was important for a far-voyaging author to keep his distance, not only from 'invention', but from even the 'appearance of invention'. The difficulty faced by the author of a real voyage, like Dampier, that his reader's belief must depend principally on his text, was an opportunity welcomed by the author of an imaginary voyage, like Defoe or Swift, who naturally adopted Dampier's solution: a plain and simple style designed as a medium to convey strange and distant 'facts' to a sceptical and civilized reader, half a world away.

The circumstantial manner of *Gulliver's Travels* has frequently been noticed by Swift's critics. One comments that 'we are overwhelmed by the impression of Gulliver's commitment to hard, undeniable fact', and compares his style to the Royal Society's ideal of 'so many *things*, almost in an equal number of *words*'.[197] Another remarks that 'Gulliver arrives in Lilliput in a shower of circumstantial detail, most of it apparently accurate on its 1 : 12 scale', while the first one records that 'the pages are peppered with citations of numbers, figures, dimensions: I count over thirty such citations in the last paragraph of Chapter One'.[198] The same could be said of the 'Voyage to Brobdingnag', and it is of course of the essence that exotic pygmies and giants, Lilliputian and Brobdingnagian man and nature, should be a matter for scientific accuracy and a style of mathematical plainness, and of the essence that Swift's pygmies and giants should be as accurately measured as Dampier's shark.

Sprat's ideal language of the Royal Society, which resembles that of Bacon, whose ideal words were nouns, is also that of the Academy of Lagado, Balnibarbi, where the scientific projectors and professors aim 'to prevent the Growth of Wool' on sheep, extract 'Sun-Beams out of Cucumbers', 'reduce human Excrement to its original Food', and improve the language by 'leaving out Verbs and Participles, because in reality all things imaginable are but Nouns'.[199] As a further improvement, 'many of the most Learned and Wise adhere to the New Scheme of expressing themselves by *Things*', which is a *reductio ad absurdum* of the Royal Society's scheme.[200]

Swift's sources for the scientific theories and inventions described in Gulliver's 'Voyage' to Laputa and Balnibarbi have mostly been traced, not to the accounts of real or imaginary voyages, but to the accounts of contemporary scientific experiments and inventions that appear, side by side with the accounts of far-voyagers, in the *Philosophical Transactions of the Royal Society*.[201] The apparently coincidental presence of Swift's scientific sources and accounts of voyages together in the *Philosophical Transactions* seemed so striking to the discoverers of the scientific sources that they conjectured that the coincidence may have led Swift 'to the general idea of the travels of Gulliver' and that the accounts of voyages in the *Philosophical Transactions* may have been Swift's sources in the same way that the scientific accounts were.[202] But science and travel are linked by more than striking coincidence in both the *Philosophical Transactions* and *Gulliver's Travels*, and Swift possessed his own copy of Dampier's *New Voyage*, for example, and had no need to avail himself of the digest of its contents in the *Philosophical Transactions*.[203] *Gulliver's Travels* satirizes the scientific tendency of voyages as well as the voyaging tendency of science, and the Academy of Lagado satirizes, not only the utopian science of the Royal Society, but also the scientific utopia of Salomon's House.

It is fitting that the Royal Society, discovered by Bacon in the fictional Pacific, should be rediscovered there by Swift, and all the more so because in the next chapter we shall see the real Royal Society send out a scientific expedition which would discover, in the real Pacific, the last islands of romance.

4

The Observation of Venus

I said I was certain that a great part of what we are told by the travellers to the
South Sea must be conjecture . . . Dr. Johnson was of the same opinion. He
upon another occasion, when a friend mentioned to him several extraordinary
facts, as communicated to him by the circumnavigators, slily observed, 'Sir, I
never before knew how much I was respected by these gentlemen; they told
me none of these things.'

(Boswell, *Life of Johnson*)[1]

The 'Terra Australis' of Hall's *Mundus* and of the French eighteenth-century
utopists was, in geographical theory, no fiction. Formed out of the classical Antipodes, the biblical Ophir, and also Polo's reports of Lukak, south-south-west of
Chamba (Cambodia), it awaited its Columbus.[2] In 1765 Charles de Brosses's *Histoire
des navigations aux terres australes* took the form of a manifesto, with detailed plans
for the exploration and colonization of the southern continent, and the next year
there appeared the first of the three volumes of John Callander's *Terra Australis
Cognita* (1766–8), pirating de Brosses's work and translating the argument for a
French colony into an argument for a British colony—no mere utopia:

It is very certain that the discovery of *Terra Australis Incognita* is considered, by many wise
and knowing people, as a kind of philosopher's stone, perpetual motion, or, in plain *English*,
as a chimera, fit only to take up the empty brains of wild projectors. Yet there seems to be
no sufficient reason, why such as are competent judges of the matter in dispute, should
decide, peremptorily, that there is no such country: or, if there be, that it is not worth the
finding. These sort of hasty conclusions are extremely fatal to science in general and to the
art of navigation in particular.[3]

Those who deemed his project 'idle and chimerical' should reflect, argued Callander,
'that they will hardly be able to say so much against it, as was urged against the
noble attempt of *Columbus*'.[4] Alexander Dalrymple, a Fellow of the Royal Society,
was another believer in the southern continent. He corresponded with de Brosses,
and made his case, as de Brosses did, in the form of a tendentious history, *An Account
of the Discoveries made in the South Pacifick Ocean, Previous to 1764*, printed in
1767, but not published until 1769.[5]

The first voyage of exploration in what was to be a new phase of British activity
in the Pacific was commanded by Captain John Byron—the 'grand-dad' of the
author of *Don Juan*, and the discoverer of Patagonian giants—who turned his back

on his orders to search for the North-West Passage, and sailed across the Pacific in 1765.[6] Apart from the Patagonians, 'who in size come the nearest to Giants I believe of any People in the World', Byron made only a few, minor discoveries, but he was the first British explorer for almost a quarter of a century to cross that ocean.[7] The following year, 1766, the British Admiralty took up the search for the southern continent officially, sending out Captain Samuel Wallis in what had been Byron's ship, the *Dolphin*, accompanied by Philip Carteret in the unseaworthy *Swallow*, with which Wallis parted company on entering the Pacific. Wallis's secret instructions were: 'to discover and obtain a complete knowledge of the Land or Islands supposed to be situated in the Southern Hemisphere.'[8]

Forced north into the tropics by contrary winds after a perfunctory search of the southerly latitudes of the Pacific, Wallis sailed from the history of geographical theory into the history of discovery. On 18 June 1767, the sailors saw 'a great high mountain covered with clouds on the tope' and in the evening, 'at Sun Set, we now suposed we saw the long wishd for Southern Continent, which has been often talkd of, but neaver before seen by any Europeans'.[9] This was not, they soon realized, the southern continent, which Cook would dismiss from most of the ocean, but it was its replacement on the utopist's map, a real island, a more tangible fantasy: Tahiti.[10] The historian J. C. Beaglehole describes Wallis's discovery in the context of the history of the Pacific:

So almost suddenly, so overwhelmingly, was the idea of the Pacific at last to enter into the consciousness, not of seamen alone but of literate Europe, in the form of this remarkable, this—as it were—symbolic island. It was not singular in its characteristics. Its primacy in natural beauty has been contested. One may exercise, in our later day, all due reserve. But it was the heart of Polynesia. Geographically, therefore, it was important. A few years more, and its importance would also be psychological. For Wallis had not merely come to a convenient port of call. He had stumbled on a foundation stone of the Romantic Movement. Not as continent, not as vast distances, was the ocean henceforth in common thought to be known. The unreal was to mingle with the real, the too dramatic with the undramatic; the shining light was to become a haze in which every island was the one island, and the one island a Tahitian dream.[11]

That is how the discovery of Tahiti appears to Beaglehole, the Captain Cook of Pacific historiography, but not, of course, how it appeared to Captain Wallis and his men, whose discovery should be seen in their own words rather than through the haze which soon enveloped the island its inhabitants called 'Tahiti-nui mare'are'a', Great Tahiti of the Golden Haze.[12] The fullest account from the British point of view is given in the journal of George Robertson, the master of the *Dolphin*. The Tahitian point of view, which played its part in determining events at Tahiti, and therefore British perceptions, is, unfortunately, if not beyond conjecture, at least beyond the scope of reliable ethnohistory.[13]

On the morning of 19 June, as the *Dolphin* approached Tahiti, 'the weather was very thick and hazy all round', so that the island vanished from view. When the haze lifted the sailors found themselves surrounded by over a hundred canoes, containing men who 'lookt at our ship with great astonishment'.[14] Signs of friendship were exchanged. The British 'show'd them several trinkets' and the Tahitians held up 'Branches of plantain trees' and came aboard.[15] The British expressed their desires: 'some of the men Grunted and Cryd lyke a Hogg then pointed to the shore'. The Tahitians expressed theirs: they 'began to pull and hall at the Iron stanchons and Iron ring balls in order to carie them off'. When they were shown some nails, 'which they appeard very fond of', they became so fiercely importunate that the *Dolphin* fired a nine pound shot to scare them off the ship.[16]

Thus Anglo-Tahitian relations took shape. The scurvy-ridden British wanted fresh food and the stone-age Tahitians wanted iron. It would take more than a nine pound shot to settle the terms on which their mutual desires could be satisfied, and even then the British would have other desires. These the Tahitians soon recognized and, after the first Tahitian had been killed in an attack, so 'they now understood the use of musketry', they tried a new tactic, displaying to the *Dolphin*, from a safe distance, 'a good many fine young Girls . . . —this new sight Attract our mens fance a good dale, and the natives observed it, and made the Young Girls play a great many droll wanting [wanton] tricks'.[17] This ploy was repeated the next day, by which time the *Dolphin* had found an anchorage in Matavai Bay. About three hundred canoes came off from the shore, ostensibly to trade, and there was 'a fair young Girl in Each Canoe, who playd a great many droll wanton tricks'.[18] These the British rightly guessed were to serve as a distraction, and they feared an attack, which duly came.[19] The *Dolphin* responded with its guns, as Robertson says, 'and gave them a few round and Grape shot, which struck such terror amongs the poor unhappy croad that it would require the pen of Milton to describe, therefor too mutch for mine'.[20]

Emboldened, the British landed 'to take possesion of this Beautyfull Island'— which Wallis named 'King George the thirds Island'—by planting a pendant on the shore.[21] Two venerable natives of King George's new island then paddled out to the *Dolphin* in a canoe and presented the ship with 'two fine fatt Hoggs', for which they seemed unwilling, for some reason, to accept any payment. On returning to the shore, however, the venerable Tahitians 'struck the pendant and caried it clear off'.[22] At 7.30 the next morning the *Dolphin*'s crew 'observed a great number of large canoes, coming towards the ship . . . and all full of men, at the same time we saw several thousands of Men comeing allong shore . . . with our pendant flying at the end of a long pole, amongst the middle of them'.[23] The Tahitians wanted more lessons in the power and range of the *Dolphin*'s guns, which they duly received. Only then, on 26 June, after the deaths of many Tahitians, 'toar to peces in such a manner as I am certain they never beheald before', was peace finally established and the island of their desires finally discovered to the hungry, exclusively male strangers.[24] Now a regular market for exchanging provisions and nails was opened and soon food was in plentiful supply. That same day, 26 June, the Tahitians made available the island girls:

The old men made them stand in Rank, and made signs for our people to take which they lyked best, and as many as they lyked and for fear our men hade been Ignorant and not known how to use the poor young Girls, the old men made signs how we should behave to the Young women.[25]

These 'young Girls' understood the value of nails and, as Robertson remarks, 'a new sort of trade' was established, which 'might be more properly called the old trade'.[26]

As 'the old trade went on merrily' it soon became apparent that it was spoiling the trade for provisions and reducing the value of nails.[27] It was time to lecture the sailors, 'who gives too high a price for all sorts of curiositys they deal in', and to 'put a very necessary Question to the Doctor, who Affirmed on his Honour that no man onbd. was affected with any sort of disorder, that they could communicate to the Natives of this beautiful Island'.[28]

About 10 July 'a fine well lookt woman' appeared on the scene, whom the *Dolphin*'s crew took to be 'the Queen of the Country', but who was in fact Purea, the wife of the chief of the southern district of Papara.[29] Known to the British as Queen Oberea, she was to preside over the events of the *Dolphin*'s final fortnight at Tahiti. She invited the ailing Captain ashore, according to his log, had 'four young Girls' undress and massage him, clothed him 'after their Manner' in a robe of tapa, presented him with 'a very large Sow Big with Young', and then escorted him back to the ship, lifting him 'over every slough with as much ease as I could (when in health) a child'.[30]

When Wallis announced his departure (by which time most of the men were sleeping on the deck for want of nails to their hammocks) 'the Queen' at first tried to dissuade him and then 'burst out in Tears, and Cryed and Weept in such a manner that few men could have helpt pitying her'.[31] She spent the last night of the *Dolphin*'s stay camped on the beach and, on the sailors' departure, 'she wept and cryd, in my oppinion with as mutch tenderness and Affection as any Wife or Mother, could do, at the parting with their Husbands or children'.[32] Others were more suspicious than Robertson and indeed there seems reason to believe that Purea's affection for Wallis and his ship was more political than maternal—if we can judge, that is, by the subsequent history of the *Dolphin*'s pendant, which, according to the *Memoirs* of Purea's great-great-grandniece, Purea 'seems to have converted . . . into the *Maro ura* [high-chiefly red feather girdle] with which her son was to be invested'.[33] She hoped to use the power and prestige of the *Dolphin* to further the career of her son, for whom her maternal affection was real.

The Tahiti discovered by the *Dolphin*'s crew was not Beaglehole's 'symbolic island'. Robertson wrote that the island 'hade the most Beautiful appearance its posable to Imagin' and the corresponding beauty of the island girls was universally acknowledged: 'the sailors swore they never saw handsomer made women in their lives.'[34] Wallis, writing up his log, concurred, but considered the cost: 'The women in General are very handsome, some really great Beauties, yet their Virtue was not proof against a Nail.'[35] If he 'had stumbled on a foundation stone of the Romantic Movement' he was naturally not aware of it, but was well aware of the force that had been required to place that stone in position: 'notwithstanding all their civility, I doubt not but it was more thro' fear than love that they respected us so much'.[36] The journals of Wallis and Robertson were not published, however, and the next visitors to Tahiti, who would benefit from the impression made by the *Dolphin*'s 'Great Guns', were not to know why Tahitian policy, in subsequent encounters with Europeans, was to make love not war.

Louis-Antoine de Bougainville, courtier, savant, soldier, sailor, sighted the high volcanic peak of Tahiti on 2 April 1768. Although he came to the Pacific in command of the *Boudeuse* and the *Étoile* under the influence of de Brosses, with official instructions to search for a southern continent, he would find no such continent, but the island which Wallis had labelled 'King George the thirds Island' and which Bougainville himself would name 'la Nouvelle-Cythère'.[37] If Robertson had not 'the pen of Milton' at his disposal neither had Wallis. If they had read the classics or the modern philosophers it did not show. Bougainville stayed only ten days at Tahiti but he had read enough literature and philosophy to interpret his experience accordingly.[38] Not that he was an admirer of Rousseau. Of the Patagonians he had written in his journal, with reference to that philosopher's self-confessed disability: 'Ceux-ci pissent accroupis, seroit-ce la façon de pisser la plus naturelle? Si cela étoit, Jean-Jacques Rousseau qui pisse très mal à notre manière, auroit dû adopter celle là. Il nous renvoye tant à l'homme sauvage.'[39]

As his ships steered carefully through the Tahitian reefs and anchored, on 6 April, they were surrounded by canoes 'dans plusieurs desquelles il y avoit des femmes'.[40] Bougainville's own journal does not record these details—except to mention that 'il est venue dans une des pirogues une jeune et jolie fille presque nue, qui montroit son sexe pour de petits clouds'—so I quote from the fullest account of the French discovery of 'la Nouvelle-Cythère', given in the journal of Charles-Félix Fesche, a young 'volontaire' on Bougainville's own ship, the *Boudeuse*, who describes a 'nouvelle Vénus' who came aboard from a canoe:

Elle étoit grande, bien faite et avoit un tein que la plus grande partie des espagnolles ne désavoueroient pas pour sa blancheur. Plusieurs françois gourmet et à qui un jeûne forcé de plusieurs mois donnoit un appétit dévorant s'approchent, regardent, admirent, touchent. Bientôt le voile qui dérobait à leur yeux les appas qu'une pudeur blâmable sans doute ordonne de cacher, ce voile dis-je est bientôt levé, plus promptement il est vrai par la divinité indienne elle-même que par eux, elle suivoit les usages de de son pays, usage hélas que la corruption de nos moeurs a détruit ché nous. Quel pinceau pouroit décrire les merveilles que nous découvrons à la chute heureuse de ce voile importun, une retraite destiné à l'amour lui seul, il lui seroit impossible d'y loger un second avec lui, un bosquet enchanteur que ce dieu avoit sans doute lui même planté.[41]

Such was the Tahiti discovered by the French: 'une retraite destiné à l'amour lui seule', an idea as well as an island.

When the ships had anchored Bougainville himself went ashore, where 'une foule d'indiens nous a reçu sur le bord du rivage avec les démonstrations de joye les plus décisives', as he wrote in his journal. An invitation was made by the local chief and, sitting on the ground in the open air, served with fish, fruit, and water, 'nous avons fait un repas de l'âge d'or avec des gens qui en sont encore à ce siècle fortuné.'[42] On the following day, according to the next entry in Bougainville's journal, the French sailors wandered freely on the island, to be received by Tahitian Didos, like epic voyagers from Troy:

En entrant dans des maisons, on leur a présenté de jeunes filles, on a jonché la terre de feuillage et grand nombre d'indiens et d'indiennes faisant un cercle autour d'eux, on a célébré l'hospitalité, tandis qu'aux accords de la flutte, un des assistans chantoit une hymne de jouissance. 'O Venus, hospitibus nam te dare jura loquuntur, hunc loetum Tyriisque diem Trojaque profectis esse velis nostrosque hujus meminisse minores.' Didon fait ensuitte les honneurs de chez elle à la façon de cette isle . . . Ce peuple ne respire que le repos et les plaisirs des sens. Vénus est la déesse que l'on y sert. La douceur du climat, la beauté du paisage, la fertilité du sol partout arrosé de rivières et de cascades, la pureté de l'air . . . tout inspire la volupté. Aussi l'ai-je nommé la Nouvelle-Cythère.[43]

Fesche gives a more detailed account of such Tahitian hospitality in his journal, rendered in prose more erotic than ethnographic, but prefaced with an insistence that 'les choses que je dirai avoir vu sont dans la plus exacte vérité': 'Une main hardie et conduite par l'amour se glisse sur deux pommes naissantes ennemies l'une de l'autre . . . La main glissa bientôt . . . [La fille] écarta ces deux obstacles qui empêchent l'entrée de ce temple . . .'. But, faced with a young girl 'avec le seul habillement que portoit Eve avant son péché', and also 'la présence de 50 Indiens qui l'environnoient', the civilized Adam falls a victim to postlapsarian shame, 'nos préjugés'. Fesche draws his conclusion: 'La corruption de nos moeurs nous a fait trouver du mal dans une action dans laquelle ces gens avec raison ne trouvent que du bien.'[44] The young Prince of Nassau-Siegen, sent round the world to keep him from the temptations of Paris, played a leading role in a very similar scene with a young girl and a crowd of Tahitian spectators, remarking in his journal that 'la jeune fille étoit très jolie mais les préjugés européens exigent plus de mistère', and concluding: 'Heureuse nation qui ne connoit point les noms odieux de honte et de scandale.'[45]

The ships' naturalist, Commerson, also went on shore, to botanize with his servant Jean Baré, as Bougainville relates:

M. de Commerçon étoit descendu à terre avec Baré qui le suivoit dans toutes ses herborisations . . . A peine le domestique est-il sur le rivage que les Cythéréens l'entourent, crient que c'est une femme et veulent lui bien faire les honneurs de l'isle. Il fallut que l'officier de garde vint le dégager.[46]

Jean Baré, as the Tahitians discovered, was Jeanne Baré. After her Tahitian discovery she was interviewed by Bougainville and 'les larmes aux yeux m'a avoué qu'elle étoit fille'.[47]

On 10 April a Tahitian was found shot dead.[48] On the 12th three others were bayoneted by soldiers from the *Boudeuse*, who were apprehended by the Prince and arrested.[49] Bougainville feared retaliation and there was danger, too, for the ships, as the French had not found the safe anchorage of Matavai. It was time to leave the Tahitians, all 'pleurant amèrement', except for a young man named Aotourou who was going all the way to Paris, so much further than he knew.[50] Bougainville's account closes with a long farewell to 'la Nouvelle-Cythère':

Je ne saurois quitter cette isle fortunée sans renouveller ici les éloges que j'en ai déjà faits. La nature l'a placée dans le plus beau climat de l'univers, embellie des plus rians aspects, enrichie de tous ses dons, couverte d'habitans beaux, grands, forts. Elle-même leur a dicté des loix, ils les suivent en paix et forment peut-être la plus heureuse société qui existe sur ce globe. Legislateurs et philosophes, venez voir ici tout établi ce que votre imagination n'a pu même rêver . . . Ils n'ont besoin que des fruits que la terre y prodigue sans culture, le reste, en nous attirant, leur attireroit tous les maux du siècle de fer. Adieu peuple heureux et sage, soyez toujours ce que vous êtes. Je ne me rappellerai jamais sans délices le peu d'instans que j'ai passés au milieu de vous et, tant que je vivrai, je célèbrerai l'heureuse isle de Cythère. C'est la véritable Eutopie.[51]

Some weeks after leaving Tahiti Bougainville made a less pleasant discovery: 'Il s'est déclaré à bord des deux navires ces jours-ci plusieurs maladies vénériennes prises à Cythère . . . Colomb l'a rapporté d'Amérique. La voilà dans un isle isolée au milieu des mers.'[52] In time he learned that Wallis had anticipated his discovery of Tahiti and in his published account of his voyage he laid the blame for the Cytherean venereal disease on the British sailors, starting a long controversy.[53] He also learned more about Tahitian society from Aotourou and what he learned caused him somewhat to modify the account of Tahiti he would give to the world. But his first impressions of Tahiti, as we have seen, are of classical myth and literature rediscovered in reality, of the golden age revived, and, like Montaigne in 'Des cannibales', Bougainville contrasts this reality with the imaginary societies dreamed of by legislators and philosophers. Tahiti is no utopia, no 'not place', but the real 'beautiful place': 'la véritable Eutopie'.

Bougainville's published *Voyage* would make its contribution to literature, would repay the debt it owed, but his voyage would contribute little to science beyond some islands and plants found and named, including, of course, that tropical vine with red and purple flowers in which Bougainville gallantly placed 'l'espoir de ma renommée.'[54] Bougainville's was the first voyage of discovery equipped with a travelling scientist, but Commerson's collection and notes were never properly catalogued and published.[55] On the return voyage the clerk, Saint-Germain, grumbled into his journal:

Que pouvons-nous . . . dire sur Cyterre? Avons-nous vu l'intérieur du pays? M. de Commerson aporte-il la notte des trésors qu'elle renferme ou peut renfermer en fait d'histoire naturelle, plante ou mines? Y avons-nous sondé le long de la cotte? . . . A quoy se réduit l'utilité de ce voyage pour la nation?[56]

Bougainville's was the first of a new kind of voyage in which the amateur scientist, like Dampier, was replaced by a professional. We shall now consider the second such voyage, which was to enable the Fellows of the Royal Society to do for themselves what they had been directing the far-voyagers to do for them: 'to study *Nature* rather than *Books*'.[57] The transit of the planet Venus across the sun was due in 1769, according to the predictions of Edmund Halley, and would not recur for more than a century. The event, if observed from various specific points on the earth's surface, could determine the earth's distance from the sun, and one of these points on the earth's surface happened to be in the middle of the Pacific. The Royal Society petitioned the King, who promised funds and a naval ship for the necessary voyage. Alexander Dalrymple, who was a Fellow of the Society, now saw the prospect of turning his theory of the southern continent into reality, of studying it in nature rather than in books, and was recommended by the Society for the captaincy. The Admiralty also thought a search for the southern continent a useful subsidiary function for the voyage, but refused to appoint Dalrymple to command a naval vessel, informing the Society 'that such appointment was totaly repugnant to the rules of the navy' and choosing James Cook instead, early in April 1768.[58]

Naval regulations did not, of course, preclude the Society's right to appoint the scientific personnel, although Dalrymple flatly refused any role except that of command. Naturally the Society appointed an astronomer, but they took consideration also of other branches of science and recommended 'Joseph Banks Esq. Fellow of this Society, a Gentleman of large fortune, who is well versed in natural history'.[59] Banks was qualified not only as a natural historian, a Fellow, and a gentleman who had decided that 'my Grand Tour shall be one round the whole globe', but also by his 'large fortune'—an income of £6,000 p.a.—which enabled him to furnish the expedition lavishly with scientific gadgetry and to employ a team of servants, artists, and scientific assistants, notably Dr Solander, an able botanist and a Fellow of the Society.[60] As another Fellow reported to Linnaeus, Solander's teacher, in Sweden: 'No people ever went to sea better fitted out for the purpose of Natural History.'[61]

In May 1768 Wallis returned with the news of his discovery of Tahiti, a hospitable island conveniently located in the area from which Venus was to be observed, so the destination of the voyage was easily decided. Cook's instructions stipulated that, after the observation of Venus, he was to search the Pacific south of Tahiti, where 'there is reason to imagine that a Continent or Land of great extent may be found'.[62] In fact Cook's voyage would exclude this imaginary continent from a great part of the Pacific and his second voyage would nearly eliminate it, severing it from Australia and shrinking it to the size of Antarctica.[63] In a few decades the vast continent would be exploded, mostly by its anti-Columbus, James Cook, and crumbled into a multitude of islands in a vast ocean.

The *Endeavour* sailed on 26 August 1768, and anchored in Matavai Bay on 13 April 1769. The observation of the transit of Venus was to prove less than perfect for various reasons, chiefly because Venus was clothed, as Cook reported, in 'an

Atmosphere or dusky shade round the body of the Planet', but the three months the *Endeavour* stayed at Tahiti gave considerable time for observation of the Tahitians.[64] Banks's journal gives a more detailed account than Cook's journal, for botany at Tahiti took second place to ethnography, and Banks had much more contact with the Tahitians than Cook, who noted that Banks was 'always very alert upon all occations wherein the Natives are concern'd'.[65] His amiability and authority were appreciated and respected by the Tahitians and he entered into their culture in ways a man of Cook's responsibilities and temperament could not, 'sleeping continualy in their houses in the woods', 'stripping off my European cloths' to make a participant observation of a Tahitian mourning ceremony, and observing everything from the tattooing of a girl's buttocks to the construction of a fishing hook.[66]

On the day the *Endeavour* anchored Banks went ashore to receive his first impression of Tahiti: 'the scene we saw was the truest picture of an arcadia of which we were going to be kings that the imagination can form.'[67] The next day the kings of Arcadia were

attended by the ladies who shewd us all kind of civilities our situation could admit of, but as there were no places of retirement, the houses being intirely without walls, we had not an opportunity of putting their politeness to every test that maybe some of us would not have faild to have done had circumstances been more favourable; indeed we had no reason to doubt any part of their politeness, as by their frequently pointing to the matts on the ground and sometimes by force seating themselves and us upon them they plainly shewd that they were much less jealous of observation than we were.[68]

To the evident displeasure of his hostess, a chief's wife, but 'ugly enough in con science', Banks applied himself to 'a very pretty girl with a fire in her eyes', while Dr Solander had his spy glass stolen from his pocket.[69] Purea, 'the Dolphins Queen', reappeared on the scene, her power and circumstances much reduced for reasons the British could not fully comprehend: after the *Dolphin*'s departure her political rivals had violently taken objection to her ambitious plans for her son.[70] She remained none the less a notable character and Banks called upon 'her majesty but was surprizd to find her in bed [in her canoe] with a hansome lusty young man'. He noted that 'I am offerd if I please to supply his place, but I am at present otherwise engag'd; indeed was I free as air her majesties person is not the most desireable'.[71] It is clear that Banks does not refer here to his betrothed, Miss Harriet Blosset, busily employed in working waistcoats for him, far away, but then it is by no means clear to whom he does refer. Perhaps to Purea's 'attendant Othéothéa . . . (my flame)', but she was not the one 'with a fire in her eyes', nor one of the '3 hansome girls [who] with very little perswasion' agreed to share a tent with Banks on a later occasion.[72]

It is perhaps Banks's interest in Tahitian ladies that explains why he and not Cook was given a leading role in a curious Tahitian ceremony that does not yield much to anthropological analysis beyond the conclusion that Banks's admiration for Tahitian ladies was reciprocated.[73] The participants, apart from Banks, were some ladies and a man equipped with nine pieces of cloth.

Three were first laid. The foremost of the women, who seemed to be the principal, then stept upon them and quickly unveiling all her charms gave me a most convenient opportunity of admiring them by turning herself gradualy round: 3 peices more were laid and she repeated her part of the ceremony: the other three were then laid which made a treble covering of the ground between her and me, she then once more displayed her naked beauties and immediately marchd up to me . . .[74]

Cook's account of this 'ceremony' is, understandably, more objective. He does not speak of the lady's 'unveiling all her charms' or of 'a most convenient opportunity for admiring them', but reports that the lady 'step'd upon the Cloth and with as much Innocency as one could possibly conceve, expose'd herself intirely naked from the waist downwards, in this manner she turn'd her Self once or twice round, I am not certain which'.[75]

On the following Sunday Cook proposed a divine service in the fort he had constructed to protect the Observatory on 'Point Venus, so called from the Observation being made there'.[76] Banks was keen that some of 'our Indian freinds . . . should be present that they might see our behaviour and we might if possible explain to them (in some degree at least) the reasons of it.' His guests, however, politely 'imitated my motions' but would not 'attend at all to any explanation'.[77] The symbolic significance for Tahitian society, if any, of the 'Scene' that followed later the same day has never been satisfactorily explained, but in Britain this 'Scene' would become symbolic of Tahiti, that 'symbolic island', and of the whole South Seas.[78] The Point Venus 'Scene' is described by Cook, but not by Banks, who may have been 'otherwise engag'd'.

This day we perform'd divine Service in one of the Tents in the Fort where several of the Natives attended and behaved with great decency the whole time: this day closed with an odd Scene at the Gate of the Fort where a young fellow above 6 feet high lay with a little Girl about 10 or 12 years of age publickly before several of our people and a number of the Natives. What makes me mention this, is because, it appear'd to be done more from Custom than Lewdness, for there were several women present particularly Obarea [Purea] and several others of the better sort and these were so far from shewing the least disaprobation that they instructed the girl how she should act her part, who young as she was, did not seem to want it [i.e to require such instruction].[79]

Inevitably, during three months of contact between the British and the Tahitians, relations were not always amicable and amorous. The inhabitants of 'King George the third's Island' respected the value of European property but not the European idea of the rights to possess it. A Tahitian was shot within days of the *Endeavour*'s arrival, while stealing a musket. Banks's attractive 'white jacket and waistcoat, with silver frogs' changed hands while he slept, chastely, in Purea's canoe, and so did the the carefully guarded astronomical quadrant, essential for the observation of Venus, which had to be hunted across the island, retrieved in pieces and reassembled.[80]

The British learned from the Tahitians of the previous, non-British visitors to 'King George the third's Island', who had brought 'on board their ships a woman', and also, according to Cook, 'the Venerial distemper . . . now as common as in any part of the world'.[81] Even so, two young marines preferred Tahiti to Europe and, when the time of the *Endeavour*'s departure drew near, they deserted, Cook's enquiries revealing that 'they were gone to the Mountains & that they had got each of them a Wife & would not return'.[82] He had to threaten the lives of the local chiefs before the Tahitians would cooperate in the arrest of the deserters, who were, however, recaptured in time for the *Endeavour*'s departure on 13 July, 'not without plenty of tears', to circumnavigate New Zealand, discredit the southern continent, and discover the east coast of Australia.[83]

It was probably not until after they had sailed from Tahiti that Cook and Banks had the opportunity to compose the reports of Tahiti that follow the narratives of events in both their journals. To what extent, we may ask, do these reports confirm or contradict Bougainville's as yet unpublished description of a Eutopian, Elysian Eden or, indeed, Banks's own initial impression, on the first day he went ashore on Tahiti, that 'the scene we saw was the truest picture of an arcadia'? To what extent, in other words, was the discovery of Tahiti recorded in Cook's and Banks's journals a rediscovery, as in the journals of Bougainville and his men, of the lost paradises of biblical and classical myth? Because Cook's report is heavily indebted to Banks's report, we should attend principally to Banks:

In the article of food these happy people may almost be said to be exempt from the curse of our forefather; scarcely can it be said that they earn their bread with the sweat of their brow when their cheifest sustenance Bread fruit is procurd with no more trouble than that of climbing a tree and pulling it down.[84]

What about the other concomitant of the Fall: shame? To quote Banks again: 'all privacy is banishd even from those actions which the decency of Europaeans keep most secret.'[85] Neither Cook nor Banks expresses shock at the Tahitian customs. Word for word they describe a dance which they call the 'Timorodee', perhaps a rendering of the Tahitian 'ti moro-iti', meaning 'copulation':

they dance especialy the young girls whenever they can collect 8 or 10 together, singing most indecent words using most indecent actions and setting their mouths askew in a most extrordinary manner, in the practise of which they are brought up from their earlyest childhood; in doing this they keep time to a suprizing nicety.

The dance is doubly 'indecent', according to Banks, but nicely timed. Cook agrees exactly, and adds that it is an 'indecent dance'.[86]

After the description of the 'Timorodee', however, both reports give an account of a Tahitian institution that was indeed shocking to Banks and Cook: the society, or rather, religious order, of the 'Arioi', who toured Tahiti and the adjacent islands giving exhibitions of dance, drama, and music, 'like Homer of old', says Banks, 'poets as well as musicians'.[87] Here is Banks, fresh from the 'Timorodee':

One amusement more I must mention tho I confess I hardly dare touch upon it as it is founded upon a custom so devilish, inhuman, and contrary to the first principles of human nature that tho the natives have repeatedly told it to me, far from concealing it rather looking upon it as a branch of freedom upon which they valued themselves, I can hardly bring myself to beleive it much less expect that any body Else shall. It is this that more than half of the better sort of the inhabitants of the Island have like Comus in Milton enterd into a resolution of enjoying free liberty in love without a possibility of being troubled or disturbd by its consequences; these mix together with the utmost freedom seldom cohabiting together more than one or two days by which means they have fewer children than they would otherwise have, but those who are so unfortunate as to be thus begot are smotherd at the moment of their birth.[88]

So there was death even in 'arcadia', and Comus in paradise after all.

When Banks returned from his global grand tour, landing in England on 12 July 1771, it was to find himself a lion. We have Lady Mary Coke's authority for this: 'the people who are most talk'd of at present are Mr Banks & Doctor Solander: I saw them at Court & afterwards at L[ad]y Hertford's, but did not hear them give any account of their Voyage round the world, which I am told is very amusing.'[89] More or less garbled accounts of Tahiti appeared in the papers for those without Lady Mary's opportunities: 'The women are extremely lascivious . . . dance in the most indecent manner . . . a thousand obscene gesticulations [etc.]'.[90]

The Admiralty, with other things to consider, had possession of Cook's journal, as well as those of Byron, Wallis, Robertson, and Carteret, and was anxious to publish an official account of the voyages in order to establish British claims in the South Seas.[91] The Admiralty, in fact, was in need of an author. So, when Lord Sandwich happened to encounter Dr Burney in September 1771, the latter 'had a happy opportunity of extremely obliging Dr. Hawkesworth', as Fanny Burney relates:

His Lordship was speaking of the late voyage round the world and mentioned his having the papers of it in his possession; for he is First Lord of the Admiralty; and said that they were not arranged, but mere rough draughts, and that he should be much obliged to any one who could recommend a proper person to *write the Voyage*. My father directly named Dr. Hawkesworth, and his Lordship did him the honour to accept his recommendation.[92]

Dr Hawkesworth wrote in early October to thank the extremely obliging Dr Burney and to report that: 'the property of the work will be my own. Accept my best Thanks, dear Sir, for the Advantage which this work must necessarily procure me, which will be very considerable'.[93] The advantage amounted to the considerable sum of £6,000, which Hawkesworth, after applications from half the booksellers in London and some hard bargaining, obtained in return for the copyright to his *Voyages*.[94]

Hawkesworth's *Voyages* was eagerly awaited. 'So much for what we *have* been reading', wrote Walpole to a correspondent; 'at present our ears listen and our eyes are expecting . . . Mr Banks's voyage'.[95] Boswell and Johnson, who provide a running commentary on Tahitian affairs in London, anticipated the forthcoming event in their different ways. Boswell spoke with enthusiasm of 'the people of Otaheite who have the bread tree'. Johnson would have none of this nonsense about 'ignorant savages' and refuted Boswell as he had refuted Berkeley: 'No, Sir, (holding up a slice of a good loaf,) this is better than the bread tree.'[96] His opinion of his old friend Dr Hawkesworth's forthcoming work was equally characteristic:

'Sir, if you talk of it as a subject of commerce, it will be gainful; if as a book that is to increase human knowledge, I believe there will not be much of that. Hawkesworth can tell only what the voyagers have told him; and they have found very little, only one new animal, I think.' Boswell: 'But many insects, Sir.'[97]

What kind of *Voyages* was Dr Hawkesworth—poet, critic, essayist, adaptor and expurgator of Southerne's *Oroonoko*, author of *Almoran and Hamet*, translator of Fénelon's *Aventures de Télémaque*—going to write? Sandwich, according to Fanny Burney, regarded the original journals as 'mere rough draughts'. He wanted 'a proper person', a man of letters, not a seaman, 'to *write the Voyage*'. Cook admitted that he himself had 'neither natural or acquired abilities for writing', but his claim to represent what he reported 'with undisguised truth and without gloss' is justified by his journal, written in the 'naked natural' prose Sprat had recommended for the Royal Society.[98] As a recorder of his travels Cook was Montaigne's man. Nevertheless Hawkesworth had been employed 'to write the Voyage' and to adapt the journals of Cook, Wallis, Robertson, and others to form a continuous and homogeneous narrative. He also obtained for this purpose the journal of Banks, promising Sandwich, who had supplied it, to 'satisfy the utmost Delicacy of a Gentleman to whom I shall be so much obliged'.[99] This obligation Hawkesworth proudly acknowledged in his introduction to his account of the voyage of the *Endeavour*, pointing out that 'few philosophers have furnished materials for accounts of voyages undertaken to discover new countries'.[100]

In his General Introduction to his *Voyages* Hawkesworth gives us a glimpse of himself discussing narrative technique with the Admiralty. It was 'readily acknowledged on all hands', he says, that the work should be written 'in the first person', as this would 'more strongly excite an interest, and consequently afford more entertainment'.[101] Lest this impersonation of 'the several Commanders' should restrict Hawkesworth to a merely 'naked narrative', it was also agreed that he should be at liberty to 'intersperse such sentiments and observations as my subject should suggest'.[102] As his manuscript would be submitted to the persons in whose names Hawkesworth would express his sentiments, and their approval secured, 'it would signify little who conceived the sentiments that should be expressed'.[103] This promise was properly kept, Hawkesworth assures the reader:

That no doubt might remain of the fidelity with which I have related the events recorded in my materials, the manuscript account of each voyage was read to the respective Commanders at the Admiralty . . . The account of the voyage of the Endeavour was also read to Mr. Banks and Dr. Solander, in whose hands, as well as in those of Captain Cook, the manuscript was left for a considerable time after the reading.[104]

Hawkesworth may have believed this but it is difficult to reconcile with the statements of Cook and others to the contrary. Carteret indignantly denied having seen or approved the manuscript and Cook recorded that 'I never had the perusal of the Manuscript nor did I ever hear the whole of it read in the mode it was written, notwithstanding what Dr Hawkesworth has said to the Contrary in the Interduction'.[105]

The resulting *Voyages*, inevitably, was not a 'naked narrative'. Hawkesworth's narrator, a composite character, speaking in the names of Byron, Wallis, Carteret, and Cook, and combining, in the account of the *Endeavour*'s voyage, Cook's resolution, Banks's sympathy, and Hawkesworth's sententiousness, is a creation with a past in Homeric epic and a future in boys' adventure, his roots in Odysseus and his flowering in Captain Hornblower.[106] Hawkesworth's novelistic treatment of his material—diligently characterizing and dramatizing, supplying comedy, pathos, and continual grandiloquence—can be illustrated briefly with reference to Wallis's and Robertson's accounts of Tahiti. On at least two occasions Hawkesworth provides gratuitous humour, regaling his reader with stories of a Tahitian butted by the *Dolphin*'s goat and another astonished by the removal of a wig, incidents comically illustrative of primitive simplicity, but without any manuscript authority, though amusing enough to find their way into several twentieth-century historical accounts.[107] Wallis, Hawkesworth's narrator, and Purea are inevitably central characters, and their relationship, although quite proper, is so very proper that it is elevated to heroic heights. Purea becomes 'my princess' to Hawkesworth's gallant Captain, who is so moved by Robertson's opinion of the 'tenderness and Affection' of her tearful farewell that he becomes quite emotional himself: 'our Indian friends, and particularly the queen, once more bade us farewel, with such tenderness of affection and grief, as filled both my heart and my eyes.'[108]

Wallis's voyage, however, received much less attention from Hawkesworth than Cook's, which occupied volumes two and three of the three quarto volumes of Hawkesworth's *Voyages* and contained, as Hawkesworth announced in his General Introduction, most of his 'sentiments and observations'.[109] So what did Hawkesworth observe about Tahiti, a pivotal point in his *Voyages*, first discovered by Odysseus–Wallis and then lingeringly revisited by Odysseus–Cook? To what extent did he transform or distort the firsthand observations of Cook and Banks? Was he the expurgator of Tahiti, as of Southerne's *Oroonoko*, or did he discover, like Telemachus in his translation of Fénelon's *Aventures de Télémaque*, 'that there was yet a people in the world, who, by a perfect conformity to the law of nature, were so wise and so happy'?[110]

Hawkesworth's 'observations' are frequently comparative, as described in his General Introduction, where he outlines a grandly Frazerian role for himself, learnedly 'noting the similitude or dissimilitude between the opinions, customs, or manners of the people now first discovered, and those of nations that have been long known'.[111] He is a philosopher as well as a comparative anthropologist. A Tahitian's passionate response to a false accusation of theft, for example, moves him to comment that: 'Upon this occasion it may be observed, that these people have a knowledge of right and wrong from the mere dictates of natural conscience.'[112] The remark is inconsistent with some of Hawkesworth's other observations, which arise as he is inspired by this or that 'occasion' rather than from a considered judgement on Tahitian society as a whole, and it is not meant to license all Tahitian behaviour, but it is obviously in the tradition of primitivism and Deism. On another occasion, ruminating about the Tahitian custom of exposing their dead, Hawkesworth even seems to take up the position of Montaigne, suggesting that 'perhaps no better use can be made of reading an account of manners altogether new' than to lift 'the veil of prejudice and custom' from the 'follies' of European manners. But the review of civilized customs Hawkesworth intends is not very radical. The example of a European 'folly' given is the belief of some 'honest' Catholics that they will 'secure the happiness of a future state by . . . dying with the slipper of St. Francis upon their foot'.[113]

Hawkesworth's Tahitians are not Montaigne's 'cannibales'. When he allows a consideration of comparative happiness to arise from a discussion of Tahitian tears—'like those of children', easily provoked and quickly forgotten—the question of Tahitian happiness is raised only to be dismissed, because: 'if we admit that they are upon the whole happier than we, we must admit that the child is happier than the man, and that we are losers by the perfection of our nature, the increase of our knowledge, and the enlargement of our views'.[114] Clearly the reader is not encouraged to admit that 'we are losers by the perfection of our nature'. Indeed the whole observation seems intended to supply the reader with material for 'the increase of [his] knowledge, and the enlargement of [his] views', and in particular with the knowledge and the view that such knowledge and views are superior to any childish happiness he may lose 'by the perfection of [his] nature'.

Those are Hawkesworth's closest approaches to primitivism and an examination of them shows him not guilty of any programme to transform the Tahitians into exemplars of natural virtue and ideal bliss. Indeed most of his observations have little to do with directing his reader's response to the Tahitians. Banks's description of how 'the Indians amuse or excercise themselves in a manner truly surprizing', by surfing, sends Hawkesworth off, after repeating it, on a wave of uplifting sentiments about the latent abilities of all mankind, exemplified by the thrilling skills of rope-dancers, the acute hearing of the blind, etc., leaving the reader to draw the conclusion, if he can remember the original topic, that he has an un-discovered but unsurprising talent for surfing.[115]

It is the comments of Cook and in particular of Banks that are more significant in forming the public view of Tahiti that Hawkesworth would present. As we know, he had the authority of Banks for stating that the Tahitian scene 'realized the poetical fables of Arcadia'.[116] In informing the British that the Tahitians 'seem to be exempted from the first general curse, that "man should eat his bread in the sweat of his brow"', he was following the journals of Banks and Cook, preferring the qualification 'seem' in place of Banks's and Cook's 'almost'.[117] If Tahiti was discovered to the British public as a prelapsarian Arcadia, biblical and classical, it was because those who had seen Tahiti had said as much and Hawkesworth had repeated what they had said.

The indecent and nicely timed 'Timorodee' is described as it is in Banks's and Cook's journals, with 'wanton' replacing 'indecent', and without the addition of any shock or comment.[118] The Arioi practice of infanticide, however, which did shock Banks (and Cook, presumably, who copies some of Banks's reaction), is not viewed with complacency by Hawkesworth. Licensed by his sources to express some disgust and horror, he confuses Arioi infanticide and Arioi promiscuity, condemns both, and fulminates sensationally about 'a scale in dissolute sensuality, which these people have ascended, wholly unknown to every other nation whose manners have been recorded from the beginning of the world to the present hour, and which no imagination could possibly conceive'. The reader's pity is evoked for 'the poor infant . . . smothered the moment it is born' and satisfaction is exacted by applying the adjectives 'diabolical' (to the 'prostitution'), 'horrid' (to the infanticide), and 'accursed' (to the Arioi society in general), these condemnations excelling Banks's 'devilish' and 'inhuman' (applied specifically to the custom of infanticide).[119]

As well as presenting his views and those of his sources, Hawkesworth supplied narrative entertainment, finding in Banks's journal the necessary characters and incidents, such as the welcoming attentions of the Tahitian women, the theft of Banks's clothes, and his encounter with Purea *in flagrante*, Banks's sketch becoming a royal portrait of the 'Queen', her canoe decorously provided with an 'antichamber', and her lover still 'handsome' but no longer 'lusty'.[120] Faithful, though, to his promise to Sandwich, Hawkesworth omits the compromising references to Banks's own amorous relations. We are told of his attentions to the girl 'with a fire in her eyes', but not that this was the motive for his attentions, the fire being safely extinguished. Purea's royal offer to Banks is not mentioned, nor his being 'otherwise engag'd', and Purea's 'attendant Othéóthéa', Banks's 'flame', is merely and vaguely 'an agreeable girl'.[121]

The 'ceremony' of the lady 'unveiling all her charms' to Banks was not compromising, however, and was duly revealed to the British public, although Hawkesworth prefers Cook's more detached description of the incident, taking up the suggestion that the lady's action displayed her 'Innocency' rather than her 'charms', and adding the information that she revolved 'with great composure and deliberation', with the result that Hawkesworth's lady, 'taking up her garments all round her to the waist, turned about, with great composure and deliberation, and with an air of perfect innocence and simplicity'.[122]

These 'uncommon Ceremonies' on Friday were followed by more material for Hawkesworth on Sunday. His chapter heading shows the close connection, as well as juxtaposition, of events, and gives an idea of the kind of Tahitian entertainment his readers would receive for their three guineas: 'Some Ladies visit the Fort with very uncommon Ceremonies: The Indians attend Divine Service, and in the Evening exhibit a most extraordinary Spectacle . . .'.[123] Hawkesworth moves from the fuller account of the divine service given in Banks's journal to the following 'Spectacle'—the 'odd Scene' recorded only by Cook—with editorial agility but without resisting the temptation to link the two events (which are merely juxtaposed in Cook's journal) by way of an amusing but irreverent metaphor. His description of the 'Spectacle' is taken from Cook without much significant revision other than a slight reduction to the man's height, a slight increase in the girl's age, and a substitution of the phrase 'performed the rites of Venus with' for Cook's naked 'lay with', and it is predictably followed by one of Hawkesworth's own 'observations'. The passage is best judged in its entirety, including Hawkesworth's introductory witticism (which is underlined in Banks's copy of the *Voyages*):

Such were our Matins; the Indians thought fit to perform Vespers of a very different kind. A young man, near six feet high, performed the rites of Venus with a little girl about eleven or twelve years of age, before several of our people, and a great number of the natives, without the least sense of its being indecent or improper, but, as appeared, in perfect conformity to the custom of the place. Among the spectators were several women of superior rank, particularly Oberea [Purea], who may properly be said to have assisted at the ceremony; for they gave instructions to the girl how to perform her part, which, young as she was, she did not seem much to stand in need of.

This incident is not mentioned as an object of idle curiosity, but as it deserves consideration in determining a question which has been long debated in philosophy; Whether the shame attending certain actions, which are allowed on all sides to be in themselves innocent, is implanted in Nature, or superinduced by custom? If it has its origin in custom, it will, perhaps, be found difficult to trace that custom, however general, to its source; if in instinct, it will be equally difficult to discover from what cause it is subdued or at least over-ruled among these people, in whose manners not the least trace of it is to be found.[124]

The public spectacle in Hawkesworth's text is ultimately no more explicable than the one in Tahiti, but we can at least make some observations and consider whether the man of letters in his study has distorted the 'odd Scene' the seaman described in Tahiti. Clearly, Hawkesworth's euphemistic 'rites of Venus', in combination with his editorial jest about Tahitian 'Vespers', gives an impression which Cook had not intended of a Tahitian religion of sexual love, but this is not to be attributed simply to the ignorance or fancy of the man of letters, his head full of myth and his eyes far from the truth. We have already seen Hawkesworth's imagery much more deliberately and consistently employed by Bougainville, a first hand observer, in his account of a Tahitian cult of Venus in 'la Nouvelle-Cythère'. Nor can it be said that Hawkesworth, in his concern for the letter of his sources, has completely forgotten to consider his reader. While the 'odd Scene' is in its essentials unchanged, Hawkesworth's substitution for Cook's 'lay with' and his slight changes to Cook's estimates of the man's height (Cook's 'above 6 feet' becomes 'near six feet') and the girl's age (Cook's 'about 10 or 11' becomes 'about eleven or twelve') do suggest some concern to moderate, if not expurgate, the 'Spectacle' for the British public.

We can also observe, which Hawkesworth's public could not, that he has a justification for displaying the 'Spectacle', and for his phrase 'without the least sense of its being indecent or improper', and also for raising the philosophical issue, in Cook's own words: 'What makes me mention this, is because, it appear'd to be done more from Custom than Lewdness'. The philosophical question itself, which Hawkesworth leaves open without pressing Montaigne's conclusion that shame is unnatural, but also without preventing the reader from inferring it, is obviously in keeping with Hawkesworth's sense of his editorial duty to supply philosophical reflections and cultural comparisons, but has the rather more important functions of clothing the 'Spectacle', otherwise a 'naked narrative', and of distancing it as well as justifying it—no mere 'object of idle curiosity'—by placing it in what Hawkesworth presumably believed was a safely balanced and neutral philosophical context. It was perhaps to excuse the public description rather than the public performance of 'certain actions', perhaps to cover himself rather than the Tahitians, that Hawkesworth added his 'observation' to Cook's observation at Point Venus.

So, in summing up the evidence of Hawkesworth's Tahiti, we can observe, as he would say, that while he provided entertainment and information from Cook's and Banks's journals and added literary and philosophical embellishments with the intention of elevating the styles of his sources and the minds of his readers, he cannot justly be accused of censoring or significantly misrepresenting the matter of Tahiti as described at first hand by his sources. Andrew Kippis, who produced his own account of Cook's life and voyages fifteen years later, in 1788, gives a full account of the divine service at Tahiti, introduced, pointedly, as 'an instance . . . of the inattention of the natives to our modes of religion', but makes no mention of either the 'ceremony' before or the 'Scene' after that event.[125] In describing that 'ceremony' and that 'Scene' Hawkesworth omitted nothing and invented nothing, but closely followed his sources, Cook and Banks—all too closely, perhaps, and without sufficiently reflecting that what was public in Tahiti 'without the least sense of its being indecent or improper' was now, by himself, to be made public in Britain. Nevertheless, if Hawkesworth did not expurgate the prelapsarian, publicly sexual Tahitian, neither did he invent him. That Tahitian was discovered by Cook and Banks in Tahiti, as he—or she—had been by Bougainville.

The eagerly awaited publication of Hawkesworth's *Account of the Voyages undertaken by the order of his present Majesty for making Discoveries in the Southern Hemisphere* took place on 9 June 1773, and Walpole 'waded through' the volumes to conclude that they lacked 'entertaining matter'.[126] But a second edition was required before the end of the year, which also saw an American edition, followed by French and German translations in 1774 and a third English edition in 1785, by which time shilling and sixpenny parts were on sale.[127] Mrs Charlotte Hayes recognized that Hawkesworth's *Voyages* contained not only 'entertaining matter' but matter for entertainment, and invited her clients to observe for themselves in London what Cook had observed in Tahiti:

Mrs. Hayes presents her most respectful compliments to Lord––, and takes the liberty to acquaint him, that to-morrow evening, precisely at seven, a dozen beautiful Nymphs, unsullied and untainted, and who breathe health and nature, will perform the celebrated rites of Venus, as practised at *Otaheite*, under the instruction and tuition of Queen Oberea; in which character Mrs. Hayes will appear upon this occasion.[128]

An eyewitness account of Mrs Hayes's 'rites of Venus'—which were apparently attended by several distinguished observers, some of whom became participant observers—reports that the twelve 'beautiful Nymphs' were partnered by twelve young men who 'presented each of their mistresses', before performing, 'with a Nail'.[129]

While Walpole registered his disappointment with 'an account of the fishermen on the coasts of forty islands', and Mrs Hayes supervised the 'celebrated rites', and the *Covent-Garden Magazine; or Amorous Repository* choicely excerpted, featuring what 'we think will be worthy the perusal of *our* readers'—particularly the Tahitian 'rites of Venus' and Dr Hawkesworth's 'own truly philosophical observations'—other responses to Hawkesworth's book included disbelief and outrage.[130] A man calling himself 'A Christian' harangued and castigated Hawkesworth in the press, sustaining for ten weeks a tirade of which this is only a sample:

Our Women may find *in Dr. Hawkesworth's Book* stronger Excitements to vicious Indulgences than the most intriguing French Novel could present to their Imaginations [and] our Libertines may throw aside the *Woman of Pleasure* [i.e. Cleland's pornographic novel, better known as *Fanny Hill*], and gratify their impure Minds with the Perusal of infinitely more lascivious Recitals than are to be found in that scandalous Performance!'[131]

John Wesley, a better Christian, took refuge in disbelief. Any text which contradicted the biblical account of postlapsarian shame must necessarily be fictional: '"Men and women coupling together in the face of the sun, and in the sight of scores of people!" . . . Hume or Voltaire might believe this, but I cannot . . . I cannot but rank this narrative with that of Robinson Crusoe.'[132]

Some ladies were not excited by the *Voyages*. Mrs Elizabeth Montagu, for example, doyenne of the Blue Stockings, wrote to her sister:

I cannot enter into the prudery of the Ladies, who are afraid to own they have read the Voyages, and less still into the moral delicacy of those who suppose the effronterie of the Demoiselles of Ottaheité will corrupt our Misses; if the girls had invented a surer way to keep intrigues secret, it might have been dangerous, but their publick amours will not be imitated.[133]

One of Mrs Montagu's friends, however, did not feel that the proud disclaimer she made of any firsthand knowledge of the *Voyages* should prevent her from expressing a widely held opinion: 'It gives one great pleasure to find that this nation has still virtue enough to be shocked and disgusted by . . . an outrage against decency, such as Dr. Hawkesworth's last performance, which I find is most universally disliked.'[134]

Dr Hawkesworth, author of Tahitian indecency, for which he was held as guilty as if he had invented it or even perpetrated it, survived the publication of his 'last performance' by less than six months. It was generally agreed that his *Voyages* had brought him not only fortune but ill fame, ill health, and death. After a dinner Hawkesworth attended at the Burneys' in Queen Square in October 1773, Fanny remarked in her journal that the abuse of his *Voyages* 'has really affected his health'.[135] She, whose father had been so helpful, was certain of the cause of his death the next month, which she explained afterwards in a letter:

The death of poor Dr. Hawkesworth is most sincerely lamented by us all, the more so as we do really attribute it to the abuse he has met with . . . His book was dearly purchased at the price of his character, and peace . . . He dined with us about a month before he died, and we all agreed we never saw a man more altered, thin, livid harassed![136]

Another acquaintance of Hawkesworth's contributes 'high living' in the fast company of Sandwich to the reasons for the livid appearance and sad disappearance of Dr Hawkesworth, who 'became careless and luxurious; hurt his constitution by high living'.[137] The critic and scholar Edmond Malone added opium and suicide to the melancholy tale of pious Dr Hawkesworth, tempted to indecency by £6,000 and, as debauched Dr Hawkesworth, nearly Tahitian Dr Hawkesworth, meeting his inevitable end. Attacks on his *Voyages*, according to Malone,

affected him so much that, from the low spirits he was seized with a nervous fever, which on account of the high living he had indulged in had the more power on him; and he is supposed to have put an end to his life by intentionally taking an immoderate dose of opium.[138]

Hawkesworth's literary efforts were not completely obscured by his indecency, however. Walpole was quick to remark upon Hawkesworth's epic treatment of Wallis and Purea, scoffing in one of his letters that 'an old black gentlewoman of forty carries Capt. Wallis cross a river, when he was too weak to walk, and the man represents them as a new edition of Dido and Aeneas'.[139] But Walpole's scorn was another man's praise. A sympathetic writer in the *Monthly Review* found Hawkesworth's 'occasional reflections' on some of the 'curious facts' in his *Voyages* to be 'ingenious, philosophical and well-expressed'. There was, he suggested, a resemblance between Tahitian society and the ideal condition of man depicted in Rousseau's *Discours sur l'inégalité*, 'la véritable jeunesse du Monde', and he admired Purea's 'most tender attachment to our adventurers'. She seemed, he thought, 'as susceptible as Queen Dido'.[140] The *Gentleman's Magazine* also detected the influence of Virgil in a voyage 'so elegantly written', and considered 'the parting of the Captain and his Indian Queen' to be 'very similar to that of Dido and Aeneas'.[141]

If the similarity between Purea and Dido was beautiful, the disparity was ridiculous, and Walpole was not the only one to notice it. In the wake of Hawkesworth's *Voyages* came a series of anonymous poetical pamphlets, the mock-heroic and mock-scholarly style of which is clearly in honour of Hawkesworth's literary and editorial endeavours. To the authors of these nudging and winking verses, Banks seemed an obvious choice for a hero. Hawkesworth had been discreet, but he had not been nearly discreet enough. The pamphleteers read between his lines and, failing to find Banks's real 'flame', they came up with a better character, Purea, as a suitable partner for Banks. The first of the pamphlets to appear, at the price of one shilling, probably in September 1773, was *An Epistle from Oberea, Queen of Otaheite, to Joseph Banks, Esq. Translated by T. Q. Z. Esq. Professor of the Otaheite Language in Dublin, and of all the Languages of the undiscovered Islands in the South Sea*, a work which is nowadays attributed to John Scott, at the time a young army officer.[142]

Spurning Virgil's Dido and Aeneas, Scott turned instead to Ovid and took Oenone's complaint to Paris in the *Heroides* as a model for his *Epistle*. The pastoral setting of Mount Ida, scene of Oenone's past happiness with Paris, is transferred to Tahiti, where Purea recalls to Banks how:

> . . . oft with me you deign'd the night to pass,
> Beneath yon bread-tree on the bending grass.[143]

This parodic account of Purea's idyll with Banks serves as Scott's excuse for developing, with the firm support of footnotes from Hawkesworth's text, all the parts of the *Voyages* that most interested him: Banks's discovery of a rival in Purea's bed ('what streams of scalding tears I shed'); the famous 'Timorodee' (which she dances to impress Banks); the theft of Banks's clothes (which predictably become his 'breeches'); the 'ceremony' of Banks and the unveiling lady; venereal disease; and, of course, the notorious 'Spectacle' at Point Venus, with the answer to Hawkesworth's philosophical question made plain:

> Scarce twelve short years the wanton maid had seen,
> The youth was six foot high, or more I ween.
> Experienc'd matrons the young pair survey'd,
> And urg'd to feats of love the self-taught maid;
> With skill superior she perform'd her part,
> And potent nature scorn'd the tricks of art.[144]

A reply to Purea's *Epistle* followed in a few months: *An Epistle from Mr. Banks, Voyager, Monster-hunter, and Amoroso, to Oberea, Queen of Otaheite. Transfused by A. B. C. Esq. Second Professor of the Otaheite, and of every other unknown Tongue*.[145] The author may again be John Scott, as is sometimes supposed, but this seems unlikely, for the work is in a different vein from Purea's *Epistle*, pseudo–satire and titillation replacing comedy and literary pastiche.[146] The frontispiece, by way of advertising the author's interest to his readers, displays a Tahitian female displaying her tattooed posterior to an audience of keenly observing British males. Pointing out that 'What's vice in us, in you is virtue clear', the author's narrator, Banks, runs through all the memorable Tahitian events, substantiated by footnotes from the *Voyages*: the lover 'in the royal bed', the 'Temeredee', the stolen breeches, the 'ceremony' illustrated in the frontispiece, the Point Venus 'Spectacle'. He then turns, still in the character of Banks, to condemn the *Endeavour*'s voyage and its author:

> O shame! were we, great George, thy gallant crew,
> And had we—damn it—nothing else to do,
> But turn thy great design to filthy farce,
> And search for wonders on an Indian's a— — —?
> But then to print our tale! O curse the thought!
> Curse those who sold,—a blush for those who bought.
> Fine tales for misses!—charming table-talk!
> Delightful too in each meandring walk,
> Through Britain's ample plains!—The lustful 'squire
> With ease may quench his unsubdu'd desire:—
> One page of Hawkesworth, in the cool retreat,
> Fires the bright maid with more than mortal heat;
> She sinks at once into the lover's arms,
> Nor deems it vice to prostitute her charms;
> 'I'll do,' cries she, 'what Queens have done before;'
> And sinks, *from principle*, a common whore.[147]

A continuing interest in the matter of Tahiti was demonstrated in the new year, 1774, by the appearance of *An Epistle (Moral and Philosophical) from an Officer at Otaheite to Lady Gr*s**n*r*, perhaps by John Courtenay, an MP with a reputation as a wit, who addresses his *Epistle* to a notorious divorcee whose scandalous trial in 1772 does not, however, take up his attention.[148] This time the initiation at Point Venus, Hawkesworth's 'Spectacle', emerges more clearly as the most interesting and significant of the stock Tahitian topics and is given a lingering introduction, too long to quote in full:

> Lo here, *whence* frozen Chastity retires,
> Love finds an altar for his fiercest fires.
> The throbbing virgin loses ev'ry fear,
>
>   .   .   .   .
>
> Unerring instinct prompts her golden dreams;
> Her bed, like Eve's (a), with choicest flowers blooms.[149]

The scholarly footnote (a) quotes Milton's lines describing the dubious delights of postlapsarian copulation in *Paradise Lost*.[150] The 'throbbing virgin', needless to say, after very lengthy and patently unnecessary instructions from Purea, proceeds to enact the 'Scene' originally witnessed in Tahiti and now described in full detail in London.

The author then calls for the expansion of Purea's 'empire, Love, from shore to shore' and, continuing in this apparently libertine vein, approaches the issues raised by Hawkesworth's philosophical commentary (which he quotes in a footnote):

> here no shame imprest,
> Heaves with alarming throbs the female breast;
> Naked and smiling every nymph we see,
> Like Eve unapron'd 'ere she *robb'd the tree.*
> Immodest words are spoke without offence,
> And want of decency shews innocence.
> A problem hence Philosophers advance,
> Whether shame springs from Nature or from chance.
> The contest lasts; kept up by human pride;
> Where Sages differ, how can I decide?'[151]

The philosophical argument continues for a further forty-two lines, the sarcasm becomes more blatant, and it becomes obvious which side of Hawkesworth's question the author espouses—and obvious, too, that his celebration of libertine Tahiti has been ironic as well as (hypocritically) erotic. 'Is it great Nature's voice,' he asks,

> Or is it custom?—dubious is the choice?
> No; modest instinct proves *its* source divine
>
> . . . . .
>
> Tho' lewdness and unbridled lust combine,
> To counteract the Deity's design;
>
> . . . . .
>
> Yet babbling fools into the notion fall,
> If Vice destroy *it* [Virtue], 'there *was* none at all.'
>
> . . . . . .
>
> Custom indeed corrupts the human heart.[152]

The references to Eve and *Paradise Lost* should have prepared us to expect a changed note in this author's treatment of Tahiti, a note which sounds even more clearly towards the end of the poem, with the introduction of a new Tahitian topic from Hawkesworth:

> Still must I sing the lewd promiscuous joy,
> Which boundless reigns amidst their *Arreoy.*
> Can the fond mother act Medea's part?
> Can she expose the darling of her heart?
> Without a tear, her infant, cherub doom,
> And stab the smiling offspring of her womb?
> O dire effect of passions unrestrain'd,
> O dire effect of Nature's laws profan'd.
> From such black scenes, the Muse indignant turns,
> Where lust deprav'd, the mad'ning female burns.[153]

So this *Epistle* is indeed *Moral and Philosophical* as promised. We have seen the 'throbbing virgin' and her 'valves of Venus' examined too closely and with too little evidence of irony for us to believe in the author's complete sincerity, but his moral and philosophical theme is nevertheless quite clear, the corruption of Nature by Tahitian custom: *un*natural lust leads to death in a Tahitian paradise lost.[154] A new reading of Hawkesworth's Tahiti has revealed—not Venus, but Medea.

It is not possible to prove that the still unidentified author of *Otaheite: A Poem*, published in London the same year, had read *An Epistle (Moral and Philosophical)*, but it does seem likely, although *A Poem* marks a new departure in these Tahitian pamphlets, with sentimental piety replacing satire and titillation. The poet begins by praising the scientific voyagers, the 'Sons of Science':

> Not their's the fatal Triumph to explore
> Climes rich with latent Gems or golden Ore;
> To bear, exulting, the rich Spoils away,
> And curse their Country with a baneful Prey.
> Their's be the Task, with unpolluted Hand,
> Nature's mysterious Volume to expand.[155]

We then turn to the page of this 'Volume' which the 'Sons of Science' have recently opened, the poem's subject, 'The CYPRUS of the SOUTH, the Land of Love', where the inhabitants enjoy continual spring while 'Nature their vegetable Bread supplies':

> Their Ev'ning Hours successive Sports prolong,
> The wanton Dance, the Love-inspiring Song.
> Impetuous Wishes no Concealment know,
> As the Heart prompts, the melting Numbers flow:
> Each OBEREA feels the lawless Flame,
> Nor checks Desires she does not blush to name.[156]

But, after Oberea, here comes Medea:

> Can cruel Passions these calm Seats infest,
> And stifle Pity in a Parent's Breast?
> Does here MEDEA draw the vengeful Blade,
> And stain with filial Gore the blushing Shade;
> Here, where Arcadia should its Scenes unfold,
> And past'ral Love revive an Age of Gold!'[157]

The author's answer to his question is, with a great deal of pathetic detail, emphatically in the affirmative. Where Arcadia should be, and a Golden Age revived, there is indeed 'MEDEA'. The proper Tahitian genre is tragedy not pastoral. This time it is Hawkesworth's description of the Arioi infanticide rather than the Point Venus 'Spectacle' which inspires the pamphleteer's imagination:

> Ah! see in vain the little Suppliant plead
> With silent Eloquence to check the Deed:
> He smiles unconscious on th'uplifted Knife,
> And courts the Hand that's arm'd against his Life.[158]

The author takes the new Tahitian theme to its logical conclusion:

> On Minds which thus untaught thus darkling stray,
> To pour the radiant Beams of heav'nly Day;
> To point where Nature the great Outline draws,
> Where Truth reveal'd gives Sanction to her Laws;
> To bid th'intemp'rate Reign of Sense expire,
> And quench th'unholy Flame of loose Desire;
> Teach them their Being's Date, its Use and End,
> And to immortal Life their Hopes extend,
> How great the Triumph!—But to whom assign'd?
> What Nations rise the Teachers of Mankind?[159]

This call for a new kind of voyage to Tahiti was prophetic, but not yet to be heard, and not to be answered until the close of the century. Meanwhile, in July 1774, Walpole wrote to keep a correspondent up to date: 'Africa is indeed coming into fashion . . . Otaheite and Mr Banks are quite forgotten.'[160] In the few years since Wallis's discovery in 1767, the European idea of Tahiti had developed rapidly. Wallis had not discovered a paradise, but with the *Dolphin*'s 'Great Guns' had created the conditions for Bougainville, Cook, and Banks to be received with open arms by charming women, not savage men with spears and clubs, and to discover a new kind of noble savage, the nubile savage, erotic as well as exotic, inhabiting an Eden, it seemed, of prelapsarian innocence and bliss. But this Eden described by Cook and Banks and publicized by Hawkesworth, where the inhabitants, in Hawkesworth's words, 'seem to be exempted from the first general curse' and showed 'not the least trace' of 'the shame attending certain actions', was indeed an odd Eden, where 'the poor infant is smothered the moment it is born'. The pamphleteers reading and rewriting the Tahitian Eden revealed by Hawkesworth soon discovered the presence of death. Hawkesworth's Tahiti may have 'realized the poetical fables of Arcadia', but even in Arcadia there is Medea. In the seven years from the discovery of Tahiti to the publication of *Otaheite: A Poem*, then, a paradise had been found and lost again, and the Tahiti that was to be discovered by the missionaries who would answer the call and sail there twenty years later, in 1796, had already been discovered by the pamphleteers in Hawkesworth's version of the journals of those who had discovered and described an Eden.

Tahiti and Mr Banks may be 'quite forgotten' for the moment, but we cannot conclude without taking some notice of questions which persisted about some of the 'extraordinary facts' about that distant island.[161] When Cook returned from a second voyage to the South Seas in 1775—a voyage without Banks, whose entourage and equipment had overloaded the ship—he was himself something of a lion, and so Boswell was pleased to meet 'the celebrated Circumnavigator' at a dinner given by Sir John Pringle, the President of the Royal Society, on 2 April 1776. Boswell 'talked a good deal' with Cook and found that he 'was a plain and sensible man with an uncommon attention to veracity', who 'did not try to make theories out of what he had seen to confound virtue and vice'. Naturally the subject of Hawkesworth's *Voyages* was raised. Cook, according to Boswell, 'said it was not true that Mr. Banks and he had revised all the book . . . and he said Hawkesworth's story of an *Initiation* he had no reason to believe', which is odd, as of course Cook himself had witnessed and described the famous 'Initiation', as Boswell calls it, Hawkesworth's 'Spectacle', Cook's very own 'Scene' at Point Venus. But Boswell's response to Cook reflects informed contemporary opinion: ' "Why, Sir," said I, "Hawkesworth has used your narrative as a London tavern keeper does wine. He has *brewed* it." '[162]

The following morning Boswell called on Johnson and 'found him putting his books in order', enveloped in 'clouds of dust': 'I gave him an account of a conversation which had passed between me and Captain Cook, the day before, at dinner at Sir John Pringle's; and he was much pleased with the conscientious accuracy of that celebrated circumnavigator.' Boswell's scepticism about the 'exaggerated accounts given by Dr. Hawkesworth of his [Cook's] Voyages' was congenial to Johnson, but Boswell combined his scepticism about Hawkesworth's *Voyages* with enthusiasm about Cook's voyages: 'I told him that while I was with the Captain, I catched the enthusiasm of curiosity and adventure, and felt a strong inclination to go with him on his next voyage.' 'Why, Sir', replied Johnson, 'a man *does* feel so, till he considers how very little he can learn from such voyages.'[163]

5

Aotourou and Omai

Ne pouvant voiager, je me suis mis à lire le voiage autour du monde de
Messieurs Banks et Solander. Je ne connais rien de plus instructif. Je vois avec
un plaisir extrême que Mr De Bougainville nous a dit la vérité. Quand les
Français et les Anglais sont d'accord il est démontré qu'ils ne nous ont point
trompés.

(Voltaire, *Correspondence*)[1]

Bougainville reached Saint-Malo on 16 March 1769, and was soon with Aotourou
in Paris, from where the news spread rapidly. The Duchesse de Choiseul wrote to
inform Voltaire at Ferney on the 20th, reporting Bougainville's arrival with 'son
sauvage', whom she was 'curieuse' to see, and on the 23rd the chronicler Bachaumont
was recording in his *Mémoires secrets* the latest tattle of the salons about a 'nouveau
Robinson':

M. de Bougainville raconte beaucoup de choses de son voyage, il prétend entr'autres
merveilles avoir découvert aux Terres Australes une nouvelle Isle, dont les moeurs sont
admirables, dont l'administration civile fait honte aux Gouvernemens les plus policés de
l'Europe: il ne tarit point sur les détails charmans qu'il en raconte. Il est bien à craindre que
ce nouveau Robinson n'ait acquis ce goût du merveilleux, si ordinaire aux voyageurs, & que
son imagination exaltée ne lui fasse voir les objets tout autres qu'ils ne sont.[2]

Thus, more than a year before the publication of Bougainville's *Voyage*, the tale
of Tahiti was being told. Bachaumont was sceptical but the 'nouveau Robinson'
had brought a Friday with him. If it was 'une chose bien extraordinaire' to be
Persian, it was all the more so to be Tahitian, especially if you were real.[3] In April
the far-traveller and savant La Condamine came with the royal interpreter Pereire,
expert in articulation, to observe Aotourou chez Bougainville in the rue Basse-du-
Rempart. They found 'l'Insulaire de la mer du Sud' in a costume with gold frogs,
easily bored, and they took notes of their 'Observations', Pereire remarking that
Aotourou:

n'a pû absolument articuler aucune des consonnes qui commencent les syllabes *ca da fa ga
sa za*, non plus que le son qu'on nomme *l* mouillée, ni pas une des voyelles appellées
nazales. Ce n'est pas tout; il n'a pas sçu faire la distinction entre les articulations *cha* & *ja*,
& n'a prononcé qu'imparfaitement le *b* & l'*l* ordinaire, & plus imparfaitement encore la
double *r*, c'est-à-dire l'*r* forte ou initiale.[4]

La Condamine's 'Observations' were of a different kind:

J'ai vu notre insulaire [faire des signes très énergiques] qui n'avoient rien d'équivoque à l'aspect d'un tableau qui représentoit une Vénus presque nue; il fit semblant d'abord d'écarter le linge qui la couvroit très légèrement. Ici je me trouve embarrassé à décrire les autres signes que fit le jeune sauvage . . .[5]

Overcoming his embarrassment, La Condamine went on to describe in detail an elaborate mime of smelling, tasting, grimacing, and smiling, which he tentatively guessed to be a representation of Aotourou's prodigious ability to diagnose female venereal infection by smell and taste. Aotourou was not unintelligent, it seemed, for in addition to communicating the wonderful acuity of his senses to La Condamine, he recognized that La Condamine's spectacles and hearing-trumpet were aids to the deficiencies of La Condamine's own. At a dinner with Bougainville and Aotourou, Charles de Brosses, champion of the French Pacific, was able to confirm La Condamine's interpretation of Aotourou's performance, and made a note of Bougainville's information that:

le Sauvage accoutumé à suivre la simple impulsion de la nature et fort ardent pour les femmes, alloit le soir en chercher sur le rempart ou dans les rues: qu'on lui fit entendre qu'il risquoit beaucoup avec ces sortes de coureuses, pour la plupart gâtées: qu'il fit entendre à son tour qu'il les laissoit quand elles étoient mal saines: qu'il savoit les discerner en portant son doigt à l'endroit suspect, puis à son nez ou sur sa langue. On connoît que cette qualité de l'odorat ou du goût, quoiqu'elle nous sois inconnue, n'a rien d'impossible.[6]

A few days after La Condamine's observations, Aotourou was presented to the King and the princes at Versailles, and seems to have kept good company in Paris as well as bad, accompanying Bougainville, apparently, to the philosophes—Buffon, d'Alembert, Helvétius, Holbach—and to the theatre, where he made the acquaintance of the singer Sophie Arnould, the actress Mademoiselle Clairon, and the young German dancer, Mademoiselle Heinsel, whose bottom he wanted to tattoo.[7] Bougainville complained that the curious saw in Aotourou only what they wanted to satisfy their prejudices:

L'empressement pour le voir a été vif, curiosité stérile qui n'a servi presque qu'à donner des idées fausses à des hommes persifleurs par état, qui ne sont jamais sortis de la capitale, qui n'approfondissent riens, & qui, livrés à des erreurs de toute espece, ne voyent que d'après leurs préjugés.[8]

But the conclusions drawn about Aotourou by that dedicated 'persifleur', Bachaumont, are not so very different from Bougainville's. Bachaumont reported about Aotourou and his country that:

sa grande passion est celle des femmes, auxquelles il se livre indistinctement. Elle est généralement celle de ses compatriotes. M. de Bougainville prétend que dans le pays où il a pris ce sauvage, un des principaux chefs du lieu, hommes & femmes se livrent sans pudeur au péché de la chair; qu'à la face du ciel & de la terre ils se copulent sur la premiere natte offerte, d'où lui est venu l'idée d'appeler cette Isle l'*Isle de Cythere*, nom qu'elle mérite également par la beauté du climat, du sol, du site, du lieu, & de ses productions.[9]

While Bachaumont's idea that Aotourou was 'un des principaux chefs' was inaccurate, his report of Aotourou's 'grande passion' is more than corroborated by the Tahitian's shipmates on the voyage from Tahiti. The surgeon Vivez describes Aotourou's assiduous attentions to Jeanne Baré, 'fort gênante pour elle et pour son maitre' (Commerson), and Fesche suggests that France was as arousing for Aotourou as Tahiti was for the French, noting that Aotourou's 'principal mobil' in leaving Tahiti was his desire for 'des femmes blanches'.[10] A few days after leaving Tahiti, and after receiving repeated 'signes non équivoques' from Aotourou, Bougainville recorded in his journal:

Notre Indien ne pense qu'à ses femmes, il nous entretient sans cesse, c'est son unique idée ou du moins toutes les autres chez lui se rapportent à celles là. Il nous fait entendre que s'il n'y a point de femmes pour lui ou nous allons, il faut lui couper le col.[11]

Bougainville was more discreet in his published *Voyage*, telling us that Aotourou's great passion in Paris was for the opera, that he was very fond of Voltaire's correspondent, the Duchesse de Choiseul, and that his knowledge of French was elementary.[12] But, even if Aotourou could not manage *ca da fa ga sa za*, there were others who would speak for him, and to understand why they said what they did we must turn from the reality of Aotourou to the theory of 'l'Homme Sauvage'. We must turn in particular to the ruminations of Rousseau, 'enfoncé dans la forêt' at Saint-Germain some years before, in a warm November 1754, with some women to look after him and cook, while he planned his *Discours sur l'origine et les fondemens de l'inégalité parmi les hommes* (1755).[13]

Rousseau's *Discours* differed from previous philosophers' accounts of man's original condition by positing a state of nature which was more rigorously natural:

Les Philosophes qui ont examiné les fondemens de la société, ont tous senti la nécessité de remonter jusqu'à l'état de Nature, mais aucun d'eux n'y est arrivé ... Enfin tous, parlant sans cesse de besoin, d'avidité, d'oppression, de desirs, & d'orgueil, ont transporté à l'état de Nature, des idées qu'ils avoient prises dans la société; Ils parloient de l'Homme Sauvage, & ils peignoient l'homme Civil.[14]

This, then, was Rousseau's revolution: to place natural man ('l'Homme Sauvage') in a state of nature which was not simply the culture of savages, but ideally natural, and therefore pre-cultural, prehistorical, and—inevitably—hypothetical: 'un Etat qui n'existe plus, qui n'a peut-être point existé'.[15] 'Commençons donc par écarter tous les faits', he proposed, thus avoiding the charge of contradicting the biblical 'faits' of Genesis, but also giving his imaginary 'Homme Sauvage' the scientific appearance of a hypothesis or model and, moreover, the romantic appeal of a creature of inspiration and introspection in the forest.[16] 'O Homme', he addressed his reader, 'Voici ton histoire telle que j'ai cru la lire, non dans les Livres de tes semblables qui sont menteurs, mais dans la Nature qui ne ment jamais.'[17]

In the state of nature thus revealed to Rousseau by nature itself, not culture, his 'Homme Sauvage', whom he narrowly but necessarily distinguishes from an animal by endowing him with free will and the fateful capacity for self-improvement ('perfectibilité'), is naturally happy and good, having, like Adam and Eve, no knowledge of good or evil and, unlike cultural man, no artificial sentiments of love or its corollary, jealousy. Strong and independent, homeless and promiscuous, this unreflecting solitary wanderer is, 'quand il a diné' and copulated, 'avec plus de plaisir que de fureur', at peace with the world.[18] 'Qu'en scais-tu'? asked Voltaire in the margin of his copy of Rousseau's *Discours*. 'As-tu vu des sauvages faire l'amour'?[19] But Rousseau, who returned to amuse himself with his women 'aux heures des repas', from the forest where he sought and found 'l'image des premiers temps', knew something of the nature of natural man.[20]

Having constructed his state of nature with the aim, above all, of demonstrating that 'l'homme est naturellement bon', Rousseau then proceeds in his *Discours*, over immeasurable 'multitudes de Siécles', to a later stage which he calls 'la Société naissante', in which man, no longer a solitary wanderer, has come to recognize merit and beauty, and hence inequality, and come to experience love, and hence jealousy, rivalry, and cruelty.[21] The negative aspects of 'la Société naissante' are the evils observable in contemporary savages and mistakenly associated by previous philosophers (this is 'la faute que Hobbes & d'autres ont commise') with a state of nature:

Voilà précisement le degré où étoient parvenus la plûpart des Peuples Sauvages qui nous sont connus; & c'est faute d'avoir suffisamment distingué les idées, & remarqué combien ces Peuples étoient déjà loin du premier état de Nature, que plusieurs se sont hâtés de conclure que l'homme est naturellement cruel.[22]

The positives, however, must seem to Rousseau to outweigh the negatives, for he declares 'la Société naissante', despite its evils, to be the happiest and best of all conditions of man. That it is a better state than man's natural state we must accept simply because Rousseau says that it is 'le meilleur', but that it is better than man's subsequent, civilized state is made plain:

Plus on y réflechit, plus on trouve que cet état [la Société naissante] étoit le moins sujet aux révolutions, le meilleur à l'homme, & qu'il n'en a du sortir que par quelque funeste hazard qui pour l'utilité commune eût dû ne jamais arriver. L'exemple des Sauvages qu'on a presque tous trouvés à ce point semble confirmer que le Genre-humain étoit fait pour y rester toujours, que cet état est la véritable jeunesse du Monde, & que tous les progrès ultérieurs ont été en apparence autant de pas vers la perfection de l'individu, & en effet vers la décrépitude de l'espéce.[23]

This 'Société naissante', the state in which most savages have been discovered, is of course a version of the primitivist paradise or golden age of the savage before his decline and fall ('quelque funeste hazard'), which Rousseau associates, as Ovid did the ends of the Golden and Bronze Ages, with the inventions of agriculture and metallurgy.[24] The differences in Rousseau's revised version are that he has conceded that the contemporary savage condition is not purely natural or good,

and has preceded it by an earlier paradise or golden age, his original and hypothetical state of nature, in which man could more credibly be presented as 'naturellement
bon'. So Rousseau has, in order to save the goodness of nature and the naturalness
of goodness, depicted an earlier and more primitive condition than that of contemporary savages, but he has nevertheless reserved his preference for cultural rather
than chronological primitivism, for the myth of the superiority of contemporary
savagery to civilization, even though the necessity of refuting Hobbes has obliged
him to admit the contemporary savages' partial decadence and degeneration from
the state of nature happily inhabited by Montaigne's 'cannibales', for example,
whose idyll was untroubled by Hobbes. So Rousseau has been obliged to admit a
difference between nature and savage culture, and indeed this difference is a
significant discovery, but his criticisms of civilization at the conclusion of the
Discours are the same that came from the mouths of Montaigne's 'cannibales',
spoken now by Rousseau in the name of nature: 'il est manifestement contre la Loi
de Nature, de quelque maniére qu'on la définisse, qu'un enfant commande à un
vieillard, qu'un imbécille conduise un homme sage, & qu'une poignée de gens
regorge de superfluités, tandis que la multitude affamée manque du nécessaire.'[25]

Chateaubriand's remark that Rousseau's *Discours* 'n'est qu'une paraphrase
éloquente' of Montaigne's 'Des cannibales' would seem to have some justice,
therefore, but it ignores the originality of Rousseau's relocation of the state of
nature in a hypothetical history, beyond the possibility of contradiction by facts or
books, except the book of nature itself, 'qui ne ment jamais'.[26] Nevertheless, for all
the romantic and scientific ideality of his original 'Homme Sauvage', this creature
of Rousseau's imagination is abundantly supplied with textual and empirical support, partly derived by adaptation of the information about animals in Buffon's
Histoire naturelle, but mostly by selection from the textual observations by voyagers
of existing real savages. Rousseau's most frequent references are to the Hottentots
and the American Indians, particularly 'les Caraïbes, celui de tous les Peuples
existans, qui jusqu'ici s'est écarté le moins de l'état de Nature', and his principal
source is the fifth volume of Prévost's compendious *Histoire générale des voyages*
(1748), particularly the descriptions of Hottentots by the German traveller Kolben,
who is quoted five times in the *Discours* and its copious notes.[27] Thus, for example,
Rousseau writes in support of the physical strength and prowess of his 'Homme
Sauvage':

Les relations des voyageurs sont pleines d'exemples . . . 'Les Hottentots', dit Kolben . . . 'Les
Hottentots', dit encore le même Auteur . . . Le P. du Tertre dit à peu près sur les Sauvages
des Antilles les mêmes choses qu'on vient de lire sur les Hottentots du Cap de Bonne
Esperance . . . Les Sauvages de l'Amérique Septentrionale . . . [Les] Indiens de l'Amérique
Meridionale . . .[28]

Even when no textual sources are cited, Rousseau repeatedly assures his reader
that the state of 'l'Homme Sauvage' is, 'selon le rapport des Voyageurs, celui de la
plûpart des Peuples Sauvages . . . les Hottentots . . . les Sauvages de l'Amérique . . .'.[29]

Rousseau's 'Homme Sauvage' is thus constructed from selected parts of Hottentots and American Indians, and is thus, one could argue, the creature of
books, not nature, derived from the pages of the voyagers, who provide the documentation for Rousseau's imagination. If Rousseau's state of nature was 'un bien
mauvais roman', as Voltaire protested in the margin, it was a novel filled with
facts.[30]

The culture of Rousseau's 'Société naissante' is also documented from the
voyagers' observations, again of Hottentots and American Indians. The superiority
of the 'Société naissante' to civilization, for example, is demonstrated in a note
which supports the words 'le meilleur à l'homme' by giving two accounts of savages who disdained civilization. The first is an anecdote about an American chief
unimpressed by the court of England, after the manner of Montaigne's 'cannibales'
at the court of France, and the second, which is illustrated as the frontispiece of
the *Discours*, is a story quoted from Kolben about an educated Hottentot who
renounced civilization to revert to his preferable Hottentot savagery.[31]

Although both Rousseau's 'état de Nature' and his 'Société naissante' are substantiated and supported by the evidence Rousseau derives from the voyagers, he
fiercely attacks his eyewitnesses as prejudiced and poor observers, criticizing Andrew
Battell and Dapper, quoted in Rousseau's favourite fifth volume of Prévost's
Histoire générale, for describing as apes what to Rousseau are more probably
primitive men (the hairy West African 'Pongos'), a specific complaint that leads to
a general condemnation:

Depuis trois ou quatre cens ans que les habitans de l'Europe inondent les autres parties du
monde & publient sans cesse de nouveaux recueils de voyages & de rélations, je suis
persuadé que nous ne connoissons d'hommes que les seuls Européens . . . La cause de ceci
est manifeste, au moins pour les contrées éloignées: Il n'y a guéres que quatre sortes
d'hommes qui fassent des voyages de long cours; les Marins, les Marchands, les Soldats, &
les Missionnaires; Or on ne doit guéres s'attendre que les trois premiéres Classes fournissent
de bons Observateurs, et quant à ceux de la quatriéme, [ils sont trop] occupés de la vocation
sublime qui les appelle.[32]

Rousseau calls, instead, for 'deux hommes bien unis, riches, l'un en argent, l'autre
en genie', to circumnavigate the world and study man, a call that has been acclaimed
as a prophecy of social anthropology.[33] Then, again castigating 'des voyageurs
grossiers' and thus Montaigne's ideal voyager, 'simple et grossier', and forgetting
his own principled rejection of the civilized sophistries of 'livres scientifiques',
Rousseau makes another appeal for voyaging philosophers:

toute la terre est couverte de Nations dont nous ne connoissons que les noms, & nous nous
mêlons de juger le genre-humain! Supposons un Montesquieu, un Buffon, un Diderot, un
Duclos, un d'Alembert, un Condillac, ou des hommes de cette trempe, voyageant pour
instruire leurs compatriotes, observant & décrivant comme ils savent faire . . . nous verrions
nous mêmes sortir un monde nouveau de dessous leur plume, & nous apprendrions ainsi à
connoître le nôtre.[34]

To M. Philibert Commerson must go the honour, as he sailed before Banks and Solander, of being the first scientist to travel as Rousseau had wished. Well connected in scientific circles, Commerson had edited a description of rare Mediterranean fish for Linnaeus, and was said by his own brother-in-law to have gone for weeks without sleep or food, except 'pain, légumes et fromage', in a 'passion' for natural history 'poussée à des excès incroiables', the same passion 'pour aprofondir et augmenter les connoissances de la nature et ses productions' which led him, according to a sarcastic shipmate, to embark 'à cet effet pour son domestique une fille déguisée'.[35] Commerson did not return to France with Bougainville, disembarking with Baré at the Ile de France (Mauritius), where the fruits of his far-flung researches were sadly neglected, though some of his collection of fish found its way after his death to the attic of Buffon, where various pickled corpses were eventually discovered in their boxes.[36] He did however produce a description of Tahiti in a letter which was published in the *Mercure de France* of November 1769. Here, then, is the first published account by a scientist of Tahiti—or, rather, Utopia: 'Je lui avais appliqué le nom d'*Utopie* que Thomas Morus avait donné à sa république idéale, en le dérivant des racines grecques (*eus* et *topus, quasi felix locus*).' He was unable to divulge the latitude and longitude of Utopia,

mais je puis vous dire que c'est le seul coin de la terre où habitent des hommes sans vices, sans préjugés, sans besoins, sans dissensions. Nés sous le plus beau ciel, nourris des fruits d'une terre féconde sans culture, régis par des pères de famille plutôt que par des rois, ils ne connaissent d'autre dieu que l'Amour. Tous les jours lui sont consacrés, toute l'isle est son temple, toutes les femmes en sont les autels, tous les hommes les sacrificateurs. Et quelles femmes, me demanderez-vous? les rivales des Géorgiennes en beauté, et les sœurs des grâces toutes nues. Là, ny la honte, ny la pudeur n'exercent point leur tyrannie: la plus légère des gazes flotte toujours au gré des vents et des désirs: l'acte de créer son semblable est un acte de religion; les préludes en sont encouragés par les vœux et les chants de tout le peuple assemblé, et la fin célébré par des applaudissements universels, tout étranger est admis à participer à ces heureux mystères; c'est même un des devoirs de l'hospitalité que de les inviter, de sorte que le bon Utopien jouit sans cesse ou du sentiment de ses propres plaisirs ou du spectacle de ceux des autres. Quelque censeur à double rabat ne verra peut-être en tout cela qu'un débordement de moeurs, une horrible prostitution, le cynisme le plus effronté; mais il se trompera grossièrement lui-même en méconnaissant l'état de l'homme naturel, né essentiellement bon, exempt de tout préjugé et suivant, sans défiance comme sans remords, les douces impulsions d'un instinct toujours sûr, parce qu'il n'a pas encore dégénéré en raison.[37]

Commerson's report is clearly inspired by his reading of Rousseau's *Discours*, though not a very careful reading, perhaps, for Commerson seems to be mistaken about the 'état de l'homme naturel', in which, according to Rousseau, 'les mâles & les femelles s'unissoient fortuitement selon la rencontre, l'occasion, & le desir', while love came only at a later stage, with 'la Société naissante', and came only at a cost, for 'la jalousie s'éveille avec l'amour'.[38] We can be sure that Commerson had read Rousseau's note attacking the voyagers, however, for Commerson concludes his description of Tahiti with an account of how he protected Aotourou from the cruelty of the French sailors, remarking: 'Telle est l'âme des marins, sur laquelle Jean-Jacques Rousseau place judicieusement un point de doute et d'interrogation'.[39]

It was probably Commerson's letter which provided an obscure writer, Nicolas Bricaire de La Dixmerie, with the matter for his ventriloquial writings of Aotourou, *Le Sauvage de Taïti aux Français; avec un envoi au philosophe ami des sauvages* (1770), published before Bougainville's own *Voyage*. The author tells the French about Tahiti in the introduction, and then Aotourou tells them about France: 'Chacque jour est pour nous un jour de fête et le Dieu qu'on y célèbre, c'est l'amour. A peine avez-vous le loisir de le connaître. L'ambition, l'intrigue, le faste, la dissipation, voilà les Dieux à qui vous sacrifiez.'[40] 'Le Sauvage de Taïti' had also something to say to the 'philosophe ami des sauvages', for the pseudo-Aotourou's reading of Rousseau's *Discours* was closer than Commerson's and he had noticed that Rousseau's 'état de Nature' would, by definition, exclude Tahiti. This gap between the state of nature and the state of contemporary savages which Rousseau's *Discours* had opened Aotourou wished to close, with particular reference to his own country: 'Vous dites que tout ce qui n'est point dans la nature a des inconvénients, et la Société plus que tout le reste. Nous vivons en Société, et l'instinct seul de la nature nous y fait vivre en paix.'[41]

Although Bougainville was not d'Alembert (who had been one of Rousseau's nominees for the post of travelling philosopher), he had been taught mathematics by d'Alembert, had published a *Traité de calcul intégrale*, had been admitted to the Royal Society of London and, in the opinion of Diderot (another of Rousseau's candidates), 'il a de la philosophie'.[42] His *Voyage autour du monde*, published in May 1771, confirmed much of the gossip about Tahiti and delivered it with authority and charm, not to the Admiralty like the firsthand accounts of Robertson, Wallis, and Cook, but directly to the public of the Paris salons, to the 'littérateurs' as well as the 'savants' and 'philosophes'.[43] Nevertheless, Bougainville chose to present himself in his *Voyage* as a sailor leading a 'vie errante & sauvage' rather than as a civilized savant or man of letters. 'Je suis maintenant bien loin du sanctuaire des Sciences & de Lettres', he declared; 'mes idées & mon style n'ont que trop pris l'empreinte de la vie errante & sauvage'.[44] He disclaimed also the role of philosopher, preferring to stress again that he was a voyager and a sailor, and therefore—he added sarcastically—an imbecile and a liar in the opinion of certain armchair-travelling philosophers. This is, of course, an allusion to Rousseau's criticism of the voyagers in his note to the *Discours*, with which Bougainville had taken issue more explicitly in his journal, mocking Rousseau's scheme for a travelling 'paire d'amis, l'un bête et riche, l'autre pauvre et bel esprit'. 'Dieu me garde toutefois d'aller en tiers avec les deux amis', he added.[45] He was no philosopher, he maintained in the 'Discours préliminaire' to his *Voyage*, and had no desire to prove or disprove 'aucune hypothèse':

Je suis voyageur & marin; c'est à dire, un menteur, & un imbécille aux yeux de cette classe d'écrivains paresseux & superbes qui, dans les ombres de leur cabinet, philosophent à perte de vûe sur le Monde & ses habitans, & soumettent impérieusement la nature à leurs imaginations. Procédé bien singulier, bien inconcevable de la part de gens qui, n'ayant rien observé par eux mêmes, n'écrivent, ne dogmatisent que d'après des observations empruntées de ces mêmes voyageurs auxquels ils refusent la faculté de voir & de penser.[46]

But Bougainville was not Montaigne's 'homme simple et grossier'.

In his *Voyage* he describes how his ships were surrounded as they approached Tahiti by canoes 'remplies de femmes'.[47] Then, omitting the girl in his journal 'qui montroit son sexe pour de petits clouds', he describes a scene which is not mentioned in his journal, but which took place on the following day, according to the *Voyage*, while the *Boudeuse* was anchoring, the description in the *Voyage* probably deriving either from the description of the 'nouvelle Vénus' in the journal of Fesche, or from Bougainville's own recollection of the actual scene that Fesche describes.[48] That the scene described by Fesche (and subsequently by Bougainville in his *Voyage*) has its basis in an actual scene can be inferred from the much more prosaic description in the Prince of Nassau-Siegen's journal of what is almost certainly the same scene, featuring a Tahitian girl who came aboard the *Boudeuse* just after it had anchored, according to Nassau-Siegen, and displayed 'de son plein gré toutes les perfections d'un beau corps'.[49] In any case the scene Bougainville describes in his *Voyage* is not, in its bare essentials, much different from the one he mentions himself in his journal—a girl 'montroit son sexe'—but it is very differently described. According to the *Voyage* a young girl came from a canoe onto the deck of the *Boudeuse*, 'malgré toutes les précautions que nous pûmes prendre', and stood in front of the sailors who were lowering the anchor. Then: 'La jeune fille laissa tomber négligemment une pagne qui la couvroit & parut aux yeux de tous, telle que Vénus se fit voir au berger Phrygien. Elle en avoit la forme céleste.'[50] Thus Tahiti discovered herself to the city of Paris, in Bougainville's *Voyage*, as Venus did to the shepherd in classical myth. Thus the Tahiti of myth and literature was publicly revealed.

Bougainville's *Voyage* then describes the welcome he received on shore, but adds a detail absent from his—or any other—journal. Although the Tahitians 'ne savoient comment exprimer leur joie de nous recevoir', one dignified and venerable old man remained unmoved: 'son air rêveur & soucieux, sembloit annoncer qu'il craignoit que ces jours heureux, écoulés pour lui dans le sein du repos, ne fussent troublés par l'arrivée d'une nouvelle race.'[51] With the exception of this symbolic figure, however, a typical, traditional 'philosophe nu', the Tahitian men, unarmed, are as pleased to see the 'nouvelle race' as the Tahitian women are. Although Bougainville leaves out the reference made in his journal to Dido, he retains his analogy with the *Aeneid* by placing at the head of a chapter a quotation referring to Aeneas' visit to the Elysian Fields, and he describes Tahitian hospitality in terms much the same as those in the journal:

Chacque jour nos gens se promenoient dans le pays sans armes, seuls ou par petites bandes. On les invitoit à entrer dans les maisons, on leur y donnoit à manger; mais ce n'est pas à une collation légere que se borne ici la civilité des maîtres de maisons; ils leur offroient de jeunes filles; la case se remplissoit à l'instant d'une foule curieuse d'hommes & de femmes qui faisoient un cercle autour de l'hôte & de la jeune victime du devoir hospitalier; la terre se jonchoit de feuillage & de fleurs, & des musiciens chantoient aux accords de la flûte une hymne de jouissance. Vénus est ici la déesse de l'hospitalité, son culte n'y admet point de mysteres, & chaque jouissance est une fête pour la nation. Ils étoient surpris de l'embarras qu'on témoignoit; nos moeurs ont proscrit cette publicité.[52]

Bougainville completely omits, however, his call in his journal to legislators and philosophers to see their utopian dreams made real in a 'véritable Eutopie' and, later in the *Voyage*, he introduces information (obtained from Aotourou on the return voyage) which flatly contradicts his own earlier description of the perfection of Tahitian society:

J'ai dit plus haut que les habitans de Taiti nous avoient paru vivre dans un bonheur digne d'envie. Nous les avions cru presque égaux entre eux, ou du-moins jouissant d'une liberté qui n'étoit soumise qu'aux loix établies pour le bonheur de tous. Je me trompois; la distinction des rangs est fort marquée à Taiti, & la disproportion cruelle.[53]

While Bougainville adds these and other ethnographic facts, however, which clearly invalidate the initial impression he has given in the *Voyage* of Tahitians enjoying 'un bonheur digne d'envie', that initial impression is nevertheless given in the *Voyage*, much as Bougainville had received it at Tahiti and recorded it in his journal before learning the facts from Aotourou. The two views of Tahiti recorded in the journal, then, the first idyllic and the second realistic, are not integrated in the *Voyage* to produce a single composite picture of Tahiti, and there are in the *Voyage*, therefore, two Tahitis, the one to which Bougainville had given the name 'la nouvelle Cythère' and the other which 'reçoit de ces habitans celui de Taiti', the one derived from Bougainville's impression and the other from Aotourou's information, the one literary and mythic and the other ethnographic and scientific.[54] It is of course the former Tahiti, Bougainville's own 'la nouvelle Cythère', which is much the more impressive to the reader of the *Voyage*: Tahiti 'où règne encore la franchise de l'âge d'or'; where, in addition, 'Je me croyois transporté dans le jardin d'Eden'; where, above all, Venus was 'la déesse de l'hospitalité'; Tahiti, the land of Venus reborn, 'la nouvelle Cythère'.[55] This was the Tahiti of firsthand personal experience and these were the words of an eyewitness who despised those who 'philosophent à perte de vûe sur le Monde & ces habitans, & soumettent impérieusement la nature à leurs imaginations'.

Diderot, whose hand in the *Discours sur l'inégalité* Rousseau acknowledges in his *Confessions*, seems to have been undeterred by these criticisms of chairbound philosophizing.[56] In an unpublished review of Bougainville's *Voyage*, Diderot approves of the character of the author, the explorer with charm and 'la philosophie', with Virgil 'dans la tête ou dans la malle', but his review consists mainly in an appeal to the very civilized Bougainville to leave the happily primitive Tahitians alone, an appeal much like Ronsard's to Villegagnon, two hundred years before: 'Ah! monsieur de Bougainville, éloignez votre vaisseau des rives de ces innocents et fortunés Taïtiens; ils sont heureux et vous ne pourrez que nuire à leur bonheur.'[57] Noting Bougainville's information that the Tahitians make love in all innocence in public, but not Bougainville's celebration of this innocence, Diderot tells him that 'vous allez empoisonner leurs âmes de vos extravagantes et fausses idées et réveiller en eux des notions de vice, avec vos chimériques notions de pudeur.'[58] He concludes that Bougainville's was 'le seul voyage dont la lecture m'ait inspiré du gout pour une autre contrée que la mienne'.[59] The Tahitian theme, to Diderot, was clear. Tahiti was a paradise before the fall which Europeans would bring with their 'chimériques notions de pudeur'.

This review, intended for the *Correspondence littéraire*, the newsletter edited and circulated by Diderot's friend, Grimm, never appeared there, perhaps because Diderot reworked it to become his *Supplément au voyage de Bougainville, ou dialogue entre A et B, sur l'inconvénient d'attacher des idées morales à certaines actions physiques qui n'en comportent pas*, which did appear in Grimm's *Correspondence*, in instalments in 1773 and 1774, and which Diderot further revised in manuscript before his death.[60] The *Supplément*, with a feeble, playful gesture to the realistic utopian tradition, was cast in the form of a speech by a venerable Tahitian, supposedly transcribed and translated by an improbably literate Tahitian called Orou (after Aotourou, perhaps), followed by a journal supposedly kept by a priest on Bougainville's expedition, recording this priest's conversations with the remarkable Orou. These documents, supposedly suppressed by Bougainville, had come into the hands of the character B, whose conversations with A form a frame to the supplementary Tahitian material.

B announces that Bougainville's 'fable d'Otaïti' is no fable, as will be confirmed if A will read the 'Supplément', which he suggests they do together.[61] Thus we read, and A and B read, first the speech of the venerable Tahitian 'viellard', who is clearly inspired by the Tahitian 'philosophe nu' in Bougainville's *Voyage*—but not in his original journal—who fears 'l'arrivée d'une nouvelle race'. Bougainville's 'philosophe nu', happily at home in Diderot's fiction, speaks eloquently and profusely the warning to the Tahitians that Bougainville had imagined running through his mind. He then turns to Diderot's imaginary Bougainville and addresses to him an extended version of the plea Diderot had made to the real Bougainville in his review:

Et toi, Chef des brigands qui t'obéissent, écarte promptement ton vaisseau de notre rive. Nous sommes innocens, nous sommes heureux, et tu ne peux que nuire à notre bonheur. Nous suivons le pur instinct de la Nature, et tu as tenté d'effacer de nos ames son caractere. Ici tout est à tous, et tu nous a prêché je ne sais quelle distinction du tien et du mien . . . Nous sommes libres, et voilà que tu as enfoui dans notre terre le titre de notre futur esclavage [i.e. Bougainville's deed of possession].[62]

This Golden Age liberty and equality plainly contradict, of course, the actual facts reported by Bougainville in his *Voyage* when correcting his earlier belief that the Tahitians were 'presque égaux entre eux' and noting instead what Aotourou had told him, the cruel inequality that actually existed in Tahiti.[63] But such facts will not do for Diderot, who has informed us, via B, that 'l'Otaïtien touche à l'origine du monde' and, via the Tahitian 'philosophe nu', that the Tahitians follow 'le pur instinct de la Nature'.[64] Inequality cannot exist in Diderot's Tahiti because he is now revising the *Discours sur l'inégalité*, bridging the gap of immeasurable centuries Rousseau had opened up between the state of nature and that of contemporary savages, rescuing the state of nature from the lost past, and reviving the pre-cultural, prelapsarian savage of Montaigne. For Montaigne, the savage's shameless nudity symbolized his prelapsarian condition; for Diderot, the savage's shameless sexuality would have this function. The fall, in Diderot's version, was not to be 'quelque funeste hazard', as in Rousseau's version, but, specifically, the advent of European civilization, bringing its false and poisonous sense of shame and its real and poisonous venereal disease ('tu as infecté notre sang') to the island of innocent sexuality.[65] This the Tahitian 'philosphe nu' makes clear as he harangues Bougainville: 'L'idée du crime et le péril de la maladie sont entrés avec toi parmi nous. Nos jouissances autrefois si douces sont accompagnées de remords et d'effroi.'[66]

We then turn, with A and B, to Diderot's fictitious priest, who has spent his time at Tahiti as the guest of the remarkable Orou and has kept a verbatim record of their dialogue. Orou's hospitality is naturally Tahitian and he offers his wife and daughters to the priest (thereby casting some doubt on the alleged freedom and equality of Diderot's Tahitian females). To this hospitable offer the priest replies feebly 'que sa religion, son état, les bonnes moeurs et l'honnêteté ne lui permettaient pas d'accepter ces offres'.[67] Thus Diderot causes the shameless sexuality of his Tahitians to open up for criticism the morality of European civilization. The priest's excuses for not enjoying 'un plaisir innocent auquel Nature, la souveraine maitresse, nous invite tous' are quickly subjected to the remorseless logic of the redoubtable and philosophical Orou, who then gives an account of the sexual laws of Tahiti and the 'lois de la Nature', which are, supposedly, identical.[68]

These natural and Tahitian laws, it becomes clear, are concerned with procreation rather than pleasure. Thus, although Nature and the Tahitians have no objections, as Orou explains, to promiscuity, adultery, and incest, those Tahitian females who are sterile, congenitally or through old age, are obliged—by Nature, with the full co-operation of the Tahitian law—to wear a black veil. Any sterile female 'qui quitte ce voile et se mêle avec les hommes est une libertine' and any male 'qui releve ce voile et s'approche de la femme stérile est un libertin'.[69] The punishment for these sterile women, if they are convicted of the crime of sexual intercourse, is 'l'exil au nord de l'Ile ou l'esclavage'.[70] Similarly those females who are experiencing 'la maladie périodique' must wear grey veils and abstain or else be called 'libertines'. Theirs, however, is not so serious an offence and requires no more punishment than 'le blâme'.[71] In addition, all Tahitian girls must wear a white veil until puberty, while all the young men, until they are, at 26, considered sufficiently virile, must have 'les reins ceints d'une petite chaîne'.[72] Shame is considered insufficient as a punishment for offenders in these cases, so any 'filles précoces' behaving unnaturally are locked up, while the parents of any guilty 'jeunes hommes qui déposent leur chaîne avant le temps prescrit par la Nature et par la Loi', are reprimanded.[73] Theirs are not innocent pleasures, and so Nature, with the assistance of the law of Tahiti and some little chains and punishments, including enslavement—which is not, therefore, a European innovation—makes sure that such unnatural desires are kept under control.

Clearly Diderot's Tahiti is no paradise of sexual pleasure for pleasure's sake, but then that is consistent with Diderot's own practical rather than liberal view of sexuality. His eloquent article on 'jouissance' in the *Encyclopédie* defended sexual pleasure because, as he reminded his reader, 'c'est le plaisir qui t'a tiré du néant'.[74] In the supplementary chapter, 'Des voyageurs', which he added in manuscript to his youthful *Bijoux indiscrets* (1748), the islanders discovered by the voyagers check the male and female sexual 'bijoux' for compatibility at a sacred and public ceremony with the practical purpose of ensuring marital happiness, an admirable purpose with the less admirable consequence, however, that the union of incompatible 'bijoux' is considered 'un véritable péché contre nature', and prevented by the enforcement of a list of laws and prohibitions.[75] Diderot's daughter Angélique was instructed in the machinery of sexuality, but quite rightly enjoined by her loving father to look after her sexual property in French society.[76]

In imaginary Tahiti, Diderot's priest finds Orou's arguments convincing and reasonable, and conforms to the ways of Nature and Tahiti, accepting Orou's offer of the favours of his wife and daughters. He is not, however, completely convinced by Orou's logic, for he cries out many times in the night: 'mais ma religion! mais mon état!'[77] A and B draw our conclusions for us. B has read the 'Supplément' correctly, for he says: 'je croirais volontiers le Peuple le plus sauvage de la terre, l'Otaïtien qui s'en est tenu scrupuleusement à la loi de Nature, plus voisin d'une bonne législation qu'aucun Peuple civilisé.'[78]

So the contemporary savage has been restored to his former home in a state of nature supposedly real—not lost forever in the past—and thus a viable alternative to civilized culture. This much Diderot has achieved on the basis of Bougainville's discovery of the shameless sexuality of Tahiti, merely 'un simple appetit physique', as B says, to be satisfied by 'le frottement voluptueux de deux intestins'.[79] Hence the subtitle of Diderot's *Supplément*, 'sur l'inconvénient d'attacher des idées morales à certaines actions physiques qui n'en comportent pas', an idea with which we are already familiar. For Diderot has discovered for himself in Bougainville's *Voyage* the Tahitian theme suggested by Hawkesworth's 'question which has been long debated in philosophy; Whether the shame attending certain actions, which are allowed on all sides to be in themselves innocent, is implanted in Nature, or superinduced by custom?'—to which Diderot in his *Supplément* has given his answer.[80]

Voltaire took an interest in Tahitian affairs in England as well as France, and checked the two versions of Tahiti for discrepancies. In a letter of June 1774, not long after the publication of the French translation of Hawkesworth's *Voyages*, Voltaire tells a correspondent that:

Ne pouvant voiager, je me suis mis à lire le voiage autour du monde de Messieurs Banks et Solander [i.e. Hawkesworth's *Voyages*]. Je ne connais rien de plus instructif. Je vois avec un plaisir extrême que Mr De Bougainville nous a dit la vérité. Quand les Français et les Anglais sont d'accord il est démontré qu'ils ne nous ont point trompés.[81]

We can be sure which island in Hawkesworth's *Voyages* most interested Voltaire and which aspect of that island. He continues:

Je suis encor dans l'île de Taïti. J'y admire la diversité de la nature. J'y vois avec édification la Reine du païs assister à une communion de l'église anglicane, et inviter les Anglais au service divin qu'on fait dans son roiaume; ce service divin consiste à faire coucher ensemble un jeune homme et une jeune fille tout nuds en présence de Sa Majesté et de cinq cent courtisans et courtisanes. On peut assurer que les habitans de Taïti ont conservé dans toute sa pureté la plus ancienne religion de la terre.[82]

Voltaire's Eldorado in *Candide* (1759) is a utopia in which Candide does not wish to stay; his Huron in *L'Ingénu* (1767) is only half a Huron. His sarcastic comment on Rousseau's 'état de Nature' is well known ('Il prend envie de marcher à quatre pattes quand on lit votre ouvrage') and he made his comment on the happy savages of Rousseau's 'Société naissante' in the margin of his text: 'Quelle chimere . . . !'[83] Yet he was capable, in the article on 'Anthropophages' in his *Dictionnaire philosophique* (1764), of echoing the sentiment of Montaigne's 'Des cannibales', that European cruelty to the living was worse than the savage custom of eating the dead.[84] As his letter shows, Voltaire had immediately recognized the main Tahitian topic. So what would he make of it?

The answer came the next year, 1775, Voltaire's eightieth, with the publication of his *Les Oreilles du comte de Chesterfield et le chapelain Goudman*, so named because the priest, Goudman, through the deafness of Lord Chesterfield, loses his chance of a good living and with it his prospect of marrying the desirable Miss Fidler. Goudman complains of his poverty and Chesterfield thinks he has complained of his health and, instead of offering him the lucrative appointment, sends him, as a favour, to Mr Sidrac, his personal physician. While Goudman is at the doctor's, a rival makes himself heard, receives the living and, inevitably, Miss Fidler. Chesterfield promptly dies, before his mistake can be rectified, and Goudman, disconsolate and convinced that 'la fatalité gouverne irrémissiblement toutes les choses de ce monde', decides to take the advice of Mr Sidrac and become a philosopher.[85]

Goudman and Sidrac, himself something of a philosopher, discuss several topics: nature, procreation, the soul, God, fate, and, with reference to these, Miss Fidler. Goudman reflects that, if things had turned out differently and he had been given his appointment, he would never have considered these important issues, but now that he is idle he should improve his philosophical knowledge. 'Eh bien!' says Sidrac, and invites him to dinner the following day to meet Dr Grou, who has 'fait le tour du monde avec MM. Banks et Solander', and therefore knows 'Dieu et l'âme, le vrai et le faux, le juste et l'injuste, bien mieux que ceux qui ne sont jamais sortis de Covent-Garden'.[86]

In the course of the discussion the next evening Dr Grou avers that, of all the religions he has encountered in the world, the religion of Tahiti is the best. In that remarkable island there is the bread tree, and therefore no need for cannibalism, but there is a human need more natural, more gentle, more universal, which the religion of Tahiti requires be satisfied in public. This, the most respectable of all religious ceremonies, he has witnessed for himself, and so has the whole crew of his ship. It is no fable, no fiction, and 'le docteur Jean Hakerovorth' has just printed an account of it.[87] After coffee Dr Grou relates Voltaire's version of Hawkesworth's version of Cook's version of the scene at Point Venus, not forgetting to stress its religious solemnity:

Une jeune fille très jolie, simplement parée d'un déshabille galant, était couchée sur une estrade qui servait d'autel. La reine Obéira ordonna à un beau garçon d'environ vingt ans d'aller sacrifier. Il prononça une espèce de prière, et monta sur l'autel. Les deux sacrificateurs étaient à demi nus. La reine, d'un air majestueux, enseignait à la jeune victime la manière la plus convenable de consommer le sacrifice. Tous les Otaïtiens étaient si attentifs et si respectueux qu'aucun de nos matelots n'osa troubler la cérémonie par un rire indécent. Voilà ce que j'ai vu, vous dis-je, voilà tout ce que notre équipage a vu. C'est à vous d'en tirer les conséquences.[88]

Goudman draws the conclusion that this Tahitian rite is very admirable and he hopes it will please God 'que je pusse sacrifier avec miss Fidler devant la reine Obéira en tout bien et en tout honneur!'[89] It would certainly be the most beautiful day and the most beautiful action of his life, he believes. Sidrac agrees that Queen Obéira and her religion are indeed admirable. But he has heard, he says, that the Europeans who have visited Tahiti have taken with them the venereal disease. As a doctor, he admits, he owes most of his fortune to this disease, but he detests it all the same, because his wife infected him with it on his wedding night. As a philosopher, he wonders what 'ce qu'on appelle *la nature*' was thinking of when she spilled this poison into the sources of life.[90] Man was said to have been made in the image of God, he reflects, 'et c'est dans les vaisseaux spermatiques de cette image qu'on a mis la douleur, l'infection, et la mort!'[91] Goudman draws the new conclusion that he should perhaps thank Providence that he did not marry his dear Miss Fidler, 'car sait-on ce qui serait arrivé?'[92]

On the following day the three meet again to discuss the question of the primary cause of all human actions. Goudman naturally suggests love and ambition; Grou suggests money; and Sidrac is certain that the primary cause of all human actions is the commode. While Sidrac is proving this hypothesis with a number of examples from history of the momentous consequences of the constipation of men such as Cromwell and Charles IX of France, Goudman is called to the door to receive some news. The steward of the late Lord Chesterfield announces to him that the circumstances which occurred on the marriage night of Mr and Mrs Sidrac have repeated themselves in the case of Miss Fidler and her husband. The couple have quarrelled and separated and the husband has lost his job. The steward is aware of Goudman's feelings for Miss Fidler, but he himself is also partial to the desirable lady and, if he can have her, Goudman can have the profitable job. Remarking that commodes are not so very important in human affairs, Goudman consults his two friends, who advise him to choose the job and the money rather than Miss Fidler, for with the job and the money he can have all the women in the parish and Miss Fidler as well. Goudman takes their advice, the job, the money—and Miss Fidler whenever he likes—and becomes one of the fiercest priests in England, 'plus persuadé que jamais de la fatalité qui gouverne toutes les choses de ce monde'.[93]

Thus Voltaire, who controls 'la fatalité qui gouverne toutes les choses' in his plot, has shown how a Goudman, because of the venereal disease, and despite the ears of Lord Chesterfield, can fulfil his ambition and sacrifice with Miss Fidler according to the commandment of Queen Obéira of Tahiti. In *Candide*, ever-optimistic Pangloss, suffering the 'enfer' of venereal disease as a consequence of enjoying the sexual 'délices du paradis', points out to Candide the providential light at the end of a tunnel of consequences: 'si Colomb n'avais pas attrapé, dans une île de l'Amérique, cette maladie qui empoisonne la source de la génération, qui souvent même empêche la génération, et qui est évidemment l'opposé du grand but de la nature, nous n'aurions ni le chocolat, ni la cochenille.'[94] The plot of *Les Oreilles* parodies such explanations, reversing the usual sequences of sex and disease, paradise and fall. If there were no venereal disease there would be no Tahitian ceremonies for Goudman with Miss Fidler. 'C'est à vous d'en tirer les conséquences', as Grou said of Cook's 'odd Scene' at Point Venus. Voltaire had drawn his conclusions and shown the consequences.

But what of Aotourou, the real Tahitian from the island Diderot and Voltaire had imagined? According to Diderot, speaking through his mouthpiece B in the *Supplément*, Aotourou would be regarded as a liar if he ever returned to Tahiti to tell the tale of his travels, because the Tahitians 'aimeront mieux prendre Aotourou pour un menteur que de nous croire si fous'.[95] But how could Aotourou return to Tahiti? When the eager Tahitian had sailed away with the French, Fesche had written gloomily in his journal that 'je regarde comme impossible son retour dans sa patrie'.[96] In France the poet Delille describes the savage from Tahiti, 'Où l'amour, sans pudeur, n'est pas sans innocence', coming across a plant from his native country in the botanical gardens at Versailles, and weeping as

> son ame attendrie,
> Du moins pour un instant, retrouva sa patrie.[97]

Bougainville was determined that Aotourou should see Tahiti again and contributed a large sum to equip a ship for the purpose. 'Puisse Aotourou revoir bientôt ses compatriotes!' he wrote in his *Voyage*.[98]

Aotourou sailed from France late in March 1770, and reached the Ile de France in October, an island he had visited before on his passage with Bougainville to France, and named 'Enoua erao piri piri', 'country miserly with cunts'.[99] The future author of *Paul et Virginie*, Bernardin de Saint-Pierre, compared 'cet insulaire de Taïti' before and after his experience of 'les moeurs de l'Europe': 'Je l'avois trouvé à son passage, franc, gai, un peu libertin. A son retour, je le voyois réservé, poli & maniéré.' Aotourou had acquired a watch, according to Bernardin de Saint-Pierre, and knew the hours by his Paris habits: the hours for rising, for eating, for walking, for going to the opera. He seemed greatly bored at the Ile de France and 'se promenoit toujours seul'.[100]

Eventually, after much debate and delay, an expedition was organized at the Ile de France, with the pretext of repatriating Aotourou and the incentives of rediscovering the 'Terra Austrialis' of Quirós, perhaps, or at least profiting from the spices of the Moluccas. Marion du Fresne was appointed to command, in his younger days the rescuer of Bonnie Prince Charlie from Scotland after Culloden.[101] Five days after sailing, in October 1771, Aotourou complained of a fever and the symptoms soon declared themselves of the smallpox he had contracted at the Ile de France, where an 'épidémie faisoit les plus cruels ravages'.[102] Marion anchored off the coast of Madagascar in hope of a recovery but, according to the ship's surgeon, Aotourou 'était épuisé par les débauches, ayant, en outre, une dartre . . . qui occupait tout le scrotum'.[103] On the evening of 6 November he died and was buried at sea off the south-east coast of Madagascar, wrapped in a sail and weighted with a ball, never to see his home again. Marion sailed on into the Pacific, but he was never to see his home again either, killed with twenty-five of his men at the Bay of Islands, New Zealand, and allegedly eaten. Crozet, his second-in-command, was bitter in his anger at 'les philosophes panégyristes de l'homme naturel', who had proved himself more savage than 'un tigre ou un lion'. 'Voilà cependant ces hommes naturels si vantés par ceux qui ne les connoissent pas', he wrote. 'Je parle d'après ce que j'ai vu.'[104] When he dined with Cook and his officers aboard the *Resolution* at the Cape of Good Hope in March 1775, Crozet told them of the massacre at New Zealand and of Rousseau's response: 'Is it possible that the good Children of Nature can really be so wicked?'[105]

The *Resolution* was returning from Cook's second voyage when Crozet came aboard at the Cape, but her companion ship, the *Adventure*, captained by Tobias Furneaux, was already in England, having arrived on 14 July 1774, just four days after Walpole had announced the end of the Tahitian fashion and the beginning of the African, with the return of the explorer James Bruce, 'who has lived three years in the Court of Abyssinia, and breakfasted every morning with the maids of honour on live oxen'.[106] Furneaux had lost ten men, killed in New Zealand—by cannibals, according to the report of his officer, James Burney, who was 'convinced by most horrid & undeniable proofs—a great many baskets . . . of roasted flesh'.[107] And in case this was not news Furneaux had brought with him a Tahitian, Able Seaman Omai of the *Adventure*, 'dark, ugly and a downright blackguard' in Cook's opinion, a young man of about 20, born a member of the second social class, the *raatira*, on Raiatea in the Society Islands, and displaced as a refugee to Tahiti on the invasion of Raiatea by men from Borabora, but a noble Tahitian for the British public, none the less.[108]

Mai—or Omai, as he was known with the usual European confusion of the Tahitian ''o', meaning 'it is', with the proper name—was immediately placed by the Admiralty in the care of Joseph Banks at New Burlington Street, from where Banks's sister heard (via his housekeeper) of Omai's intentions: 'to return with men and guns in a ship to drive the Bola Bola usurpers from his property' and then to wed 'a young & handsome English Woman 15 years old'.[109] He began his stay in England by being presented, fresh from the lower decks at Plymouth, to the King and Queen at Kew, and then dined with the Duke of Gloucester in the company of Mr Bruce, 'lately returned from Abyssinia', as the *General Evening Post* reported.[110] 'As every Circumstance relative to the Native of Otaheite, now amongst us, engages the Attention of Philosophers', the newspapers kept the public well informed, the *St. James's Chronicle* predicting that, 'all his Observations leading to immediate corporeal Gratifications', Omai would soon take some exercise in the parks, 'after the Manner of his own Country'.[111] In August Fanny Burney, sister of James of the *Adventure*, sorted out priorities in her diary: 'The present *Lyon* of the times . . . is Omy, the native of Otaheite; and next to him, the present object is Mr. Bruce, a gentleman who has been abroad twelve years, and spent four of them in Abyssinia.'[112]

The lion was busy meanwhile, being vaccinated against smallpox by a Baron, portrayed in flowing robes of Tahitian tapa by Nathaniel Dance, dined and observed by the Royal Society, awed by the 'Doctors and Professors' at Cambridge ('supposing them in a near relation to the Deity', according to the *General Evening Post*), and entertained at Hinchingbrooke, the country house of the First Lord of the Admiralty, Lord Sandwich.[113] Fanny's father was also invited by Lord Sandwich, 'to meet Lord Orford and the Otaheitan at Hinchinbrook', and 'to bring with him *his son, the Lieutenant*', whose shipboard acquaintance with Able Seaman Omai might now, Fanny hoped, be the making of him: 'This has filled us with hope for some future good to my sailor-brother, who is the capital friend and favourite of Omai.'[114]

It was not until 30 November that 'this *Lyon* of lyons', as Fanny now called him, found time, between a visit to the House of Lords and an appointment 'to see no less than 12 Ladies', to dine with the Burneys in their new home in St. Martin's Street, off Leicester Square, where he arrived wearing 'a Suit of Manchester velvet, lined with white satten, a *Bag*, lace Ruffles, & a very handsome Sword which the King had given to him'.[115] 'He makes *remarkable* good Bows', wrote

Fanny to a friend the next day. 'Indeed he seems to Shame Education, for his manners are so extremely graceful.' When he spilled a little of his drink, 'he was *shocked* extremely'. Compared to Lord Chesterfield's son, 'a meer *pedantic booby*', Omai was 'thoroughly well bred!' Fanny drew—at last—her conclusion: 'I think this shews how much more *Nature* can do without *art*, than art with all her refinement, unassisted by *Nature*.'[116]

Samuel Johnson had also 'been in company with Omai', as Boswell tells us, and

was struck with the elegance of his behaviour, and accounted for it thus: 'Sir, he had passed his time, while in England, only in the best company; so that all that he had acquired of our manners was genteel. As a proof of this, Sir, Lord Mulgrave and he dined one day at Streatham; they sat with their backs to the light fronting me, so that I could not see distinctly; and there was so little of the savage in Omai, that I was afraid to speak to either, lest I should mistake one for the other.'[117]

The translator of Father Lobo's *Voyage to Abyssinia* (1735) and author of *Rasselas* (1759) did not have as good an opinion of Omai's rival Abyssinian lion. In his preface to the former work Johnson wrote with approval that Lobo had 'consulted his Senses, not his Imagination'.[118] This was not the case with Mr Bruce, Johnson had obviously decided, for, as Boswell reports, Johnson had also 'been in the company' of Bruce, but 'had not listened to him with that full confidence, without which there is little satisfaction in the society of travellers'.[119]

Johnson's opinion of Bruce was commonly held. It was those breakfasts of live oxen referred to by Walpole that no one could swallow. Walpole himself regarded Bruce as a liar, but having given his opinion in a letter he asked his correspondent not to repeat it. He had no wish, he said, to be engaged in 'a duel'.[120] Bruce, mocked on stage as 'Macfable', was indeed notoriously sensitive on the subject of the Abyssinian diet.[121] In his published account of his *Travels to Discover the Source of the Nile* (1790) he wrote:

When first I mentioned this in England . . . I was told by my friends it was not believed. I asked the reason of this disbelief, and was answered, that people who had never been out of their own country, and others well acquainted with the manners of the world, for they had travelled as far as France, had agreed the thing was impossible, and therefore it was so.[122]

This, then, was the opinion commonly held of Fanny's lesser lion when she encountered him at the home of his distant relative, Mrs Strange, in March 1775. The conversation turning naturally to Omai, Mr Bruce spoke with feeling about Omai's probable reception at Tahiti: 'he will only pass for a consummate liar when he returns; for how can he make them believe half the things he will tell them? He can give them no idea of our houses, carriages, or any thing that will appear probable.' At this Mrs Strange made a suggestion which Fanny considered 'well worth being tried': '"Troth, then," cried Mrs. Strange, "they should give him a set of dolls' things and a baby's house, to show them; he should have everything in miniature".'[123]

By now Omai had awakened the pamphleteers, and *An Historic Epistle, from Omiah, to the Queen of Otaheite; being his Remarks on the English Nation* appeared anonymously in June 1775.[124] 'Omiah' is, predictably, the savage of nature satirizing the arts of civilization:

> Can *Europe* boast, with all her pilfer'd wealth,
> A larger share of happiness, or health?
> What then avail her thousand arts to gain
> The stores of every land, and every main:
> Whilst we, whom love's more grateful joys enthral,
> Profess one art—to live without them all.[125]

'Omiah' himself plays little part in what follows, as the author, in his name, passes his 'Remarks on the English Nation'. Nor are there many comparative references to Tahitian society as the topics come and go: the church, the law, the world of letters, and the Royal Society—

> This wond'rous race still pry, in nature's spite,
> Through all her secrets, and *Transactions* write.[126]

The only Tahitian topic brings 'Omiah' briefly into action:

> When stranger first I sought their Monarch's Court,
> A nymph I saw, just ripe for amorous sport;
> Struck with her air and shape, I blaz'd desire,
> And long'd to quench the heav'n descended fire;
>
> .   .   .   .
>
> When, strange to tell, the court appear'd amaz'd,
> The young folks titter'd, and the old ones gaz'd:
> The virgin's cheeks a crimson glow display'd.[127]

'Omiah' wonders 'what reason could such conduct cause'. The answer is that the author wants to mention the venereal disease:

> I knew but one and fancy instant drew,
> BOUGAINVILLE'S horrors to my pitiying view.[128]

After all this 'Omiah', like the reader, is tired of 'senseless art', and would like to return to 'a willing maid' and 'extatic flames' in Tahiti,

> Where nature only rules the lib'ral mind
> Unspoil'd by art, by falsehood unrefin'd.[129]

Some who had been observing Omai's progress in civilized society took the view that he should not be returned to Tahiti totally 'unspoil'd by art'. A London philanthropist, Granville Sharp, obtained the permission of the First Lord of the Admiralty, and undertook the instruction of Omai in the English language on 14 February 1776, though it appears from Sharp's notes that, after about thirteen lessons, Omai 'had no time for a lesson', then only 'a very short time', and then 'was so taken up with engagements that I could have no more opportunity of giving him lessons'.[130] No doubt Omai really was busy, but one is not convinced of this by turning the pages of Sharp's *An English Alphabet, for the Use of Foreigners: wherein the Pronunciation of the Vowels, or Voice-Letters, is explained in Twelve short general Rules, With their several Exceptions, as abridged (For the Instruction of Omai) from a larger Work* (1786).[131] These short rules and their several exceptions were intended, of course, to form a medium for the communication of higher things to the South Seas. According to his account, Sharp expounded the ten commandments to Omai, up to number seven, when his pupil asked, 'Adultery! what that? what that?', whereupon Sharp explained that adultery was 'contrary to the first principle of the law of nature'. 'First principle of the law of nature . . . what that? what that?' Sharp explained the seventh commandment more clearly and was gratified when Omai demonstrated his full comprehension by means of three pens, representing the First Lord of the Admiralty, the First Lord of the Admiralty's wife, and the First Lord of the Admiralty's mistress, Miss Ray.[132]

Cook returned aboard the *Resolution* from his voyage to the South Seas and towards the South Pole in late July 1775, a year after Omai's arrival aboard the *Adventure*. Cook had been wiping out the Southern Continent, sailing south 'not only further than any other man has been before me, but as far as I think it possible for man to go', and he had also been prodigiously writing, producing during the course of his voyage three variant versions, nearly complete, of his journal.[133] The most likely explanation for—to quote Cook's modern editor—'the vast amount of drafting and redrafting, expanding, abbreviating and recasting, correction, substitution, interlineation, a million words or so of it, that Cook committed to paper between July 1772 and July 1775', is that Cook had been writing—not a journal merely, or several versions of a journal, but—a book.[134] And indeed the authorship of this second voyage was not to be entrusted to some new Hawkesworth. The Admiralty appointed John Douglas, Canon of Windsor, as an editor, not an author, of what was to be Cook's own book, which Cook continued to revise in England, yet again deleting, redrafting, and adding, filling in the spaces between the lines, spilling into the margins, taking to the crammed pages with red ink.[135] Canon Douglas, mindful of Tahiti, must have made some 'remarks' to his author, to which Cook replied in January 1776, 'with respect to the Amours of my people at Otaheite & at other places: I think it will not be necessary to mention them attall'.[136] Douglas was to rest assured of Cook's desire that his book should be 'unexceptionable to the nicest readers' and contain 'nothing indecent'.[137]

Cook was indeed busy and it was not until 2 April 1776, a few months before 'the celebrated Circumnavigator' was to depart on his third and final voyage, that Boswell made his acquaintance. It was on this occasion that Boswell interviewed Cook about Hawkesworth's *Voyages*, and they also discussed Omai and his forthcoming departure with Cook, who reported that the two things Omai wanted above all else to take back to Tahiti with him were 'port wine, which he loved the best of any liquor, and gunpowder'. It was Cook's opinion, according to Boswell,

'that for some time after Omai's return home he would be a man of great consequence, as having many wonders to tell', but 'that when he had told all he had to
tell, he would sink back into his former state'.[138]

Cook also had wonders to tell, but pleased Boswell at a Royal Society dinner a
fortnight later by admitting 'that he and his companions who visited the South Sea
Islands could not be certain of any information they got, or supposed they got,
except as to objects falling under the observation of the senses'.[139] This admirable
empiricism Cook demonstrated to Boswell with an account of an experiment he
had conducted aboard the *Resolution* at Queen Charlotte Sound, New Zealand,
shortly before the 'horrid & undeniable proofs' James Burney of the *Adventure* had
observed there a few weeks later. Tired, according to his journal, of being asked by
sceptics in England 'if I had actualy seen them eat human flesh my self', and
'desireous of being an eye wittness to a fact which many people had their doubts
about', Cook had ordered Lieutenant Clerke to cook a piece of flesh from a boy's
head (purchased ashore for two nails) which was then served 'on the quarter deck
where one of these Canibals eat it with a seeming good relish' (deleted and revised
to 'a surprising avidity').[140] The controversy about Pacific cannibalism—though
not the controversy about public copulation—was effectively settled for Boswell,
who found Cook's experiment convincing: 'He gave me a distinct account of a
New Zealander eating flesh in his presence and in that of many more aboard, so
that the fact of cannibals is now certainly known.'[141]

Cook was still at work on the journal of his second voyage when he received his
orders from the Admiralty to prepare the *Resolution* for his third voyage, and one
of his many corrections, in view of Omai's social progress since his appointment as
an Able Seaman, was the excision of the words 'dark, ugly and a downright
blackguard' from his text.[142] A few weeks before sailing he wrote to thank Douglas
for his past and prospective assistance with the production of *A Voyage towards the
South Pole, and Round the World . . . Written by James Cook* (1777), which would be
presented to the public, after Douglas had improved Cook's grammar, syntax,
spelling, and punctuation, with Cook's Introduction (considerably reorganized by
Douglas), 'desiring the reader to excuse the inaccuracies of style' in 'a work
designed for information, and not merely for entertainment', which 'is the production of a man, who has not had the advantages of much school education, but who
has been constantly at sea from his youth'.[143] The reviewer of the *Gentleman's
Magazine* responded on behalf of that public by drawing the intended conclusion
that Cook had expressed himself 'with a plain natural strength and clearness,
and an unaffected modesty which schools cannot teach', thus celebrating another
triumph in the manner of Omai, of nature over art.[144]

Cook was never to see the book he had so laboriously prepared for the public,
sailing for the Pacific with the *Resolution* and the *Discovery* on 12 July 1776, with
the duties of repatriating Omai and settling, if possible, the old question about a
North-West Passage. As the *Resolution* approached Tahiti a year later, in August
1777, having sailed by way of Tasmania, New Zealand, and Tonga, Lieutenant

King was expectant, knowing that 'many in England envy'd us the sight of Omai's return to his Countrymen'.[145] When 'the Husband of Omai's Sister' and a chief came aboard from a canoe, however, Omai 'was receiv'd rather Coldly than cordially' until he produced some of the valuable red feathers he had acquired in the Tongan Islands, 'which work'd a most surprising alteration'.[146] Cook had hoped that 'with the property he was master of' (European as well as Tongan) Omai would have 'made himself respected and even courted by the first persons in the island' but on shore, to Cook's annoyance, Omai 'suffered himself to be duped by every designing knave'.[147] Indeed Omai in Tahiti, unlike Omai in England, 'kept company with the lowest people', according to King, associating 'with the black guards of the Island', according to the surgeon's mate Samwell, 'acting the part of a merry Andrew, parading about in ludicrous Masks & different Dresses to the great admiration of the Rabble'.[148] He failed to impress the rabble, however, on the astonishing imported horses (see Plate 3), being 'thrown off before he got himself seated', as Cook noticed, and even when 'Omai put on his Suit of Armour [supplied by Lord Sandwich], mounted a stage in one of the Canoes and was paddled all along the shore of the bay, so that every one had a full View of him . . . it did not draw their attention so much as might be expected'.[149] The journals of Samwell and the astronomer Bayly reveal that Cook planned to marry Omai to a sister of the chief Tu, Cook's supposed 'Otoo the King', but the sister had a man of her own, Bayly tells us, who supplied Omai with a substitute girl and then, with other 'raskels', attempted to rob him in the night. 'Omi fired a Pistol at him, but mis'd him: & they all quarreled & the girl left him but not till she had in a manner strip'd him of his most valuable things, & to crown all she gave him the foul disease.'[150]

While this farce which Hawkesworth would have relished went unrecorded by Cook, the prospective author of the official account was mindful of his duty as an anthropologist and, hearing a human sacrifice advertised, 'thought this a good oppertunity to see something of this extraordinary and Barbarous custom', observing also the part played in the barbarous custom by 'the English Pendant [of] Captain Wallis'.[151] After the dispassionate field-work, Omai protested on behalf of the British to the chief responsible and, as Cook recorded, 'entered into our arguments with so much Spirit that he put the Cheif out of all manner of patience, especially when he was told that if he a Cheif in England had put a Man to death as he had done this he would be hanged for it'. 'Maeno maeno', the chief cried out, appalled, 'How evil, how vile!' (see Plate 4).[152]

There was clearly no secure place for Omai among the royalty of Tahiti, Cook decided, as his protégé had 'conducted himself in such a manner as not only to lose the friendship of Otoo but that of every other person of note in the island'.[153] The ships sailed on to Huahine in the nearby Society Islands, where Able Seaman Omai had come aboard four years before, and where Cook, now better pleased with Omai's 'prudence', decided to settle him, quashing his ambition to return to his native Raiatea to lead a revolution against the usurpers from Borabora, and employing the ships' carpenters on the construction, 'with as few nails as possible', of a house that would not be pillaged and pulled apart, 'for Omai to secure his property in'.[154]

When the house was ready to safeguard Omai's exotic property and the door had been provided with a lock and Omai with a key, his boxes and casks of imports were taken ashore and unpacked in 'a grand exhibition before a great multitude of the Natives The Young King & most of the Chiefs being present'.[155] But Omai, 'being a man of pleasure', according to Bayly, had left his provisioning and packing 'entirely to other people', so that when he 'came to examine the contents of his Boxes & Casks, he was very near going out of his Senses'.[156] There were 'only 8 Spike-nails', hatchets of 'the very worst' kind, some glass beads of such poor quality that no one 'would give Cocoanuts' for them, an 'Organ', an 'Electrifying machine', and, by contrast with the contemptible hatchets and beads, 'two exceeding good Drums'.[157] The advice of Mrs Strange had not been forgotten, for—as Cook recorded—'amongst many other useless things, was a box of Toys which when exposed to publick view seemed to please the gazing Multitude very much', consisting, according to a more enthusuastic report, of 'whole Regiments of Soldiers, Coaches Horses and The Figure of Almost Every creature we know of'.[158] In addition there were, of course, Sandwich's suit of armour, some fireworks supplied by the Royal Ordnance at Woolwich, and, according to Banks's manuscript list of 'Presents for Omai', men's and women's clothing, tools, furniture (a bed, table and chair), pots, plates, and cutlery, 'Hankerchiefs with Great Britain printed on them', 'Soap', 'Straw hatts ornamented', 'the Kings picture', 'the Queens do', and, last on the list, 'Medecines for the Venereal disease'.[159]

Civilization also supplied Omai with an armoury of pistols, guns, swords, and cutlasses and, to make him 'happy', Cook added a stock of gunpowder and ammunition.[160] Of more use than all these mostly 'useless things', in Cook's opinion, and of more use than Omai himself—indeed 'the greatest benifit these islands will receive from Omais travels'—were a pair of horses, a pregnant goat, a family of pigs, and, according to an unofficial report from below decks, a monkey.[161] Over and above all these, but included in the sum, were two boys from New Zealand, whose 'most violent & poignant grief' at their abandonment distracted some observers from the simple farewell of Omai, who remained aboard the *Resolution* till she had cleared the reef on 2 November, and then 'threw his Arms round Captn Cook, bid him adieu and walked into the Boat weeping'.[162]

The *Resolution* and the *Discovery* sailed north after leaving the Society Islands and on 18 January 1778 sighted Oahu and Kauai of the Hawaiian Islands, thus discovered to Europeans and 'named *Sandwich Islands*' by Cook.[163] 'The very instant' he stepped ashore on Kauai, 'they all fell flat on their faces', a mark of respect which he understood (correctly) was paid 'to their great chiefs'.[164] He was surprised to find people so far north belonging to 'the same Nation as the people of Otahiete' and banned 'connection' with the women in an attempt to prevent the spread of venereal infection to another group of Polynesian islands.[165] It was an attempt without much hope of success, he recognized, and indeed the women 'used all their arts' and even 'force', as Samwell recorded.[166] After visiting the nearby island of Niihau, Cook continued his interrupted voyage north to search for the imaginary Passage in the North Pacific and the Arctic Ocean, and then returned south in late October to winter in the Hawaiian Islands.

The island of Maui was sighted on 26 November but Cook kept his ships at sea to maintain the value of iron by controlling the trade with canoes, which came out from the island bringing provisions and women, still banned, who 'by no means took the refusal Patiently, but by their Manners & gestures abusd & ridiculed us'.[167] It became evident that Cook's previous measures to control the venereal trade had failed, however, for three men from Maui who came aboard 'had a Clap', as King reported. 'Their Penis was much swell'd, & inflamed', and 'they consider'd us as the Original authors'.[168] Perhaps because the damage was already done, Cook lifted the ban on women on 7 December and, thereafter, at a mere gesture, according to the poetical Samwell, 'a handsome Girl in a Canoe' would swim aboard to be received 'in our arms like another Venus just rising from the Waves'.[169] The sailors' frustration was only partly relieved, however, for Cook still kept the ships at sea, circling the main island of Hawaii until 17 January, when he entered Kealakekua Bay to be greeted by crowds lining the shore, filling canoes and swimming 'like shoals of fish' in the sea, to quote from the last entry in Cook's log.[170] His writings—or what remains of them—run out on this day, when he went ashore to be received by prostrations and repetitions of 'a sentence, wherein the word Erono was always mention'd', as we learn from King's journal.[171] This 'Erono' was Cook himself, taken for the Hawaiian *akua* or god Rono, or Lono, and—patient and 'quite passive', according to King—he was guided by priests through a 'long, & rather tiresome ceremony, of which we could only guess at its Object & Meaning'.[172] Certainly it was 'highly respectful', King thought, and might also be useful, as indeed it was, for ample provisions and generally good relations accompanied the respect for Cook that 'seemd to approach to Adoration'.[173]

His ships watered and well stocked, Cook sailed from Kealakekua Bay on 4 February, but a gale a few days later badly damaged the foremast of the *Resolution*, so the ships sailed back into Kealakekua Bay for repairs on 11 February. The reception of the reappearing Lono was still respectful but less rapturous, perhaps because, as King reported, some of the Hawaiian laity believed the ships came from a country without provisions, with no other purpose than 'filling our bellies'.[174] Some Hawaiians were 'troublesome' and 'insolent' according to King, while Captain Clerke of the *Discovery* reported 'a stronger propensity to theft than we had reason to complain of during our former stay'.[175] On the morning of 14 February the theft of a large cutter was discovered and Cook, following a long-established practice, went ashore with nine marines under the command of Lieutenant Phillips to take the Hawaiian 'king' aboard the *Resolution* as a hostage for the cutter's return. There were prostrations 'as usual' on the way to the village, where the old King Kalaniopuu was wakened and came willingly until they reached the shore, but there a royal wife and two chiefs stopped him while a large crowd formed.[176] Cook was threatened with 'a long Iron Spike' ('furnish'd them by ourselves'), a fight started and, amid what Phillips's report called 'a most miserable scene of confusion', Cook was felled in the sea and killed.[177]

Some weeks after Omai's departure from England the event was the excuse for the publication of *Omiah's Farewell; Inscribed to the Ladies of London* (1776). In a Preface the anonymous author laments that Omai during his time in England was not given some useful instruction, particularly of a medical (i.e. venereological) nature, that might have been of use to his afflicted countrymen, rather than dressed up 'in a bag and sword' and taken 'to all public spectacles'.[178] He reports that 'Omiah is now returning to his native isle, fraught by royal order with squibs, crackers, and a various assortment of fireworks, to show to the wild untutored Indian the great superiority of an enlighted Christian prince'.[179] The verses that follow these sharp satirical barbs are not concerned with Omiah's useful instruction:

> Oft LADY ******* hast thou promise made,
> To sleep with me beneath the *Bread-tree's* shade,
> For brighter suns, to leave this clouded sky,
> And with OMIAH share Eternity.
> For thee, her stores shall *Otaheitée* pour,
> And VENUS guide each gay delicious hour.[180]

So it goes on, as 'Omiah' says his goodbyes regretfully to Lady ***** and 'beauteous B******' and others, until finally the versifier finds a more specific target in the form of naughty Lord Sandwich and his mistress, the 'coelestial *Ray*'.[181]

In April 1779, while the tubercular and dying Captain Clerke was dutifully continuing Cook's search for the illusive Passage, Martha Ray was shot and killed leaving Covent Garden Opera House by James Hackman, a man infatuated with her, and the opportunity was taken of manufacturing and publishing *Love and Madness* (1780), pretending to be a series of letters exchanged between Ray and Hackman and enrolling Omai as an observer of their supposed affair at Hinchingbrooke, and a potential informer of Lord Sandwich.[182] 'Come then tomorrow', Ray surreptitiously writes to Hackman, 'and surely Omiah will not murder love! ... What will Oberea and her coterie say to this, Omiah ... What would Rousseau say to it ... ?'[183]

News of Cook's death reached the bereaved Sandwich and thence the newspapers and the public in January 1780, and Oberea and Omai were not forgotten in the most popular literary response, Anna Seward's pompous and woeful *Elegy on Captain Cook* (1780), which called upon the islanders of the 'Gay Eden of the south' to pay their funerary respects 'in pomp of woe':

> Come Oberea, hapless fair-one! come,
> With piercing shrieks bewail thy Hero's doom!
> .   .   .   .
> Bid mild Omiah bring his choicest stores,
> The juicy fruits, and the luxuriant flow'rs.[184]

The *Resolution* and *Discovery* finally returned in October 1780, having lost both Captains Cook and Clerke and found no North-West Passage. Sandwich appointed Douglas in 1781 to prepare the account of the voyage for publication and the task of narrating the events after Cook's death was given, on the advice of Banks, by now President of the Royal Society, to James King on his return in 1782, tubercular, from duty in the West Indies. The whole work was to be supervised by Douglas, who admitted in his autobiographical notes some years later that he 'took more Liberties' than he had with Cook's account of his second voyage.[185] Although faithful to 'the facts', he had allowed himself greater freedom 'in cloathing them with better Stile', and had made use of the journal of the surgeon Anderson, another victim of tuberculosis, as 'a fruitful Source of important Additions'.[186]

These additions do not include Anderson's conscientious description of a Tahitian dance featuring the shameless exposure by young women of 'those parts' and the male spectators' 'most anxious curiosity to see that part just mentioned', but Douglas made frequent use of Anderson's journal to supplement—and sometimes to substitute for—Cook's account of the human sacrifice at Tahiti, for example, to which Anderson had accompanied Cook to obtain additional 'ocular proof'.[187] Contributing a sarcastic interpolation of his own, so that Cook's plain 'this' becomes 'this act of worship', Canon Douglas preferred Anderson's simple 'scaffold' to Cook's too generously ecumenical 'alter' as a term for the repository for sacrificial dogs, dogs' entrails, and dead pigs, and also Anderson's more genteel 'emitted an intolerable stench' to Cook's 'stunk most intolerably'.[188] As a man who could be relied upon to eschew philosophy as well as pornography, Douglas was careful to leave no questions open about cultural relativity and, finding Cook's observations too coldly anthropological and insufficiently expressive of the right kind of revulsion, he supplied some suitable comments of Anderson's upon 'a practice so horrid'.[189]

Omai was a subject more to the taste of his readers, Douglas knew, remarking that: 'The history of Omai will, perhaps, interest a very numerous class of readers, more than any other occurrence of a voyage, the objects of which do not, in general, promise much entertainment'.[190] To Cook's comments on the installation of Omai at Huahine and the benefit the islands would derive from his travels because of the animals that accompanied him from England, Douglas appended some loftier reflections from the journal of James King, about the ridiculous nature of Omai's vengeful 'Schemes' against the 'Bora-Bora men', and the doubtful nature of his 'future ease & happiness' in view of his inability to compensate with 'some useful Knowledge' for his 'defect in rank' in a society so rigidly ruled by class distinctions.[191] Douglas concluded these reflections by commenting that knowledge of Omai's fate would have to await the observations of 'future navigators of this Ocean; with whom it cannot but be a principal object of curiosity to trace the future fortunes of our traveller'.[192]

The product of Douglas's editorial attentions, *A Voyage to the Pacific Ocean*, which eventually appeared in 1784 under the names of Cook and King, was a success.

The first edition sold out in days and, in the following year, which saw a second edition and a third, the proprietors of the Theatre Royal, Covent Garden, requiring a subject for a Christmas pantomime, undertook a production of Cook's last voyage in the form of a spectacular travelogue.[193] They seemed to share Douglas's sense of what would provide 'entertainment' and 'interest a very numerous class', for it was a pantomime called *Omai: Or, A Trip Round the World* that opened on 20 December 1785. The spectacle was provided by Phillipe de Loutherbourg, a French stage designer resident in England, who was responsible for the costumes and scenery, and the pantomime was the work of the undistinguished dramatist John O'Keeffe, who concocted a plot, dialogue, and lyrics for the music composed by a Mr Shield.

To achieve the realistic effect of a trip round the world, Loutherbourg consulted John Webber, the draughtsman employed on Cook's last voyage, and the playbill for *Omai* boasted of 'Exactly representing the Dresses, Weapons, and Manners, of the Inhabitants of Otaheite, New Zealand', etc.[194] Certainly the effect pleased the reviewer of the *Morning Chronicle*, who praised the 'spectacle' fulsomely, although he was less pleased with the pantomime, which he recognized to be merely a vehicle for the spectacle.[195] O'Keeffe also consulted Webber, but in the main he consulted Cook and King's *A Voyage to the Pacific Ocean* and his own imagination, with this result: Omai, son of Otoo and heir to the throne of Tahiti, comes to England where, despite the machinations of his Spanish rival, Don Struttolando, he wins the hand of the fair Londina, whom he escorts back to Tahiti by way of various locations visited by Cook, affording Loutherbourg with opportunities for representing 'A *Village* in *Tongataboo*', 'A *consecrated Place* in the Sandwich Islands', and so forth.[196] Back in Tahiti Omai ousts a Tahitian rival, despite the machinations of Oberea, an enchantress, and is crowned and married to Londina in the bay of Otaheite, a ceremony that culminates in the descent from the clouds of a gigantic picture of the 'Apotheosis of Captain Cook' (the British hero, not the Hawaiian Lono).[197] To this confection O'Keeffe added a layer of pantomime in the form of Harlequin and Colombine (the servants of Omai and Londina) and a Clown (the servant of Don Struttolando), and a rich coating of 'comic Business'.[198]

Omai's story had popular appeal, as Canon Douglas had predicted. *Omai* won the hand of Londina and was performed fifty times during the Christmas season of 1785–6, once by royal command, and was revived again in the autumn of 1786 and yet again in 1788.[199] A more critical view of the production was taken by a young Frenchman in London who sent a report of it back to his friend Joseph Joubert, an enthusiast who believed that 'à force de philosophie' he could become 'ce qu'est naturellement un jeune Otahitien' and slept in Paris facing Tahiti so that his thoughts would turn to the island of his dreams:

Otahiti, que tes filles sont belles et que tes hommes sont doux! Tu es la merveille des tropiques, dans les mers qui sont sous nos pieds. Cette moitié de l'océan que tu partages en deux autres moitiés te doit son plus grand ornement. Le néant est à ses deux bouts; l'âge d'or est dans tes bocages. J'aime à dormir tourné vers toi.[200]

Naturally Joubert's friend kept him in touch with Tahitian affairs in England:

Ils [the English] viennent de faire une pantomime d'Omai. C'était un sujet charmant. Le génie de Cook devait les élever. Eh bien! ils ont donné Arlequin pour domestique à Omai. Ils peignent l'Otahitien débarquant à Portsmouth poursuivi par les officiers de douane et la justice en grand panier. La scène change. Le jeune insulaire retourne dans sa patrie. On attend quelque chose. C'est un matelot qui, voulant reprendre son habit, trouve dans le panier où il l'a laissé, un crabe immense qui lui dévore toute la tête.[201]

Obviously *Omai*, despite its carefully authentic settings and costumes, had a ridiculously fantastic plot, but O'Keeffe did make some use of Cook and King's *A Voyage to the Pacific Ocean*, which not only provided him with the basis for his improbable plot (Omai's political 'schemes') and a reminder, if he needed one, of Omai's popular appeal, but also with realistic exotic colour of the kind displayed in Loutherbourg's costumes and scenery. Some idea of O'Keeffe's contribution to *Omai*, with some portions of his text, can be derived from his *A Short Account of the New Pantomime called Omai, or, A Trip Round the World* (1785), which reveals that, in addition to the 'comic Business' deplored by Joubert's correspondent, Omai's arrival in England was greeted by two 'Airs by an old *Water-cress Woman, or Fairy*' and his departure, with Londina, Harlequin, and others, was preceded by another 'Air', sung by the 'Master of a Raffling Toy-Shop'.[202]

O'Keeffe's use of South Sea material can be illustrated by a sample of his text, a passage he quotes from 'A *Moon-light Scene* in a sequester'd part of *Otaheite*'.[203] Oberea sings, to the accompaniment of footnotes:

> Soft and lightly tread, as falling snow upon the Hoohoo's(a) wing,
> In this delicious spot
> By sweet Kabulla's(b) op'ning odours richly perfum'd,
> Where creeping taro(c) and choee(d) spring;
> Where dancing shadows chequer the carpet of this green alcove,
> Favor'd retreat of wild Omai, Londina fair, and love.[204]

O'Keeffe supplies the following glosses to Oberea's song: (a) 'A beautiful bird of these islands'; (b) 'A delicate and fragrant flower'; (c) 'Bread-fruit'; (d) 'An aromatic shrub'.[205] His glosses are somewhat vague and uninformative, but his exotic terms are indeed authentic. Passing over the improbability of snow falling on the Hawaiian 'Hoohoo', and avoiding the springing and creeping 'ehoee', we can take 'Kabulla' and 'taro' as examples of O'Keeffe's researches in *A Voyage to the Pacific Ocean*, where we find, if not 'Kabulla' exactly, at least 'various sweet-smelling flowers, which go under the general name of *kahulla*', and also an explanation for O'Keeffe's confusion of 'creeping taro' with 'Bread-fruit', which is not taro and cannot, even in O'Keeffe's poetry, creep: 'roots which they call *taro* (the *coccos* of other countries); a bread-fruit; and . . .'.[206]

O'Keeffe was not the only author with a professional interest in Cook and King's *A Voyage to the Pacific Ocean*. In June 1784, the month of its publication, William Cowper, writing from rural Olney to his evangelical friend John Newton, mentioned that he had requested a loan from London of 'Cook's last voyage which I have a great curiosity to see'.[207] By August he was reporting to another correspondent that 'I find myself a voyager in the Pacific Ocean' and that 'these volumes furnish much matter of philosophical speculation', which found its way, in due course, into the first book of his poem, *The Task*, published in 1785.[208] In this meandering work Cowper contrasts the city and the country, which he prefers because it seems to him more civilized. London is 'slack in discipline', disrespectful of 'sabbath rites', and the cause of 'public mischief', perhaps even of the collapse—presaged by the loss of the American colonies—of 'Our arch of empire'.[209] There could be little virtue in a place as barbarous and disorderly as London, so, truly, 'God made the country, and man made the town'.[210] But what about Tahiti? Well, 'the favor'd isles, So lately found',

> Can boast but little virtue; and inert
> Through plenty, lose in morals, what they gain
> In manners, victims of luxurious ease.[211]

Clearly God did not make Tahiti, which seems to be rather like London, where 'rank abundance breeds . . . sloth and lust'.[212] But Cowper does not pity Londoners, he pities Tahitians, 'plac'd remote From all that science traces, art invents', and most of all he pities Omai, who has seen civilization and knows what he is missing (not, we are to understand, 'sloth and lust').[213] Now, for Omai, 'the gentle savage':

> The dream is past. And thou hast found again
> Thy cocoas and bananas, palms and yams,
> And homestall thatch'd with leaves. But hast thou found
> Their former charms? And having seen our state,
> Our palaces, our ladies, and our pomp
> Of equipage, our gardens, and our sports,
> And heard our music; are thy simple friends,
> Thy simple fare, and all thy plain delights,
> As dear to thee as once? And have thy joys
> Lost nothing by comparison with ours?
> Rude as thou art (for we return'd thee rude
> And ignorant, except of outward show)
> I cannot think thee yet so dull of heart
> And spiritless, as never to regret
> Sweets tasted here, and left as soon as known.
> Methinks I see thee straying on the beach,
> And asking of the surge that bathes thy foot
> If ever it has wash'd our distant shore.
> I see thee weep, and thine are honest tears,
> A patriot's for his country. Thou art sad
> At thought of her forlorn and abject state,
> From which no power of thine can raise her up.

> Thus fancy paints thee, and though apt to err,
> Perhaps errs little, when she paints thee thus.[214]

Let us not ask of Cowper's fancy why she paints Omai's 'simple fare, and . . . plain delights' in contrast to the debilitating 'plenty' of other Tahitians, and Londoners for that matter, nor ask why Omai is to be pitied and not envied his rural life and diet. If Cowper's heart is muddled, his mind is nevertheless made up: the country is better than the city, civilization is better than savagery, and Omai is a matter for sympathy. Only a few years before, Delille had pictured Aotourou weeping in France for:

> Ces bananiers chargés & de fruits & d'ombrage
> Et le toit paternel, & les bois d'alentour.[215]

Now Cowper pictures Omai in just those circumstances weeping for:

> Our palaces, our ladies, and our pomp
> Of equipage, our gardens, and our sports.

But what matters to these two poets is not a Tahitian weeping for civilization or for Tahiti. What matters to them—what moves them—is a man whose past is so completely lost.

In the summer of 1785, the year of *Omai* and *The Task*, the French response to Cook set out to examine the Pacific, surveying, collecting, classifying, under the command of Jean-François de Lapérouse and the personal orders of Louis XVI, which informed Lapérouse that one of the best measures of the expedition's success would be its completion without the loss of a single life, whether of a sailor or a savage.[216] Lapérouse was a little less enlightened than his monarch and the squalor of the Indians he encountered at Alaska occasioned sarcasm in his journal about 'ces peuples qu'on nous peint si bons, parcequ'ils sont trèz prèz de la Nature'. He contrasted the authority of the 'philosophes' with his own experience: 'ils font leurs livres au coin de leur feu, et je voyage depuis trente ans.'[217]

The Samoan Islands, however, seemed as charming as Bougainville's Tahiti. 'Quelle imagination ne se peindroit le bonheur dans un cite aussi ravissant', wrote Lapérouse on the island of Tutuila. The climate and the natural abundance of food made clothing and work superfluous. 'Nous nous disions "ces insulaires sont les plus heureux habitans de la terre".' Surrounded by their women, the islanders were as blissfully idle as Adam in Paradise, their only care, 'comme le premier homme de ceuillir des fruits qui croissent sur leurs têtes sans aucun travail'. But, although there were no weapons to be seen, the men's bodies were scarred and their features showed signs of a ferocity which seemed ominous to Lapérouse: 'la Nature en avoit sans doute laissé l'empreinte pour avertir que malgré les académies qui courronent les paradoxes des phylosophes l'homme presque sauvage et dans l'anarchie est un être plus méchant que les loups et les tigres des forets.'[218] On 11 December 1787, twelve men were massacred on that Samoan island, including

Lapérouse's old friend and second-in-command, de Langle, and the scientist Lamanon. In his last letter from Botany Bay, before vanishing into the Pacific, Lapérouse expressed his anger: 'Je suis cependant mille fois plus en colère contre les philosophes qui exaltent tant les sauvages, que contre les sauvages eux-mêmes. Ce malheureux Lamanon, qu'ils ont massacré, me disait la veille de sa mort, que ces hommes valaient mieux que nous.'[219]

Exactly what fate Lapérouse encountered is unknown. News of his shipwreck only came, with 'the silver guard of a sword', from the island of Vanikoro in the Santa Cruz group, in 1826.[220] After his ships failed to return, as they should have done, at about the time of the fall of the Bastille, the Revolutionary authorities appointed an editor, Milet-Mureau, to undertake the publication of Lapérouse's journals, the last of which had been returned from Botany Bay by the British, and Milet-Mureau began questioning the various committees of the new Republic. Could the King's titles be used? Would it be permissible to illustrate Lapérouse's ships without the revolutionary tricolour?[221] When Milet-Mureau finally produced the *Voyage de La Pérouse autour du monde* in 1797, it was without Lapérouse's uncomplimentary reference at Tutuila to the author of the *Discours sur l'inégalité*, which Milet-Mureau had nervously removed.[222] The utopian charm of the South Seas survived the massacre of Lapérouse's crew, however, as can be seen from another last letter, from the revolutionary Dantonist, Camille Desmoulins, to his wife, on the morning he was taken to the guillotine: 'O ma chère Lucile! j'étois né pour faire des vers, pour défendre les malheureux, pour te rendre heureuse, pour composer, avec ta mère et ton père, et quelques personnes selon notre coeur, un Otaïti. J'avois rêvé une république que tout le monde eût adorée.'[223]

6

Such a Revolution

It may be asked what could be the cause for such a Revolution. In Answer to
which I have only to give a description of Otaheite, which has every allurement
both to luxury and ease, and is the Paradise of the World.

(Bligh, letter to Banks)[1]

Early in 1787 Joseph Banks convinced the British Government of the case for
transplanting the breadfruit from Tahiti to the West Indies. Eighteen years previously, at Tahiti, he had remarked in his journal that the breadfruit fed the Tahitians with 'no more trouble than that of climbing a tree' and that therefore 'these
happy people may almost be said to be exempt from the curse of our forefather;
scarcely can it be said that they earn their bread with the sweat of their brow'.[2]
Now this almost paradisal plant could usefully feed the slaves in the West Indies,
who would not as a consequence be exempted from the curse of work, but would
produce cheaper sugar for the planters and merchants in the West Indies, with
whom Banks had been corresponding, and on whose behalf he had been lobbying,
for years. There would inevitably be more trouble initially than climbing a tree,
but Banks persuaded the Government of the ultimate benefits of an expedition and
in May the Government instructed the Admiralty accordingly, although it was
Banks himself who chose the ship, supervised her refitting to accommodate the
breadfruit plants, and recommended an officer with experience on Cook's last
voyage to command.

The *Bounty* sailed on 27 December 1787, under the command of Lieutenant
William Bligh, and anchored in Matavai Bay, Tahiti, on 26 October 1788. Bligh
had found the carpenter 'insolent' and the Master 'troublesome' on the voyage out,
and he had also been frustrated by bad weather at the Horn, which had forced the
Bounty to turn back and take the passage to the Pacific via the Cape of Good
Hope.[3] The consequent delay in reaching Tahiti would necessitate a long stay at
the island to await the westerly winds required for the return voyage, as instructed,
through Torres Strait.[4]

On arrival at Matavai Bay Bligh asked immediately for news of Omai, and heard
that Omai was no more. After arranging for the collection of the breadfruit plants,
he usefully occupied himself by filling his log with anthropological reports of his
observations and conversations with Cook's Otoo (Tu), now called Tynah (Taina),
who dined frequently aboard the *Bounty* with his consort Iddeah (Itia), who 'kept

a Gallant' who also 'fed Tynah at dinner'.⁵ His guests enquired after Bligh's own customs and religious beliefs, at which 'they laughed exceedingly. You have a God then who never had a Father or Mother and has a Child without a Wife . . .'.⁶ Some details were obtained about Omai: that he had been victorious in inter-island feuding but had not thereby raised his status, and that he and the elder New Zealand boy 'died Natural deaths about 30 Months after Captn. Cook left them'.⁷ Bligh learned from Itia about the Tahitian transvestites, the *mahu*, and about 'many other as uncommon ways' the Tahitians had 'of gratifying their beastly inclinations'.⁸ He noticed that the *Bounty*'s female figurehead was much admired, and entertained the Tahitians with a trick. A dummy was dressed as a woman and then brought up on deck, to be greeted by the Tahitians with 'a general shout of "Huheine no Pretanee Myty" '. 'Tynah and other Cheifs were mad after' the excellent British lady, 'even when they knew it was not real', and Bligh 'was enjoined to bring some English Women out when I came again'.⁹ As a respectful 'compliment', he was treated to a special performance of an entertainment, 'a Grand Heivah' featuring three men who 'suddenly took off what cloathing they had' and got down to 'the whole business', which consisted 'of distorting the Penis and Testicles, making at the same time wanton and lascivious motions'. The first man effected an erection by tightly binding his penis, the second squeezed his testicles into the top of his penis, and the third surpassed the others, in Bligh's opinion: 'The Third Person was more horrible than the other two, for with both hand seizing the extremity of the Scrotum he pulled it out with such force, that the penis went in totally out of sight and the Scrotum became Shockingly distended.'¹⁰

On 4 April the *Bounty* sailed from 'the Paradise of the World', as Bligh called Tahiti in his log, and steered for the island of Huahine, where Bligh hoped for 'farther knowledge concerning Omai'.¹¹ A canoe came out with a man aboard who confirmed the 'natural death' of Omai and the two New Zealand boys and supplied some more particular information about Omai's monkey, which had 'created great mirth' but had 'fallen from a Cocoa Nutt Tree and was killed'.¹² The *Bounty* continued on her journey towards Torres Strait, discovering Aitutaki in the Cook Group and making a stop at Nomuka in the Tongan Group for wood and water, sailing again on 26 April. Relations between Bligh and Fletcher Christian, whom Bligh had appointed Acting Lieutenant on the voyage out, were becoming tense and fractious. On 21 April 'Mr Bligh and Mr Christain had some words', according to the Master, John Fryer, and at Nomuka Bligh called Christian 'a Cowardly rascal', according to James Morrison, the boatswain's mate.¹³ On the 27th an incident took place which is not mentioned in Bligh's log but is reported by both Fryer and Morrison. When Bligh came on deck in the morning he noticed that a pile of coconuts acquired at Nomuka seemed suspiciously smaller. He called for the Master 'and said Mr Fryer dont you think those Cocoanuts are shrunk since last Night?'¹⁴ The gentlemen and men were all assembled and interrogated in turn about the missing coconuts, Christian replying that he hoped Bligh did not 'think me so mean as to be Guilty of Stealing'. 'Yes you dam'd Hound I do', said Bligh.

'God dam you, you Scoundrels, you are all thieves alike.'[15] Bligh then harangued the crew and threatened to reduce the allowance of yams.

That afternoon Christian was seen by the carpenter coming from Bligh with tears 'running fast from his eyes in big drops' and that evening, as they sailed through a calm sea thirty miles to the south of the Tongan island of Tofua, Fletcher Christian prepared to abandon the *Bounty*, supplying himself with roast pig and with nails and beads for barter, lashing staves and a plank into a crude raft and 'tearing some letters to peices in the Fore chains', saying 'he would not wish every Body to see his letters'.[16] He was unable to put his plan into effect that night, as there were too many on deck watching the erupting volcano on Tofua, so he slept at about 3.30 a.m. and was roused for his watch at 4 a.m. by his friend Stewart, who 'begd him not to attempt swimming away, saying "the People are ripe for any thing" '.[17] On this, according to Christian's own account as reported by Morrison, Christian 'resolved to seize the ship'.[18] Wearing 'a deep sea lead concealed' beneath his jacket, in readiness to jump and drown 'should his plan fail', he recruited men to mutiny.[19]

Then, according to the 'Remarks' in Bligh's log for 28 April:

Just before Sun rise Mr Christian, Mate, Chas Churchill, Ships Corporal, John Mills, Gunners Mate, and Thomas Burkett, Seaman, came into my Cabbin while I was a Sleep and seizing me tyed my hands with a Cord behind my back and threatned me with instant death if I spoke or made the least noise.[20]

Bligh 'was forced on Deck in my Shirt' and kept under guard, 'Christian holding me by the Bandage that secured my hands with one hand, and a Bayonet in the other'.[21] The *Bounty*'s launch was hoisted out and Bligh's clerk, Samuel, stocked it with bread, rum, and wine, a quadrant, a compass, and Bligh's log, while others supplied a large cask of water, ropes, sails, and equipment. The unpopular midshipmen Hayward and Hallet were ordered aboard the launch by Christian, and the armourer and two assistant carpenters, who would be useful, were ordered to remain aboard the *Bounty*, but most of the men went or stayed by their own choice, though some remained aboard the *Bounty* not because they chose either Christian's mutiny or the *Bounty*'s safety as such, but because there was no more room in the 23 foot launch, crowded to capacity. Bligh himself remained on deck under guard and pleaded with Christian:

'Consider, Mr Christian, I have a wife and four children in England, and you have danced my children upon your knee.' Christian replied, 'You should have thought of them sooner yourself, Captain Bligh; it is too late to consider now. I have been in hell for weeks past with you.'[22]

Bligh was then forced into the launch, which was veered to the stern of the *Bounty*, from where a quantity of pork and four cutlasses were handed over with some abuse for Bligh: 'shoot the Bugger . . . now let the Bugger see if he can live on three Quarters of a pound of Yams.'[23]

Those aboard the launch cast off and rowed for the island of Tofua, about thirty miles away, while cries of 'Huzza for Otaheite' came from the *Bounty* and Bligh considered, according to his log, 'what could be the reason for such a revolt'.[24] This reason was, in a word, Tahiti:

It is certainly true that no effect could take place without a Cause, but here it is equally certain that no cause could justify such an effect. It however may very naturally be asked what could be the reason for such a revolt, in answer to which I can only conjecture that they have Idealy assured themselves of a more happy life among the Otaheitans than they could possibly have in England, which joined to some Female connections has most likely been the leading cause of the Whole business . . . [W]hat a temptation it is to such Wretches when they find it in their power, however illegally it can be got at, to fix themselves in the midst of plenty in the finest Island in the World where they need not labour, and where the alurements of disipation are more than equal to any thing that can be conceived.

At Tofua Bligh and his eighteen men landed at a stony cove where they were eventually discovered by the islanders, who 'began to encrease in their Number'.[25] 'The Beach was now lined with the Natives', Bligh wrote in his log on 3 May, 'and we heard nothing but the knocking of Stones together.'[26] The log, which he had been 'writing up' in a cave at the head of the cove, 'was nearly taken away'.[27] He planned to escape that evening and, while the islanders 'kept knocking their Stones together', he informed the chiefs that he was going to spend the night in the launch.[28] With this explanation, he took one of them, Nageete, 'by the hand and we walked down the Beach, every one in a silent kind of horror'.[29] Nageete slipped away before Bligh, with Purcell the carpenter at his side, reached the boat, 'when the stones began to fly', according to Fryer's account, and 'Mr Purcel lifted' Bligh, and Fryer 'hauld him into the Boat'.[30] A sailor who had run ashore to cast off was knocked down and beaten on the head with stones while the men aboard the launch rowed for the open sea, pursued by canoes and pelted with stones. Convinced of the dangers of Pacific landings without firearms, Bligh dropped a plan to make for the island of Tongataboo, heading instead for the distant island of Timor in the Dutch East Indies, sustaining his men with rations of pork, bread, coconut milk or water, and occasional teaspoons of rum.

At one in the morning of 28 May, the man at the helm heard the sound of breakers on the Great Barrier Reef, and a passage was found, when day came, into the calm waters off the coast of (Queensland) New Holland, where the launch landed on a small island about a quarter of a mile from the mainland. 'On first landing', wrote Fryer, 'we were like so many drunken men', and Bligh reported the 'General complaints' of dizziness, weakness, 'and violent Tenesmus, most of us having had no evacuation since we left the Ship'.[31] Fryer and some others went to collect oysters, from which a soup was made, but Bligh complained in his log that Fryer disagreed with him about how much water should be added to the oyster soup 'and showed a turbulent disposition'.[32] Fryer complained later that Bligh 'did nothing but make a great Noise and write his remarks' in his log.[33]

They continued their journey north along the Australian coast the next day and stopped at another island on 31 May, where Purcell 'began to be insolent to a high degree, and at last told me with a mutinous aspect he was as good a Man as I was'.[34] Fryer's account gives more details than Bligh's:

I heard a great noise in the boat, Captain Bligh calling some body a damn scoundrel &c what have I brought you here when if I had not been with you, you would have all aperished, yes Sir the carpenter said, if it had not been for you we should not have been here—what's that you say Sir—I say Sir if it had not been for you we should not have been here—you damn'd scoundrel what do you mean—I am not a scoundrel Sir the carpenter said. I am as good a man as you in that respect—when Captain Bligh snatch up a cutlass and went forward in the Boat and told the carpenter to take another the carpenter said no Sir you are my officer.[35]

Fryer intervened at this point, Purcell stopped his insinuations, and tempers cooled. They sailed on up the coast, stopping off at islands to avoid unarmed encounters with the Aborigines who shouted and waved ambiguously from the mainland, and reached the northern tip of the Australian coast on 3 June. They entered the open sea that evening and, after another ordeal of hunger and exposure, 'at 3 in the Morning' on 12 June, 'with an excess of Joy we discovered Timor'.[36]

It took two more days to reach the town of Coupang, where the Dutch governor was ill and dying but kindly provided a house for Bligh and his 'Spectres of Men', who now suffered 'the excruciating torture from not being able to void the faecis'.[37] Bligh quarrelled again with Purcell and Fryer, who carefully made his own note of the incident, concluding: 'This is the sort of treatment the Officers in general have received from Mr Bligh in the course of the Voyage which in my opinion has been the cause of all our misfortunes.'[38] The gardener, Nelson, who had been in charge of the breadfruit, died of a fever, and Bligh purchased, on the Admiralty's credit, a small schooner in which to sail to Batavia, capital of the Dutch East Indies, where passages could be obtained, by way of Capetown, to Europe. They sailed for Batavia on 20 August, in the schooner named *Resource*, with the *Bounty*'s launch on tow, and reached Sourabaya on 12 September. There another mutiny nearly took place, recorded in a log Bligh kept for the *Resource* but did not submit to the Admiralty, and also in another note taken by Fryer. The trouble started with a row between Bligh and Fryer, whom Bligh accused of 'insolence'.[39] 'It is no insolence', answered Fryer.[40] 'You not only use me Ill but every Man in the Vessel and every Man will say the same.'[41] 'A muttering now began' among the men: 'Yes by God we are used damned Ill, nor have we any right to be used so.'[42] Bligh was obliged to restore his authority by brandishing a bayonet and calling in the Dutch authorities at Sourabaya. Fryer and Purcell were placed under arrest, Purcell until he reached England, and Fryer until he apologized and provided Bligh with a letter declaring that 'you never have behaved with the least partical of Tyrranny or oppression'.[43]

They reached Batavia on 1 October, where Bligh sold the schooner and the

Bounty's launch, and wrote to inform the Admiralty and Banks of what had happened and why: 'In Answer to which I have only to give a description of Otaheite, which has every allurement both to luxury and ease, and is the Paradise of the World.'[44] Bligh was ill at Batavia and took the first available berths on a ship for the Cape, on 16 October, for himself, his clerk, Samuel, and his cook. Of the others left to follow, three died at insalubrious Batavia, and another two on the voyage home. Bligh himself reached Portsmouth, after sailing from the Cape, on 14 March 1790, and 'took post Chaise for [London] Town where I arrived that Night'.[45]

Rumours of Bligh's news spread and reports were soon in the papers. The *General Evening Post* gave an account of the 'Mutiny on board the Bounty' on 16 March, praising Bligh's 'seamanship' in the launch, sympathizing with his 'distresses' (which 'entitle him to every reward') and giving, as the 'most probable' explanation for the mutiny, that the young mutineers, led by Fletcher Christian, 'were so greatly fascinated by the Circean blandishments of the Otaheitean women, they took this desperate method of returning to scenes of voluptuousness unknown, perhaps, in any other country.'[46] In April Fanny Burney visited her brother James, who had served with Bligh on Cook's last voyage, and she and James 'read a good deal of Captain Bligh's interesting narrative', which James may have been helping Bligh prepare for publication.[47] A few weeks later, on 11 May, she reports James and a friend discussing a manuscript of the narrative, the friend enthusing about 'this Captain Bligh', who had performed such feats and defied such dangers, 'with such cool, manly skill'.[48] By this time a play was in performance at the Royalty Theatre, London, entitled *The Pirates: or, The Calamities of Capt. Bligh*, billed as 'a fact, told in action', and featuring 'an Otaheitean dance', the 'Attachment of the Otaheitean Women to, and their Distress at parting from, the British Sailors' and 'An Exact Representation of the Seisure of Capt. Bligh, in the Cabin of the Bounty, by the Pirates', all 'Rehearsed under the immediate Instruction of a Person who was on-board the Bounty'.[49]

Bligh's own account, *A Narrative of the Mutiny, on board His Majesty's Ship 'Bounty'; and the subsequent voyage of part of the crew in the ship's boat, from Tofoa . . . to Timor*, was published in June. Based on his log, it gave an account of the voyage only from 4 April 1789, when the *Bounty* sailed from Tahiti, and repeated Bligh's case that the mutiny was caused by Tahiti:

It will very naturally be asked, what could be the reason for such a revolt? in answer to which, I can only conjecture that the mutineers had assured themselves of a more happy life among the Otaheiteans, than they could possibly have in England; which, joined to some female connections, have most probably been the principal cause of the whole transaction.[50]

There was no reference in the *Narrative* to the coconut incident, which had not been mentioned in Bligh's log, and there was no reference to Christian's feelings about Bligh, with the exception of a passage in the *Narrative* which had not appeared in the log:

Notwithstanding the roughness with which I was treated, the remembrance of past kindnesses produced some signs of remorse in Christian. When they were forcing me out of the ship, I asked him, if this treatment was a proper return for the many instances he had received of my friendship? he appeared disturbed at my question, and answered, with much emotion, 'That,—captain Bligh,—that is the thing;—I am in hell—I am in hell.'[51]

To set beside the paradise of Tahiti, therefore, there was the hell—not of Bligh's behaviour—but of Christian's conscience. The quarrels with Fryer and Purcell on the islands off the Queensland coast, recorded in the log, were not repeated in the *Narrative*, except for a brief account of Purcell's protest that 'he was as good a man as myself', and nothing at all was said about the trouble at Sourabaya, so the reader was not to see how far Bligh's difficulties with his men, or theirs with him, extended beyond the possible range of even Tahitian charms.[52]

Bligh's Tahitian explanation of the mutiny was unchallenged by any other public account, and was a popular story, inspiring in 1790 the first of three editions of *An Account of the Mutinous Seizure of the Bounty: with the succeeding Hardships of the Crew: to which are added Secret Anecdotes of the Otaheitean Females*, an anonymous work which combined its piracy of Bligh's account of the mutiny with an endorsement of his attractive explanation. Indeed, as 'the Circean blandishments' of the Tahitian females were the cause of the mutiny, 'we think it necessary (in order to prove that there is no absurdity in the supposition) to offer our readers some authentic anecdotes respecting them'.[53] The ensuing 'Secret Anecdotes of the Otaheitean Females', thinly dressed up with some sentiments about Rousseau and 'a state of pure nature', consisted of select but hardly secret excerpts from Hawkesworth's *Voyages*: Banks's discovery of Oberea *in flagrante*, the story of Banks and the unveiling lady, and, for conclusion, the Point Venus scene, complete with Hawkesworth's philosophical question.[54] The work had one piece of real news to add to its borrowings from Bligh and Hawkesworth: the information, dated 20 June 1790, received from a man whose ship had called at Tahiti since the mutiny, 'that Christian and his crew had visited that island' but had 'left it' before the informant's ship reached it.[55]

The Admiralty, meanwhile, had not forgotten the *Bounty*, and in August 1790 Captain Edward Edwards was appointed to command the *Pandora* in search of the mutineers. The mandatory court martial of Bligh, as a captain who had lost a naval ship, acquitted him of any responsibility, and was followed, on the same day, 22 October 1790, by the trial of Purcell on charges of misconduct brought by Bligh, which were found 'in part proved', so that Purcell was reprimanded, while Bligh was promoted, to Commander and then Post-Captain.[56] There were no charges against Fryer, but he was sufficiently provoked by Bligh's *Narrative* to write his own manuscript account of the voyage, 'the best my memory will allow me'.[57] This gave Fryer's side of the quarrels with Bligh before and after the mutiny, reported that Christian's 'hell' was not in his conscience but in the person of his captain, and responded directly to the explanation of the mutiny given in Bligh's *Narrative*:

It will very reasonabely be ask what could be the cause for such a revolt—in answer to which I can only say that Christain was not particular attach to any Woman at Otaheite nor any of them except Mr Stewart and Jame Morrison Boatswain Mate—who were the only two that had there particular Girls—so that from what they said I suppose they did not like their Captain.[58]

After the mutiny on the *Bounty* the men who did not like their captain made a collective decision to sail for Tahiti, according to the journal of James Morrison, boatswain's mate, written up later, in 1792.[59] It was probably Christian's own decision, however, to sail for Tahiti via the island of Tubuai in the Austral Group, 300 miles to the south of Tahiti. Tubuai had been discovered by Cook on his third voyage, although he did not land there as it 'appeared to be of little consequence', as Christian would probably have read with interest in the *Bounty*'s copy of Cook's *A Voyage to the Pacific Ocean*.[60] On 1 May most of the breadfruit plants were 'thrown overboard' and 'Uniform Jackets' were made from sails for the whole crew—to impress the islanders, Christian said, though Morrison noticed that they would have the useful function of impressing the crew, too, by reminding them of naval discipline.[61] On 25 May the *Bounty* anchored at Tubuai, but the people in canoes, although speaking a Polynesian dialect similar to Tahitian, could not be induced to board the ship. On the following day, however, eighteen 'young and handsom' girls came aboard with 'fine long hair which reachd their Waists in waving ringlets' and with five male accomplices who set about pilfering, while fifty canoes full of men awaited an opportunity to attack.[62] Fighting followed the pilfering, and the Tubuaians learnt the effects of firearms. Twelve of them were killed in the bay which the *Bounty*'s men named Bloody Bay.

Christian had decided to settle on Tubuai, nevertheless, knowing very well that there could be no safety from the Admiralty at Tahiti, and at the end of May the *Bounty* sailed for Tahiti with the aim of acquiring women and livestock.[63] On 6 June the *Bounty* anchored at Matavai, where Christian had forbidden any mention of Tubuai. Taina was told that Cook (who Bligh had pretended was still living) had encountered Bligh and, intending to form a settlement on 'an Island call'd Whytootackee' (Aitutaki), had deposited Bligh and the breadfruit plants there and sent Christian to Tahiti to obtain 'a good stock of Hogs & fowls' for the new colony.[64] After about ten days the *Bounty* sailed for Tubuai with a large number of pigs, goats, and chickens, and a smaller number of Tahitians, some of them stowaways, '9 Men 8 Boys 10 Weomen & one female Child', by Morrison's count.[65] One of the Tahitian women was Teehuteatuaonoa, known as Jenny, and another, described in Jenny's recollections of Tubuai as 'Christian's wife', was probably Mauatea, called Isabella by Christian, and nicknamed Mainmast.[66]

Anchoring in Bloody Bay on 26 June, the prospective colonizers now found the Tubuaians friendly and Christian formed an alliance with Tamatoa, chief of the western district incorporating Bloody Bay. When he found a more suitable location for settlement in the north-eastern district of another chief, Taroatohoa, he alienated

Tamatoa, however, who combined with the chief of the third, south-eastern district, Tinarou, to harass and oppose Christian and restrict supplies of food and women to his men, who thus became embroiled in the endemic inter-district feuding that was still in process when a missionary came to Tubuai in 1822, to find 'the whole of the small population of the island engaged in war'.[67] The *Bounty*'s crew was not peacefully united either. Early in July, according to the journal kept by the young midshipman, Peter Heywood, 'Some of the people began to be mutinous'.[68] Able Seamen Sumner and Quintal spent the night ashore without permission, informing Christian that 'we are now our own Masters', whereupon Christian brandished Bligh's pistol, which he kept in his pocket, and told them: 'I'll let you know who is Master.'[69] He seems to have been ruling democratically, however, for Heywood says that the rebels 'were put in Irons by a Majority of Votes'.[70] They expressed themselves repentant and on the following day, according to an account kept by another of the young gentlemen, George Stewart, 'Articles were drawn up by Christian & Churchill specifying a mutual forgiveness of all past grievances', which everyone signed except the perpetually obstreperous Able Seaman Thompson.[71]

To relieve the sailors' needs, Christian made arrangements for overnight shore leave and then inaugurated the construction of a fort, patriotically named 'Fort George', by hoisting the Union Jack.[72] 'Nor was Mr. Christian an Idle Spectator', writes Morrison, 'for He always took a part in the Most laborious part of the Work'.[73] In August the sailors' needs for food and women began to interfere with progress, however, and feuding broke out between the Tubuaians and British. A Tubuaian was shot dead in a dispute about coconuts and then, according to Morrison, some of the *Bounty*'s men 'were decoyd by the Weomen into Tinnarows district where they were Strip'd'.[74] Christian responded by seizing the 'Carved Images' of Tinarou's 'Houshold Gods' as hostages—to bargain for peace, in Morrison's account, for 'Wives', in Heywood's.[75] Those of the *Bounty*'s men who were womanless 'began to Murmur', and there were proposals 'to make slaves' of the Tahitians and 'to procure Women by force, but Christian would not agree to either Scheme'.[76] An argument went on for three days, during which the locked supply of grog was broken into, until finally Christian called a proper conference and a vote was taken. Sixteen of the twenty-five voted for a return to Tahiti, 'where they might get Weomen without force', but it was agreed that the other nine, who included Christian, should have possession of the *Bounty* and 'take her to whatever place they shd. think fit'.[77]

Preparations for departure were made but, before the *Bounty* left Tubuai, the trouble with Tinarou culminated in a battle between the British and Tahitian men, armed with guns, and several hundred of Tinarou's people, of whom over fifty were killed.[78] In the aftermath, a Tubuaian named Taroamiva (a younger brother of Christian's ally, the chief Taroatohoa) and two other Tubuaian men asked and received permission to accompany the *Bounty*, which sailed on 15 September and anchored at Matavai in the afternoon of the 20th.[79]

The sixteen sailors who had voted for Tahiti, who included three Bligh acknowledged had been detained on the *Bounty* against their wishes (two carpenter's mates and the armourer) and four others with good claims to be innocent of the mutiny (the young gentlemen, Stewart and Heywood, the boatswain's mate, Morrison, and the nearly blind fiddler, Byrne), went ashore with their belongings and the captured Tubuaian 'Houshold Gods' on the following day.[80] Night had fallen before the unloading was completed and, according to Morrison,

Mr. Christian told us that He intended to stay a day or two, and hoped that we would assist him to fill some water, as he intended to Cruize for some Uninhabited Island where he would . . . set fire to the Ship, and where he hoped to live the remainder of His days without seeing the face of a European but those who were already with him.[81]

According to Heywood, however, Christian revealed to Stewart and Heywood that he intended to sail immediately and, indeed, Morrison and the other members of the crew 'were all much surprized' that night when 'we found the Ship under way, standing out of the Bay'.[82]

The *Bounty* men who landed at Matavai were welcomed and accommodated according to their Tahitian as well as their British ranks and relationships. Stewart had a Tahitian 'Wife' called Peggy (his particular girl from the *Bounty*'s original visit) and he and Heywood remained a little aloof from the common sailors, leading a gentrified life in the Matavai household of Peggy's father, 'an old landed proprietor', as Heywood later explained to his mother.[83] Another group formed around Morrison, who had a Tahitian alliance, a *taio* friendship, with a chief at Matavai, and who provides a detailed record of events on Tahiti which says nothing about his own female connection or connections, although he was one of those Fryer named as having a particular girl. Morrison's team began building a schooner and reverting to British customs, hoisting 'the Collours' and reading 'Divine Service' on Sundays, and flogging Tahitians who interfered with boat-building by stealing.[84]

In February 1790 Thompson 'ill used a young Girl, for which her brother in revenge knock'd Him down'.[85] Enraged by this humiliation, Thompson fired at some passing Tahitians whose curiosity about his exotic British behaviour was not reduced by his shouting at them in English to go away. His shot killed a man and the child in the man's arms and wounded another man and woman. Churchill, the *Bounty*'s master-at-arms, offered to organize the British defence against the expected Tahitian reprisals, but the other sailors refused to associate themselves with Thompson's murders, and Churchill and Thompson left the group at Matavai for the Taiarapu Peninsula on the other side of the island. There, in March, Churchill inherited the title of chief on the death of his *taio* and fired at some people who disturbed the ducks he was hunting, wounding a man and a boy who died when his wound became infected. In April Churchill quarrelled with Thompson, who shot him dead and was then himself attacked by Churchill's men, who revenged the murder of their chief by holding Thompson down and crushing his head with a large stone.

In July 1790 the schooner, about 34 feet by 9 feet, was blessed by a Tahitian priest, launched and named the *Resolution*. Although many difficulties in its construction had been resolved by Crusoe-like ingenuity and labour, its sails remained a problem, Tahitian mats being usable for the purpose but insufficiently strong. In August or September the British men's Tahitian hosts called upon their guests' fire-power to further the political ambitions of the young chief, Taina's son, to whom Taina had transferred his status and his name, Tu, and to whom the *Bounty* men had ceremoniously presented the imported Tubuaian 'Houshold Gods'. Morrison's party and also Heywood and Stewart assisted, lending themselves and their guns to help Tu's men quash some western districts of Tahiti, a cause the British understood as the suppression of a 'Rebellion' against Tahiti's rightful ruler.[86] In October or November Morrison's team sailed the *Resolution* to the nearby island of Moorea but concluded that escaping in her to Batavia, which had been Morrison's intention, was too dangerous—because of doubts about the durability of the sails of matting, according to Morrison, because of doubts about Morrison's 'abilities as a Navigator', Heywood was told.[87]

Taina's programme for subjugating the whole of Tahiti under the rule of his son proceeded in February of the following year, 1791, with his son's ceremonial investiture, accompanied by human sacrifices and the symbolic offering of the victims' eyes to the young chief, and in March plans for conquering another district, the Taiarapu Peninsula, involved the *Resolution* in a trip round the coast to the district of Papara, from where the attack was to be launched. Having left four men (Heywood, Stewart, Coleman, and Skinner) behind at Matavai, the other ten British men were ashore at Papara for breakfast with the district chief, 'but were scarcely sat down', says Morrison, when a messenger 'arrived in haste, telling us that a ship had anchord at Maatvye since we had left it, that those we had left there were gone on board', and that armed boats were coming in pursuit of the *Bounty* men who remained on the island.[88]

The *Pandora* had been seen approaching Matavai at daybreak on the morning of 23 March and a Tahitian came running with the news to Heywood, who sent a messenger to inform Coleman, the *Bounty*'s armourer, who set off for the *Pandora* in a canoe immediately and went aboard before the ship had even anchored.[89] Heywood and Stewart, 'tanned', 'tattooed', and 'dressed in the country manner', then paddled out by canoe, 'made ourselves known' and 'were ordered to be put in irons, and looked upon—oh, infernal words!—as *piratical villains*'.[90] Coleman, one of those who Bligh had declared in his log and published *Narrative* had been detained aboard the *Bounty* 'contrary to their inclination', was also put in irons by Captain Edwards, who treated all the *Bounty*'s men as guilty until a court martial should decide their cases, and Skinner who came aboard that afternoon was also taken prisoner.[91] Two of the *Pandora*'s boats were sent that morning to apprehend the other 'Pirates', as Edwards called them in his log.[92]

Four of these, Byrne, Morrison, Ellison, and Norman, made their way across the island to give themselves up, and were placed with 'both legs in Irons' beside

Heywood, Stewart, Coleman, and Skinner, from whom they learned that their guards had orders 'not to suffer any of the Natives to speak to us' and to shoot any one of them 'that spoke to another in the Taheite Language'.[93] Edwards meanwhile perused the 'journals kept on board the *Bounty*, which were found in the chests of the pirates at Otaheite'—the journals of Heywood and Stewart, from which 'Extracts' were copied—but these, although outlining events at Tubuai and Tahiti, gave no clues to the whereabouts of Christian and the *Bounty*.[94] Supplied with 'plenty of Cocoa Nuts' by their Tahitian friends, and with 'Handcuffs' added to their leg-irons, the prisoners were joined by their companions, who were rounded up, and then the fourteen *Bounty* men, including those declared innocent by Bligh, were confined in a prison constructed by the *Pandora*'s carpenters on deck, measuring 11 feet by 18 feet, which 'we Stiled Pandoras Box'.[95] While the prisoners sweated in Pandora's Box, with maggots and lice for 'troublesome Neighbours and the two necessary tubbs which were Constantly kept in the place', the *Pandora*'s crew was treated to an entertainment by 'two men, who vied with each other in filthy lascivious attitudes', and 'two ladies, pretty fancifully dressed', who engaged in 'half an hours hard exercise' before closing the proceedings by 'exposing that which is better felt than seen', in the opinion of George Hamilton, the *Pandora*'s doctor.[96] Hamilton, a reader of 'Captain Cook's Voyages', reflected that Tahiti 'may well be called the Cytheria of the southern hemisphere'.[97] 'What poetic fiction has painted of Eden, or Arcadia, is here realized', he wrote, 'where the earth without tillage produces both food and cloathing', not to mention 'fair ones ever willing to fill your arms with love'.[98] He also noticed aboard the *Pandora* 'too moving a scene for any feeling heart', which is better described by Morrison, suddenly revealing an aspect of Anglo-Tahitian relations he has hardly mentioned hitherto:

During the time we staid, the Weomen with whom we had cohabited on the Island Came frequently under the Stern (bringing their Children of which there were 6 born, Four Girls & two Boys, & several of the Weomen big with Child) Cutting their Heads till the Blood discolloured the water about them.[99]

These 'Mourning rites' continued till Edwards sailed on 8 May 1791, accompanied by the *Resolution* (which he renamed *Matavy* and 'supplied with canvas sails' and a crew from the *Pandora*), to perform his appointed duty of searching for Christian 'in an immense ocean strewed with an almost innumerable number of known and unknown islands', as he described it to the Admiralty.[100] He investigated 'Why-to-tackee' (Aitutaki), the island Christian had mentioned as a blind to the Tahitians, lost one of his boats and five men in a storm off Palmerston Island, an atoll in the Cook Group, and then on 22 June, near Tutuila in the Samoan Islands, became separated from the *Matavy*, with its crew of nine. On 13 August, heading for Torres Strait and home, *Pandora* passed within a mile of the reef of an island where 'we saw smoke very plain, from which it may be presumed that the island is inhabited'.[101] This was Vanikoro, where Lapérouse had been shipwrecked three years before and where, according to some of the reports received in 1826 by

1. The Hereford Mappa Mundi (c.1300), with Jerusalem at the centre and Paradise an island at the eastern end of the world (at the top of the map).

2. 'A Sailor giving a Patagonian Woman some Biscuit for her Child', the illustrator's generous rendering of the Patagonians averaging 'about eight feet', in *A Voyage Round the World in His Majesty's Ship the Dolphin* (1767).

3. 'Omai's Public Entry on his first landing at Otaheite', the illustrator's rendering of Rickman's flattering and fanciful description of Omai in his suit of armour riding with Cook, in [J. Rickman], *Journal of Captain Cook's Last Voyage* (1781).

4. Cook (holding his hat) and Omai (at extreme right) in 'A Human Sacrifice, in a Morai, in Otaheite', in Cook and King, *A Voyage to the Pacific Ocean* (1784).

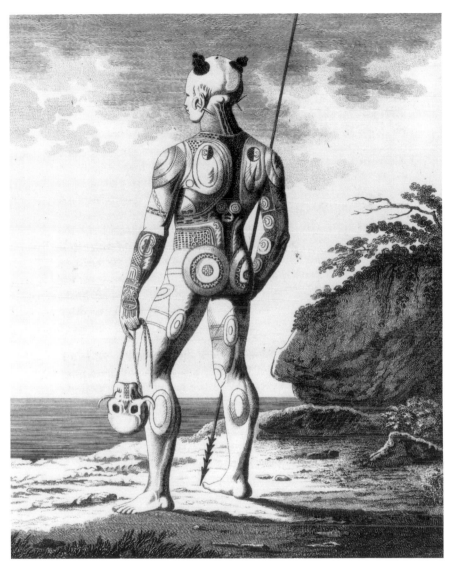

5. 'A Young Nukuhiwan not completely Tattooed', showing the head 'shaved, with the exception of a small spot above each ear, where the long hair is tied up in such a manner as nearly to resemble horns', in G. H. von Langsdorff, *Voyages and Travels* (1813).

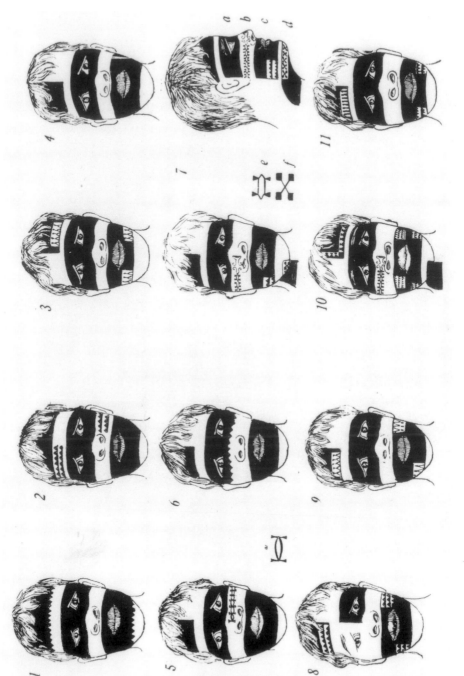

6. 'Face Patterns for Men', in W. C. Handy, *Tattooing in the Marquesas* (1922).

7. 'Portrait of Jean Baptiste Cabri', in G. H. von Langsdorff, *Voyages and Travels* (1813).

8. A Tahitian girl, probably Taatamata, a snapshot by Rupert Brooke.

Peter Dillon, who solved the mystery of the lost expedition, some survivors may still have been living.[102]

In the early evening of 28 August the *Pandora* struck the Great Barrier Reef and started taking water fast. The men were ordered to the pumps but the hold was still filling and the prisoners 'broke our Irons', writes Morrison, 'that we might be ready to assist ourselves'.[103] The three whom Bligh had declared innocent were released from the Box to help man the pumps, but the others were 'handcuffd and leg Irond again', by Edwards's orders, and placed under armed guard.[104] Twelve hours after she had struck, the *Pandora* was awash 'and we began to leap overboard and take to the boats', according to Edwards's report, which makes no mention of his prisoners.[105] He and the other officers were at this point standing on top of Pandora's Box, about to board the boats, and from within the Box, says Heywood, 'we again implored his mercy'.[106] At Edwards's orders the *Pandora*'s armourer's mate now released some of the prisoners from their irons and handcuffs and let three of them out of the Box, one still with his handcuffs on, whereupon the opening of the Box was bolted shut again, leaving eight men still trapped 'when the Ship took a Sally and a general cry of "there she Goes" was heard'.[107] 'She now took a very heavy heel', according to Hamilton's account, and one of the officers told Edwards 'that she was then going; and, bidding him farewell, jumped' and Edwards 'jumped after him' and Morrison and the others in the Box now 'saw through the Stern Ports Captain Edwards astern swiming to the Pinnace'.[108] Water was beginning 'to flow in upon us' when one of the *Pandora*'s crew, scrambling over the Box, heard the desperate cries from within and unbolted the opening.[109] All but one of the prisoners escaped from the Box as the ship went down, but two were struck by a falling gangway and went to the bottom. The survivors were able to swim to the *Pandora*'s boats and were landed 'on a small sandy Key on the Reef' where 'we found that Four of our fellow prisoners were drown'd, two of which, Skinner and Heildbrandt, with their Handcuffs on, and Stuart and Sumner were struck by the Gangway'.[110] They 'also learnt that 31 of the Pandoras Ships Company were lost', says Morrison, 'but all the Officers were Saved'.[111]

The *Pandora*'s boats eventually reached Coupang, Timor, where the men transferred to a Dutch ship, the *Rembang*, which sailed for Batavia, encountering en route at Samarang the lost *Matavy*, which had sailed via the Fiji Islands to Sourabaya, and been detained there on the suspicion that its crew were 'part of the Pirates who had seized on the *Bounty*'.[112] The *Rembang* and the *Matavy* sailed together from Samarang, arriving on 7 November at Batavia, where the prisoners received permission to smoke to protect their health from the noxious air, and wove hats for cash, and Heywood surreptitiously wrote a long letter to his mother defending his conduct and narrating his adventures.[113] From Batavia the *Pandora*'s crew and the *Bounty* prisoners were despatched in various ships to the Cape, where the prisoners were placed aboard HMS *Gorgon* and at last received humane treatment. They reached Spithead on 19 June 1792, and were transferred to HMS *Hector* to await trial.

When the prisoners arrived in England, Bligh was at Tahiti. After promotion to Post-Captain he had been appointed, in April 1791, with Banks's continued support, to command a second voyage to transplant the breadfruit, and had anchored in Matavai Bay a year later, on 9 April 1792, to hear from the Tahitians of Christian's two visits in the *Bounty* and his disappearance into the Pacific, and of the arrests made by Edwards: 'It may readily be believed that I found great satisfaction and pleasure to hear of these Wretches all being taken by Captain Edwards except two who were killed by the Indians [i.e. Thompson and Churchill].'[114] In Bligh's absence his log of occurrences on the *Bounty* prior to the mutiny (promised to follow his *Narrative of the Mutiny* 'as soon as it can be got ready') was being edited by James Burney, with the assistance of Banks, for publication as *A Voyage to the South Sea*.[115] From the correspondence between Burney and Banks in September and October 1791, it emerges that a proposal in Bligh's *Voyage* for ending Arioi infanticide—supposedly a form of population control—by giving Tahitians the opportunity of 'emigrating to New Holland' was Burney's own idea.[116] Burney's other editorial contributions were more modest: the arrangement of Bligh's log into chapters, some rephrasings of his sentences and sentiments, and the removal of such anthropological passages as those describing the various 'beastly acts of gratification' practised by Tahitians and their displays of gymnastics featuring 'the Penis and Testicles'.[117] The account of the mutiny given in *A Voyage to the South Sea* (1792) did not significantly differ from the account in Bligh's *Narrative of the Mutiny* (1970), however, and it was this account which the prisoners at Spithead had returned to face.[118]

The court martial opened on 12 September 1792, aboard HMS *Duke* at Portsmouth, and continued daily. Bligh was in Torres Strait, with a cargo of breadfruit for the West Indies, and his account of the mutiny written to the Admiralty from Coupang on 18 August 1789 was read out as evidence.[119] Fryer, Cole, Peckover, and Purcell (who had accompanied Bligh in the launch) gave evidence from which there seemed no doubt that Coleman, Norman, and McIntosh had been detained aboard the *Bounty* by the mutineers and that Byrne was also innocent. It also emerged that Burkett, who was one of those who arrested Bligh in his cabin, was clearly a mutineer and under arms, and that Millward had also been armed, though this seemed to have been at the orders of the mutineer Churchill. Ellison, only seventeen at the time, had also been seen carrying arms and—according to Cole—Muspratt too. The witnesses seemed favourable to Heywood and Morrison, but then Purcell revealed, under questioning from the court, that he had seen Heywood with his hand on a cutlass, though 'it was not in his Hand', and he had seemed 'confused' and not one of the mutineers.[120]

The court martial was not concerned with establishing the causes of the mutiny, only with determining innocence or guilt, but in the course of narrating the events Fryer quoted Christian saying, 'I have been in Hell for Weeks past—Captain Bligh has brought all this on himself.'[121] Purcell also mentioned that Christian had said to Bligh, 'I have been in Hell for weeks past with you', and Cole remembered him saying 'he had been in Hell for Weeks and weeks past'.[122] Fryer was questioned by the court on this point:

What did you suppose to be Mr. Christian's meaning when he said he had been in Hell for a fortnight?—From the frequent Quarrels that they had had, and the Abuse which he had received from Mr. Bligh.

Had there been any very recent Quarrel?—The Day before Mr. Bligh challenged all the young Gentlemen and People with stealing his Cocoanuts.[123]

The evidence of the two midshipmen who had been consigned to the launch, Hayward and Hallet, was less sympathetic to the prisoners and tended to incriminate Morrison as well as Heywood. Hayward remembered Burkett, Millward, and Muspratt carrying arms and Ellison, 'as a Centinel with a Bayonet in his hand, over Captain Bligh, saying damn him I will be Centinel over him'.[124] He also testified that Ellison and Millward were among those at the stern of the *Bounty* insulting Bligh in the launch, and that Millward 'jeered us saying, "Go and see if you can live upon a Quarter of a lb. of Yams pr. Day." '[125] Morrison, in Hayward's opinion, was on the side of the mutineers. The reason for his opinion, which the court asked him to justify, was the expression on Morrison's face. Hallet said he had seen Ellison, Millward, and Burkett armed, and that Morrison, 'with a Musquet', looking over the stern at the launch, had 'called out in a jeering Manner, "If my friends enquire after me, tell them I am somewhere in the South Seas." '[126] He had not seen Heywood armed but he recalled that when Bligh had spoken to Heywood, 'he laughed, turned round, and walked away'.[127]

The witnesses were questioned by the prisoners, Morrison earning the admiration of the author of a letter published in the *Gentleman's Magazine* who had seen the whole trial and wrote that the *Bounty*'s boatswain's mate 'questioned all the evidences, and in a manner so arranged and pertinent, that the spectators waited with impatience for his turn to call on them, and listened with attention and delight during the discussion'.[128] Prepared speeches were also read in the prisoners' defence, Morrison's denying that he had been armed or jeering, and reminding the court, and Hayward, 'that the face is *too often* a bad index to the Heart'.[129] Heywood, who had been sixteen at the time of the mutiny, argued his 'extreme youth', denied that he had laughed at Bligh, and maintained that if he had handled a cutlass he had done so innocently and in a 'stupor' of confusion.[130] Ellison also argued his youth, but with less hope of a reprieve in view of so much evidence that he was armed. He stressed his 'terror' at 'the site of Mr. Christain; he looked like a Madman, is long hair was luse, is shirt Collair open'.[131] Muspratt argued that he had taken up a musket only to assist Mr Fryer in an attempt to retake the ship (which Fryer had indeed contemplated). Burkett, who had been involved from the beginning of the mutiny, argued unconvincingly that he had taken up arms only under compulsion by Christian, and Millward, who had been asleep when the ship was taken, as the witnesses had testified, argued more plausibly that he had been bullied into taking up arms.

On 18 September the court delivered its verdicts: Norman, Coleman, McIntosh, and Byrne were acquitted, as expected, but all the others—Heywood, Morrison, Ellison, Burkett, Millward, and Muspratt—were found guilty and sentenced 'to suffer Death by being hanged by the Neck', although 'the Court, in consideration of various Circumstances, did humbly and most earnestly recommend the said Peter Heywood and James Morrison to His Majesty's Royal Mercy'.[132]

Back on board HMS *Hector*, sentenced to death but recommended to mercy, Heywood and Morrison were busy. In the form of a letter to a 'Reverd. Mr. Howell', dated 'Hector 10th Octr. 1792', Morrison gave an account of 'the particulars of the Treatment' received by the prisoners when under the care of Captain Edwards, and in the same month, probably, Morrison also wrote his 'Memorandum and Particulars respecting the Bounty and her Crew', containing a number of charges against Bligh's conduct on the *Bounty*: of embezzling cheeses, fiddling expenses, skimping on the sailors' provisions, and unjustly accusing the officers of stealing coconuts.[133] Meanwhile Heywood was 'employing [his] leisure Hours in making a Vocabulary of the Otaheitean Language', as he told his sister, Nessy, in a letter of 16 October.[134] This Vocabulary, now lost, consisted of 'one hundred full-written folio pages', according to a description in 1831.[135] Heywood had also been writing some 'Remarks' on the evidence against him at the court martial, which Nessy forwarded to the First Lord of the Admiralty on 11 October, while she awaited with trepidation the outcome of the recommendation to the King's mercy.[136] On 24 October the King's warrant was despatched from the Admiralty granting pardons to Heywood and Morrison, and a reprieve for Muspratt on a point of legal procedure, and authorizing the executions of Burkett, Millward, and Ellison.[137] Heywood reached his lawyer's house in Great Russell Street, London, on the morning of 29 October, from where Nessy wrote to her mother at 'half-past ten o'clock—the brightest moment of my existence!' and Heywood signed the letter with her.[138] That same day, aboard HMS *Brunswick* at Portsmouth, in front of men assembled from the crews of the other naval ships at Portsmouth and Spithead, to whom they were to serve as an example, Burkett, Millward, and Ellison were hanged.[139]

Heywood wrote from Great Russell Street to Edward Christian, Fletcher's brother, on 5 November, offering to see him

and endeavour to prove, that your brother was not that vile wretch, void of all gratitude, which the world had the unkindness to think him: but, on the contrary, a most worthy character; ruined only by having the misfortune, if it can be so called, of being a young man of strict honour, and adorned with every virtue; and beloved by all (except one, whose ill report is his greatest praise) who had the pleasure of his acquaintance.[140]

Heywood's letter was published in the *Cumberland Packet* of 20 November 1792, with an accompanying commentary, no doubt by Edward Christian, to say that Fletcher Christian, of Cumberland, was 'not that detestable and horrid monster of wickedness' he had falsely been represented as, and promising an account of the recent court martial which would permit members of the public to 'correct the erroneous opinions, which, from certain false narratives, they have long entertained'.[141]

On 25 November the Revd William Howell, the clergyman who had attended the *Bounty* prisoners aboard HMS *Hector*, wrote to his former ship-mate, James and Fanny Burney's brother-in-law, Captain Molesworth Phillips, whom Howell addressed c/o Sir Joseph Banks at Soho Square, to say that he was unable to send 'Morrison's narrative', as Phillips had requested, because it was 'at present in the Isle of Wight', from where Howell would have it in a few days.[142] This 'narrative' is very probably Morrison's 'Memorandum', because Howell informs Phillips that 'Morrison is getting very forward' with another narrative, identifiable as his so-called 'journal', 'which will be ready for the press in about six or seven Weeks', and which, if Sir Joseph cares to, he can see before publication.[143] As well as indicating a probable date for the composition of Morrison's journal, Howell's letter to Phillips reveals how opinions about Bligh were changing now that the accounts in his *Narrative* and *Voyage* were being challenged by other accounts:

It is very natural for Sir Joseph Banks not to think so unfavorably of Bligh as you or I may— there was a time when no one could have an higher opinion of an officer than I had of him— so many circumstances however have arisen up against him attended with such striking marks of veracity That I have been compelled to change that idea of him into one of a very contrary nature.[144]

Although Morrison had 'writing Utincils paper &c' on Tahiti, it is unlikely that he could have preserved a journal, or even notes, when swimming from the sinking *Pandora* with his loins wrapped in 'a Sash or Marro after the Taheite Manner'.[145] If he did keep a journal it must have been lost with the *Pandora*, as Stewart's and Heywood's journals almost certainly were (except for the extracts from them made by Edwards, which were saved with Edwards's own log).[146] The work known as Morrison's journal was most probably written from recollection, despite the quantity and accuracy of the information it contains.[147] Morrison's narrative of events on the *Bounty*, Tubuai, Tahiti, and the *Pandora* is followed in his journal by an account of Tahiti and the Tahitians which is of anthropological value because of the length of Morrison's contact and his consequent knowledge of the language, and also, he argues, because he had been able to observe Tahitian culture undisturbed by the presence of a visiting ship: 'as their whole system was overturned by the arrival of a ship, their Manners were then as much altered from their Common Course, as those of our own Country are at a Fair, which might as well be given for a specimen of the Method of living in England.'[148] Unlike 'former Voyagers', Morrison had never seen the Tahitians 'holding Carnal Conversation in Publick' and he disputes 'the Idea formd' of the Tahitians by those former voyagers.[149] As the 'Famous Queen Pbooraya' (Purea) was one of the Arioi, it was only to be expected that her followers were such as preferd the Rites of Venus to those of Mars and as she saw that they were also more agreeable to her Visitors (the general Case with Sailors after a long Voyage) they were no doubt practiced and carried to the utmost verge of their lattitude . . . However the ladys who act these parts are not to be taken as a standard for the Whole no more than the Nymphs of the Thames or Syrens of Spithead are to be taken as Samples of our own fair Country Weomen.[150]

Morrison closes his account of the Tahitian people, 'who are without doubt the Happiest on the Face of the Globe', by referring the reader to 'a Vocabulary' (perhaps Heywood's) which is missing from the manuscript of his journal.[151]

In December 1792 Phillips obtained Morrison's 'Memorandum' from Howell in Portsmouth and sent it on 12 December to Banks, mentioning another 'account to be published amplified & corrected by a clergyman' (almost certainly Morrison's journal) but adding 'I imagined you would prefer the genuine unsophisticated story so I have sent you this, in the mans own writing'.[152] From 16 December Edward Christian was also writing to Banks, raising questions about Bligh's conduct on the *Bounty*.[153]

Bligh returned from delivering the breadfruit to the West Indies on 7 August 1793, and on that day Heywood's uncle, Captain Pasley, wrote to Matthew Flinders—who had served, on Pasley's recommendation, as a midshipman on Bligh's second breadfruit voyage—informing him that 'Your Capt. will meet a very hard reception—he has Dam'd himself'.[154] Another of Bligh's officers, George Tobin, noticed the effect of the court martial of the *Bounty* mutineers on Bligh's reputation: 'it was not difficult to discover on our arrival that impressions had been received by many in the service, by no means favourable to him.'[155] Indeed Bligh does not seem to have been warmly welcomed at the Admiralty, for he complained to Banks about the First Lord, Lord Chatham's 'unaccountable conduct'.[156]

In 1794, at the request of Edward Christian, Stephen Barney, the lawyer who had successfully defended Muspratt, published the minutes he had taken at the court martial as *Minutes of the Proceedings of the Court Martial . . . on Ten Persons charged with Mutiny on board His Majesty's Ship the Bounty*, which was accompanied by an *Appendix containing a full account of the real Causes and Circumstances* by Edward Christian.[157] As a Professor of Law at Cambridge, Edward Christian was careful to assure the reader that he had no 'wish to insinuate a vindication of the crime', but only 'to state facts as they are', which he had obtained from interviews with members of the *Bounty*'s crew conducted before 'several respectable gentlemen' acting as witnesses.[158] The eleven men from the *Bounty* who were interviewed included six of those who had returned in the launch with Bligh and all of those who had been acquitted at or pardoned after the court martial, except Norman and Morrison, the latter having communicated with Christian by letter. The 'respectable' witnesses, who were also named, included several of Christian's connections from Cumberland. The *Minutes* and Edward Christian's *Appendix* based on his interviews made public the coconut incident, Fletcher Christian's tearful reaction to Bligh's treatment on the eve of the mutiny (although 'he was no milk-sop') and his plan to abandon ship.[159] The minutes and interviews also transferred Christian's 'hell' from his conscience, where Bligh's *Narrative* had located it, to the person of Bligh himself.[160] The men interviewed denied Bligh's 'Huzza for Otaheite!' (although there is independent evidence for it) and, with reference to Bligh's Tahitian explanation of the mutiny, declared that Christian 'never had a female favourite at Otaheite, nor any attachment or particular connection among the women'.[161]

In July and August 1794 Bligh gathered material for his response to Edward Christian, which was published in December 1794 as *An Answer to Certain Assertions contained in the Appendix to a Pamphlet* (1794). This attempted to refute Edward Christian's case by publishing a collection of documents from the *Bounty* and 'testimonials, without further remark'.[162] Some of these documents and testimonials had little relation to the 'assertions' they were supposed to 'answer', but others were clearly intended to discredit Edward Christian's evidence from his interviews. Affidavits were produced from three sailors maintaining that they had not made some of the unattributed statements in Christian's *Appendix* and stating that: 'I remember Christian having a girl' (Coleman); 'I remember he had a girl' (Smith); 'I remember Christian had a girl, who was always with him' (Lebogue).[163] The final 'testimonial' was a letter from a man who had sailed with Bligh and Christian to the West Indies before the *Bounty* voyage, and declared that Christian 'was then one of the most foolish young men I ever knew in regard to the sex'.[164]

The debate continued the following year with *A Short Reply to Captain W. Bligh's Answer* (1795), in which Edward Christian defended his method in the *Appendix* of presenting evidence and names of informants without attributing particular statements—a method which Bligh's *Answer* had impugned—and criticized Lawrence Lebogue's affidavit in Bligh's *Answer*, citing the respectable witnesses who confirmed what Lebogue had told Edward Christian.[165] That same year, however, as the argument between Bligh and Christian about the mutiny was ending in these quibbles, events were taking place, as if in answer at last to the call made by the author of *Otaheite: A Poem* in 1774, for a new kind of voyage to Tahiti to replace the scientific voyage—a voyage not to learn the truths of nature, but to teach the truths of scripture:

> On Minds which thus untaught thus darkling stray,
> To pour the radiant Beams of heav'nly Day.[166]

It was 'reading the voyages to the South Seas, and especially to Otaheite', that inspired the preacher and scholar, Dr Haweis, 'to make some effort to send some [missionaries] to Otaheite and the Southern Isles'.[167] In 1795 the London Missionary Society was formed, a Society which would send—on the crest of the wave of the Evangelical Movement—a voyage to the islands which the Royal Society had 'abandoned to their primitive oblivion'.[168] In a sermon preached at the formation of the Society on 22 September 1795, Dr Haweis unveiled to his audience an inviting prospect of good and evil, of:

innumerable islands, which spot the bosom of the Pacific Ocean, . . . many of them full of inhabitants,—occupying lands, which seem to realize the fabled Gardens of the Hesperides,— where the fragrant groves, which cover them from the sultry beams of day, afford them food, and clothing; whilst the sea offers continual plenty of its inexhaustible stores; and the day passes in ease and affluence, and the night in music and dancing. But amidst these enchanting scenes, savage nature still feasts on the flesh of its prisoners—appeases its Gods with human sacrifices—whole societies of men and women live promiscuously, and murder every infant born amongst them; whilst every turpitude, committed in the face of open day, proclaims, that shame is as little felt, as a sense of sin is known.[169]

Innocence of sin and shame was evidence of paradise lost, not paradise, to Dr Haweis, but 'No region of the world', he said, 'affords us happier prospects'.[170]

In a speech two days later, Dr Haweis did not confront his Society with the anthropological horrors of the Arioi society, but concentrated on the classical delights of the Hesperidean South Sea Islands. The Society should begin its mission 'where the difficulties are least', where 'the cold of winter is never known', among 'groves, odoriferous, as loaded with abundance', where the 'natives, not harassed by labour for daily bread, . . . are always sure to have abundant time for instruction', and where 'we have more to apprehend from being caressed and exalted, than from being insulted and oppressed'.[171] Of the evils of Tahiti he said nothing, and of the dangers he mentioned only 'one, perhaps, as hard to endure as a fiery ordeal'.[172] He had been more explicit in an article in the *Evangelical Magazine* in July 1795, entitled 'The very probable success of a proper Mission to the South Sea Islands': 'No-where are the prospects of success more flattering, or the dangers and difficulties of the Missionaries less to be apprehended, except, as the worthy Admiral Bligh informed me, such as may arise from the fascination of beauty, and the seduction of appetite.'[173]

The *Duff* sailed from London down the Thames at six in the morning of 10 August 1796, those on board singing 'Jesus, at thy command, We launch into the deep'.[174] They were 'haild in the night by a Man of War', according to a journal kept by Dr Haweis: 'Whither bound?—Otaheite.—What cargo?—Missionaries & Provisions'.[175] The *Duff* was actually bound for Spithead, where Haweis's own missionary voyage was safely to terminate when the *Duff* sailed from England, but the missionaries found they had missed the convoy they intended to sail with, and were obliged to spend several weeks waiting for another. During this time Haweis continued his journal, noting that on 16 September a Mr Howell came aboard the *Duff* and 'communicated to me a vast store of knowledge, respecting the South-sea Islands, having been the Chaplain who attended the Mutineers condemned for running away with the Bounty'.[176] Better still, Howell 'hath kindly entrusted me with his papers': Morrison's 'Journal' and 'a vocabulary' of the Tahitian language.[177] Howell 'had proposed publishing his [Morrison's] papers', we learn from a note made by Haweis's colleague Samuel Greatheed, 'but suppressed them on condition that Morrison should be provided for by the Government', as their publication 'would have reflected some discredit on Captain Bligh'.[178] Over the following days Haweis was busy transcribing for the missionaries 'many pleasing particulars out of the Mutineer's Journal'.[179] The prospective missionaries were also provided with a copy of the Tahitian Vocabulary (probably the one compiled by Heywood) and, when the *Duff* eventually sailed from Spithead on 24 September, these papers were 'of unspeakable service to the missionaries', the Vocabulary 'for the help it afforded them to learn before their arrival much of this unknown tongue', and Morrison's journal 'as giving the most inviting and encouraging description of the natives, and of the cordial reception which they might expect'.[180] As the author of a history of *Maritime Discovery and Christian Missions, considered in their Mutual Relations* (1840) was later to remark: 'In connexion with the future evangelization of the islands of the South Sea, therefore, the mutiny of the Bounty was one of those events in Providence, which plainly indicate the finger of God.'[181]

In the month that the *Duff* sailed from Spithead there appeared in London what seemed to be the answer at last to an unresolved question: *Letters from Mr. Fletcher Christian, containing a Narrative of the Transactions on board His Majesty's Ship Bounty, Before and After the Mutiny, with his subsequent Voyages and Travels in South America* (1796). But the account given in the *Letters* of the *Bounty*'s stay at Tahiti prior to the mutiny more than coincidentally resembles the account in Bligh's *Voyage*, and the description of the tempting women of 'this terrestrial paradise' echoes the words used in Bligh's explanation of the mutiny in his *Narrative*, with which the supposed Fletcher Christian is in very close agreement.[182] The 'sensibility', 'delicacy', and 'allurements' of 'the women at Otaheite' result in 'connexions' for everyone, including Christian himself: 'I shall candidly acknowledge, that I had my favourite as well as the rest. Indeed, it is but justice to confess, that our subsequent conspiracy in a great measure owed its rise to these connexions.'[183] 'It is but justice' also, it seems to Christian, that he 'should acquit Captain Bligh' of any blame for having contributed to the causes of this conspiracy 'by any harsh or ungentleman like conduct on his part'.[184]

After the mutiny, the *Bounty* returns directly to Tahiti, where descriptions of the island's tattooing, dancing, venereal disease, soil, and bananas, supplemented by one or two details from George Hamilton's *A Voyage Round the World, in His Majesty's Frigate Pandora*, fill and conceal the gap left in the *Letters* by the absence of any particulars of individuals or incidents.[185] Leaving some of the *Bounty*'s men at Tahiti, Christian and nine others, with some Tahitian women, then proceed vaguely across the Pacific until they are shipwrecked by the author's flagging imagination off the coast of South America. A truly 'tedious' journey north, from Chile to Panama, by Christian, the only survivor, then fills the *Letters* with the contents of some plagiarized traveller's guide, and Christian is left finally in Spain to write his *Letters* to some unnamed person in England.[186]

Bligh received a copy of *Letters from Mr. Fletcher Christian* from his publisher and, surprisingly, seemed to afford the work some degree of belief, despite its obvious debt to his own account, or perhaps because of this debt, which kept its explanation of the mutiny in agreement with his own. On 16 September he wrote to Banks with his response to 'a Pamphlet called Christian's Letters': 'is it possible that Wretch can be at Cadiz and that he has had intercourse with his Brother, that sixpenny Professor, who has more Law about him than honor[?]'[187]

William Wordsworth knew better. He had been at Cockermouth School with Fletcher Christian, although six years his junior, and at Hawkshead School under the headmastership of Edward Christian. More recently, his cousin, Captain John Wordsworth, and uncle, the Revd William Cookson, had been two of the 'respectable gentlemen' present at Edward Christian's interviews with the *Bounty* men. He had particular reason to know, therefore, what any reader of Edward Christian's *Appendix* could know, that Christian had made a settlement at Tubuai, and that the ignorance of this in the *Letters* was sufficient proof, apart from any others, that the *Letters* were not authentic.[188] It is not surprising, then, that when some excerpts from the *Letters* were printed in the Sherborne *Weekly Entertainer* of 26 September 1796, under the heading 'Christian's own Account of the Mutiny on Board his Majesty's Ship Bounty', Wordsworth wrote from Racedown, Dorset, on 23 October, a letter which the *Weekly Entertainer* published on 7 November:

There having appeared in your Entertainer an extract from a work purporting to be the production of Fletcher Christian, who headed the mutiny on board the Bounty, I think it proper to inform you, that I have the best authority for saying that this publication is spurious. Your regard for the truth will induce you to apprize your readers of this circumstance.[189]

Nor is it surprising that, in a notebook kept by Coleridge from 1795 to 1800, there is listed—among twenty-seven other projected works, between 'Ode to a Moth' and 'Military Anecdotes'—'Adventures of CHRISTIAN, the mutineer'.[190]

These unsurprising facts may lead us to consider the impact of the South Sea discoveries on the generation of poets—Wordsworth, Coleridge, and Southey— born in the years of Cook's voyages. Cook's biographer, Andrew Kippis, in his reverential account of Cook's life and voyages, *The Life of Captain James Cook* (1788), had remarked that Cook's discoveries had opened up the Pacific, not only for science, but also for literature: 'Captain Cook's discoveries, among other effects, have opened up new scenes for a poetical fancy to range in, and presented new images to the selection of genius and taste.'[191] The poetical works Kippis quotes are the woeful odes and elegies that gushed forth in response to Cook's death in Hawaii, from which I give merely a sample from the most popular, Anna Seward's *Elegy on Captain Cook* (1780), in which, while 'the lurid atmosphere portentous lours', Mrs Cook plays a tragic role:

> Ill-fated matron!—for, alas! in vain
> Thy eager glances wander o'er the main!—
> 'Tis the vex'd billows, that insurgent rave,
> Their white foam silvers yonder distant wave,
> 'Tis not his sails!—thy husband comes no more!
> His bones now whiten an accursed shore![192]

Miss Seward's verse requires no comment, and Kippis hoped that the subject opened up by Cook 'may hereafter call forth the genius of some poet of the stronger sex'.[193] So what was the impact, then, of Cook's 'new scenes' on the young Romantics?

Tahiti may perhaps have played a modest part in Southey's conception of the utopian community he and Coleridge planned and called 'Pantisocracy'. In a letter of February 1793, imagining 'the most delightful theory of an island', Southey remarked: 'If the *Bounty* mutineers had not behaved so cruelly to their officers I should have been the last to condemn them. Otaheitia independent of its women had many inducements not only for the sailor but the philosopher.'[194] In 'To a Young Lady with a Poem on the French Revolution' (1794), Coleridge recalled briefly and irrelevantly how in his early youth he had mourned the fate of 'Prince' Lee Boo, a chief's son from the Palau Islands in the Caroline Group, who was brought to London in the 1780s, died of smallpox, and was buried in the churchyard of St Mary's, Rotherhithe:

> My soul amid the pensive twilight gloom
> Mourn'd with the breeze, O Lee Boo! o'er thy tomb.[195]

But, despite the interest taken by these poets, notably Coleridge, in the literature of travel, they seem to have taken little advantage of the opportunities afforded them by Cook's 'new scenes', though 'The Ancient Mariner' might seem to be something of an exception, as the poem's 'Argument' tells us that the Mariner's ship sailed in 'the Great Pacific Ocean'.[196] Indeed it is quite possible, as searchers for Coleridge's sources have suggested, that he found hints for the imagery of his poem in some of the details in accounts of Cook's voyages, such as the luminous sea-creatures described in the account of the last voyage, *A Voyage to the Pacific Ocean* (1784), and also that Christian's remark, as reported by Bligh, 'I am in hell', may have contributed to the portrayal of the tormented Mariner, his 'soul in agony', but even this much, though possible, is so much speculation.'[197] There was, despite 'The Ancient Mariner' and Coleridge's appetite for travel literature, something parochial about 'the Lakers', as Byron called them, wishing they would change their 'lakes for ocean'.[198] We may conclude that the impact of Cook's 'new scenes' on the work of the early Romantic poets was nearly negligible, though Southey's sympathy with the *Bounty* mutineers' attraction to Tahiti and Coleridge's for the noble Lee Boo are worthy of notice, particularly as Southey, who had remarked in 1793 on the 'many inducements' of Tahiti, had decided by 1803 that the Tahitians were 'the most degraded of the human species'.[199]

Some reason for Southey's changed opinion can be found by resuming the voyage of the *Duff*, with its cargo of thirty missionaries—artisans and tradesmen for the most part, with only four ordained ministers.[200] Eighteen of them, with five wives and three children, were landed at Matavai Bay, Tahiti, on 5 March 1797, and the others were taken on in the *Duff* to the Tongan Group and the Marquesas. The official account of the *Duff*'s voyage, *A Missionary Voyage to the Southern*

Pacific Ocean (1799), explained the motives which had led the London Missionary Society to undertake a voyage to the islanders who had been 'abandoned' when their island had served the needs of the naturalist to explore 'the peculiar subject of his researches' and of the astronomer to advance the study of his 'celestial science':

Reflections on their unhappy situation had dropped from the pen of the humane, and pity had often swelled the bosom of the compassionate: a few felt for them, not only as men, but as Christians, and wished some mode could be devised of communicating to them the knowledge of that inestimable book, compared with which all beside is pompous ignorance.[201]

First impressions of Tahiti were favourable, although, inevitably, the customs of Tahiti were not observed with philosophical enthusiasm, or scientific exactitude, in the missionaries' journal: 'Many *unnatural crimes*, which we dare not name, are committed daily without the idea of shame or guilt.'[202] On 13 August 1797 John Jefferson, a minister, recorded his considered opinion in his personal journal: 'The more I see of the customs, temper, and conduct of this people, the more I am confirmed in an opinion that I have some time formed; viz. that our success will not be speedy.'[203] In November a pressing question was raised by a young shoe-maker, Francis Oakes: 'If any brother should find himself disposed to marry one of the native women, would it be thought by the society a proper act?'[204] The answer, it was decided, was 'that to marry an heathen woman was directly contrary to the Word of God'.[205] This, however, did not prevent John Cock, a carpenter, from experiencing 'various temptations'—the 'allurements of dissipation' described in Bligh's *Narrative of the Mutiny*, about which he had warned Dr Haweis.[206] The missionaries had indeed 'more to apprehend from being caressed', as Dr Haweis had said, but they were also 'insulted and oppressed'. The young chief, Tu (son and heir of Cook's Tu, Bligh's Taina, who now called himself Pomare), furious because the missionaries prevented him from obtaining guns from a visiting ship, the *Nautilus*, stripped a delegation from the mission naked.[207] Most of the missionaries left immediately on the *Nautilus*, in search of seals, leaving only seven men and one wife on 31 March 1798.[208] One of these, Thomas Lewis, a minister, abandoned the mission station at Matavai in July, writing to his colleagues on 1 August 1798, to 'inform you that it is my fixed determination to take to wife one of these natives'.[209] Whereupon, as John Jefferson reported to the Society in England, Lewis 'sunk into the arms of a poor idolatress'.[210] Benjamin Broomhall followed this example in June 1800, telling the assembled brethren who tried to dissuade him that: 'The soul is mortal.'[211]

Reinforcements arrived from England, however, aboard the *Royal Admiral* in July 1801, and the mission survived, although making no conversions and suffering more defections for various reasons. One of the new arrivals, William Waters, gave cause for concern by announcing 'that he had committed murder on the body of a man on board the Royal Admiral in the shape of a dog' and by professing his love for Tu's wife and his zeal to teach the Tahitians Hebrew.[212] Meanwhile Tu, whose father Pomare died in 1803, accumulated muskets and established himself as King Pomare II of Tahiti. When he was defeated in a rebellion of 1808, he feared 'the people would cut off his head as the people of France had done with their king' (as he told the missionaries) and therefore fled the island.[213] The missionaries, identified with Tu's faction and his fate, followed him, giving up their mission on Tahiti late in 1808.

Earlier that year, in February, Captain Mayhew Folger of the *Topaz*, from Boston, called at a small Pacific island to hunt seals. The island was apparently uninhabited, so he was surprised when a canoe came off from the shore, and even more surprised when he was hailed in English by a young man in the canoe, who asked him who he was, to which he replied that he was an American from Boston. 'You are an American; you come from America; where is America? Is it in Ireland?' 'Who are you?' asked Folger.

'We are Englishmen.'—'Where were you born?'—'On that island which you see.' 'How then are you Englishmen, if you were born on that island, which the English do not own, and never possessed?'—'We are Englishmen because our father was an Englishman.'— 'Who is your father?'— . . . 'Aleck.'—'Who is Aleck?'—'Don't you know Aleck?'—'How should I know Aleck?'—'Well then, did you know Captain Bligh of the Bounty?'[214]

Folger went ashore on Pitcairn Island and met Aleck, the only survivor of the men who had sailed with Christian from Tahiti, John Adams, alias Alexander Smith, Able Seaman of the *Bounty*, from whom Folger received a brief and slightly garbled account of the later history of the *Bounty* and, by way of evidence, the ship's chronometer.[215] Folger reported his discovery to the British authorities at Valparaiso, and the Admiralty received a report in May 1809, but no official action was taken, though the report to the Admiralty was published in the *Quarterly Review*, early in 1810.[216] In 1814, in the course of the Anglo-American War of 1812, two British ships, HMS *Briton* and HMS *Tagus*, unaware of Folger's news, were in the Pacific in pursuit of an American ship, the *Essex*, and called by chance at Pitcairn to make what was, for them, a new discovery. Again the visitors were asked if they knew 'one William Bligh, in England'. They responded by asking the speaker if he knew one Fletcher Christian. ' "Oh yes," said he, "very well, his son is in the boat there coming up, his name is Friday Fletcher October Christian. His father is dead now—he was shot by a black fellow." '[217]

The fuller story that emerged then—and was expanded and clarified when Captain Beechey of HMS *Blossom* visited Pitcairn in 1825, and was later corroborated and supplemented by an interview with the Tahitian woman, Jenny, who returned from Pitcairn to Tahiti—had something like a moral.[218] Aboard the *Bounty* on her last night at Matavai Bay, in September 1789, were nine of her original crew, including Christian, four Tahitian men, two Tubuaian men, and about nineteen Tahitian women, some of whom had been invited aboard 'with the feigned purpose of taking leave'.[219] While these crucial females were at supper below, the *Bounty*'s cable was cut and she was taken out to sea, not to sail to another part of the island, as the women were told, but to sail away forever.[220] One woman who discovered the deception jumped overboard and swam for the shore, although the *Bounty* was by then about a mile outside the reefs.[221] The next morning, six women who were 'rather ancient', according to Jenny, were allowed ashore at Moorea, but the remainder sailed on in the *Bounty*, westward, to an island Jenny remembers was called Purutea, probably one of the Cook Islands, where Christian gave a man who came aboard his jacket, and another of the *Bounty*'s men wantonly shot the new owner of the jacket dead.[222] The *Bounty* sailed on to one of the Tongan Islands, and then continued west to a small island that seemed promising for colonization, but turned out to be inhabited.[223] After this Christian ceased his westward search for an ideal island, habitable but prefer-ably uninhabited, by contrast with Tubuai, and turned the *Bounty* round, perhaps because, studying the books in Bligh's cabin, he had found what he wanted, as Adams told Beechey, in Hawkesworth's *Voyages*—a reference to Carteret's dis-covery, in 1767, of the island he named 'Pitcairn's Island':

It appeared like a great rock rising out of the sea: it was not more than five miles in circumference, and seemed to be uninhabited; it was, however, covered with trees, and we saw a small stream of fresh water running down one side of it. I would have landed upon it, but the surf, which at this season broke upon it with great violence, rendered it impossible.[224]

The *Bounty* was two months out of sight of land and there had been talk of returning to Tahiti when Pitcairn was found, one evening, in windy weather that made landing impossible until the third day following, as Jenny recalled.[225] Christian and some others went ashore and returned to the *Bounty* to report that the island abounded with coconuts and sea birds and was indeed uninhabited, although there were signs that man had been there before: the stone foundations of houses, some carved boards.[226] The *Bounty*'s crew and passengers, nine British and six Polynesian men and twelve Polynesian women, one with a young female child, went ashore, and the *Bounty* was emptied of everything of use, while a debate took place about what to do with her, which ended when Matthew Quintal set fire to her, on 23 January 1790.[227] 'During the night all were in tears at seeing her in flames', Jenny remembered.[228]

Now Pitcairn was divided up, 'into equal portions, but to the exclusion of the poor blacks', the Polynesian men, who were thus reduced from 'friends' to 'slaves', as Captain Beechey comments.[229] The women, it seems, had already been divided up, or had divided themselves up, so that the nine British men had one Polynesian woman each, and the six Polynesian men had three Polynesian women between them.[230] Christian's first son was born to his woman, Mauatea, in October of the first year, but when Williams's woman died, that same year, one of the Polynesian men was compelled to surrender his woman to Williams, and the Polynesian men, with some justification, now plotted a mutiny.[231] This plot the women betrayed to the British, supposedly by means of a song with the refrain 'Why does black man sharpen axe? to kill white man', and the Tahitian Tararo, who had been deprived of his woman, fled to the woods with Oopee, one of the Tubuaians.²³² The remaining four Polynesian men purchased their pardons by arranging the murders of these two fugitives. One of the Tubuaian men treacherously killed the other, his uncle, Oopee, and Tararo was likewise killed by two other Tahitians, with the help of his former woman, now Williams's woman, Nancy.²³³

These brutalities bought peace for a few years more, but the Polynesian men were still oppressed, particularly by Quintal and McCoy, and they planned another, more successful revolution. Williams was murdered first, then one of the Tahitians, Manarii, shot Christian in the back while he was clearing his yam plot. He exclaimed 'Oh dear!' and fell to the ground, where an axe put an end to his life.²³⁴ Mills, Martin, and Brown were also killed, but Quintal, McCoy, and Adams escaped to the woods, while Young (asthmatic and, it seems, attractive, though Bligh said he had 'rather a bad look') was protected by the women.²³⁵ After returning, being wounded and escaping again, Adams was allowed back to live with Young and the Polynesian women and the Polynesian men, who now began to quarrel over the women whose men they had murdered. Teimua was shot dead as he sat by Young's woman, Susan, accompanying her song on the flute. His murderer, Manarii, fearing retribution, then fled to join the fugitives, Quintal and McCoy, in hiding in the woods. The British men now planned to kill all the Polynesian men. Adams connived with Quintal and McCoy, who shot Manarii. The Tubuaian Tetaheite (formerly Taroamiva) was massacred with an axe by Susan, as he slept beside Jenny, and simultaneously, as planned, Young shot Nehow.²³⁶

Only when they were shown the heads and hands of the murdered Polynesians did Quintal and McCoy agree to return to the village, which they did on 3 October 1793, according to Beechey.²³⁷ At this point the population of Pitcairn consisted of Adams, Young, Quintal, McCoy, some children, and ten or eleven Polynesian women, who were now at last in surplus and lived in various combinations with the men. About two months after the return of Quintal and McCoy, Young began a journal, which records the discontent of the women, who refused to bury the murdered *Bounty* men. 'Going over to borrow a rake', wrote Young on 12 March 1794, 'I saw Jenny having a skull in her hand.'²³⁸ He also recorded that 'since the massacre' most of the women desired 'to leave the island'.²³⁹ On 14 April 1794, the men began to build the women a boat, Jenny enthusiastically tearing up the boards of her house to serve the purpose.²⁴⁰ The boat was completed on 13 August 1794, and launched on 15 August, when, Young wrote, 'according to expectation she upset', fortunately before the women had set out upon the ocean.²⁴¹ The women's dissatisfaction continued, especially with their treatment by Quintal and McCoy, who frequently beat them, Quintal proposing 'not to laugh, joke, or give any thing to any of the girls'.²⁴² On 11 November 1794, a conspiracy of the women to mutiny and murder the men in their sleep was discovered and, according to Young's journal, the men agreed to kill any woman who misbehaved in future 'until we could discover the real intentions of the women'.²⁴³ A few days later, on 30

November, the women revealed their real intentions by attacking the men, but without causing any deaths or receiving any punishment.

McCoy, who had been employed in a distillery in Scotland, experimented with the root of the ti plant and succeeded in producing a bottle of spirits on 20 April 1798. Frequent intoxication followed this success, until in a fit of delirium McCoy tied his hands and feet and threw himself from a cliff into the sea, the survivors drawing a moral from his fate.[244] Young's journal was discontinued before McCoy's death but Adams told Beechey that Quintal's woman died in a fall while searching for birds' eggs, about 1799, and that Quintal, despite the ample supply of spare women, insisted on replacing her with one belonging to Adams or Young, which caused another outbreak of quarrelling, coming to an end with Quintal's life, when Adams 'split his scull with an Axe'.[245]

The survivors, Young and Adams, now turned 'to repentance', Beechey relates, and 'resolved to have morning and evening family prayers, to add afternoon service to the duty of the Sabbath, and to train up their own children, and those of their late unfortunate companions, in piety and virtue'.[246] When Young died of his asthma about a year after Quintal, Adams became patriarch of the Pitcairn community of women and children and, with the aid of the *Bounty*'s Bible, carried on the good work. So it was that, astonished to discover the last resort of the mutineers, Lieutenant Shillibeer of the *Briton* was astonished again, and ashamed, when the young men of Pitcairn attended breakfast aboard the *Briton* in 1814:

I must here confess I blushed when I saw nature in its most simple state, offer that tribute of respect to the Omnipotent Creator, which from an education I did not perform, nor from society had been taught its necessity. 'Ere they began to eat; on their knees, and with hands uplifted did they implore permission to partake in peace what was set before them.

'Here nature was triumphant', concluded Shillibeer.[247] Beechey, a decade later, noted that the islanders worshipped several times a day and 'five times on Sunday', that they never joked, that 'irony was considered a falsehood', and that they rarely indulged in music or dancing.[248] His request for an entertainment was only reluctantly complied with:

three *grown-up* females stood up to dance, but with a reluctance which showed it was done only to oblige us, as they consider such performances an inroad upon their usual innocent pastimes. The figure consisted of such parts of the Otaheitan dance as were thought most decorous, and was little more than a shuffling of the feet, sliding past each other, and snapping their fingers . . . They did not long continue these diversions, from an idea that it was too great a levity to be continued long.[249]

Such was the Tahitian dance of Pitcairn. At Adams's earnest request, Beechey married him to his blind, bedridden Tahitian woman.

The young author Mary Russell Mitford did not have the details of these later accounts of Pitcairn at her disposal, but she had read in the *Quarterly Review* of

1810 the report of Folger's interview with Adams (calling himself Smith). Although confusing Christian's fate with McCoy's (stating that Christian 'threw himself off the rocks into the sea'), this report gave a brief but basically accurate summary of the mutineers' history, and mentioned that the islanders had now been educated by Adams 'in a religious and moral way'.[250] These facts formed the basis of Mary Russell Mitford's poem *Christina, the Maid of the South Seas* (1811), which Coleridge himself kindly corrected, adding some of 'his own beautiful lines' and removing some stanzas of compliments to Scott.[251] The eponymous Christina is a creature of Mary Russell Mitford's imagination, but the fictional story of Christina forms a sequel to the factual story of Christian, which occupies most of the poem, and is narrated by Adams, whose 'unpoetical appellation' (of Smith) Mary Russell Mitford changed to Fitzallan.[252] In an 'Advertisement' to her readers the author assured them that, although 'irresistibly attracted by the character of the gallant and amiable Christian', she had no wish 'to extenuate his crime' and had erred, if at all, 'on the side of authority'.[253] She also advanced her poem's claim to a basis in fact: '"Fitzallan's Narrative," romantic and improbable as it appears, is entirely founded on facts; the authentic document, from which it is taken, is inserted in one of the notes to the third Canto.'[254] Besides the whole report from the *Quarterly Review* (the 'authentic document'), these notes to the poem, prepared with the help of James Burney, contained extensive quotations from Bougainville, Hawkesworth, Bligh's *Voyage to the South Sea*, and Cook and King's *A Voyage to the Pacific Ocean*.[255]

The poem itself begins with the discovery by Folger (renamed Seymour) of Pitcairn:

> Fair as the fabled isles it rose,
> Where erst Ulysses found repose.[256]

A young Englishman aboard the American ship, Henry, finds himself attracted to Christina, the orphaned daughter of Christian, and uses a different figure for Pitcairn: 'An Eden blooming in the wild.'[257] Christina, however, is betrothed to Fitzallan's son, Hubert, and the reader, like Henry, must await the outcome of Mary Russell Mitford's plot while attending to 'Fitzallan's Narrative', delivered by an Adams endowed with bardic 'eloquence of song'.[258]

He begins at the beginning, with the first arrival of the *Bounty*'s crew at Tahiti, to encounter the women's 'merry glance' and 'wanton dance'.[259] Christian loves 'the sister of the king', the princess Iddeah (her name borrowed from Taina's consort), but as the hour of the *Bounty*'s departure draws near he becomes 'wild and frantic' and tells his 'tale of crime and woe' to his close friend, Fitzallan:

> Iddeah—O what frenzied tears!
> A living pledge of love she bears,—
> Slaves to their superstition wild,
> Th'Arreoys will destroy my child![260]

When Bligh refuses Christian's request to take Iddeah to England, Christian formulates his 'purpose dread' and, setting Bligh adrift, explains the principle of poetic justice to him:

> Iddeah! mercy such as thou
> Hast shown to her, such feel'st thou now![261]

Back at Tahiti, the mutineers are soon:

> In beauty's soft enchantment wrapt,
> In love, in joy, in pleasure lapt.[262]

But Christian, like Odysseus and Aeneas, is called to 'higher duties' than 'Basking in woman's sunny eye':

> No! far from that enfeebling land,
> To seek some fair, yet lonely strand,
> Where comrades, servants, children, wives,
> Might gild with tranquil beams our lives,
> Where joys, which virtue can bestow,
> Where piety's diffusive glow,
> Where years to peaceful duty given,
> Might lead each wandering soul to Heaven,
> Was Christian's plan.[263]

Already determined to leave Tahiti's 'soft voluptuous clime', Christian is shocked by a new Tahitian topic, the human sacrifice described in Cook's *A Voyage to the Pacific Ocean* and now turned into couplets:

> Hair from each bleeding victim torn!
> Eyes from their lifeless sockets borne![264]

Not for another moment would Christian 'among these pagans stay' and so he sails away from Tahitian sex and violence—not British justice—to find a utopian home for his people and their 'servants'.[265]

Pitcairn, 'A silent world of faëry!', delighted all those who formed its colony,

> Save one alone, condemn'd to bear
> The pangs of conscience and despair,
> Save Christian![266]

When Iddeah gave birth to the initial cause of all these events, it 'feebly gasp'd—and died!'.[267] This circumstance Christian interprets as a punishment for his crime and, when 'Iddeah's girdle' gives another 'pledge of Christian's love', in the shape of Christina, Mary Russell Mitford is able to explain the cause of Christian's death, as reported in the *Quarterly Review*:

> 'I'll save this one!' he cried
> 'Take me!' then plunged into the tide.

> Vain was all help;—the sudden shock
> Scatter'd his brains upon the rock.[268]

Now the ringleader of the 'servants' (the Polynesian men) 'serpent-like' incites 'his faithless comrades' to rebel against the 'tyrants' (the British men) 'To win life, land, and liberty'.[269] Of the British, only Fitzallan survives the violent effects of this twisted rhetoric, but all the treacherous—and libidinous—'servants' are poisoned and stabbed to death by the 'chaste matrons' of the British.[270]

Now 'Fitzallan's Narrative' is coming to an end and it remains for Mary Russell Mitford, freed from the constraints of facts, to provide an appropriate end for his tale on a Pitcairn at last given over, as its founding father—according to Mary Russell Mitford—had intended, to piety and virtue. Christina's wedding to Hubert is imminent, as is the departure of Henry, and Christina must keep her promise to Hubert and say farewell to Henry. As she is dressed for her wedding, we witness the ideal South Sea female as turned out by Mary Russell Mitford, carefully arranging the pareo:

> What wily art of courtly dress
> Could add to that form's loveliness?
> No art was there. The Parou wound
> In light and graceful folds, around.
> Above the slender ancle, free
> Floated that nymph-like drapery;
> Her round and polish'd arm reveal'd
> Her bosom's swelling charms conceal'd;
> For virtue here with beauty join'd,
> And modesty with grace combin'd.[271]

The charms of romantic love and the demands of duty are reconciled at the last moment, when Hubert appears with Henry, saying 'Take her, bright stranger, she is thine!', thus granting to Henry the permission Bligh had refused to Christian, and bringing to a happy resolution the story of Christina.[272] If the circumstances of Christina and Iddeah are somewhat different, and the 'Maid of the South Seas' is not in the condition of her mother when Christian wished to take her from Tahiti, that is because Pitcairn is not a 'soft voluptuous clime' where nature and virtue are at odds. Pitcairn is not Tahiti.

Mary Russell Mitford's concluding verses expose the contradictions in a South Sea romance based on South Sea facts. 'Oh! it is sweet', she says,

> To 'scape awhile life's sad realities,
> Where history weeps o'er the recording page.[273]

These 'sad realities' of history are not those recorded in her poem, which is the sweet escape, from 'sad realities' in Europe, of 'Fancy, to that Southern isle', there to contemplate 'her theme':

Connubial love . . .
Perfect, as joy in Eden's happy vale.[274]

Pitcairn is 'Eden's happy vale'—paradise regained in a poem 'founded on facts' but far from 'sad realities'.

Although Byron's poem, *The Island, or Christian and His Comrades*, published in June 1823, has certain themes in common with Mary Russell Mitford's poem, there is no reason to believe that Byron had read *Christina*, for these themes are such as would naturally flow from the combination of Byron's own fancy with the known facts of the South Seas. At the head of his poem Byron announced its factual sources—Bligh's account of the mutiny and a traveller's account of the Tongan Islands: 'The foundation of the following Story will be found partly in the account of the Mutiny of the Bounty in the South Seas (in 1789) and partly in "Mariner's Account of the Tonga Islands".'[275]

William Mariner, aged fifteen, had survived a massacre aboard a ship at the Tongan Islands in 1806 and then lived for four years as a Tongan before obtaining a passage back to England, where he met John Martin, a London doctor with an interest in the South Seas, who persuaded him to provide, in the form of his personal story, the material for *An Account of the Natives of the Tonga Islands, in the South Pacific Ocean. With an original grammar and vocabulary of their language. Compiled and arranged from the extensive communications of Mr. William Mariner, several years resident in those islands* (1817), written by John Martin. At the head of the book Martin quoted Alexander von Humboldt's observation of 1814 that 'les sauvages de l'Amérique . . . inspirent moins d'intérêt, depuis que des voyageurs célèbres nous a fait connoître [les] habitans des îles de la mer du Sud', and indeed the ethnographic content of the work is nowadays considered to be essentially accurate because of Mariner's identification with, and absorption in, Tongan culture.[276] There is some truth in Martin's claim that: 'Having been thrown upon those islands at an early age, his young and flexible mind had so accorded itself with the habits and circumstances of the natives, that he evinced no disposition to overrate or to embellish what to him was neither strange nor new.'[277] While Tonga was not a strange new world to Mariner, it was, however, inevitably strange and new to Martin, and he is no doubt responsible for the romantic appearance of some aspects of Tongan reality in the work. Martin's hand can be seen in the portrayal of Tongan landscape, for example, and his own taste is even ascribed to the Tongan chief, Moegagogo, who was 'passionately delighted with romantic scenery'.[278]

According to George Clinton, in his *Life and Writings of Lord Byron* (1825), Byron was fascinated by Mariner's account of Polynesian life, 'was never tired of talking of it to his friends', and employed Bligh's account of the mutiny merely as a vehicle for Mariner's Polynesian material.[279] It is hard to believe that Byron's interest in the story of the *Bounty* was so limited, however, and the question arises whether he made use of any other source than Bligh's *A Voyage to the South Sea* (which appeared in shortened form as an Appendix to Byron's poem). As the

'Island' of Byron's title is 'Toobonai', which is presumably derived from Tubuai, it seems likely that he may have seen or heard something of Edward Christian's *Appendix*, for example, but that he was unaware of, or chose to ignore, the subsequent history of Christian and his comrades on Pitcairn is confirmed by his note describing 'Toobonai' as 'the last island where any distinct account is left of Christian and his comrades'.[280] In any case, Byron's treatment of Bligh and Christian in *The Island* cannot be explained as the consequence of his knowing only Bligh's version of events. As *The Island* makes plain, Byron was well aware of Christian's potential as a ready-made, real-life Romantic hero, but chose to portray him in a less than sympathetic light, perhaps for aesthetic reasons as much as for the reason he gave in a letter to Leigh Hunt: that he should not 'run counter to the reigning stupidity altogether—otherwise they will say that I am eulogizing *Mutiny*'.[281]

Certainly the first canto of *The Island* describes the mutiny from the point of view of Bligh's *Voyage*, which Byron follows closely, describing Bligh as 'gallant' and 'bold' without a mention of tyranny or anything of the sort.[282] The lack of fair balance in Bligh's version is more than compensated for, however, by the Miltonic contrast it provides between the 'hell' of Christian's conscience and the paradise of Tahiti. Thus Byron's Christian cries out in guilt, as Bligh reported, 'I am in Hell! in Hell!' and Byron elaborates on Bligh's poetical picture of the tempting delights of Tahiti for rootless sailors 'void of connections' other than 'female connections' at Tahiti:

> Young hearts, which languished for some sunny isle,
> Where summer years and summer women smile;
> Men without country, who, too long estranged,
> Had found no native home, or found it changed,
> And, half uncivilized, preferred the cave
> Of some soft savage to the uncertain wave—
> The gushing fruits that Nature gave untilled;
> The wood without a path but where they willed;
> The field o'er which promiscuous plenty poured
> Her horn; the equal land without a lord.[283]

Byron adds to Bligh's poetical picture the political delights of Tahiti, 'the equal land', but he contrasts the liberty acquired by the guilty mutineers with the liberty naturally possessed by the innocent South Sea islanders:

> 'Huzza! for Otaheite!' was the cry;
> How strange such shouts from sons of Mutiny![284]

The guilty sailors who

> preferred the cave
> Of some soft savage to the uncertain wave

will all, with one exception, find a South Sea 'grave', not a South Sea 'cave'. The rhyme 'wave/cave' is used nine times in the poem, the rhyme 'wave/grave' three times, and the rhyme 'cave/grave' once.[285] Only one sailor, or man of the 'wave', will find a cave, as we shall see, a cave beneath the waves, and thus escape the grave.

Byron passes over his mutineers' stay at Tahiti, and his second canto opens with a song 'taken', as he acknowledges in a note, 'from an actual song of the Tonga Islanders, of which a prose translation is given in Mariner's Account of the Tonga Islands'.[286] Byron's song, we learn, is not sung on the Tongan Islands, but on Toobonai, in the 'tropic afternoon', when the wind began

> to urge the wave
> All gently to refresh the thirsty cave,
> Where sat the songstress with the stranger boy,
> Who taught her passion's desolating joy.[287]

The 'stranger boy', the refreshing wave, is Torquil, raised in the Hebrides, a detail that allows Byron to identify with him by way of a personal digression on his own childhood memories of the Highlands.[288] The songstress of the 'thirsty cave' is Neuha, once a ferocious Tongan chief in Martin and Mariner's *Account*, now the first full-blooded Polynesian girl of European romance.[289] The Oberea of the versifiers of the 1770s was full-blooded but not a heroine of romance, while Christina, very much the heroine of romance, was the daughter of an Englishman. Neuha is neither a prim Christina nor a wanton Oberea:

> Voluptuous as the first approach of sleep;
> Yet full of life—for through her tropic cheek
> The blush would make its way, and all but speak;
> The sun-born blood suffus'd her neck, and threw
> O'er her clear nut-brown skin a lucid hue,
> Like coral reddening through the darkened wave,
> Which draws the diver to the crimson cave.[290]

The image of the cave, representing the South Sea island refuge, is here extended by Byron so that Neuha herself is a cave. This suggests the sexual connection between Neuha, 'the thirsty cave', and Torquil, the refreshing wave, and also the powerful presence in *The Island* of one of the two fundamental, archetypal metaphors of the imaginary South Seas, in which the South Sea island is symbolized either by the nubile, welcoming island girl, or by the threatening, cannibal male. In Byron's treatment of Torquil the relationship between the stranger 'wave' and the island 'cave' is sexual but innocent, although in Byron's references to the other mutineers the ocean wave is associated with the mutineers' crime and is incompatible with the natural innocence of the island cave. Torquil and Neuha, however, 'the half savage and the whole', are

> Both children of the isles, . . .
> Both nourish'd amidst Nature's native scenes.[291]

Byron sustains the South Sea idyll of Torquil and Neuha at length and without irony, but it is abruptly interrupted by comedy, in the form of Torquil's fellow-mutineer, Ben Bunting, identifiable by his dress as a beachcomber—a sailor turned South Sea islander—and notable as the first of his kind in fiction. 'A seaman in a savage masquerade', Ben Bunting wears a 'somewhat scanty mat' in place of 'inexpressibles and hat'.[292] His comic appearance serves to divide the idyllic from the tragic, however, for he brings news to Torquil that a ship has come to capture the mutineers and they must stand and fight.

The third canto opens when the 'fight was o'er' and only a few surviving mutineers remain uncaptured, including the interesting ones, whose hopes that

> their distant caves
> Might still be missed amidst the world of waves

are dashed:

> Their sea-green isle, their guilt-won paradise,
> No more could shield their virtue or their vice.[293]

The men of the waves drink and wash their wounds in a South Sea island stream,

> Close on the wild, wide ocean, yet as pure
> And fresh as innocence.[294]

Christian at least reappears in the poem, heroic but guilty, like Milton's Satan, his 'locks . . . like startled vipers o'er his brow', and Neuha arrives with islanders and canoes to effect the mutineers' escape.[295] Hotly pursued by boats into the fourth canto, the canoes take separate directions and Neuha, who accompanies Torquil, takes him, not to a paradisal isle, but up to a rock so forbidding that Torquil wonders:

> Is this a place of safety, or a grave,
> And yon huge rock the tombstone of the wave?[296]

Calling to him to follow, she dives and disappears without trace into the sea, and he dives after her. When they resurface, out of sight of their baffled pursuers, Neuha explains:

> Around she pointed to a spacious cave,
> Whose only portal was the keyless wave.[297]

Byron explains in a note: 'Of this cave (which is no fiction) the original will be found in the 9th chapter of "Mariner's Account of the Tonga Islands". I have taken the poetical liberty to transplant it to Toobonai.'[298] Not only the cave, to which Mariner himself dived, but its use, according to Tongan legend, as a secret refuge for lovers pursued by enemies, is derived from Martin and Mariner's account of Tonga.[299] So the Tongan cave '(which is no fiction)' has provided the central image of *The Island*, the image of the South Sea cave from which Byron has formed the pattern 'wave/cave/grave' to be found in his plot as well as in his rhymes.

Christian and the others find another 'rock', but no cave, and, dismissing their native allies, prepare for their last stand—and fall:

> They stood, the three, as the three hundred stood
> Who dyed Thermopylae with holy blood.
> But, ah! how different! 'tis the *cause* makes all,
> Degrades or hallows courage in its fall.[300]

With Torquil safely hidden in his cave, Byron can now open the grave that befits a 'guilt-won paradise':

> Their life was shame, their epitaph was guilt.
> And this they knew and felt, at least the one,
> The leader of the band he had undone;
>
> .   .   .   .
>
> The chances were in favour of his fall:
> And such a fall![301]

Preserved till last, heroic but guilty, Christian,

>   like a serpent, coiled
> His wounded, weary form, to where the steep
> Looked desperate as himself along the deep;
> Cast one glance back, and clenched his hand, and shook
> His last rage 'gainst the earth which he forsook;
> Then plunged: the rock below received like glass
> His body crushed into one gory mass.[302]

Whether or not Christian's fall was suggested by the mistaken account in the *Quarterly Review*, it certainly suits Byron's theme, itself suggested by the implied contrast in Bligh's *Voyage* between the hell of Christian's guilt and the paradise of Tahiti. But we should not forget Torquil and Neuha, the wave and the cave suggested by Mariner's *Account*, for theirs is another story, with another theme, and *The Island* closes with their return to Toobonai to a feast of celebration:

> A night succeeded by such happy days
> As only the yet infant world displays.[303]

Thus Byron is able to combine in *The Island* the two major South Sea island themes: the paradise lost (by Christian) and the paradise regained (by Torquil). While Christian is very much the Byronic hero, Byron's identification with Torquil stretched further than their common Highland childhood. Sailing, a few months after writing *The Island*, to his death in Greece, Byron told a travelling companion that, if his Greek venture failed, he intended 'to obtain by purchase, or otherwise, some small island in the South Sea, to which . . . he might retire for the remainder of his life'.[304] In a more flippant mood, he had no doubt that the public would also prefer the idyll of Torquil to the tragedy of Christian. 'I will bet you a flask of Falernum', he wrote to Leigh Hunt, 'that . . . the most *pamby* portions of the Toobonai Islanders—will be the most agreeable to the enlightened Public.'[305]

But the story of the *Bounty* was also agreeable to the public. John Barrow, the Second Secretary at the Admiralty, wrote in his own historical account, *The Mutiny and Piratical Seizure of H.M.S. Bounty* (1831):

The story in itself is replete with interest. We are taught by *The Book* of sacred history, that the disobedience of our first parents entailed on our globe of earth a sinful and a suffering race: in our time there has sprung up from the most abandoned of this sinful family—from pirates, mutineers, and murderers—a little society which, under the precepts of that sacred volume, is characterized by religion, morality, and innocence. The discovery of this happy people, as unexpected as it was accidental, and all that regards their condition and history, partake so much of the romantic, as to render the story not ill adapted for an epic poem. Lord Byron, indeed, has partially treated the subject; but by blending two incongruous stories, and leaving both of them imperfect, and by mixing up fact with fiction, has been less felicitous than usual.[306]

What Barrow found infelicitous in *The Island* is Byron's mixture of fact and fiction and of 'two incongruous stories': the stories of Christian and Torquil, of paradise lost and paradise regained. But Barrow's own view of the literary potential of the historical facts is clearly rather similar, except that the fictitious idyll of Toobonai is to be replaced by the true parable of Pitcairn. In Barrow's view the story of the *Bounty* mutineers is a story of paradise lost by 'the disobedience of our first parents', an act of disobedience symbolically repeated by the mutiny, followed by paradise regained on Pitcairn—'a little society which . . . is characterized by religion, morality, and innocence'. As we have noticed, Mary Russell Mitford also rendered the story of the *Bounty* as a story of paradise lost and regained.

While Pitcairn seemed to Barrow an 'enviable little Eden', he had heard quite different reports of Tahiti and the Tahitians:

All their usual and innocent amusements have been denounced by the missionaries, and, in lieu of them, these poor people have been driven to seek for resources in habits of indolence and apathy: that simplicity of character, which atoned for many of their faults, has been converted into cunning and hypocrisy; and drunkenness, poverty, and disease have thinned the island of its former population to a frightful degree . . . —and there is but too much reason to ascribe this diminution to praying, psalm-singing, and dram-drinking.[307]

The missionaries who had retreated from Tahiti to Port Jackson, Australia, began to return in 1811, to the neighbouring island of Moorea, where Pomare lived in exile and sought conversion and the support of the white man's God in regaining his kingdom. Inspired, his forces defeated the pagan forces and, at the end of 1815, King Pomare and the missionaries were re-established, victorious, in Tahiti. This was a turning point, and the victory was followed by mass conversions and enthusiasm, a number of new missionaries—notably William Ellis, who brought a

printing press, and John Williams, who would become a powerful propagandist for
the mission back in Britain—arriving in 1817 to cater for the demand. Pomare
himself regally turned the press on the first page of the first text to be printed in
the South Seas, in June 1817, a spelling primer, soon followed by a catechism and
the Tahitian translation, with which Pomare also assisted, of the Gospel according
to St Luke.[308] But old Tahitian habits died hard and some new ones were all too
easily acquired. Depravity, promiscuity, and dancing continued to distress the
missionaries, as did Pomare's own royal behaviour, described in a passage from
the missionary William Crook's journal which was omitted from publication in the
Transactions of the Missionary Society:

One painful thing is the spiritual & temporal state of the King who arrived this
morning . . . looking very gloomy & sulky as usual, under the influence of two bottles of
spirits . . . At dinner his detestable pander [a *mahu*, a transvestite] sat along side of him on
a low seat . . . Mr Nott reports that . . . when he is translating the Scriptures with the King,
he (Mr. N) on one couch & the King on another this detestable wretch is frequently between
them, and he is obliged to turn his head from them to his book to avoid seeing what passes
& still gets his ears shocked with that he hears.[309]

Southey took an early interest in the Tahitian mission, which explains why the
poet who had once written of the 'many inducements' of Tahiti had decided by
1803 that the Tahitians were 'the most degraded of the human species'.[310] He
rejoiced at Pomare's conversion: 'His letters are in my last Evangelical Magazine
. . . This conversion may, very probably, lead to [Tahiti's] complete civilisation.
Human sacrifices would, of course, be abolished, and schools established. His
Majesty himself writes a remarkably good hand.'[311] Chateaubriand, however, like
Barrow, portrayed missionary Tahiti as a version of paradise lost, mourning its fate
in the introduction to his *Voyage en Amérique* (1826):

Otaïti a perdu ses dances, ses choeurs, ses moeurs voluptueuses. Les belles habitantes de la
nouvelle Cythère, trop vantées peut-être par Bougainville, sont aujourd'hui, sous leurs
arbres à pain et leurs élégants palmiers, des puritaines qui vont au prêche, lisent l'Ecriture
avec des missionnaires méthodistes, controversent du matin au soir, et expient dans un
grand ennui la trop grande gaîté de leurs mères. On imprime à Otaïti des Bibles et des
ouvrages ascétiques.[312]

The Russian explorer, Otto von Kotzebue, who visited Tahiti in 1824, gave in
his account of his voyage, translated into English as *A New Voyage Round the
World* (1830), a report of the kind that Barrow and Chateaubriand had heard:

By order of the Missionaries, the flute, which once awakened innocent pleasure, is heard no
more. No music but that of the psalms is suffered in Tahiti: dancing, mock-fights, and
dramatic representations are no longer permitted. Every pleasure is punished as a sin,
among a people whom Nature destined to the most cheerful enjoyment.[313]

'False!' retorts a commentator in the margin of the London Missionary Society's
copy of Kotzebue's *Voyage*, which registers the missionaries' indignation at the

'tremendous lies' and 'diabolical falsehood' of Kotzebue and his 'debauched & unprincipled' crew.[314] Kotzebue's *Voyage* did indeed contain many errors, as the missionary William Ellis was able to point out in his *A Vindication of the South Sea Missions from the Misrepresentations of Otto von Kotzebue* (1831), but Ellis's main dispute with Kotzebue was over a matter of opinion: the good or bad effects of the missionaries on the Tahitians. Ellis attributed Kotzebue's bad opinion, in 'real fact', to his 'mortification' at the discovery that the Tahitians were no longer the 'lascivious race' described by Wallis (i.e. Hawkesworth), Bougainville, and others.[315] This 'change in character and manners' was undoubtedly an improvement, according to Ellis:

No one can have read the accounts of the most transient visits of early voyagers, without disgust at the manners they describe; . . . deeds, in broad open day, so gross and horrid, that the slightest notice of them would be to outrage every feeling of delicacy and propriety implanted by nature, or cherished by religion . . . Now what is the fact? In 1815, 16, and 17, the people embraced Christianity . . . The virtue of chastity was inculcated and maintained; Christian marriage was instituted soon after; . . . and whatever deviations may have arisen, the great principle is uniformly maintained to this day.[316]

It was indeed 'the fact' that the Tahitians had changed—for the worse, according to Kotzebue, for the better, according to Ellis, who suggested that, in their re-formed conditions, 'there is a striking resemblance between the inhabitants of Pitcairn's Island and those of Tahiti'.[317]

Ellis had previously published his *Polynesian Researches* (1829), combining a history of the South Sea mission with a quantity of information about the indigenous cultures of the Polynesian islands. 'A more interesting book than this, in all its parts, we have never perused', began Southey's review of *Polynesian Researches*, initiating a connection with the literary missionary, who visited the poet laureate at Keswick and received his criticisms and corrections of an unpublished epic poem which Ellis produced on the subject of Pomare's victory and the defeat of idolatry in Tahiti.[318] Ellis's London Missionary Society colleague, William Henry, one of those who came on the *Duff*, was also something of a poet, and in May 1822 he penned 'Lines composed on the building of a Christian Church . . . upon the ruins of the Royal Marae', which contains some observations (elucidated by a page of anthropological footnotes) on the rites formerly practised on the site of the new church:

Just now a *human victim* fresh arrives,
And the sage Priest plucks from it both its eyes,
And on his blood stain'd hand doth rudely place,
And them present before his Sovereign's face.

His royal mouth the Sovereign opens wide,
The priest obsequious doth the morsel guide
Quite near his lips; then gently turning round,
Doth cast the eye-balls on the sacred ground.

According to Henry's 'Notes explanatory of some allusions etc. in the above lines':
'Sometimes the right eye only was plucked out & presented on these occasions.'[319]

Coleridge, during the course of a two and three-quarter hour conversational
monologue at Highgate, made it clear that he felt that his youthful tears over the
grave of the South Sea Island prince had been shed in error:

Christianity brings immense advantages to a savage. It is an evident preferment for him.
The missionaries have done a great deal for us in clearing up our notions about savage
nations. What an immense deal of harm Captain Cook's *Voyages* did in that way! Sailors,
after being a long time at sea, found a fertile island, and a people of lax morals, which were
just the things they wanted; and of course there never were such dear, good, kind, amiable
people. We know now that they were more detestably licentious than we could have
imagined.[320]

In a letter Southey tells of Coleridge's scheme for putting an end to Tahitian
wickedness once and for all, 'by extirpating the bread-fruit from their island, and
making them live by the sweat of their brows'.[321]

7

Of the Cannibals

Il semble que nous n'avons autre mire de la verité et de la raison que l'exemple
et idée des opinions et usances du païs où nous sommes.

(Montaigne, 'Des cannibales')[1]

As Coleridge noticed, the missionaries who came to the South Seas at the end of
the eighteenth century had changed the image of the South Sea savage. This
change he understood as fact replacing fiction: 'The missionaries have done a great
deal for us in clearing up our notions about savage nations ... of course there
never were such dear, good, kind, amiable people. We know now that they were
more detestably licentious than we could have imagined.'[2]

Thus Coleridge reviewed the South Sea savage from the vantage point of
Highgate Hill, placing his faith in one kind of text rather than another. The kind
he believed to be fact can be represented by the report of an American missionary,
Richard Armstrong, who spent eight months in an attempt to establish a mission
on the island of Nukuhiva in the Marquesas, and later published 'A Sketch of
Marquesian Character' in the *Hawaiian Spectator* of January 1838. Much of
Armstrong's own experience could not be given as evidence, because 'the scenes
of licentiousness' he observed 'were too shocking ever to be narrated by either pen
or tongue'.[3] Even the most mundane facts could not be written or read: 'Were we
to give a *matter of fact* account of the common every-day talk of those islanders,
our reader would cast the paper away from him as though his very fingers were
polluted by it.'[4] But conclusions could be drawn from the unmentionable evidence:

In point of morals, the Marquesians must be classed with the lowest of our species. Nothing
we have ever beheld in the shape of depravity in other parts of the world will compare for
a moment with their shameful and shameless iniquities. The blackest ink that ever stained
paper is none too dark to describe them ... In attempting to form a correct conception of
Marquesian character, you ... must imagine a human being, in mere physical qualities
equal to any of the race, but in morals, barren of every thing that adorns human nature;
destitute of regard for the authority of God or man, honor or law, decency or propriety.
Unaccountably mean in his dealings, filthy in his habits and conversation, savage in his
temper, a cannibal by education, ungrateful for favors, cruel to his enemies, treacherous to
his friends.[5]

The same number of the *Hawaiian Spectator* contained a discussion of 'Reports
on the condition of the unevangelized' by R. Tinker, another missionary. He
considered the difficulty of describing peoples of other cultures and called for

empirical evidence: 'Let a writer state what he sees, what he knows, what he hears—but not give us inferences and conclusions for facts, especially when he reasons from erroneous data.'[6] He had in front of him 'two sketches of Marquesian character', one 'by the master of a merchantman which anchored there a few years since', which he quoted:

The Nuuhivans . . . are decidedly the finest looking and best disposed natives in the South Seas. Nor can civilization in my opinion make them either better or happier. They are like children of one family dwelling in unity and peace, generous to an extreme; they would divide what they got in trade, and share it with all around them . . . if there be a terrestrial Paradise, or happiness in this mundane sphere, it is there.[7]

Tinker ridiculed this report of 'Paradise, and beings dwelling in it beautiful and pure as the primitive pair', subjected each phrase to fierce analysis, and then asked: 'But are there no better reporters abroad? Yes, there are. To them we turn. The second sketch of Marquesian character to which reference has been made, is in this number of the Hawaiian Spectator . . . It speaks for itself.'[8]

But the ignoble savage did not simply displace the noble savage. The missionaries, far from 'clearing up our notions about savage nations', as Coleridge believed, had intensified civilized confusion about the savage. In the first half of the nineteenth century, savages from the same islands were described very differently. A. J. von Krusenstern, commander of a Russian ship which visited Nukuhiva in 1804, reported of the Nukuhivans:

that they have neither social institutions, religion, nor humane feelings in any degree whatever,—in a word, that no traces of good qualities are to be found among them; that they undoubtedly belong to the very worst of mankind, and at at any rate that no one can quarrel with me for calling them savages.[9]

According to the missionary Robert Thomson, a member of a London Missionary Society team which followed the American mission to the Marquesas in the 1830s, with no better success,

In lying and theft the Marquesan finds few competitors; in licentiousness he is unrivalled. Every dark crime wh[ich] contaminates the mind, sweeps from the heart every tender and noble feeling, stains the polluted soul of the Marquesan; haughty and vindictive; cruel and ungrateful, he stands forth a most revolting character, a living blot on Natures brow. Mercy is a stranger to his bosom and his hand is often wet with blood. Selfishness is his ruling passion, the mainspring of every action; hospitality he never knew, and if one spark of kindness is ever struck from his flinty bosom, it is in hopes of an equivalent in return.[10]

An American naval officer, David Porter, took a different view of the Marquesan character, as he observed it on the island of Nukuhiva in 1813:

a more honest, or friendly and better disposed people could not exist under the sun. They have been stigmatized by the name of savages; it is a term wrongly applied; they rank high in the scale of human beings, whether we consider them morally, or physically. We find them brave, generous, honest, and benevolent, acute, ingenious, and intelligent, and the beauty and regular proportions of their bodies correspond with the perfections of their minds.[11]

Obviously these contradictory reports cannot be representations of fact. To adapt Coleridge's conclusion: 'Of course there never were such dear, good, kind, amiable . . . detestably licentious' people. There were no people so bad *and* so good at Nukuhiva, and no people so bad *or* so good. Yet these travellers' descriptions, so particular on the issue of the savage character, were not fictions in any ordinary sense. They were the reports of eyewitnesses, not of imaginary travellers like Gulliver or Crusoe. Because of the controversy about the savage it was crucial that travellers, whether sailors or missionaries, should act as scientific observers, reporters of fact, who would once and for all 'clear up our notions'. Thus Porter's account aims to present the real truth about the Marquesans, who 'have been stigmatized by the name of savages'. Thus another American sailor who visited Nukuhiva reacted, not only to the Marquesan character, but to previous 'tales' about them:

So pure and upright were they in all the relations of life, that entering their valley, as I did, under the most erroneous impressions of their character, I was soon led to exclaim in amazement: 'Are these the ferocious savages, the blood-thirsty cannibals of whom I have heard such frightful tales!'[12]

So, once again, fact about the savages replaced fiction—'frightful tales'. But was it fact? The publisher's reader reported to the house of Harper in New York that 'this work if not as good as Robinson Crusoe seems to be not far behind it'.[13] And Harper rejected the first work of the great American novelist, Herman Melville, because 'it was impossible that it could be true and therefore was without real value'.[14] The author of ' "Typee" "Piddledee" &c' (as he called his own early works) came to resent the fame of his South Sea books and the name they brought him of 'Mr. Typee'.[15] As he wrote to Nathaniel Hawthorne in 1851, the year of the publication of *Moby-Dick*: 'What "reputation" H.M. has is horrible. Think of it! To go down to posterity is bad enough, any way; but to go down as a "man who lived among the cannibals"!'[16]

But, at the very beginning of his literary career, it was exactly this reputation that Melville sought to establish. In London his brother Gansevoort, recently appointed Secretary to the American Legation, took Melville's manuscript to the publisher John Murray, who considered including the work in his 'Colonial and Home Library' of authentic travel narratives. But Murray was suspicious of Melville's narrative, which seemed to him to be the work of 'a practised writer' rather than of a man who had truly lived among the cannibals.[17] While Gansevoort assured the sceptical publisher that the author was 'a mere novice in the art' and that 'the adventurer, and the writer of the adventure are one & the same person', Melville supplied 'three new chapters' which Gansevoort told Murray would 'go far to give a more life-like air to the whole, an[d] parry the incredulity of those who may be disposed to regard the work as an ingenious fiction'.[18] Murray accepted

Gansevoort's assurances and Melville's book, and so *Typee* ('the title I always intended', said Melville) was published as *Narrative of a Four Months' Residence Among
the Natives of a Valley of the Marquesas Islands; or, A Peep at Polynesian Life* on 21
February 1846.[19] Meanwhile Gansevoort, probably with the help of Washington
Irving, had interested Irving's American publishers, Wiley and Putnam, in *Typee*.
In Mr Putnam's opinion, 'it had all the interest of Robinson Crusoe, superadded
to that of being a work of fact', and an American edition followed the British
edition on 17 March 1846, with the title *Typee: A Peep at Polynesian Life During
a Four Months' Residence in a Valley of the Marquesas.*[20]

Some of the reviewers regarded Melville's first work as fact, some of them
regarded it as fiction and some were undecided, but few of them ignored the
issue.[21] The London *Spectator* was undecided:

Much of the book is not beyond the range of invention, especially by a person acquainted
with the Islands, and with the fictions of De Foe; and we think that several things have been
heightened for effect, if indeed this artistical principle does not pervade the work. Many of
the incidents, however, seem too natural to be invented by the author.[22]

The New York *Gazette and Times* spoke of 'our American Crusoe' while, in
London, *Douglas Jerrold's Shilling Magazine* believed in 'a *real* Robinson Crusoe'
and the reviewer of the *John Bull* wrote that, 'if there be really such a person as
Herman Melville, he has either employed a Daniel Defoe to describe his adventures, or is himself both a Defoe and an Alexander Selkirk'.[23] Although the Christian press was critical as well as sceptical, resenting Melville's unflattering portrayal
of the missionaries, most of Melville's first reviews were favourable. The *Almanack
of the Month* lampooned the critical debate and its conclusion:

Alleged Forgery.—An individual who gave the name of Herman Melville was brought up
on a charge of having forged several valuable documents relative to the Marquesas, in which
he decribed himself to have been formerly resident. A good deal of conflicting evidence was
brought forward on both sides, and it was obvious that whether the papers were forgeries
or not, the talent and ingenuity of Herman Melville were of themselves sufficient to
recommend him very favourably to a literary tribunal.[24]

In the midst of this controversy, on 1 July 1846, one of Melville's characters
came forward to defend him, his companion in *Typee*, Richard Tobias Greene,
who announced in a letter to the Buffalo *Commercial Advertiser* that: 'I am the true
and veritable "Toby", yet living, and I am happy to testify to the entire accuracy
of the work so long as I was with Melville, who makes me figure so very largely in
it.'[25] This announcement was followed ten days later by the publication in the
Commercial Advertiser of a further letter from Greene, giving 'Toby's Own Story'
of events after his separation from Melville on the island of Nukuhiva.[26]

Melville was delighted and wrote to Murray a few days after the publication of
'Toby's Own Story':

to inform you that 'Toby' who figures in my narrative has come to life—tho' I had long supposed him to be dead . . . Toby's appearance has produced quite a lively sensation here—and 'Truth is stranger than Fiction' is in every body's mouth . . . The impression which Toby's letter has produced is this—ie—that every thing about it bears the impress of truth.—Indeed, the whole Typee adventure is now regarded as a sort of Romance of Real Life.[27]

Murray, however, was still not satisfied, as we can tell from Melville's letter of 2 September 1846:

You ask for 'documentary evidences' of my having been at the Marquesas—in Typee.— Dear Sir, how indescribably vexatious, when one really feels in his very bones that he has been there, to have a parcel of blockheads question it!—Not (let me hurry to tell you) that Mr John Murray comes under that category—Oh no—Mr Murray I am ready to swear stands fast by the faith, beleiving 'Typee' from Preface to Sequel—He only wants something to stop the mouths of the senseless sceptics—men who go straight from their cradles to their graves & never dream of the queer things going on at the antipodes.[28]

He had written to the owners of the whaling ship *Acushnet*, he assured Murray, and hoped to receive 'a copy of that part of the ship's log which makes mention of two rascals running away at Nukuheva—to wit Herman Melville and Richard T. Greene'.[29] But Murray was still asking for 'documentary evidence' in 1848, as we can tell from Melville's correspondence with Murray, in which his exasperation with his publisher's persistent requests is mingled with promises of his fantastical third book, *Mardi*, which 'shall afford the strongest presumptive evidence of the truth of Typee & Omoo [his second book] by the sheer force of contrast'.[30]

Modern scholars eventually procured the 'documentary evidence' that Melville had failed to supply, their researches revealing in 1935 that the autobiographical basis for *Typee* was confirmed by Captain Pease of the *Acushnet*, who had testified to John Stetson, American vice-commercial agent at Lahaina, Hawaii, that: 'Richard T Greene & Herman Mellvile deserted at Nukehiva July 9th 1842'.[31] Then, in 1940, evidence was found and published which settled a question that had been a matter of—as it transpired—fairly accurate speculation by literary historians. This evidence came to light indirectly, as a result of the discovery, amongst the records of the British Consulate at Papeete, Tahiti, of a 'packet of papers, rather badly insect-holed, but otherwise in good condition', which established the historical reality of the mutiny Melville described in *Omoo*, the sequel to *Typee*.[32] Amongst these papers were the 'affidavits' referred to in *Omoo*, which were produced at the trial of Melville and the other mutineers, and also a certificate written by the acting British consul, Wilson, which lists the men who mutinied, including 'Herman Melville Able Seaman, as per Articles Signed at the Island of Nukahiva, Marquesas, on the 9th day of August, 1842'.[33] Thus Melville's stay on shore at Nukuhiva can be precisely dated, from 9 July 1842, until 9 August: a period of thirty-one days. If we accept the internal evidence of *Typee*, that Melville spent six days in the

mountains of Nukuhiva before descending to the valley where he lived with its
inhabitants, then his residence in that valley can have lasted only twenty-five days.
The six days spent in covering a distance 'not over five miles' are easily credible—
as Melville would not have known the 'well-known trail' taken twenty-five years
later by a curious explorer of his text—but, even if we reject, as fictitious, the six
days spent in the mountains, the period of Melville's residence in the valley is a
maximum of thirty-one days, which is about four weeks, not the 'Four Months'
Residence' of his title.[34]

The biographical evidence confirms the partial, if not total, truth of *Typee*, but
what of the ethnographic evidence? James Frazer, in *The Belief in Immortality and
the Worship of the Dead* (1922), was pleased to accept the testimony of 'a runaway
American sailor, Hermann Melville', on a number of occasions.[35] He cites *Typee* on
Marquesan tattooing, marriage customs, mourning rites, ancient monuments, and,
of course, on the Marquesan afterlife, explaining to the interested reader how the
Marquesan 'soul sailed away in a coffin shaped like a canoe' (like Queequeg's in
Moby-Dick, another work by the 'runaway American sailor').[36]

Frazer, like Coleridge, had never seen the South Seas, but the facts about
Marquesan culture are obscured from modern anthropologists—who travel to
observe the cultures they describe—by a gulf of time instead of space. Civilization
has made the savage cultures of the South Seas more accessible, but it has also
made them less savage. By the beginning of the twentieth century the population
of Nukuhiva, about 6,000 at the time of Melville's visit, had declined to 682, and,
with the passing of the Marquesans, their culture too was dying.[37] Under the French
colonial rule Melville saw being established at Nukuhiva in 1842, indigenous
Marquesan culture was discouraged and gradually destroyed. First native dress—
or undress—was banned and then, as a modern anthropologist says, 'native dances,
musical instruments, songs and even tattooing were banned also, so that by 1890
the culture was well broken'.[38] In the first decade of this century Jack London
came to Melville's Marquesan valley and wrote: 'He saw a garden. We saw a
wilderness.'[39] The 'valley of Typee', he reported in 1908, 'is the abode of some
dozen wretched creatures, afflicted by leprosy, elephantiasis, and tuberculosis'.[40]
By the time the anthropologists came to the Marquesas the culture they came to
study had almost vanished, surviving mainly in the memories of a few aged
Marquesans and in the texts of travellers like Melville.[41]

In 1920 a Mr and Mrs Handy from the Bernice P. Bishop Museum, Honolulu,
came and spent nine months in the Marquesas, examining the remnants of the
native culture and the travellers' texts. In her study, *Tattooing in the Marquesas*, Mrs
Willowdean Handy was sceptical of some of Melville's information and suspected
him of invention, although her reason for doubting him, that 'no memory [of such
practices] is discoverable today', is far from conclusive.[42] More positively, she also
suspected him of plagiarizing some of his ethnography from the accounts of
previous travellers.[43] That this latter suspicion was fully justified has been demonstrated by Russell Thomas and, at greater length, by Charles Anderson, whose

Melville in the South Seas (1939) contains the most detailed study of Melville's debt to the texts of previous travellers.[44] That Melville borrowed some of his information is not surprising, now that we know his own time for observation was much more limited than he pretended. When Frazer quoted the testimony of one traveller, Charles Stewart, on Marquesan polygamy, and added that 'Melville describes the custom in substantially the same way', he believed his comparison of the texts had confirmed the facts about Marquesan polygamy. Anderson compared the same texts in 1939 and came to a different conclusion: that 'Melville, as he wrote, apparently had Stewart's treatise open before him'.[45]

The 'two chief volumes to which *Typee* is indebted', as Anderson amply demonstrated, were Captain David Porter's *Journal of a Cruise Made to the Pacific Ocean* (1815) and the Reverend Charles Stewart's *A Visit to the South Seas* (1831).[46] Melville himself cites these two works in *Typee* as the two most important accounts of the Marquesas, although he denies any acquaintance with Porter's work:

Of this interesting group, but little account has ever been given . . . and all that we know about them is from a few general narratives. Among these, there are two that claim particular notice. Porter's 'Journal of the Cruise of the U.S. frigate Essex in the Pacific, during the late War', is said to contain some interesting particulars concerning the islanders. This is a work, however, which I have never happened to meet with; and Stewart, the chaplain of the American sloop of war Vincennes, has likewise devoted a portion of his book, entitled 'A Visit to the South Seas', to the same subject.[47]

Captain David Porter came to Nukuhiva in 1813 to refit his ship, the USS *Essex*. In order to do this in safety he was obliged, so he explains, to suspend his Anglo-American tribal war (the War of 1812) and engage in a Marquesan one. Having allied himself with the tribe, the Teii, inhabiting the valley where he landed, Porter found himself challenged by a rival tribe, who 'exposed their posteriors' to the Americans and were duly defeated.[48] He was then challenged by another tribe, Melville's future hosts, who 'said we were the posteriors and the privates of the Taeehs [the Teii]', and felt himself obliged to respond by invading their valley, encountering 'in our way several beautiful villages, which were set on fire', and killing several of its 'happy and heroic people'.[49] 'Peace now being established throughout the island, and the utmost harmony reigning', according to Porter, the people of 'Madison's Island' were 'all much pleased at being *Melleekees* [Americans], as they called themselves', and delighted to acknowledge President Madison as 'their new chief', until Porter sailed away.[50] These conflicts with the Marquesans, whom Porter admired very romantically ('They have been stigmatized by the name of savages'), he frequently regretted in his published *Journal of a Cruise*, but, so he argued, his attacks on them were necessary for the protection of his men (and also to ensure his supplies of supplicatory fruit and pigs):

Many may censure my conduct as wanton and unjust . . . But let such reflect a moment on our peculiar situation—a handful of men residing among numerous warlike tribes, liable every moment to be attacked by them, and all cut off; our only hopes of safety was in convincing them of our great superiority over them, and from what we had already seen, we must either attack them or be attacked.[51]

There is an apparent contradiction, then, in Porter's account, between his romantic sensibility and his military duty, but this contradiction is only apparent, because the more Porter battles, heroically and regretfully, with the 'happy and heroic' Marquesans, the more romantic the 'unhappy and heroic' Marquesans become.[52]

The missionary Charles Stewart came to Nukuhiva in 1829 as chaplain of the USS *Vincennes*. Although he had spent two years with the American mission at Hawaii, Stewart was by no means a typical missionary of the kind caricatured in cannibals' cooking pots, famous for their 'missionary position' and their opinion that 'Every prospect pleases, And only man is vile', an opinion Stewart quotes and rejects in his published account of his travels with the *Vincennes*, *A Visit to the South Seas*.[53] Certainly the exotic prospect pleased Stewart, for whom a Marquesan valley was 'more like a highly-wrought fancy sketch for a romance of the stage, than a scene in nature'.[54] The people were as pleasing as the prospect, however, and just as much a work of art:

Amidst objects at once so soft and sylvan, so unique and wild, and surrounded by a people whose admirably modeled figures and unclad limbs were in strict unison with the whole— I experienced feelings of admiration never excited by the novelty and romance of any circumstances in which I had before been placed. It seemed almost a fairy land; scarce less fascinating in its features, than the imaginary haunts pictured by the pens of genius as the abode of Calypso, or the happy valley of the Abyssinian prince.[55]

Amidst these scenes, 'scarce less fascinating' than those in the *Odyssey* or Samuel Johnson's *Rasselas*, some 'belles' caught Stewart's eye:

belles who need not fear a comparison, either in feature or form, with most who are the admiration of fairer circles at home. The whole scene formed a subject worthy of the pencil of a Murillo or a Wilkie. I would have given much for the talent of seizing it en passant, and did make the attempt.[56]

Of course there were aspects of the Marquesas that were not so romantic or artistic. Attending a festival in the territory of the Hapaa tribe, where he found himself, as usual, in 'fairy land', and 'transported' by the exotic novelty 'to the times of Cook', Stewart was suddenly shocked and 'hurried away in a horror of disgust'.[57] But this 'horror of disgust' came after seven pages of gushing admiration—for the scene (a grove 'which the muses themselves might covet'), the women ('their eyes have a rich brilliancy, softened by long glossy eyelashes'), the principal dancer ('his whole style more that of an Adonis than of an Apollo')—when, suddenly, Stewart was distracted from his sketching by some unmentionable 'licentiousness' and 'the charm at first felt from the novelty and wild beauty of the scene, was speedily broken'.[58] Only 'missionary instruction', he believed, could make Nukuhiva 'not only what it is now by nature—one of the most romantic

spots on the globe—but morally and spiritually *"the happy valley"* '.[59] Stewart's
report of his visit in the *Vincennes* was influential in sending the unsuccessful
American missionaries to Nukuhiva in 1833, and the *Vincennes*'s visit was perhaps
influential in sending Melville there, too, for his cousin Thomas Melville was a
midshipman on the *Vincennes*, and accompanied Stewart on a trip ashore to the
valley where Melville later lived.[60]

In their military and missionary roles, Porter and Stewart held appropriate
civilized opinions which were not to them incompatible with the Romantic, even
Rousseauist, opinions which are clearly manifest in their admiration for the
uncorrupted 'state of nature' which they both believed Marquesans to inhabit.
Porter compared the Nukuhivans to the Polynesians of other islands who

had long resided with white men; they had fallen into their vices, and indulged in the same
food; they were no longer in a state of nature; they had, like us, become corrupt, and while
the honest guileless face of the Nooaheevan shone with benevolence, good nature, and
intelligence, the downcast eye and sullen looks of the others marked their inferiority and
degeneracy.[61]

Stewart, probably with Porter's text before him, wrote:

The inhabitants [of Nukuhiva] are now, as they then [at the time of Porter's visit] were, in
an entire state of nature: and their primeval condition is in every respect unchanged, except
it may be in addition of corruption—among those in the immediate vicinity of the harbor
occasionally visited by ships—from a licentious intercourse with unprincipled white men
from civilized and Christian countries.[62]

And Melville, with Stewart's text before him (from which he was adapting a long
passage), wrote:

Its [Nukuhiva's] inhabitants have become [since the time of Porter's visit] somewhat corrupted, owing to their recent commerce with Europeans; but so far as regards their peculiar
customs and general mode of life, they retain their original primitive character, remaining
very nearly in the same state of nature in which they were first beheld by white men.[63]

Although Gansevoort Melville was correct in assuring Murray that 'the adventurer' of *Typee* 'and the writer of the adventure are one & the same person',
Melville was indeed, as the critic of the *John Bull* suggested, 'both a Defoe and an
Alexander Selkirk'. It is necessary to distinguish, therefore, rather awkwardly,
between Melville, the writer, and 'Melville', his adventurer. Melville the writer
was engaged in shaping his adventurer's story, as well as in adding details from
Porter and Stewart, and a literary critic pointed out some years ago that Melville
alludes in *Typee* to Milton's *Paradise Lost*.[64]

'Melville' and his companion 'Toby', while escaping from their ship and crawl-
ing up to the 'infernal' region of the mountains, are likened by Melville to 'a
couple of serpents', and 'Melville's' first glimpse of the valley of his residence
resembles Satan's first glimpse of Earth on his journey from Hell to Paradise.[65] As
Satan's first sight of Earth is likened by Milton to a 'prospect of some foreign land'

from 'some high-climbing hill', so 'Melville's' first sight of his valley from the mountains is likened by Melville to a prospect of Paradise: 'Had a glimpse of the gardens of Paradise been revealed to me I could scarcely have been more ravished with the sight'.[66] On entering the valley, starving after their days in the mountains, the fugitive sailors' 'first thought' is of 'the fruit', but now the predictable tendency of the imagery is interrupted, for they find 'the fruit, but to our chagrin they proved to be much decayed'.[67] Then 'Toby' recoils 'as if stung by an adder' when they see for the first time some savages of the potentially paradisal valley:

They were a boy and a girl, slender and graceful, and completely naked, with the exception of a slight girdle of bark, from which depended at opposite points two of the russet leaves of the bread-fruit tree. An arm of the boy, half screened from sight by her wild tresses, was thrown about the neck of the girl, while with the other he held one of her hands in his.[68]

The literary critic noticed that this passage 'recalls the famous scene in which Satan first views Adam and Eve', but he did not notice 'the exception of a slight girdle' and some leaves, which take us from Milton's prelapsarian Adam and Eve to his postlapsarian Adam and Eve:

> O how unlike
> To that first naked glory. Such of late
> Columbus found the American so girt . . .[69]

Thus Melville begins to confuse the alternative South Sea images of paradise and paradise lost, suggesting one and then the other. The young Adam and Eve in *Typee* are far from innocent: 'a couple of wilier young things than we afterwards found them to have been on this particular occasion never probably fell in any traveller's way.'[70] Sometimes 'Melville' is a 'poor devil' in *Typee*; sometimes it is the Marquesans who are 'so many demons'.[71]

Melville treats the image of childhood in *Typee* in much the same way. Often it is used, as one might expect, conventionally, to describe the primitive savages, who are 'childish'.[72] Thus Porter's opinion that 'in religion these people are mere children; their morais are their baby-houses, and their gods are their dolls' is echoed in *Typee*: 'The whole of these [religious] proceedings were like those of a parcel of children playing with dolls and baby houses.'[73] But, much more often, the image is reversed, so that 'Melville' is seen by the Marquesans as a 'child' and hand fed 'as if I were an infant' by the 'childish' savages who 'regard me as a froward child'.[74]

In time *Typee* ceased to be regarded as factual, the work of the runaway American sailor, and came to be regarded as symbolical, the work of the great American novelist, but fact and symbol are not incompatible in *Typee*. If 'Melville's' Marquesan servant and keeper, Kory-Kory, has 'the appearance of being decorated with a pair of horns', it was because of his Marquesan hairstyle, which can be seen clearly in a print in Langsdorff's *Voyages and Travels* (1813) (see Plate 5) and, as the missionary Thomson wrote in his unpublished report, 'gives them the appearance of being horned'.[75] If Kory-Kory, treating 'Melville' 'as if I were an infant, insisted upon feeding me with his own hands', it was because this was a Polynesian practice with a person under a taboo.[76] Kory-Kory's motherly care, like his devilish hair-style, had its foundation in fact.

This brings us to a central theme in *Typee*, a symbolic theme in which Melville neatly captures 'Melville's' ambivalence about his Marquesan life, in which he is continually being fed and often in fear of being eaten. 'Toby' points out the ambiguity of savage hospitality to 'Melville': 'Look at that Kory-Kory there!—has he not been stuffing you with his confounded mushes, just in the way they treat swine before they kill them? Depend upon it, we will be eaten.'[77] Page after page of Melville's documentation of the Marquesan diet has an artistic purpose in *Typee*, suggesting the delights of Marquesan life and also the potential danger. As Kory-Kory tells 'Melville': 'Ah, Typee! isn't it a fine place though!—no danger of starving here . . .'.[78] Ethnographic chapters promising the reader 'The Feast of the Calabashes' and 'A Midnight Banquet' hint at possible dangers other than starvation. Such are implied, for example, in this brief passage from a chapter on the Marquesan diet: 'Raw fish! Shall I ever forget my sensations when I first saw my island beauty devour one? Oh, heavens! Fayaway, how could you ever have contracted so vile a habit?'[79] As the missionary William Ellis wrote in his chapter on the Marquesas in *Polynesian Researches* (a work to which Melville refers in *Typee*): 'Even the tender-looking female will join, if permitted, in the horrid repast.'[80] Ellis was referring, of course, to cannibalism, and so, by implication, is Melville, expressing 'Melville's' fear that his lovely 'island beauty' might even love to eat him. When his ship first set its course for the Marquesas, 'Melville' had mixed expectations of a South Sea island: 'Naked houris—cannibal banquets'.[81] Now, as he looks at his 'naked houri', Fayaway (whose name, suggesting a fairy far away, is more plausibly rendered in a manuscript draft as 'Faaua'), the alternative possibility of 'cannibal banquets' is still running through his mind.[82]

'Melville's' divided feelings are correlated with his physical condition, for during much of his time in the valley he is incapacitated by a painful and swollen leg. It is to get medical help for 'Melville' that his companion 'Toby' leaves the valley, but he never returns and 'Melville', who was not allowed to leave, remains alone to ponder his fate. His leg hinders his chances of escaping, but, when it 'suddenly healed' and he is 'enabled to ramble', he no longer wishes to escape: 'I began to experience an elasticity of mind which placed me beyond the reach of those dismal forebodings to which I had so lately been a prey.'[83] Echoing Montaigne, who suggested in 'Des cannibales' that the civilized practice of torturing the living was more barbarous than the savage practice of eating the dead ('qu'il y a plus de barbarie à manger un homme vivant qu'à le manger mort'), 'Melville' now questions 'whether the mere eating of human flesh so very far exceeds in barbarity' the punishments and tortures 'which only a few years since [were] practised in enlightened England'.[84] 'The term "Savage" is', he thinks, 'often misapplied.'[85] The language of 'a certain tribe in the Pacific' (unspecified, and perhaps not unrelated to Montaigne's Brazilian Indians) 'is almost entirely destitute of terms to express the delightful ideas conveyed by our endless catalogue of civilized crimes'.[86] Indeed, 'four or five Marquesan Islanders sent to the United States as Missionaries might be quite as useful as an equal number of Americans despatched to the Islands in a similar capacity'.[87] A long catalogue of some of 'those thousand sources of irritation that the ingenuity of civilized man has created' duly follows, in the primitivist tradition Montaigne passed on from Ovid.[88]

In his 'altered frame of mind' 'Melville' is enthusiastic about the notorious Marquesan tribe he is living with:

I began to distrust the truth of those reports which ascribed so fierce and belligerent a character to the Typee nation . . . I could not avoid thinking that I had fallen in with a greatly traduced people, and I moralized not a little upon the disadvantage of having a bad name, which in this instance had given a tribe of savages, who were as pacific as so many lambkins, the reputation of a confederacy of giant-killers.[89]

Now free from 'disagreeable thoughts', he compares himself with Johnson's Rasselas: 'When I looked around the verdant recess in which I was buried, and gazed up to the summits of the lofty eminence that hemmed me in, I was well disposed to think that I was in the "Happy Valley".'[90] Melville's understanding of *Rasselas* is better than Stewart's, however, and there is irony in his language and in his allusion to the captivity of Rasselas, also 'hemmed . . . in', if not 'buried', in Johnson's original 'Happy Valley': 'When he looked round about him, he saw himself confined by the bars of nature which had never been broken.'[91]

'Melville's' physical well-being and corresponding 'frame of mind' are brought to an end by his hosts' insistence that he have his face tattooed, so that, as he says, he would never again 'have the *face* to return to my countrymen'.[92] He has to resist sustained pressure from the Marquesans: 'The only consolation afforded me was a choice of patterns: I was at perfect liberty to have my face spanned by three horizontal bars, after the fashion of my serving man's; or to have as many oblique stripes slanting across it.'[93] The reference to the 'fashion of my serving man's' tattoo (i.e. Kory-Kory's) makes the symbolic significance plain: 'His countenance . . . always reminded me of those unhappy wretches whom I have sometimes observed gazing out sentimentally from behind the grated bars of a prison window.'[94] The illustrations of Marquesan tattoo designs in Willowdean Handy's *Tattooing in the Marquesas* demonstrate vividly the factual basis of Melville's symbolism, depicting eleven faces all spanned by variations on the pattern of three bars (see Plate 6).[95]

As 'Melville' says, 'all my former desire to escape from the valley now revived with additional force', and his former mental and physical condition also returned: 'It was during the period I was in this unhappy frame of mind that the painful malady under which I had been laboring—after having almost completely subsided—began again to show itself, and with symptoms as violent as ever.'[96] In this 'unhappy frame of mind' his Marquesan hosts appear again as 'evil beings' and, almost immediately, 'Melville' discovers 'three human heads' in a package hanging 'over my head': 'I had discovered enough to fill me, in my present state of mind, with the most bitter reflections.'[97] It is in this 'state of mind', in which his 'imagination ran riot', that 'Melville' confirms his worst fears by discovering, in a 'vessel . . . which resembled in shape a small canoe', the 'disordered members of a human skeleton'.[98] This convinces 'Melville' (the character in the book, that is, not necessarily the author) that the people whose valley he is inhabiting are, in fact, cannibals, though a passage preceding his discovery of the 'evidence' might lead a careful reader to doubt this: 'It is a singular fact, that in all our accounts of cannibal tribes we have seldom received the testimony of an eye-witness to the revolting practice.'[99] 'Melville' has not been an eyewitness to the practice. He has had a 'slight glimpse' of the remains of a dead body in a canoe-shaped 'vessel' (which may be funerary, like Queequeg's, not culinary) while in an 'unhappy frame of mind' in which his 'imagination ran riot'.[100] That is how Melville presents the evidence for Marquesan cannibalism.

But what is the evidence for Marquesan cannibalism? There were many more beachcombers than Melville in the Marquesas. The missionary Robert Thomson, who spent some months at Nukuhiva in 1840, two years before Melville's visit, wrote in his report to the London Missionary Society that 'upon Nuuhiva there are at present from 20 to 30 such characters'.[101] Between Cook's rediscovery of the Marquesas in 1774 and the French appropriation of the islands in 1842, the year of Melville's visit, there were probably more than 150 Europeans and Americans who spent varying amounts of time, with varying degrees of assimilation, living with Marquesans.[102]

A. J. von Krusenstern and G. H. von Langsdorff, the commander and the naturalist of a Russian expedition which spent ten days at Nukuhiva in 1804, both affirmed Marquesan cannibalism as 'a well-established fact' in their published accounts, and Krusenstern was Ellis's authority for the cannibal *femme fatale*: 'Even the tender looking female, whose eyes beam nothing but beauty, will join, if permitted, in this horrid repast.'[103] But Krusenstern's and Langsdorff's accounts of Marquesan cannibalism depended entirely on the information they received from two beachcombers. One of these was the Frenchman, Joseph (or Jean) Kabris (or Cabri), who lived among the tribe in Melville's valley, was married and extensively tattooed (see Plate 7), and had almost forgotten his own name and language. 'All that he was able to say was, "Oui moi beaucoup François, Americanish ship, ah dansons la Carmagnole!" '[104] Kabris stayed too long aboard Krusenstern's ship and was thus transported by accident to Russia, where, Langsdorff informs us, he became 'teacher of swimming to the corps of marine cadets at Cronstadt' before returning to roam France exhibiting his tattoos.[105] On 22 September 1822, at Valenciennes, between the 'jeune fille pesant 400 livres' and the 'veau à trois têtes', he felt ill, and died on the 23rd, aged 42, and was buried between two other corpses to hide his skin from a local 'amateur de choses rares'.[106] A pamphlet published in Paris briefly and unreliably details his life and things Marquesan, including cannibalism.[107] The Russians' other beachcomber informant, Edward

Robarts, also married and tattooed, was one of the very few who (like Melville) wrote an account of his Marquesan life, before vanishing from historical knowledge at Calcutta.[108] In his simple and credible story, unpublished in his lifetime, Robarts tells of seeing a Marquesan priest gobble the remains of a young woman: 'He took a stone and broke the skull and took the Brains out and eat them raw.'[109]

David Porter was assured by his beachcomber authority, James Wilson, 'that the natives of this island were cannibals', although it appeared that Wilson had not actually 'seen them in the act of eating human flesh'.[110] 'Desirous of clearing up in my own mind a fact which so nearly concerned the character of a whole people', Porter investigated and reported that the Nukuhivans 'did not deny that they sometimes ate their enemies, at least so we understood them; but it is possible we may have misunderstood'.[111] He concluded generously that the Nukuhivans 'do not appear to deserve the stain which has been cast upon them'.[112] The missionary Thomson 'never witnessed' cannibalism himself, but he believed in it, and met a Spanish beachcomber at Nukuhiva who said he 'saw the body cooked and eaten'.[113] Thomson admitted, though, with judicious fairness, that: 'So little dependence can we place upon the statements even of the natives, that we are at a loss what to say upon this subject.'[114] A ship's doctor named John Coulter spent some time with the Marquesans on the island of Hiva Oa in 1833, and published his *Adventures in the Pacific* in Dublin in 1845, a year before Melville's *Typee*. According to his *Adventures*, Coulter submitted to his Marquesan hosts' keen desire that he 'be "tatooed", provided that neither my face nor hands should be touched'.[115] He also says that he witnessed the preparations for a feast after a tribal skirmish: 'they cut up the dead bodies of their enemies into convenient sizes, and rolled the pieces up in banana or plantain leaves' before placing them 'on the hot stones' for cooking.[116] But then he says: 'I must throw a veil over the feast of the following day, as I had only one look at the beginning of it, and left the arena sick to loathing: went off to the house, and did not leave it until the horrid scene was ended.'[117] We may not be wholly convinced by this 'one look'.

In *The Man-Eating Myth: Anthropology and Anthropophagy* (1979), the anthropologist Walter Arens surveyed some of the basic historical evidence of cannibalism and found that much of this evidence was merely circumstantial in modern accounts and highly suspect in older accounts. He found no account by a modern anthropologist who had actually been an eyewitness of the practice, and the rare accounts he found by travellers of former times almost always occurred in contexts where the account served to justify some civilized practice with regard to the 'cannibals', such as conversion to Christianity, enslavement, or colonial conquest. Arens's work pays too little attention to the Pacific evidence, and the opinion of the specialist ethnohistorians is that the Marquesans probably were cannibals, but there is nevertheless much truth in Arens's conclusion that 'cannibalism' was a civilized myth, having little relation to reality but great significance for those who believed in it, for whom it defined the savagery of others.[118]

Whatever the facts were about cannibalism in the Marquesas, certainly Melville in *Typee* has defined cannibalism as the product of a civilized observer's 'frame of mind'. For Melville has dramatically portrayed in the reactions of his protagonist, 'Melville', civilized ambivalence about the savage, ambivalence that depends, not on facts, but on fictions, on stories like his own. The missionary Stewart also recognized that the reputation of savages was based on fictions—the accounts of other travellers, of course, not his own. Thus he recounts a story which he has heard from the Nukuhivans about a French captain who kidnapped and maltreated a Marquesan chief in order to obtain food, his cruelty being followed by Marquesan reprisals and the slaughter of a member of his crew. Stewart comments:

it is in such aggression and barbarity, on the part of civilized and nominally Christian men, that more than half the reputed savageness of the heathen world has its origin . . . But the facts on which this assertion rests seldom reach the public ear or meet the public eye, unless it be in a version somewhat similar to that, which we may rightly suppose, the Frenchman in the case above related, to have given of the circumstance—communicated to us with all the freshness and feeling of just indignation—on his arrival at some one of his native ports. 'The ship——commanded by——has just entered our harbor, from a long voyage in the Pacific ocean. She has been peculiar[l]y unfortunate in the loss of several of her crew at the Washington Islands [the Marquesas], where she touched at Nukuhiva for refreshments. The islanders, it appears, are a very treacherous and ferocious people—a boat sent on shore for water was suddenly attacked by a party in ambush, and unhappily one of the crew perished; and the rest barely made their escape after being severely wounded!''[19]

Because the savages were the stuff of fictions it was the duty of every traveller to report what Stewart calls the 'facts'. Stewart realized that these 'facts' could depend on the observer's point of view, but he believed that, if only one took great care to avoid the extremes of primitivist and anti-primitivist points of view, one could actually arrive at the 'facts':

In every observation I have made on the genius and condition of the people, I have endeavoured to free myself from any bias, that might interfere with a candid exposition of their true character. There is a double danger to be guarded against on this point. A man of nice moral sensibility, and one alive to the purity of affection essential to genuine piety, is exposed, in a disgust at the licentiousness unavoidably obtruded on his notice, to lose sight of all that is pleasing and praiseworthy in the nature and condition of the inhabitants, and to think and speak of them only, as associated, in his mind, with a moral deformity and vileness that, in some respects, can scarce be equalled. On the other hand, the depraved and the guilty, regarding such traits with a lenient eye, or screening them from view with a mantle of brotherly kindness, are in hazard of imposing on the world a belief that none are so happy or so fair—that the islands themselves are an elysium, and their inhabitants a race exempt from the ordinary ills of life, who pass their time in uninterrupted joys—ignorant of sorrow and strangers to anxiety and care.

Both these extremes I would avoid; and have given you undisguised facts, so far as they could with propriety be presented, by which to prove, on the one hand, that . . . in general [the Marquesans] appear amiable and kind in their domestic and social relations, and in their intercourse with those who visit their distant shores. But on the other, that . . . they most unquestionably are deceitful and treacherous, vindictive and blood-thirsty, delighting in devastation and war, and accustomed to riot on the flesh of their fellows.[120]

So those are—without 'bias', and avoiding 'extremes'—the 'facts': the Marquesans appear 'amiable and kind' and are unquestionably 'vindictive and blood-thirsty'.

Like Stewart, Melville recognized that savages were the stuff of fiction: 'Even before visiting the Marquesas, I had heard from men who had touched at the group on former voyages some revolting stories in connection with these savages [the Typees].'[121] He proceeds to relate two of these 'stories' about 'the perfidious Typees'.[122] Later, among the people themselves, in his favourable 'frame of mind', 'Melville' considers 'all these terrible stories . . . nothing more than fables':

So pure and upright were they in all the relations of life, that entering their valley, as I did, under the most erroneous impressions of their character, I was soon led to exclaim in amazement: 'Are these the ferocious savages, the blood-thirsty cannibals of whom I have heard such frightful tales!'[123]

But then, in a different 'frame of mind', he discovers the 'evidence' to confirm these 'frightful tales'.

Melville's own tale dramatizes the civilized ambivalence about savages that results in 'amiable and kind' and 'vindictive and blood-thirsty' savages: those are the 'facts', and the fictions. Travellers' narratives like Stewart's were quests, as he says, for the 'undisguised facts' about the 'true character' of savages, savages about whom so many different stories were told, who inhabited a distant, different culture from which facts were inevitably far-fetched. But fact, that which is verifiable, cannot be far-fetched, and is confined to the culture of civilization, of which it is a product. In *Typee* Melville writes of the 'scientific voyager' who returns to civilization and 'attempts, perhaps, to give a description of some of the strange people he has been visiting': 'were the book thus produced to be translated into the tongue of the people of whom it purports to give the history, it would appear quite as wonderful to them as it does to the American public, and much more improbable.'[124]

The object of the traveller's quest, like Stewart's, for the 'facts' about the 'true character' of savages, is the subject of Melville's *Typee*, which dramatizes the two 'extremes' which Stewart sought to 'avoid' and shows how the ambiguous savage is the consequence of civilized ambivalence, the observer's point of view depending on his 'frame of mind'. The ambiguous savage, extremely good and extremely bad, is the consequence of civilized man's ambivalence and ultimately, perhaps, of his desire to escape—both from civilization and from savagery, as 'Melville' does in *Typee*, escaping first from civilization, in the form of Captain Vangs (as the real Captain Pease was renamed), and then from savagery, in the form of chief Mow-Mow, who pursues 'Melville' in his final flight from Typee valley. Civilization has its 'cannibal' horrors, in the form of Captain Vangs, or Fangs, just as savagery has, in the form of chief Mow-Mow, or Mouth-Mouth, and the result is ambivalence and alternating 'frames of mind' in which the savage state appears, by contrast with civilization, now as a refuge, now as a prison. The savage state is thus presented as a subjective state of mind, its objective reality incomprehensible.

Among the Typees, says 'Melville', 'I saw everything, but could comprehend nothing'.[125] As he documents the culture of the Typees his adjectives qualify the ethnographic findings of his own (and other travellers') observations: 'unintelligible', 'inexplicable', 'incomprehensible', 'mysterious', 'perplexing', 'inscrutable'.[126] In the words of Melville's Preface: 'There are some things related in this narrative which will be sure to appear strange, or perhaps entirely incomprehensible, to the reader; but they cannot appear more so to him than they did to the author at the time.'[127]

One recent critic who has noticed 'Melville's' statement that he 'could comprehend nothing' has commented that these words, 'when they are seen in the light of the later fiction, assume a special significance which is only vaguely suggested by the context of the novel [*Typee*] itself'.[128] Similarly, another critic has remarked that: 'Melville seems to be suggesting that the Typees, like Moby Dick, are animated nature—a phenomenological whole that baffles inquiry. But these patterns of intimation can be detected only by comparing them to the later works.'[129] But, when *Typee* is read 'in the light' of contemporary travellers' accounts of the 'true character' of the Marquesans, its meaning is clear, and can be detected without comparing *Typee* to 'the later works'.

It may be worth remarking, in conclusion, that Melville was aware of an affinity between the Typees and that 'Red race' of American Indians whom the Puritans had misread in terms of the Bible, as 'types'.[130] Whether Melville intended an ironical pun we cannot be sure, but there is no doubt that his narrative—a captivity narrative in the American Puritan tradition—demonstrates that the Typees, those savages with 'a bad name', cannot be comprehended as types of the devil in the biblical garden of Eden, or even as types of Adam and Eve.[131] The savages with 'a bad name' are not types—of malevolence or of innocence. Pun or no pun, the Typees are not types, as Melville discovered by living among the Taipi (as the name is nowadays spelled).[132]

8

The Palm-Tree Shall Grow

[The Tahitian chief Tati said that] all the low lands were formerly fully inhabited and in a good state of cultivation; but now the Fau and other bushes and trees covered the land, and the remnant of the people inhabited merely the sea side. This led him to mention a prophecy or rather a threating of the prophets in former times when there appeared a backwardness in the people to observe the injunctions of the gods, the prophet used to cry out. E tupu te fau, e toro te farero E ore te taata i.e. The Fau shall grow and overspread the land, and the branching coral the deep, but the race of man shall be extinct.

(John Davies, 29 October 1816, 'Journal of a preaching tour round Tahiti')[1]

The *Lucy Ann* sailed from Sydney on 18 February 1842, for whales in the Pacific, and lost eight of its crew and its second mate on the island of Tahuata in the Marquesas, where they deserted in June.[2] Two other men were 'mutinous', according to the captain, and were put in irons and handed over to the recently established French forces, for shipment to the British naval authorities at Valparaiso.[3] Then, at Nukuhiva, three more of the *Lucy Ann*'s crew escaped, one of them, John Troy, making off with 'several medicines' from the ship's chest.[4] These men were recaptured, however, and the *Lucy Ann* signed on two new sailors at Nukuhiva on 8 August and, on the following day, another, Herman Melville, escaping from the Taipi.[5]

The pattern more obviously present in *Typee*, of escape and captivity, can also be discerned beneath the surface of its sequel, *Omoo: A Narrative of Adventures in the South Seas* (1847), an apparently unpatterned, wandering narrative with a title Melville glossed in his Preface as follows: 'The title of the work—Omoo—is borrowed from the dialect of the Marquesas Islands, where, among other uses, the word signifies a rover, or rather, a person wandering from one island to another, like some of the natives, known among their countrymen as "Taboo kannakers".'[6] The principal rover in *Omoo* is 'Melville', and one of the objects of the book, according to Melville's Preface, is 'to convey some idea' of the wild and uncivilized behaviour of sailors, which can be seen nowhere 'under wilder aspects, than in the South Seas', where 'the most reckless seamen of all nations' are inspired by 'a spirit of the utmost license'.[7] Besides a portrayal of the savage lives led by civilized sailors, 'another object proposed' in *Omoo* is to show the effects of civilization on the lives of the Polynesian savages themselves: 'to give a *familiar* account of the present condition of the converted Polynesians, as affected by their promiscuous intercourse with foreigners, and the teachings of the missionaries, combined.'[8]

This second object makes *Omoo* into a complement to *Typee*. The first book had been concerned with the true character of savages, and the second was to concern itself with the true character of savages in contact with civilization. The question of civilization, in other words, was to follow the question of savagery. Melville explained this relation between *Typee* and *Omoo* in a letter to Murray: 'I think you will find it a fitting successor to "Typee"; inasmuch as the latter book delineates Polynisian Life in its primitive state—while the new work, represents it, as affected by intercourse with the whites.'[9]

Omoo begins where *Typee* ends, with 'Melville's' escape from Nukuhiva in the *Julia* (in reality the *Lucy Ann*), and deviates into fiction by describing the *Julia*'s return to the Marquesan island of Tahuata 'for the purpose of obtaining eight seamen, who, some weeks before, had stepped ashore there from the Julia', as indeed they had in reality from the *Lucy Ann*.[10] At Tahuata more of the *Julia*'s crew desert, but are recaptured with the assistance of the French, as are five of the original deserters. The real *Lucy Ann* made no such return to Tahuata, but the imaginary episode—inspired by the actual events at Tahuata before Melville joined the *Lucy Ann*—provides *Omoo* with an extra thematic chapter of escape and recapture, and reveals Melville's authorial hand at work, steering the *Julia* away from the facts of the *Lucy Ann*'s voyage.

On leaving Tahuata, the *Julia* proceeds to the nearby island of Hiva Oa, where the *Lucy Ann* did indeed call with Melville aboard after leaving Nukuhiva.[11] There, at Hiva Oa, in the bay of Hanamenu, the *Julia* is met, according to *Omoo*, by a canoe containing some Marquesans and a white man who is reminiscent of the symbolism of *Typee*: 'With them also came a stranger, a renegado from Christendom and humanity—a white man, in the South Sea girdle, and tattooed in the face.'[12] This character, 'an Englishman, Lem Hardy he called himself', a deserter who has successfully established himself in Marquesan society and is 'perfectly satisfied with his circumstances', was probably inspired by the accounts of Joseph Kabris and Edward Robarts in Langsdorff's *Voyages and Travels*, and certainly there is no mention of Lem Hardy in the account by a visitor who came to Hanamenu only two months before Melville.[13] In any case, whether fiction or fact, Lem Hardy serves an aesthetic purpose, as an image of what 'Melville' might have been in *Typee*, and of what he might become in *Omoo*. 'It is just this sort of men', says Melville of Hardy, men 'without ties, reckless, and impatient of the restraints of civilization, who are occasionally found quite at home upon the savage islands of the Pacific.'[14] The white man gone native is the counterpart, in *Omoo*, of the Polynesian gone civilized.

The 'restraints of civilization' and the wild South Sea sailors' desire to escape them are behind the mutiny of the crew of the *Julia* on its arrival at Tahiti, a mutiny that has its factual basis in the mutiny of the crew of the *Lucy Ann* in September 1842. Captain Guy of the *Julia* is ill, according to *Omoo*, and needs medical attention at Tahiti, which had indeed been the case with Captain Ventom of the *Lucy Ann*, who was suffering from 'a deep Seated abcess . . . in the perineum', according to a medical certificate written by a Dr Johnstone (Johnson in *Omoo*) who treated him at Tahiti.[15] Captain Guy of the *Julia*, like Captain Ventom of the *Lucy Ann*, is resolved that his whaling voyage should continue nevertheless, while he remains at Tahiti for treatment, and that his unruly and evasive crew should not be allowed ashore. The mutiny, Melville implies in *Omoo*, is provoked by this frustration of the sailors' 'pleasant anticipations' of Tahiti as much as by their 'grievances' about their shipboard conditions, and is a mutiny, in effect, against the 'restraints of civilization'.[16]

The consular records show that Melville was not among the original mutineers who were temporarily imprisoned aboard the French frigate, the *Reine Blanche*, as 'Melville' is, but joined them five days later, when the men appeared for judgement before the acting British consul, Charles Wilson.[17] The 'restraints of civilization' then take the form of the 'Calabooza Beretanee', the so-called 'British' gaol or lock-up near Papeete, where 'Melville' is for a time confined to the stocks with his fellow mutineers and, like them, proceeds to escape the 'restraints of civilization' in the Calabooza by 'getting boozy' with the help of intoxicating medicines obtained under false pretences from Dr Johnson.[18] The reality of Melville's Tahitian captivity was confirmed by a Lieutenant Henry A. Wise, who quotes in his *Los Gringos: or an Inside View of . . . Polynesia* (1849) a passage from Dr Johnstone's 'dose book', which records that 'Melvil Herman. Stocks' was supplied on 15 and 19 October 1842 with 'Embrocation'.[19]

The gaoler at the Calabooza, according to *Omoo*, is an indulgent Tahitian known as Captain Bob, and the restraints of civilization are soon relaxed enough for 'Melville' to visit the port of Papeete, which had replaced Matavai as the favoured harbour for passing ships, and would soon become the capital of the island which the French had recently seized (not on the 'morning' of the *Julia/Lucy Ann*'s arrival, as Melville conveniently has it in *Omoo*, but actually only a few days before).[20] 'Melville's' rovings from the Calabooza enable him to make his 'observations' of the condition of Tahitians undergoing civilization, a topic that develops as he observes, among other things, a missionary church service, a nominally Christian Tahitian girl (whose name, Ideea, Melville probably borrowed from Bligh's Iddeah) and the 'religious police' employed to enforce the recalcitrant Tahitians' 'spiritual well-being'.[21] For some of 'Melville's' 'observations', however, Melville was indebted to a source of 'information' he rather inadequately acknowledged in his Preface: 'the "Polynesian Researches" of Ellis'.[22] Thus, for example, Ellis's descriptions of well-built Tahitians in second-hand 'European clothing', with 'imprisoned and pinioned arms occasionally struggling for liberty, and the perspiration oozing from the pores of the skin, indicating the laborious confinement of the body', provided Melville with ready-make instances of the constraints of civilization for his chapter 'How They Dress in Tahiti'.[23]

In the following chapter, entitled 'Tahiti As It Is', Melville directly addresses the question to which his previous chapters of observations have been tending, the question of civilization, as revealed by its effects on the Polynesians. Tahiti, as he says, was a test case:

Of the results which have flowed from the intercourse of foreigners with the Polynesians, including the attempts to civilize and christianize them by the missionaries, Tahiti, on many accounts, is obviously the fairest practical example. Indeed, it may now be asserted, that the experiment of christianizing the Tahitians, and improving their social condition by the introduction of foreign customs, has been fully tried.[24]

This was, indeed, the Tahitian question. As the Marquesan question was the nature of the savage, so the Tahitian question was the nature of the civilized savage—and thus of civilization itself—and every traveller to Tahiti was expected to participate in the debate, and expected to come to a conclusion. This Tahitian debate had already been taking shape around the opposing views of Kotzebue and Ellis, and it had continued with Captain Beechey, who had been disappointed by the dancing on Pitcairn, and 'greatly disappointed' by the forbidden but inoffensive dancing on Tahiti, predictably taking the side of Kotzebue.[25]

Like many before him, Charles Darwin, who came to Tahiti aboard the *Beagle* in 1835, attempted an objective assessment of the conflicting textual evidence:

From the varying accounts which I had read before reaching these islands, I was very anxious to form, from my own observation, a judgement of their moral state—although such judgement would necessarily be very imperfect. A first impression at all times very much depends on one's previously-acquired ideas. My notions were drawn from Ellis's 'Polynesian Researches'—an admirable and most interesting work, but naturally looking at every thing under a favourable point of view; from Beechey's Voyage; and from that of Kotzebue, which is strongly adverse to the whole missionary system. He who compares these three accounts will, I think, form a tolerably accurate conception of the present state of Tahiti.[26]

Darwin's assessment of the texts shows an admirable impartiality but an inadequate recognition of the extent to which a judgement of the Tahitians' 'moral state' must ultimately be a matter of opinion, or point of view, and Darwin's own observations on Tahiti show his own opinion, which favours the 'favourable point of view' of Ellis.

Melville, too, makes a display of objectivity in his Preface to *Omoo*:

In every statement connected with missionary operations, a strict adherence to facts has, of course, been scrupulously observed; and in some instances, it has even been deemed advisable to quote previous voyagers, in corroboration of what is offered as the fruit of the author's own observations.[27]

Melville's use of the texts of previous voyagers is, however, prejudiced and tendentious.[28] He cites Kotzebue and Beechey, two unfavourable 'authorities' cited in the Right Revd Michael Russell's *Polynesia: or, An Historical Account of the Principal Islands in the South Sea* (1842), making much of Russell's comment that they 'cannot fail to have much weight with the public', but making no mention of Russell's own attempt to refute such 'authorities' by deploying the arguments of Ellis.[29]

Russell himself, a bishop of Glasgow and Galloway who wrote several accounts of places he had never seen—Palestine, Egypt, Nubia, Abyssinia, North Africa, Iceland, Greenland, the Faroe Islands—had manifested in his *Polynesia* a concern for objectivity and an understanding of the philosophical problem presented by the subjectivity of European observers' opinions:

> a great question remains to be solved as to the result of missionary exertion on the character of the natives, and the permanence of the change which has been effected by the advent of a civilized people among them. In attempting to arrive at truth on these interesting points, we are impeded by the difficulty which arises from the marked disagreement prevailing among voyagers in regard to the actual condition of the inhabitants, both at the Society and Sandwich Islands [i.e. Tahiti and Hawaii]. Such discrepancy, we are satisfied, does not arise so much from want of candour, as from the different aspect under which the same objects are contemplated by two classes of persons who have so little in common as seamen and ministers of the gospel.[30]

This recognition of the 'different aspect', or point of view, of seamen and of ministers of the gospel, did not prevent the Right Revd Russell from preferring the point of view of a minister of the gospel, and he cites the opinions of the missionary, Ellis, to contradict those of the seaman, Kotzebue, who has 'a strong prejudice', says Russell, and makes 'some important mistakes'.[31] Melville, on the other hand, cites the seaman Beechey to contradict the missionary Ellis:

> Captain Beechey, in alluding to the 'Polynesian Researches' of Ellis, says, that the author has impressed his readers with a far more elevated idea of the moral condition of the Tahitians, and the degree of civilization to which they have attained, than they deserve; or, at least, than the facts which came under his observation, authorized.[32]

What this debate reveals, of course, is the disparity of visitors' opinions, the 'facts' about 'civilized' Tahitians being as difficult to determine as the 'facts' about 'savage' Marquesans. But Melville's aim in *Omoo* is not that in *Typee*, of demonstrating the subjectivity of civilized views of the 'savage' object. In *Omoo* he is concerned to present a case against civilization and it is to this end alone that he presents the testimony of other travellers, 'in corroboration', as he says, of his own 'observations' of the 'facts'. In the chapter following 'Tahiti As It Is', entitled 'Same Subject Continued', Melville develops his case:

> Calculated for a state of nature, in a climate providentially adapted to it, they [the Polynesians] are unfit for any other. Nay, as a race, they can not otherwise long exist.
>
> The following statement speaks for itself.
>
> About the year 1777, Captain Cook estimated the population of Tahiti at about two hundred thousand. By a regular census, taken some four or five years ago, it was found to be only nine thousand.[33]

The causes of this depopulation, according to Melville, are the evils of civilization:

These evils, of course, are solely of foreign origin. To say nothing of the effects of drunkenness, the occasional inroads of the small-pox, and other things, which might be mentioned, it is sufficient to allude to a virulent disease, which now taints the blood of at least
two thirds of the common people of the island; and, in some form or other, is transmitted
from father to son.[34]

Melville, of course, has chosen his figures to fit his argument.[35] Thus, the source
he cites for a Tahitian population of 9,000, Charles Wilkes's *Narrative of the
United States Exploring Expedition* (1844), points out that:

When this is compared with the estimates of the navigators who first visited these islands,
an enormous decrease would appear to have taken place. The first estimates were, however,
based on erroneous data, and were unquestionably far too high; yet there is no doubt that
the population has fallen off considerably in the interval.[36]

Cook's population figure, then, as Melville would have known, was regarded as
erroneous, not only by Ellis and Russell (who followed Ellis's refutation of Cook's
figure almost verbatim), but by Wilkes, who was not a minister of the gospel.[37]
This view, that Cook's estimate of 1774 was 'a gross exaggeration', is also held
today, and two modern studies, based on what little evidence there is, agree that
the population of Tahiti at the time of discovery was, more plausibly, about
35,000.[38] As the population of Tahiti at the time of Melville's visit was actually
between eight and nine thousand, so that Wilkes's and Melville's figure of nine
thousand was very nearly correct, the decline in the Tahitian population in the
years since discovery was certainly considerable, as Wilkes remarked, but by no
means as spectacularly steep as Melville made it appear.[39]

Melville, though, was not one to let statistics stand in his way. If he did not scoff
at Wilkes's scientific South Sea expedition as Thoreau did, who remarked that 'It
is not worth the while to go round the world to count the cats in Zanzibar', it was
because Wilkes's figures, combined with Cook's, gave Melville a factual basis for
his theme, by no means new, of death in paradise.[40] He closes his case against the
effects of civilization in Tahiti with:

the prediction of Teearmoar, the high-priest of Paree; who lived over a hundred years ago.
I have frequently heard it chanted, in a low, sad tone, by aged Tahitians:—

> 'A harree ta fow,
> A toro ta farraro,
> A mow ta tararta.'
> The palm-tree shall grow,
> The coral shall spread,
> But man shall cease.[41]

In reality, Melville heard this prophecy from his copy of Ellis's *Polynesian Researches*, Ellis in his turn having derived it from the missionary John Davies's
account of his tour of Tahiti in 1816.[42] Melville has adapted Ellis's version of the

prophecy, however, by replacing Ellis's authentic 'The *fau* (hibiscus) shall grow' with the more picturesquely emblematic 'The palm-tree shall grow', and he has altered Ellis's Tahitian text to match, by inserting the Tahitian for 'palm', 'ha'ari', but in place of the Tahitian for 'grow', 'tupu', not in place of the Tahitian for 'hibiscus', 'fau'. Melville has thus produced his own original version of the old Tahitian dictum, credible in English but nonsensical in Tahitian.

Having presented his case about Tahiti, Melville returns to the plot of *Omoo* to narrate, appropriately, the escape of 'Melville' and a companion, Long Ghost (John Troy of the *Lucy Ann*), from Tahiti to the neighbouring island of Moorea, or Eimeo, less civilized than Tahiti. Under the aliases of Peter and Paul they are employed by two white potato farmers, a Yankee and a Cockney, on a plantation in the valley of 'Martair', or Maatea, where the indigenous islanders, 'secluded, in great measure, from the ministrations of the missionaries, . . . gave themselves up to all manner of lazy wickedness'.[43] This 'wickedness' consists mostly in 'napping' and 'smoking' and Melville concludes that: 'Upon the whole, they were a merry, indigent, godless race.'[44] 'Melville' and Long Ghost are similarly remiss, concerned mostly with eating, napping, and smoking. Soon tiring of the drudgery of farming, they resolve 'to visit Tamai, a solitary inland village'.[45] Tamai has 'delicious fish', 'the finest fruit of the islands' and, besides:

in Tamai dwelt the most beautiful and unsophisticated women in the entire Society group [of Tahiti and adjacent islands]. In short, the village was so remote from the coast, and had been so much less affected by recent changes than other places that, in most things, Tahitian life was here seen, as formerly existing in the days of young Otoo, the boy-king, in Cook's time.[46]

The purpose of the expedition to Tamai is clear, therefore: a further escape from civilization, to a Tahiti of the past, rediscovered in the present. Tamai is not 'Tahiti as it is' and the travellers find 'a happy little community, comparatively free from many deplorable evils to which the rest of their countrymen are subject'.[47] The young girls of Tamai are 'far fresher and more beautiful' than their more civilized compatriots, and 'Melville' and Long Ghost look forward, in a place 'so remote from ecclesiastical jurisdiction', to 'the prospect of seeing an old-fashioned "hevar", or Tahitian reel'.[48] Their hopes are fulfilled and by moonlight they witness the chanting and dancing and the 'throbbing bosoms and glowing cheeks' of 'the backsliding girls of Tamai'.[49] 'Melville' and Long Ghost decide to 'settle down' amidst the old-fashioned attractions of Tamai, but—just as they are discussing 'various plans for spending our time pleasantly'—they are disturbed by some women who 'hurriedly besought us to *heree! heree!* (make our escape), crying out something about the *mickonarees*'.[50] As 'Melville' and Long Ghost run off to make their 'escape' from the missionaries, and thus from civilization, they are in effect reversing the direction of *Omoo*. In running away from ideally primitive Tamai, they are inevitably running towards civilization.

It is worth remarking, in view of the significance of primitive Tamai as a foil to civilized Tahiti, that the 'dance of the backsliding girls of Tamai' actually took place in the Marquesas—or, more precisely, in *Typee*. Melville provides the evidence himself, in a letter to Murray:

You will perceive that there is a chapter in the book [*Omoo*] which describes a dance in the valley of Tamai. This discription has been modified & adapted from a certain chapter which it was thought best to exclude from Typee. In their dances the Tahitians much resembled the Marquesans (the two groups of islands are not far apart) & thus is the discription faithful in both instances.[51]

The two groups of islands were not far apart in space, but the progress of civilization had separated their cultures, leaving their resemblance in the past tense. The Marquesan dance in the Society Islands was not a backsliding dance, therefore, but an anachronism, a nostalgic fiction.

While the dance at Tamai derived from *Typee*, Tamai itself may have come from *Polynesian Researches*, where Ellis refers to it twice, rather than from Melville's own personal experience of Moorea.[52] As Ellis each time describes Tamai as 'sequestered', it would have suited Melville as a place where he could pretend that 'many heathenish games and dances still secretly lingered', instead of the Christian 'meditation and secret prayer' described there by Ellis.[53] In his *Rovings in the Pacific . . . By a Merchant long Resident at Tahiti* (1851), Edward Lucett protested that 'the valley which he [Melville] describes in Moorea . . . has existence only in the region of his imagination', and it is more likely that Lucett was referring to Melville's improbable valley of Tamai than to his credible valley of Maatea.[54] Another indication that Melville's Tamai is an invention may be his placing it near 'the very heart of the island' and 'not far' from Taloo (Tareu), a bay 'on the western side of the island', when Tamai was actually located, as Ellis said, 'on the north-eastern side' of the island, 'between the mountains and the sea'.[55] Melville's Tamai is probably a utopian fiction. 'Tahiti as it is' is a paradise lost in *Omoo*, and Tahiti 'as formerly existing'—and its beguiling dancing girls—can exist only in fiction. Melville used such fiction to heighten the contrast between the lost Tahiti and the found, but he also needed it, more mundanely, to fill his book. Despite the claim of his Preface that he 'spent about three months' on Tahiti and Moorea, Melville spent only about forty days on those two islands, or about six weeks, and of those six weeks he probably spent less than three on Moorea.[56]

After their 'escape' from Tamai, the roving 'Melville' and Long Ghost return to the plantation at Martair (or Maatea) and then, Melville depending more and more on Ellis, they proceed along the coast to the port of Taloo (or Tareu), where 'Melville', according to Melville, 'at last pined for the billows'.[57] Leaving Long Ghost (in reality John Troy) on Moorea, 'Melville' (like Melville) sailed on the whaler 'the Leviathan' (in reality the *Charles and Henry*, in the first week of November 1842) and *Omoo* closes by echoing the departure of Milton's Adam and Eve from their lost paradise, with the fallen world 'all before them'.[58] 'And all before us', says Melville, 'was the wide Pacific'.[59]

For the final development of postlapsarian 'Tahiti as it is', visited by the 'evils' of civilization and by death, it was logical, almost inevitable, that the beguiling island girl, symbol of prelapsarian Tahiti 'as formerly existing', should suffer personally the 'evils' of civilization and thus become the dying island girl, symbol of postlapsarian 'Tahiti as it is'. This perfected version of the South Sea paradise lost, *Le Mariage de Loti—Rarahu* (1880), was the work of a man who was, like Melville, a sailor turned author: Julien Viaud, a French naval officer better known by his *nom de plume*, Pierre Loti. The Rarahu of his title is a Tahitian girl and the epigraph on the title page is a 'vieux dicton de la Polynésie' with which we are already familiar in its distinctive Melvillean version, which is undoubtedly Viaud–Loti's unacknowledged source:

> *E hari te fau,*
> *E toro te faaro,*
> *E no te taata.*
> Le palmier croîtra,
> Le corail s'étendra,
> Mais l'homme périra.[60]

Le Mariage de Loti tells the story of a relationship, 'un mariage tahitien', between the narrator, Harry Grant, a British naval officer familiarly known by his Tahitian name of Loti, and the young Rarahu.[61] They meet 'en-dessous du vieux monde' at the waterfall of Fataoua, which falls 'en sens inverse des cascades du bois de Boulogne et de Hyde-Park', and share an idyll.[62] When Grant–Loti's naval duties take him away for a month to Nukuhiva, however: 'L'idylle était finie . . . Contre nos prévisions humaines, ces heures de paix et de frais bonheur écoulées au bord du ruisseau de Fataoua, s'en étaient allées pour ne plus revenir.'[63] On his return to Tahiti, he finds that the foster-parents of Rarahu have died and he accedes to her wish to live with him in Papeete, the capital and centre of civilizing influence on the island: 'C'est ainsi que joyeusement elle franchit le pas fatal. Pauvre petite plante sauvage, poussée dans les bois, elle venait de tomber comme bien d'autres dans l'atmosphère malsaine et factice où elle allait languir et se faner.'[64] Rarahu is soon 'assez civilisée déjà pour aimer quand je l'appelasse "petite sauvage"' and she develops 'une toute petite toux sèche'.[65] The grand-daughter of the ageing Queen Pomare also manifests the symptoms of tuberculosis, of civilization, and in the Queen herself (granddaughter of Cook's Tu) Grant–Loti sees: 'surtout une immense tristesse,—tristesse de voir la mort lui prendre l'un après l'autre tous ses enfants frappés du même mal incurable,—tristesse de voir son royaume, envahi par la civilisation, s'en aller à la débandade,—et son beau pays dégénérer en lieu de prostitution.'[66]

In due course Rarahu's 'petite toux caractéristique, pareille à celle des enfants de la reine, devenait chez elle plus fréquente', and Grant–Loti indicates her symbolic significance: 'Elle était une petite personnification touchante et triste de la race polynésienne, qui s'éteint au contact de notre civilisation et de nos vices, et ne sera plus bientôt qu'un souvenir dans l'histoire d'Océanie.'[67] At this point Grant–Loti has to leave Tahiti again for California. When he returns to Rarahu after some months, 'la petite toux si redoutée sortait souvent de sa poitrine'.[68] Forseeing her fate when he leaves Tahiti forever, Grant–Loti begs Rarahu to leave Papeete when he himself returns to civilization: 'Pars, toi aussi, lui disais-je, à genoux; va, loin de cette ville de Papeete; va vivre avec Tiahoui, ta petite amie, dans un district éloigné où ne viennent pas les Européens.'[69] Grant–Loti and Rarahu pay a last visit to the pool at Fataoua:

Tout était bien resté tel qu'autrefois, dans cet endroit où l'air avait toujours la fraîcheur de l'eau courante; nous connaissions là toutes les pierres, toutes les branches . . .

Nous suspendîmes nos vêtements aux branches,—et puis nous nous assîmes dans l'eau, savourant le plaisir de nous retrouver encore, et pour la dernière fois, en parée, au baisser du soleil, dans le ruisseau de Fataoua . . .

Nous ne nous disions rien tous deux;—assis près l'un de l'autre, nous devinions mutuellement nos pensées tristes, sans avoir besoin de troubler ce silence pour nous les communiquer . . .

Tout ce pays et ma petite amie bien-aimée allaient disparaître, comme s'évanouit le décor de l'acte qui vient de finir . . .

Celui-là était un acte de féerie au milieu de ma vie,—mais il était fini sans retour! . . . Finis les rêves, les émotions douces, enivrantes, ou poignantes de tristesse,—tout était fini, était mort . . .'[70]

Rarahu promises to leave Papeete and Grant–Loti returns to 'Brightbury, Comté de Yorkshire (Angleterre)', where he receives letters from Rarahu, ill and pleading with him to return to her.[71] 'Pourquoi m'oublies-tu?' she asks, closing quaintly and abruptly with 'J'ai fini de te parler'.[72] Then, in Regent Street, London, he meets a friend with news of Rarahu and hears that she returned to Papeete six or eight months after Grant–Loti's departure and 'devint la maîtresse d'un jeune officier français'.[73] The little granddaughter of Queen Pomare has died and the old Queen is not expected to survive the shock. A footnote informs us that: 'La reine Pomaré est morte en 1877 . . . Elle avait survécu environ deux ans à sa petite-fille.—On peut considérer qu'à dater de ce jour commence la fin de Tahiti, au point de vue des coutumes, de la couleur locale, du charme et de l'étrangeté.'[74] Rarahu remains at Papeete, Grant–Loti's friend tells him, and she leads there 'une vie absolument déréglée et folle'.[75] Finally, a year later, in Malta, Grant–Loti learns that Rarahu, who 's'était mise à boire de l'eau-de-vie', has died.[76]

Grant–Loti has played a part in the fall of Rarahu, of course, and his responsibility is acknowledged in the book when Rarahu calls him 'long lézard sans pattes', a designation explained as follows: 'Le serpent étant un animal tout à fait inconnu en Polynésie, la métis qui avait éduqué Rarahu, pour lui expliquer sous quelle forme le diable avait tenté la première femme, avait eu recours à cette périphrase.'[77] There is more to *Le Mariage de Loti*, however, than a simple tale of satanic civilization bringing death to a young savage girl, 'une petite personnification touchante et triste de la race polynésienne'. The beguiling island girl, although dying in a paradise lost, loses none of her charms. Grant–Loti is attracted to Rarahu not just because she is Tahitian and 'sauvage', but also because she is doomed: 'C'était peut-être pour moi un charme de plus, le charme de ceux qui vont mourir, et plus que jamais je me sentais l'aimer.'[78] When Rarahu coughs her 'petit toux', her face appears to Grant–Loti to take on 'ce charme ultra-terrestre de ceux qui vont mourir'.[79] That other little personification of the fate of Tahiti, that 'délicieuse petite malade', Queen Pomare's granddaughter, has a similar attraction: 'Cette maladie prévue et cette mort certaine donnaient un charme de plus à cette petite créature, la dernière des Pomaré, la dernière des reines des archipels tahitiens.'[80] This appears to be the real charm of Tahiti for Grant–Loti, the charm, not of paradise, but of paradise lost.

Grant–Loti's author, Viaud–Loti, had his personal reasons for associating ultra-terrestrial charm with Tahitian, for seeing Tahiti as another world. When he was an eight-year-old at Rochefort, his older and only brother Gustave had given him a book called *Voyage en Polynésie* and had then made that voyage, while Julien, as he recalled in his memoirs, coloured in its illustrations of garlanded, bare-breasted 'jeunes filles tahitiennes au bord de la mer', carefully and incorrectly: 'oh! blanches et roses.'[81] Letters came to Rochefort from Gustave, one enclosing a dried flower for Julien, which had bloomed at the window of Gustave's house in Tahiti. In a letter to Julien himself, Gustave spoke of a delightful valley in Tahiti called Fataüa, and wished that the 'île délicieuse' had a door that opened into the courtyard of the family house in Rochefort.[82] That night young Julien dreamed that he went down in the deathly light of dusk to the courtyard in Rochefort, and flew through the air to the valley of Fataüa, where in disbelief he clutched at the tangible reality of the tropical ferns. When he woke: 'Ma main vide restait encore fermée, crispée, les ongles presque marqués sur la chair, pour mieux garder l'imaginaire bouquet de Fataüa, l'impalpable rien du rêve . . .'.[83] Gustave died in 1865, and was buried at sea in the Bay of Bengal, but his delicious isle remained tangibly real in the imagination of Julien, who came there in January 1872, to find his treasured, dried flower at his brother's ruined Tahitian house, blooming 'dans l'intérieur abandonné'.[84]

On arrival at Tahiti in *Le Mariage de Loti*, Harry Grant, soon to become Loti, writes to his sister at Brightbury in England: 'Me voici devant cette île lointaine que chérissait notre frère, point mystérieux qui fut longtemps le lieu des rêves de mon enfance.'[85] At first he is disappointed—'la civilisation y est trop venue'—but soon he rediscovers the paradise of his lost brother: 'Me voilà sous le charme, moi aussi—sous le charme de ce pays qui ne ressemble à aucun autre.—Je crois que je le vois comme jadis le voyait Georges, à travers le même prisme enchanteur . . .'.[86] With Rarahu he lives

cette vie exotique, tranquille et ensoleillée, cette vie tahitienne telle que jadis l'avait menée mon frère Rouéri [the Tahitian name of his brother Georges], telle que je l'avais entrevue et désirée, dans ces étranges rêves de mon enfance qui me ramenaient sans cesse vers ces lointains pays du soleil.[87]

On two occasions when he is about to leave Rarahu, to go to California and to leave Tahiti forever, Grant–Loti neglects her to seek out his dead brother's Tahitian mistress, Taïmaha, and search for his dead brother's abandoned half-Tahitian children. The search climaxes in his last days at Tahiti, when he leaves Rarahu to visit the island of Moorea, where, according to Taïmaha, his brother's elder child is living. After a long, hurried journey he at last finds the boy: 'C'était un délicieux enfant, mais je retrouvais dans sa figure ronde les traits seuls de sa mère, le regard noir et velouté de Taïmaha.'[88] The boy also seems 'bien jeune' and 'un doute amèrement triste me traversa l'esprit'.[89] A messenger is sent to obtain the records of the children's birth and these prove that they are too young to be Grant–Loti's dead brother's: 'c'était comme s'il fût mort une seconde fois.—Et il semblait que ces îles fussent devenues subitement désertes,—que tout le charme de l'Océanie fût mort du même coup, et que rien ne m'attachât plus à ce pays.'[90]

The whole episode is implausibly romantic and melodramatic, but true. Among Viaud–Loti's papers is a copy of a letter he addressed from San Francisco, California, to a missionary on Tahiti, requesting his help in tracing Gustave's Tahitian mistress and children.[91] Viaud–Loti's journal records his visit to Moorea in almost identical terms to those in *Le Mariage de Loti*, with the difference that the original names are used. Thus, for example, he records his discovery of the child he believes to be his brother's: 'C'était un délicieux enfant, mais je retrouvai chez lui tous les traits de Tarahu [Gustave's mistress], et rien de plus, je l'aurais aussi cru plus grand, et pour la première fois un doute amèrement triste me traversa l'esprit.'[92] His doubts are confirmed in the same way as in *Le Mariage* and with the same result: 'Il semblait qu'un vide immense venait de se faire autour de moi, que ces îles étaient désertes, que tout le charme de Tahiti était mort du même coup, et que rien ne m'attachait plus à ce pays.'[93]

A significant part of *Le Mariage de Loti* has no basis in Viaud–Loti's journal, however, as can be seen if we compare, for example, Grant–Loti's last visit to the pool at Fataoua, described in a passage already quoted from *Le Mariage*, with the description of Viaud–Loti's last visit to the pool in his journal:

Tout était bien tel que je l'avais laissé, dans cet endroit où l'air avait toujours la fraîcheur de l'eau courante; je connaissais là toutes les pierres, toutes les branches ...

Je suspendis mes vêtements aux branches et puis je savourai le plaisir de me retrouver encore pour la dernière fois, en pareo, au baiser [?baisser] du soleil, dans l'eau de Fautaua ...

Tout ce pays allait disparaître, comme s'évanouit le décor de l'acte qui vient de finir; celui-là était un acte de féerie au milieu de ma vie, mais il était fini sans retour ... Fini, les rêves, les émotions douces ou poignantes de tristesse, tout était fini, tout était mort...[94]

The text of *Le Mariage de Loti* repeats the text of the journal almost word for word, but the pool at Fataoua (or Fautaua) contained, in reality, no Rarahu. 'Tout ce pays allait disparaître' in the journal becomes 'Tout ce pays et ma petite amie bien-aimée allaient disparaître' in the novel. Viaud–Loti himself described *Le Mariage de Loti* in a letter to a friend as 'des notes anciennes que j'ai rassemblées', but pointed out that 'le fond de l'histoire n'est pas vrai' because Rarahu herself, although 'une étude assez fidèle de la jeune femme maorie', was a fiction.[95] He added, however, that 'Tout ce qui concerne Taïmaha est rigoureusement vrai'.[96] Taïmaha, the dead brother's Tahitian mistress in the novel, was Tarahu in reality, a name, of course, not unlike Rarahu.

The fictional story of Rarahu and Grant–Loti has its precedent, however, and its possible source, in a true story set in Nukuhiva in the 1840s, and told by Max Radiguet, who came to the Marquesas with the French forces aboard the *Reine Blanche*, on which 'Melville', but not Melville, was briefly detained.[97] In his book, *Les Derniers Sauvages, souvenir de l'occupation française aux îles Marquises, 1842– 1859*, first published in 1861, and republished in 1882, by the publisher of *Le Mariage de Loti*, Radiguet recounts the romantic tale of 'une jeune insulaire, nommée Taha', a young Nukuhivan, 'mariée suivant la coutume du pays, avec un officier français, auquel je laisserai son nom polynésien de Teapo'.[98] Living with Teapo at the French colonial centre of Taiohae, young Taha develops a 'toux sèche' and dies, leaving Teapo wondering 'si son rôle dans l'existence de cette créature de Dieu avait été bienfaisant ou fatal'.[99]

Melville and Loti came to the South Seas as sailors, but Stevenson came as a writer. He had already discovered the South Seas in fiction, and even in fiction of his own, not forgetting the 'beautiful girl'. At the age of twelve he had written 'Creek Island, or Adventures in the South Seas'. The *Shark* is wrecked in the South Seas in 1720 and two midshipmen are taken captive by the natives:

They had a council which pronounced death, but which death would I have to suffer? It was to be burned alive . . . Next morning very early we had to get up and prepare to be burned alive. When we arrived at the place of execution, we shuddered to think of being killed so soon. But I forgot to tell you that I had made love to beautiful girl [*sic*] even in one day, and from all I knew she loved me. The next thing they did was to build round us sticks and rubbish of all kinds till we could hardly see what they were doing. At last they finished. They then set fire to it, and after it had got hold well, they began to dance, which is called a war-dance. (To be continued.)[100]

A few years later, as a boy of fifteen in Edinburgh, Stevenson introduced himself, one Sunday after church, to R. M. Ballantyne—'Ballantyne the brave', as he was to call him in the verses prefacing *Treasure Island*.[101] The young Stevenson declared himself an admirer of *The Coral Island*, which he had read twice, he told Ballantyne, and hoped to read twice more.[102] The idea for *The Coral Island: A Tale of the Pacific Ocean* (1858) came to Ballantyne while he was looking out of the window of a lodging house, one sunny day, across the Firth of Forth to the island of Inchkeith.[103] He procured some reference books, but they did not prevent a notorious error in *The Coral Island*, in which coconuts grow without husks, an error Ballantyne explained as follows:

Despite the utmost care of which I was capable, while studying up for *The Coral Island*, I fell into a blunder through ignorance in regard to a familiar fruit. I was under the impression that cocoa-nuts grew on their trees in the same form as that in which they are usually presented to us in grocers' windows.[104]

As a result of this blunder, which was pointed out to him time and again, Ballantyne 'formed the resolution always to visit—when possible—the scenes in which my stories were laid'.[105] The boy who has been 'studying up' in *The Coral Island* is Jack, and his companion Peterkin, like the young reader, is duly impressed:

'I say, Jack, how does it happen that you seem to be up to everything? You have told us the names of half-a-dozen trees already, and yet you say that you were never in the South Seas before.'

'I'm not up to *everything*, Peterkin, as you'll find out ere long,' replied Jack with a smile; 'but I have been a great reader of books of travel and adventure all my life, and that has put me up to a good many things that you are, perhaps, not acquainted with.'

'Oh, Jack, that's all humbug. If you begin to lay everything to the credit of books, I'll quite lose my opinion of you,' cried Peterkin, with a look of contempt. 'I've seen a lot 'o fellows that were *always* poring over books, and when they came to try to *do* anything, they were no better than baboons!'

'You are quite right,' retorted Jack; 'and I have seen a lot of fellows who never looked into books at all, who knew nothing about anything except the things they had actually seen, and very little they knew even about those. Indeed, some were so ignorant that they did not know that cocoa nuts grew on cocoa-nut trees!'[106]

Stevenson knew *The Coral Island* long before he encountered *Typee* and *Omoo* in 1879–80, and long before he sailed from San Francisco into the Pacific in June 1888, on a South Sea cruise to be paid for with South Sea 'Letters' to be syndicated in the papers.[107] Accompanying him on board were his widowed mother, his wife Fanny, his stepson Lloyd, and with the hired schooner, the *Casco*, came Captain Otis, who had read *Treasure Island*, but no further in Stevenson's works.[108] Their first island encounter was with Anaho Bay in the north of Nukuhiva, where a Marquesan girl told Stevenson 'All the Kanaks die; then no more' and he formulated in his journal what he called 'the Highland metaphor': 'if I am to call these men savages (which no bribe could induce me to do) what name should I find for a Hebridean man. The Highlands and Islands somewhat more than a century back were in much the same convulsive and transitory state as the Marquises today.'[109] This analogy with another, more familiar, vanishing culture Stevenson retained in the published account of his visit to the Marquesas, in which the prevailing mood of elegiac melancholy is enhanced by the addition of an old Tahitian saying, borrowed without acknowledgement to its author: ' "The coral waxes, the palm grows, but man departs", says the sad Tahitian proverb.'[110]

The account in Stevenson's journal does not significantly differ from that given in the South Sea 'Letters' published in the British and American press and, posthumously, as *In the South Seas* (1896).[111] Melville's Tahitian proverb was an afterthought, but the passages quoted above from the journal reappear, revised, in the published versions, and there are no discrepancies of the kind that would suggest the addition of fiction or the suppression of fact. Indeed Stevenson was not so much writing a journal as drafting an account for publication, as is plainly revealed by his use in the journal of the words: 'difficult to describe in a work intended for the general reader.'[112] The theme marked by the chapter headings of *In the South Seas*, 'Death' and 'Depopulation', was implicit in the journal, even if Melville's sad Tahitian proverb was added later. It appears twice in the published work, ascribed, on the second occasion, to the Marquesans: ' "The coral waxes, the palm grows, and man departs", says the Marquesan; and he folds his hands.'[113]

Melville was on Stevenson's mind as he sailed 'past Typee' (deleted and replaced with 'Taipi') to Taiohae, the capital of Nukuhiva.[114] In a passage of his journal which did not reach *In the South Seas* he reflected that Melville's South Sea writing 'leaves upon the mind of a reader the durable impression of good fiction; and for that very reason, I believe, fills him with doubts of its veracity. But how easy it is to raise doubts! and how easy often, if our information were complete, to lay them!'[115] The absence of sandflies from *Typee*, for instance, and their abundance at Taipi, did not prove that 'Herman Melville cannot have stayed at Taipi', as might be supposed, because the sandflies came only with civilization.[116] As he sailed among the Marquesas, Stevenson also recalled the narrator of Tennyson's 'Locksley Hall' (published in 1842, the year of Melville's Taipi adventure), who rejected his own fantasy of escape to 'Summer isles of Eden', sternly reminding himself: 'Better fifty years of Europe . . .'.[117] 'When you sit in the wide verandah', wrote Stevenson at Tahauku, Hiva Oa (not far from where Gauguin died, fifteen years later), 'you may say to yourself if you are able: "Better fifty years in Europe . . ." '.[118] Sailing from the Marquesas to the Tuamotus, in September, Stevenson wrote to his old friend Charles Baxter of his high hopes for his South Sea travel writings: 'I shall have a fine book of travels, I feel sure; and will tell you more of the South Seas after very few months than any other writer has done—except Herman Melville perhaps, who is a howling cheese [i.e. an exemplar of smartness and cleverness].'[119]

From the Tuamotus the *Casco* sailed for Tahiti, where Stevenson spent some days unhappily at Papeete, near the ruins of Melville's old Calabooza, and several weeks blissfully at the village of Tautira on the other side of the island, where he exchanged names with a hospitable chief, Ori a Ori (or Teriitera), and suspended his journal.[120] Then from Tahiti the *Casco* proceeded to Honolulu, where Stevenson dismissed her and took a house near the beach at Waikiki, 'connected by telephone with the chief shops', he informed his friend Sidney Colvin at the British Museum, 'and the tramway runs to within a quarter of a mile of us'.[121] At Waikiki he completed *The Master of Ballantrae* and chatted with King Kalakaua, who had read *Dr Jekyll and Mr Hyde* as well as *Treasure Island*, and from there he made trips to the island of Hawaii and to the leper colony on Molokai, keeping notes for future South Sea 'Letters'.[122]

From Honolulu Stevenson's mother returned to Scotland and he and his American family sailed again as passengers aboard a trading ship, the *Equator*, in June 1889, for the Gilbert Islands, and more South Sea material. On the intoxicated island of Butaritari, Stevenson negotiated between the traders and the local 'king' a taboo on the sale of alcohol, and observed the politics of 'the beach', the community of beachcombers, traders, and others who formed an outpost of civilization in the Micronesian islands, as in other parts of the Pacific.[123] 'The beachcomber is perhaps the most interesting character here', he wrote to Colvin, and filled several pages of his journal with the grim stories he heard about the Gilbert Island traders: Jim, whose 'element' was 'drink', and Tom, a murderer with a devoted 'New Hebrides woman' for a wife and three delightful daughters in 'three sizes of Rob Roy Macgreggor Frocks'.[124] These characters with their guns and gin were of interest to Stevenson the story-teller as well as Stevenson the traveller, who admired the Gilbertese dancing (which he described almost identically in his journal and in *In the South Seas*). In return he entertained the islanders with biblical magic lantern slides lent by a missionary, noting their reaction: ' "Why then", the word went round, "the bible is true after all!" '[125]

From Butaritari Stevenson sailed on to Abemama, where the 'king' was excellent material. 'The king is a great character', he reported to Colvin, 'the great attraction'.[126] The despotic High Chief Tem Binoka looms large in the journal and in the published book, 'blue-spectacled' in the glaring sun with his talk of 'Mo' betta' ' and his gun, composing romantic songs (songs like lies) about 'Sweethearts and trees and the sea. No all the same true; all the same lie'.[127] He took a liking to his visitor. 'You good man; you no lie', he told Stevenson, who added, in print, that this was 'a doubtful compliment to a writer of romance'.[128]

From the Gilberts the *Equator* took Stevenson and family on to Apia, Samoa, where a local missionary, 'making my way along the "Beach" ', encountered a tanned woman wearing a Gilbertese straw hat and carrying a mandolin, a thin man with a cigarette, and a younger man wearing dark glasses and carrying a concertina and a ukelele, a trio he took for 'a party of vaudeville artists *en route* to Australia or the States'.[129] Stevenson bought the site of Vailima and they sailed then for Sydney, Australia, from where Stevenson planned to visit England, but where he took ill. They set out again for the revitalizing South Seas, therefore, as passengers aboard the trading steamer *Janet Nichol*, revisiting Samoa and the Gilberts, and calling at Penrhyn and New Caledonia and many other islands.[130] From Noumea, New Caledonia, Stevenson returned to Sydney and then to Samoa where, after nearly three years of cruising in the South Seas, he settled at Vailima, late in 1890.

While at Waikiki in May 1889, Fanny Stevenson had written to Colvin telling him of the proposed trip to the Gilberts, and of her concern at Stevenson's planned travel book:

Louis has the most enchanting material that any one ever had in the whole world for his book, and I am afraid he is going to spoil it all. He has taken into his Scotch Stevenson head that a stern duty lies before him, and that his book must be a sort of scientific and historical impersonal thing, comparing the different languages (of which he knows nothing, really) and the different peoples . . . Think of a small treatise on the Polynesian races being offered to people who are dying to hear about Ori a Ori, the making of brothers with cannibals, the strange stories they told, and the extraordinary adventures that befell us:—suppose Herman Melville had given us his theories as to the Polynesian language and the probable good or evil results of the missionary influence instead of *Omoo* and *Typee* . . .[131]

Fanny forgets that Melville's works do contain arguments about the missionary influence as well as accounts of adventures, but anyway the book that Stevenson outlined in a letter to Colvin while sailing to Samoa from the Gilberts, in December 1889, does not seem to be the 'sort of scientific and historical impersonal thing' that she had feared. Indeed, as Stevenson's comments to Colvin indicate, the book's basis was firmly in Stevenson's own travels:

My book is now practically modelled: if I can execute what is designed, there are few better books now extant on this globe, bar the epics, and the big tragedies, and histories, and the choice lyric poetics and a novel or so—none. But it is not executed yet; and let not him that putteth on his armour, vaunt himself. At least, nobody has had such stuff; such wild stories, such beautiful scenes, such singular intimacies, such manners and traditions, so incredible a mixture of the beautiful and the horrible, the savage and the civilised . . . I propose to call the book *The South Seas*: it is rather a large title, but not many people have seen more of them than I, perhaps no one—certainly no one capable of using the material.[132]

Stevenson's letters to Colvin from Vailima (published as *Vailima Letters* in 1895) give frequent reports of progress 'with the South Sea book', while Fanny also wrote, telling of her 'desperate engagements with the man of genius':

He has always had a weakness for teaching and preaching, so here was his chance. Instead of writing about his adventures in these wild islands, he would ventilate his own theories on the vexed questions of race and language. He wasted much precious time over grammars and dictionaries, with no results, for he was able to get an insight into hardly any native tongue. Then he must study the coral business. That, I believe, would have ruined the book but for my brutality.[133]

She describes returning to the shore after 'having some odd adventures and seeing many curious things' on an island visited by the *Janet Nichol*, to find the man of genius

on the reef, halfway between the ship and shore, knee-deep in water, the tropical sun beating on his unprotected head, hammering at the reef with a big hatchet. His face was purple and his eyes injected with blood. 'Louis, you will die,' I cried, 'come away out of the sun quickly.' 'No,' he answered, 'I must get specimens from this extraordinary piece of coral . . . '. 'Louis,' I said, 'how ignorant you are! Why, that is only the common brain coral. Any schoolboy in San Francisco will give you specimens if you really want them.'[134]

As Stevenson revised and shaped his journal, forming thematic connections and making inter-island comparisons instead of following strict chronological order, he was sending off parts of the work to Colvin in London for comment, and to the publisher S. S. McClure in New York for serialization in the British and American press as 'Letters' from the South Seas. These 'Letters' were not to be confused with the planned book, Stevenson insisted to Colvin in April 1891:

No one ever seems to understand my attitude about that book; the stuff sent was never meant for other than a first state; I never meant it to appear as a book . . . I hoped some day to get a 'spate of style' and burnish it—fine mixed metaphor. I am now so sick that I intend, when the Letters are done and some more written than will be wanted, simply to make a book out of it by the pruning knife . . . which will not be what I had hoped to make, but must have the value it has and be d——d to it. I cannot fight longer; . . . [and] really five years were wanting, when I could have made a book; but I have a family, and—perhaps I could not make a book after all, and anyway, I'll never be allowed for Fanny has strong opinions and I prefer her peace of mind to my ideas.[135]

Colvin removed the reference to Fanny from the published edition of the *Vailima Letters*, but, whether or not Fanny was to blame, the work published posthumously as *In the South Seas* (1896), edited by Colvin from some of the serialized 'Letters', was not *The South Seas* that Stevenson had imagined, Fanny had feared and, for whatever reasons, Stevenson had been unable to write.[136] The grand inter-island comparisons and anthropological speculations decrease as *In the South Seas* proceeds from the Marquesas to the Gilberts, with less and less disruption of the narrative of personal adventures, while Stevenson's researches on the coral reef, far from wrecking the book, are barely mentioned at all.[137]

In any case the 'scientific' South Seas of the projected book was already, in the early months at Vailima, taking second place in Stevenson's mind to the romantic South Seas of fiction. The idea for a story 'shot through me like a bullet', Stevenson told Colvin early in November 1890.[138] 'It is really good', he wrote in April 1891, 'well fed with facts, true to the manners, and (for once in my works) rendered pleasing by the presence of a heroine who is pretty'.[139] He had not forgotten the 'beautiful girl'. In September 1891, he read through the sixteen pages he had written, and reported to Colvin: 'I never did a better piece of work, horrid, and pleasing, and extraordinarily *true*; it's sixteen pages of the South Seas; their essence.'[140] Later that month the story had its name, *The Beach of Falesá*, and an ending. Its realism pleased him:

There is a vast deal of fact in the story, and some pretty good comedy. It is the first realistic South Sea story; I mean with real South Sea character and details of life . . . You will know more about the South Seas after you have read my little tale than if you had read a library.[141]

Stevenson's little tale was no substitute for his failure to transcribe the South Sea facts in his projected *The South Seas*, but 'the beach' he had observed in the Gilberts did contribute to the realism of *The Beach of Falesá*.[142] The story is narrated by an island trader, Wiltshire, who has, as Stevenson told Colvin, 'under his beast-ignorant ways, right noble qualities'.[143] Arriving at the village of Falesá on an imaginary South Sea island, Wiltshire 'marries' an island girl, Uma, in a fraudulent ceremony arranged and staged by Case, a local trader. Wiltshire soon discovers that his own trade-store is taboo to the natives, who have a superstitious fear of Uma. Realizing that Case has tricked him, and ashamed of his own role in the fraudulent marriage, Wiltshire asks a passing missionary to conduct a proper marriage between himself and Uma, and then proceeds to investigate the deceptions practised by Case, who controls the islanders by playing upon their superstitions. In the melodramatic climax of the story—'melodramatic' is Stevenson's own word—Wiltshire exposes Case's trickery and blows up his collection of 'queer figures, idols, or scare-crows' and a luminous painted mask.[144] Case 'was a good forger of island curiosities'.[145] After the explosion in the bush, Wiltshire lies wounded there with Uma until the timely arrival of Mr Tarleton, the missionary.

This is very like the conclusion of *The Coral Island*—although with a difference. In Ballantyne's book the South Sea heroine of the romantic sub-plot, Avatea, is a Christian—as Uma is—but is destined by Ballantyne to be married to an islander, not to any one of the three white boy-heroes, who are not designed for such a purpose. At the end of *The Coral Island* the boys are suddenly released by their cannibal captors and conducted to a native village:

The scene that met our eyes here was one that I shall never forget. On a rude bench in front of his house sat the chief. A native stood on his left hand, who, from his dress, seemed to be a teacher. On his right stood an English gentleman, who, I at once and rightly concluded, was a missionary. He was tall, thin, and apparently past forty, with a bald forehead, and thin gray hair. The expression of his countenance was the most winning I ever saw, and his clear gray eye beamed with a look that was frank, fearless, loving, and truthful. In front of the chief was an open space, in the centre of which lay a pile of wooden idols, ready to be set on fire; and around these were assembled thousands of natives, who had come to join in or to witness the unusual sight . . . 'And what of Avatea?' inquired Jack. The missionary replied by pointing to a group of natives in the midst of whom the girl stood. Beside her was a tall, strapping fellow, whose noble mien and air of superiority bespoke him a chief of no ordinary kind [he is a Christian].[146]

Peterkin refuses to leave for 'dear old England' until 'I see these fellows burn their gods': 'Peterkin had his wish, for, in a few minutes afterwards, fire was put to the pile, the roaring flames ascended, and, amid the acclamations of the assembled thousands, the false gods of Mango were reduced to ashes!'[147]

Stevenson has achieved much the same conclusion—the victory of Christianity, marked by the arrival of the missionary, the marriage of the Christian island girl, and the burning of the false gods—but he has made the false gods of Falesá the creation, not of the islanders, but of Case, a white man, 'a good forger of island curiosities'. The conflict between islanders and missionaries is thus made into a conflict between traders and missionaries, which is to recognize the new realities of power in the Pacific, but to pass over the continuing and more fundamental conflict between the indigenous cultures and civilization in all its manifestations.

The Beach of Falesá was sold for serialization in all countries to S. S. McClure in December 1891, but at the end of January 1892 Stevenson received a request from S. S. McClure's brother, Robert McClure, to alter the the story so that Uma and Wiltshire should be properly, not fraudulently, married. What was troubling Robert McClure was the following passage in Stevenson's manuscript, in which Wiltshire describes the ceremony staged by Case and his accomplice:

I thought shame I say; for the mountebank [Case's accomplice] was dressed with a big paper collar, the book he made believe to read from was an odd volume of a novel, and the words of his service not fit to be set down. My conscience smote me when we joined hands; and when she got her certificate, I was tempted to throw up the bargain and confess. Here is the document: it was Case that wrote it, signatures and all, in a leaf out of the ledger: 'This is to certify that *Uma* daughter of *Faavao* of Falesá island of——, is illegally married to *Mr John Wiltshire* for one night, and Mr John Wiltshire is at liberty to send her to hell next morning.'[148]

McClure's 'plaintive request', as Stevenson called it, he refused.[149] 'You will see what would be left of the yarn, had I consented', he told Colvin.[150] Nevertheless, the editor of the *Illustrated London News* believed, as he later explained, that the editors of 'journals for general family reading' had responsibilities which were more important than 'the feelings of an author, however great', and Stevenson's story first appeared in the *Illustrated London News* in July and August 1892, with the text of the marriage certificate omitted (and the words 'Here is the document' replaced by 'What a document it was!'), as Stevenson discovered when he received a copy of the first instalment of the story from a visitor to Samoa in August 1892.[151] He wrote to Colvin to insist that when *Falesá* appeared in book form he would not 'have the marriage contract omitted'.[152] But the publishers, Cassell and Company, were anxious to avoid the terms of the marriage contract and proposed a compromise, which was eventually adopted when the story was published in *Island Nights' Entertainments* (1893), in which edition, and for many subsequent editions, the text read that Uma 'is illegally married to Mr. John Wiltshire for one week, and Mr. John Wiltshire is at liberty to send her to hell when he pleases'.[153] When this compromise was put to Stevenson, via Colvin, he replied: 'Well, well, if the dears prefer a week, why, I'll give them ten days, but the real document, from which I have scarcely varied, ran for one night.'[154]

This 'real document' was mentioned in one of Stevenson's South Sea 'Letters' published in the New York *Sun* in 1891, and subsequently in the posthumous *In the South Seas* (1896), in a description of the relations between traders and Gilbertese women that is clearly based on information Stevenson received in the Gilberts, though it does not appear in Stevenson's original journal.[155] Remarking that the trader 'often makes a kind and loyal husband', Stevenson describes five native wives and adds:

All these women were legitimately married. It is true that the certificate of one, when she proudly showed it, proved to run thus, that she was 'married for one night', and her gracious partner was at liberty to 'send her to hell' the next morning; but she was none the wiser or the worse for the dastardly trick. Another, I heard, was married on a work of mine in a pirated edition; it answered the purpose as well as a hall Bible.[156]

Although Stevenson claimed that *Falesá* was 'well fed with facts', and contained 'a vast deal of fact', the marriage certificate is the only case of an actual, textual overlap between the factual *In the South Seas* and the fictional *Falesá*, and was cut and altered for the fiction. In Stevenson's South Sea writings, the account of his own experience, *In the South Seas*, is almost completely separate from his fiction, *The Beach of Falesá*. Of the two works it is *In the South Seas* that is closer to the works of Melville and Loti, not only in its basis in true experience, but also in its relation to the theme of paradise lost, the theme of Stevenson's Marquesas, marked by his use of Melville's very own Tahitian saying.

Both Loti and Stevenson had used Melville's Tahitian saying to lament the passing of paradise in the Pacific, but paradise could still be found there as well as paradise lost, even in the twentieth century. On 15 October 1913 Rupert Brooke checked into the five-storey Moana Hotel on Waikiki Beach, near Honolulu. He remembered his broken heart 'by some other sea' and expressed his feelings in a South Sea poem:

> Plangent, hidden from eyes,
> Somewhere an *eukaleli* thrills and cries
> And stabs with pain the night's brown savagery.[157]

From Hawaii he sailed to Samoa, where he preferred the moonlight, 'not sticky, like Honolulu moonlight, not to be eaten with a spoon'.[158] He watched a 'tropical and savage' Samoan dance and visited the grave of Stevenson, as he told Stevenson's friend Edmund Gosse on hotel writing-paper decorated by the management with natives, sailing boat, and palm trees.[159] To his own friend, Edward Marsh, Churchill's private secretary, he wrote that he felt himself 'becoming indistinguishable from R.L.S., both in thinness, in literary style, & in dissociation from England'.[160] He had been in the South Seas only a few weeks, but the literary associations were established and the speed of travel had increased. He was getting to know the islands rapidly. On the boat to Fiji he wrote to Marsh again a few days later:

Oh, Eddie, it's all true about the South Seas! I get a little tired of it at moments, because I am just too old for Romance, & my soul is seared. But there it is: there it wonderfully is: heaven on earth, the ideal life, little work, dancing, singing & eating, naked people of incredible loveliness, perfect manners, & immense kindliness, a divine tropical climate, & intoxicating beauty of scenery.[161]

In a letter to Violet Asquith written a few weeks later 'in the mountains of Fiji' Brooke reported his new discovery, that death had come to paradise. The South Sea islanders, he told the Prime Minister's daughter:

are—under our influence—a dying race. We gradually fill their lands with plantations and Indian coolies. The Hawaians, up in the 'Sandwich Islands', have almost altogether gone, and their arts and music with them, and their islands are a replica of America. A cheerful thought, that all these places are to become indistinguishable from Denver and Birmingham and Stuttgart, and the people of dress and behaviour precisely like Herr Schmidt, and Mr Robinson and Hiram O. Guggenheim. And now they're so . . . it's impossible to describe how far nearer the Kingdom of Heaven—or the Garden of Eden—these good naked laughing people are than oneself or one's friends.[162]

From Fiji he sailed—via New Zealand—to Tahiti, where, at a guest-house in the village of Mataia, he 'found the most ideal place in the world, to live and work in . . . A wide verandah over a blue lagoon'.[163] Diving in the 'blue lagoon' he scratched his leg on coral and the wound became infected. On the 'wide verandah' he worked on poems, one of them, 'Tiare Tahiti', addressed to Mamua, Brooke's fictional name for a Tahitian girl, Taatamata, now known only from some old photographs in the library of King's College, Cambridge (see Plate 8).[164] When Brooke's 'beastly coral-poisoning' from the lagoon 'came on bad', he was 'nursed & waited on by a girl with wonderful eyes', as he told Edward Marsh.[165] 'The South Seas', he wrote to Phyllis Gardner, 'have got into my blood'.[166]

On his return to England in June 1914, Brooke heard that Quiller-Couch wanted his assistance for the next term at Cambridge. 'At last I shall have to read *The Faerie Queene*', he said, but another fate was awaiting him.[167] One night in December 1914, at an army camp near Blandford, Dorset, Brooke had a nightmare, which he described in a letter to his friend Dudley Ward:

I dreamt I landed at Papeete, and went up between the houses, and the air was heavy with sunshine. I went into the house of a half-caste woman I know and she gave me tea, and talked. And she told me about everyone. And at last I said 'And how and where's Taatamata?' And she said 'Oh—didn't you know?' And I said 'No'. She said 'She's dead.' I asked (knowing the answer) 'When did she die?' 'Months ago, just after you left.' She kept evading my eye. After a long silence I asked (feeling very sick) 'Did she kill herself?' The half-caste nodded. I went out of the house and out to the lagoon, feeling that a great friendliness—all the place—had gone against me. Then I woke with a dry throat, and found a frosty full moon blazing in at the window, and the bugle hammering away at the 6.30 *Reveille*.[168]

A month later, in January 1915, he received a letter, dated 'Le 2 Mai 1914': 'forwarded by the Dead Letter Office from Ottawa, "recovered" by divers from the wreck of the Empress of Ireland. Rather frayed at the edges, and the ink much washed out. But it was a letter from Taatamata . . . I think Life's FAR more romantic than any books.'[169] The dying island girl of Brooke's dream was really alive and well. She wrote:

Sweetheart you know I alway thinking about you that time when you left me I been sorry for long time. whe [we] have good time when you was here I always remember about you forget me all readly oh! mon cher bien aimé je t'aimerai toujours . . . je me rappeler toujour votre petite étroite figure et la petite bouche qui me baise bien tu m'a percea mon cœur et je t'aime toujours ne m'oubli pas mon cher maintenant je vais finir ma lettre . . .

> I send my kiss to you darling
> xxxxxxxxxxxxxxxx mille kiss
> Taatamata[170]

But Brooke had not forgotten Taatamata, the Mamua of 'Tiare Tahiti'. The South Seas were still in his blood. When a mosquito bite became infected, septicaemia set in at sea on the way to Gallipoli. His resistance to infection dangerously weakened by the coral-poisoning at Tahiti, Brooke died and was buried on Skyros.[171] In a letter written a few weeks before his death to Dudley Ward, a letter written in case of death, Brooke made a last request: 'Try to inform Taata of my death. Mlle Taata, Hotel Tiare, Papeete, Tahiti. It might find her. Give her my love.'[172]

Taatamata–Mamua was not the last of her kind, that line of South Sea island girls that began with Byron's Neuha and reached its apogee in Viaud–Loti's Rarahu, the 'petite personnification' of the dying South Sea island. The South Sea girl lived on, but in literature not destined for immortality. Almost every modern novel with 'Paradise' in the title and a woman on the cover is probably set in the 'South Seas', an ocean of kitsch that has little relation to the modern Pacific.

The South Sea stories of Somerset Maugham are better than that, but they could have been set almost anywhere hot. Maugham came to the South Seas in 1916, visiting Hawaii, Samoa, and Tahiti, and taking notes. The main characters of the stories he collected in *The Trembling of a Leaf: Little Stories of the South Sea Islands* (1921) were sketched from life and are easily recognizable in *A Writer's Notebook*. 'All you have to do is just sit here in the bar', advised the proprietor of the Central Hotel, Apia, 'and you'll get all the stories you need.'[173] In this way Maugham encountered the colonial officer with a passion for roads who appears in 'Mackintosh', and 'L.', the original of Lawson, the man who married a half-caste and drowned himself in 'The Pool'.[174] The captain of the ship from Honolulu to Apia inspired the captain in 'Honolulu' and among the passengers Maugham found the principals of 'Rain', a missionary couple and an American prostitute on the run from the brothels of Honolulu, whom he also described in his notebook: 'Miss Thompson. Plump, pretty in a coarse fashion, perhaps not more than twenty-seven: she wore a white dress and a large white hat, and long white boots from which her calves, in white cotton stockings, bulged.'[175]

Miss Thompson, calves bulging from white boots, is the heroine of 'Rain': 'She was twenty-seven perhaps, plump, and in a coarse fashion pretty. She wore a white dress and a large white hat. Her fat calves in white stockings bulged over the tops of long white boots in glacé kid.'[176] To engage this portrait in action, Maugham has imagined a fatal confrontation between Miss Thompson and the missionary couple, horrified and fascinated by her public sexuality, to which the Revd Davidson falls victim, like some of his pioneering predecessors on Tahiti. This is, of course, a South Sea plot, but the heroine is an American prostitute, not an innocent island girl, and the South Seas setting does not seem essential. The islands in *Little Stories of the South Sea Islands* are an exotic backdrop from which 'the natives' emerge only occasionally, to serve 'kava' or 'the Honolulu cocktail', play 'the ukalele' or proffer a garland of flowers, to the colonial regulars or to passing tourists, like Maugham himself.[177]

Of course Maugham's stories reflect the facts of the changed Pacific, but they also reflect Maugham's own limitations as a traveller and a writer. That it is not just the indigenous cultures which have degenerated can be seen from Maugham's portrait of the captain's ukelele-playing island girl in 'Honolulu', who was:

a very pretty person. She was a good deal taller than the captain, and even the Mother Hubbard, which the missionaries of a past generation had, in the interests of decency, forced on the unwilling natives, could not conceal the beauty of her form. One could not but suspect that age would burden her with a certain corpulence, but now she was graceful and alert. Her brown skin had an exquisite translucency and her eyes were magnificent. Her black hair, very thick and rich, was coiled round her head in a massive plait. When she smiled in a greeting that was charmingly natural, she showed teeth that were small, even, and white. She was certainly a most attractive creature.[178]

It is not the missionaries who have robbed this descendant of Neuha, Fayaway, and Rarahu of her character and culture. The only thing that distinguishes Maugham's magnificent-eyed, translucent-skinned, black-haired, white-toothed creature as a native of the South Seas—rather than of, say, Trinidad, Curitiba, or Timbuktu—is her Mother Hubbard.

Meanwhile the South Seas had been popularized in America by a play called *A Bird of Paradise* which opened on Broadway in January 1912, featuring a young actress named Laurette Taylor, trained to hula by a big Hawaiian who 'moved', she remembered, 'like a fat little wave'.[179] Described as 'geography made easy and poetry realized in the everyday', *A Bird of Paradise* toured America in the second decade of the century with its advertised attractions:

the play of a woman's soul . . . beautiful, intensely atmospheric . . . Hawaii with its shores girdled by lazy waves in languorous moonlight . . . Hawaii with its laughing, dancing maidens crowned and garlanded with brilliant flowers, maidens casting eyes of witchery on white strangers.[180]

Hawaii with its shores girdled and its maidens garlanded was popular with 'white strangers', and the South Sea island and its 'petite personnification', the island girl—or island-girl—became a part of American culture and international culture, inspiring such songs as 'I Want Some More of Samoa' and 'Honolulu Moon', treacly and coy, strummed on the ukelele and consumed in spoonfuls.[181]

Alec Waugh, whose travels round the world to Tahiti began 'in the spring of 1925, with the reading of *The Trembling of a Leaf*', concluded in his own travel book, *The Coloured Countries* (1930), that it had become 'difficult to write otherwise than conventionally' about the South Seas: 'It is as hard not to echo Loti as it is for the writer of detective stories to avoid parallels with Sherlock Holmes.'[182] The Tahiti he found had already been discovered: 'The South Seas are terribly *vieux jeux* . . . Long before you get to them you know precisely what you are to find. There have been Maugham and Loti and Stevenson and Brooke . . . Everything about the islands is *vieux jeu*.'[183]

The South Seas were indeed 'vieux jeu', but even in the modern Pacific the ancient commonplaces of travel literature found new ways to reassert their claims to be facts about real places. Thus Margaret Mead's anthropological study of young girls *Coming of Age in Samoa* (1928) revealed that in Samoa, unlike civilized America, 'Sex is a natural, pleasurable thing.'[184] Malinowski also, unknowingly, was giving new life to an old story when he regretted, in *Argonauts of the Western Pacific* (1922), that: 'Just now, when the methods and aims of scientific field ethnology have taken shape, when men fully trained for the work have begun to travel into savage countries and study their inhabitants—these die away under our very eyes.'[185]

The islanders survived but their indigenous cultures did not. Hawaiian culture was exterminated and then reanimated as a fiction, reduced by tourism to 'aloha' and 'hula', the greeting of 'love' and the welcoming dance so attractive to 'white strangers'.[186] A former president of the Hawaiian Visitors Bureau describes the process of creation: 'Since real cultural events do not always occur on schedule, we invented pseudo-events for the tour operators who must have a dance of the vestal virgins precisely at 10.00 a.m. every Wednesday.'[187] We may recall that Melville's 'dance of the backsliding girls of Tamai' was also a pseudo-event.[188] Advertisements for Tahiti, meanwhile, make a point of emphasizing the 'fatal impact' of civilization on rival Hawaii:

Tahiti is special. The Tahitians make sure it will always be so. They want their island to be truly Polynesian. They go to such lengths as to forbid constructions above the height of a coconut tree. They won't worry if Tahiti gets less tourists than Hawaii. They rather reserve Tahiti for the connoisseurs. Connoisseurs who will enjoy their wide sandy beaches and lagoons, their 'Tiare' and frangipani, their lush green mountains and their 'joie de vivre' with a special possessive pleasure. Discover it with UTA.[189]

A photograph of a garlanded, grass-skirted, dancing island girl illustrates the 'special possessive pleasure' that awaits those who will follow in the wake of Wallis, Cook, and Bougainville and 'discover' Tahiti. The palm-tree shall grow, the coral shall spread, and the island girl shall dance on Wednesdays.

Notes

PREFACE

1. John Martin, *An Account of the Natives of the Tonga Islands, in the South Pacific Ocean. With an original grammar and vocabulary of their language. Compiled and arranged from the extensive communications of Mr. William Mariner* (London, 1817), i. 124.

CHAPTER 1

1. Descartes, *Discours de la méthode*, in *Œuvres et lettres de Descartes*, ed. A. Bridoux (Pléiade edn., 1953), 129.
2. Joseph Banks, *The 'Endeavour' Journal of Joseph Banks*, ed. J. C. Beaglehole (Sydney, 1962), ii. 54.
3. 1 Kings, 9: 28, *Authorised Version of the English Bible, 1611*, ed. W. A. Wright (Cambridge, 1909).
4. See Columbus, 'Narrative of the voyage which the admiral, Don Christopher Columbus, made the third time that he came to the Indies', in *Select Documents Illustrating the Four Voyages of Columbus*, trans. and ed. Cecil Jane, ii (London, 1932), 6.
5. Samuel Purchas, *Purchas His Pilgrimes* (Glasgow, 1905–7), i. 66. On speculation about Ophir, see R. R. Cawley, *Unpathed Waters* (London, 1967), 31 ff., and P. Herrmann, *Conquest by Man*, trans. M. Bullock (London, 1954), 67 ff.
6. Jonson, *The Alchemist*, ed. F. H. Mares (London, 1971), ii. i. 1–5.
7. See L. Casson, *Travel in the Ancient World* (London, 1974), 62; also E. H. Bunbury, *A History of Ancient Geography* (reprinted, New York, 1959), i. 318 ff., and J. O. Thomson, *History of Ancient Geography* (Cambridge, 1948), 73 ff.
8. 'The Periplus of Hanno', in *The Ancient Fragments*, ed. I. P. Cory (London, 1828), 129.
9. See B. Heuvelmans, *On the Track of Unknown Animals* (Paladin edn., London, 1970), 27, and *OED*, 'Gorilla'.
10. Andrew Battell, 'The strange adventures of Andrew Battell of Leigh in Essex, sent by the Portugals prisoner to Angola', in Purchas, *Pilgrimes*, vi. 398. Rousseau, *Discours sur l'origine de l'inégalité* (Amsterdam, 1755), 222. Rousseau found Battell's account of the 'Pongos' in *Histoire générale des voyages*, ed. A.-F. Prévost, v (Paris, 1748), 88–9.
11. James Burnett, Lord Monboddo, *Of the Origin and Progress of Language*, i (Edinburgh, 1773), 175; *Of the Origin and Progress of Language*, i (2nd edn., Edinburgh, 1774), 254, 255.
12. See Heuvelmans, *Unknown Animals*, 26, and *Encyclopaedia Britannica*, xii (Cambridge, 1910), 'Gorilla'.
13. For Eratosthenes on Anaximander, see Strabo, *The Geography*, trans. H. L. Jones (Loeb edn., 1917–32), i. 23. For Herodotus, see R. E. Dickinson and O. J. R. Howarth, *The Making of Geography* (Oxford, 1933), 9, and Herodotus, *The Histories*, trans., A. de Selincourt (Penguin edn., 1954), 328.

14. On the Pythagoreans, see Diogenes Laertius, *The Lives of the Philosophers*, trans. R. D. Hicks (Loeb edn., 1925), ii. 343. On Plato and Aristotle, see D. R. Dicks, *Early Greek Astronomy to Aristotle* (Bristol, 1970), 72.

15. Herodotus, *Histories*, 218.

16. Strabo, *Geography*, i. 5.

17. See 'The Shipwrecked Sailor', *Egyptian Tales: Translated from the Papyri, 1st ser.: IVth to XIIth Dynasty*, ed. Flinders Petrie (4th edn., London, 1926), 81–96.

18. Eratosthenes, quoted in Strabo, *Geography*, i. 87. On Eratosthenes and Homeric geography, see Rudolf Pfeiffer, *History of Classical Scholarship from the Beginnings to the End of the Hellenistic Age* (Oxford, 1968), 166.

19. Strabo, *Geography*, i. 73.

20. See Thucydides, *History of the Peloponnesian War*, VI, trans. C. F. Smith (Loeb edn., rev. 1928–35), iii. 183.

21. Theocritus, *Idylls*, XI. 7, trans. A. S. F. Gow (Cambridge, 1950), 87.

22. Karl Baedeker, *Southern Italy and Sicily* (Leipzig, 1930), 420.

23. See J. V. Luce. 'The Wanderings of Ulysses', in W. B. Stanford and J. V. Luce, *The Quest for Ulysses* (London, 1974), 134, 118.

24. See John H. Finley, Jr., *Homer's Odyssey* (Cambridge, Mass., 1978), 59.

25. Homer, *The Odyssey*, trans. E. V. Rieu (Penguin edn., repr. 1981), 181.

26. Ibid. 136.

27. In Ithaca, his own home, Odysseus conceals and then reveals his identity from and to, in turn, Telemachus, Eumaeus, the Suitors, Penelope, and Laertes. It is discovered by Argus and Eurycleia and tested by Penelope and Laertes.

28. Homer, *Odyssey*, 149.

29. Ibid. 210.

30. Ibid. 293.

31. Ibid. 181, 272.

32. See M. I. Finley, *The World of Odysseus* (Penguin 2nd. rev. edn., 1979), 162.

33. Homer, *Odyssey*, 144 (cf. 105, 138).

34. Ibid. 25.

35. Ibid. 142. See J. Ferguson, *Utopias of the Classical World* (London, 1975), 13–14.

36. The influential distinction between 'chronological primitivism' and 'cultural primitivism' made by A. O. Lovejoy and G. Boas in their *Primitivism and Related Ideas in Antiquity* (Baltimore, 1935), 1–11, is valid in so far as it can serve to indicate a historical rather than a geographical distance from 'civilization', but it should not be allowed to obscure the interrelation between chronology and culture implicit in 'primitivism' of any kind.

37. Hesiod, *Works and Days*, trans. D. Wender (Penguin edn., 1973), 62.

38. See Ovid, *Metamorphoses*, trans. M. M. Innes (Penguin edn., 1955), 31–3.

39. Hesiod, *Works and Days*, 63.

40. Ibid. 64.

41. Although the passage referring to Kronos may not be Hesiodic, at least some classical interpolator thought it appropriate that Kronos should rule the Blessed Isles.

42. Homer, *Odyssey*, 79.

43. See Lovejoy and Boas, *Primitivism*, 292.

44. Horace, *Epodes*, xvi, *Odes and Epodes*, trans. C. E. Bennett (Loeb edn., 1927), 411, 413. See Horace, *Odes*, II. xvi, trans. J. Michie (London, 1964), 125, 126.

45. Strabo, *Geography*, i. 7.
46. Pliny, *Natural History*, VI. xxvii, trans. H. Rackham (Loeb edn., 1938–62), ii. 489, 491.
47. See Lovejoy and Boas, *Primitivism*, 303; and R. R. Cawley, *Unpathed Waters*, 3.
48. F. E. and F. P. Manuel, *Utopian Thought in the Western World* (Oxford, 1979), 77–8.
49. See Lovejoy and Boas, *Primitivism*, 303.
50. See Pindar, 'Pythian', x, *The Odes*, trans. C. M. Bowra (Penguin edn., 1969), 22–3; and also Diodorus Siculus, *Library of History*, trans. C. H. Oldfather (Loeb edn., 1933–67), ii. 39.
51. Homer, *Iliad*, XIII. 6, trans. A. T. Murray (Loeb edn., 1925), ii. 3. See Lovejoy and Boas, *Primitivism*, 315.
52. Strabo, *Geography*, iii. 199.
53. Lovejoy and Boas, *Primitivism*, 327
54. See e.g. Horace, *Odes*, III. xxiv.
55. See e.g. Diogenes Laertius, *Lives of Philosophers*, i. 43–4.
56. See G. Chinard, *L'Exotisme américain dans la littérature française au XVIᵉ siècle* (Paris, 1911), 19.
57. Tertullian, *The Five Books of Quintus Sept. Flor. Tertullianus Against Marcion*, trans. Peter Holmes, *Ante-Nicene Christian Library*, ed. A. Roberts and J. Donaldson, vii (Edinburgh, 1868), 2.
58. Lovejoy and Boas, *Primitivism*, 7.
59. On the opposition between νόμος and φύσις, see W. K. C. Guthrie, *A History of Greek Philosophy*, iii (Cambridge, 1969), 55 ff.
60. Diogenes Laertius, *Lives of Philosophers*, ii. 75, and see 55, 41, 25, 47.
61. Plato, *Republic*, 372a–c, 372d, 372–373a, trans. P. Shorey, in Plato, *The Collected Dialogues*, ed. E. Hamilton and H. Cairns (Princeton, 1961).
62. Ibid. 592a.
63. Plato, *Timaeus*, 19b, 26e, trans. B. Jowett, *Collected Dialogues*.
64. Ibid. 20d.
65. Plato, *Critias*, 108e, trans. A. E. Taylor, *Collected Dialogues*.
66. Ibid. 111c–d, and see 110d, 112c.
67. See R. R. Cawley, *Unpathed Waters*, 43, and e.g. Richard Eden, *The History of Travayle in the West and East Indies* (London, 1577), 5 ff.
68. See F. E. and F. P. Manuel, *Utopian Thought*, 23, 86–7.
69. See Diodorus Siculus, *Library of History*, ii. 65–83.
70. See E. Rohde, *Der Griechische Roman und Seine Vorläufer* (Leipzig, 1914), 258–9, and J. Ferguson, *Utopias*, 126–7.
71. Lucian, *A True Story*, trans. A. M. Harmon, in *Works* (Loeb edn., 1913–67), i. 249–51.
72. Ibid. 321.
73. Ibid. 337.
74. See ibid. 357 n. 1.
75. Ibid. 281.
76. Ibid. 251.
77. Ibid. 253.
78. Diogenes Laertius, *Lives of Philosophers*, ii. 343.
79. See J. O. Thomson, *Ancient Geography*, 338 ff.

80. St Ambrose, quoted in Dickinson and Howarth, *Making of Geography*, 40.
81. Cosmas Indicopleustes, *The Christian Topography*, trans. and ed. J. W. McCrindle (London, 1897), 17, and see 86, and Acts 17: 26.
82. See A. P. Newton, 'The Conception of the World in the Middle Ages', in A. P. Newton (ed.), *Travel and Travellers of the Middle Ages* (London, 1926), 8.
83. Genesis 2: 8, and see 3: 24. On medieval Christian belief in the terrestrial Paradise, see G. H. T. Kimble, *Geography in the Middle Ages* (London, 1938), 184–5.
84. See illustration of detail in Meryl Jancey, *Mappa Mundi: The Map of the World in Hereford Cathedral: A Brief Guide* (Hereford, 1987), 10.
85. See F. E. and F. P. Manuel, 'Sketch for a Natural History of Paradise', *Daedalus* (Winter, 1972), 117.
86. Dante is unconventional in situating the terrestrial Paradise in the southern hemisphere rather than in the East. See Kimble, 'Dante's Geographical Knowledge', *Geography in the Middle Ages*, 243–4; J. O. Thomson, *Ancient Geography*, 389; and Dante Alighieri, *Inferno*, XXXIV, *La Divina Commedia*, ed. Natalino Sapegno (Florence, 1968), i.
87. See Amerigo Vespucci, 'Letter from Seville', trans. F. J. Pohl, in J. H. Parry (ed.), *The European Reconnaissance: Selected Documents* (London, 1968), 178.
88. Dante Alighieri, *Purgatorio*, XXVIII. 139 ff., *La Divina Commedia*, ii.
89. See H. Levin, *The Myth of the Golden Age in the Renaissance* (New York, 1972), 177, 35.
90. See R. R. Cawley, *Unpathed Waters*, 5.
91. *Navigatio Sancti Brendani*, as given in *The Anglo-Norman Voyage of St. Brendan*, ed. E. G. R. Waters (Oxford, 1928), 89–90, trans. in G. Boas, *Essays on Primitivism and Related Ideas in the Middle Ages* (Baltimore, 1948), 159.
92. See A. P. Newton, '"Travellers' Tales" of Wonder and Imagination', in A. P. Newton (ed.), *Travel and Travellers*, 162.
93. The 'Letter of Prester John' is translated in Boas, *Essays on Primitivism*, 161–4, and in E. Denison Ross, 'Prester John and the Empire of Ethiopia', in A. P. Newton (ed.), *Travel and Travellers*, 174–8. Prester John was transferred to Africa from Central Asia early in the 14th cent., as a consequence of increasing familiarity with the East. (See Vsevolod Slessarev, *Prester John: The Letter and the Legend* (Minneapolis, 1959), 84.)
94. See J. R. S. Phillips, *The Medieval Expansion of Europe* (Oxford, 1988), 60–1.
95. See Henri Baudet, *Paradise on Earth: Some Thoughts on European Images of Non-European Man*, trans. Elizabeth Wentholt (New Haven, Conn., 1965), 17, 18.
96. See Leonardo Olschki, *Marco Polo's Asia*, trans. John Scott (Berkeley, Calif., 1960), 40 ff.
97. René Grousset, *Histoire de l'Asie*, iii. *Le Monde mongol* (Paris, 1922), 130.
98. E. Power, 'The Opening of the Land Routes to Cathay', in A. P. Newton (ed.), *Travel and Travellers*, 132.
99. See R. Dawson, *The Chinese Chameleon: An Analysis of European Conceptions of China* (London, 1967), 11; Donald F. Lach, *Asia in the Making of Europe*, i. *The Century of Discovery*, Book One (Chicago, 1965), 36; and Marco Polo, *The Travels*, trans. Ronald Latham (Penguin edn.,1958), 256, 258. Polo's name of Milione does not certainly refer to his reputation for exaggeration, however. (See Marco Polo, *The Description of the World*, ed. A. C. Moule and Paul Pelliot (London, 1938), Introduction, i. 31–3.)
100. Polo, *Travels*, 33–4.

101. See Olschki, *Marco Polo's Asia*, 120–1. There are a few details about Rustichello in Giorgio del Guerra, *Rustichello da Pisa* (Pisa, 1955).

102. See Marco Polo, *Il Milione*, ed. L. F. Benedetto (Florence, 1928), p. xix.

103. Ibid. p. xx.

104. Ibid. p. xxvi.

105. Ibid. p. xx.

106. Gillian Beer, *The Romance* (London, 1970), 6.

107. Ibid. 5.

108. I will not enter into the complications of the authorship, sources, and dating of *Mandeville's Travels*.

109. According to J. W. Bennett, 'Mandeville' used Carpini at second hand in the version in Vincent de Beauvais's *Speculum*. (See J. W. Bennett, *The Rediscovery of Sir John Mandeville* (New York, 1954), 21, 38.)

110. *Mandeville's Travels*, ed. M. C. Seymour (London, 1968), 15. I quote from Seymour's 1968 edn., with modernized spelling, of the Cotton manuscript translation of a French original. When I make reference to the notes in Seymour's 1967 edn., with original spelling, I shall cite *Mandeville's Travels*, ed. Seymour (Oxford, 1967).

111. *Mandeville's Travels* (1968), 243.

112. See D. R. Howard, *Writers and Pilgrims: Medieval Pilgrimage Narratives and their Posterity* (Berkeley, Calif., 1980), 59.

113. *Mandeville's Travels* (1968), pp. xiv, 3, 244.

114. See *Mandeville's Travels* (1968), pp. xiii, xv, and J. H. Parry, *The Age of Reconnaissance* (New York, 1964), 23.

115. [Richard Steele] ('Isaac Bickerstaff'), *Tatler*, 254 (21–3 Nov. 1710).

116. See *Ancient India as Described by Ktêsias the Knidian; being a translation of the abridgement of his 'Indika' by Phôtios, and of the fragments of that work preserved in other writers*, trans. and ed. J. W. McCrindle (London, 1882); Rudolf Wittkower, 'Marvels of the East: A Study in the History of Monsters', in *Allegory and the Migration of Symbols* (London, 1977), 45 ff.; and John B. Friedman, *The Monstrous Races in Medieval Art and Thought* (Cambridge, Mass. 1981).

117. *Mandeville's Travels* (1968), 122. See B. Penrose, *Travel and Discovery in the Renaissance, 1420–1620* (Cambridge, Mass., 1952), 10–11; Bennett, *Sir John Mandeville*, 37; *Mandeville's Travels* (Oxford, 1967), 249 n.

118. *Mandeville's Travels* (1968), 151 (cf. Polo, *Travels*, 258), 156, 154.

119. Sir Thomas Browne, *Pseudodoxia Epidemica*, ed. R. Robbins (Oxford, 1981), i. 237.

120. Sir Walter Raleigh, 'The Discovery of Guiana', in Richard Hakluyt, *The Principal Navigations, Voyages, Traffiques and Discoveries of the English Nation* (Glasgow, 1903–5), x. 406.

121. Shakespeare, *Othello*, I. iii. 144 ff., and see Shakespeare, *The Tempest*, Names of the Actors, and III. iii. 46 ff.

122. Spenser, *The Faerie Queene*, ed. A. C. Hamilton (London, 1977), IV. vii. 6.

123. *Mandeville's Travels* (1968), 168.

124. See M. Letts, *Sir John Mandeville: The Man and his Book* (London, 1949), 77–8.

125. *Mandeville's Travels* (1968), 234, and see Letts, *Sir John Mandeville*, 99.

126. *Mandeville's Travels* (1968), 234.

127. Ibid. 242.

128. See Bennett, *Sir John Mandeville*, 246.

129. Purchas, *Pilgrimes*, xi. 363.
130. See George B. Parks, *Richard Hakluyt and the English Voyages* (New York, 1928), 46.
131. Robert Burton, *The Anatomy of Melancholy* (Oxford, 1651), 244.
132. Richard Brome, *The Antipodes*, ed. A. Haaker (London, 1967), i. vi. 30 ff.
133. See *Mandeville's Travels* (1968), p. xvi, and Bennett, *Sir John Mandeville*, 2–3. The phrase 'the Father of English Prose' was used by William Minto in his *A Manual of English Prose Literature* (1872), but the perception of 'Mandeville' as the first writer of English prose is common in the years following Samuel Johnson's praise of 'Mandeville's' 'force of thought and beauty of expression'. (William Minto, *A Manual of English Prose Literature* (Edinburgh, 1872), 211; Samuel Johnson, Introductory essay on 'The History of the English Language', *A Dictionary of the English Language* (London, 1755); and see Bennett, *Sir John Mandeville*, 2–3.)
134. *Mandeville's Travels* (1968), p. xvi; Bennett, *Sir John Mandeville*, 4.
135. Parry, *The Age of Reconnaissance*, 24.
136. *Mandeville's Travels* (1968), 139, 141.
137. See Andrés Bernáldez, *Historia de los Reyes Católicos D. Fernando y Doña Isabel* (Seville, 1870), i. 357–8. On the association between Columbus's voyage to the 'gran Kan' and the book of 'el noble caballero inglés Juan de Mandavilla', see also ibid. ii. 43.
138. A. P. Newton, Introduction, Newton (ed.), *The Great Age of Discovery* (repr. New York, 1970), 6. See also Luis Weckmann, 'The Middle Ages in the Conquest of America', *Speculum*, 26 (1951), 130–41.
139. Antonio Pastor, 'Spanish Civilization in the Great Age of Discovery', in Newton (ed.), *The Great Age of Discovery*, 19.
140. Ibid. 41.
141. Bernal Díaz del Castillo, *The True History of the Conquest of New Spain*, trans. A. P. Maudslay, ii (London, 1910), 37.
142. See *American Place Names, A Concise and Selective Dictionary*, ed. G. R. Stewart (New York, 1970), 'California'. The romance was *Las Sergas de Esplandián*, by Garci Ordóñez de Montalvo, who was also the author of the extant version of *Amadís*. He is quoted in Pastor, 'Spanish Civilization', 19.
143. J. R. Hale, *Renaissance Exploration* (London, 1968), 90. See also H. M. Jones, *O Strange New World: American Culture: The Formative Years* (New York, 1964), 24 ff.
144. Spenser, *The Faerie Queene*, II, Proem, 1–2.
145. Columbus, journal, quoted by Las Casas in *The 'Diario' of Christopher Columbus's First Voyage to America 1492–1493*, transcribed and trans. Oliver Dunn and James E. Kelley, Jr. (Norman, Okla., 1989), 17.
146. Fernando Colón, *Historie del S. D. Fernando Colombo; nelle quali s'ha particolare, & vera relatione della vita, & de' fatti dell' Ammiraglio D. Cristoforo Colombo, suo padre*, trans. Alfonso Ulloa (Venice, 1571), 15, translation (from the Italian translation of Fernando's lost manuscript in Spanish) mine.
147. See *El libro de Marco Polo anotado por Cristóbal Colón*, ed. Juan Gil (Madrid, 1987). I can see no basis for the statement in Carlos Sanz, *El gran secreto do la Carta de Colón* that Columbus possessed and annotated a 1483 edition of Polo's *Travels* bound with *Mandeville's Travels*. (See Carlos Sanz, *El gran secreto de la Carta de Colón* (Madrid, 1959), 55.)
148. S. E. Morison, *Admiral of the Ocean Sea: A Life of Christopher Columbus* (Boston, 1942), i. 129 n.

149. *Mandeville's Travels* (1968), 142.
150. Andrés Bernáldez, *Historia*, i. 358, in *The Voyages of Christopher Columbus, Being the Journals of his First and Third, and the Letters concerning his First and Last Voyages, to which is added the Account of the Second Voyage written by Andrés Bernáldez*, trans. and ed. Cecil Jane (London, 1930), 309.
151. Columbus, journal, quoted by Las Casas in *The 'Diario'*, 19.
152. Ibid. 109, but I have slightly adapted the translation, preferring, for example, to translate 'toda via tengo determinado' as 'anyway I am still determined' rather than as 'I have already decided'. (Ibid. 108, 109, and, for an alternative translation, see *The Journal of Christopher Columbus*, trans. Cecil Jane, rev. L. A. Vigneras (London, 1960), 41.)
153. Marco Polo, *Marci Pauli de Venecijs de consuetudinibus et condicionibus orientalium regionum* (Antwerp, 1485), 3rd bk., 2nd chap., translation mine.
154. Columbus, in *El libro de Marco Polo*, 132, translation mine.
155. Polo, *Marci Pauli de Venecijs*, 2nd bk., 64th chap., and Columbus, in *El libro de Marco Polo*, 122, translations mine.
156. Amerigo Vespucci, *Mundus Novus* ('Letter to Lorenzo Pietro di Medici'), trans. G. T. Northrup (Princeton, 1916). Some scholars consider the *Mundus Novus* a forgery, though partly based on genuine letters by Vespucci. His writings and voyages are controversial. Compare A. P. Newton, *The Great Age of Discovery*, 118 and Parry, *European Reconnaissance* 173, who differ as to which of Vespucci's writings are authentic. The question is discussed in F. J. Pohl, *Amerigo Vespucci: Pilot Major* (London, 1966), 147 ff., but I do not find Pohl's arguments convincing or his conclusions satisfactory. That Vespucci did recognize a 'new world' seems a reasonable conclusion to draw from his statement in his 'Letter from Lisbon' of 1502 (not discovered till the eighteenth century, but generally considered authentic): 'we arrived at a new land which . . . we observed to be a continent'. (Vespucci, in *European Reconnaissance*, ed. Parry, 186.) [Martin Waldseemüller], *Cosmographiae Introductio* (Saint Dié, Lorraine, 1507), translation mine.
157. Columbus, journal, quoted by Las Casas in *The 'Diario'*, 104, and quoted by Fernando Colón, *Historie del S. D. Fernando Colombo*, 62, translation mine. See E. R. Curtius, *European Literature and the Latin Middle Ages*, trans. W. R. Trask (Princeton, 1973), 159 ff., and also L. Olschki, 'What Columbus Saw on Landing in the West Indies', *Proceedings of the American Philosophical Society*, 84/5 (July 1941), 633–59.
158. Columbus, journal, quoted by Las Casas in *The 'Diario'*, 65, 67, 69, translation slightly adapted with the assistance of *The Journal*, 24.
159. Columbus, 'Letter', in *Select Documents*, i. 4, 12.
160. Ibid. 12.
161. Ibid. 8.
162. Ibid. 12, 14, and Columbus, journal, quoted by Las Casas, *The 'Diario'*, 217, and 216 for the transcript, reading 'Caniba no es otra cosa sino la gente dl grā Can'. See 'Letter', *Select Documents*, i. 16, and *Mandeville's Travels* (1968), 119 ff. On Columbus, 'Canibales', and the Khan, see Peter Hulme, *Colonial Encounters: Europe and the native Caribbean, 1492–1797* (London, 1986), 22, and Tzvetan Todorov, *La Conquête de l'Amérique: la question de l'autre* (Paris, 1982), 37.
163. Columbus, 'Letter', *Select Documents*, i. 14, but I have preferred the translation in 'Letter of Columbus', in *The Four Voyages of Christopher Columbus*, trans. J. M. Cohen (Penguin edn., 1969), 121.

164. See Giuliano Dati, *Lettera delle isole che ha trovato il re di Spagna* (Florence, 1493). This is the 2nd edn., the 1st, which I have not seen, being published four months earlier in Rome. (See Martin Davies, *Columbus in Italy: An Italian Versification of the Letter on the discovery of the New World* (London, 1991) and Hugh Honour, *The New Golden Land: European Images of America* (New York, 1975), 6–7.)

165. See J. H. Elliott, *The Old World and the New, 1492–1650* (Cambridge, 1972), 10.

166. See Girolamo Fracastoro, *Syphilis sive Morbus Gallicus* (Verona, 1530), in which Columbus is not actually named, and H. M. Jones, *O Strange New World*, 400, and Leicester Bradner, 'Columbus in Sixteenth-Century Poetry', in *Essays Honoring Lawrence C. Wroth* (Portland, Me., 1951), 15–30, and Francisco Guerra, 'The Problem of Syphilis', in F. Chiappelli (ed.), *First Images of America: The Impact of the New World on the Old* (Berkeley, Calif., 1976), ii. 845–51.

167. See J. H. Elliott, *The Old World and the New*, 11–12, and Hugh Honour, *Romanticism* (London, 1979), 262–4.

168. Columbus, 'Narrative of the voyage', in *Select Documents*, ii. 16, 30, 31.

169. Ibid. 42, 46, 38. For the 'indications' Columbus refers to, corresponding with the descriptions of the terrestrial Paradise in Pierre d'Ailly's *Imago Mundi*, annotated by Columbus, see Morison, *Admiral of the Ocean Sea*, i. 121.

170. Columbus, digested by Las Casas, *The 'Diario'*, 383.

171. Vespucci, 'Letter from Seville', in *European Reconnaissance*, ed. Parry, 176.

172. Vespucci, 'Letter from Lisbon', trans. F. J. Pohl, in *European Reconnaissance*, ed. Parry, 187.

173. See A. P. Newton, 'Christopher Columbus and his First Voyage', *The Great Age of Discovery*, 97 ff.

174. Pietro Martire d'Anghiera, *The Decades of the newe worlde or west India*, trans. Richard Eden (London, 1555), 8.

175. Ibid. 17.

176. See Vespucci, *Mundus Novus*, 5–6. (Vespucci's 'Letter from Lisbon' gives a similar account of the Indians and is generally accepted as authentic, but was not discovered till the eighteenth century. See *European Reconnaissance*, ed. Parry, 187.)

177. Pierre de Ronsard, 'Complainte contre Fortune', *Œuvres complètes*, ed. P. Laumonier, x (Paris, 1939), 33–4.

178. Michael Drayton, 'To the Virginian Voyage', *Poems* (London, 1619), 295–6.

179. Ronsard, 'Complainte contre Fortune', *Œuvres*, x. 34.

180. Chinard, *L'Exotisme américain*, 119–20.

181. Sir Thomas More, *The Utopia of Sir Thomas More, in Latin from the edition of March 1518, and in English from the first edition of Ralph Robynson's translation in 1551*, ed. J. H. Lupton (Oxford, 1895), 27–8. On the *Four Voyages*, see Pohl, *Amerigo Vespucci*, ix.

182. See F. E. and F. P. Manuel, *Utopian Thought*, 123.

183. More, *The Utopia*, 216.

184. Ibid. 34.

185. Ibid. 33.

186. Ibid. 220, 112–13.

187. Ibid. 239.

188. Ibid. pp. xcix–c.

189. Michel de Montaigne, 'Des cannibales', *Essais*, ed. M. Rat (Paris, 1948), i. 234.

190. Montaigne, 'Of the Caniballes', *The Essayes*, trans. John Florio (London, 1603), 102.

191. Edward Capell pointed out Shakespeare's debt to Montaigne, but not Florio's (probable) part in the transaction. (See [Edward Capell], *Notes and Various Readings to Shakespeare* (London, 1779–80), II. iv. 63).

192. Shakespeare, *The Tempest*, II. i. 143–64.

193. Ibid. IV. i. 188–9.

194. Spenser, *The Faerie Queene*, IV. vii. 5; VI. v. 2.

195. Columbus, journal, quoted by Las Casas, *The 'Diario'*, 281, and 'Letter', *Select Documents*, i. 14.

196. See R. A. Billington, *Land of Savagery, Land of Promise: The European Image of the American Frontier in the Nineteenth Century* (New York, 1981), 5.

197. Arthur Barlowe, 'Discourse of the First Voyage', in *The Roanoke Voyages 1584–1590*, ed. D. B. Quinn (London, 1955), i. 93–4, 108.

198. See Arthur Barlowe, 'The first voyage to Virginia', in Hakluyt, *Principal Navigations*, viii. 298, 305. On Drayton and Hakluyt, see Joan Rees, 'Hogs, Gulls, and Englishmen: Drayton and the Virginian Voyages', *The Yearbook of English Studies*, 13 (1983), 20–31.

199. John Smith, *The Generall Historie of Virginia, New England, and the Summer Isles* (London, 1624), 42, 47, 48.

200. William Bradford, *History of Plymouth Plantation*, reproduced in facsimile from the original document (London, 1896), 113.

201. Ibid. 91.

202. Edward Taylor, 'Preparatory Meditations' 2nd ser., 1, *The Poems of Edward Taylor*, ed. D. E. Stanford (New Haven, Conn., 1960), 83.

203. Cotton Mather, *The Wonders of the Invisible World* (Boston, 1693), 29.

204. Mary Rowlandson, *The Soveraignty & Goodness of God, Together with the Faithfulness of His Promises Displayed; Being a Narrative of the Captivity and Restauration of Mrs. Mary Rowlandson* (2nd edn., corrected and augmented, Cambridge, Mass., 1682), 20, 6.

205. 'The Preface to the Reader', in Mary Rowlandson, *The Soveraignty & Goodness of God*.

206. Cotton Mather, *Magnalia Christi Americana*, bks. i and ii, ed. K. B. Murdock (Cambridge, Mass., 1977), 337; James Fenimore Cooper, *The Last of the Mohicans; A Narrative of 1757*, ed. J. F. Beard *et al.* (New York, 1983), 57.

207. Ibid. 349.

208. Montaigne, 'Des cannibales', *Essais*, i. 244.

209. John Milton, *Paradise Lost*, ed. A. Fowler (London, 1971), ii. 362–8, 403.

210. Ibid. ii. 1015–19, iv. 390–1.

211. Ibid. ii. 891–2.

212. Ibid. iii. 543 ff.

213. Ibid. iv. 159 ff.

214. Samuel Purchas, *Purchas his Pilgrimage, or Relations of the World and the Religions observed in all Ages and Places Discovered, from the Creation unto this Present* (London, 1613), 13.

215. Milton, *Paradise Lost*, ix. 1115 ff.

216. Ibid. xi. 834.

217. Gonzalo Fernández de Oviedo, *Historia general y natural de las Indias*, ed. Juan Pérez de Tudela Bueso (Madrid, 1959), iii. 212, trans. Parry, in *European Reconnaissance*, ed. Parry, 233.

218. It is generally accepted that Magellan named the Pacific, though this is not stated in any of the records of the voyage. See O. H. K. Spate, ' "South Sea" to "Pacific Ocean": A Note on Nomenclature', *Journal of Pacific History*, 12 (1977), 205–11.
219. Montaigne, 'Apologie de Raimond Sebond', *Essais*, ii. 287.
220. Abraham Cowley, 'To the Royal Society', in Thomas Sprat, *History of the Royal Society*, ed. J. I. Cope and H. W. Jones (Saint Louis, Mo., 1958).

CHAPTER 2

1. Montaigne, 'Des cannibales', *Essais*, i. 235.
2. François Rabelais, *Le Quart Livre des faicts & dictz heroïques du bon Pantagruel* (Lyon, 1552), 4.
3. François Rabelais, *Le Cinquiesme et Dernier Livre des faits & dits heroïques du bon Pantagruel* (Lyon, 1571), 108.
4. See A. Lefranc, *Les Navigations de Pantagruel: étude sur la géographie rabelaisienne* (Geneva, 1967), 57–65.
5. Jacques Cartier, 'Au Roy treschrestien', in *Brief recit, & succinte narration, de la navigation faicte es ysles de Canda, Hochelage & Saguenay & autres, avec particulieres meurs, langaiges, & cerimonies des habitans d'icelles: fort delectable à veoir* (Paris, 1545).
6. Vespucci, 'Letter from Seville', in *European Reconnaissance*, ed. Parry, 180.
7. Francisco López de Gómara, *Historia General de las Indias* (Madrid, 1922), i. 20, and Fernández de Oviedo, *Historia general*, i. 39, both quoted and translated in Elliott, *The Old World and the New*, 52, 40.
8. Parry, *The Age of Reconnaissance*, 17.
9. Antonio Pigafetta, *Magellan's Voyage Around the World*, the (Italian) Ambrosian MS, ed. James A. Robertson (Cleveland, Ohio, 1906), i. 40, translation mine. J. H. Elliott, in *The Discovery of America and the Discovery of Man* (London, 1972) applied Michelet's famous phrase to the discovery of America.
10. Jean-Jacques Rousseau, *Essai sur l'origine des langues*, ed. Charles Porset (Bordeaux, 1968), 89.
11. Shakespeare, *The Tempest*, v. i. 183–4.
12. G. Atkinson, *Les Nouveaux Horizons de la Renaissance française* (Paris, 1935), 63.
13. Columbus, journal, quoted by Las Casas, *The 'Diario'*, 65; Milton, *Paradise Lost*, ix. 1116. I refer to a historical fact, what Columbus found, not a multiplicity of ethnographic facts (what the various American Indians wore, or did not wear).
14. Étienne Jodelle, 'Ode à M. Thevet', in André Thevet, *Les Singularitez de la France Antarctique, autrement nommée Amerique* (Paris, 1558).
15. Montaigne, 'Au lecteur', *Essais*, i. 1.
16. Montaigne, 'Du repentir', *Essais*, iii. 19; 'De la praesumption', ibid. ii. 368; 'Sur des vers de Virgile', ibid. iii. 113.
17. Montaigne, 'De la coustume', 'De l'usage de se vestir', *Essais*, i. 113, 255.
18. Jean de Léry, *Histoire d'un voyage fait en la terre du Bresil, autrement dite Amerique* (La Rochelle, 1578), 130, 110, 130.
19. Burton, *Anatomy of Melancholy*, 469.
20. Léry *Histoire d'un voyage*, 80.
21. Montaigne, 'De la coustume', *Essais*, i. 113, 116–17.

22. See Montaigne, 'Apologie de Raimond Sebond', *Essais*, ii. 224, 196, and (editor's n. 416) 547; also P. Villey, *Les Essais de Montaigne* (Mayenne, 1972), 62.

23. Sextus Empiricus, *Outlines of Pyrrhonism*, trans. R. G. Bury (Loeb edn., 1933), 113 ff.

24. Ibid. 25.

25. Ibid. 25, 89, 93.

26. Montaigne, 'De la coustume', *Essais*, i. 123.

27. Montaigne, 'Des cannibales', *Essais*, i. 234.

28. See Montaigne, 'De la coustume' and 'Apologie de Raimond Sebond', *Essais*, i. 125, ii. 197.

29. Montaigne, 'Des cannibales', *Essais*, i. 232. G. Chinard demonstrates beyond doubt Montaigne's use of G. Benzoni, *La Historia del Mondo Nuovo* (1565), trans. and adapted, U. Chauveton, *Histoire nouvelle du nouveau monde* (1579). (See Chinard, *L'Exotisme américain*, 198 ff.)

30. Montaigne, 'Des cannibales', *Essais*, i. 233.

31. Ibid.

32. Ibid. 233–4.

33. See ibid. 234.

34. Ibid. 235.

35. Ibid. 234.

36. A. O. Lovejoy, *Essays in the History of Ideas* (New York, 1955), 238.

37. Léry, *Histoire d'un voyage*, 198.

38. Montaigne, 'Des cannibales', *Essais*, i. 244–5.

39. M. T. Hodgen, *Early Anthropology in the Sixteenth and Seventeenth Centuries* (repr. Philadelphia, 1971), 191–2. On Montaigne's knowledge of the literature on the new world, see Pierre Villey, *Les Livres d'histoire moderne utilisés par Montaigne* (Paris, 1908) and, particularly, Chinard, *L'Exotisme américain*, 194 ff.

40. Montaigne, 'Des cannibales', *Essais*, i. 245.

41. La Mothe Le Vayer, quoted in Richard H. Popkin, *The History of Scepticism from Erasmus to Descartes* (rev., New York, 1968), 17 n. See also: A. M. Boase, *The Fortunes of Montaigne: A History of the Essays in France, 1580–1669* (repr. New York, 1970), 91, 260 ff.; S. Landucci, *I filosofi e i selvaggi, 1580–1780* (Bari, 1972), 44 ff.

42. See: Popkin, *History of Scepticism* 17 n.; Boase, *Fortunes of Montaigne*, 425; G. Atkinson, *Les Relations de voyages du XVIIᵉ siècle et l'évolution des idées* (Paris, 1924), 191 ff.; Paul Hazard, *La Crise de la conscience européenne, 1680–1715* (Paris, 1935), 10–11.

43. See Atkinson, *Les Relations de voyages*, 12.

44. See Boase, *Fortunes of Montaigne*, p. xxi.

45. Descartes, *Discours de la méthode*, in *Œuvres*, 129, 132.

46. Ibid. 131.

47. Bacon, 'Of Truth', in *The Essayes or Counsels, Civill and Morall* (London, 1625), 1.

48. Bacon, 'The New Organon' ('Novum Organum'), in *The Works of Francis Bacon*, ed. J. Spedding, R. L. Ellis, and D. D. Heath (London, 1857–74), iv. 53.

49. Ibid. 114.

50. See Montaigne, 'Des coches', *Essais*, iii. 137.

51. Bacon, 'An Advertisement Touching an Holy War', in *Works*, vii. 34.

52. Bacon, 'Of Plantations', in *The Essayes*, 203.

53. On Bacon in the wake of the voyagers, see R. L. Ellis, Preface to Bacon, 'Sylva Sylvarum', in *Works*, i. 327.

54. Bacon, 'The Refutation of Philosophies' ('Redargutio Philosophiarum'), in B. Farrington, *The Philosophy of Francis Bacon* (Liverpool, 1964), 131.
55. Bacon, *The Advancement of Learning*, ed. A. Johnston (Oxford, 1974), 131; 'The New Organon', in *Works*, iv. 181, 207.
56. Bacon, 'The New Organon', in *Works*, iv. 179; 'Sylva Sylvarum', in *Works*, i. 348.
57. Bacon, 'The New Organon', in *Works*, iv. 73.
58. Pigafetta, *Magellan's Voyage*, i. 57, 85, 89, 95, 99. Shakespeare could have read of the Patagonian giants who 'cryed uppon theyr greate devyll *Setebos*' in the translation of Pigafetta's account included in Richard Eden, *The Decades of the newe worlde* (London, 1555), 219. On the Ladrones as Guam and Rota, see A. Sharp, *The Discovery of the Pacific Islands* (Oxford, 1960), 6.
59. Pigafetta, *Magellan's Voyage*, i. 109.
60. Drake (1577) and Cavendish (1586–8) were, respectively, the second and the third, after del Cano, to circumnavigate the world.
61. Bacon, *Advancement of Learning*, 77.
62. Ibid. 78.
63. See, for example, in addition to passages quoted here: Bacon, 'Thoughts and Conclusions' ('Cogitata et Visa'), in Farrington, *Philosophy of Francis Bacon*, 94; Bacon, 'The New Organon', in *Works*, iv. 82.
64. Bacon, 'The Refutation of Philosophies', in Farrington, *Philosophy of Francis Bacon*, 131.
65. The frontispiece is reproduced in Bacon, *Works*, i. 119. See Daniel, 12: 4.
66. Bacon, 'Of the Dignity and Advancement of Learning' ('De Augmentis Scientiarum'), in *Works*, iv. 283.
67. Bacon, 'Of Vicissitude of Things', in *The Essayes*, 330–1. On America as Atlantis, see Cawley, *Unpathed Waters*, 43.
68. Bacon, *New Atlantis*, ed. A. Johnston (Oxford, 1974), 215.
69. See C. Jack-Hinton, *The Search for the Islands of Solomon, 1567–1838* (Oxford, 1969), 24.
70. See Brome, *The Antipodes*. W. T. James sees 'echoes of Hall's work' in *The Antipodes*. (W. T. James, 'Nostalgia for Paradise: Terra Australis in the Seventeenth Century', in I. Donaldson (ed.), *Australia and the European Imagination* (Canberra, 1982), 70.)
71. On the maps in Hall's work, see J. Hall, *Mundus Alter et Idem*, trans. J. Healey as *The Discovery of a New World*, ed. H. Brown (Cambridge, Mass., 1937), pp. xx–xxi.
72. Milton, 'An Apology Against a Pamphlet', in *Complete Prose Works* (New Haven, Conn., 1953–74), i. 881.
73. J. Hall, *Mundus Alter et Idem*, 14.
74. Ibid. 12.
75. Ibid. 17.
76. Burton, *Anatomy of Melancholy*, 244.
77. Hernando Gallego, 'A True and Correct Account of the Voyage to the Western Isles in the Southern Ocean', in *The Discovery of the Solomon Islands*, ed. Lord Amherst of Hackney and B. Thomson (London, 1901), i. 5, 3.
78. Ibid. 17.
79. Gomez Hernández de Catoira, 'An Account of the Voyage and Discovery which was made in the South Sea', trans. in *Discovery of the Solomon Islands*, ed. Amherst and Thomson, ii. 235.

80. See: Jack-Hinton, *Search for the Islands*, 82; *Discovery of the Solomon Islands*, ed. Amherst and Thomson, i, p. lviii.

81. J. C. Beaglehole, *The Exploration of the Pacific* (rev. 3rd edn., London, 1966), 53.

82. Pedro Fernández de Quirós (and Luis de Belmonte Bermúdez), 'History of the Discovery of the Austrial Regions', in *The Voyages of Pedro Fernández de Quirós, 1595 to 1606*, ed. Sir Clements Markham (London, 1904), i. 15–16.

83. Ibid. 20.

84. Ibid. 16, 27, 21.

85. Ibid. 17.

86. Ibid. 29, 23.

87. Ibid. 23.

88. Ibid. 21, 25.

89. Ibid. 26.

90. See O. H. K. Spate, *The Pacific Since Magellan*, i. *The Spanish Lake* (London, 1979), 218.

91. Quirós, 'History of the Discovery', in *Voyages*, ed. Markham, i. 38.

92. Ibid. 85. Hence the title of Robert Graves's novel, *The Isles of Unwisdom* (London, 1950). For other works of modern literature inspired by the Mendaña-Quirós voyages, see Spate, *Spanish Lake*, 320 n., and A. Grove-Day, *Pacific Islands Literature: One Hundred Basic Books* (Honolulu, 1971), 17.

93. Quirós, 'History of the Discovery', in *Voyages*, ed. Markham, i. 110.

94. Juan de Torquemada, 'Monarquia Indiana', in *Voyages*, ed. Markham, ii. 424, 428; Quirós, 'History of the Discovery', in *Voyages*, ed. Markham, i. 213. On the identification of Quirós's discovery as Rakahanga, see: H. E. Maude, 'Spanish Discoveries in the Central Pacific', in *Of Islands and Men: Studies in Pacific History* (Melbourne, 1968), 75; A. Sharp, *Discovery of the Pacific Islands*, 62; Jack-Hinton, *Search for the Islands*, 142.

95. Quirós, 'History of the Discovery', in *Voyages*, ed. Markham, i. 227.

96. Ibid. 234. See Jack-Hinton, *Search for the Islands*, 153 n.

97. Quirós, 'History of the Discovery', in *Voyages*, ed. Markham, i. 249.

98. Ibid. 251. Quirós seems to have named his discovery 'la Austrialia', as a compliment to the King of Spain, who held the title of archduke of Austria. A later hand has changed the 'ia' in the manuscript to an 'a', rendering the name 'Australia'. But, with or without the compliment to the King, there is no doubt Quirós considered he had discovered 'las tierras Australes'. (See *La Austrialia del Espíritu Santo*, ed. C. Kelly (Cambridge, 1966), Introduction, i. 6 n.; and Jack-Hinton, *Search for the Islands*, 154.)

99. Quirós, 'History of the Discovery', in *Voyages*, ed. Markham, i. 253–4; Martín de Munilla, 'Journal', in *La Austrialia*, ed. Kelly, i. 223.

100. Quirós, 'History of the Discovery', in *Voyages*, ed. Markham, i. 259–60, 262.

101. Ibid. 262–3.

102. Quirós, 'Eighth Memorial', etc., in *Voyages*, ed. Markham, ii. 485, 478, 481, 479.

103. Ibid. 483–4.

104. Ibid. 486.

105. Burton, *Anatomy of Melancholy*, 241.

106. Charles Clerke, in *The Journals of Captain James Cook on His Voyages of Discovery*, ed. J. C. Beaglehole, ii. *The Voyage of the 'Resolution' and 'Adventure' 1772–1775* (Cambridge, 1961), 516–17 n.

107. Bacon, 'Preparative towards a Natural and Experimental History' ('Parasceve ad Historiam Naturalem et Experimentalem'), in *Works*, iv. 261. An account of Quirós's voyage appeared in 1612 in Henry Hudson's *Descriptio ac Delineato Geographica* and in 1617 there was published in London *Terra Australis Incognita, or a new Southerne Discoverie, containing a fifth part of the World, lately found out by Ferdinand de Quir.* (See the bibliography in *Voyages*, ed. Markham, i, pp. xlv, xlvii.) On communication in Spanish and sailing from Peru, see Cawley, *Unpathed Waters*, 45, and Bacon, *New Atlantis*, 215, 216, 239.

108. Henry Hawks, 'A Relation of the commodities of Nova Hispania, and the maners of the inhabitants, written by Henry Hawks merchant, which lived five yeeres in the sayd countrey', etc., in Hakluyt, *Principal Navigations*, ix. 392. On early English interest in the Solomon Islands, see Jack-Hinton, *Search for the Islands*, 107 ff., 184 ff.

109. Bacon, *New Atlantis*, 229.

110. [Steele], *Tatler*, 254 (21–3 Nov. 1710).

111. Burton, *Anatomy of Melancholy*, 60.

112. Bacon, 'Of Truth', *The Essayes*, 2.

113. Bacon, Preface, 'Of the Wisdom of the Ancients' ('De Sapientia Veterum') in *Works*, vi. 698. Cf. Bacon's views on 'feigned history' and poesy 'allusive and parabolical' in *Advancement of Learning*, 80–1.

114. Bacon, *New Atlantis*, 215.

115. Ibid.

116. Ibid. 221.

117. Ibid. 226, 225

118. Ibid. 225, 226.

119. Ibid. 227.

120. Ibid.

121. Ibid. 225.

122. Ibid. 227, 225.

123. Ibid. 228, 229.

124. Ibid. 230.

125. See Plato, *Laws*, 949e–952d, trans. A. E. Taylor, in *Collected Dialogues*, 1495–7.

126. Bacon, *New Atlantis*, 237; More, *The Utopia*, 220; Burton, *Anatomy of Melancholy*, 63.

127. Bacon, *New Atlantis*, 229.

128. Ibid.

129. Ibid. 223.

130. Ibid. 220.

131. Ibid. 247, 237.

132. Ibid. 237, 238.

133. Ibid. 247.

134. Ibid. 238.

135. Ibid. 239.

136. Ibid. 243–5.

137. Ibid. 241.

138. Ibid.

139. Ibid. 247.

140. Montaigne, 'Des cannibales', *Essais*, i. 244.

141. Bacon, *Advancement of Learning*, 6.

142. Bacon, *New Atlantis*, 221. Cf. Psalms, 137: 6.

143. Bacon, *New Atlantis*, 246.
144. Ibid. 245.
145. Burton, *Anatomy of Melancholy*, 62–3.
146. Bacon, 'The New Organon', in *Works*, iv. 91.
147. Ibid. 102.
148. W. Rawley, 'To the Reader', in Bacon, *New Atlantis*, 214. The title is from the original edition: [Francis Bacon], 'New Atlantis. A Worke unfinished', published with *Sylva Sylvarum or A Natural History in ten Centuries* (London, 1627).
149. [Bacon], 'New Atlantis', 47.
150. Cowley, 'To the Royal Society', in Sprat, *History of the Royal Society*.
151. Sprat, *History of the Royal Society*, 35.
152. The *OED* gives 1659 as the date of the first recorded use of the word 'romantic'. On its early history, see L. Pearsall Smith, 'Four Romantic Words', in *Words and Idioms* (London, 1943), 169–70.
153. Joseph Glanvill, 'Modern Improvements of Useful Knowledge', in *Essays on Several Important Subjects in Philosophy and Religion* (London, 1676), 36.
154. John Evelyn, dedication to *Instructions Concerning Erecting of a Library*, trans. by Evelyn from the French of Gabriel Naudeus (London, 1661). On Evelyn, see G. B. Parks, 'Travel as Education', in R. F. Jones *et al.*, *The Seventeenth Century: Studies in the History of English Thought and Literature from Bacon to Pope* (Stanford, Calif., 1951), 257.
155. See [Samuel Hartlib], *A Description of the Famous Kingdome of Macaria* (London, 1641), and R. F. Jones, *Ancients and Moderns: A Study of the Rise of the Scientific Movement in Seventeenth Century England* (St Louis, Mo., 1961), 174, 171.
156. S. Hartlib, letter to Worthington, in John Worthington, *Diary*, ed. J. Crossley, i. 163; quoted in R. F. Jones, *Ancients and Moderns*, 172.
157. Abraham Cowley, 'A Proposition for the Advancement of Experimental Philosophy', in *Essays and Other Prose Writings*, ed. A. B. Gough (Oxford, 1915), 28, 33.
158. Ibid. 34.
159. *Philosophical Transactions: Giving Some Accompt of the Present Undertakings, Studies, and Labours of the Ingenious in many Considerable Parts of the World* (London), 1/8 (8 January 1665/6), 140–1.
160. Bacon, 'Description of a Natural and Experimental History', in 'Preparative towards a Natural and Experimental History', in *Works*, iv. 251; Bacon, 'The New Organon', in *Works*, iv. 62–3.
161. Henry Stubbe, *The Lord Bacon's Relation of the Sweating-sickness Examined, in a Reply to George Thomson, Pretender to Physick and Chymistry. Together with a Defence of Phlebotomy* (London, 1671), 41. See R. F. Jones, *Ancients and Moderns*, pp. x–xi.
162. Samuel Purchas, 'To the Reader', in *Purchas his Pilgrimage*.
163. Sprat, *History of the Royal Society*, 113.
164. Ibid. 112.
165. See *Seventeenth-Century Prose*, ed. B. Vickers (London, 1969), 208.
166. Montaigne, 'De l'institution des enfans', *Essais*, i. 186.
167. Bacon, 'The Great Instauration' ('Instauratio Magna'), in *Works*, iv. 22.
168. Sprat, *History of the Royal Society*, 327.
169. Vespucci, 'Letter from Lisbon', in *European Reconnaissance*, ed. Parry, 187.
170. Purchas, 'To the Reader', in *Purchas His Pilgrimes*, i, p. xl.
171. See: Atkinson, *Les Relations de voyages*; R. W. Frantz, *The English Traveller and the Movement of Ideas, 1660–1732* (repr. New York, 1968).

172. See Frantz, *English Traveller*, 85, 86, 88, 89, 94.

173. Robert Drury, *Madagascar: or, Robert Drury's Journal, during Fifteen Years Captivity on that Island* (London, 1729), 72, 399.

174. Thomas Hobbes, *Leviathan or the Matter, Forme and Power of a Commonwealth Ecclesiasticall and Civil* (London, 1651), 62, 63.

175. John Locke, *Two Treatises of Government*, ed. Peter Laslett (New York, 1965), 309.

176. Ibid. 318, 381, 343.

177. John Locke, *An Essay Concerning Humane Understanding* (London, 1690), 28–9.

178. Léry, *Histoire d'un voyage*, 259. The English traveller, Sir Thomas Roe, Locke cites from Thévenot's *Relations de divers voyages curieux*. On Locke and French travel literature, see Gabriel Bonno, *Les Relations intellectuelles de Locke avec la France* (Berkeley, Calif., 1955), 82–7, 141–5, 251.

179. Locke, *An Essay Concerning Humane Understanding*, 18.

180. Montaigne, 'De la coustume', *Essais*, i. 121.

181. Montaigne, 'Apologie de Raimond Sebond', *Essais*, ii. 288.

182. Montaigne, 'Des cannibales', *Essais*, i. 234.

183. Montaigne, 'Apologie de Raimond Sebond', *Essais*, ii. 286, 287.

184. Edward Stillingfleet, *The Bishop of Worcester's Answer to Mr. Locke's Letter, Concerning Some Passages Relating to his Essay of Humane Understanding* (London, 1697), 89–90.

185. John Locke, *Mr. Locke's Reply to the Right Reverend the Lord Bishop of Worcester's Answer to his Second Letter* (London, 1699), 449, 450.

186. Edward Stillingfleet, *Origines Sacrae: or a Rational Account of the Grounds of Natural and Reveal'd Religion: Wherein the Foundations of Religion, and the Authority of the Scriptures are asserted and clear'd; with an Answer to the Modern Objections of Atheists and Deists* (Cambridge, 1701), 76 and ff.

187. Charles Gildon, letter 'To Dr. R. B.——of a God', in Charles Blount, 'The Oracles of Reason', in *The Miscellaneous Works of Charles Blount, Esq.* (London, 1695), 180.

188. William Anstruther, *Essays, Moral and Divine; in Five Discourses* (Edinburgh, 1701), 24.

189. [A. A. Cooper, 3rd Earl of Shaftesbury], *Several Letters Written by a Noble Lord to a Young Man at the University* (London, 1716), Letter 8, 3 June 1709, 39–40.

190. [A. A. Cooper, 3rd Earl of Shaftesbury], *Soliloquy: or, Advice to an Author* (London, 1710), 183–4.

191. Ibid. 179.

192. [A. A. Cooper], *Several Letters*, Letter 8, 40.

193. John R. Moore, *Defoe's Sources for 'Robert Drury's Journal'* (Bloomington, Ind., 1943), 11.

194. [Daniel Defoe], Preface, *The Life and Strange Surprizing Adventures of Robinson Crusoe, of York, Mariner* (London, 1719).

CHAPTER 3

1. [Defoe], Preface, *The Life and Strange Surprizing Adventures of Robinson Crusoe, of York, Mariner* (London, 1719).

2. Drury, *Drury's Journal* (1729), title-page, p. [ii].

3. Ibid. p. [iii].
4. Ibid.
5. Ibid. pp. iv, vi.
6. Ibid. pp. xiv, xv.
7. Ibid. 3, 428, 429.
8. Ibid., title-page.
9. *Critical Review, or, Annals of Literature*, 14 (May 1808), 92; *Monthly Review; or Literary Journal*, 63 (Sept. 1810), 110. Writing in the margins of a copy of the 1807 edition, the *Degrave*'s captain's great grandson, Hughes Minet—'whose maternal Great Grandfather Captain Young the Father was, & who am now reading these Narratives above a Century after they happened and at 80 years of age'—found that what was said about Captain Young in the book accorded with what he himself had heard from his mother, the Captain's granddaughter. (Marginal comments in a British Library copy of *The Adventures of Robert Drury, during fifteen years captivity on the island of Madagascar* (Hull, 1807), 61, and see 60.) On eighteenth- and nineteenth-century confidence in *Drury's Journal*, see also P. Oliver, Introduction, *Madagascar: or, Robert Drury's Journal, during Fifteen Years Captivity on that Island*, ed. P. Oliver (London, 1890), 9–15; and A. W. Secord, *'Robert Drury's Journal' and Other Studies* (Urbana, Ill., 1961), 4.
10. On nineteenth-century belief in the factual basis of *Drury's Journal*, see also Revd J. Richardson, 'Drury's "Vocabulary of the Madagascar Language", with Notes', *Antananarivo Annual* for 1875, repr. in *Drury's Journal* (1890), ed. Oliver, 316 ff.; and P. B. Gove, *The Imaginary Voyage in Prose Fiction* (New York, 1941), 274–5.
11. *Collections des ouvrages anciens concernant Madagascar*, ed. Alfred and Guillaume Grandidier, iv. *Les Aventures de Robert Drury* (Paris, 1906), 364 n. The Grandidiers were convinced of the authenticity of *Drury's Journal*. (See *Les Aventures*, 6 n.)
12. See the list of 'Authorities' in the article 'Madagascar', *Encyclopaedia Britannica*, xvii (Cambridge, 1911).
13. Oliver, Introduction, *Drury's Journal* (1890), 22.
14. J. R. Moore, *Defoe in the Pillory and Other Studies* (Bloomington, Ind., 1939), 104.
15. Moore, *Defoe's Sources*, 11.
16. Ibid. 20.
17. Ibid. 37, 38.
18. Ibid. 55.
19. Ibid. 55, 57.
20. Ibid. 57, 58.
21. Ibid. 85.
22. Secord, *'Robert Drury's Journal'*, 46.
23. Ibid. 71.
24. A. W. Secord, 'Defoe in Stoke Newington', *Publications of the Modern Language Association*, 66 (Mar. 1951), 222.
25. See Secord, *'Robert Drury's Journal'*, 1, and 'Defoe in Stoke Newington', 221–5. I allude to [Defoe], *A True Relation of the Apparition of one Mrs. Veal* (London, 1706).
26. W[illiam] D[uncombe], 'An Account of William Benbow, son to the Admiral', *Gentleman's Magazine*, 39 (April 1769), 172.
27. St Clement Danes records the burial of Robert Drury, and King's College, London, is built on the site of St Clement Danes's burial ground. (See Secord, *'Robert Drury's*

Journal', 43, and 'St Clement Danes', in *The London Encyclopaedia*, ed. Ben Weinreb and Christopher Hibbert (London, 1983).) For speculation about Defoe's acquaintance with Drury, see Secord, 'Defoe in Stoke Newington', 224–5.

28. See P. N. Furbank and W. R. Owens, *The Canonisation of Daniel Defoe* (New Haven, Conn., 1988).

29. See J. R. Moore, *A Checklist of the Writings of Daniel Defoe* (rev. edn., Bloomington, Ind., 1971) and, for Moore's hand in the British Library catalogue, Furbank and Owens, *Canonisation*, 117 and, for an example of a critic routinely assuming Defoe's authorship of *Drury's Journal*, see M. E. Novak, 'Defoe's Theory of Fiction', *Studies in Philology*, 61 (1964), 655.

30. Drury, *Drury's Journal* (1729), 73.

31. Ibid. 173, 241, and see 233–5, 239–43.

32. Ibid. 457, 460, 462, 463.

33. See G. R. Crone and R. A. Skelton, 'English Collections of Voyages and Travels, 1625–1846', in Edward Lynam (ed.), *Richard Hakluyt and His Successors* (London, 1946), 67–8, 78; and also W. H. Bonner, *Captain William Dampier, Buccaneer-Author: Some Account of a Modest Buccaneer and of English Travel Literature in the Early Eighteenth Century* (Stanford, Calif., 1934), 12 n.

34. [Steele], *Tatler*, 254 (21–3 Nov. 1710); [A. A. Cooper], *Soliloquy*, 178.

35. [Swift], 'A Project, For the universal benefit of Mankind', *Miscellaneous Works, Comical & Diverting: by T.R.D.J.S.D.O.P.I.I.* (London, 1720), 264.

36. See Bonner, *Captain William Dampier*, 35; Frantz, *English Traveller*, 11; Crone and Skelton, 'English Collections', in Lynam (ed.), *Hakluyt*, 74.

37. See N. M. Penzer, Preface to William Dampier, *A New Voyage Round the World*, ed. Sir Albert Gray (London, 1927), p. v.

38. Evelyn dined with Dampier chez Pepys on 6 August 1698. (See John Evelyn, *The Diary*, ed. E. S. de Beer (Oxford, 1955), v. 295.)

39. Beaglehole, *Exploration of the Pacific*, 177.

40. See J. C. Shipman, *William Dampier: Seaman-Scientist* (Lawrence, Kan., 1962), 49, 52.

41. William Dampier, *A New Voyage Round the World* (London, 1697).

42. William Dampier, Preface, *A Voyage to New Holland* (London, 1703).

43. James Burney, *A Chronological History of the Discoveries in the South Sea or Pacific Ocean*, iv (London, 1816), 486.

44. Dampier, *A Voyage* (1703), 125–6.

45. See Shipman, *William Dampier*, 53.

46. [Swift], *Travels into Several Remote Nations of the World. By Lemuel Gulliver* (London, 1726), II. iv. 2.

47. Dampier, 'Voyages to the Bay of Campeachy', in *Voyages and Descriptions* (London, 1699), 34.

48. For the suggestion, see A. W. Secord, *Studies in the Narrative Method of Defoe* (Urbana, Ill., 1924), 61.

49. Dampier, 'Voyages to the Bay of Campeachy', in *Voyages and Descriptions*, 59–60.

50. It must be said against the monkeys in Lionel Wafer's *A New Voyage* that they are merely 'pissing', but in their favour that they are in a book we know was in Swift's possession. (Lionel Wafer, *A New Voyage and Description of the Isthmus of America* (London, 1699), 108, and see R. W. Frantz, 'Swift's Yahoos and the Voyagers',

Modern Philology, 29 (Aug. 1931), 52, and Arthur Sherbo, 'Swift and Travel Literature', *Modern Language Studies*, 9 (1979), 121.)

51. [Swift], 'A Letter from Capt. Gulliver, to his Cousin Sympson', in *Travels into Several Remote Nations of the World*, in *The Works of J. S[wift]* (Dublin, 1735), ii, p. [i].

52. [Swift], *Travels* (1726), II. iv. 7–9.

53. Ibid. 7, 8.

54. Dampier, Preface, *A New Voyage* (1697).

55. Ibid. 16. Dampier's journal is presumed lost. A MS of an earlier version of *A New Voyage* exists, in the hand, probably, of a copyist, with additions in the margin by Dampier. The reference to the journal in the 'Joint of Bambo' does not appear in context in the MS. (See British Library, Sloane MS 3236, and, for some comments on the MS, Gray, Introduction, *A New Voyage* (1927), p. xxxvii.)

56. Dampier, *A New Voyage* (1697), 84. The description of the 'Muskito Indian' in the Sloane MS is consistent with that in *A New Voyage*, but much less detailed. There is a brief mention of the same Indian in William Cowley's account of his 'Voyage round the Globe', in *A Collection of Original Voyages*, ed. William Hacke (London, 1699), 7.

57. Dampier, *A New Voyage* (1697), 86; Woodes Rogers, *A Cruising Voyage Round the World: First to the South-Seas, thence to the East-Indies, and homewards by the Cape of Good Hope* (London, 1712), 130. For Will as a possible source for Crusoe, see Secord, *Studies in the Narrative Method*, 54, 57, and Bonner, *Captain William Dampier*, 86.

58. [Defoe], *Robinson Crusoe* (1719), 148.

59. Dampier, *A New Voyage* (1697), 84–6.

60. Ibid. 462. The same words are used in the Sloane MS.

61. Dampier, *A New Voyage* (1697), 468. See Frantz, 'Swift's Yahoos', 52 (*re* monkeys) and Bonner, *Captain William Dampier*, 179–80 (*re* New Hollanders and Hottentots) and M. R. James, 'Swift's Copy of Dampier', *Times Literary Supplement*, 26 Feb. 1925, 138.

62. Dampier, *A New Voyage* (1697), 464. This passage does not appear in context in the Sloane MS.

63. [Swift], *Travels* (1726), II. iv. 8.

64. [Defoe], *Robinson Crusoe* (1719), 176.

65. Dampier, *A New Voyage* (1697), 496, 497.

66. Ibid. 513, 519.

67. 'Prince *Giolo* Son to the King of *Moangis* or *Gilolo*' (a handbill in the British Library), and see Dampier, *A New Voyage* (1697), 549, and Shakespeare, *The Tempest*, II. ii. 28–34. A fuller account of Jeoly, with a portrait, and 'Romantick' excesses at which Dampier expresses amusement, is in *An Account of the Famous Prince Giolo, son of the King of Gilolo, Now in England: with an Account of his Life, Parentage, and his strange and Wonderful Adventures . . . Written from his own Mouth* (London, 1692). The reference to 'the Naked Prince' in Congreve's *Love for Love* is probably to Jeoly. Dampier heard 'that he died of the Small-pox at *Oxford*'. (Dampier, *A New Voyage* (1697), 517, 549; William Congreve, *Love for Love: A Comedy* (London, 1695), III. i, p. 38.)

68. Dampier refers to having 'what I write, Revised and Corrected by Friends' in the Preface to *A Voyage* (1703).

69. See Dampier, *A Voyage* (1703), 120–9, 144–54.

70. Dampier, *A Continuation of a Voyage to New Holland* (London, 1709), 196, and, for the verdict on Dampier, see Gray, Introduction, *A New Voyage* (1927), p. xxix; J. A.

Williamson, Introduction, *A Voyage to New Holland*, ed. J. A. Williamson (London, 1939), p. xlix; C. Lloyd, *William Dampier* (London, 1966), 93–6.

71. Dampier, *A Continuation*, 148, and see Andrew Sharp, *Discovery of the Pacific Islands*, 92.

72. For the case for Dampier's influence on Defoe's *A New Voyage*, see Bonner, *Captain William Dampier*, 141–2, and for the case for Dampier's influence on Defoe's *Captain Singleton*, see Secord, *Studies in the Narrative Method*, 153–4.

73. Woodes Rogers, *A Cruising Voyage*, 125. According to Edward Cooke, Selkirk 'enquir'd whether a certain Officer that he knew was Aboard; and hearing that he was, would rather have chosen to remain in his Solitude, than come away with him, 'till inform'd that he did not command'. (Edward Cooke, *A Voyage to the South Sea, and Round the World* (London, 1712), ii, p. xx.) There is no evidence of animosity between Selkirk and Dampier, but Dampier does fit the description, and the modern biographers of Rogers and of Selkirk speculate that Dampier was indeed the 'certain Officer'. (See Bryan Little, *Crusoe's Captain: Being the Life of Woodes Rogers, Seaman, Trader, Colonial Governor* (London, 1960), 72, and R. L. Mégroz, *The Real Robinson Crusoe, Being the Life and Strange Surprising Adventures of Alexander Selkirk of Largo, Fife, Mariner* (London, 1939), 97–8.)

74. The origin of the tradition associating Selkirk and Crusoe is unknown, but Secord writes that by 1744 an editor of Rogers's *Voyage* assumed the association 'to be common knowledge'. (Secord, *Studies in the Narrative Method*, 31.)

75. [Defoe], *Robinson Crusoe* (1719), 158.

76. Richard Steele, *The Englishman*, no. 26 (Thur., 3 Dec. 1713), ed. Rae Blanchard (Oxford, 1955), 106. For Defoe's knowledge of travel and geography, see J. N. L. Baker, 'The Geography of Daniel Defoe', *Scottish Geographical Magazine*, 47/5 (Sept. 1931), 257–69, and Peter Earle, *The World of Defoe* (London, 1976), 45–74.

77. Defoe, 'On Learning', in W. Lee, *Daniel Defoe: His Life, and Recently Discovered Writings* (London, 1869), iii. 436.

78. Defoe, 'The Compleat English Gentleman', in *Selected Writings*, ed. J. T. Boulton (Cambridge, 1975), 255.

79. [Defoe], *Robinson Crusoe* (1719), title-page.

80. Unsigned letter, *Weekly Journal; or, British Gazetteer*, Sat., 1 Nov. 1718.

81. [Defoe], Preface, *Serious Reflections during the Life and Surprising Adventures of Robinson Crusoe* (London, 1720).

82. [Defoe], *Robinson Crusoe* (1719), 84; [Defoe], *The Life, Adventures, and Pyracies, Of the Famous Captain Singleton* (London, 1720), 132.

83. Dampier gives the seals on Selkirk's island, about forty degrees further south, a one-and-a-half page description. (See Dampier, *A New Voyage* (1697), 89–90.) Charles Gildon mocks the improbability of Friday's familiarity with a bear, 'since that is a Creature, which is never found in such a warm Climate, as *Friday's* Country must needs be, since it was so near the *Equinox*', but the critic Paul Dottin notes that 'there are bears in the mountains of Venezuela and British Guiana, so that Friday might have seen some during the wanderings of his tribe'. ([Charles Gildon], *The Life and Strange Surprizing Adventures of Mr. D——DeF——, of London, Hosier* (London, 1719), 28; Paul Dottin, *Robinson Crusoe Examin'd and Criticis'd or A New Edition of Charles Gildon's Famous Pamphlet now Published with an Introduction and Explanatory Notes together with an Essay on Gildon's Life* (London, 1923), 165; and see [Defoe], *Robinson Crusoe* (1719), 352.)

84. [Theophilus Cibber?], 'The Life of Daniel De Foe', in *The Lives of the Poets of Great Britain and Ireland* (London, 1753), iv. 322.
85. Edward Cooke, *A Voyage*, ii, pp. xviii–xix.
86. [Henry Neville], *The Isle of Pines, or, A late Discovery of a fourth Island in Terra Australis, Incognita* (London, 1668).
87. Ibid. 5.
88. [Henry Neville], *The Isle of Pines, or, A late Discovery of a fourth Island near Terra Australis, Incognita by Henry Cornelius Van Sloetten* (London, 1668), 1. The sequel was *A New and further Discovery of the Isle of Pines* (London, 1668) but I quote from the combined, complete version. For bibliographical details, see W. C. Ford, *The Isle Of Pines 1668: An Essay in Bibliography* (Boston, 1920), 40–1.
89. [Neville], *Isle of Pines near Terra Australis*, 1.
90. Ibid. 2, 4, 6.
91. Ibid. 17.
92. Ibid. 30.
93. The German interpreter is quoted in Ford, *Isle of Pines*, 38; Anthony à Wood, *Athenae Oxonienses, an Exact History of all the Writers and Bishops who have had their Education at the University of Oxford*, ed. Philip Bliss, iv (London, 1820), 410. Most modern interpretations of Henry Neville's short novel are based on the evidence of the first part and on Neville's reputation as a wayward republican, and ignore the emphasis of its conclusion, and of its sequel, on propriety and religion. Such are the views that it is 'a cheerfully happy polygamous utopia' (Christopher Hill); 'an actual defence of polygamy [or] a burlesque defence' (Aldridge, 1950); 'a piece of social and political propaganda, since the only man is a servant' (W. T. James); a 'pornographic novel' (Aldridge, 1985). There is perhaps some truth in some of these views—though polygamy was suppressed in the first part and is irrelevant to the second part, the servant's grandson has become a 'Prince' with a 'Pallace' in the second part, and the opinion that it is 'pornographic' must be that of a scholar with a very low threshold of arousal. (See: Christopher Hill, *The World Turned Upside Down* (Penguin edn., 1975), 314; A. O. Aldridge, 'Polygamy in Early Fiction: Henry Neville and Denis Veiras', *Publications of the Modern Language Association*, 65 (March 1950), 468; W. T. James, 'Nostalgia for Paradise', in Ian Donaldson (ed.), *Australia*, 77–8; A. O. Aldridge, 'Feijoo, Voltaire, and the Mathematics of Procreation', *Studies in Eighteenth-Century Culture*, ed. Harold E. Pagliaro, 4 (1975), 133.)
94. John Dryden, *The Kind Keeper; or, Mr. Limberham* (London, 1680), III. i, p. 24. On continental editions of *The Isle of Pines*, see Ford, *Isle of Pines*, 13–17.
95. Benito Gerónimo Feijoo y Montenegro, 'Senectud del Mondo, Discurso XII', in *Theatro crítico universal, o discursos varios en todo genero de materias, para desengaño de errores comunes*, i (Madrid, 1733), 253–4.
96. [Neville], *Isle of Pines in Terra Australis*, 4; Masauji Hachisuka, *The Dodo and Kindred Birds, or, The Extinct Birds of the Mascarene Islands* (London, 1953), 'The Dodo of Mauritius', 'Historical Evidences', 49 ff.
97. Hachisuka, *The Dodo*, 53, 125, 231.
98. [Neville], *Isle of Pines in Terra Australis*, 4; Hachisuka, *The Dodo*, 125; and see Sir Edward Newton and Hans Gadow, 'On additional Bones of the Dodo and other Extinct Birds of Mauritius obtained by Mr. Théodore Sauzier', *Transactions of the Zoological Society of London*, 13 (London, 1895), 281–302.

99. Jean Chapelain to Carrel de Sainte-Garde, 15 Dec. 1663, in *Lettres de Jean Chapelain*, ed. Tamizey de Larroque, ii (Paris, 1883), 340–1.

100. See Gilbert Chinard, *L'Amérique et le rêve exotique dans la littérature française au XVIIe et au XVIIIe siècles* (Paris, 1913), 195. Jean Garagnon lists twelve French utopias of the seventeenth and eighteenth centuries located in Austral lands in 'French Imaginary Voyages to Austral Lands in the Seventeenth and Eighteenth Centuries', in Ian Donaldson (ed.), *Australia*, 87–107.

101. [Gabriel Foigny], 'Au Lecteur', in *La Terre Australe connue: c'est à dire, la description de ce pays inconnu jusqu'ici, de ces moeurs & de ces coûtumes. Par Mr Sadeur, avec les avantures qui le conduisirent en ce continent, & les particularitez du sejour qu'il y fit durant trente-cinq ans & plus, & de son retour. Reduites & mises en lumiere par les soins & la conduite de G. de F.* (Vannes, 1676).

102. Ibid.

103. Ibid. 103–4, 80.

104. Ibid. 184–5

105. On Denis Vairasse d'Alais, see Geoffroy Atkinson, *The Extraordinary Voyage in French Literature Before 1700* (New York, 1920), 89–91, and Emanuel von der Mühll, *Denis Veiras et son Histoire des Sévarambes* (Paris, 1938), 6–31.

106. [Denis Vairasse d'Alais], 'Au Lecteur', in *Histoire des Sevarambes, peuples qui habitent une partie du troisième continent, communément appellé La Terre Australe. Contenant une relation du gouvernement, des moeurs, de la religion, & du langage de cette nation, inconnuë jusques à present aux peuples de l'Europe* (Amsterdam, [1680?]).

107. 'Au Lecteur', ibid. On the influence of Bacon, and of the account of Francis Pelsart's shipwreck, in 'La Terre Australe descouverte par le Capitaine Pelsart, qui y fait naufrage', in *Relations de divers voyages curieux*, ed. M. Thévenot (Paris, 1663), see Atkinson, *Extraordinary Voyage Before 1700*, 100, 101, 104, 95–6.

108. *Le Journal des Sçavans* (1678), 47.

109. [Simon Tyssot de Patot], 'Lettre de L'editeur, a M***', in *Voyages et avantures de Jaques Massé* (Bordeaux, 1710).

110. [Tyssot de Patot], *Voyages et avantures*, 235–6. On Tyssot de Patot, see Geoffroy Atkinson, *The Extraordinary Voyage in French Literature from 1700 to 1720* (Paris, 1922), 67–70.

111. See J. R. Moore, 'A New Source for *Gulliver's Travels*', *Studies in Philology*, 38 (1941), 66–80.

112. [Tyssot de Patot], *Voyages et avantures*, 103. See Atkinson, *Extraordinary Voyage from 1700 to 1720*, 85–6, and Chinard, *L'Amérique et le rêve exotique*, 210.

113. See E. A. Baker, *The History of the English Novel*, iii (London, 1929), 148, 156–8; Secord, *Studies in the Narrative Method*, 23; W. A. Eddy, *'Gulliver's Travels': A Critical Study* (Princeton, 1923), 37–9, 66–7; and *Travels into Several Remote Nations of the World. By Capt. Lemuel Gulliver*, iii (London, 1727), pt. 2, 'A Voyage to Sevarambia, &c.'.

114. [Foigny], *La Terre Australe connue*, 189.

115. Hazard, *La Crise de la conscience européenne*, 28.

116. The French edition is dated 1708, like the English, but in his 'Check List' of eighteenth-century imaginary voyages P. B. Gove argues that the French edition was actually published in 1707. (See Gove, *Imaginary Voyage*, 207–9.)

117. [François Leguat], *Voyage et avantures de François Leguat et de ses compagnons, en deux isles desertes des Indes Orientales* (London, 1708 [1707?]), i. 103.

118. Ibid. 102.

119. Ibid. 147–8.

120. Ibid. p. xxix.

121. Casimir Freschot, *Nouvelle relation de la ville & république de Venise* (Utrecht, 1709), 441. Freschot's *Remarques historiques et critiques* is attacked in the Preface to the *Voyage de Leguat*, p. xxi; and the *Voyage de Leguat* is reviewed in the *Supplément du Journal des Sçavans* (1707), 521–8.

122. Maximilien Misson, 'To the Reader', in *A New Voyage to Italy* (4th edn., London, 1714), i, pt. 1, p. xviii. A. A. Bruzen de la Martinière, *Le Grand Dictionnaire géographique, historique et critique* (Paris, 1768), i, p. viii.

123. *Bibliothèque britannique, ou Histoire des ouvrages des savans de la Grande-Bretagne*, v (La Haye, 1735), 424, which is quoted in Henri Du Quesne, *Un projet de république à l'île d'Eden (l'île Bourbon) en 1689. Réimpression d'un ouvrage disparu, publié en 1689, intitulé: Recueil de quelques mémoires servans d'instruction pour l'établissement de l'isle d'Eden. Précédé d'une notice, par Th. Sauzier* (Paris, 1887), 24. There is a reference to the will of Leguat, which was registered in London on 5 Sept. 1735, in I. H. Van Eeghen, 'The Voyages and Adventures of François Leguat', *Proceedings of the Huguenot Society of London*, 18/5 (1951), 405.

124. See Pasfield Oliver, Introduction, *The Voyage of François Leguat*, ed. Pasfield Oliver (London, 1891), i, p. xlix.

125. See ibid. p. li.

126. See *Philosophical Transactions of the Royal Society*, 168 (extra vol.) (1879).

127. See *Voyage of François Leguat*, ed. Oliver, i. 81 n. 3.

128. A. Milne-Edwards, 'Notes from a Memoir on the Ancient Fauna of the Mascarene Islands', and Alfred Newton and Edward Newton, 'Notice of a Memoir on the Osteology of the Solitaire', in *Voyage of François Leguat*, ed. Oliver, ii. 341, 354. Although Oliver recognized the 'scientific interest' of Leguat's 'circumstantial delineation . . . of the curious bird fauna then extant', which rendered his 'personal observations . . . invaluable to naturalists, marked as they [the observations] are by such evident simplicity and veracity', he did notice evidence of Misson's hand in the narrative, as well as the Preface, of the *Voyage*, in the form of recurring verbal parallels with Misson's works. (Oliver, Preface, *Voyage of François Leguat*, ed. Oliver, i, p. ix. On Misson, see ibid. p. xxxii and, for suggestive, but not conclusive, parallels with Misson's writings, see 'Misson' in Oliver's Index.)

129. Atkinson, *Extraordinary Voyage from 1700 to 1720*, 37. See 'Rodrigues', *Encyclopaedia Britannica*, xxiii (Cambridge, 1911) and 'Leguat' and 'Solitaire' in Pierre Larousse, *Grand Dictionnaire universel*, x (Paris, 1873) and xiv (Paris, 1875).

130. Atkinson, *Extraordinary Voyage from 1700 to 1720*, 47 n. 31.

131. Ibid. 56.

132. See ibid. 41, 61–2.

133. Ibid. 63.

134. Pat Rogers, *Robinson Crusoe* (London, 1979), 28; P. G. Adams, *Travelers and Travel Liars 1660–1800* (Berkeley, Calif., 1962), 103; and see E. A. Baker, *History of the English Novel*, iii. 155, and Secord, *Studies in the Narrative Method*, 93, and, e.g. (in addition to Pat Rogers, *Robinson Crusoe*), Peter Earle, *The World of Defoe* (London, 1976), 47.

135. P. G. Adams, *Travel Literature and the Evolution of the Novel* (Lexington, Ky., 1983), 74.

136. Letter signed by D. Deodati and others, 'in the Fort Frederick Hendrik, on the island Mauritius, 2nd July, 1694', in H. C. V. Leibbrandt, *Precis of the Archives of the Cape of Good Hope: Letters Received, 1695–1708* (Capetown, 1896), 27.

137. Ibid. 51, 80, 82, and see 27, 28, 81. These letters were published in English after Oliver's edition of Leguat's *Voyage* in 1891, but well before Atkinson's laborious exposure of the *Voyage* as a fiction. Adams ended his account of Misson's 'invention' in *Travelers and Travel Liars* by capping Atkinson's conclusions with the statement that 'most surprising of all is the fact that at least two writers—both in the 1920's and both without real evidence—can be found who refused to accept the convincing conclusions of Oliver and Atkinson' (though it was not Oliver's case that Leguat's *Voyage* was a novel). Adams's evidence for 'without real evidence' is a reference, not to the work of the 'two writers', but to the discussion of Leguat's *Voyage* in Gove's *Imaginary Voyage*, where Gove notes that Atkinson's work has not been accepted 'without dispute' and refers to 'two articles (which I have not seen)' and another author's statement 'on the basis of secondary opinion'. One of the two articles that Gove said that he had not seen is Henri Dehérain, 'Le Voyage de François Leguat', which refers to the evidence of the letters in the Capetown archives and cites them in detail to provide 'la preuve éclatante que le voyage de Leguat est réel et non pas imaginaire'. (See: Adams, *Travelers and Travel Liars*, 104, 251; Gove, *Imaginary Voyage*, 210; Henri Dehérain, 'Le Voyage de François Leguat dans l'Océan Indien (1690–1698) est-il imaginaire?', *Comité des Travaux historiques et scientifiques, Bulletin de la section de géographie*, 41 (1926), 159–77.)

138. Secord, *Studies in the Narrative Method*, 92, 107.

139. See ibid. 123–4, and [Defoe], *Captain Singleton*, 54–6, and François Leguat, *A New Voyage to the East-Indies by Francis Leguat and His Companions* (London, 1708), 96–8.

140. Secord, *Studies in the Narrative Method*, 111 (and E. A. Baker called *Robinson Crusoe* 'a fictitious narrative of travel', Baker, *History of the English Novel*, iii. 150); J. Paul Hunter, *The Reluctant Pilgrim* (Baltimore, 1966), 19.

141. Woodes Rogers, *A Cruising Voyage*, 126.

142. Ibid. 130.

143. *Providence Display'd, Or a very Suprizing Account of one Mr. Alexander Selkirk . . . Written by his own Hand* (London, 1712).

144. Dampier, *A New Voyage* (1697), 497; Drury, *Drury's Journal* (1729), 3.

145. Oliver, Introduction, *Drury's Journal* (1890), pp. liv–lv.

146. Columbus, 'Letter', in *Select Documents*, i. 18.

147. Bernal Díaz del Castillo, *True History of the Conquest*, v (London, 1916), 275.

148. [Swift], *Travels* (1726), II. iv. 192–3.

149. James Joyce, 'Daniel Defoe', trans. Joseph Prescott, *Buffalo Studies*, 1/1 (Dec. 1964), 24; F. H. Ellis, Introduction, F. H. Ellis (ed.), *Twentieth Century Interpretations of 'Robinson Crusoe'* (Englewood Cliffs, NJ, 1969), 18, and see [Defoe?], *An Historical Account of the Voyages and Adventures of Sir Walter Raleigh* (London, 1719), 42 ff. On *Robinson Crusoe* and *The Tempest*, see J. R. Moore, '*The Tempest* and *Robinson Crusoe*', *Review of English Studies*, 21 (1945), 52–6.

150. See Little, *Crusoe's Captain*, 156–8. Defoe is deliberately vague in *An Essay on the South-Sea Trade* about the location of the colony he is advocating, speaking of 'a good footing on the *South-Sea* Coast of America' and trailing a further publication, which

'may give you an Essay at the Great Question *Where* this Settlement may, or can, or must be made'. ([Defoe], *An Essay on the South-Sea Trade* (London, 1712), 39, 46.)

151. See [Defoe], *An Essay on the South-Sea Trade*, and J. H. Jack, '*A New Voyage Round the World*: Defoe's "Roman à Thèse" ', *Huntington Library Quarterly*, 24 (1960–1), 323–36. Jack argues that *A New Voyage* 'is remarkably unified' by its 'thèse' of colonizing South America, but it is only the second part of the book which is unified in this remarkable way, and among the events in the first part, which Jack refers to as 'many setbacks', is Defoe's exploration of the South Seas, occupying about seventy pages and having nothing to do with the 'thèse' of colonizing Chile, or Patagonia. On the relation between *A New Voyage* and propaganda for a South American colony, see also Peter Earle, *World of Defoe*, 55–7, and J. A. Downie, 'Defoe, Imperialism, and the Travel Books Reconsidered', *Yearbook of English Studies*, 12 (1983), 66–83.

152. [Defoe], *A New Voyage Round the World* (London, 1725), 204, 202.

153. Ibid. 188.

154. Ibid. 175.

155. Ibid. 176, 177.

156. On the economic motive, see, e.g., Glyndwr Williams, *The Expansion of Europe in the Eighteenth Century* (London, 1965), 5.

157. [Defoe], *Robinson Crusoe* (1719), 44.

158. Voltaire, *Le Mondain*, in *Mélanges*, ed. Jacques van den Heuvel (Pléiade edn., 1961), 203.

159. See Secord, '*Robert Drury's Journal*', 35.

160. M. E. Novak, *Economics and the Fiction of Daniel Defoe* (Berkeley, Calif., 1962), 65.

161. Ian Watt, '*Robinson Crusoe* as a Myth', *Essays in Criticism*, 1 (1951), 101; Novak, *Economics*, 58.

162. [Defoe], *Robinson Crusoe* (1719), 139.

163. R. Quintana, *The Mind and Art of Jonathan Swift* (repr. London, 1953), 298.

164. [Swift], *Travels* (1726), II. iv. 124.

165. Ibid. 124, 41.

166. Ibid. 147.

167. Ibid. 37.

168. Lucian, *A True Story*, in *Works*, i. 259. See Eddy, '*Gulliver's Travels*', 54, 159, 124.

169. Rabelais, *Le Cinquiesme et Dernier Livre* (1571), ch. 22. See Pope, *The Dunciad*, i. 22, in *The Poems of Alexander Pope*, ed. John Butt (University Paperback edn., 1968), 721; and, for example, Gargantua's 'pissefort', [Rabelais], *La Vie inestimable du grand Gargantua pere de Pa[n]tagruel, jadis co[m]posée par l'abstracteur de quinte essence* (Lyon, 1537), 34. For Voltaire on Swift, and for Rabelais's experimenters and Swift's, see Eddy, '*Gulliver's Travels*', 59, 161–2.

170. See Boase, *The Fortunes of Montaigne*, 257–9, and Eddy, '*Gulliver's Travels*', 61.

171. Cyrano de Bergerac, *Estats et empires de la lune*, in *Œuvres complètes*, ed. Jacques Prévot (Paris, 1977), 376, 390.

172. *Mandeville's Travels* (1968), 161.

173. Walpole to Sir Horace Mann, 22 May 1766, in *Correspondence*, ed. W. S. Lewis, xxii (London, 1960), 421, and [Walpole], *An Account of the Giants Lately Discovered* (London, 1766), 23.

174. *A Voyage Round the World, in His Majesty's Ship the Dolphin . . . By an Officer on Board* (London, 1767), 45; *Gentleman's Magazine*, 37 (April 1767), 147; and see Charles

Clarke [i.e. Clerke], 'An Account of the very tall Men, seen near the Streights of Magellan', *Philosophical Transactions*, lvii (London, 1768), 75–9.

175. [Swift], *Travels* (1726), I. ii. 11.

176. John Arbuthnot to Swift, 5 Nov. 1726, in *The Correspondence of Jonathan Swift*, ed. Harold Williams, iii (Oxford, 1963), 180.

177. 'A Voyage into *England*' is listed, among other works, as a treatise by the author of *A Tale of a Tub*, and is probably related to the hypothetical work referred to by Swift in his *Journal to Stella*, 28 April 1711: 'Yesterday it [the *Spectator*] was made of a noble hint I gave him [Steele] long ago for his *Tatlers*, about an Indian supposed to write his travels into England. I repent he ever had it. I intended to have written a book on that subject'. ([Swift], *A Tale of a Tub* (London, 1704), facing title-page, and Swift, *Journal to Stella*, ed. Harold Williams (Oxford, 1948), i. 254–5.) J. R. Moore has looked at his map and reported that, although Gulliver's discoveries are documented, like real discoveries, with maps and longitudes and latitudes, the (commonly held) 'assumptions of the essential accuracy of *Gulliver's Travels* are groundless'. Essentially accurate or not, the geography of *Gulliver's Travels* is nevertheless realistic. (J. R. Moore, 'The Geography of *Gulliver's Travels*', *Journal of English and Germanic Philology*, 40 (1942), 215–16.)

178. [Swift], *Travels* (1726), I. i. 5.

179. John Gay to Swift, 17 Nov. 1726, in *Correspondence of Swift*, iii. 182.

180. [Swift], 'A Letter from Capt. Gulliver', in *Travels*, in *Works* (1735), iii, p. [i].

181. John Arbuthnot to Swift, 5 Nov. 1726, in *Correspondence of Swift*, iii. 180.

182. Swift to Alexander Pope, [27] Nov. 1726, ibid. 189.

183. E. A. Baker argued that Swift, in *Gulliver's Travels*, was 'undeniably, a borrower of Defoe's methods', an argument denied but not refuted by J. F. Ross. (Baker, *History of the English Novel*, iii. 231; and see J. F. Ross, *Swift and Defoe: A Study in Relationship* (Berkeley, Calif., 1941), 70–1, 142.) As Claude Rawson has pointed out, Swift leaves us in doubt about the extent to which his realism is parodic, and also about whether he is parodying real or fictitious travel books. (See C. J. Rawson, *Gulliver and the Gentle Reader: Studies in Swift and Our Time* (London, 1973), 10.)

184. [Swift], *Travels* (1726), I. ii. 2, 3–4.

185. Ibid. 5.

186. Captain Samuell Sturmy, *The Mariners Magazine or Sturmys Mathematicall and Practical Arts* (London, 1669), 17. Swift's debt to Sturmy was first pointed out by E. H. Knowles, *Notes and Queries*, 4th Ser. 1 (7 Mar. 1868), 223.

187. Dampier, *A Voyage* (1703), 109. See [Swift], *Travels* (1726), I. i. 4; and A. W. Secord, review of W. H. Eddy, '*Gulliver's Travels*', in *Journal of English and Germanic Philology*, 23 (1924), 460–2; and A. W. Secord, '*Gulliver* and Dampier', *Modern Language Notes*, 51 (Mar. 1936), 159.

188. [Swift], 'A Letter from Capt. Gulliver', in *Travels*, in *Works* (1735), iii, p. [i]. See M. R. James, 'Swift's Copy of Dampier', 138.

189. See William Symson, *A New Voyage to the East Indies* (London, 1715), 35–6 (a book partly plagiarized from John Ovington, *Voyage to Suratt* (1696)) and [Swift], *Travels* (1726), I. i. 94; and *Voyage of François Leguat*, ed. Oliver, ii. 284–5 n. The source, its fictitiousness, and its use in Oliver's edition of Leguat's *Voyage* are pointed out in R. W. Frantz, 'Gulliver's "Cousin Sympson" ', *Huntington Library Quarterly*, 1 (1938), 329–34.

190. [Swift], *Travels* (1726), II. iv. 184–5.
191. Ibid. 186.
192. Ibid.
193. [Swift], 'The Publisher to the Reader', in *Travels* (1726), I, p. vii.
194. Ibid.
195. W. Scott, 'Memoirs of Jonathan Swift', in *The Works of Jonathan Swift . . . with Notes, and A Life of the Author*, ed. W. Scott (Edinburgh, 1814), i. 340.
196. James Burney, *A Chronological History of the Discoveries in the South Sea*, iv (London, 1816), 486.
197. R. C. Elliott, 'The Satirist Satirized', in Frank Brady (ed.), *Twentieth Century Interpretations of 'Gulliver's Travels'* (Englewood Cliffs, NJ, 1968), 47; Sprat, *History of the Royal Society*, 113.
198. Brady, Introduction, Brady (ed.), *Twentieth Century Interpretations of 'Gulliver's Travels'*, 6; R. C. Elliott, 'Satirist Satirized', in Brady (ed.), *Twentieth Century Interpretations of 'Gulliver's Travels'*, 47.
199. [Swift], *Travels* (1726), II. iii. 70, 63, 64, 75.
200. Ibid. 76.
201. See M. Nicolson and N. M. Mohler, 'The Scientific Background of Swift's "Voyage to Laputa" ', *Annals of Science*, 2 (1937), 299–334, and 'Swift's "Flying Island" in the "Voyage to Laputa" ', *Annals of Science*, 2 (1937), 405–30.
202. Nicolson and Mohler, 'The Scientific Background', 304.
203. See 'An Account of a New Voyage round the World, by William Dampier', *Philosophical Transactions*, 19 (Feb. 1697), 426–33, and, for the *Transactions'* hospitality to other accounts of voyages, see Frantz, *The English Traveller*, 18–19.

CHAPTER 4

1. James Boswell, *The Life of Samuel Johnson*, ed. G. B. Hill, rev. L. F. Powell (Oxford, 1934), iii. 8.
2. See Marco Polo, *Travels*, 251.
3. John Callander, *Terra Australis Cognita*, quoted in J. C. Beaglehole, *Exploration of the Pacific*, 191.
4. John Callander, *Terra Australis Cognita, or Voyages to the Terra Australis* (Edinburgh, 1766–8), iii. 745.
5. See A. C. Taylor, 'Charles de Brosses, the Man behind Cook', in B. Greenhill (ed.), *The Opening of the Pacific—Image and Reality* (London, 1971), 9; also J. Dunmore, *French Explorers in the Pacific*, i. *The Eighteenth Century* (Oxford, 1965), 50, and O. H. K. Spate, *The Pacific Since Magellan*, iii. *Paradise Found and Lost* (London, 1988), 70–6.
6. George Gordon, Lord Byron, *Don Juan*, ii. 137, in *The Complete Poetical Works*, ed. J. J. McGann, v (Oxford, 1986), 132. See 'Byron's Secret Instructions', in John Byron, *Byron's Journal of his Circumnavigation 1764–1766*, ed. Robert E. Gallagher (Cambridge, 1964), 7.
7. Byron, *Byron's Journal of his Circumnavigation*, 46. See A. Sharp, *Discovery of the Pacific Islands*, 104, and J. A. Williamson, *Cook and the Opening of the Pacific* (London, 1946), 56, 88.

8. Wallis's instructions, quoted in G. Robertson, *The Discovery of Tahiti, A Journal of the Second Voyage of H.M.S. 'Dolphin' round the World*, ed. H. Carrington (London, 1948), p. xxiii.

9. Robertson, *Discovery of Tahiti*, 135.

10. On Cook's dismissal of the southern continent, see Beaglehole, *The Journals of Captain Cook*, ed. Beaglehole, i. *The Voyage of the 'Endeavour' 1768–1771* (rev., Cambridge, 1968), p. cxv.

11. Ibid. pp. xciv–xcv.

12. See Teuira Henry, *Ancient Tahiti* (Honolulu, 1928), 70.

13. The so-called *Memoirs of Arii Taimai* (Paris, 1901) give some account of the Tahitian view, but one obscured by the passage of more than a century, by Arii Taimai's position as a member of the Teva dynasty descending from Purea (Arii Taimai's great-great-great-aunt), and by the historian Henry Adams, who ghosted the *Memoirs*. He was said to have 'become more Teva than the Tevas', and his knowledge of the published European accounts is evident in the *Memoirs*. (John La Farge, *Reminiscences of the South Seas* (London, 1914), 351.) Teuira Henry, *Ancient Tahiti*, is also a source contaminated by the European sources, specifically Hawkesworth. (See [Henry Adams], *Memoirs of Arii Taimai* (Paris, 1901), and Teuira Henry, *Ancient Tahiti*, and also Niel Gunson, 'A Note on the Difficulties of Ethnohistorical Writing, with Special Reference to Tahiti', *Journal of the Polynesian Society*, 72 (1963), 415–19.)

14. Robertson, *Discovery of Tahiti*, 136.

15. Ibid.

16. Ibid. 137.

17. Ibid. 148.

18. Ibid. 154.

19. See ibid.

20. Ibid.

21. Ibid. 159; Samuel Wallis, entry for Friday, 26 June, 'His Majestys Ship Dolphin's Log Book', MS, Public Record Office, London, Adm. 55/35.

22. Robertson, *Discovery of Tahiti*, 162.

23. Ibid. 162–3.

24. Ibid. 156.

25. Ibid. 166.

26. Ibid. 180.

27. Ibid.

28. Ibid. 200, 186.

29. Ibid. 187, 203.

30. Samuel Wallis, entry for Monday, 13 July, 'His Majestys Ship Dolphin's Log Book'.

31. Robertson, *Discovery of Tahiti*, 225, and see 207.

32. Ibid. 227.

33. [Henry Adams], *Memoirs of Arii Taimai*, 137. On his third voyage Cook observed the ceremonial function of the *Dolphin*'s pendant at a human sacrifice. (See Cook, *Journals of Captain Cook*, ed. Beaglehole, iii. *The Voyage of the 'Resolution' and 'Discovery' 1776–1780* (Cambridge, 1967), 203.) On Purea, the *Dolphin*, and Tahitian politics, see W. H. Pearson, 'European Intimidation and the Myth of Tahiti', *Journal of Pacific History*, 4 (1969), 212–14.

34. Robertson, *Discovery of Tahiti*, 139, 167.

35. Samuel Wallis, 'Remarks made at Georges Island', in 'His Majestys Ship Dolphin's Log Book'.

36. Ibid.

37. Wallis, entry for Friday, 26 June, 'His Majestys Ship Dolphin's Log Book'; L. A. de Bougainville, 'Journal de Bougainville', in *Bougainville et ses compagnons autour du monde 1766–1769: Journaux de navigation*, ed. Étienne Taillemite (Paris, 1977), i. 318. On de Brosses's influence on Bougainville, see Dunmore, *French Explorers in the Pacific*, i. 50; and for Bougainville's instructions see ibid. 67.

38. On Bougainville's knowledge of literature and philosophy, classical and modern, see Taillemite, Introduction, *Bougainville et ses compagnons*, ed. Taillemite, i. 49, and J. E. Martin-Allanic, *Bougainville navigateur et les découvertes de son temps* (Paris, 1964), i. 64.

39. Bougainville, 'Journal', i. 269. On Rousseau's urinary problem, see Jean-Jacques Rousseau, *Les Confessions* (London/Neuchâtel, 1786–90), e.g. 2nd Part, Book 8, iv 208–9; also J. Starobinski's essay, 'Sur la maladie de Rousseau', in J. Starobinski, *Jean-Jacques Rousseau: La transparence et l'obstacle* (Paris, 1971), 430 ff.

40. Charles-Félix Fesche, 'Journal de Fesche', in *Bougainville et ses compagnons*, ed. Taillemite, ii. 80.

41. Bougainville, 'Journal', i. 315; Fesche, 'Journal', ii. 80. Fesche may have written his journal in collaboration with Starot de Saint-Germain, a fellow voyager. (See Taillemite, *Bougainville et ses compagnons*, ed. Taillemite, i. 126–7, and É. Taillemite, 'Le séjour de Bougainville à Tahiti: Essai d'étude critique des témoignages', *Journal de la Société des Océanistes*, 24/24 (Dec. 1968), 7.)

42. Bougainville, 'Journal', i. 316.

43. Ibid. 317–18. Bougainville quotes (or, rather, misquotes) from Virgil, *Aeneid*, 1. 731–3.

44. Fesche, 'Journal', ii. 81–2.

45. Charles-Nicolas de Nassau-Siegen, 'Journal de Nassau-Siegen', in *Bougainville et ses compagnons*, ed. Taillemite, ii. 395–6. On the Prince's 'tentations parisiennes', see Taillemite, *Bougainville et ses compagnons*, ed. Taillemite, i. 76.

46. Bougainville, 'Journal', i. 349.

47. Ibid. For an account of Baré, or Baret, see H. Jacquier, 'Jeanne Baret, la première femme autour du monde', *Bulletin de la Société des Études Océaniennes*, 12/141 (1962), 150–6.

48. See Bougainville, 'Journal', i. 320–1.

49. See ibid. 322, and Nassau-Siegen, 'Journal', ii. 397.

50. Bougainville, 'Journal', i. 326.

51. Ibid. 326–8.

52. Ibid. 342.

53. See Bougainville, *Voyage autour du monde, par le frégate du roi la Boudeuse et la flûte l'Étoile; en 1766, 1767, 1768 & 1769* (Paris, 1771), 242. The controversy continues: see, e.g., H. M. Smith, 'The Introduction of Venereal Disease into Tahiti: a Re-examination', *Journal of Pacific History*, 10 (1975), Part 1, 38–45.

54. Bougainville, quoted in Martin-Allanic, *Bougainville navigateur*, ii. 887.

55. See Taillemite, *Bougainville et ses compagnons*, ed. Taillemite, i. 134–5. On the contribution to science of Bougainville's voyage, see also Dunmore, *French Explorers in the Pacific*, i. 99–100, 108–9.

56. Louis-Antoine Starot de Saint-Germain, 'Journal de Saint-Germain' (extracts), in *Bougainville et ses compagnons*, ed. Taillemite, ii. 109 n. 2.

57. *Philosophical Transactions: Giving Some Accompt of the Present Undertakings, Studies, and Labours of the Ingenious in many Considerable Parts of the World* (London), 1/8 (8 Jan. 1665/6), 140–1.

58. 'Transactions of the Royal Society relative to the sending out people to Observe the transit of Venus in 1769', in *Journals of Captain Cook*, ed. Beaglehole, i. Appendix ii. 'The Royal Society and the Voyage', 513.

59. 'Minutes of the Council of the Royal Society', quoted in J. C. Beaglehole, Introduction, *The 'Endeavour' Journal of Joseph Banks*, ed. J. C. Beaglehole (Sydney, 1962), i. 22.

60. Banks, quoted in ibid. 23.

61. John Ellis to Linnaeus, 19 Aug. 1768, quoted in ibid. 30.

62. Cook's Instructions, quoted in *Journals of Captain Cook*, ed. Beaglehole, i, p. cclxxxii.

63. See ibid. p. cxx.

64. Cook, *Journals of Captain Cook*, i. 97. O. H. K. Spate has disputed Beaglehole's assessment of the observation as a 'failure'. (See *Journals of Captain Cook*, ed. Beaglehole, i, p. cxliv, and Spate, *Paradise Found and Lost*, 100.)

65. Cook, *Journals of Captain Cook*, i. 87.

66. Banks, *Journal of Joseph Banks*, i. 334, 289.

67. Ibid. 252.

68. Ibid. 254.

69. Ibid. 255.

70. Ibid. 266.

71. Ibid. 267, 279.

72. Ibid. 276, 285.

73. See Beaglehole's notes in *Journal of Joseph Banks*, ed. Beaglehole, i. 276, and *Journals of Captain Cook*, ed. Beaglehole, i. 93.

74. Banks, *Journal of Joseph Banks*, i. 275.

75. Cook, *Journals of Captain Cook*, i. 93.

76. Ibid. 119.

77. Banks, *Journal of Joseph Banks*, i. 277.

78. The popular anthropologist Bengt Danielsson's account of the Point Venus 'Scene' is a muddle of assertion, assumption, and factual inaccuracy about 'what Cook, Banks and Solander had witnessed'. (Bengt Danielsson, *Love in the South Seas*, trans. F. H. Lyon (New York, 1956), 180.) Douglas Oliver, who should know better, confuses Cook's and Hawkesworth's accounts of the 'Scene' and quotes with approval 'Danielsson's judgement', lacking any anthropological sense, or any relevance, that acts of public copulation between Tahitian 'women and European sailors were doubtless due to the Polynesians' curiosity and, like all instances of sexual intercourse in public, must be regarded as a special form of entertainment'. (Douglas Oliver, *Ancient Tahitian Society* (Canberra, n.d.), i. 363; Danielsson, *Love in the South Seas*, 64.)

79. Cook, *Journals of Captain Cook*, i. 93–4. It is possible that Cook did not mean that, 'although she was young, she did not seem to require instruction in the sexual act', but, on the contrary, that, 'because she was young, she did not desire the part in the sexual act'. To the psychological and cultural mystery of the mind of that young Tahitian girl is added the ambiguity of 'want' ('desire'/'require') in eighteenth-century usage. The girl's not desiring the part might correspond better with the remarks made about the Point Venus 'Scene' by William Wales, but his remarks are at second hand and in the tendentious context of defending the virtue of Tahitian women from the

alleged misrepresentations of published accounts: 'I have been informed from the authority of a gentleman who was in the *Endeavour*, and saw the transaction here alluded to, that it is very imperfectly, and in some measure erroneously, related by Dr. Hawkesworth. Oberea *obliged* the two persons to *attempt* what is there said to have been done, but they were exceedingly terrified, and by no means able to perform it.' (William Wales, *Remarks on Mr. Forster's Account of Captain Cook's last Voyage round the World, In the Years 1772, 1773, 1774, and 1775* (London, 1778), 52 n.) Hawkesworth probably read Cook correctly, however, as meaning that the young girl did not seem to require instruction.

80. Sydney Parkinson, *A Journal of a Voyage to the South Seas, in his Majesty's Ship, the 'Endeavour'* (London, 1773), 31.

81. Banks, *Journal of Joseph Banks*, i. 287; Cook, *Journals of Captain Cook*, i. 98–9.

82. Cook, *Journals of Captain Cook*, i. 114–15.

83. Banks, *Journal of Joseph Banks*, i. 313.

84. Ibid. 341. Cf. Cook, *Journals of Captain Cook*, i. 121.

85. Banks, *Journal of Joseph Banks*, i. 340.

86. Ibid. 351; Cook, *Journals of Captain Cook*, i. 127. Beaglehole's footnote to Cook's text suggests the possible Tahitian meaning of the word 'Timorodee'.

87. Banks, *Journal of Joseph Banks*, i. 290. For an account of the 'Arioi', see Oliver, *Ancient Tahitian Society*, ii. 913 ff.

88. Banks, *Journal of Joseph Banks*, i. 351. Cf. Cook, *Journals of Captain Cook*, i. 127–8.

89. Lady Mary Coke, *Letters and Journals*, ed. J. A. Home (Edinburgh, 1889–96), iii. 435.

90. 'An Authentic Account of the Natives of OTAHITEE, or GEORGE'S ISLAND: Together with some of the Particulars of the three years voyage lately made by Mr. *Banks*, and Dr. *Solander*, in the years 1768, 1769, and 1770. Being the Copy of an original Letter from — —, on board the ENDEAVOUR, to his friend in the country', *General Evening Post* (Sat., 27 July to Tues., 30 July 1771).

91. See Cook, *Journals of Captain Cook*, i. 479, and H. Wallis, 'John Hawkesworth and the English Circumnavigators', *Commonwealth Journal*, 6 (1963), 167.

92. Frances Burney, *The Early Diary of Frances Burney, 1768–1778*, ed. A. R. Ellis (London, 1889), i. 133–4.

93. Hawkesworth to Burney, 6 Oct. 1771, quoted in J. L. Abbott, *John Hawkesworth, Eighteenth-Century Man of Letters* (Madison, Wis., 1982), 144.

94. Cf. the £1,575 that Johnson was paid for his *Dictionary*. (See Boswell, *Life of Johnson*, i. 183.) Beaglehole gives other comparative figures: £1,940 for the first two volumes of Hume's *History*; £3,400 for William Robertson's *Charles V*. (See *Journals of Captain Cook*, ed. Beaglehole, i, p. ccxliii.) Abbott cites a letter from Hawkesworth to Garrick which shows Hawkesworth's dealings with the booksellers. (See Abbott, *John Hawkesworth*, 148.)

95. Walpole to Mason, 15 May 1773, in Walpole, *Correspondence*, xxviii (London, 1955), 86.

96. Boswell, *Life of Johnson*, ii. 248.

97. Ibid. 247.

98. Cook, quoted in *Journals of Captain Cook*, ed. Beaglehole, i, pp. cxciii, cxciv. Cook's literary ability is assessed in J. C. Beaglehole, *Cook the Writer* (Sydney, 1970).

99. Hawkesworth to Sandwich, 19 Nov. 1771, quoted in Abbott, *John Hawkesworth*, 145.

100. John Hawkesworth, *An Account of the Voyages undertaken by the order of his present Majesty for making Discoveries in the Southern Hemisphere, And successively performed by*

Commodore Byron, Captain Wallis, Captain Carteret, and Captain Cook, in the Dolphin,
the Swallow, and the Endeavour: drawn up from the Journals which were kept by the several
Commanders, And from the Papers of Joseph Banks, Esq. (London, 1773), ii, p. xiii.

101. Hawkesworth, *Voyages*, i, p. iv.
102. Ibid. p. v.
103. Ibid.
104. Ibid. p. vi.
105. Cook, *Journals of Captain Cook*, ii. 661. On Carteret's complaints about Hawkesworth, which moved him to prepare his own account of his voyage, not published, however, until modern times, see H. Wallis, 'John Hawkesworth and the English Circumnavigators', 169, and Abbott, *John Hawkesworth*, 159.
106. On the character of Hawkesworth's narrator, see W. H. Pearson, 'Hawkesworth's Alterations', *Journal of Pacific History*, 7 (1972), 64, and E. H. McCormick, *Omai, Pacific Envoy* (Auckland, 1977), 81.
107. See Hawkesworth, *Voyages*, i. 434, 463. W. H. Pearson pointed out these divergences by Hawkesworth from his sources. (See 'Hawkesworth's Alterations', 58–9.) Hawkesworth's comic business can be found recorded as history, e.g., in Beaglehole, *Exploration of the Pacific*, 202, 204, and in Teuira Henry, *Ancient Tahiti*, 11, and, disgracefully, in *An Account of the Discovery of Tahiti From the Journal of George Robertson*, ed. Oliver Warner (London, 1955), 22, 94, where Hawkesworth's verbose jokes are quoted from 'Captain Wallis's Journal'.
108. Robertson, *Discovery of Tahiti*, 227; Hawkesworth, *Voyages*, i. 462, 479. Cf. Samuel Wallis, entry for Mon., 27 July, 'His Majestys Ship Dolphin's Log Book'.
109. Hawkesworth, *Voyages*, i, p. v.
110. François de Salignac de la Mothe-Fénelon, *The Adventures of Telemachus, the Son of Ulysses*, trans. John Hawkesworth (London, 1795), i. 149.
111. Hawkesworth, *Voyages*, i, p. v.
112. Ibid. ii. 101.
113. Ibid. 145.
114. Ibid. 103, 105.
115. Banks, *Journal of Joseph Banks*, i. 283. See Hawkesworth, *Voyages*, ii. 135–7.
116. Ibid. 83.
117. Ibid. 186.
118. Ibid. 206.
119. Ibid. 207–9.
120. Ibid. 107.
121. Ibid. 125.
122. Ibid.
123. Ibid. 124, chapter heading.
124. Ibid. 128.
125. A. Kippis, *The Life of Captain James Cook* (London, 1788), 34.
126. Walpole to Mason, 5 July 1773, in Walpole, *Correspondence*, xxviii. 96.
127. See *Journals of Captain Cook*, ed. Beaglehole, i, pp. ccliii, 642, and H. Wallis, 'John Hawkesworth and the English Circumnavigators', 168.
128. Mrs Hayes's invitation, quoted in *Nocturnal Revels: or, The History of King's-Place, and other Modern Nunneries* (London, 1779), ii. 21–2.
129. The account of Mrs Hayes's 'rites of Venus', in *Nocturnal Revels*, ii. 26.

130. Walpole to Mason, 5 July 1773, in Walpole, *Correspondence*, xxviii. 96; *Covent-Garden Magazine; or, Amorous Repository*, 2 (June 1773), 203, 204.
131. 'A Christian', 'To Dr. Hawkesworth', *Public Advertiser* (Sat., 3 July 1773).
132. John Wesley, 17 Dec. 1773, *The Journal of the Rev. John Wesley*, ed. Nehemiah Curnock (London, 1909–16), vi. 7.
133. Elizabeth Montagu to her sister, in *Mrs. Montagu, 'Queen of the Blues': Her Letters and Friendships from 1762 to 1800*, ed. Reginald Blunt (London, n.d.), i. 279.
134. Elizabeth Carter to Mrs Montagu, 14 Aug. 1773, in Elizabeth Carter, *Letters from Mrs. Elizabeth Carter to Mrs. Montagu between the years 1755 and 1800*, ed. Montagu Pennington (London, 1817), ii. 209.
135. Burney, *The Early Diary*, i. 255.
136. Burney, 'Remnant of an Old Letter to Mr. Crisp', in *The Early Diary*, i. 262–3.
137. Joseph Cradock, *Literary and Miscellaneous Memoirs* (London, 1828), iv. 185.
138. Edmond Malone, in Sir James Prior, *Life of Edmond Malone, editor of Shakespeare, with selections from his Manuscript Anecdotes* (London, 1860), 441.
139. Walpole to Lady Ossory, 21 June 1773, in Walpole, *Correspondence*, xxxii (London, 1965), 127–8.
140. *Monthly Review*, 49 (Aug., Dec., and Oct. 1773), 140, 487, 298; Rousseau, *Discours sur l'origine et les fondemens de l'inégalité parmi les hommes* (Amsterdam, 1755), 116.
141. *Gentleman's Magazine*, 43 (Dec. and Nov. 1773), 590, 541.
142. The date of publication given on the title-page is 1774 but, as J. C. Beaglehole has suggested, this work was probably postdated. (See *Journal of Joseph Banks*, ed. Beaglehole, i. 101.) The Introduction, dated 20 Sept. 1773, probably gives a better indication of its publication date. On John Scott, the supposed author, see C. Roderick, 'Sir Joseph Banks, Queen Oberea and the Satirists', in W. Veit (ed.), *Captain James Cook: Image and Impact, South Sea Discoveries and the World of Letters* (Melbourne, 1972), 71.
143. [John Scott?], *An Epistle from Oberea, Queen of Otaheite, to Joseph Banks, Esq. Translated by T.Q.Z. Esq. Professor of the Otaheite Language in Dublin, and of the Languages of the undiscovered Islands in the South Sea; And enriched with Historical and Explanatory Notes* (London, 1774 [1773?]), 5.
144. Ibid. 7, 9, 11–12.
145. The work is, allegedly, 'Printed at Batavia, for Jacobus Opano' (i.e. Joseph Banks) and undated, but the Introduction is dated 'Grub Street, Dec., 20, 1773' and that year is assigned to the work in the British Library catalogue.
146. Beaglehole ascribed the work to Scott, but C. Roderick gives reasons to doubt this. (See *Journal of Joseph Banks*, ed. Beaglehole, i. 102, and Roderick, 'Sir Joseph Banks', 77.)
147. *An Epistle from Mr. Banks, Voyager, Monster-hunter, and Amoroso, to Oberea, Queen of Otaheite. Transfused by A.B.C. Esq. Second Professor of the Otaheite, and of every other unknown Tongue* [London, 1773?], 12, 8, 13.
148. On Courtenay, see Roderick, 'Sir Joseph Banks', 82, 84.
149. [J. Courtenay?], *An Epistle (Moral and Philosophical) from an Officer at Otaheite to Lady Gr*s**n*r with Notes, Critical and Historical* (London, 1774), 2, 3, 4.
150. Ibid. 4. (See Milton, *Paradise Lost*, ix. 1034 ff.)
151. [J. Courtenay?], *An Epistle (Moral and Philosophical)*, 8, 10.
152. Ibid. 11, 12.

153. Ibid. 28–30.
154. Ibid. 2, 3.
155. *Otaheite: A Poem* (London, 1774), 9–10.
156. Ibid. 12, 13, 13–14.
157. Ibid. 15.
158. Ibid.
159. Ibid. 16.
160. Walpole to Sir Horace Mann, 10 July 1774, in Walpole, *Correspondence*, xxiv. 21.
161. Ibid.; Boswell, *Life of Johnson*, iii. 8.
162. Boswell, *Boswell: The Ominous Years 1774–1776*, ed. C. Ryskamp and F. A. Pottle (London, 1963), 308–9.
163. Boswell, *Life of Johnson*, iii. 7.

CHAPTER 5

1. Voltaire to Jean Baptiste Nicolas de Lisle, 11 June 1774, in Voltaire, *Correspondence*, ed. T. Besterman, xli (Banbury, 1975), 17.
2. Duchesse de Choiseul to Pierre Jacques Claude Dupuits, [20 Mar.] 1769, in Voltaire, *Correspondence*, xxiv (Banbury, 1974), 352; [Louis-Pétit de Bachaumont], *Mémoires secrets pour servir à l'histoire de la république des lettres en France, depuis MDCCLXII jusqu'à nos jours; ou Journal d'un observateur*, iv (London, 1777), 249–50.
3. [Montesquieu], *Lettres persanes* (2nd edn., Cologne, 1721), i. 118.
4. Pereire, 'Observations sur l'articulation de l'Insulaire de la mer du Sud', in Bougainville, *Voyage autour du monde*, 403.
5. La Condamine, 'Observations de Mr. de la Condamine sur l'insulaire de la Polynésie amené de l'isle de Taiti en France par Mr. de Bougainville', MS, Bibliothèque Nationale, Paris, accompanying Charles de Brosses's personal copy of his *Histoire des navigations aux terres australes*. I would like to thank my friend Patrick von Richthofen for transcribing the MS.
6. De Brosses, MS marginal note on La Condamine, 'Observations'.
7. Information about Aotourou's acquaintances from Martin-Allanic, *Bougainville navigateur*, ii. 970–1, which cannot be checked because no sources are given.
8. Bougainville, *Voyage autour du monde*, 224.
9. [Bachaumont], *Mémoires secrets*, iv. 309–10.
10. Vivez, 'Journal de Vivez' (Manuscrit de Versailles), in *Bougainville et ses compagnons*, ed. Taillemite, ii. 240; Fesche, 'Journal', ii. 92.
11. Bougainville, 'Journal', i. 331, 332.
12. See Bougainville, *Voyage*, 226.
13. Rousseau, *Confessions*, 2nd Part, Book 8, iv. 277.
14. Rousseau, *Discours*, 4–5.
15. Ibid. p. lviii.
16. Ibid. 6.
17. Ibid. 7–8.
18. Ibid. 208 n. 7, 80.
19. Voltaire, in G. R. Havens, *Voltaire's Marginalia on the Pages of Rousseau: A Comparative Study of Ideas* (Columbus, Ohio, 1933), 13.

20. Rousseau, *Confessions*, iv. 277.
21. Rousseau, *Discours*, 205, 104, 115.
22. Ibid. 248–9 n. 10, 113–14.
23. Ibid. 116.
24. I differ from the conclusion of A. O. Lovejoy's influential essay, 'The Supposed Primitivism of Rousseau's *Discourse on Inequality*', that the *Discours* is not primitivist, a conclusion that, with respectful reference to Lovejoy's essay, is frequently repeated— by Starobinski, for example, who agrees that Rousseau, in the *Discours*, 'n'est pas un primitiviste'. (J. Starobinski, 'Sur l'origine de l'inégalité', in *Jean-Jacques Rousseau*, 345, and see A. O. Lovejoy, 'The Supposed Primitivism of Rousseau's *Discourse on Inequality*', in *Essays in the History of Ideas*, 14–37.) To avoid a lengthy argument with Lovejoy's essay, and a lengthier quibble about the word 'primitivism', I shall confine myself to expressing the opinion that a proper reading of Rousseau's *Discours* cannot but suggest that it fits the definition of primitivism given by Lovejoy himself in his work with Boas: 'the discontent of the civilized with civilization'. (Lovejoy and Boas, *Primitivism*, 7.)
25. Rousseau, *Discours*, 184. Cf. Montaigne in my chapter 2.
26. Chateaubriand, quoted by Pierre Villey, who gives no source, in Montaigne, *Les Essais*, ed. P. Villey and V.-L. Saulnier (Paris, 1965), 1140.
27. Rousseau, *Discours*, 81. The version of Kolben's account of the Hottentots in *Histoire générale des voyages*, ed. Prévost, v (Paris, 1748) derives from an English translation, *The Present State of the Cape of Good Hope: or, A Particular Account of the several Nations of the Hottentots . . . Written Originally in High German, by Peter Kolben . . . Done into English . . . by Mr. Medley* (London, 1731). In his Preface, Guido Medley writes of Kolben: 'His Reasoning is sometimes very bad, and often very tedious. I have therefore retrench'd him . . . and have here and there alter'd him' (p. xvii).
28. Rousseau, *Discours*, 197–200 n. 5. 'Le P. du Tertre' is Père du Tertre, *Histoire générale des Antilles* (Paris, 1667–71). (See G. Pire, 'Jean-Jacques Rousseau et les relations de voyages', *Revue d'histoire littéraire de la France*, 56 (1956), 355–78.)
29. Rousseau, *Discours*, 29.
30. Voltaire, in Havens, *Voltaire's Marginalia*, 14.
31. See Rousseau, *Discours*, 254–9 n. 13, and *Histoire générale des voyages*, ed. Prévost, v. 175. We learn from Medley's breezy translation that Kolben remonstrated with the recalcitrant Hottentot: 'I met with this Spark several Times up in the Country, and had a great deal of Talk with him' (Kolben, *The Present State of the Cape*, i. 107). But Kolben had no success in persuading the Hottentot to reconsider his renunciations of civilization and Christianity. He is illustrated in the frontispiece of the *Discours* abandoning a group of baffled Dutchmen and captioned 'Il retourne chez ses Egaux'.
32. Rousseau, *Discours*, 231–2 n. 8; see *Histoire générale des voyages*, ed. Prévost, v. 87–9. There seems no evidence that Rousseau was deploying in the *Discours* any knowledge of other volumes of the *Histoire générale des voyages*. His erroneous reference to vol. iii (instead of vol. iv) is copied from the same error made in a note to the passage he is quoting from vol. v, which refers the reader incorrectly to vol. iii. Rousseau has silently omitted from his 'quotation' from the *Histoire générale* Purchas's report that Battell said the Pongos were twice the size of a man, which is correctly translated in the *Histoire générale* from Purchas's note: 'He said, their highth was like a mans, but their bignesse twice as great' (*Purchas His Pilgrimes*, vi. 398).

33. Rousseau, *Discours*, 234; see Claude Lévi-Strauss, 'Jean-Jacques Rousseau, fondateur des sciences de l'homme', in *Anthropologie structurale deux* (Paris, 1973), 45–6.

34. Rousseau, *Discours*, 237, p. lxiv, 236–7.

35. Commerson's brother-in-law, François Beau, quoted in Taillemite, 'Le séjour de Bougainville à Tahiti', 38; Vivez (who disliked Commerson), 'Journal de Vivez' (Manuscrit de Rochefort), in *Bougainville et ses compagnons*, ed. Taillemite, ii. 237.

36. On the fate of Commerson's fish, see 'Commerson' in *Nouvelle Biographie Générale*, ed. J. C. F. Hoefer, xi (Paris, 1855).

37. Commerson, 'Post-scriptum sur l'île de Taïti ou Nouvelle Cythère' (*Mercure de France*, Nov. 1769), repr. in F. B. de Montessus, *Martyrologie et biographie de Commerson* (Chalon-sur-Saone, 1889), 58. Commerson's published 'Post-scriptum' contrasts starkly with his more objective notes on Tahiti, published in *Bougainville et ses compagnons*, ed. Taillemite, ii. 496 ff.

38. Rousseau, *Discours*, 47, 111.

39. Commerson, 'Post-scriptum', 62.

40. [Nicolas Bricaire de la Dixmerie], *Le Sauvage de Taiti aux Français; avec un envoi au philosophe ami des sauvages* (Londres, 1770), quoted in Jean Gautier, 'Tahiti dans la littérature française à la fin du XVIIIᵉ siècle: quelques ouvrages oubliés', *Journal de la Société des Océanistes*, 3 (1947), 46.

41. [Dixmerie], *Le Sauvage*, quoted in Gautier, 'Tahiti', 47.

42. Diderot, 'Voyage autour du monde', etc. (review of Bougainville, *Voyage autour du monde*), in Denis Diderot, *Supplément au voyage de Bougainville*, ed. G. Chinard (Paris, 1935), 204; and see Martin-Allanic, *Bougainville navigateur*, i. 1.

43. On the reception of Bougainville's *Voyage*, see: Dunmore, *French Explorers in the Pacific*, i. 108–9; Martin-Allanic, *Bougainville navigateur*, ii. 1252; Taillemite, *Bougainville et ses compagnons*, ed. Taillemite, i. 111–21.

44. Bougainville, 'Discours préliminaire', in *Voyage autour du monde*, 16.

45. Bougainville, 'Journal', i. 281.

46. Bougainville, 'Discours préliminaire', in *Voyage autour du monde*, 16, 17.

47. Bougainville, *Voyage autour du monde*, 190.

48. See my chapter 4.

49. Naussau-Siegen, 'Journal', ii. 394.

50. Bougainville, *Voyage autour du monde*, 190.

51. Ibid. 192–3.

52. See ibid. 209; Virgil, *Aeneid*, 6. 673–5; Bougainville, *Voyage autour du monde*, 197–8. Cf. Bougainville, 'Journal', i. 317–18, 327.

53. Bougainville, *Voyage autour du monde*, 228.

54. Ibid. 209.

55. Ibid. 190, 198.

56. See Rousseau, *Confessions*, 2nd Part, Book 8, iv. 278; and G. R. Havens, 'Diderot, Rousseau, and the *Discours sur l'inégalité*', *Diderot Studies*, 3 (1961), 219–62, which sums up its findings in one of its sentences: 'It is, in any case, impossible to determine today the degree and the primacy of their mutual influence on each other' (250).

57. Diderot, 'Voyage autour du monde', etc. (review of Bougainville, *Voyage autour du monde*), in *Supplément*, 204, 207.

58. Ibid. 207–8.

59. Ibid. 210.

60. See Peter Jimack, *Diderot: Supplément au voyage de Bougainville* (London, 1988), 11–12. The revised manuscript of the *Supplément* was published in 1935, ed. Gilbert Chinard, and it is to this text I refer.

61. Diderot, *Supplément*, 115.

62. Ibid. 119–20.

63. Bougainville, *Voyage autour du monde*, 228.

64. Diderot, *Supplément*, 115, 119–20.

65. Rousseau, *Discours*, 116; Diderot, *Supplément*, 123.

66. Ibid. 125.

67. Ibid. 134.

68. Ibid. 134, 143.

69. Ibid. 163.

70. Ibid. 169.

71. Ibid. 164.

72. Ibid. 151.

73. Ibid. 169.

74. [Diderot], 'Jouissance', *Encyclopédie, ou dictionnaire raisonné des sciences, des arts et des métiers*, viii (Neuchâtel, 1765).

75. Diderot, *Les Bijoux indiscrets*, in *Œuvres de Denis Diderot*, publiées, sur les manuscrits de l'auteur, par Jacques-André Naigeon (Paris, 1798), x. 95.

76. See Diderot to Sophie Volland, [22 Nov. 1768], Diderot, *Correspondance*, ed. Georges Roth, viii (Paris, 1962), 231–2.

77. Diderot, *Supplément*, 176.

78. Ibid. 181.

79. Ibid. 178, 189. Cf. Chamfort's definition of love as 'nothing but the contact of two epidermises', quoted in P. Gay, *The Enlightenment: An Interpretation* (London, 1973), ii. 202.

80. Hawkesworth, *Voyages*, ii. 128.

81. Voltaire to Jean Baptiste Nicolas de Lisle, 11 June 1774, in *Correspondence*, xli. 17. Although Voltaire refers to 'le voiage autour du monde de Messieurs Banks et Solander', he does not thereby refer to a work which appeared in French as early as 1772, entitled *Supplément au voyage de M. de Bougainville; ou journal d'un voyage autour du monde, fait par MM. Banks & Solander* ... traduit de l'Anglois, par M. de Fréville (Paris, 1772), a translation of the anonymous *A Journal of a Voyage round the World* (London, 1771), which has been variously attributed to one or another of Cook's crew. (See *Journals of Captain Cook*, ed. Beaglehole, i, pp. cclvi–cclxiv.) The French translation may possibly have suggested to Diderot the title of his *Supplément*, but it is unlikely that it provided Diderot or Voltaire with much Tahitian information in its brief and bland account of that island. Certainly the scene at Point Venus is not mentioned in *Supplément au voyage* (1772), and there is no doubt that Voltaire, following the common practice of attributing Cook's voyage to the famous Banks, was indeed referring, in his letter, to Hawkesworth's *Voyages*, just recently published in a French translation, *Relation des voyages entrepris par ordre de Sa Majesté Britannique* (Lausanne and Neuchâtel, 1774), which we know was in Voltaire's possession. (See J. Dunmore, 'The Explorer and the Philosopher: Diderot's *Supplément* and Giradoux's *Supplément*', in W. Veit (ed.), *Captain James Cook: Image and Impact* (Melbourne, 1972), 58.)

82. Voltaire to Jean Baptiste Nicolas de Lisle, 11 June 1774, in *Correspondence*, xli. 17.

83. Voltaire to Jean-Jacques Rousseau, [30 Aug. 1755], in *Correspondence*, xvi (Banbury, 1971), 259; Voltaire, in Havens, *Voltaire's Marginalia*, 17.

84. See [Voltaire], 'Antropofages', in *Dictionnaire philosophique* (London, 1764), 26–8.

85. Voltaire, *Les Oreilles du conte de Chesterfield et le chapelain Goudman*, in *Romans et contes*, ed. F. Deloffre and J. van den Heuvel (Pléiade edn., 1979), 577.

86. Ibid. 586.

87. Ibid. 589.

88. Ibid. 589–90.

89. Ibid. 590.

90. Ibid. 591.

91. Ibid.

92. Ibid.

93. Ibid. 595.

94. Voltaire, *Candide ou l'optimisme*, in *Roman et contes*, 153.

95. Diderot, *Supplément*, 115.

96. Fesche, 'Journal', ii. 92.

97. Jacques Delille, *Les Jardins, ou l'art d'embellir les paysages* (Paris, 1782), 54–5.

98. Bougainville, *Voyage autour du monde*, 227.

99. Aotourou's name for the Isle de France, as transcribed and translated by Commerson, in 'Notes de Commerson', in *Bougainville et ses compagnons*, ed. Taillemite, ii. 500, translation (from Commerson's French) mine.

100. [Bernardin de Saint-Pierre], *Voyage à l'Isle de France* (Amsterdam and Paris, 1773), ii. 2, 4.

101. See Martin-Allanic, *Bougainville navigateur*, ii. 1311, and Dunmore, *French Explorers in the Pacific*, i. 168.

102. [Julien Crozet], *Nouveau voyage à la Mer du Sud . . . rédigée d'après les plans & journaux de M. Crozet*, ed. A. M. Rochon (Paris, 1783), 5.

103. 'Procès-verbal' of the *Mascarin*, quoted in Martin-Allanic, *Bougainville navigateur*, ii. 1325.

104. [Crozet], *Nouveau voyage*, 95, 128–9.

105. Rousseau, as reported by Crozet, in Anders Sparrman, *A Voyage Round the World with Captain James Cook in H.M.S. Resolution*, trans. A. Mackenzie-Grieve and H. Beamish, ed. O. Rutter (London, 1944), 187–8.

106. Walpole to Sir Horace Mann, 10 July 1774, in *Correspondence*, xxiv. 21.

107. James Burney, 'Burney's Log', in *Journals of Captain Cook*, ii. 750.

108. Cook, the Greenwich MS, quoted in *Journals of Captain Cook*, ii. 428 n. On Omai's background on Raiatea and his boyhood flight to Tahiti, see McCormick, *Omai*, 1, 3.

109. Sarah S. Banks, MS 'Memorandums', National Library of Australia, Canberra, quoted in McCormick, *Omai*, 113. On the Tahitian ''o'', see [John Davies], *A Tahitian and English Dictionary* (Tahiti, 1851), 4, 157, and D. T. Tryon, *Conversational Tahitian* (Berkeley, Calif., 1970), 10.

110. *General Evening Post*, 26–8 July 1774, [1]; and see *General Evening Post*, 21–3 July 1774, [3, 4].

111. *St. James's Chronicle*, 4–6 Aug. 1774, [1].

112. Burney, *Early Diary*, i. 311.

113. *General Evening Post*, 5–8 Nov. 1774, [4]; see *General Evening Post*, 23–6 July 1774, [4], and McCormick, *Omai*, 111, 121 and facing page.

114. Burney, *Early Diary*, i. 311.
115. Ibid. 332; Frances Burney to Samuel Crisp, 1 Dec. 1774, British Library, Egerton MS 3694.
116. Ibid.
117. Boswell, *Life of Johnson*, iii. 8.
118. [Samuel Johnson], Preface, *A Voyage to Abyssinia by Father Jerome Lobo, . . . A Portuguese Jesuit . . . From the French* (London, 1735), p. viii.
119. Boswell, *Life of Johnson*, ii. 333.
120. Walpole to Mason, 29 Feb. 1776, in *Correspondence*, xxviii (London, 1955), 250.
121. See P. G. Adams, *Travelers and Travel Liars*, 216.
122. James Bruce, *Travels to Discover the Source of the Nile* (Edinburgh, 1790), iii. 144.
123. Burney, *Early Diary*, ii. 25.
124. For the month of *An Historic Epistle*, see McCormick, *Omai*, 144.
125. *An Historic Epistle, from Omiah, to the Queen of Otaheite; being his Remarks on the English Nation. With Notes by the Editor* (London, 1775), 3.
126. Ibid. 14.
127. Ibid. 31–2.
128. Ibid. 32.
129. Ibid. 43, 44.
130. 'Mr. Sharp's manuscript notes', quoted in Prince Hoare, *Memoirs of Granville Sharp, Esq. composed from his own Manuscripts and other Authentic Documents* (London, 1820), 148.
131. See [Granville Sharp], *An English Alphabet, for the Use of Foreigners: wherein the Pronunciation of the Vowels, or Voice-Letters, is explained in Twelve short general Rules, With their several Exceptions, as abridged (For the Instruction of Omai) from a larger Work* (London, 1786).
132. Granville Sharp, 'Address to the Maroons in the new English settlement at Sierra Leone', quoted in Hoare, *Memoirs*, 150–1.
133. Cook, *Journals of Captain Cook*, ii. 322.
134. Beaglehole, *Cook the Writer*, 12. This work repeats a good deal of the dense matter of Beaglehole's 'Textual Introduction' to *Journals of Captain Cook*, ii, but with the difference that Beaglehole makes explicit the inference to be drawn from the variant texts: that Cook had been preparing a book. This conclusion is reinforced, as Beaglehole points out, by the fact that, in the second of the two extant holograph MSS of Cook's journal, Cook has changed from ship time to civil time. (See *Cook the Writer*, 14–15.)
135. See ibid. 15–16, and Cook, journal of second voyage, British Library, Additional MS 27888.
136. Cook to Douglas, 10 Jan. 1776, quoted in *Journals of Captain Cook*, ii, p. cxlvi.
137. Ibid.
138. Boswell, *Ominous Years*, 310.
139. Ibid. 341.
140. Cook, *Journals of Captain Cook*, ii. 294, 293, and, for reworking, British Library, Additional MS 27888, f. 150. Cf. 'an avidity which amazed me', William Wales, 'Journal', in *Journals of Captain Cook*, ii. 818.
141. Boswell, *Ominous Years*, 341.
142. The words are deleted in the second of Cook's two holograph MSS in the British Library, Additional MS 27888, f. 224ᵛ.
143. James Cook, General Introduction, *A Voyage towards the South Pole, and Round the*

World (London, 1777), i, p. xxxvi. For Cook's own text, see Beaglehole, *Cook the Writer*, 22.

144. *Gentleman's Magazine*, 47 (Oct. 1777), 491.
145. James King, 'King's Journal', in *Journals of Captain Cook*, iii. 1369.
146. Ibid.
147. Cook, *Journals of Captain Cook*, iii. 186.
148. King, 'King's Journal', iii. 1375; David Samwell, 'Samwell's Journal', in *Journals of Captain Cook*, iii. 1062.
149. Cook, *Journals of Captain Cook*, iii. 209, 213.
150. William Bayly, in *Journals of Captain Cook*, iii. 193 n. Cf. Samwell, 'Samwell's Journal', iii. 1059.
151. Cook, *Journals of Captain Cook*, iii. 199, 203.
152. Ibid. 206.
153. Ibid. 193.
154. Ibid. 233, 239, 235.
155. Bayly, in *Journals of Captain Cook*, iii. 237 n. 2. For the lock and key, see Samwell, 'Samwell's Journal', iii. 1070.
156. Bayly, in *Journals of Captain Cook*, iii. 193 n. 2.
157. Ibid. 237 n. 2, 193 n. 2.
158. Cook, *Journals of Captain Cook*, iii. 237; Alexander Home, in *Journals of Captain Cook*, iii. 237 n. 2.
159. Banks's list of 'Presents for Omai', in Michael Alexander, *Omai: 'Noble Savage'* (London, 1977), 143–4. For the fireworks, see Cook, *Journals of Captain Cook*, iii. 237, and Alexander, *Omai*, 145.
160. Cook, *Journals of Captain Cook*, iii. 239.
161. Ibid. 241. For the monkey, see John Ledyard, *A Journal of Captain Cook's Last Voyage* (Hartford, Conn., 1783; facsimile repr. Chicago, 1963), 59.
162. King, 'King's Journal', iii. 1387; Samwell, 'Samwell's Journal', iii. 1073.
163. Cook, *Journals of Captain Cook*, iii. 278.
164. Ibid. 269.
165. Ibid. 263–4, 265.
166. Samwell, 'Samwell's Journal', iii. 1083.
167. King, 'King's Journal', iii. 498.
168. Ibid.
169. Samwell, 'Samwell's Journal', iii. 1154. Samwell 'wrote much verse in both English and Welsh, and was by his friends esteemed an elegant poet'. (Beaglehole, 'The Ships' Companies', *Journals of Captain Cook*, iii. 1463.)
170. Cook, 'Log', in *Journals of Captain Cook*, iii. 491. What remains of Cook's journal runs only to 6 Jan. 1779, and what remains of his log runs only to 17 Jan. 1779. (See Beaglehole, *Journals of Captain Cook*, iii, p. clxxii.)
171. King, 'King's Journal', iii. 504.
172. Ibid. 506.
173. Ibid. 506–7, 509.
174. King, in James Cook and James King, *A Voyage to the Pacific Ocean* (London, 1784), iii. 26.
175. King, 'King's Journal', iii. 529; Charles Clerke, 'Clerke's Journal', in *Journals of Captain Cook*, iii. 531.

176. Samwell, 'Samwell's Journal', iii. 1195.
177. Molesworth Phillips, 'Phillips's Report', in *Journals of Captain Cook*, iii. 535, 536; Clerke, 'Clerke's Journal', iii. 538 ('furnish'd them by ourselves'). Phillips gives the only account by an eyewitness of events on the shore, and 'after being knock'd down I saw no more of Capt Cook', so the exact manner of Cook's death—whether by stabbing, clubbing, drowning, or a combination—is uncertain. Theories about the causes in the wider sense range from the psychological/medical (the deleterious effects on Cook's judgement of a vitamin B deficiency) to the anthropological/mythical (the consequences of the parallels between Cook and the Hawaiian Lono). It seems to me, however, that explanations in terms of 'colonization [of Cook's intestine] by coliform bacteria which could interfere with the absorption of the B complex of vitamins' or 'a situational set of relations, crystallized from the operative cultural categories and actors' interests [and] subject to the double structural determination of intentions grounded in a cultural scheme and the unintended consequences arising from re-cuperation in other projects and schemes' reveal more about the conditions of the medical and anthropological disciplines than about the particular 'set of relations' in the 'colonization' of Hawaii that left Cook dead at Kealakekua Bay in 1779. (Phillips, 'Phillips's Report', iii. 536; Sir James Watt, 'Medical Aspects and Consequences of Cook's Voyages', in R. Fisher and H. Johnston (eds.), *Captain James Cook and His Times* (Vancouver, 1979), 155; Marshall Sahlins, *Islands of History* (Chicago, 1985), 125 n.)
178. *Omiah's Farewell; Inscribed to the Ladies of London* (London, 1776), p. ii.
179. Ibid. p. iv.
180. Ibid. 6–7.
181. Ibid. 10.
182. See George Martelli, *Jemmy Twitcher: A Life of the Fourth Earl of Sandwich 1718–1792* (London, 1962), 165–77.
183. [Herbert Croft], *Love and Madness: A Story Too True. In a Series of Letters* (London, 1780), 6.
184. Anna Seward, *Elegy on Captain Cook* (London, 1780), 15–16.
185. John Douglas, autobiographical notes, quoted in *Journals of Captain Cook*, iii, p. cxcix.
186. Ibid.
187. William Anderson, 'Anderson's Journal', in *Journals of Captain Cook*, iii. 978.
188. Cook, *Journals of Captain Cook*, iii. 198, 202; Anderson, 'Anderson's Journal', iii. 980; Cook and King, *A Voyage*, ii. 31, and see 35.
189. Anderson, 'Anderson's Journal', iii. 983, and see Cook and King, *A Voyage*, ii. 41.
190. Cook and King, *A Voyage*, ii. 103.
191. King, 'King's Journal', iii. 1386–7. Cf. Cook and King, *A Voyage*, ii. 105–9.
192. Cook and King, *A Voyage*, ii. 108.
193. On editions and sales of Cook and King, *A Voyage*, see *Journals of Captain Cook*, iii, p. cciv. On the pantomime *Omai*, see William Huse, 'A Noble Savage on the Stage', *Modern Philology*, 33 (1936), 303–16, and Rüdiger Joppien, 'Phillipe Jacques de Loutherbourg's Pantomime *Omai, or a Trip round the World* and the Artists of Captain Cook's Voyages', in T. C. Mitchell (ed.), *Captain Cook and the South Pacific* (London, 1979), 81–136.
194. See Playbill for *Omai*, reproduced in Joppien, 'Loutherbourg's Pantomime', 119.
195. *Morning Chronicle*, 21 Dec. 1785, [3].

196. John O'Keeffe, *A Short Account of the New Pantomime called Omai, or, A Trip Round the World* (London, 1785), 14 ff.
197. See Joppien, 'Loutherbourg's Pantomime', 89, and plates 60–2, 130–1; and *Morning Chronicle*, 21 Dec. 1785, [3].
198. O'Keeffe, *A Short Account*, 7, etc.
199. See Huse, 'A Noble Savage', 303.
200. Joseph Joubert, unpublished notes, quoted in André Beaunier, 'Joseph Joubert et Tahiti', *Revue des deux mondes*, 24 (1914), 775, 769.
201. Louis de Fontanes to Joubert, 20 Jan. 1786, quoted in Beaunier, 'Joseph Joubert', 764.
202. O'Keeffe, *A Short Account*, 7, 10.
203. Ibid. 17.
204. Ibid.
205. Ibid.
206. Cook and King, *A Voyage*, i. 388, 197. For '*ehoee*' and '*hoohoo*', see, ibid. ii. 154, iii. 119.
207. William Cowper to John Newton, 21 June 1784, in *The Letters and Prose Writings of William Cowper*, ed. J. King and C. Ryskamp, ii (Oxford, 1981), 255.
208. William Cowper to William Unwin, 14 Aug. 1784, in *Letters*, ii. 270, 271.
209. William Cowper, *The Task, A Poem, in Six Books* (London, 1785), 39, 41.
210. Ibid. 40.
211. Ibid. 33.
212. Ibid. 36.
213. Ibid. 33.
214. Ibid. 34–5.
215. Delille, *Les Jardins*, 55.
216. See 'Mémoire du Roi', in Lapérouse, *Voyage de La Pérouse autour du monde*, rédigé par M. L. A. Milet-Mureau (Paris, 1797), i. 54.
217. Lapérouse, 'Journal de Lapérouse', *Le Voyage de Lapérouse 1785–1788: Récit et documents originaux*, ed. John Dunmore and Maurice de Brossard (Paris, 1985), ii. 147.
218. Ibid. 447.
219. Lapérouse to Fleurieu, 7 Feb. 1788, in *Le Voyage*, i. 279.
220. Peter Dillon, *Narrative and Successful Result of a Voyage in the South Seas, performed by order of the Government of British India, to ascertain the actual fate of La Pérouse's Expedition* (London, 1829), i. 33.
221. See Maurice de Brossard, *Lapérouse: des combats à la découverte* (Paris, 1978), 573.
222. See Lapérouse, *Voyage de La Pérouse*, ii. 191.
223. Camille Desmoulins to Lucile Desmoulins, 'Duodi germinal, 5 heures du matin', in *Correspondance inédite de Camille Desmoulins*, ed. M. Matton (Paris, 1836), 225.

CHAPTER 6

1. Bligh to Sir Joseph Banks, 13 Oct. 1789, MS, Mitchell Library, Sydney, Australia.
2. Banks, *Journal of Joseph Banks*, i. 341. For an account of events leading up to the *Bounty* breadfruit expedition, see the chapter 'Food for Slaves' in David Mackay, *In the Wake of Cook: Exploration, Science and Empire, 1780–1801* (London, 1985).
3. William Bligh, *The Log of the Bounty*, ed. O. Rutter (London, 1936), i. 295, 349.

4. See Bengt Danielsson, *What Happened on the Bounty*, trans. Alan Tapsell (London, 1962), 68–9.

5. Bligh, *Log*, i. 399.

6. Ibid. 390.

7. Ibid. 394.

8. Ibid. ii. 17.

9. Ibid. i. 386.

10. Ibid. ii. 34–5.

11. Ibid. i. 381; ii. 70.

12. Ibid. 83.

13. John Fryer, *Journal*, in *The Voyage of the Bounty's Launch as Related in William Bligh's Despatch to the Admiralty and the Journal of John Fryer*, ed. O. Rutter (London, 1934), 53; James Morrison, *The Journal of James Morrison Boatswain's Mate of the Bounty*, ed. O. Rutter (London, 1935), 37.

14. Fryer, *Journal*, 55.

15. Morrison, *Journal*, 41.

16. Edward Christian, 'The Appendix', [Stephen Barney and Edward Christian], *Minutes of the Proceedings of the Court Martial held at Portsmouth ... With an Appendix*, in *A Book of the 'Bounty'*, ed. G. Mackaness (London, 1938), 250–1; Fryer, *Journal*, 61.

17. Morrison, *Journal*, 44. Cf. [Morrison], 'Memorandum and Particulars respecting the Bounty and her Crew', MS, Mitchell Library, Sydney, 35, 37; Edward Christian, 'Appendix', 258; and F. W. Beechey, *Narrative of a Voyage to the Pacific and Bering's Strait*, pt. I (London, 1831), 53 (though denied by Heywood in Heywood to Beechey, 5 April 1830, in [John Barrow], *The Eventful History of the Mutiny and Piratical Seizure of H.M.S. Bounty: Its Cause and Consequences* (London, 1831), 90–1).

18. Morrison, *Journal*, 44.

19. George Peard, 'Account of the Mutiny', in MS 'Journal kept in H.M.S. Blossom', British Library, Additional MS 35141 (and see Beechey, *Narrative of a Voyage*, I. 53–4).

20. Bligh, *Log*, ii. 118.

21. Ibid. 118, 120.

22. Edward Christian, 'Appendix', 256, which is closer than Bligh's version to the statements by the witnesses, Fryer and Purcell, at the court-martial. (See *The Court-Martial of the 'Bounty' Mutineers*, ed. O. Rutter (Edinburgh, 1931), 73, 102, and William Bligh, *A Narrative of the Mutiny, on board His Majesty's Ship 'Bounty'; and the subsequent voyage of part of the crew in the ship's boat, from Tofoa ... to Timor ...* (London, 1790), 8.)

23. Fryer, *Journal*, 60.

24. Bligh, *Log*, ii. 122, 123. The cries of 'Huzza for Otaheite' were denied by Edward Christian, as never heard by the witnesses he interviewed, but are confirmed in the account given by Adams to Beechey. (See Edward Christian, 'Appendix', 256, and Beechey, *Narrative of a Voyage*, I. 56.)

25. Bligh, *Log*, ii. 130.

26. Ibid.

27. Ibid. 131.

28. Ibid.

29. Ibid.

30. Fryer, *Journal*, 65.
31. Ibid. 69; Bligh, *Log*, ii. 186.
32. Ibid.
33. Fryer, *Journal*, 70.
34. Bligh, *Log*, ii. 192.
35. Fryer, *Journal*, 71.
36. Bligh, *Log*, ii. 221.
37. Ibid. 227, 230.
38. Fryer, note dated 8 July 1789, in *The Voyage of the Bounty's Launch*, 80.
39. William Bligh, 'Particular transactions at Sourabya', 'Log of the *Resource*', in *Bligh's Voyage in the 'Resource' from Coupang to Batavia, together with the Log of his subsequent passage to England in the Dutch Packet 'Vlydt' and his Remarks on Morrison's Journal*, ed. O. Rutter (London, 1937), 64.
40. Ibid.
41. Ibid.
42. Ibid. 64–5. Cf. Fryer, note dated 16 Sept. 1789, in *The Voyage of the Bounty's Launch*, 80 ff.
43. Fryer, letter to Bligh, copied in Bligh, 'Remarks at Samarang', in *Bligh's Voyage in the 'Resource'*, 82.
44. Bligh to Sir Joseph Banks, 13 Oct. 1789, MS, Mitchell Library, Sydney.
45. Bligh, 'Log' of his passage to England, in *Bligh's Voyage in the 'Resource'*, 149.
46. 'Mutiny on board the Bounty Armed Ship', *General Evening Post*, 16–18 Mar. 1790, [4].
47. [Frances Burney], *Diary and Letters of Madame d'Arblay*, ed. by her niece (London, 1842–6), v. 101. For the suggestion that James Burney edited Bligh's *Narrative of the Mutiny*, see G. E. Manwaring, *My Friend the Admiral: The Life, Letters, and Journals of Rear-Admiral James Burney* (London, 1931), 198.
48. [Burney], *Diary and Letters*, v. 114.
49. See facsimile of the playbill, in George Mackaness, *The Life of Vice-Admiral William Bligh* (new and rev. edn., London, 1951), facing p. 176.
50. Bligh, *Narrative of the Mutiny*, 9.
51. Ibid. 8.
52. Ibid. 55.
53. *An Account of the Mutinous Seizure of the Bounty: with the succeeding Hardships of the Crew: to which are added Secret Anecdotes of the Otaheitean Females* (London, 1792), 13, 43.
54. Ibid.; and see 44–7.
55. Ibid. 42.
56. Minutes of the court martial of William Purcell, PRO, London, quoted in Mackaness, *The Life of Bligh*, 188.
57. John Fryer, *Journal*, 63. As Fryer's account refers to Purcell's court martial (p. 65), it must have been written after Oct. 1790. On Fryer, see Rolf E. Du Rietz, *Fresh Light on John Fryer of the 'Bounty'* (Uppsala, 1981).
58. Fryer, *Journal*, 58, 60–1.
59. For the decision to sail for Tahiti, see James Morrison, *Journal*, 45. On the date of composition of Morrison's journal, see Rolf E. Du Rietz, 'Note sur l'histoire des manuscrits de James Morrison', in James Morrison, *Journal de James Morrison*, trans.

B. Jaunez (Paris, 1966), pp. ix–xiii, and Rolf E. Du Rietz, *Peter Heywood's Tahitian Vocabulary and the Narratives by James Morrison: Some Notes on their Origin and History* (Uppsala, 1986), 15.

60. James Cook and James King, *A Voyage to the Pacific Ocean* (London, 1784), ii. 5 (with a map showing Tubuai on the facing page). Lieutenant Shillibeer of the *Briton* reports the presence on Pitcairn of 'several books belonging to Captain Bligh which were taken out of the *Bounty*' and saw a copy of Hawkesworth's *Voyages* in which 'Christian had written his name immediately under [Bligh's] without running his pen through, or defacing in the least that of Captain Bligh'. (Lieut. J. Shillibeer, RM, *A Narrative of the Briton's Voyage, to Pitcairn's Island* (Taunton, 1817), 96–7.)

61. Morrison, *Journal*, 47 (breadfruit) and see George Stewart, 'Stewart's Journal' and Peter Heywood, 'Heywood's Journal', MSS, Ministry of Defence Library, London; Stewart, 'Stewart's Journal' (uniforms) and see Morrison, *Journal*, 48. Notes taken from the journals of Peter Heywood and George Stewart, 'Extracts from Peter Heywood's Journal' and 'From Stewarts Journal', are among the papers of Edward Edwards in the Ministry of Defence Library, London. As Heywood's and Stewart's original journals, presumably lost on the *Pandora*, were probably written contemporaneously with events, I have sometimes preferred their dates, when they agree, to Morrison's.

62. Morrison, *Journal*, 49.

63. See ibid. 50 and Heywood, 'Heywood's Journal', and the account Adams gave to Moerenhout, in which 'manque de femmes' is crucial. (J. A. Moerenhout, *Voyages aux îles du Grand Océan* (Paris, 1837), ii. 291.)

64. Heywood, 'Heywood's Journal', and see Morrison, *Journal*, 51.

65. Morrison, *Journal*, 52. Heywood, 'Heywood's Journal' gives a slightly lower number of Tahitian passengers.

66. Jenny, in *United Service Journal* (1829), pt. II, p. 589. Jenny dictated an account to the missionary, Henry Nott, on Tahiti, which was given to the *Bengal Hurkaru* by Peter Dillon, discoverer of the fate of Lapérouse, and published in the *Bengal Hurkaru* (2 Oct. 1826) and reprinted in *United Service Journal* (1829) pt. II.

67. William Ellis, *Polynesian Researches*, iii (London, 1833), 385. I have adopted the spelling of Tubuaian personal names used by H. E. Maude. (See H. E. Maude, *Of Islands and Men* (Melbourne, 1968), 7 n.)

68. Heywood, 'Heywood's Journal'.

69. Morrison, *Journal*, 55.

70. Heywood, 'Heywood's Journal'.

71. Stewart, 'Stewart's Journal'.

72. See Morrison, *Journal*, 56.

73. Ibid. 57.

74. Ibid. 58.

75. Ibid.; Heywood, 'Heywood's Journal'.

76. Morrison, *Journal*, 60; Heywood, 'Heywood's Journal'.

77. Morrison, *Journal*, 61; Heywood, 'Heywood's Journal' (and see also Edward Christian, 'Appendix', 260).

78. See Morrison, *Journal*, 63, and Heywood, 'Heywood's Journal'.

79. For the Tubuaians accompanying the *Bounty*, see Morrison, *Journal*, 63–4 and, for the dates, see 'Heywood's Journal' and 'Stewart's Journal'. Morrison's journal and Edward

Christian's 'Appendix' give differing dates and I have preferred the chronology of the journals of Heywood and Stewart. These sometime differ, too, so the dating of these events is only conjectural.

80. Bligh's log records the detention 'Contrary to their inclinations' of Coleman, McIntosh, and Norman. (See Bligh, *Log*, ii. 120.)

81. Morrison, *Journal*, 76.

82. Ibid. For Christian's telling Heywood and Stewart that he intended to sail immediately, see Edward Christian, 'Appendix', 261. Heywood refers to a last meeting with Christian, on the eve of his departure from Tahiti, in Heywood to Beechey, 5 Apr. 1830, in [Barrow], *The Eventful History*, 90–1, and Lady Belcher's account gives further details (which may or may not be based on good evidence) in [Diana] Belcher, *The Mutineers of the Bounty and their Descendants in Pitcairn and Norfolk Islands* (London, 1870), 50–1.

83. Morrison, *Journal*, 76; Heywood to his Mother, 20 Nov. 1791, in [Barrow], *The Eventful History*, 182. On the continuity of Stewart's relationship with Peggy, see Bligh, journal on the *Providence*, published as *Return to Tahiti: Bligh's Second Breadfruit Voyage*, ed. Douglas Oliver (Honolulu, 1988), 87.

84. Morrison, *Journal*, 81.

85. Ibid. 87.

86. Heywood, 'Heywood's Journal'. On the Tahitian politics underlying these events, see Douglas Oliver, *Ancient Tahitian Society*, iii. *The Rise of the Pomares* (Canberra, n.d., originally published Honolulu, 1974), particularly ch. 28, 'Wars of the *Bounty* Mutineers'.

87. Heywood, 'Heywood's Journal'. I equivocate about dates in this paragraph because those given by Morrison and Heywood are inconsistent and the extract 'From Stewarts Journal' ends with the separation from the *Bounty* and cannot therefore be used as a check.

88. Morrison, *Journal*, 119.

89. See Heywood to his Mother, 15 Aug. 1792, in Edward Tagart, *A Memoir of the late Captain Peter Heywood, R. N. with extracts from his Diaries and Correspondence* (London, 1832), 82–3; and the entry for Wednesday, 23 Mar. 1791, in the log of the *Pandora*, MS, Ministry of Defence Library, London.

90. Heywood to his Mother, 15 Aug. 1792, in Tagart, *Memoir*, 83; Heywood to his Mother, 20 Nov. 1791, in [Barrow], *The Eventful History*, 182–3. Heywood and Stewart were both tattooed at Tahiti, even before the mutiny, as can be seen from Bligh's 'Description of the Pirates' in his *Log*, ii. 124.

91. Bligh, *Narrative of the Mutiny*, 4, and see Bligh, *Log*, ii. 120. Edwards's orders were 'to keep the mutineers as closely confined as may preclude all possibility of their escaping, having, however, proper regard to the preservation of their lives, that they may be brought home to undergo the punishment due to their demerits' (PRO, Adm. 2/120), quoted in *Voyage of H.M.S. 'Pandora'*, ed. Basil Thomson (London, 1915), 41, and in Geoffrey Rawson, *'Pandora''s Last Voyage* (London, 1963), 5.

92. Edward Edwards, log of *Pandora*, MS, Ministry of Defence Library, London, and see Edwards's report from 'Batavia, the 25th November, 1791', in *Voyage of H.M.S. 'Pandora'*, 31, and George Hamilton, *A Voyage Round the World, in His Majesty's Frigate Pandora* (Berwick, 1793), 25.

93. Morrison, *Journal*, 122.
94. Edwards, report from 'Batavia, the 25th November, 1791', 34. That the 'journals' referred to by Edwards were those of Heywood and Stewart can be inferred from the fact that the extracts from their journals are with Edwards's papers in the Ministry of Defence Library, and is confirmed by the fact that the account Edwards gives, based on these 'journals', derives its dates and figures from the 'Extracts from Peter Heywood's Journal'.
95. Morrison, *Journal*, 122.
96. Ibid. 123, and, for the lice, see James Morrison to William Howell, 10 Oct. 1792 [46], MS, Mitchell Library, Sydney; Hamilton, *Voyage Round the World*, 36.
97. Ibid. 36, 37.
98. Ibid. 37.
99. Ibid. 34; Morrison, *Journal*, 123.
100. Ibid.; David Renouard, midshipman of the *Pandora* and one of the crew of the *Resolution/Matavy*, 'Renouard's Narrative', in H. E. Maude, 'The Voyage of the *Pandora*'s Tender', *Mariner's Mirror*, 50 (Aug. 1964), 222; Edwards, report from 'Batavia, the 25th November, 1791', 38.
101. Ibid. 67–8 (and see George Hamilton, *Voyage Round the World*, 99).
102. Dillon spoke to a man in 1826 who, about six years previously, 'had seen and conversed with two old men who belonged to the ships' of Lapérouse. (Peter Dillon, *Narrative and Successful Result of a Voyage in the South Seas*, i. 34.)
103. Morrison, *Journal*, 126 (and see Heywood to his Mother, 20 Nov. 1791, in [Barrow], *The Eventful History*, 185).
104. Morrison, *Journal*, 126 (and see Heywood to his Mother, 20 Nov. 1791, in [Barrow], *The Eventful History*, 185).
105. Edwards, report from 'Batavia, the 25th November, 1791', 73.
106. Heywood to his Mother, 20 Nov. 1791, in [Barrow], *The Eventful History*, 185.
107. Morrison, *Journal*, 127.
108. Hamilton, *Voyage Round the World*, 107; Morrison, *Journal*, 127.
109. Ibid.
110. Ibid. 128.
111. Ibid.
112. David Renouard, 'Renouard's Narrative', 229.
113. See Morrison, *Journal*, 134, 135.
114. Bligh, journal on the *Providence, Return to Tahiti*, 55.
115. 'Advertisement', *Narrative of the Mutiny*, p. iii. Burney's editorial assistance with Bligh, *A Voyage to the South Sea . . . for the purpose of Conveying the Bread-fruit Tree to the West Indies* (London, 1792) was surmised by G. E. Manwaring, *My Friend the Admiral: The Life, Letters, and Journals of Rear-Admiral James Burney* (London, 1931), 198–201, on the evidence of Bligh to Burney, 26 July 1791 (in Mackaness, *The Life of Bligh*, 18–19) and proved conclusively by three letters, of Sept. and Oct. 1791, from Burney to Banks, in Rolf E. Du Rietz, 'Three letters from James Burney to Sir Joseph Banks', *Ethnos*, 27 (1962), 115–25.
116. Burney to Banks, 13 Oct. 1791, in 'Three letters', 123; [Bligh], *Voyage to the South Sea*, 80.
117. Bligh, *Log*, ii. 17, 35.

118. See Bligh, *Narrative of the Mutiny*, 1 ff. and *Voyage to the South Sea*, 154 ff.

119. See *The Court-Martial of the 'Bounty' Mutineers*, ed. O. Rutter, which publishes the official Minutes (PRO Adm. 1 5330), 68.

120. Ibid. 107.

121. Ibid. 73.

122. Ibid. 102, 83.

123. Ibid. 80.

124. Ibid. 119.

125. Ibid. 115.

126. Ibid. 127.

127. Ibid. 126.

128. *Gentleman's Magazine*, 62 (Dec. 1792), 1097.

129. *The Court-Martial*, ed. Rutter, 166.

130. Ibid. 139.

131. Ibid. 175.

132. Ibid. 199.

133. James Morrison to William Howell, 10 Oct. 1792, [43], MS, Mitchell Library, Sydney, and see [Morrison], 'Memorandum and Particulars'. Bligh's response to Morrison's 'Memorandum and Particulars'—confusingly entitled 'Remarks on Morrison's Journal' —was published in *Bligh's Voyage in the 'Resource'*.

134. Peter Heywood to Nessy Heywood, 16 Oct. 1792, MS transcript of the Heywood family correspondence and poetry 1790–3, Newberry Library, Chicago, quoted in Du Rietz, *Peter Heywood's Tahitian Vocabulary*, 12.

135. [Barrow], *The Eventful History*, 258. Heywood's Tahitian Vocabulary was listed in 1842 among the holdings of the Royal United Service Institution, London, but subsequently disappeared. (See Du Rietz, *Peter Heywood's Tahitian Vocabulary*, 14.)

136. See Tagart, *Memoir*, 143, 152–3.

137. See [Barrow], *The Eventful History*, 271.

138. Nessy Heywood to Mrs Heywood, 29 Oct. 1792, in Tagart, *Memoir*, 159.

139. See [Barrow], *The Eventful History*, 271, and 'Particulars of the late Execution on-board the *Brunswick*', *Gentleman's Magazine*, 62 (Dec. 1792), 1097–8.

140. Heywood to Edward Christian, 5 Nov. 1792, published in the *Cumberland Packet*, 20 Nov. 1792, quoted in William Bligh, *An Answer to Certain Assertions contained in the Appendix to a Pamphlet* (London, 1794), 17.

141. [Edward Christian?], *Cumberland Packet*, quoted in Bligh, *An Answer to Certain Assertions*, 16.

142. William Howell to Molesworth Phillips, 25 Nov. 1792, quoted in Du Rietz, *Peter Heywood's Tahitian Vocabulary*, 20 (and see Ida Leeson, 'The Morrison Myth', *Mariner's Mirror*, 25 (1939), 433–8). Howell is identifiable as the clergyman who attended the *Bounty* men from Thomas Haweis, 'A Journal of a Visit to Portsmouth and its Environs, in the Ship Duff', MS, Council for World Mission archives, School of Oriental and African Studies, London, South Sea Journals, Box 1, and as 'a shipmate also of Colonel Phillips' from James Burney to John Payne, May 1821, in Manwaring, *My Friend the Admiral*, 279. Bligh and Phillips (of the Marines) were also former shipmates, aboard the *Resolution* on Cook's last voyage.

143. Howell to Phillips, 25 Nov. 1792, quoted in Du Rietz, *Peter Heywood's Tahitian Vocabulary*, 20.

144. Ibid.
145. Morrison, *Journal*, 111, 128.
146. Heywood told his sister that he had lost in the wreck 'my little all of property' (Heywood to Nessy Heywood, 31 July 1792, in Tagart, *Memoir*, 75). The wreck of the *Pandora* has been located and some items retrieved but it is impossible that any journals could have been preserved in a legible condition. (See Du Rietz, *Peter Heywood's Tahitian Vocabulary*, 11, and on the wreck of the *Pandora*: Ronald A. Coleman, 'Tragedy of the Pandora', in *Mutiny on the Bounty 1789–1989* (National Maritime Museum exhibition catalogue, London, 1989), 116 ff., and Luis Marden, 'Tragic Sequel to *Bounty* Mutiny: Wreck of the *Pandora* Found on Australia's Great Barrier Reef', *National Geographic* (Oct. 1985), 423 ff.)
147. Attempts to suggest a very late date for the composition—or 'concoction'—of Morrison's journal are attempts to discredit it as an alternative version of the *Bounty*'s voyage from Bligh's. It is plausible—and probable, in the light of Howell's letter to Phillips—that Morrison was working on his journal late in 1792. Those regarding the journal as a concoction have not been able to find any convincing evidence of fiction in it, and those supporting the veracity and authenticity of the journal have not been able convincingly to explain how it could contain so much detailed information which can be confirmed by checking with other accounts to which Morrison could not have had access. There is no doubting the journal's basic reliability, but its reticence about Morrison's personal affairs seems remarkable when we consider that Fryer named Morrison as one of the few before the mutiny 'that had there particular Girls'. This reticence may have something to do with the circumstances in which the journal was probably written—for publication with the assistance of a sympathetic clergyman, and by way of resistance to Bligh's Tahitian explanation of the mutiny—but Morrison's journal is so obviously written as a historical and anthropological record that personal matters may have seemed out of place, merely, rather than spiritually and legally compromising. For argumentation about Morrison's journal, see H. S. Montgomerie, *The Morrison Myth* (London, 1938); Ida Leeson, 'The Morrison Myth', 433–8; H. S. Montgomerie, 'The Morrison Myth', *Mariner's Mirror*, 27 (1941), 69–76.
148. Morrison, *Journal*, 235.
149. Ibid. 235, 236. It could also be argued that the 'former Voyagers' were observing a Tahitian culture that, at an earlier stage of contact with Europeans, was less disturbed rather than more. In any case it is possible that Morrison's concern to defend the morals of the Tahitians may have some connection with his more immediate concern to defend himself and others from Bligh's Tahitian explanation of the mutiny.
150. Ibid. 237.
151. Ibid. 240.
152. Molesworth Phillips to Sir Joseph Banks, 12 Dec. 1792, British Library, Additional MS 33979.
153. Edward Christian's letters to Banks seem to be lost but their existence and something of their substance can be deduced from William Bligh, 'Rems. on Mr. Christian's Letters.—The 1st. dated Decr. 16. 1792', MS, Mitchell Library, Sydney.
154. Thomas Pasley to Matthew Flinders, 7 Aug. 1793, quoted in James D. Mack, *Matthew Flinders 1774–1814* (Melbourne, 1966), 11.
155. George Tobin, 'Journal of a Voyage in H.M.S. *Providence*', MS in Mitchell Library, Sydney, quoted in Mackaness, *The Life of Bligh*, 301.

156. Bligh to Banks, MS in Mitchell Library, Sydney, quoted ibid. 302.

157. Barney's *Minutes* did not cover the whole proceedings, but contained the significant testimony of Fryer and Purcell, among others.

158. Edward Christian, in [Stephen Barney and Edward Christian], *Minutes of the Proceedings*, 247, 248.

159. Ibid. 251.

160. Ibid. 256.

161. Ibid. 256, 262, and see Beechey, *Narrative of a Voyage*, I. 56.

162. William Bligh, *An Answer to Certain Assertions contained in the Appendix to a Pamphlet* (London, 1794), 2.

163. Ibid. 19, 22, 35.

164. Edward Lamb to Bligh, 28 Oct. 1794, ibid. 30.

165. See Edward Christian, *A Short Reply to Captain W. Bligh's Answer* (London, 1795).

166. *Otaheite: A Poem* (London, 1774), 16.

167. Thomas Haweis, MS memorandum, quoted in Richard Lovett, *The History of the London Missionary Society 1795–1895* (London, 1899), i. 117.

168. [William Wilson *et al.*], *A Missionary Voyage to the Southern Pacific Ocean, performed in the years 1796, 1797, 1798, in the Ship Duff, commanded by Captain James Wilson* (London, 1799), 2.

169. Revd T. Haweis, 'Sermon I. The Apostolic Commission, preached at the Spa Fields Chapel, September 22, 1795', in *Sermons Preached in London, at the formation of the Missionary Society, September 22, 23, 24, 1795* (London, 1795), 12.

170. Ibid. 13.

171. Revd T. Haweis, 'A Memoir on the Most Eligible Part to Begin a Mission, and the most probable means of accomplishing it: being the Substance of a Discourse delivered in Surry-Street Chapel, before the Missionary Society, September 24, 1795', in *Sermons Preached*, 163, 168, 169, 170.

172. Ibid. 170.

173. T. H. [Revd T. Haweis], 'The very probable success of a proper Mission to the South Sea Islands', *Evangelical Magazine* (July 1795), 262.

174. Thomas Haweis, 'A Journal of a Visit to Portsmouth and its Environs, in the Ship Duff with the Missionaries, who were embarked for the South Seas', MS, Council for World Mission archives, School of Oriental and African Studies, London, South Sea Journals, Box 1.

175. Ibid.

176. Ibid.

177. Ibid.

178. Samuel Greatheed, MS notes, quoted in John Campbell, *Maritime Discovery and Christian Missions, considered in their Mutual Relations* (London, 1840), 156.

179. Haweis, 'A Journal of a Visit to Portsmouth'.

180. [Wilson *et al.*], *A Missionary Voyage*, 14.

181. Campbell, *Maritime Discovery*, 156.

182. *Letters from Mr. Fletcher Christian, containing a Narrative of the Transactions on board His Majesty's Ship Bounty, Before and After the Mutiny, with his subsequent Voyages and Travels in South America* (London, 1796), 21.

183. Ibid. 24–5. Cf. Bligh, *Narrative of the Mutiny*, 9–10.

184. *Letters from Mr. Fletcher Christian*, 29.

185. Compare, for example, the descriptions of Omai's venereal fate in Hamilton, *Voyage Round the World*, 62 and in *Letters from Mr. Fletcher Christian*, 49.
186. Ibid. 144, 148, etc.
187. Bligh to Banks, 16 Sept. 1796, MS, Mitchell Library, Sydney.
188. The *Letters from Mr. Fletcher Christian* mention Tubuai only in passing, although Christian's visit to Tubuai after the mutiny, before returning to Tahiti, and his attempt at settlement there, were facts publicly available in Edward Christian's 'Appendix'. A modern editor who believes that 'the letters bear every mark of authenticity' has, as his only possible excuse, the statement in the *Letters from Mr. Fletcher Christian* that 'Fletcher Christian' has, in some 'very rare' instances, taken the precaution of the 'omission or occasional alteration of certain proper names, after my separation from Captain Bligh'. (*The Saga of the Bounty: Its Strange History as related by the Participants Themselves*, ed. Irvin Anthony (New York, 1935), 30; *Letters from Mr. Fletcher Christian*, 6.) For the connections at Cockermouth and Hawkshead Schools between William Wordsworth and Fletcher and Edward Christian, who subsequently acted for William and Dorothy Wordsworth in their suit for debt against Lord Lonsdale in 1791, see Glynn Christian, *Fragile Paradise: The Discovery of Fletcher Christian, Bounty Mutineer* (London, 1982), 32, 34, and Mary Moorman, *William Wordsworth: A Biography: The Early Years* (Oxford, 1957), 15, 90; and for William Wordsworth's relationship to Edward Christian's 'respectable gentlemen', see Moorman, *William Wordsworth*, 300. *Letters from Mr. Fletcher Christian* was reprinted, with a new title page, as *Voyages and Travels of Fletcher Christian, and a Narrative of the Mutiny, on board His Majesty's Ship Bounty, at Otaheite* ([London], 1798).
189. William Wordsworth to the *Weekly Entertainer*, 23 Oct. 1796, in the *Weekly Entertainer*, 28 (7 Nov. 1796), 377. See 'Christian's own Account of the Mutiny on Board his Majesty's Ship Bounty, commanded by Captain Bligh, of which he was the Ringleader', *Weekly Entertainer; or Agreeable and Instructive Repository*, 27 (26 Sept. 1796), 255–6.
190. S. T. Coleridge, *The Notebooks*, ed. K. Coburn, i (London, 1957), 174, G. 169.
191. Andrew Kippis, *The Life of Captain James Cook* (London, 1788), 510.
192. Anna Seward, *Elegy on Captain Cook* (London, 1780), 17, quoted in Kippis, *Life of Captain Cook*, 509–10.
193. Kippis, *Life of Captain Cook*, 511.
194. Southey to G. C. Bedford, 8 Feb. 1793, *New Letters of Robert Southey*, ed. Kenneth Curry (New York, 1965), i. 19.
195. Coleridge, 'To a Young Lady with a Poem on the French Revolution', *The Poetical Works of S. T. Coleridge*, ed. E. H. Coleridge (London, 1912), 64. On Lee Boo, see Daniel J. Peacock, *Lee Boo of Belau: A Prince in London* (Honolulu, 1987).
196. Coleridge, 'The Rime of the Ancient Mariner', *Poetical Works*, 186.
197. For these suggestions, see J. L. Lowes, *The Road to Xanadu* (Boston & New York, 1927), 46, 27–8. In *The Wake of the Bounty*, C. S. Wilkinson takes up one of them and finds a 'strong likeness' between the courses sailed by the Mariner's ship and the *Bounty*, as both ships sail south, then north, then into the Pacific, where Wilkinson admits the 'strong likeness' is at an end. He then revives an old rumour of Christian's return to England, and points out that, if this rumour were true, then 'the whole scheme of the "Ancient Mariner"' would 'be accounted for', because the 'Argument' of the poem, including 'in what manner the Ancyent Marinere came back to his own

Country', would be 'an accurate summary of the story of the *Bounty* and Fletcher Christian'. Wilkinson spends the rest of his book attempting to demonstrate that Christian not only returned to England, but told his story to Wordsworth, who passed it on to Coleridge, the conclusive proof of all this being the fact that both Wordsworth and Coleridge maintained throughout their lives, on Christian's behalf, a strict and total silence on the subject—except, of course, for the revelation hidden in 'The Ancient Mariner'. In a lengthy and circumstantial paper, Bernard Smith argues, without reference to Wilkinson's book, that the course followed by the Ancient Mariner is that of Cook's second voyage, and that Coleridge made use in the poem of information derived from the headmaster of his school, William Wales, who sailed with Cook on that voyage. Smith's research is thorough but his argument that Wales told Coleridge something that appears in the text of 'The Ancient Mariner' is no more than a series of speculations interspersed with the words 'doubtless', 'may well have', 'presumably', 'it is probable', 'not unreasonable to suppose', 'may be inferred', 'not at all unlikely', etc., all of which is admirably cautious but completely inconclusive, not to say doubtful, improbable, etc. (C. S. Wilkinson, *The Wake of the Bounty* (London, 1953), 92–3, 122; Coleridge, 'The Rime of the Ancient Mariner', 186; Bernard Smith, 'Coleridge's "Ancient Mariner" and Cook's Second Voyage', *Journal of the Warburg and Courtauld Institutes*, 19 (1956), 120, 121, 122, 123, 127, 129, 138.) In another paper, Neal B. Houston takes up Wilkinson's research into the rumoured return of Christian, repeats it with some errors, peers deeply into the text of 'The Ancient Mariner' and finds Wilkinson's theory fully proved. (See Neal B. Houston, 'Fletcher Christian and "The Rime of the Ancient Mariner"', *Dalhousie Review*, 45 (Winter, 1965–6), 431–46.) We have Wordsworth's own word for it that a passage from Shelvocke's *Voyage round the World by the Way of the Great South Sea* (1726) played a part in the conception of 'The Ancient Mariner', but links between the Mariner's voyage and those of Cook or Bligh are, to say the least, tenuous. (See J. L. Lowes, *Road to Xanadu*, 233; William Wordsworth, in Christopher Wordsworth, *Memoirs of William Wordsworth* (London, 1851), i. 107.)

198. Byron, *Don Juan*, Dedication, 1, 5, *Poetical Works*, v. 3, 4.

199. Southey to John Rickman, 23 Dec. 1803, *Life and Correspondence*, ed. C. C. Southey, ii (London, 1850), 243.

200. See Lovett, *History*, i. 127.

201. [Wilson *et al.*], *A Missionary Voyage*, 2.

202. 'Journal of the Tahitian mission', 13 Apr. 1797, quoted in Lovett, *History*, i. 142.

203. John Jefferson, 'Journal', 13 Aug. 1797, quoted in Lovett, *History*, i. 147–8.

204. 'Otaheitean Journals', 20 Nov. 1797, in *Transactions of the Missionary Society*, i (London, 1804), 15–16.

205. Ibid. 16.

206. 'Otaheitean Journals', 25 Jan. 1798, i. 24; Bligh, *Narrative of the Mutiny*, 10 (and *Log*, ii. 123).

207. See 'Otaheitean Journals', 26 Mar. 1798, i. 35.

208. See 'Otaheitean Journals', 31 Mar. 1798, i. 42.

209. Thomas Lewis, letter, 1 Aug. 1798, in 'Otaheitean Journals', i. 57.

210. John Jefferson, letter for the Society, Otaheite, 1 Feb. 1799, MS, Council for World Mission archives, School of Oriental and African Studies, London, South Sea Letters, Box 1.

211. Benjamin Broomhall, quoted in John Jefferson *et al.*, 'A Journal of the Missionaries proceedings on Otaheite 1800', 16 June 1800, MS, Council for World Mission archives, School of Oriental and African Studies, South Sea Journals, Box 1.

212. John Jefferson *et al.*, 'A Journal of the Missionaries Proceedings on Otaheite 1802–1803', 8 Dec. 1802, MS, Council for World Mission archives, School of Oriental and African Studies, South Sea Journals, Box 1. See also Lovett, *History*, i. 180.

213. John Davies, *The History of the Tahitian Mission 1799–1830*, ed. C. W. Newbury (Cambridge, 1961), 121.

214. Folger's account, as told to Amasa Delano, and reported in Amasa Delano, *A Narrative of Voyages and Travels, in the Northern and Southern Hemispheres* (Boston, 1817), 139.

215. In Lieutenant Fitzmaurice's report of Folger's discovery, sent on from Rio de Janeiro and received by the Admiralty, 14 May 1809, the second mate of the *Topaz* is reported as saying that Christian became insane, soon after arrival at Pitcairn, and threw himself into the sea, and Delano reports Folger as saying that he was told that Christian had died a natural death some years later, but both reports are contradicted by several subsequent accounts. (See Lieutenant Fitzmaurice's report, quoted in [Barrow], *The Eventful History*, 283–4, and Amasa Delano, *Narrative of Voyages*, 140.)

216. See [John Barrow], review of *Voyage à la recherche de La Pérouse*, *Quarterly Review*, 3/5 (Feb. 1810), 23–4.

217. Shillibeer, *Narrative of the Briton's Voyage*, 82.

218. The report by Sir Thomas Staines (of the *Briton*) to the Admiralty, a letter by Captain Pipon (of the *Tagus*) to John Barrow, and the published account by Lieut. Shillibeer (of the *Briton*) are in agreement that Christian was killed by a Polynesian man. (See: Sir Thomas Staines to the Admiralty, 18 Oct. 1814, quoted in [Barrow], *The Eventful History*, 285–7, and published as 'Account of the Descendants of Christian and other Mutineers of the Bounty', *Naval Chronicle*, 33 (1815), 217–18; Captain Pipon to John Barrow, partly quoted in [Barrow], *The Eventful History*, 287 ff. and at greater length (from the MS in the Mitchell Library, Sydney) in Mackaness, *The Life of Bligh*, 216–19; Shillibeer, *Narrative of the Briton's Voyage*.) My account of events on Pitcairn is based on the fuller and franker accounts in Beechey, *Narrative of a Voyage*, i. 59 ff., and Lieutenant George Peard, 'Account of the Mutiny', in 'Journal kept in H. M. S. Blossom', British Library, Additional MS 35141, and (as independent corroboration) the interview with Jenny (Teehuteatuaonoa) at Tahiti, published in the *Bengal Hurkaru* (2 Oct. 1826) and subsequently in the *United Service Journal* (1829), pt. II, pp. 589–93.

219. Beechey, *Narrative of a Voyage*, i. 59, who says that the account he gives 'is compiled almost entirely from Adams' narrative' (51).

220. See Jenny, *United Service Journal*, pt. II, p. 590.

221. See ibid.

222. Ibid. For an intelligent attempt to place the *Bounty*'s movements on the map, see H. E. Maude, 'In Search of a Home', *Of Islands and Men: Studies in Pacific History* (Melbourne, 1968), 1–34.

223. See Jenny, *United Service Journal*, pt. II, p. 590.

224. Hawkesworth, *Voyages*, i. 561 (with 'A Chart and Views of Pitcairn's Island' on the facing page). Adams told Beechey that it was 'Carteret's account of Pitcairn' (i.e. in Hawkesworth's *Voyages*) that determined Christian's choice of the island. (Beechey, *Narrative of a Voyage*, i. 59.) Shillibeer of the *Briton* saw Bligh's copy of Hawkesworth's

Voyages, with Christian's name written beneath Bligh's in each of the volumes. (See Shillibeer, *Narrative of the Briton's Voyage*, 96–7.)

225. See Jenny, *United Service Journal*, pt. II, p. 590.

226. See ibid. 590–1.

227. The figures for the *Bounty*'s and hence Pitcairn's initial population are from Peard, 'Account of the Mutiny', which agree with the figures in Jenny's narrative. The date for the burning of the *Bounty* is given in Beechey, *Narrative of a Voyage*, I. 59.

228. Jenny, *United Service Journal*, pt. II, p. 591.

229. Beechey, *Narrative of a Voyage*, I. 60.

230. See G. Peard, 'Account of the Mutiny', and Jenny, *United Service Journal*, who says the Polynesian men had only two women (pt. II, p. 591). The correspondences between the accounts, despite the discrepancies over numbers, are marked.

231. See Jenny, *United Service Journal*, pt. II, p. 591, Beechey, *Narrative of a Voyage*, I. 60, and Peard, 'Account of the Mutiny', which all agree about the basic facts.

232. Beechey, *Narrative of a Voyage*, I. 61, with which Peard is consistent. I have used the rendering of the Polynesian names given in Jenny's narrative, as the men involved in the translation of her narrative—the missionary, Henry Nott, and Peter Dillon—were likely to have a better comprehension of Polynesian names than either Peard or Beechey of the *Blossom*.

233. Peard, 'Account of the Mutiny', gives more details of these treacherous murders than Beechey, *Narrative of a Voyage*.

234. Peard, 'Account of the Mutiny', and see Jenny, *United Service Journal*, pt. II, p. 592, and Beechey, *Narrative of a Voyage*, I. 62.

235. Bligh, 'Description of the Pirates', *Log*, ii. 124.

236. See: Beechey, *Narrative of a Voyage*, I. 64; Peard, 'Account of the Mutiny'; Jenny, *United Service Journal*, pt. II, pp. 592–3. The Polynesian names not supplied by Jenny are rendered in the spelling used by Beechey.

237. See Beechey, *Narrative of a Voyage*, I. 65.

238. Edward Young, journal, quoted in Beechey, *Narrative of a Voyage*, I. 65.

239. Ibid.

240. See Beechey, *Narrative of a Voyage*, I. 65.

241. Young, journal, quoted in Beechey, *Narrative of a Voyage*, I. 65–6.

242. Ibid. 66.

243. Ibid.

244. See: Beechey, *Narrative of a Voyage*, I. 68; Jenny, *United Service Journal*, pt. II, p. 593.

245. Peard, 'Account of the Mutiny', and see Beechey, *Narrative of a Voyage*, I. 68. Jenny places Quintal's murder before McCoy's death, and states simply that Quintal was murdered by the three other men 'in a drunken affray' (Jenny, *United Service Journal*, pt. II, p. 591).

246. Beechey, *Narrative of a Voyage*, I. 69.

247. Shillibeer, *Narrative of the Briton's Voyage*, 88.

248. Beechey, *Narrative of a Voyage*, I. 90, 89, 81.

249. Ibid. 82.

250. *Quarterly Review*, 3/5 (Feb. 1810), 24.

251. Mary Russell Mitford to Dr Mitford, 3 Mar. 1811, in *The Life of Mary Russell Mitford, Related in a Selection from her Letters to her Friends*, ed. A. G. L'Estrange (London, 1870), i. 119.

252. Mary Russell Mitford, *Christina, the Maid of the South Seas; a Poem* (London, 1811), 318 n.
253. Ibid. p. viii.
254. Ibid.
255. Mary Russell Mitford thanks Captain Burney for his assistance 'in arranging and revising her notes' (ibid. pp. ix–x).
256. Ibid. 8
257. Ibid. 31.
258. Ibid. 143.
259. Ibid. 67.
260. Ibid. 69, 74, and see 318 n.
261. Ibid. 75, 80.
262. Ibid. 83.
263. Ibid. 83, 84.
264. Ibid. 85, 86.
265. Ibid. 88.
266. Ibid. 117.
267. Ibid. 118.
268. Ibid. 120, 121.
269. Ibid. 123, 124.
270. Ibid. 130.
271. Ibid. 174–5.
272. Ibid. 185.
273. Ibid.
274. Ibid. 187, 186.
275. George Gordon, Lord Byron, *The Island, or Christian and His Comrades*, in *The Complete Poetical Works*, vii (Oxford, 1993), 26.
276. Alexander von Humboldt, *Voyage aux régions équinoxiales du nouveau continent* (Paris, 1814), i. 33, and see J. Martin, *An Account of the Natives of the Tonga Islands* (London, 1817), title-page.
277. Ibid. i, p. vii.
278. Ibid. ii. 42. On the Romantic element in Martin's *Account of the Natives*, see Bill Pearson, *Rifled Sanctuaries: Some Views of the Pacific Islands in Western Literature* (Auckland, 1984), 37–8.
279. George Clinton, *Memoirs of the Life and Writings of Lord Byron* (London, 1825), 656.
280. Byron, *The Island*, 146–7 n.
281. Byron to Leigh Hunt, 25 Jan. 1823, *Byron's Letters and Journals*, ed. L. A. Marchand, x (London, 1980), 90.
282. Byron, *The Island*, Canto I, ll. 17, 51.
283. Ibid. Canto I, l. 164; [Bligh], *Voyage to the South Sea*, 162, and see 161; Byron, *The Island*, Canto I, ll. 27–36.
284. Ibid. Canto I, ll. 105–6.
285. Ibid. 'wave/cave': Canto I, ll. 31–2, 169–70, Canto II, ll. 109–10, 139–40, 155–6, 386–7, Canto III, ll. 35–6, Canto IV, ll. 97–8, 121–2; 'wave/grave': Canto II, ll. 364–5, Canto IV, ll. 55–6, 85–6; 'cave/grave': Canto IV, ll. 221–2.
286. Ibid. 144 n.
287. Ibid. Canto II, ll. 106, 109–12.

288. See ibid. Canto II, ll. 280 ff.
289. See J. Martin, *Account of the Natives*, i. 83.
290. Byron, *The Island*, Canto II, ll. 134–40.
291. Ibid. Canto II, ll. 304, 274, 276.
292. Ibid. Canto II, ll. 463, 482, 483.
293. Ibid. Canto III, ll. 1, 35–6, 39–40.
294. Ibid. Canto III, ll. 67–8.
295. Ibid. Canto III, ll. 89–90.
296. Ibid. Canto IV, ll. 55–6.
297. Ibid. Canto IV, ll. 121–2.
298. Ibid. 146 n.
299. See J. Martin, *Account of the Natives*, i. 268–79.
300. Byron, *The Island*, Canto IV, ll. 259–62.
301. Ibid. Canto IV, ll. 270–2, 276–7.
302. Ibid. Canto IV, ll. 336–42.
303. Ibid. Canto IV, ll. 419–20.
304. James H. Browne, 'Voyage from Leghorn to Cephalonia with Lord Byron, and a Narrative of a Visit, in 1823, to the seat of the War in Greece', *Blackwood's Edinburgh Magazine*, 25/217 (January, 1834), 64.
305. Byron to Leigh Hunt, 25 Jan. 1823, *Letters and Journals*, x. 90.
306. [Barrow], *The Eventful History*, pp. ix–x.
307. Ibid. 341, 38.
308. See Lovett, *History*, i. 215.
309. William Crook, journal, 6 Feb. 1821, MS, Council for World Mission archives, School of Oriental and African Studies, South Sea Journals, Box 4.
310. Southey to G. C. Bedford, 8 Feb. 1793, *New Letters*, i. 19; Southey to John Rickman, 23 Dec. 1803, *Life and Correspondence*, ii (London, 1850), 243.
311. Southey to Herbert Hill, 28 Dec. 1813, *Life and Correspondence*, iv (London, 1850), 55–6.
312. François-René de Chateaubriand, *Voyage en Amérique*, ed. R. Switzer (Paris, 1964), i. 46–7.
313. Otto von Kotzebue, *A New Voyage Round the World, in the years 1823, 24, 25, and 26* (London, 1830), i. 172.
314. MS annotations in the margin of the LMS copy of Kotzebue, *New Voyage*, i. 172, 163, 169, 197, Council for World Mission archives, School of Oriental and African Studies, London.
315. William Ellis, *A Vindication of the South Sea Missions from the Misrepresentations of Otto von Kotzebue* (London, 1831), 78–9.
316. Ibid. 78, 89, 90, 91.
317. Ibid. 110.
318. [Southey], review of W. Ellis, *Polynesian Researches, Quarterly Review*, 43 (May & Oct. 1830), 1, and see John E. Ellis, *Life of William Ellis* (London, 1873), 150, 204–5, and Southey to William Ellis, 7 Aug. 1830, in Ellis, *Life of William Ellis*, 205 ff.
319. W. H. [William Henry], 'Lines composed on the building of a Christian Church, in the District of Papetoai, Island of Eimeo; upon the ruins of the Royal Marae in that District', Eimeo, 21 May 1822, MS, Council for World Mission archives, School of Oriental and African Studies, London, South Sea Letters, Box 3.

320. Coleridge, in conversation recorded in John Sterling, *Essays and Tales*, ed. J. C. Hare (London, 1848), i, pp. xx–xxi.
321. Southey to John Rickman, 23 Dec. 1803, *Life and Correspondence*, ii (London, 1850), 243.

CHAPTER 7

1. Montaigne, 'Des cannibales', *Essais*, i. 234.
2. Coleridge, in conversation recorded in John Sterling, *Essays and Tales*, i, pp. xx–xxi.
3. Richard Armstrong, 'A Sketch of Marquesian Character', *Hawaiian Spectator*, 1/1 (Honolulu, Jan. 1838), 12.
4. Ibid.
5. Ibid. 11, 16.
6. R. Tinker, 'Correspondence and Reports on the condition of the unevangelized', *Hawaiian Spectator*, 1/1 (Honolulu, Jan. 1838), 87.
7. Unidentified 'master of a merchantman', remarks on 'a manuscript chart of Porter's Bay', Nukuhiva, quoted in Tinker, 'Correspondence and Reports', 87.
8. Tinker, 'Correspondence and Reports', 87, 90.
9. A. J. von Krusenstern, *Voyage Round the World, in the years 1803, 1804, 1805, & 1806*, trans. Richard Belgrave Hoppner (London, 1813), i. 182.
10. Robert Thomson, 'Marquesas. Their Discovery, and Early History', MS, Council for World Mission archives, School of Oriental and African Studies, London, South Sea Journals, Box 9, 20–1.
11. David Porter, *Journal of a Cruise Made to the Pacific Ocean, in the U.S. Frigate Essex, in the years 1812, 1813, and 1814* (Philadelphia, 1815), ii. 96.
12. Herman Melville, *Typee: A Peep at Polynesian Life*, ed. H. Hayford *et al.* (Chicago, 1968), 203.
13. Recollections of Frederick Saunders, reader for Messrs Harper and Bros., quoted in J. Leyda, *The Melville Log: A Documentary Life of Herman Melville, 1819–1891* (New York, 1969), i. 196.
14. Ibid.
15. Melville to Allan Melville, 22 May 1860, *Correspondence*, ed. Lynn Horth (Chicago, 1993), 343.
    On Melville as 'Mr Typee', see Charles Anderson, *Melville in the South Seas* (New York, 1939), 284.
16. Melville to Nathaniel Hawthorne, [1 June?] 1851, *Correspondence*, 193.
17. John Murray, quoted by G. Melville, letter to John Murray, 21 Oct. 1845, in Leyda, *The Melville Log*, i. 199.
18. G. Melville, letters to John Murray, 21 Oct. 1845, and 6 Dec. 1845, quoted in Leyda, *The Melville Log*, i. 199, 200–1.
19. Melville to John Murray, 15, July 1846, *Correspondence*, 57.
20. G. P. Putnam, in conversation with G. Melville, 11 Jan. 1846, Gansevoort Melville, *London Journal*, ed. Hershel Parker (New York, 1966), 22.
21. My comments on the critical reception of *Typee* are based on sixteen reviews in the year of its publication, reprinted in *Melville: The Critical Heritage*, ed. W. G. Branch (London, 1974).

22. Unsigned review, London *Spectator* (28 Feb. 1846), in *Melville*, ed. Branch, 55.

23. Charles Fenno Hoffman, unsigned review, New York *Gazette and Times* (30 Mar. 1846), in *Melville*, ed. Branch, 69; unsigned review, London *Douglas Jerrold's Shilling Magazine*, 3 (Jan.–June 1846), 382; unsigned review, London *John Bull* (7 Mar. 1846), in *Melville*, ed. Branch, 65.

24. Gilbert Abbott À Beckett, unsigned lampoon, *Almanack of the Month*, 1 (June 1846), in *Melville*, ed. Branch, 84.

25. Richard T. Greene to the Editor, *Buffalo Commercial Advertiser*, 1 July 1846, reprinted in Melville, *Correspondence*, 579.

26. See Richard T. Greene, 'Toby's Own Story', *Buffalo Commercial Advertiser*, 11 July 1846, reprinted in Melville, *Correspondence*, 580–4.

27. Melville to John Murray, 15 July 1846, *Correspondence*, 55.

28. Melville to John Murray, 2 Sept. 1846, *Correspondence*, 65–6.

29. Ibid. 66.

30. Melville to John Murray, 25 Mar. 1848, *Correspondence*, 106–7.

31. Captain Pease, declaration in John Stetson, certificate of 2 June 1843, quoted in Leyda, *The Melville Log*, i. 130. Stetson's certificate was first published in Robert S. Forsythe, 'Herman Melville in Honolulu', *New England Quarterly*, 8/1 (Mar. 1935), 102.

32. Ida Leeson, 'The Mutiny on the *Lucy Ann*', *Philological Quarterly*, 19/4 (Oct. 1940), 371.

33. Melville, *Omoo: A Narrative of Adventures in the South Seas*, ed. H. Hayford *et al.* (Chicago, 1968), 139; Charles B. Wilson, certificate, 'Documents on the *Lucy Ann* Revolt', in *Omoo: A Narrative of Adventures in the South Seas*, ed. H. Hayford and W. Blair (New York, 1969), 330.

34. Titus Coan, *Life in Hawaii, an Autobiographic Sketch of Mission Life and Labors (1835– 1881)* (New York, 1882), 200. R. S. Forsythe estimated 8 August 1842 as the day of Melville's escape from Taipi valley, and Charles Anderson estimated 8 or 15 August. As they were unaware that he signed articles on 9 August, their guesses were remarkably accurate. (See R. S. Forsythe, 'Herman Melville in the Marquesas', *Philological Quarterly*, 15/1 (Jan. 1936), 10; Anderson, *Melville in the South Seas*, 466 n.)

35. James G. Frazer, *The Belief in Immortality and the Worship of the Dead*, ii. *The Belief among the Polynesians* (London, 1922), 330.

36. Ibid. 363, and see 333, 338, 354, 361.

37. See Norma McArthur, *Island Populations of the Pacific* (Canberra, 1967), 284, 286.

38. Robert C. Suggs, *The Island Civilizations of Polynesia* (New York, 1960), 130.

39. Jack London, *The Cruise of the Snark* (New York, 1908), 167.

40. Ibid. 170. See also the report, repeating the paradise lost topos, of Frederick O'Brien, *White Shadows in the South Seas* (London, 1919), 223.

41. See: Robert C. Suggs, *The Hidden Worlds of Polynesia* (London, 1963), 58–9; Irving Goldman, *Ancient Polynesian Society* (Chicago, 1970), 126–7; Greg Dening, *Islands and Beaches: Discourse on a Silent Land: Marquesas 1774–1880* (Honolulu, 1980), 278–9.

42. W. C. Handy, *Tattooing in the Marquesas*, Bernice P. Bishop Museum Bulletin 1 (Honolulu, 1922), 5.

43. See ibid. n.

44. See Russell Thomas, 'Yarn for Melville's *Typee*', *Philological Quarterly*, 15/1 (Jan. 1936), 16–29; Anderson, *Melville in the South Seas*.

45. Frazer, *Belief in Immortality*, ii. 338; Anderson, *Melville in the South Seas*, 142.

46. Ibid. 118.
47. Melville, *Typee*, 5–6.
48. Porter, *Journal of a Cruise* (1815), ii. 40.
49. Ibid. 73, 105, 102.
50. Ibid. 110, 82. For what happened subsequently, see 'Transactions at Nooaheevah, after Captain Porter's Departure: Compiled from the Journal of Lt. Gamble', ch. xix in David Porter, *Journal of a Cruise Made to the Pacific Ocean* (New York, 1822), ii.
51. Porter, *Journal of a Cruise* (1815), ii. 99.
52. Ibid. 102, 108.
53. See Charles Stewart, *A Visit to the South Seas, in the U.S. Ship Vincennes, during the years 1829 and 1830* (New York, 1831), i. 355.
54. Ibid. 280.
55. Ibid. 285 6.
56. Ibid. 294.
57. Ibid. 253, 262.
58. Ibid. 253, 255, 259, 261.
59. Ibid. 295.
60. For Stewart's stimulus to the American mission to the Marquesas, see Dening, *Islands and Beaches*, 175, and T. Walter Herbert, Jr., *Marquesan Encounters: Melville and the Meaning of Civilization* (Cambridge, Mass., 1980), 64. For Thomas Melville's presence in Herman Melville's valley, see Stewart, *Visit to the South Seas*, i. 316.
61. Porter, *Journal of a Cruise* (1815), ii. 183.
62. Stewart, *Visit to the South Seas*, i. 212–13.
63. Melville, *Typee*, 11.
64. See Robert Stanton, '*Typee* and Milton: Paradise Well Lost', *Modern Language Notes*, 74 (May 1959), 407–11.
65. Melville, *Typee*, 47, 39.
66. Milton, *Paradise Lost*, iii. 548, 546; Melville, *Typee*, 49.
67. Ibid. 66, 67.
68. Ibid. 68.
69. Stanton, '*Typee* and Milton', 409; Milton, *Paradise Lost*, ix. 1114–16.
70. Melville, *Typee*, 69.
71. Ibid. 31, 93.
72. Ibid. 77, 144, 174, etc.
73. Porter, *Journal of a Cruise* (1815), ii. 119; Melville, *Typee*, 176.
74. Ibid. 80, 88, 247.
75. Ibid. 83; Thomson, 'Marquesas', 22.
76. Melville, *Typee*, 88. See E. S. C. Handy, *Polynesian Religion*, Bernice P. Bishop Museum Bulletin 34 (Honolulu, 1927), 44; Franz Steiner, *Taboo* (Pelican edn., 1967), 46.
77. Melville, *Typee*, 94.
78. Ibid. 103.
79. Ibid. 208. A Melville critic has suggested that this passage refers to fellatio, which was indeed a Marquesan practice, as were, probably, cannibalism and, more mundanely, the eating of raw fish. (See David Williams, 'Peeping Tommo: *Typee* as Satire', *Canadian Review of American Studies*, 6/1 (Spring 1975), 41, and Robert C. Suggs, *Marquesan Sexual Behaviour* (London, 1966), 117, etc.) I see the passage as hinting at the second practice but not the first.

80. William Ellis, *Polynesian Researches*, iii (London, 1833), 313. For Melville's reference to *Polynesian Researches*, see *Typee*, 6.

81. Ibid. 5.

82. Herman Melville, 'First Draught of Typee', MS, New York Public Library, Melville Family Papers, fos. 12ʳ, 13ʳ, 14ᵛ, etc.

83. Melville, *Typee*, 123.

84. Montaigne, 'Des cannibales', *Essais*, i. 239; Melville, *Typee*, 125. Melville purchased an edition of Montaigne in Jan. 1848, but *Typee* suggests some prior acquaintance with 'Des cannibales'. (See Leon Howard, *Herman Melville: A Biography* (Berkeley, Calif., 1951), 115.)

85. Melville, *Typee*, 125.

86. Ibid. 126.

87. Ibid. 125–6.

88. Ibid. 126.

89. Ibid. 126, 128.

90. Ibid. 124.

91. Samuel Johnson, *The History of Rasselas*, ed. G. Tillotson and B. Jenkins (London, 1971), 13.

92. Melville, *Typee*, 219.

93. Ibid. 220.

94. Ibid. 83.

95. See also Karl von den Steinen, *Die Marquesaner und ihre Kunst*, i. *Tatauierung* (Berlin, 1925), 111, 146, etc.

96. Melville, *Typee*, 220, 231–2.

97. Ibid. 227, 232, 233.

98. Ibid. 233, 238.

99. Ibid. 237, 234. In relation to my distinction between Melville and 'Melville', it may be significant that, when the author of an article on Melville (published in 1901, ten years after his death) submitted the proposed text of the article to Melville's widow for correction, her principal objection, according to the author of a note to the published article, was that 'Mr. Melville would not have been willing to call his old Typee entertainers "man-devouring", as he has stated that whatever might have been his suspicions, he never had evidence that it was the custom of the tribe'. (Note to Mary L. D. Ferris, 'Herman Melville', *Bulletin of the Society of American Authors*, 6 (Sept. 1901), 316, quoted in William H. Gilman, *Melville's Early Life and 'Redburn'* (New York, 1951), 343 n.)

100. Melville, *Typee*, 238, 231, 233. For the coffin-canoe (the prototype of Queequeg's), see 171–3. For illustrations, see Karl von den Steinen, *Die Marquesaner und ihre Kunst*, iii. *Die Sammlungen* (Berlin, 1928), p. aX.

101. Thomson, 'Marquesas', 48.

102. See Dening, *Islands and Beaches*, 130.

103. G. H. von Langsdorff, *Voyages and Travels in Various Parts of the World, during the years 1803, 1804, 1805, 1806, and 1807* (London, 1813), i. 149, and see 140 ff.; Krusenstern, *Voyage Round the World*, i. 181, and see 180 ff.

104. Charles Espenberg, 'Journal of the Voyage from Brazil to Kamchatka; extracted from a Letter of Dr. Espenberg, dated the Harbour of St. Peter and St. Paul, August 24, 1804', *Philosophical Magazine*, 22 (1805), 8.

105. Langsdorff, *Voyages and Travels*, i, p. xiv.
106. Aimé Leroy, 'Kabris (Joseph)', in *Les Hommes et les choses du Nord de la France et du Midi de la Belgique*, ed. Aimé Leroy and Arthur Dinaux (Valenciennes, 1829), 133.
107. See A. F. Dulys, *Précis historique et veritable du séjour de Joseph Kabris, natif de Bordeaux, dans les îles de Mendoça, situées dans l'Ocean Pacifique* (Paris, 1817), reprinted in English translation in Jennifer Terrell, 'Joseph Kabris and his notes on the Marquesas', *Journal of Pacific History*, 17 (Jan. 1982), 102–12.
108. See *The Marquesan Journal of Edward Robarts 1797–1824*, ed. Greg Dening (Canberra, 1974), 1–29.
109. Robarts, *The Marquesan Journal*, ed. Dening, 116.
110. Porter, *Journal of a Cruise* (1815), ii. 45.
111. Ibid. 45, 49.
112. Ibid. 50.
113. Thomson, 'Marquesas', 28.
114. Ibid. 29.
115. John Coulter, *Adventures in the Pacific* (Dublin, 1845), 208.
116. Ibid. 231.
117. Ibid. 232.
118. See W. Arens, *The Man-Eating Myth: Anthropology and Anthropophagy* (New York, 1979), which is justly criticized for neglecting Pacific evidence in Spate, *Paradise Found and Lost*, 52. For the opinion of the specialist ethnohistorians, see Dening, *Islands and Beaches*, 248–9, and Nicholas Thomas, *Marquesan Societies: Inequality and Political Transformation in Eastern Polynesia* (Oxford, 1990), 169 and 229 n. 4.
119. Stewart, *A Visit to the South Seas*, i. 298–9.
120. Ibid. 354–6.
121. Melville, *Typee*, 25.
122. Ibid.
123. Ibid. 128, 203.
124. Ibid. 170–1.
125. Ibid. 177.
126. Ibid. 103, 120, 139, 141, 160, 171.
127. Ibid. p. xiv.
128. E. A. Dryden, 'Portraits of the Artist as a Young Man', in Milton R. Stern (ed.), *Critical Essays on Herman Melville's 'Typee'* (Boston, 1982), 176.
129. J. Seelye, *'Typee*: The Quixotic Pattern', in Stern (ed.), *Critical Essays on Herman Melville's 'Typee'*, 199.
130. That Melville associated the Polynesians with the American Indians is clear from *Typee*, in which he predicts that civilization would destroy the South Sea islanders, just as it had 'extirpated the greater portion of the Red race'. (Melville, *Typee*, 195.) That he knew of the Puritan typological interpretation of the American Indian is clear from his description of Tashtego in *Moby-Dick*: 'To look at the tawny brawn of his lithe snaky limbs, you would almost have credited the superstitions of some of the earlier Puritans, and half believed this wild Indian to be a son of the Prince of the Powers of the Air'. (Melville, *Moby-Dick*, ed. H. Hayford, H. Parker, and G. T. Tanselle (Chicago, 1988), 120.)
131. Melville, *Typee*, 128.
132. The spelling of Marquesan names naturally varied in the first half of the nineteenth

century. In his MS, Melville wrote of the 'Tipiis', whereas Stewart writes of 'the Taipiis' and Porter of 'the Typees', the form which Melville adopted and, possibly, employed in a punning sense. The name is, however, nowadays correctly spelled 'Taipi', that form being used both for the valley and the tribe inhabiting it—as Jack London discovered, travelling in Melville's wake: ' "Taipi" the chart spelled it, and spelled it correctly, but I prefer "Typee" and I shall always spell it "Typee". When I was a little boy, I read a book spelled in that manner—Herman Melville's *Typee*.' (London, *The Cruise of the Snark*, 154.)

CHAPTER 8

1. John Davies, 29 Oct. 1816, 'Journal of a preaching tour round Tahiti', MS, Council for World Mission archives, School of Oriental and African Studies, London, South Sea Journals 1807–16, Box 3.
2. See Henry Ventom, deposition, in 'Documents on the *Lucy Ann* Revolt', in Melville, *Omoo* (1969), 319.
3. Ventom, ibid.
4. James German, deposition, in 'Documents', in Melville, *Omoo* (1969), 324.
5. See ibid. and Charles Wilson, Notes, 'Documents', in Melville, *Omoo* (1969), 318.
6. Melville, *Omoo* (1968), p. xiv. Hayford and Blair note in their edition, with reference to the word 'omoo', that: 'We cannot find a word of similar sound and meaning in any Polynesian glossary'. ('Explanatory Notes', in Melville, *Omoo* (1969), 347.)
7. Melville, *Omoo* (1968), p. xiii.
8. Ibid.
9. Melville to John Murray, 29 Jan. 1847, *Correspondence*, 78.
10. Melville, *Omoo* (1968), 15.
11. The *Lucy Ann* took on some men at Hiva Oa on 26 Aug. 1842. See Charles Wilson, certificate, 'Documents', in Melville, *Omoo* (1969), 330.
12. Melville, *Omoo* (1968), 27.
13. Ibid. 27, 28. For the absence of Lem Hardy from Hanamenu, see Max Radiguet, *Les Derniers Sauvages: la vie et les moeurs aux Îles Marquises (1842–1859)* (Paris, 1929), 45–6. There were beachcombers at Hanamenu before and after Melville's visit, however, and Lem Hardy is far from impossible. Camille de Roquefeuil met Charles Person, from 'une famille connue de Boston', at Hanamenu in 1818, and in 1852 E. H. Lamont encountered an Irishman there, 'named George'. (Camille de Roquefeuil, *Journal d'un voyage autour du monde, pendant les années 1816, 1817, 1818 et 1819* (Paris, 1823), i. 269; E. H. Lamont, *Wild Life among the Pacific Islanders* (London, 1867), 40.)
14. Melville, *Omoo* (1968), 28.
15. F. Johnstone, certificate, in 'Documents', in Melville, *Omoo* (1969), 314.
16. Melville, *Omoo* (1968), 68, 74.
17. See Wilson, Notes and certificate, and James German, deposition, in 'Documents', in Melville, *Omoo* (1969), 318, 328, 324.
18. Melville, *Omoo* (1968), 116, 136.
19. Dr Johnstone's 'dose book', quoted in Lieut. (Henry A.) Wise, *Los Gringos: or an Inside View of Mexico and California, with Wanderings in Peru, Chili, and Polynesia* (London, 1849), 358.

20. Melville, *Omoo* (1968), 69. For dates concerning the *Lucy Ann*, see the 'Documents', in Melville, *Omoo* (1969), and for an account of the French seizure of Tahiti see Colin Newbury, *Tahiti Nui: Change and Survival in French Polynesia 1767–1945* (Honolulu, 1980), 106–8.

21. Melville, *Omoo* (1968), 127, 179. Hayford and Blair suggest that the name of Melville's Ideea (*Omoo* (1968), 178) was probably taken from (Bligh's) Iddeah, or Itia, who is often mentioned, as 'Idia', in Ellis, *Polynesian Researches*, ii (London, 1834), 7, 69, etc. See 'Explanatory Notes', in Melville, *Omoo* (1969), 387. On the Tahitian code of laws, the 'Ture no Tahiti', see Newbury, *Tahiti Nui*, 50 ff., and for its enforcement see 66.

22. Melville, *Omoo* (1968), p. xiv. On Melville's considerable debt to Ellis, see Anderson, *Melville in the South Seas*, ch. x, and Hayford and Blair, Introduction and 'Explanatory Notes', in Melville, *Omoo* (1969), pp. xxv–xxvi, 375 ff.

23. Ellis, *Polynesian Researches*, ii. 395. Cf. Melville, *Omoo* (1968), 182. On the debt of Melville's chapter to Ellis, see Anderson, *Melville in the South Seas*, 277, and 'Explanatory Notes', in Melville, *Omoo* (1969), 389–90.

24. Melville, *Omoo* (1968), 184.

25. Beechey, *Narrative of a Voyage*, I. 210.

26. Charles Darwin, 'Journal and Remarks, 1832–1836', (included as vol. iii) in Robert Fitzroy, *Narrative of the Surveying Voyages of His Majesty's Ships Adventure and Beagle, between the years 1826 and 1836, describing their Examination of the southern shores of South America, the Beagle's Circumnavigation of the Globe* (London, 1839), iii. 492–3. The passage occurs in the entry for 22 Nov. 1835 in Darwin's original journal, *Charles Darwin's Diary of the Voyage of H.M.S. 'Beagle'*, edited from the MS by Nora Barlow (Cambridge, 1933), 355.

27. Melville, *Omoo* (1968), p. xiv.

28. On Melville's use of the textual evidence in the case of Tahiti, see Anderson, *Melville in the South Seas*, ch. x, and 'Explanatory Notes', in Melville, *Omoo* (1969), 391 ff.

29. Melville, *Omoo* (1968), 186; Michael Russell, *Polynesia: or, An Historical Account of the Principal Islands in the South Sea, including New Zealand; the Introduction of Christianity; and the actual condition of the inhabitants in regard to civilization, commerce, and the arts of social life* (Edinburgh, 1842), 111. Russell's comment does not specifically refer to Beechey as well as Kotzebue, which Melville implies, but Russell does, as Melville says, quote Beechey (e.g. 394–5). For Russell's use of Ellis's *Vindication* against Kotzebue, see Russell, *Polynesia*, 111–30.

30. Russell, *Polynesia*, 394. (As Russell makes clear, the point he makes about the varying views of seamen and missionaries derives from Beechey, *Narrative of a Voyage*, I. 197–8.) On Russell, see *The Dictionary of National Biography*, ed. Leslie Stephen and Sidney Lee, 49 (London, 1897), 467–8.

31. Russell, *Polynesia*, 114.

32. Melville, *Omoo* (1968), 188, rather inexactly quoting Beechey, *Narrative of a Voyage*, I. 197. Russell correctly cites the same passage from Beechey (see Russell, *Polynesia*, 394).

33. Melville, *Omoo* (1968), 190–1.

34. Ibid. 191.

35. See Anderson, *Melville in the South Seas*, 279 ff., and 'Explanatory Notes', in Melville, *Omoo* (1969), 397 ff.

36. Charles Wilkes, *Narrative of the United States Exploring Expedition, during the years 1838, 1839, 1840, 1841, 1842* (Philadelphia, 1844), ii. 51.

37. For Ellis and Russell (clearly following Ellis) on Cook's figures, see Ellis, *Polynesian Researches*, i. 101, and Russell, *Polynesia*, 410.
38. McArthur, *Island Populations*, 261 (on Cook's figures) and see (on population at the time of discovery) 260, and Oliver, *Ancient Tahitian Society*, i. *Ethnography*, 33–4. Oliver and McArthur reach their figures from the same starting point but by different routes, and Oliver very properly recognizes 'the imperfections, in data and in assumptions,' of his figures (Oliver, *Ancient Tahitian Society*, i. 33).
39. See McArthur, *Island Populations*, Table 53, 261.
40. Henry David Thoreau, *Walden*, ed. J. L. Shanley (Princeton, 1971), 322.
41. Melville, *Omoo* (1968), 192.
42. '*E tupu te fau, e toro te farero, e mou te taata*: "The *fau* (hibiscus) shall grow, the *farero* (coral) shall spread or stretch out its branches, but man shall cease."' (Ellis, *Polynesian Researches*, i. 103.) Davies's MS account of his tour, quoted at the head of this chapter, was published in the *Quarterly Chronicle of Transactions of the London Missionary Society*. Melville's spelling of Tahitian words is his own, but, as Hayford and Blair pointed out, Ellis is nevertheless Melville's source. He would have found 'the *haari*, or cocoa-nut' in Ellis's account of Polynesian flora at i. 50, and elsewhere, and, as Hayford and Blair suggest, he also obtained his priest from Ellis, who mentions 'Tairimoa, one of the priests' at iii. 109. (See 'Explanatory Notes', in Melville, *Omoo* (1969), 402.) Ellis's own source, as he implies, is the missionary John Davies, and the prophecy is quoted in 'Mr. Davies's Journal of a Preaching Tour around Otaheite, in the Year 1816', *Quarterly Chronicle of Transactions of the London Missionary Society in the years 1815, 1816, 1817, 1818, and 1819*, i (London, 1821), 325–6. Melville's muddle of the Tahitian is careless, as Ellis's gloss clearly identifies *fau*, not *tupu*, as 'hibiscus', but Russell, who (as Melville would have known) also quotes the prophecy, without acknowledging his source, Ellis, has rendered the English as 'the fan (bulrush) shall grow', which may or may not have suggested to Melville that, if 'bulrush' were possible as an alternative to 'hibiscus', then 'palm' would do too. (See Russell, *Polynesia*, 411, where 'fan' for 'fau' is probably a typesetter's error, and where the substitution of 'bulrush' for 'hibiscus' is probably the result of Russell's careless reading and misunderstanding of Ellis's explanation of the tendency of spreading coral to block the passage of canoes, etc.) The American and English first editions of *Omoo* (1847) have 'now' (in the line 'A mow ta tararta') which Hayford and Blair suggest is probably a typesetter's error for Melville's 'mow', rendering Ellis's '*mou*'.
43. Melville, *Omoo* (1968), 203.
44. Ibid.
45. Ibid. 234.
46. Ibid.
47. Ibid. 238–9.
48. Ibid. 238, 239.
49. Ibid. 241, 242.
50. Ibid. 245.
51. Melville to John Murray, 29 Jan. 1847, *Correspondence*, 78.
52. See Ellis, *Polynesian Researches*, i. 19, ii. 244. Anderson suggested that Melville's Tamai may be a fiction based on Ellis, and Hayford and Blair are sure of this. (See Anderson, *Melville in the South Seas*, 295, and Introduction and 'Explanatory Notes', in Melville, *Omoo* (1969), pp. xxix, 410.)

53. Ellis, *Polynesian Researches*, i. 19, ii. 244; Melville, *Omoo* (1968), 239.

54. [Edward Lucett], *Rovings in the Pacific, from 1837 to 1849, with a Glance at California. By a Merchant long Resident at Tahiti* (London, 1851), i. 296. Anderson assumes that Lucett was referring to Melville's 'valley' of Martair. (See Anderson, *Melville in the South Seas*, 286–7.)

55. Melville, *Omoo* (1968), 237, 246; Ellis, *Polynesian Researches*, i. 19. Another sign that Melville's Tamai is a fiction may be its location on the wrong side of Moorea in the map Melville told Murray had been 'drawn expressly' for *Omoo*, but this map is so inaccurate as to render it almost meaningless. 'Typee' and 'Hapaar', for example, are placed on the opposite side of Nukuhiva from their actual location, an error repeated from the map in the original edition of *Typee*, which has 'Typee' at the north-east of Nukuhiva instead of the south-east. (Melville to John Murray, 29 Jan. 1847, *Correspondence*, 78; and see the map from the original edition of *Omoo*, reproduced in *Omoo* (1968), 380, and the map in Herman Melville, *Narrative of a Four Months' Residence Among the Natives of a Valley of the Marquesas Islands; or, A Peep at Polynesian Life* (London, 1846).)

56. Melville, *Omoo* (1968), p. xiv. Charles Wilson, the acting British consul, records that the *Lucy Ann* came into Papeete on 28 Sept. (29 by the Tahitian calendar Wilson uses) and Melville was still on Tahiti (at the Calabooza) on 19 Oct. (if the dates in Dr Johnstone's 'dose book' are reliable). He left Moorea on the *Charles and Henry*, which was at Moorea on 2 Nov. and was reported off Tahiti (having sailed from Moorea) on 7 Nov. (See: Charles Wilson, Notes and certificate, 'Documents', in Melville, *Omoo* (1969), 318, 328; Johnstone, 'dose book', quoted in Wise, *Los Gringos*, 358 (and Wise's MS, quoted in 'Explanatory Notes', in Melville, *Omoo* (1969), 378); John B. Coleman, master of the *Charles and Henry* to Charles and Henry Coffin, 2 Nov. 1842, Eimeo (Moorea), in Leyda, *The Melville Log*, i. 155–6; Wilson L. Heflin, 'Melville's Third Whaler', *Modern Language Notes* (Apr. 1949), 241–5; Howard, *Herman Melville: A Biography*, 64.)

57. Melville, *Omoo* (1968), 312. For evidence of Melville's increasing dependence on Ellis, see 'Explanatory Notes', in Melville, *Omoo* (1969), 414 ff.

58. Melville, *Omoo* (1968), 312; Milton, *Paradise Lost*, xii. 646.

59. Melville, *Omoo* (1968), 316.

60. [Pierre Loti (Julien Viaud)], *Le Mariage de Loti—Rarahu* (Paris, 1880), [–1]. Loti's source is betrayed, despite his revision of Melville's spelling, by his repetition of Melville's distinctively garbled Tahitian.

61. Ibid. 21.

62. Ibid. 139.

63. Ibid. 94.

64. Ibid. 116.

65. Ibid. 133, 132.

66. Ibid. 155.

67. Ibid. 181.

68. Ibid. 217.

69. Ibid. 253–4.

70. Ibid. 264–6.

71. Ibid. 5.

72. Ibid. 282, 284.

73. Ibid. 286.
74. Ibid. 287 n.
75. Ibid. 287.
76. Ibid. 293.
77. Ibid. 69.
78. Ibid. 179.
79. Ibid. 218.
80. Ibid. 62, 28.
81. Pierre Loti, *Le Roman d'un enfant* (Paris, 1890), 110. Gustave Viaud, naval surgeon, was stationed at Tahiti 1859–1862. (See Georges Taboulet and Jean-Claude Demariaux, *La Vie dramatique de Gustave Viaud, frère de Pierre Loti* (Paris, 1961).)
82. Loti, *Le Roman*, 195.
83. Ibid. 197.
84. Ibid. 127. Loti made a drawing of his brother's ruined house, which is mentioned but not reproduced in Pierre Loti, *Cent dessins de Pierre Loti*, commentés par Claude Farrère (Tours, 1948), 59.
85. [Loti], *Le Mariage*, 5. This passage in the letter in *Le Mariage* closely resembles a passage in Viaud's letter to his sister of 30 Jan. 1872, in Pierre Loti, *Correspondance inédite 1865–1904*, ed. Nadine Duvignaux and N. Serban (Paris, 1929), 128.
86. [Loti], *Le Mariage*, 7, 41.
87. Ibid. 119.
88. Ibid. 231.
89. Ibid.
90. Ibid. 242.
91. See Julien Viaud to Frederic Vernier, quoted in Emile Vedel, 'A propos de Pierre Loti à Tahiti', *Bulletin de la Société d'Etudes Océaniennes*, 5/50 (Mar. 1934), 288, and in Taboulet and Demariaux, *La Vie dramatique*, 264.
92. Julien Viaud, 'Journal intime de Pierre Loti à Tahiti', ed. André Ropiteau, *Bulletin de la Société d'Etudes Océaniennes*, 5/50 (Mar. 1934), 307–8.
93. Ibid. 318. See also Viaud's account of his disappointment in his letter to his sister of 18 July 1872, *Correspondance inédite*, 136. Georges Taboulet and Jean-Claude Demariaux suggest, however, that the documents Julien Viaud saw may have misled him about the ages of the two boys and that the elder boy may possibly have been Gustave's. (See Taboulet and Demariaux, *La Vie dramatique*, 265 n.)
94. Viaud, 'Journal intime', 329, 330–1.
95. Julien Viaud, 'de Pierre Loti à Plumkett' (i.e. Lucien Hervé Jousselin), 24 Feb. 1879, in Pierre Loti, *Journal intime, 1878–1881*, ed. Samuel Viaud (Paris, 1925), 62. Claude Farrère quotes Loti saying to him that 'Pour *le Mariage de Loti*, je dus inventer beaucoup, pour "faire une histoire", car, dans les pages de mon Journal, je crois bien qu'il n'y en avait pas' (Loti, *Cent dessins de Pierre Loti*, 78).
96. Viaud, 'de Pierre Loti à Plumkett', 24 Feb. 1879, in Loti, *Journal intime*, 62–3.
97. See 'Taha et Teapo', in Max Radiguet, *Les Derniers Sauvages, souvenir de l'occupation française aux îles Marquises, 1842–1859* (Brussels, 1861), 253–82. Another edition was published (according to a catalogue of the Bibliothèque Nationale, Paris) by Calmann-Lévy, Viaud–Loti's publisher, as *Les Derniers Sauvages: la vie et les mœurs aux îles Marquises* (Paris, 1882).

98. Radiguet, *Les Derniers Sauvages* (1929), 181.

99. Ibid. 185, 201.

100. Robert Louis Stevenson, 'Creek Island, or Adventures in the South Seas', MS, quoted in Graham Balfour, *The Life of Robert Louis Stevenson* (London, 1901), i. 66. On Stevenson's 'Creek Island', see also R. G. Swearingen, *The Prose Writings of Robert Louis Stevenson: A Guide* (London, 1980), 2–3.

101. R. L. Stevenson, 'To the Hesitating Purchaser', *Treasure Island* (London, 1883), p. [vi].

102. See Eric Quayle, *Ballantyne the Brave: A Victorian Writer and His Family* (London, 1967), 217.

103. See ibid. 113–14.

104. R. M. Ballantyne, *Personal Reminiscences in Book-Making* (London, [1893]), 13. On Ballantyne's research for *The Coral Island*, see Eric Quayle, *The Collector's Book of Boys' Stories* (London, 1973), 52, and Pearson, *Rifled Sanctuaries*, 52.

105. Ballantyne, *Reminiscences*, 15.

106. R. M. Ballantyne, *The Coral Island: A Tale of the Pacific Ocean* (London, 1858), 39–40.

107. For Stevenson's encounter with *Typee* and *Omoo*, see Balfour, *Life of Stevenson*, ii. 171, and the fictional scene in R. L. Stevenson and Lloyd Osbourne, *The Wrecker* (2nd edn., London, 1892), 125–6. Stevenson's copy of *Omoo* was inscribed by his stepdaughter, Belle, 'The book that took Louis Stevenson to the S. Seas—given to him in San Francisco by Charles Warren Stoddard' (quoted in Melville, *Omoo* (1969), p. 1). For Stevenson's agreement with S. S. McClure for syndication of South Seas 'Letters', see Samuel S. McClure, *My Autobiography* (London, 1914), 191–2.

108. For Captain Otis's knowledge of Stevenson's works, see Arthur Johnstone, *Recollections of Robert Louis Stevenson in the Pacific* (London, 1905), 24.

109. R. L. Stevenson, 'Cruise of the *Casco*', MS journal, The Huntington Library, San Marino, Calif., HM 2412: 26, 46, 44–5. Cf. R. L. Stevenson, *In the South Seas*, in *The Works of Robert Louis Stevenson*, Edinburgh edn., xx (Edinburgh, 1896), 28, 16, 12. The 'Highland metaphor' had also been employed, of course, by Byron in *The Island*.

110. Stevenson, *In the South Seas* (1896), 6.

111. There are many parts and versions, in manuscript and in print, of the South Sea material best known as *In the South Seas*. My comments are based on comparisons between the MS original journal, in the Huntington Library, and the first publicly available version in book form, edited by Sidney Colvin as *In the South Seas*, in *The Works of R. L. Stevenson*, Edinburgh edn., xx (Edinburgh, 1896). (A version entitled *The South Seas: A Record of Three Cruises* was printed in an edition of twenty-two copies by Cassell and Company, London, 1890, to secure copyright.) For an account of the various scattered manuscripts and published versions, see Swearingen, *Prose Writings*, 134–43.

112. Stevenson, 'Cruise of the *Casco*', 53.

113. Stevenson, *In the South Seas* (1896), 36.

114. Stevenson, 'Cruise of the *Casco*', 61.

115. Ibid. 66.

116. Ibid.

117. Alfred Tennyson, 'Locksley Hall', *Poems* (London, 1842), ii. 108, 110.

118. Stevenson, 'Cruise of the *Casco*', 91. Cf. Stevenson, *In the South Seas* (1896), 116, 2. On Gauguin, see Bengt Danielsson, *Gauguin in the South Seas*, trans. Reginald Spink (London, 1965).

119. Stevenson to Charles Baxter, 6 Sept. 1888, *The Letters of Robert Louis Stevenson*, ed. Sidney Colvin (London, 1911), iii. 65.

120. See: Margaret Stevenson, *From Saranac to the Marquesas and Beyond, being Letters written by Mrs. M. I. Stevenson during 1887–8, to her sister, Jane Whyte Balfour*, ed. M. C. Balfour (London, 1903), 172; Fanny Stevenson to Sidney Colvin, 4 Dec. 1888, in *The Letters of Robert Louis Stevenson*, iii. 82; Stevenson to Sidney Colvin, Sept. 1891, *Vailima Letters, being Correspondence addressed by Robert Louis Stevenson to Sidney Colvin, Nov. 1890–Oct. 1894* (London, 1895), 90.

121. Stevenson to Sidney Colvin, Mar. 1889, *Letters*, iii. 103.

122. For accounts of Stevenson at Honolulu, see: Lloyd Osbourne, 'Stevenson at Thirty-nine', in R. L. Stevenson, *The Ebb-Tide: A Trio and Quartette*, in *The Works of R. L. Stevenson*, Tusitala edn., xiv (London, 1923); Johnstone, *Recollections*; Martha M. McGaw, *Stevenson in Hawaii* ([1950] repr. Westport, Conn., 1978); Margaret Mackay, *The Violent Friend: The Story of Mrs Robert Louis Stevenson 1840–1914* (abridged edn., London, 1970), 191–202. For some of Stevenson's Hawaiian writings, see R. L. Stevenson, *Travels in Hawaii*, ed. A. Grove Day (Honolulu, 1973).

123. Fanny Stevenson writes of 'the entire island' of Butaritari being 'wildly drunk on "sour toddy"', while Stevenson makes the story of the drunken island turn on imported alcohol sold by foreign traders. (Fanny Stevenson, *The Cruise of the 'Janet Nichol' Among the South Sea Islands: A Diary by Mrs. Robert Louis Stevenson* (New York, 1914), 4.) For 'the beach' in general, see Caroline Ralston, *Grass Huts and Warehouses: Pacific Beach Communities of the Nineteenth Century* (Canberra, 1977).

124. Stevenson to Sidney Colvin, 22 Aug. 1889, *Letters*, iii. 133–4; R. L. Stevenson, Cruise of the *Equator*, MS journal beginning 'Butaritari, July', The Huntington Library, San Marino, Calif., HM 2412: 41, 43, 45.

125. Ibid. 31. Cf. Stevenson, *In the South Seas* (1896), 288.

126. Stevenson to Sidney Colvin, Oct. 1889, *Letters*, iii. 135.

127. Stevenson, Cruise of the *Equator*, 50, 49, 55. Cf. Stevenson, *In the South Seas* (1896), 340, 316, 335. For a historical account of Tem Binoka, see H. E. Maude, 'Baiteke and Binoka of Abemama: arbiters of change in the Gilbert Islands', in J. W. Davidson and Deryck Scarr (eds.), *Pacific Island Portraits* (Canberra, 1970).

128. Stevenson, Cruise of the *Equator*, 47; Stevenson, *In the South Seas* (1896), 321.

129. W. E. Clarke, 'Robert Louis Stevenson in Samoa', *Yale Review*, 10/2 (Jan. 1921), 275–6. Clarke speaks of Lloyd carrying 'a banjo', which was probably the 'native instrument' Fanny said he was taking aboard the *Equator* at Honolulu, 'something like a banjo, called a taropatch fiddle', which is the name for a larger, five-stringed kind of ukelele. (Fanny Stevenson to Sidney Colvin, 21 May 1889, in *Letters of Robert Louis Stevenson*, iii. 122, and see John Henry Felix, Leslie Nunes, and Peter F. Senecal, *The 'Ukulele: A Portuguese Gift to Hawaii* (Honolulu, 1980), 3.)

130. See R. L. Stevenson, 'A Pearl Island: Penrhyn', in *Vailima Papers, The Works of Robert Louis Stevenson*, Skerryvore edn., xiv (London, 1925), 341–52, and Fanny Stevenson, *The Cruise of the 'Janet Nichol'*.

131. Fanny Stevenson to Sidney Colvin, 21 May 1889, in *Letters of Robert Louis Stevenson*, iii. 122–3.

132. Stevenson to Sidney Colvin, 2 Dec. 1889, *Letters*, iii. 139.
133. Stevenson to Sidney Colvin, 2 Nov. 1890, *Vailima Letters*, 4; Fanny Stevenson to Sidney Colvin [and Fanny Sitwell, later Mrs Colvin], [Jan. 1891], 'More Letters of Mrs. R. L. Stevenson', ed. Sidney Colvin, *Scribner's Magazine*, 75 (1924), 416–17. Colvin dates the letter January 1890, which is impossible, and comparison with the entry in Fanny Stevenson's diary for January 1891 confirms that date for the letter. (See Fanny and Robert Louis Stevenson, *Our Samoan Adventure: with a Three-year Diary by Mrs. Stevenson now published for the first time*, ed. Charles Neider (London, 1956), 93–7.)
134. Fanny Stevenson, 'More Letters', 417. Stevenson's researches on the reef of Arorae on 9 June 1890, dramatized by Fanny to display Stevenson's scientific folly to Colvin, are more briefly and comically described by Fanny in *The Cruise of the 'Janet Nichol'*, 112–14.
135. Stevenson to Sidney Colvin, 18–22 Apr. 1891, quoted (from the MS in the Widener Collection, Harvard University) in Swearingen, *Prose Writings*, 143. Cf. Stevenson, *Vailima Letters*, 68, and Stevenson, *Letters*, iii. 254–5.
136. Exactly what sources Colvin drew upon for his text of *In the South Seas* (1896) is a complex question that I am in no position to determine. For some comments by Colvin himself, see Stevenson, *Letters*, iii. 137, and for some bibliographical details, see: Swearingen, *Prose Writings*, 138; and *A Stevenson Library: Catalogue of a Collection of Writings by and about Robert Louis Stevenson formed by Edwin J. Beinecke*, compiled by George L. McKay (New Haven, 1951–64), i. 230–1; and *Robert Louis Stevenson: A Catalogue of the Henry E. Gerstley Stevenson Collection of Victorian Novelists, and Items from Other Collections of the Princeton University Library*, compiled by Alexander D. Wainwright (Princeton, NJ, 1971), p. 102.
137. The coral researches at Arorae in the Gilberts are conflated in *In the South Seas* with previous coral researches by Stevenson at Funafuti in the Ellice Islands, where he found the worm-infested coral he describes in *In the South Seas*. (See Fanny Stevenson, *The Cruise of the 'Janet Nichol'*, 94, 112–13; Stevenson, *In the South Seas* (1896), 175–6.)
138. Stevenson to Sidney Colvin, 6? Nov. 1890, *Vailima Letters*, 16. I have preferred a relatively detailed consideration of *The Beach of Falesá* to an inevitably cramped and inadequate consideration of Stevenson's other South Sea fictions (written in collaboration with Lloyd Osbourne), *The Wrecker* and *The Ebb-Tide*.
139. Stevenson to Sidney Colvin, 29 Apr. 1891, *Vailima Letters*, 70–1.
140. Stevenson to Sidney Colvin, 5? Sept. 1891, *Vailima Letters*, 86.
141. Stevenson to Sidney Colvin, 28 Sept. 1891, *Vailima Letters*, 94–5.
142. There are, in particular, several grisly pages of notes in Stevenson's manuscript journal of the Cruise of the *Equator* that justify his comment to Colvin that the dissolute figure of Randall in *The Beach of Falesá* was not 'the whole truth—for I did extenuate there'. (Stevenson to Sidney Colvin, 17 May 1892, *Vailima Letters*, 170, and see Stevenson, Cruise of the *Equator*, 41–6, 52–4, 57–9, 67, 68.)
143. Stevenson to Sidney Colvin, 17 May 1892, *Vailima Letters*, 170.
144. Stevenson to Sidney Colvin, 28 Sept. 1891, *Vailima Letters*, 95; Stevenson, *The Beach of Falesá*, in Barry Menikoff, *Robert Louis Stevenson and 'The Beach of Falesá': A Study in Victorian Publishing, with the Original Text* (Edinburgh, 1984), 168. This edition prints Stevenson's manuscript, now in the Huntington Library, HM 2391.

145. Ibid.

146. Ballantyne, *The Coral Island*, 431–2.

147. Ibid. 434.

148. Stevenson, *The Beach of Falesá* (1984), 123–4 (and see photograph of manuscript, 101).

149. Stevenson to Sidney Colvin, 1 Feb. 1892, *Vailima Letters*, 136. That the request was Robert McClure's—not Clement Shorter's, as Swearingen has it—appears likely from the letters from Lemuel Bangs, Scribner's representative, to Charles Scribner, which are quoted in Menikoff's commentary accompanying his edition of *The Beach of Falesá*. (See Swearingen, *Prose Writings*, 154, and Menikoff, *Stevenson and 'The Beach of Falesá'*, 18, 19.) It is possible that Robert McClure's request was made on behalf of Clement Shorter, of course, and indeed all the facts are not in yet in the confused case of the publication of *The Beach of Falesá*.

150. Stevenson to Sidney Colvin, 1 Feb. 1892, *Vailima Letters*, 136.

151. Clement Shorter, Foreword, R. L. Stevenson, *Letters to an Editor* [London?, 1914], p. iv; R. L. Stevenson, 'Uma; or The Beach of Falesá (being the narrative of a South-Sea Trader)', *Illustrated London News* (2 July 1892), 11. For Stevenson's receipt of a copy, see Stevenson to Sidney Colvin, [19] Aug. 1892, *Vailima Letters*, 213.

152. Stevenson to Sidney Colvin, [19] Aug. 1892, *Vailima Letters*, 213.

153. R. L. Stevenson, 'The Beach of Falesá', *Island Nights' Entertainments* (London, 1893), 18.

154. Stevenson to Sidney Colvin, 17 May 1892, *Vailima Letters*, 170.

155. The passage from *The Sun* (11 Oct. 1891) is quoted in Menikoff, *Stevenson and 'The Beach of Falesá'*, 86.

156. Stevenson, *In the South Seas* (1896), 297, 298. I have corrected the erroneous 'Hall Bible' to 'hall Bible', following the text of *The Sun*, quoted in Menikoff, *Stevenson and 'The Beach of Falesá'*, 86.

157. Rupert Brooke, 'Waikiki', *The Poetical Works of Rupert Brooke*, ed. Geoffrey Keynes (London, 1946), 37. It is hard to tell if Brooke is thinking here of his affair with Ca Cox, or his affair with Noel Olivier, or of both. (See Christopher Hassall, *Rupert Brooke: A Biography* (London, 1964), 417, and Rupert Brooke to Noel Olivier, [27 Oct.–2 Nov., 1913], *Song of Love: The Letters of Rupert Brooke and Noel Olivier, 1909–1915*, ed. Pippa Harris (London, 1991), 255.)

158. Rupert Brooke to Violet Asquith, Dec. 1913, *The Letters of Rupert Brooke*, ed. Geoffrey Keynes (London, 1968), 542.

159. Rupert Brooke to Cathleen Nesbitt, early Nov. 1913, *Letters*, 522; and see Rupert Brooke to Edmund Gosse, from McDonald's Hotel, Fiji, 19 Nov. 1913, *Letters*, 530–2.

160. Rupert Brooke to Edward Marsh, 2? Nov. 1913, *Letters*, 524.

161. Rupert Brooke to Edward Marsh, 15? Nov. 1913, *Letters*, 525.

162. Rupert Brooke to Violet Asquith, 'Nearly half-way through December' 1913, *Letters*, 544.

163. Rupert Brooke to Cathleen Nesbitt, 7 Feb. 1914, *Letters*, 562.

164. See Rupert Brooke, 'Tiare Tahiti', *Poetical Works*, 27. A few snapshots and negatives of Taatamata are among the Rupert Brooke Papers, King's College Library, Cambridge, but one of her 'naked to the waist . . . and smiling', mentioned in Hassall, *Rupert Brooke*, 43, seems to have been lost.

165. Rupert Brooke to Edward Marsh, 7 Mar. 1914, *Letters*, 564, 565.
166. Rupert Brooke to Phyllis Gardner, Mar. 1914, *Letters*, 566.
167. Rupert Brooke, in conversation recorded in A. C. Benson's diary, quoted in Hassall, *Rupert Brooke*, 452.
168. Rupert Brooke to Dudley Ward, [before 15 Dec. 1914], *Letters*, 635.
169. Rupert Brooke to Dudley Ward, [13 or 14 Jan. 1915], *Letters*, 653–4.
170. Taatamata to Rupert Brooke, 2 May 1914, MS, Brooke Papers, King's College Library, Cambridge.
171. On the connection between Brooke's coral-poisoning at Tahiti and his death, see Hassall, *Rupert Brooke*, 507, and Philip Snow and Stefanie Waine, *The People from the Horizon: An Illustrated History of Europeans among the South Sea Islanders* (Oxford, 1979), 215.
172. Rupert Brooke to Dudley Ward, 17 Mar. 1915, *Letters*, 672.
173. The proprietor of the Central Hotel, Apia, Samoa, in conversation to Maugham, according to Maugham in conversation recorded in Wilmon Menard, *The Two Worlds of Somerset Maugham* (Los Angeles, 1965), 143.
174. See W. Somerset Maugham, *A Writer's Notebook* (London, 1949), 111–13.
175. Ibid. 106. For the captain and the missionary couple, see 109, 105–6.
176. W. Somerset Maugham, 'Rain', *The Trembling of a Leaf: Little Stories of the South Sea Islands* (London, 1921), 252.
177. Maugham, *The Trembling of a Leaf*, 28, 152, 276, etc. ('the natives'); 18, 213, 216, and see 99.
178. Maugham, 'Honolulu', *The Trembling of a Leaf*, 217.
179. Laurette Taylor, quoted in Marguerite Courtney, *Laurette: The Intimate Biography of Laurette Taylor* ([1955], repr. New York, 1984), 113.
180. Publicity for *A Bird of Paradise*, quoted in F. C. Furnas, *Anatomy of Paradise: Hawaii and the Islands of the South Seas* (London, 1950), 412, 414–15. The play itself was written by Richard Walton Tully, who was charged with plagiarism by another author, Grace A. Fendler.
181. For 'Honolulu Moon', see *Hawaiian Music and Musicians: An Illustrated History*, ed. George S. Kanahele (Honolulu, 1979), 19, and for illustrations of the island-girl, see Desoto Brown, *Hawaii Recalls: Nostalgic Images of the Hawaiian Islands: 1910–1950* (London, 1986), 15, 25, 60, 61.
182. Alec Waugh, *The Coloured Countries* (London, 1930), 2, 41.
183. Ibid. 19 20.
184. Margaret Mead, *Coming of Age in Samoa: A Psychological Study of Primitive Youth for Western Civilization* (London, 1929), 201. On Mead's *Coming of Age*, see Derek Freeman, *Margaret Mead and Samoa: The Making and Unmaking of an Anthropological Myth* (Cambridge, Mass. 1983), which is not, however, a balanced work.
185. Bronislaw Malinowski, *Argonauts of the Western Pacific: An Account of Native Enterprise and Adventure in the Archipelagoes of Melanesian New Guinea* (London, 1922), p. xv. Anthropology has subsequently come of age and acquired a sense of history.
186. See Louis Turner and John Ash, *The Golden Hordes: International Tourism and the Pleasure Periphery* (London, 1975), 161–2.
187. Thomas Hale Hamilton, former president of the Hawaiian Visitors Bureau, quoted in Louis Turner and John Ash, *The Golden Hordes*, 162.

188. Melville, *Omoo* (1968), 242.

189. UTA advertisement, *The Far Eastern Economic Review* (25 Mar. 1972), facing 45. I allude to Alan Moorehead, *The Fatal Impact: An Account of the Invasion of the South Pacific 1767–1840* (Penguin edn., 1968), which gives a historical form to the European myth of a South Sea paradise lost.

Bibliography

ABBOTT, J. L., *John Hawkesworth, Eighteenth-Century Man of Letters* (Madison, Wis., 1982).

[À BECKETT, GILBERT ABBOTT], lampoon, *Almanack of the Month* (June 1846), i, in *Melville*, ed. Branch, 84.

An Account of the Famous Prince Giolo, son of the King of Gilolo, Now in England: with an Account of his Life, Parentage, and his strange and Wonderful Adventures . . . Written from his own Mouth (London, 1692).

An Account of the Mutinous Seizure of the Bounty: with the succeeding Hardships of the Crew: to which are added Secret Anecdotes of the Otaheitean Females (London, 1792).

[ADAMS, HENRY], *Memoirs of Arii Taimai* (Paris, 1901).

ADAMS, PERCY G., *Travelers and Travel Liars 1660–1800* (Berkeley, Calif., 1962).

—— *Travel Literature and the Evolution of the Novel* (Lexington, Ky., 1983).

ALDRIDGE, A. O., 'Polygamy in Early Fiction: Henry Neville and Denis Veiras', *Publications of the Modern Language Association*, 65 (March 1950), 464–72.

—— 'Feijoo, Voltaire, and the Mathematics of Procreation', *Studies in Eighteenth-Century Culture*, ed. Harold E. Pagliaro, 4 (1975), 131–5.

ALEXANDER, MICHAEL, *Omai: 'Noble Savage'* (London, 1977).

ALIGHIERI, DANTE, *La Divina Commedia* , ed. Natalino Sapegno (3 vols.; Florence, 1968).

ANDERSON, CHARLES, *Melville in the South Seas* (New York, 1939).

ANDERSON, WILLIAM, 'Anderson's Journal' ('A Journal of a Voyage made in His Majestys Sloop Resolution'), in *Journals of Captain Cook*, ed. Beaglehole, iii. 721–986.

ANTHONY, IRVIN, ed., *The Saga of the Bounty: Its Strange History as related by the Participants Themselves* (New York, 1935).

ANSTRUTHER, WILLIAM, *Essays, Moral and Divine; in Five Discourses* (Edinburgh, 1701).

ARENS, W., *The Man-Eating Myth: Anthropology and Anthropophagy* (New York, 1979).

ARMSTRONG, RICHARD, 'A Sketch of Marquesian Character', *Hawaiian Spectator*, 1/1 (Honolulu, Jan. 1838).

ATKINSON, GEOFFROY, *The Extraordinary Voyage in French Literature Before 1700* (New York, 1920).

—— *The Extraordinary Voyage in French Literature from 1700 to 1720* (Paris, 1922).

—— *Les Relations de voyages du XVIIᵉ siècle et l'évolution des idées* (Paris, 1924).

—— *Les Nouveaux Horizons de la Renaissance française* (Paris, 1935).

'An Authentic Account of the Natives of OTAHITEE, or GEORGE'S ISLAND: Together with some of the Particulars of the three years voyage lately made by Mr. *Banks*, and Dr. *Solander*, in the years 1768, 1769, and 1770. Being the Copy of an original Letter from —— ——, on board the ENDEAVOUR, to his friend in the country', *General Evening Post* (Sat., 27 July to Tues., 30 July 1771).

Authorized Version of the English Bible, 1611, ed. W. A. Wright (Cambridge, 1909).

[BACHAUMONT, LOUIS-PÉTIT DE, et al.], *Mémoires secrets pour servir á l'histoire de la république des lettres en France, depuis MDCCLXII jusqu'à nos jours; ou Journal d'un observateur* (36 vols.; London, 1777–89).

BACON, FRANCIS, *The Essayes or Counsels, Civill and Morall* (London, 1625).

BACON, FRANCIS, 'New Atlantis. A Worke unfinished', published with *Sylva Sylvarum or A Natural History in ten Centuries* (London, 1627).

—— 'The New Organon' ('Novum Organum'), trans. in *The Works of Francis Bacon*, ed. James Spedding, R. L. Ellis, and D. D. Heath (14 vols.; London, 1857–74), iv. 37–248.

—— 'Of the Dignity and Advancement of Learning' ('De Augmentis Scientiarum', expanded Latin version of *The Advancement of Learning*), trans. in *Works*, iv. 273–498, and v. 3–119.

—— 'Preparative towards a Natural and Experimental History' ('Parasceve ad Historiam Naturalem et Experimentalem'), trans. in *Works*, iv. 249–71.

—— 'The Great Instauration' ('Instauratio Magna'), trans. in *Works*, iv. 3–35.

—— 'Of the Wisdom of the Ancients' ('De Sapientia Veterum'), trans. in *Works*, vi. 687–764.

—— 'An Advertisement Touching an Holy War', in *Works*, vii. 9–36.

—— 'The Refutation of Philosophies' ('Redargutio Philosophiarum'), trans. in Benjamin Farrington, *The Philosophy of Francis Bacon: An Essay on its Development from 1603 to 1609 with New Translations of Fundamental Texts* (Liverpool, 1964), 103–33.

—— 'Thoughts and Conclusions' ('Cogitata et Visa'), trans. in Farrington, *Philosophy of Francis Bacon*, 73–102.

—— *The Advancement of Learning*, ed. Arthur Johnston (with *New Atlantis*) (Oxford, 1974).

—— *New Atlantis*, ed. Arthur Johnston (with *The Advancement of Learning*) Oxford, 1974).

BAEDEKER, KARL, *Southern Italy and Sicily* (Leipzig, 1930).

BAKER, E. A., *The History of the English Novel* (10 vols.; London, 1924–39).

BAKER, J. N. L., 'The Geography of Daniel Defoe', *Scottish Geographical Magazine*, 47/5 (Sept. 1931), 257–69.

BALFOUR, GRAHAM, *The Life of Robert Louis Stevenson* (2 vols.; London, 1901).

BALLANTYNE, R. M., *The Coral Island: A Tale of the Pacific Ocean* (London, 1858).

—— *Personal Reminiscences in Book-Making* (London, [1893]).

BANKS, JOSEPH, *The 'Endeavour' Journal of Joseph Banks*, ed. J. C. Beaglehole (2 vols.; Sydney, 1962).

BARLOWE, ARTHUR, 'The first voyage to Virginia', in Hakluyt, *The Principal Navigations, Voyages, Traffiques and Discoveries of the English Nation*, viii. 297–310.

—— 'Discourse of the First Voyage', in *The Roanoke Voyages 1584–1590*, ed. D. B. Quinn (2 vols.; London, 1955), i. 91–116.

[BARROW, JOHN], review of *Voyage à la recherche de La Pérouse*, *Quarterly Review*, 3/5 (Feb. 1810), 21–43.

[——] *The Eventful History of the Mutiny and Piratical Seizure of H. M. S. Bounty: Its Cause and Consequences* (London, 1831).

BATTELL, ANDREW, 'The strange adventures of Andrew Battell of Leigh in Essex, sent by the Portugals prisoner to Angola', in Purchas, *Purchas His Pilgrimes*, iv.

BAUDET, HENRI, *Paradise on Earth: Some Thoughts on European Images of Non-European Man*, trans. Elizabeth Wentholt (New Haven, Conn., 1965).

BEAGLEHOLE, J. C., *The Exploration of the Pacific* (rev. 3rd edn., London, 1966).

—— *Cook the Writer* (Sydney, 1970).

—— ed., *The 'Endeavour' Journal of Joseph Banks* (2 vols.; Sydney, 1962).

—— ed., *The Journals of Captain James Cook on His Voyages of Discovery*: i. *The Voyage of the 'Endeavour' 1768–1771* (rev., Cambridge, 1968); ii. *The Voyage of the 'Resolution' and*

'*Adventure*' *1772–1775* (Cambridge, 1961); iii. *The Voyage of the 'Resolution' and 'Discovery' 1776–1780* (2 pts.; Cambridge, 1967).

BEAUNIER, ANDRÉ, 'Joseph Joubert et Tahiti', *Revue des deux mondes*, 24 (1914).

BEECHEY, F. W., *Narrative of a Voyage to the Pacific and Bering's Strait* (2 pts.; London, 1831).

BEER, GILLIAN, *The Romance* (London, 1970).

BELCHER, DIANA, *The Mutineers of the Bounty and their Descendants in Pitcairn and Norfolk Islands* (London, 1870).

BENNETT, J. W., *The Rediscovery of Sir John Mandeville* (New York, 1954).

BERNÁLDEZ, ANDRÉS, *Historia de los Reyes Católicos D. Fernando y Doña Isabel* (2 vols.; Seville, 1869–70).

—— *Historia*, i. in *The Voyages of Christopher Columbus, Being the Journals of his First and Third, and the Letters concerning his First and Last Voyages, to which is added the Account of the Second Voyage written by Andrés Bernáldez*, trans. and ed. Cecil Jane (London, 1930).

[BERNARDIN DE SAINT-PIERRE, JACQUES-HENRI], *Voyage à l'Isle de France* (2 vols.; Amsterdam, 1773).

BILLINGTON, R. A., *Land of Savagery, Land of Promise: The European Image of the American Frontier in the Nineteenth Century* (New York, 1981).

BLIGH, WILLIAM, *A Narrative of the Mutiny, on board His Majesty's Ship 'Bounty'; and the subsequent voyage of part of the crew in the ship's boat, from Tofoa . . . to Timor . . .* (London, 1790).

[——] *A Voyage to the South Sea . . . for the purpose of Conveying the Bread-fruit Tree to the West Indies*, [ed. James Burney] (London, 1792).

—— *An Answer to Certain Assertions contained in the Appendix to a Pamphlet* (London, 1794).

—— *The Log of the Bounty*, ed. O. Rutter (2 vols.; London, 1936).

—— *Bligh's Voyage in the 'Resource' from Coupang to Batavia, together with the Log of his subsequent passage to England in the Dutch Packet 'Vlydt' and his Remarks on Morrison's Journal*, ed. O. Rutter (London, 1937).

—— Journal on the *Providence*, PRO, London, published as *Return to Tahiti: Bligh's Second Breadfruit Voyage*, ed. Douglas Oliver (Honolulu, 1988).

—— to Sir Joseph Banks, 13 Oct. 1789, MS, Mitchell Library, Sydney, Australia.

—— to Sir Joseph Banks, 16 Sept. 1796, MS, Mitchell Library, Sydney, Australia.

—— 'Rems. on Mr. Christian's Letters.—The 1st. dated Decr. 16. 1792', MS, Mitchell Library, Sydney, Australia.

BOAS, GEORGE, *Essays on Primitivism and Related Ideas in the Middle Ages* (Baltimore, 1948).

BOASE, A. M., *The Fortunes of Montaigne: A History of the Essays in France, 1580–1669* (repr. New York, 1970).

BONNER, W. H., *Captain William Dampier, Buccaneer-Author: Some Account of a Modest Buccaneer and of English Travel Literature in the Early Eighteenth Century* (Stanford, Calif., 1934).

BONNO, GABRIEL, *Les Relations intellectuelles de Locke avec la France* (Berkeley, Calif., 1955).

BOSWELL, JAMES, *The Life of Samuel Johnson*, ed. G. B. Hill, rev. L. F. Powell (6 vols.; Oxford, 1934).

—— *Boswell: The Ominous Years 1774–1776*, ed. C. Ryskamp and F. A. Pottle (London, 1963).

BOUGAINVILLE, L. A. DE, *Voyage autour du monde, par la frégate du roi la Boudeuse et la flûte l'Étoile; en 1766, 1767, 1768 & 1769* (Paris, 1771).
—— 'Journal de Bougainville', in *Bougainville et ses compagnons*, ed. Taillemite, i.
BRADFORD, WILLIAM, *History of Plymouth Plantation*, reproduced in facsimile from the original document (London, 1896).
BRADNER, LEICESTER, 'Columbus in Sixteenth-Century Poetry', in *Essays Honoring Lawrence C. Wroth* (Portland, Me., 1951), 15–30.
BRADY, FRANK (ed.), *Twentieth Century Interpretations of 'Gulliver's Travels'* (Englewood Cliffs, NJ, 1968).
BRANCH, W. G., ed., *Melville: The Critical Heritage* (London, 1974).
BROME, RICHARD, *The Antipodes*, ed. A. Haaker (London, 1967).
BROOKE, RUPERT, *The Poetical Works of Rupert Brooke*, ed. Geoffrey Keynes (London, 1946).
—— *The Letters of Rupert Brooke*, ed. Geoffrey Keynes (London, 1968).
—— and OLIVIER, NOEL, *Song of Love: The Letters of Rupert Brooke and Noel Olivier, 1909–1915*, ed. Pippa Harris (London, 1991).
BROSSARD, MAURICE DE, *Lapérouse: des combats à la découverte* (Paris, 1978).
BROWN, DESOTO, *Hawaii Recalls: Nostalgic Images of the Hawaiian Islands: 1910–1950* (London, 1986).
BROWNE, JAMES H., 'Voyage from Leghorn to Cephalonia with Lord Byron, and a Narrative of a Visit, in 1823, to the seat of the War in Greece', *Blackwood's Edinburgh Magazine*, 25/217 (Jan. 1834), 56–67.
BROWNE, Sir THOMAS, *Pseudodoxia Epidemica*, ed. R. Robbins (2 vols.; Oxford, 1981).
BRUCE, JAMES, *Travels to Discover the Source of the Nile* (5 vols.; Edinburgh, 1790).
BRUZEN DE LA MARTINIÈRE, A. A., *La Grand Dictionnaire géographique, historique et critique* (6 vols.; Paris, 1768).
BUNBURY, E. H., *A History of Ancient Geography* (repr., 2 vols.; New York, 1959).
BURNETT, JAMES, Lord MONBODDO, *Of the Origin and Progress of Language* (6 vols.; Edinburgh, 1773–92).
—— *Of the Origin and Progress of Language*, i (2nd edn., Edinburgh, 1774).
BURNEY, FRANCES (FANNY), subsequently Mme d'Arblay, *Diary and Letters of Madame d'Arblay*, ed. by her niece (7 vols.; London, 1842–6).
—— *The Early Diary of Frances Burney, 1768–1778*, ed. A. R. Ellis (2 vols.; London, 1889).
—— to Samuel Crisp, 1 Dec. 1774, British Library, Egerton MS 3694.
BURNEY, JAMES, *A Chronological History of the Discoveries in the South Sea or Pacific Ocean* (5 vols.; London, 1803–17).
—— 'Burney's Log', in *Journals of Captain Cook*, ed. Beaglehole, ii.
—— to Sir Joseph Banks, in Rolf E. Du Rietz, 'Three letters from James Burney to Sir Joseph Banks', *Ethnos*, 27 (1962), 115–25.
BURTON, ROBERT, *The Anatomy of Melancholy* (Oxford, 1651).
BYRON, GEORGE GORDON, *Don Juan*, in *The Complete Poetical Works*, ed. J. J. McGann (7 vols.; Oxford, 1980–93), v.
—— *The Island, or Christian and His Comrades*, in *The Complete Poetical Works*, vii.
—— *Byron's Letters and Journals*, ed. L. A. Marchand (11 vols.; London, 1973–81).
BYRON, JOHN, *Byron's Journal of his Circumnavigation 1764–1766*, ed. Robert E. Gallagher (Cambridge, 1964).

CAMPBELL, JOHN, *Maritime Discovery and Christian Missions, considered in their Mutual Relations* (London, 1840).

CALLANDER, JOHN, *Terra Australis Cognita, or Voyages to the Terra Australis* (3 vols.; Edinburgh, 1766–8).

[CAPELL, EDWARD], *Notes and Various Readings to Shakespeare* (3 vols.; London, 1779–80).

CARTER, ELIZABETH, *Letters from Mrs. Elizabeth Carter to Mrs. Montagu between the years 1755 and 1800*, ed. Montagu Pennington (3 vols.; London, 1817).

CARTIER, JACQUES, *Brief recit, & succinte narration, de la navigation faicte es ysles de Canada, Hochelage & Saguenay & autres, avec particulieres meurs, langaiges, & cerimonies des habitans d'icelles: fort delectable à veoir* (Paris, 1545).

CASSON, LIONEL, *Travel in the Ancient World* (London, 1974).

CATOIRA, GOMEZ HERNÁNDEZ DE, 'An Account of the Voyage and Discovery which was made in the South Sea', trans. in *The Discovery of the Solomon Islands*, ed. Lord Amherst of Hackney and B. Thomson (2 vols.; London, 1901), i.

CAWLEY, R. R., *Unpathed Waters: Studies in the Influence of the Voyagers on Elizabethan Literature* (London, 1967).

CHAPELAIN, JEAN, *Lettres de Jean Chapelain*, ed. Ph. Tamizey de Larroque (2 vols.; Paris, 1880, 1883).

CHATEAUBRIAND, FRANÇOIS-RENÉ DE, *Voyage en Amérique*, ed. R. Switzer (2 vols.; Paris, 1964).

CHINARD, GILBERT, *L'Exotisme américain dans la littérature fançaise au XVIe siècle* (Paris, 1911).

—— *L'Amérique et le rêve exotique dans la littérature fraçaise au XVIIe et au XVIIIe siècles* (Paris, 1913).

CHRISTIAN, EDWARD, 'The Appendix', [Stephen Barney and Edward Christian], *Minutes of the Proceedings of the Court Martial held at Portsmouth on Ten Persons charged with Mutiny on board His Majesty's Ship the Bounty, With an Appendix containing a full account of the real Causes and Circumstances of that unhappy Transaction, the most material of which have hitherto been withheld from the Public*, reprinted in *A Book of the 'Bounty'*, ed. G. Mackaness (London, 1938).

CHRISTIAN, GLYNN, *Fragile Paradise: The Discovery of Fletcher Christian, Bounty Mutineer* (London, 1982).

'Christian's own Account of the Mutiny on Board his Majesty's Ship Bounty, commanded by Captain Bligh, of which he was the Ringleader', *Weekly Entertainer; or Agreeable and Instructive Repository*, 27 (26 Sept. 1796), 255–6.

[CIBBER, THEOPHILUS?], 'The Life of Daniel De Foe', in *The Lives of the Poets of Great Britain and Ireland* (5 vols.; London, 1753), iv.

CLARKE, W. E., 'Robert Louis Stevenson in Samoa', *Yale Review*, 10/2 (Jan. 1921), 275–96.

CLERKE, CHARLES, 'An Account of the very tall Men, seen near the Straits of Magellan', *Philosophical Transactions*, 57 (London, 1768).

—— 'Clerke's Journal', in *Journals of Captain Cook*, ed. Beaglehole, iii. 1301–40.

CLINTON, GEORGE, *Memoirs of the Life and Writings of Lord Byron* (London, 1825).

COAN, TITUS, *Life in Hawaii, an Autobiographic Sketch of Mission Life and Labors (1835–1881)* (New York, 1882).

COKE, Lady MARY, *Letters and Journals*, ed. J. A. Home (4 vols.; Edinburgh, 1889–96).

COLEMAN, RONALD A., 'Tragedy of the Pandora', in *Mutiny of the Bounty 1789–1989* (National Maritime Museum exhibition catalogue, London, 1989), 116–23.

COLERIDGE, S. T., *The Poetical Works of S. T. Coleridge*, ed. E. H. Coleridge (London, 1912).

—— *The Notebooks*, ed. K. Coburn (4 vols.; London, 1957–90).

COLÓN, FERNANDO (Fernando Colombo/Ferdinand Columbus), *Historie del S. D. Fernando Colombo; nelli quali s'ha particolare, & vera relatione della vita, & de' fatti dell'Ammiraglio D. Cristoforo Colombo, suo padre*, trans. Alfonso Ulloa (Venice, 1571).

COLUMBUS, CHRISTOPHER (Cristoforo Colombo/Cristóbal Colón), 'Letter', in *Select Documents Illustrating the Four Voyages of Columbus*, trans. and ed. Cecil Jane (2 vols.; London, 1930, 1932), i.

—— 'Narrative of the voyage which the admiral, Don Christopher Columbus, made the third time he came to the Indies', in *Select Documents*, ii.

—— *The Journal of Christopher Columbus*, trans. Cecil Jane, rev. L. A. Vigneras (London, 1960).

—— 'Letter of Columbus', in *The Four Voyages of Christopher Columbus*, trans. J. M. Cohen (Penguin edn., 1969).

—— *El libro de Marco Polo anotado por Cristóbal Colón*, ed. Juan Gil (Madrid, 1987).

—— *The 'Diario' of Christopher Columbus's First Voyage to America 1492–1493*, transcribed and trans. Oliver Dunn and James E. Kelley, Jr. (Norman, Okla., 1989).

COMMERSON, PHILIBERT, 'Post-scriptum sur l'île de Taïti ou Nouvelle Cythère', in F. B. de Montessus, *Martyrologie et biographie de Commerson* (Chalon-sur-Saone, 1889).

—— 'Notes de Commerson', in *Bougainville et ses compagnons*, ed. Taillemite, ii. 496 ff.

CONGREVE, WILLIAM, *Love for Love: A Comedy* (London, 1695).

COOK, JAMES, *A Voyage towards the South Pole, and Round the World* (2 vols.; London, 1777).

—— *The Journals of Captain James Cook on His Voyages of Discovery*, ed. J. C. Beaglehole: i. *The Voyage of the 'Endeavour' 1768–1771* (rev. edn., Cambridge, 1968); ii. *The Voyage of the 'Resolution' and 'Adventure' 1772–1775* (Cambridge, 1961); iii. *The Voyage of the 'Resolution' and 'Discovery' 1776–1780* (Cambridge, 1967) pt. 1.

—— journal of second voyage, British Library, Additional MS 27888.

—— and KING, JAMES, *A Voyage to the Pacific Ocean* (3 vols.; London, 1784).

COOKE, EDWARD, *A Voyage to the South Sea, and Round the World* (2 vols.; London, 1712).

[COOPER, A. A., 3rd Earl of Shaftesbury], *Soliloquy: or, Advice to an Author* (London, 1710).

[——] *Several Letters Written by a Noble Lord to a Young Man at the University* (London, 1716).

COOPER, JAMES FENIMORE, *The Last of the Mohicans; A Narrative of 1757*, ed. J. F. Beard *et al.* (New York, 1983).

COSMAS INDICOPLEUSTES, *The Christian Topography*, trans. and ed. J. W. McCrindle (London, 1897).

COULTER, JOHN, *Adventures in the Pacific* (Dublin, 1845).

[COURTENAY, JOHN?], *An Epistle (Moral and Philosophical) from an Officer at Otaheite to Lady Gr*s**n*r with Notes, Critical and Historical* (London, 1774).

COURTNEY, MARGUERITE, *Laurette: The Intimate Biography of Laurette Taylor* (repr. New York, 1984).

Covent-Garden Magazine; or, Amorous Repository ('Amorous Extracts from Dr. Hawkesworth's Collection of Voyages, with natural Remarks') 2 (1773), 201–4 (June), 251–2 (July).

COWLEY, ABRAHAM, 'A Proposition for the Advancement of Experimental Philosophy', in *Essays and Other Prose Writings*, ed. A. B. Gough (Oxford, 1915).

COWLEY, ABRAHAM, 'To the Royal Society', in Thomas Sprat, *History of the Royal Society*, ed. J. I. Cope and H. W. Jones (Saint Louis, Mo., 1958).

COWLEY, WILLIAM, 'Voyage round the Globe', in *A Collection of Original Voyages*, ed. William Hacke (London, 1699).

COWPER, WILLIAM, *The Task, A Poem, in Six Books* (London, 1785).

—— *The Letters and Prose Writings of William Cowper*, ed. J. King and C. Ryskamp (3 vols.; Oxford, 1979–82).

CRADOCK, JOSEPH, *Literary and Miscellaneous Memoirs* (4 vols.; London, 1828).

Critical Review, or, Annals of Literature (review of *Adventures of Robert Drury* (1807)), 14/1 (May 1808), 84–92.

[CROFT, HERBERT], *Love and Madness: A Story Too True. In a Series of Letters* (London, 1780).

CRONE, G. R., AND SKELTON, R. A., 'English Collections of Voyages and Travels, 1625–1846', in Edward Lynam (ed.), *Richard Hakluyt and His Successors* (London, 1946).

CROOK, WILLIAM, Journal, 1821, MS, Council for World Mission archives, School of Oriental and African Studies, London, South Sea Journals, Box 4.

[CROZET, JULIEN], *Nouveau voyage à la Mer du Sud . . . rédigée d'après les plans & journaux de M. Crozet*, ed. A. M. Rochon (Paris, 1783).

CTESIAS (or Ktêsias), *Ancient India as Described by Ktêsias the Knidian; being a translation of the abridgement of his 'Indika' by Phôtios, and of the fragments of that work preserved in other writers*, trans. and ed. J. W. McCrindle (London, 1882).

CURTIUS, E. R., *European Literature and the Latin Middle Ages*, trans. W. R. Trask (Princeton, 1973).

CYRANO DE BERGERAC, SAVINIEN, *Estats et empires de la lune*, in *Œuvres complètes*, ed. Jacques Prévot (Paris, 1977).

DALRYMPLE, ALEXANDER, *An Account of the Discoveries made in the South Pacifick Ocean, Previous to 1764* (London, 1767).

DAMPIER, WILLIAM, 'An Account of a New Voyage Round the World', *Philosophical Transactions*, 19 (Feb. 1697), 426–33.

—— *A New Voyage Round the World* (London, 1697).

—— 'Voyages to the Bay of Campeachy', in *Voyages and Descriptions* (London, 1699).

—— *A Voyage to New Holland* (London, 1703).

—— *A Continuation of a Voyage to New Holland* (London, 1709).

[——] MS version of *A New Voyage* in the hand, probably, of a copyist, with marginal additions by Dampier, British Library, Sloane MS 3236.

DANIELSSON, BENGT, *Love in the South Seas*, trans. F. H. Lyon (New York, 1956).

—— *What Happened on the Bounty*, trans. Alan Tapsell (London, 1962).

—— *Gauguin in the South Seas*, trans. Reginald Spink (London, 1965).

DARWIN, CHARLES, 'Journal and Remarks, 1832–1836', (included as vol. iii) in Robert Fitzroy, *Narrative of the Surveying Voyages of of His Majesty's Ships Adventure and Beagle, between the years 1826 and 1836, describing their Examination of the southern shores of South America, the Beagle's Circumnavigation of the Globe* (3 vols., London, 1839).

—— *Charles Darwin's Diary of the Voyage of H. M. S. 'Beagle'*, edited from the MS by Nora Barlow (Cambridge, 1933).

DATI, GIULIANO, *Lettera delle isole che ha trovato il re di Spagna* (Florence, 1493).

DAVIES JOHN, 'Mr. Davies's Journal of a Preaching Tour around Otaheite, in the Year 1816',

Quarterly Chronicle of Transactions of the London Missionary Society in the years 1815, 1816, 1817, 1818, and 1819, i (London, 1821).

—— *A Tahitian and English Dictionary, with Introductory Remarks on the Polynesian Language, and a Short Grammar of the Tahitian Dialect* (Tahiti, 1851).

——*The History of the Tahitian Mission 1799–1830*, ed. C. W. Newbury (Cambridge, 1961).

—— 'Journal of a preaching tour round Tahiti', MS, Council for World Mission archives, School of Oriental and African Studies, London, South Sea Journals 1807–16, Box 3.

DAVIES, MARTIN, *Columbus in Italy: An Italian Versification of the Letter on the discovery of the New World* (London, 1991).

DAWSON, RAYMOND, *The Chinese Chameleon: An Analysis of European Conceptions of China* (London, 1967).

[DEFOE, DANIEL], *A True Relation of the Apparition of one Mrs. Veal* (London, 1706).

[——] *An Essay on the South-Sea Trade* (London, 1712).

[——?] *An Historical Account of the Voyages and Adventures of Sir Walter Raleigh* (London, 1719).

[——] *The Life and Strange Surprizing Adventures of Robinson Crusoe, of York, Mariner* (London, 1719).

[——] *Serious Relections during the Life and Suprising Adventures of Robinson Crusoe* (London, 1720).

[——] *The Life, Adventures, and Pyracies, Of the Famous Captain Singleton* (London, 1720).

[——] *A New Voyage Round the World* (London, 1725).

—— 'On Learning', in W. Lee, *Daniel Defoe: His Life, and Recently Discovered Writings* (3 vols.; London, 1869), iii.

—— 'The Compleat English Gentleman', in *Selected Writings*, ed. J. T. Boulton (Cambridge, 1975).

DEHÉRAIN, HENRI, 'Le Voyage de François Leguat dans l'Océan Indien (1690–1698) est-il imaginaire?', *Comité des Travaux historiques et scientifiques, Bulletin de la section de géographie*, 41 (1926), 159–77.

DELANO, AMASA, *A Narrative of Voyages and Travels, in the Northern and Southern Hemispheres* (Boston, 1817).

DELILLE, JACQUES, *Les Jardins, ou l'art d'embellir les paysages* (Paris, 1782).

DENING, GREG, *Islands and Beaches: Discourse on a Silent Land: Marquesas 1774–1880* (Honolulu, 1980).

DESCARTES, RENÉ, *Discours de la méthode*, in *Œuvres et lettres de Descartes*, ed. A. Bridoux (Pléiade edn., 1953).

DESMOULINS, CAMILLE, *Correspondance inédite de Camille Desmoulins*, ed. M. Matton (Paris, 1836).

DÍAZ DEL CASTILLO, BERNAL, *The True History of the Conquest of New Spain*, trans. A. P. Maudslay (5 vols.; London, 1908–16).

DICKINSON, R. E. and HOWARTH, O. J. R., *The Making of Geography* (Oxford, 1933).

DICKS, D. R., *Early Greek Astronomy to Aristotle* (Bristol, 1970).

Dictionary of National Biography, The, ed. Leslie Stephen and Sidney Lee (London, 1885–1911).

[DIDEROT, DENIS], 'Jouissance', *Encyclopédie, ou dictionnaire raisonné des sciences, des arts et des métiers*, viii (Neuchâtel, 1765).

—— *Les Bijoux indiscrets*, in *Œuvres de Denis Diderot*, publiées, sur les manuscrits de l'auteur, par Jacques-André Naigeon (15 vols.; Paris, 1798), x.

[DIDEROT, DENIS], *Supplément au voyage de Bougainville, ou dialogue entre A et B, sur l'inconvénient d'attacher des idées morales à certaines actions physiques qui n'en comportent pas* (publié d'après le manuscrit de Leningrad), ed. G. Chinard (Paris, 1935).

—— *Correspondance*, ed. Georges Roth (16 vols.; Paris, 1955–70).

DILLON, PETER, *Narrative and Successful Result of a Voyage in the South Seas, performed by order of the Government of British India, to ascertain the actual fate of La Pérouse's Expedition* (2 vols.; London, 1829).

DIODORUS SICULUS, *Library of History*, trans. C. H. Oldfather *et al.* (12 vols.; Loeb edn., 1933–67).

DIOGENES LAERTIUS, *The Lives of the Philosophers*, trans. R. D. Hicks (2 vols.; Loeb edn., 1925).

DOTTIN, PAUL, *Robinson Crusoe Examin'd and Criticis'd or A New Edition of Charles Gildon's Famous Pamphlet now Published with an Introduction and Explanatory Notes together with an Essay on Gildon's Life* (London, 1923).

Douglas Jerrold's Shilling Magazine (review of Melville's *Narrative of a Four Months' Residence*), 3 (Jan.–June 1846), 380–3.

DOWNIE, J. A., 'Defoe, Imperialism, and the Travel Books Reconsidered', *Yearbook of English Studies*, 12 (1983) 66–83.

DRAYTON, MICHAEL, *Poems* (London, 1619).

DRURY, ROBERT, *Madagascar: or, Robert Drury's Journal, during Fifteen Years Captivity on that Island* (London, 1729).

DRYDEN, E. A., 'Portraits of the Artist as a Young Man', in Milton R. Stern (ed.), *Critical Essays on Herman Melville's 'Typee'* (Boston, 1982).

DRYDEN, JOHN, *The Kind Keeper; or, Mr. Limberham* (London, 1680).

D[UNCOMBE], W[ILLIAM], 'An Account of William Benbow, son to the Admiral', *Gentleman's Magazine*, 39 (April 1769), 171–2.

DUNMORE, JOHN, *French Explorers in the Pacific*, i. *The Eighteenth Century* (Oxford, 1965), ii. *The Nineteenth Century* (Oxford, 1969).

—— 'The Explorer and the Philosopher: Diderot's *Supplément* and Giradoux's *Supplément*', in W. Veit (ed.), *Captain James Cook: Image and Impact* (Melbourne, 1972).

DU QUESNE, HENRI, *Un projet de république à l'île d'Eden (l'île Bourbon) en 1689. Réimpression d'un ouvrage disparu, publié en 1689, intitulé: Recueil de quelques mémoires servans d'instruction pour l'établissement de l'isle d'Eden. Précédé d'une notice, par Th. Sauzier* (Paris, 1887).

DU RIETZ, ROLF E., 'Note sur l'histoire des manuscrits de James Morrison', in James Morrison, *Journal de James Morrison*, trans. B. Jaunez (Paris, 1966), pp. ix–xiii.

—— *Fresh Light on John Fryer of the 'Bounty'* (Uppsala, 1981).

—— *Peter Heywood's Tahitian Vocabulary and the Narratives by James Morrison: Some Notes on their Origin and History* (Uppsala, 1986).

EARLE, PETER, *The World of Defoe* (London, 1976).

EDDY, W. A., *'Gulliver's Travels': A Critical Study* (Princeton, 1923).

EDEN, RICHARD, ed. and trans., *The Decades of the newe worlde or west India* (London, 1555).

—— ed. and trans., *The History of Travayle in the West and East Indies* (London, 1577).

EDWARDS, EDWARD, report from 'Batavia, the 25th November, 1791', in *Voyage of H.M.S. 'Pandora'*, ed. Basil Thomson (London, 1915).

—— log of the *Pandora*, MS, Ministry of Defence Library, London, © Crown Copyright/ MOD. Reproduced with the permission of the Controller of HMSO.

ELLIOTT, J. H., *The Discovery of America and the Discovery of Man* (London, 1972).

ELLIOTT, J. H., *The Old World and the New, 1492–1650* (Cambridge, 1972).

ELLIOTT, R. C., 'The Satirist Satirized', in Frank Brady (ed.), *Twentieth Century Interpretations of 'Gulliver's Travels'* (Englewood Cliffs, NJ, 1968), 41–53.

ELLIS, F. H. (ed.), *Twentieth Century Interpretations of 'Robinson Crusoe'* (Englewood Cliffs, NJ, 1969).

ELLIS, JOHN E., *Life of William Ellis* (London, 1873).

ELLIS, R. L., Preface to Bacon, 'Sylva Sylvarum', *The Works of Francis Bacon*, ed. James Spedding, R. L. Ellis, and D. D. Heath (14 vols.; London, 1857–74), i.

ELLIS, WILLIAM, *A Vindication of the South Sea Missions from the Misrepresentations of Otto von Kotzebue* (London, 1831).

—— *Polynesian Researches* (4 vols.; London, 1832–4).

Encyclopaedia Britannica (29 vols.; Cambridge, 1910–11).

An Epistle from Mr. Banks, Voyager, Monster-hunter, and Amoroso, to Oberea, Queen of Otaheite. Transfused by A.B.C. Esq. Second Professor of the Otaheite, and of every other unknown Tongue [London, 1773?].

ESPENBERG, CHARLES, 'Journal of the Voyage from Brazil to Kamchatka; extracted from a Letter of Dr. Espenberg, dated the Harbour of St. Peter and St. Paul, August 24, 1804', *Philosophical Magazine*, 22 (1805), 4–13, 115–23.

EVELYN, JOHN, Dedication to *Instructions Concerning Erecting of a Library*, trans. by Evelyn from the French of Gabriel Naudeus (London, 1661).

—— *The Diary*, ed. E. S. de Beer (6 vols.; Oxford, 1955).

Far Eastern Economic Review, The [UTA advertisement] (25 Mar. 1972).

FEIJOO Y MONTENEGRO, BENITO GERÓNIMO, *Theatro crítico universal, o discursos varios en todo genero de materias, para desengaño de errores comunes* (9 vols.; Madrid, 1733–40).

FELIX, JOHN HENRY, NUNES, LESLIE, and SENECAL, PETER F., *The 'Ukulele: A Portuguese Gift to Hawaii* (Honolulu, 1980).

FÉNELON, FRANÇOIS DE SALIGNAC DE LA MOTHE-, *The Adventures of Telemachus, the Son of Ulysses*, trans. John Hawkesworth (2 vols.; London, 1795).

FERGUSON, JOHN, *Utopias of the Classical World* (London, 1975).

FERNÁNDEZ DE OVIEDO, GONZALO, *Historia general y natural de las Indias*, ed. Juan Pérez de Tudela Bueso (5 vols.; Madrid, 1959).

FESCHE, CHARLES-FÉLIX, 'Journal de Fesche', in *Bougainville et ses compagnons*, ed. Taillemite, ii.

FINLEY, JOHN H., Jr., *Homer's Odyssey* (Cambridge, Mass., 1978).

FINLEY, M. I., *The World of Odysseus* (Penguin 2nd rev. edn., 1979).

[FOIGNY, GABRIEL], *La Terre Australe connue: c'est à dire, la description de ce pays inconnu jusqu'ici, de ces moeurs & de ces coûtumes. Par Mr Sadeur, avec les avantures qui le conduisirent en ce continent, & les particularitez du sejour qu'il y fit durant trente-cinq ans & plus, & de son retour. Reduites & mises en lumiere par les soins & la conduite de G. de F.* (Vannes, 1676).

FORD, W. C., *The Isle of Pines 1668: An Essay in Bibliography* (Boston, 1920).

FORSYTHE, ROBERT S., 'Herman Melville in Honolulu', *New England Quarterly*, 8/1 (Mar. 1935), 99–105.

—— 'Herman Melville in the Marquesas', *Philological Quarterly*, 15/1 (Jan. 1936), 1–15.

FRACASTORO, GIROLAMO, *Syphilus sive Morbus Gallicus* (Verona, 1530).

FRANTZ, R. W., 'Swift's Yahoos and the Voyagers', *Modern Philology*, 29 (Aug. 1931), 49–57.

—— 'Gulliver's "Cousin Sympson"', *Huntington Library Quarterly*, 1 (1938), 329–34.

FRANTZ, R. W., *The English Traveller and the Movement of Ideas, 1660–1732* (repr. New York, 1968).

FRAZER, JAMES G., *The Belief in Immortality and the Worship of the Dead* (3 vols.; London, 1913–24).

FREEMAN, DEREK, *Margaret Mead and Samoa: The Making and Unmaking of an Anthropological Myth* (Cambridge, Mass., 1983).

FRESCHOT, C., *Nouvelle relation de la ville & république de Venise* (Utrecht, 1709).

FRIEDMAN, JOHN B., *The Monstrous Races in Medieval Art and Thought* (Cambridge, Mass., 1981).

FRYER, JOHN, *Journal*, in *The Voyage of the Bounty's Launch as Related in William Bligh's Despatch to the Admiralty and the Journal of John Fryer*, ed. O. Rutter (London, 1934).

FURBANK, P. N., and OWENS, W. R., *The Canonisation of Daniel Defoe* (New Haven, Conn., 1988).

FURNAS, F. C., *Anatomy of Paradise: Hawaii and the Islands of the South Seas* (London, 1950).

GALLEGO, HERNANDO, 'A True and Correct Account of the Voyage to the Western Isles in the Southern Ocean', trans. in *The Discovery of the Solomon Islands*, ed. Lord Amherst of Hackney and B. Thomson (2 vols.; London, 1901), i.

GARAGNON, JEAN, 'French Imaginary Voyages to Austral Lands in the Seventeenth and Eighteenth Centuries', in Ian Donaldson (ed.), *Australia and the European Imagination* (Canberra, 1982).

GAUTIER, JEAN, 'Tahiti dans la littérature française à la fin du XVIIIᵉ siècle: quelques ouvrages oubliés', *Journal de la Société des Océanistes*, 3 (1947), 43–56.

GAY, PETER, *The Enlightenment: An Interpretation* (2 vols.; London, 1973).

General Evening Post, 21–3 July 1774; 26–8 July 1774; 16–18 March 1790.

Gentleman's Magazine ('A Voyage round the World in his Majesty's Ship Dolphin'), 37 (April 1767), 147–51.

—— ('Epitome of Capt. Wallis's Voyage round the World' and 'Epitome of the Voyage round the World by Lieutenant Cook, accompanied by Mr. Banks and Dr. Solander'), 43 (Sept. 1773), 417–23; (Oct. 1773), 484–91; (Nov. 1773), 536–43; (Dec. 1773), 589–96.

—— (review of *A Voyage towards the South Pole*), 47 (Oct. 1777), 491–4.

—— ('Particulars of the late Execution on-board the *Brunswick*'), 62 (Dec. 1792), 1097–8.

GILDON, CHARLES, Letter 'To Dr. R. B.——of a God', in Charles Blount, 'The Oracles of Reason', in *The Miscellaneous Works of Charles Blount, Esq.* (London, 1695).

[——] *The Life and Strange Surprizing Adventures of Mr. D——DeF—, of London, Hosier* (London, 1719).

GILMAN, WILLIAM H., *Melville's Early Life and 'Redburn'* (New York, 1951).

GLANVILL, JOSEPH, 'Modern Improvements of Useful Knowledge', in *Essays on Several Important Subjects in Philosophy and Religion* (London, 1676).

GOLDMAN, IRVING, *Ancient Polynesian Society* (Chicago, 1970).

GOVE, P. B., *The Imaginary Voyage in Prose Fiction: A History of its Criticism and a Guide for its Study, with an Annotated Check List of 215 Imaginary Voyages from 1700 to 1800* (New York, 1941).

GRANDIDIER, ALFRED, and GRANDIDIER, GUILLAUME, eds., *Collections des ouvrages anciens concernant Madagascar*, iv. *Les Aventures de Robert Drury* (Paris, 1906).

GRAVES, ROBERT, *The Isles of Unwisdom* (London, 1950).

GRAY, ALBERT, Introduction to William Dampier, *A New Voyage Round the World*, ed. Sir Albert Gray (London, 1927).

GREENE, RICHARD TOBIAS, to the Editor, *Buffalo Commercial Advertiser*, 1 July 1846, repr. in Herman Melville, *Correspondence*, ed. Lynn Horth (Chicago, 1993), 579.

—— 'Toby's Own Story', *Buffalo Commercial Advertiser*, 11 July 1846, reprinted in Herman Melville, *Correspondence*, ed. Lynn Horth (Chicago, 1993), 580–584.

GROUSSET, RENÉ, *Histoire de l'Asie* (3 vols.; Paris, 1921–2).

GROVE-DAY, A., *Pacific Islands Literature: One Hundred Basic Books* (Honolulu, 1971).

GUERRA, GIORGIO DEL, *Rustichello da Pisa* (Pisa, 1955).

GUERRA, FRANCISCO, 'The Problem of Syphilis', in F. Chiappelli (ed.), *First Images of America: The Impact of the New World on the Old* (2 vols.; Berkeley, Calif., 1976), ii. 845–52.

GUNSON, NIEL, 'A Note on the Difficulties of Ethnohistorical Writing, with Special Reference to Tahiti', *Journal of the Polynesian Society*, 72 (1963), 415–19.

GUTHRIE, W. K. C., *A History of Greek Philosophy* (6 vols.; Cambridge, 1962–81).

HACHISUKA, MASAUJI, *The Dodo and Kindred Birds, or, The Extinct Birds of the Mascarene Islands* (London, 1953).

HAKLUYT, RICHARD, *The Principal Navigations, Voyages, Traffiques and Discoveries of the English Nation* (12 vols.; Glasgow, 1903–5).

HALE, J. R., *Renaissance Exploration* (London, 1968).

HALL, JOSEPH, *Mundus Alter et Idem*, trans. J. Healey as *The Discovery of a New World*, ed. H. Brown (Cambridge, Mass., 1937).

HAMILTON, GEORGE, *A Voyage Round the World, in His Majesty's Frigate Pandora* (Berwick, 1793).

HANDY, E. S. C., *Polynesian Religion*, Bernice P. Bishop Museum Bulletin 34 (Honolulu, 1927).

HANDY W. C., *Tattooing in the Marquesas*, Bernice P. Bishop Museum Bulletin 1 (Honolulu, 1922).

HANNO, 'The Periplus of Hanno', in *The Ancient Fragments*, ed. I. P. Cory (London, 1828).

[HARTLIB, SAMUEL], *A Description of the Famous Kingdome of Macaria* (London, 1641).

HASSALL, CHRISTOPHER, *Rupert Brooke: A Biography* (London, 1964).

HAVENS, G. R., 'Diderot, Rousseau, and the *Discours sur l'inégalité*', *Diderot Studies*, 3 (1961), 219–62.

H[AWEIS], [Revd] T[HOMAS], 'The very probable success of a proper Mission to the South Sea Islands', *Evangelical Magazine* (July 1795).

—— 'Sermon I. The Apostolic Commission, preached at the Spa Fields Chapel, September 22, 1795', in *Sermons Preached in London, at the formation of the Missionary Society, September 22, 23, 24, 1795* (London, 1795).

—— 'A Memoir on the Most Eligible Part to Begin a Mission, and the most probable means of accomplishing it: being the Substance of a Discourse delivered in Surry-Street Chapel, before the Missionary Society, September 24, 1795', in *Sermons Preached*.

—— 'A Journal of a Visit to Portsmouth and its Environs, in the Ship Duff with the Missionaries, who were embarked for the South Seas', MS, Council for World Mission archives, School of Oriental and African Studies, London, South Sea Journals, Box 1.

HAWKESWORTH, JOHN, *An Account of the Voyages undertaken by the order of his present Majesty for making Discoveries in the Southern Hemisphere, And successively performed by Commodore Byron, Captain Wallis, Captain Carteret, and Captain Cook, in the Dolphin, the Swallow, and the Endeavour: drawn up from the Journals which were kept by the several Commanders, And from the Papers of Joseph Banks, Esq.* (3 vols.; London, 1773).

HAWKESWORTH, JOHN, *Relation des voyages entrepris par ordre de Sa Majesté Britannique, pour faire des découvertes dans l'hémisphere méridional* . . . (4 vols.; Lausanne and Neuchâtel, 1774).

HAWKS, HENRY, 'A Relation of the commodities of Nova Hispania, and the maners of the inhabitants, written by Henry Hawks merchant, which lived five yeeres in the sayd countrey', in Richard Hakluyt, *The Principal Navigations, Voyages, Traffiques and Discoveries of the English Nation* (12 vols.; Glasgow, 1903–5), ix.

HAZARD, PAUL, *La Crise de la conscience européenne, 1630–1715* (Paris, 1935).

HEFLIN, WILSON L., 'Melville's Third Whaler', *Modern Language Notes* (Apr. 1949), 241–5.

HENRY, TEUIRA, *Ancient Tahiti* (Honolulu, 1928).

H[ENRY], W[ILLIAM], 'Lines composed on the building of a Christian Church, in the District of Papetoai, Island of Eimeo; upon the ruins of the Royal Marae in that District', Eimeo, 21 May 1822, MS, Council for World Mission archives, School of Oriental and African Studies, London, South Sea Letters, Box 3.

HERBERT, T. WALTER, Jr., *Marquesan Encounters: Melville and the Meaning of Civilization* (Cambridge, Mass., 1980).

HERODOTUS, *The Histories*, trans. A. de Selincourt (Penguin edn., 1954).

HERRMANN, P., *Conquest by Man: The Saga of Early Exploration and Discovery*, trans. M. Bullock (London, 1954).

HESIOD, *Works and Days*, trans. D. Wender (Penguin edn., 1973).

HEUVELMANS, BERNARD, *On the Track of Unknown Animals*, trans. Rupert Hart-Davis (London, 1970).

HEYWOOD, PETER, to Edward Christian, 5 Nov. 1792, published in the *Cumberland Packet*, 20 Nov. 1792, reprinted in William Bligh, *An Answer to Certain Assertions*.

—— 'Extracts from Peter Heywood's Journal', MS, Ministry of Defence Library, London, Papers of Edward Edwards. © Crown Copyright/MOD. Reproduced with the permission of the Controller of HMSO.

HILL, CHRISTOPHER, *The World Turned Upside Down* (Penguin edn., 1975).

An Historic Epistle, from Omiah, to the Queen of Otaheite; being his Remarks on the English Nation. With Notes by the Editor (London, 1775).

HOARE, PRINCE, *Memoirs of Granville Sharp, Esq. composed from his own Manuscripts and other Authentic Documents* (London, 1820).

HOBBES, THOMAS, *Leviathan or the Matter, Forme and Power of a Commonwealth Ecclesiasticall and Civil* (London, 1651).

HODGEN, MARGARET T., *Early Anthropology in the Sixteenth and Seventeenth Centuries* (repr. Philadelphia, 1971).

[HOFFMAN, CHARLES FENNO], review of *Typee*, New York *Gazette and Times* (30 March, 1846), in *Melville*, ed. Branch, 68–70.

HOMER, *The Iliad*, trans. A. T. Murray (2 vols.; Loeb edn., 1925).

—— *The Odyssey*, trans. E. V. Rieu (Penguin edn., repr. 1981).

HONOUR, HUGH, *The New Golden Land: European Images of America* (New York, 1975).

—— *Romanticism* (London, 1979).

HORACE, *Odes and Epodes*, trans. C. E. Bennett (Loeb edn., rev. 1927).

—— *Odes*, trans. J. Michie (London, 1964).

HOUSTON, NEAL B., 'Fletcher Christian and "The Rime of the Ancient Mariner"', *Dalhousie Review*, 45 (Winter 1965–6), 431–46.

HOWARD, D. R., *Writers and Pilgrims: Medieval Pilgrimage Narratives and their Posterity* (Berkeley, Calif., 1980).

HOWARD, LEON, *Herman Melville: A Biography* (Berkeley, Calif., 1951).

HULME, PETER, *Colonial Encounters: Europe and the native Caribbean, 1492–1797* (London 1986).

HUMBOLDT, ALEXANDER VON, *Voyage aux régions équinoxiales du nouveau continent* (3 vols.; Paris, 1814).

HUNTER, J. PAUL, *The Reluctant Pilgrim: Defoe's Emblematic Method and Quest for Form in 'Robinson Crusoe'* (Baltimore, 1966).

HUSE, WILLIAM, 'A Noble Savage on the Stage', *Modern Philology*, 33 (1936), 303–16.

JACK, J. H., '*A New Voyage Round the World*: Defoe's "Roman à Thèse"', *Huntington Library Quarterly*, 24 (1960–1), 323–36.

JACK-HINTON, C., *The Search for the Islands of Solomon, 1567–1838* (Oxford, 1969).

JACQUIER, H., 'Jeanne Baret, la première femme autour du monde', *Bulletin de la Société des Études Océaniennes*, 12/141 (1962), 150–6.

JAMES, M. R., 'Swift's Copy of Dampier', *Times Literary Supplement*, (26 Feb. 1925), 138.

JAMES, W. T., 'Nostalgia for Paradise: Terra Australis in the Seventeenth Century', in I. Donaldson (ed.), *Australia and the European Imagination* (Canberra, 1982).

JANCEY, MERYL, *Mappa Mundi: The Map of the World in Hereford Cathedral: A Brief Guide* (Hereford, 1987).

JEFFERSON, JOHN, letter for the Society, Otaheite, 1 Feb. 1799, MS, Council for World Mission archives, School of Oriental and African Studies, London, South Sea Letters, Box 1.

—— et al., 'A Journal of the Missionaries proceedings on Otaheite 1800', MS, Council for World Mission archives, School of Oriental and African Studies, London, South Sea Journals, Box 1.

—— et al., 'A Journal of the Missionaries Proceedings on Otaheite 1802–1803', MS, Council for World Mission archives, School of Oriental and African Studies, London, South Sea Journals, Box 1.

JENNY (TEEHUTEATUAONOA), Narrative in *United Service Journal* (1829), pt. II. 589–93.

JIMACK, PETER, *Diderot: Supplément au voyage de Bougainville* (London, 1988).

JODELLE, ÉTIENNE, 'Ode à M. Thevet', in André Thevet, *Les Singularitez de la France Antarctique, autremont nommée Amerique* (Paris, 1558).

[JOHNSON, SAMUEL], Preface, *A Voyage to Abyssinia by Father Jerome Lobo . . . A Portuguese Jesuit . . . From the French*, trans. Samuel Johnson from the French translation by Le Grand (London, 1735).

—— *A Dictionary of the English Language* (2 vols.; London, 1755).

—— *The History of Rasselas*, ed. G. Tillotson and B. Jenkins (London, 1971).

JOHNSTONE, ARTHUR, *Recollections of Robert Louis Stevenson in the Pacific* (London, 1905).

JONES, H. M., *O Strange New World: American Culture: The Formative Years* (New York, 1964).

JONES, R. F., *Ancients and Moderns: A Study of the Rise of the Scientific Movement in Seventeenth Century England* (St Louis, Mo., 1961).

JONSON, BEN, *The Alchemist*, ed. F. H. Mares (London, 1971).

JOPPIEN, RÜDIGER, 'Phillipe Jacques de Loutherbourg's Pantomime *Omai, or a Trip round the World* and the Artists of Captain Cook's Voyages', in T. C. Mitchell (ed.), *Captain Cook and the South Pacific* (London, 1979), 81–136.

Le Journal des Sçavans (review of *Histoire des Sevarambes*) (1678), 47–8.

Le Journal des Sçavans, Supplément (review of *Voyage de Leguat*) (1707), 521–8.

A Journal of a Voyage round the World (London, 1771).

JOYCE, JAMES, 'Daniel Defoe', trans. Joseph Prescott, *Buffalo Studies*, 1/1 (Dec. 1964).

KANAHELE, GEORGE S., ed., *Hawaiian Music and Musicians: An Illustrated History* (Honolulu, 1979).

KELLY, CELSUS, ed., *La Austrialia del Espíritu Santo* (2 vols.; Cambridge, 1966).

KIMBLE, G. H. T., *Geography in the Middle Ages* (London, 1938).

KING, JAMES, 'King's Journal', in *Journals of Captain Cook*, ed. Beaglehole, iii. 1361–455.

KIPPIS, A., *The Life of Captain James Cook* (London, 1788).

KNOWLES, E. H. (on Swift's debt to Sturmy), *Notes and Queries*, 4th Ser. 1 (7 March 1868), 223.

KOLBEN, PETER, *The Present State of the Cape of Good Hope; or, A Particular Account of the several Nations of the Hottentots*, trans. Guido Medley (London, 1731).

KOTZEBUE, OTTO VON, *A New Voyage Round the World, in the years 1823, 24, 25, and 26* (2 vols., London, 1830).

KRUSENSTERN, A. J. VON, *Voyage Round the World, in the years 1803, 1804, 1805, & 1806*, trans. Richard Belgrave Hoppner (2 vols.; London, 1813).

KTÊSIAS, see Ctesias.

LACH, DONALD F., *Asia in the Making of Europe* (2 vols. in 5 bks.; Chicago, 1965–77).

LA CONDAMINE, CHARLES-MARIE DE, 'Observations de Mr. de la Condamine sur l'insulaire de la Polynésie amené de l'isle de Taiti en France par Mr. de Bougainville', MS, Bibliothèque Nationale, Paris, accompanying Charles de Brosses's personal copy of his *Histoire des navigations aux terres australes*.

LA FARGE, JOHN, *Reminiscences of the South Seas* (London, 1914).

LAMONT, E. H., *Wild Life among the Pacific Islanders* (London, 1867).

LANDUCCI, S., *I filosofi e i selvaggi, 1580–1780* (Bari, 1972).

LANGSDORFF, G. H. VON, *Voyages and Travels in various Parts of the World, during the years 1803, 1804, 1805, & 1806* (2 vols.; London, 1813).

LAPÉROUSE, J.-F. DE GALAUP DE, *Voyage de La Pérouse autour du monde*, rédigé par M. L. A. Milet-Mureau (4 vols.: Paris, 1797).

—— 'Journal de Lapérouse', in *Le Voyage de Lapérouse 1785–1788: Récit et documents originaux*, ed. John Dunmore and Maurice de Brossard (2 vols.; Paris, 1985).

LAROUSSE, PIERRE, *Grand Dictionnaire universel* (17 vols.; Paris, 1864–90).

LEDYARD, JOHN, *A Journal of Captain Cook's Last Voyage* (Hartford, Conn., 1783; facsimile repr. Chicago, 1963).

LEESON, IDA, 'The Morrison Myth', *Mariner's Mirror*, 25 (1939), 433–8.

—— 'The Mutiny on the *Lucy Ann*', *Philological Quarterly*, 19/4 (Oct. 1940), 370–9.

LEFRANC, A., *Les Navigations de Pantagruel: étude sur la géographie rabelaisienne* (Geneva, 1967).

LEGUAT, FRANÇOIS, *Voyage et avantures de François Leguat et de ses compagnons, en deux isles desertes des Indes Orientales* (2 vols.; London, 1708 [1707?]).

—— *A New Voyage to the East-Indies by Francis Leguat and His Companions* (London, 1708).

—— *The Voyage of François Leguat*, ed. Pasfield Oliver (2 vols.; London, 1891).

LEIBBRANDT, H. C. V., *Precis of the Archives of the Cape of Good Hope: Letters Received, 1695–1708* (Capetown, 1896).

LEROY, AIMÉ, and DINAUX, ARTHUR, eds., *Les Hommes et les choses du Nord de la France et du Midi de la Belgique* (Valenciennes, 1829).

LÉRY, JEAN DE, *Histoire d'un voyage fait en la terre du Bresil, autremont dite Amerique* (La Rochelle, 1578).

Letters from Mr. Fletcher Christian, containing a Narrative of the Transactions on board His Majesty's Ship Bounty, Before and After the Mutiny, with his subsequent Voyages and Travels in South America (London, 1796).

LETTS, M., *Sir John Mandeville: The Man and his Book* (London, 1949).

LEVIN, HARRY, *The Myth of the Golden Age in the Renaissance* (New York, 1972).

LÉVI-STRAUSS, CLAUDE, *Anthropologie structurale deux* (Paris, 1973).

LEYDA, JAY, *The Melville Log: A Documentary Life of Herman Melville, 1819–1891* (2 vols.; New York, 1969).

LITTLE, BRYAN, *Crusoe's Captain: Being the Life of Woodes Rogers, Seaman, Trader, Colonial Governor* (London, 1960).

LLOYD, CHRISTOPHER, *William Dampier* (London, 1966).

LOCKE, JOHN, *An Essay Concerning Humane Understanding* (London, 1690).

—— *Mr. Locke's Reply to the Right Reverend the Lord Bishop of Worcester's Answer to his Second Letter* (London, 1699).

—— *Two Treatises of Government*, ed. Peter Laslett (New York, 1965).

LONDON, JACK, *The Cruise of the Snark* (New York, 1908).

LÓPEZ DE GÓMARA, FRANCISCO, *Historia General de las Indias* (2 vols.; Madrid, 1922).

[LOTI, PIERRE (Julien Viaud)], *Le Mariage de Loti—Rarahu* (Paris, 1880).

—— *Le Roman d'un enfant* (Paris, 1890).

—— *Journal intime, 1878–1881*, ed. Samuel Viaud (Paris, 1925).

—— *Correspondance inédite 1865–1904*, ed. Nadine Duvignaux and N. Serban (Paris, 1929).

—— 'Journal intime de Pierre Loti à Tahiti', ed. André Ropiteau, in *Bulletin de la Société d'Etudes Océaniennes*, 5/50 (Mar., 1934), 291–332.

—— *Cent dessins de Pierre Loti*, commentés par Claude Farrère (Tours, 1948).

LOVEJOY, A. O., *Essays in the History of Ideas* (New York, 1955).

—— and BOAS, G., *Primitivism and Related Ideas in Antiquity* (Baltimore, 1935).

LOVETT, RICHARD, *The History of the London Missionary Society 1795–1895* (2 vols.; London, 1899).

LOWES, JOHN LIVINGSTON, *The Road to Xanadu: A Study in the Ways of the Imagination* (Boston, 1927).

LUCE, J. V., 'The Wanderings of Ulysses', in W. B. Stanford and J. V. Luce, *The Quest for Ulysses* (London, 1974).

[LUCETT, EDWARD], *Rovings in the Pacific, from 1837 to 1849, with a Glance at California. By a Merchant long Resident at Tahiti* (2 vols.; London, 1851).

LUCIAN, *A True Story*, in *Works*, trans. A. M. Harmon and M. D. Macleod (8 vols.; Loeb edn., 1913–67).

MACK, JAMES D., *Matthew Flinders 1774–1814* (Melbourne, 1966).

MACKANESS, GEORGE, *The Life of Vice-Admiral William Bligh* (rev. edn., London, 1951).

MACKAY, DAVID, *In the Wake of Cook: Exploration, Science and Empire, 1780–1801* (London, 1985).

MACKAY, MARGARET, *The Violent Friend: The Story of Mrs Robert Louis Stevenson 1840–1914* (abridged edn., London 1970).

MALINOWSKI, BRONISLAW, *Argonauts of the Western Pacific: An Account of Native Enterprise and Adventure in the Archipelagoes of Melanesian New Guinea* (London, 1922).

MALONE, EDMOND, in James Prior, *Life of Edmond Malone, editor of Shakespeare, with selections from his Manuscript Anecdotes* (London, 1860).

Mandeville's Travels, ed. M. C. Seymour (Oxford, 1967).

Mandeville's Travels, ed. M. C. Seymour (London, 1968).

MANWARING, G. E., *My Friend the Admiral: The Life, Letters, and Journals of Rear-Admiral James Burney* (London, 1931).

MANUEL, F. E., and MANUEL, F. P., 'Sketch for a Natural History of Paradise', *Daedalus* (Winter 1972).

—— *Utopian Thought in the Western World* (Oxford, 1979).

MARDEN, LUIS, 'Tragic Sequel to *Bounty* Mutiny: Wreck of the *Pandora* Found on Australia's Great Barrier Reef', *National Geographic Magazine* (Oct. 1985), 423 ff.

MARTELLI, GEORGE, *Jemmy Twitcher: A Life of the Fourth Earl of Sandwich 1718–1792* (London, 1962).

MARTIN, JOHN, *An Account of the Natives of the Tonga Islands, in the South Pacific Ocean. With an original grammar and vocabulary of their language. Compiled and arranged from the extensive communications of Mr. William Mariner* (2 vols.; London, 1817).

MARTIN-ALLANIC, J. E., *Bougainville navigateur et les découvertes de son temps* (2 vols.; Paris, 1964).

MARTIRE D'ANGHIERA, PIETRO (Peter Martyr), *The Decades of the newe worlde or west India*, trans. Richard Eden (London, 1555).

MATHER, COTTON, *The Wonders of the Invisible World* (Boston, 1693).

—— *Magnalia Christi Americana*, ed. K. B. Murdock (Cambridge, Mass., 1977).

MAUDE, H. E., *Of Islands and Men: Studies in Pacific History* (Melbourne, 1968).

—— 'Baiteke and Binoka of Abemama: arbiters of change in the Gilbert Islands', in J. W. Davidson & Deryck Scarr (eds.), *Pacific Island Portraits* (Canberra, 1970).

MAUGHAM, WILLIAM SOMERSET, *The Trembling of a Leaf: Little Stories of the South Sea Islands* (London, 1921).

—— *A Writer's Notebook* (London, 1949).

McARTHUR, NORMA, *Island Populations of the Pacific* (Canberra, 1967).

McCLURE, SAMUEL S., *My Autobiography* (London, 1914).

McCORMICK, E. H., *Omai, Pacific Envoy* (Auckland, 1977).

McGAW, MARTHA M., *Stevenson in Hawaii* ([1950] reprinted Westport, Conn., 1978).

McKAY, GEORGE L., *A Stevenson Library: Catalogue of a Collection of Writings by and about Robert Louis Stevenson formed by Edwin J. Beinecke* (6 vols.; New Haven, 1951–64).

MEAD, MARGARET, *Coming of Age in Samoa: A Psychological Study of Primitive Youth for Western Civilization* (London, 1929).

MÉGROZ, R. L., *The Real Robinson Crusoe, Being the Life and Strange Surprising Adventures of Alexander Selkirk of Largo, Fife, Mariner* (London, 1939).

MELVILLE, GANSEVOORT, *London Journal*, ed. Hershel Parker (New York, 1966).

MELVILLE, HERMAN, *Narrative of a Four Months' Residence Among the Natives of a Valley of the Marquesas Islands; or, A Peep at Polynesian Life* (London, 1846).

—— *Typee: A Peep at Polynesian Life*, ed. H. Hayford, H. Parker, and G. T. Tanselle (Chicago, 1968).

—— *Omoo: A Narrative of Adventures in the South Seas*, ed. H. Hayford, H. Parker, and G. T. Tanselle (Chicago, 1968).

—— *Omoo: A Narrative of Adventures in the South Seas*, ed. H. Hayford and W. Blair (New York, 1969).

—— *Moby-Dick*, ed. H. Hayford, H. Parker, and G. T. Tanselle (Chicago, 1988).

—— *Correspondence*, ed. Lynn Horth (Chicago, 1993).

—— 'First Draught of Typee', MS, New York Public Library, Melville Family Papers.

MENARD, WILMON, *The Two Worlds of Somerset Maugham* (Los Angeles, 1965).

MENIKOFF, BARRY, *Robert Louis Stevenson and 'The Beach of Falesá': A Study in Victorian Publishing, with the Original Text* (Edinburgh, 1984).

MILNE-EDWARDS, ALPHONSE, 'Notes from a Memoir on the Ancient Fauna of the Mascarene Islands', in Leguat, *The Voyage of François Leguat*, ed. Oliver, ii.

MILTON, JOHN, 'An Apology Against a Pamphlet', in *Complete Prose Works* (8 vols., New Haven, Conn., 1953–74), i. 867–953.

—— *Paradise Lost*, ed. A. Fowler (London, 1971).

MINET, HUGHES, MS marginalia, British Library copy of Robert Drury, *The Adventures of Robert Drury, during fifteen years captivity on the island of Madagascar* (Hull, 1807).

MINTO, WILLIAM, *A Manual of English Prose Literature* (Edinburgh, 1872).

MISSON, MAXIMILIEN, *A New Voyage to Italy* (4th edn., 2 vols.; London, 1714).

MITFORD, MARY RUSSELL, *Christina, the Maid of the South Seas; a Poem* (London, 1811).

—— in *The Life of Mary Russell Mitford, Related in a Selection from her Letters to her Friends*, ed. A. G. L'Estrange (3 vols.; London, 1870).

MOERENHOUT, J. A., *Voyages aux îles du Grand Océan* (2 vols.; Paris, 1837).

MONTAGU, ELIZABETH, in *Mrs. Montagu, 'Queen of the Blues': Her Letters and Friendships from 1762 to 1800*, ed. Reginald Blunt (2 vols.; London, n.d.).

MONTAIGNE, MICHEL DE, *The Essayes*, trans. John Florio (London, 1603).

—— *Essais*, ed. M. Rat (3 vols.; Paris, 1948).

—— *Les Essais*, ed. P. Villey and V.-L. Saulnier (Paris, 1965).

[MONTESQUIEU, CHARLES DE SECONDAT, Baron de], *Letters persanes* (2nd edn., 2 vols.; Cologne, 1721).

MONTGOMERIE, H. S., *The Morrison Myth* (London, 1938).

—— 'The Morrison Myth', *Mariner's Mirror*, 27 (1941), 69–76.

Monthly Review; or Literary Journal (review-account of Hawkesworth, *Voyages*), 49 (Aug. 1773), 136–45; (Oct. 1773), 289–304; (Nov. 1773), 355–69; (Dec. 1773), 479–98.

—— (review of *Adventures of Robert Drury* (1807)), 63 (Sept. 1810), 110–11.

MOORE, JOHN R., *Defoe in the Pillory and Other Studies* (Bloomington, Ind., 1939).

—— 'A New Source for *Gulliver's Travels*', *Studies in Philology*, 38 (1941), 66–80.

—— 'The Geography of *Gulliver's Travels*', *Journal of English and Germanic Philology*, 40 (1942), 214–28.

—— *Defoe's Sources for 'Robert Drury's Journal'* (Bloomington, Ind., 1943).

—— 'The Tempest and Robinson Crusoe', *Review of English Studies*, 21 (1945), 52–6.

—— *A Checklist of the Writings of Daniel Defoe* (rev. edn., Bloomington, Ind., 1971).

MOOREHEAD, ALAN, *The Fatal Impact: An Account of the Invasion of the South Pacific 1767–1840* (Penguin edn., 1968).

MOORMAN, MARY, *William Wordsworth: A Biography: The Early Years* (Oxford, 1957).

MORE, Sir THOMAS, *The Utopia of Sir Thomas More, in Latin from the edition of March 1518, and in English from the first edition of Ralph Robynson's translation in 1551*, ed. J. H. Lupton (Oxford, 1895).

MORISON, SAMUEL, E., *Admiral of the Ocean Sea: A Life of Christopher Columbus* (2 vols.; Boston, 1942).

Morning Chronicle (review of *Omai*), 21 Dec. 1785.

MORRISON, JAMES, *The Journal of James Morrison Boatswain's Mate of the Bounty*, ed. O. Rutter (London, 1935).

MORRISON, JAMES, 'Memorandum and Particulars respecting the Bounty and her Crew', MS, Mitchell Library, Sydney.

—— to William Howell, 10 Oct. 1792, MS, Mitchell Library, Sydney.

MÜHLL, EMANUEL VON DER, *Denis Veiras et son Histoire des Sévarambes* (Paris, 1938).

MUNILLA, MARTÍN DE, 'Journal', trans. in *La Austrialia del Espíritu Santo*, ed. C. Kelly (2 vols.; Cambridge, 1966), i.

NASSAU-SIEGEN, CHARLES-NICOLAS DE, 'Journal de Nassau-Siegen', in *Bougainville et ses compagnons*, ed. Taillemite, ii.

Navigatio Sancti Brendani, as given in *The Anglo-Norman Voyage of St. Brendan*, ed. E. G. R. Waters (Oxford, 1928).

[NEVILLE, HENRY], *The Isle of Pines, or, A late Discovery of a fourth Island in Terra Australis, Incognita* (London, 1668).

[——] *The Isle of Pines, or, A late Discovery of a fourth Island near Terra Australis, Incognita by Henry Cornelius Van Sloetten* (London, 1668).

NEWBURY, COLIN, *Tahiti Nui: Change and Survival in French Polynesia 1767–1945* (Honolulu, 1980).

NEWTON, A. P. (ed.), *Travel and Travellers of the Middle Ages* (London, 1926).

—— (ed.), *The Great Age of Discovery* (repr. New York, 1970).

NEWTON, ALFRED, and NEWTON, EDWARD, 'Notice of a Memoir on the Osteology of the Solitaire', in Leguat, *The Voyage of François Leguat*, ed. Oliver, ii.

NEWTON, Sir EDWARD, and GADOW, HANS, 'On additional Bones of the Dodo and other Extinct Birds of Mauritius obtained by Mr. Théodore Sauzier', *Transactions of the Zoological Society of London*, 13 (London, 1895), 281–302.

NICOLSON, MARJORIE, and MOHLER, NORA M., 'The Scientific Background of Swift's "Voyage to Laputa"', *Annals of Science*, 2 (1937), 299–334.

—— 'Swift's "Flying Island" in the "Voyage to Laputa"', *Annals of Science*, 2 (1937), 405–30.

Nocturnal Revels: or, The History of King's-Place, and other Modern Nunneries (2 vols.; London, 1779).

Nouvelle Biographie Générale, ed. J. C. F. Hoefer (46 vols.; Paris, 1855–66).

NOVAK, M. E., *Economics and the Fiction of Daniel Defoe* (Berkeley, Calif., 1962).

—— 'Defoe's Theory of Fiction', *Studies in Philology*, 61 (1964), 650–68.

O'BRIEN, FREDERICK, *White Shadows in the South Seas* (London, 1919).

O'KEEFFE, JOHN, *A Short Account of the New Pantomime called Omai, or, A Trip Round the World* (London, 1785).

OLIVER, DOUGLAS, *Ancient Tahitian Society* (3 vols.; Canberra, n.d.).

OLIVER, PASFIELD, ed., *Madagascar: or, Robert Drury's Journal, during Fifteen Years Captivity on that Island* (London, 1890).

—— ed., *The Voyage of François Leguat* (2 vols.; London, 1891).

OLSCHKI, LEONARDO, 'What Columbus Saw on Landing in the West Indies', *Proceedings of the American Philosophical Society*, 84/5 (July, 1941), 633–59.

—— *Marco Polo's Asia*, trans. J. A. Scott (Berkeley, Calif., 1960).

Omiah's Farewell; Inscribed to the Ladies of London (London, 1776).

OSBOURNE, LLOYD, 'Stevenson at Thirty-nine', in R. L. Stevenson, *The Ebb-Tide: A Trio and Quartette*, in *The Works of R. L. Stevenson*, Tusitala edn., xiv (London, 1923).

'Otaheitean Journals', in *Transactions of the Missionary Society* (4 vols.; London, 1804–18).

Otaheite: A Poem (London, 1774).

OVID (Publius Ovidius Naso), *Metamorphoses*, trans. M. M. Innes (Penguin edn., 1955).

PARKINSON, SYDNEY, *A Journal of a Voyage to the South Seas, in his Majesty's Ship, the 'Endeavour'* (London, 1773).

PARKS, GEORGE B., *Richard Hakluyt and the English Voyages* (New York, 1928).

—— 'Travel as Education', in R. F. Jones *et al.*, *The Seventeenth Century: Studies in the History of English Thought and Literature from Bacon to Pope* (Stanford, Calif., 1951).

PARRY, JOHN H., *The Age of Reconnaissance* (New York, 1964).

—— ed., *The European Reconnaissance: Selected Documents* (London, 1968).

PASTOR, ANTONIO, 'Spanish Civilization in the Great Age of Discovery', in A. P. Newton (ed.), *The Great Age of Discovery*.

PEACOCK, DANIEL J., *Lee Boo of Belau: A Prince in London* (Honolulu, 1987).

PEARD, GEORGE, 'Account of the Mutiny', in 'Journal kept in H.M.S. Blossom', British Library, Additional MS 35141.

PEARSALL-SMITH, LOGAN, *Words and Idioms* (London, 1943).

PEARSON, W. H., 'European Intimidation and the Myth of Tahiti', *Journal of Pacific History*, 4 (1969), 199–217.

—— 'Hawkesworth's Alterations', *Journal of Pacific History*, 7 (1972), 45–72.

—— *Rifled Sanctuaries: Some Views of the Pacific Islands in Western Literature* (Auckland, 1984).

PENROSE, BOIES, *Travel and Discovery in the Renaissance, 1420–1620* (Cambridge, Mass., 1952).

PENZER, N. M., Preface to William Dampier, *A New Voyage*, ed. Gray.

PEREIRE, JACOB-RODRIGUE, 'Observations sur l'articulation de l'Insulaire de la mer du Sud', in Bougainville, *Voyage autour du monde*.

PFEIFFER, RUDOLF, *History of Classical Scholarship from the Beginnings to the End of the Hellenistic Age* (Oxford, 1968).

PHILLIPS, J. R. S., *The Medieval Expansion of Europe* (Oxford, 1988).

PHILLIPS, MOLESWORTH, 'Phillips's Report', in *Journals of Captain Cook*, ed. Beaglehole, iii. 534–6.

—— to Sir Joseph Banks, 12 Dec. 1792, British Library, Additional MS 33979.

Philosophical Transactions: Giving Some Accompt of the Present Undertakings, Studies, and Labours of the Ingenious in many Considerable Parts of the World (London), 1/8, (8 Jan. 1665/6).

Philosophical Transactions of the Royal Society, 168 (extra vol.) (1879).

PIGAFETTA, ANTONIO, *Magellan's Voyage Around the World*, the (Italian) Ambrosian MS, ed. James A. Robertson (Cleveland, Ohio, 1906).

PINDAR, *The Odes*, trans. C. M. Bowra (Penguin edn., 1969).

PIRE, G., 'Jean-Jacques Rousseau et les relations de voyages', *Revue d'histoire littéraire de la France*, 56 (1956), 355–78.

PLATO, *The Collected Dialogues*, ed. E. Hamilton and H. Cairns (Princeton, 1961).

PLINY, THE ELDER, *Natural History*, trans. H. Rackham *et al.* (10 vols.; Loeb edn., 1938–62).

POHL, F. J., *Amerigo Vespucci: Pilot Major* (London, 1966).

POLO, MARCO, *Marci Pauli de Venecijs de consuetudinibus et condicionibus orientalium regionum* (Antwerp, 1485).

—— *Il Milione*, ed. L. F. Benedetto (Florence, 1928).

—— *The Description of the World*, ed. A. C. Moule and Paul Pelliot (London, 1938).

POLO, MARCO, *The Travels*, trans. Ronald Latham (Penguin edn., 1958).

POPE, ALEXANDER, *The Poems of Alexander Pope*, ed. John Butt (University Paperback edn., 1968).

POPKIN, RICHARD H., *The History of Scepticism from Erasmus to Descartes* (rev., New York, 1968).

PORTER, DAVID, *Journal of a Cruise Made to the Pacific Ocean, in the U.S. Frigate Essex, in the years 1812, 1813, and 1814* (2 vols.; Philadephia, 1815).

——*Journal of a Cruise Made to the Pacific Ocean* (2 vols.; New York, 1822).

POWER, E., 'The Opening of the Land Routes to Cathay', in Newton (ed.), *Travel and Travellers*.

PRÉVOST, A.-F., ed., *Histoire générale des voyages* (20 vols.; Paris, 1746–70).

'Prince *Giolo* Son to the King of *Moangis* or *Gilolo*' (handbill in British Library).

Providence Display'd, Or a very Surprising Account of one Mr Alexander Selkirk . . . Written by his own Hand (London, 1712).

Public Advertiser (Sat., 3 July 1773).

PURCHAS, SAMUEL, *Purchas his Pilgrimage, or Relations of the World and the Religions observed in all Ages and Places Discovered, from the Creation unto this Present* (London, 1613).

——*Purchas His Pilgrimes* (20 vols.; Glasgow, 1905–7).

QUAYLE, ERIC, *Ballantyne the Brave: A Victorian Writer and His Family* (London, 1967).

——*The Collector's Book of Boys' Stories* (London, 1973).

QUINTANA, R., *The Mind and Art of Jonathan Swift* (repr. London, 1953).

QUIRÓS, PEDRO FERNÁNDEZ DE (and Luis de Belmonte Bermúdez), 'History of the Discovery of the Austrial Regions', trans. in *The Voyages of Pedro Fernández de Quirós, 1595 to 1606*, ed. Sir Clements Markham (2 vols.; London, 1904), i.

[RABELAIS, FRANÇOIS], *La Vie inestimable du grand Gargantua pere de Pa[n]tagruel, jadis co[m]posée par l'abstracteur de quinte essence* (Lyon, 1537).

——*Le Quart Livre des faicts & dictz heroïques du bon Pantagruel* (Lyon, 1552).

——*Le Cinquiesme et Dernier Livre des faits & dits heroïques du bon Pantagruel* (Lyon, 1571).

RADIGUET, MAX, *Les Derniers Sauvages, souvenir de l'occupation française aux îles Marquises, 1842–1859* (Brussels, 1861).

——*Les Derniers Sauvages: la vie et les moeurs aux Îles Marquises (1842–1859)* (Paris, 1929).

RALEIGH, Sir WALTER, 'The Discovery of Guiana', in Richard Hakluyt, *The Principal Navigations, Voyages, Traffiques and Discoveries of the English Nation* (12 vols.; Glasgow, 1903–5), x.

RALSTON, CAROLINE, *Grass Huts and Warehouses: Pacific Beach Communities of the Nineteenth Century* (Canberra, 1977).

RAWSON, CLAUDE J., *Gulliver and the Gentle Reader: Studies in Swift and Our Time* (London, 1973).

RAWSON, GEOFFREY, *'Pandora''s Last Voyage* (London, 1963).

REES, JOAN, 'Hogs, Gulls, and Englishmen: Drayton and the Virginian Voyages', *The Year-book of English Studies*, 13 (1983), 20–31.

RENOUARD, DAVID, 'Renouard's Narrative', in H. E. Maude, 'The Voyage of the *Pandora*'s Tender', *Mariner's Mirror*, 50 (August 1964), 217–35.

RICHARDSON, Revd J., 'Drury's "Vocabulary of the Madagascar Language", with Notes', *Atananarivo Annual* for 1875, repr. in Drury, *Madagascar*, ed. Oliver, 316 ff.

[RICKMAN, J.], *Journal of Captain Cook's Last Voyage to the Pacific Ocean, on Discovery; performed in the Years 1776, 1777, 1778, 1779* (London, 1781).

ROBARTS, EDWARD, *The Marquesan Journal of Edward Robarts 1797–1824*, ed. Greg Dening (Canberra, 1974).

ROBERTSON, GEORGE, *The Discovery of Tahiti, A Journal of the Second Voyage of H.M.S. 'Dolphin' round the World*, ed. H. Carrington (London, 1948).

RODERICK, C., 'Sir Joseph Banks, Queen Oberea and the Satirists', in W. Veit, (ed.), *Captain James Cook: Image and Impact, South Sea Discoveries and the World of Letters* (Melbourne, 1972).

ROGERS, PAT, *Robinson Crusoe* (London, 1979).

ROGERS, WOODES, *A Cruising Voyage Round the World: First to the South-Seas, thence to the East-Indies, and homewards by the Cape of Good Hope* (London, 1712).

ROHDE, E., *Der Griechische Roman und Seine Vorläufer* (Leipzig, 1914).

RONSARD, PIERRE DE, *Œuvres complètes*, ed. P. Laumonier (19 vols.; Paris, 1924–74).

ROQUEFEUIL, CAMILLE DE, *Journal d'un voyage autour du monde, pendant les anneés 1816, 1817, 1818 et 1819* (2 vols.; Paris, 1823).

ROSS, E. DENISON, 'Prester John and the Empire of Ethiopia', in Newton (ed.), *Travel and Travellers.*

ROSS, J. F. *Swift and Defoe: A Study in Relationship* (Berkeley, Calif., 1941).

ROUSSEAU, JEAN-JACQUES, *Discours sur l'origine et les fondemens de l'inégalité parmi les hommes* (Amsterdam, 1755).

—— *Les Confessions* (10 vols.; London / Neuchâtel, 1786–90).

—— *Essai sur l'origine des langues*, ed. Charles Porset (Bordeaux, 1968).

ROWLANDSON, MARY, *The Soveraignty & Goodness of God, Together with the Faithfulness of His Promises Displayed; Being a Narrative of the Captivity and Restauration of Mrs. Mary Rowlandson* (2nd edn., corrected and augmented, Cambridge, Mass., 1682).

RUSSELL, MICHAEL, *Polynesia: or, An Historical Account of the Principal Islands in the South Sea, including New Zealand; the Introduction of Christianity; and the actual condition of the inhabitants in regard to civilization, commerce, and the arts of social life* (Edinburgh, 1842).

RUTTER, OWEN, ed., *The Court-Martial of the 'Bounty' Mutineers* (Edinburgh, 1931).

SAHLINS, MARSHALL, *Islands of History* (Chicago, 1985).

SAINT-GERMAIN, LOUIS-ANTOINE STAROT DE, 'Journal de Saint-Germain', extracts from the lost MS, printed as notes accompanying 'Journal de Fesche', in *Bougainville et ses compagnons*, ed. Taillemite, ii.

St. James's Chronicle, 4–6 Aug. 1774.

SAMWELL, DAVID, 'Samwell's Journal' ('Some Account of a Voyage to South Sea's In 1776–1777–1778'), in *Journals of Captain Cook*, ed. Beaglehole, iii. 987–1300.

SANZ, CARLOS, *El gran secreto de la Carta de Colón* (Madrid, 1959).

[SCOTT, JOHN?], *An Epistle from Oberea, Queen of Otaheite, to Joseph Banks, Esq. Translated by T.Q.Z. Esq. Professor of the Otaheite Language in Dublin, and of the Languages of the undiscovered Islands in the South Sea; And enriched with Historical and Explanatory Notes* (London, 1774 [1773?]).

SCOTT, WALTER, 'Memoirs of Jonathan Swift', in *The Works of Jonathan Swift . . . with Notes, and A Life of the Author*, ed. W. Scott (19 vols.; Edinburgh, 1814), i.

SECORD, A. W., *Studies in the Narrative Method of Defoe* (Urbana, Ill., 1924).

—— review of W. A. Eddy, '*Gulliver's Travels': A Critical Study*, in *Journal of English and Germanic Philology*, 23 (1924), 460–2.

—— '*Gulliver* and Dampier', *Modern Language Notes*, 51 (March 1936), 159.

SECORD, A. W., 'Defoe in Stoke Newington', *Publications of the Modern Language Association*, 66 (March 1951), 211–25.

—— '*Robert Drury's Journal*' *and Other Studies* (Urbana, Ill., 1961).

SEELYE, J., 'Typee: The Quixotic Pattern', in Milton R. Stern (ed.), *Critical Essays on Herman Melville's 'Typee'* (Boston, 1982).

SEWARD, ANNA, *Elegy on Captain Cook* (London, 1780).

SEXTUS EMPIRICUS, *Outlines of Pyrrhonism*, trans. R. G. Bury (Loeb edn., 1933).

SHAFTESBURY, 3rd Earl of, *see* Cooper, A. A.

SHAKESPEARE, WILLIAM, *Othello*, ed. M. R. Ridley (Arden edn., rev. 1962).

——*The Tempest*, ed. Frank Kermode (Arden edn., rev. 1962).

SHARP, ANDREW, *The Discovery of the Pacific Islands* (Oxford, 1960).

[SHARP, GRANVILLE], *An English Alphabet, for the Use of Foreigners: wherein the Pronunciation of the Vowels, or Voice-Letters, is explained in Twelve short general Rules, With their several Exceptions, as abridged (For the Instruction of Omai) from a larger Work* (London, 1786).

SHERBO, ARTHUR, 'Swift and Travel Literature', *Modern Language Studies*, 9 (1979), 114–27.

SHILLIBEER, Lieut. J., RM, *A Narrative of the Briton's Voyage to Pitcairn's Island* (Taunton, 1817).

SHIPMAN, J. C., *William Dampier: Seaman-Scientist* (Lawrence, Kan., 1962).

'The Shipwrecked Sailor', in *Egyptian Tales: Translated from the Papyri*: 1st Ser.: *IVth to XIIth Dynasty*, ed. Flinders Petrie (4th edn., London, 1926).

SHORTER, CLEMENT, Foreword, R. L. Stevenson, *Letters to an Editor* [London?, 1914].

SLESSAREV, VSEVOLOD, *Prester John: The Letter and the Legend* (Minneapolis, 1959).

SMITH, BERNARD, 'Coleridge's "Ancient Mariner" and Cook's Second Voyage', *Journal of the Warburg and Courtauld Institutes*, 19 (1956), 117–54.

SMITH, H. M., 'The Introduction of Venereal Disease into Tahiti: a Re-examination', *Journal of Pacific History*, 10 (1975), pt. 1, pp. 38–45.

SMITH, JOHN, *The Generall Historie of Virginia, New England, and the Summer Isles* (London, 1624).

SNOW, PHILIP, and WAINE, STEFANIE, *The People from the Horizon: An Illustrated History of Europeans among the South Sea Islanders* (Oxford, 1979).

[SOUTHEY, ROBERT], review of W. Ellis, *Polynesian Researches*, *Quarterly Review*, 43 (May and Oct. 1830), 1–54.

—— *Life and Correspondence*, ed. C. C. Southey (6 vols.; London, 1849–50).

—— to William Ellis, 7 Aug. 1830, in J. E. Ellis, *Life of William Ellis* (London, 1873), 205 ff.

—— *New Letters of Robert Southey*, ed. Kenneth Curry (2 vols.; New York, 1965).

SPARRMAN, ANDERS, *A Voyage Round the World with Captain James Cook in H.M.S. Resolution*, trans. A. Mackenzie-Grieve and H. Beamish, ed. O. Rutter (London, 1944).

SPATE, O. H. K., '"South Sea" to "Pacific Ocean": A Note on Nomenclature', *Journal of Pacific History*, 12 (1977), 205–11.

—— *The Pacific Since Magellan*, i. *The Spanish Lake* (London, 1979).

—— *The Pacific Since Magellan*, iii. *Paradise Found and Lost* (London, 1988).

SPENSER, EDMUND, *The Faerie Queene*, ed. A. C. Hamilton (London, 1977).

SPRAT, THOMAS, *History of the Royal Society*, ed. J. I. Cope and H. W. Jones (Saint Louis, Mo., 1958).

STAINES, THOMAS, 'Account of the Descendants of Christian and other Mutineers of the Bounty', *Naval Chronicle*, 33 (1815), 217–18.

STANTON, ROBERT, '*Typee* and Milton: Paradise Well Lost', *Modern Language Notes*, 74 (May 1959), 407–11.

STAROBINSKI, JEAN, *Jean-Jacques Rousseau: La transparence et l'obstacle* (Paris, 1971).

[STEELE, RICHARD] ('Isaac Bickerstaff'), *Tatler*, 254 (21–3 Nov. 1710).

—— *The Englishman*, ed. Rae Blanchard (Oxford, 1955).

STEINEN, KARL VON DEN, *Die Marquesaner und ihre Kunst*, i. *Tatauierung* (Berlin, 1925).

—— *Die Marquesaner und ihre Kunst*, iii. *Die Sammlungen* (Berlin, 1928).

STEINER, FRANZ, *Taboo* (Penguin edn., 1967).

STERLING, JOHN, *Essays and Tales*, ed. J. C. Hare (2 vols.; London, 1848).

STEVENSON, FANNY, *The Cruise of the 'Janet Nichol' Among the South Sea Islands: A Diary by Mrs. Robert Louis Stevenson* (New York, 1914).

—— 'More Letters of Mrs. R. L. Stevenson', ed. Sidney Colvin, *Scribner's Magazine*, 75 (1924), 408–20.

—— and STEVENSON, R. L., *Our Samoan Adventure: with a Three-year Diary by Mrs. Stevenson now published for the first time*, ed. Charles Neider (London, 1956).

STEVENSON, MARGARET, *From Saranac to the Marquesas and Beyond, being Letters written by Mrs. M. I. Stevenson during 1887–8, to her sister, Jane Whyte Balfour*, ed. M. C. Balfour (London, 1903).

STEVENSON, ROBERT LOUIS, *Treasure Island* (London, 1883).

—— 'Uma; or The Beach of Falesá (being the narrative of a South-Sea Trader)', *Illustrated London News* (2 July–6 Aug. 1892).

—— 'The Beach of Falesá', *Island Nights' Entertainments* (London, 1893).

—— *Vailima Letters, being Correspondence addressed by Robert Louis Stevenson to Sidney Colvin, November 1890–October 1894* (London, 1895).

—— *In the South Seas: Being an Account of Experiences and Observations in the Marquesas, Paumotus and Gilbert Islands in the course of two Cruises, on the yacht 'Casco' (1888) and the schooner 'Equator' (1889)*, in *The Works of Robert Louis Stevenson*, Edinburgh edn., xx (Edinburgh, 1896).

—— 'Creek Island, or Adventures in the South Seas', in Graham Balfour, *The Life of Robert Louis Stevenson* (2 vols.; London, 1901), i.

—— *The Letters of Robert Louis Stevenson*, ed. Sidney Colvin (4 vols.; London, 1911).

—— 'A Pearl Island: Penrhyn', in *Vailima Papers, The Works of Robert Louis Stevenson*, Skerryvore edn., xiv (London, 1925), 341–52.

—— *Travels in Hawaii*, ed. A. Grove Day (Honolulu, 1973).

—— *The Beach of Falesá*, in Barry Menikoff, *Robert Louis Stevenson and 'The Beach of Falesá': A Study in Victorian Publishing, with the Original Text* (Edinburgh, 1984).

—— 'Cruise of the *Casco*', MS journal, The Huntington Library, San Marino, Calif., HM 2412.

—— Cruise of the *Equator*, MS journal beginning 'Butaritari, July', The Huntington Library, San Marino, Calif., HM 2412.

—— and OSBOURNE, LLOYD, *The Wrecker* (2nd edn., London, 1892).

STEWART, CHARLES, *A Visit to the South Seas, in the U.S. Ship Vincennes, during the years 1829 and 1830* (2 vols.; New York, 1831).

STEWART, GEORGE, 'From Stewarts Journal', MS, Ministry of Defence Library, London, Papers of Edward Edwards. © Crown Copyright/MOD. Reproduced with the permission of the Controller of HMSO.

STEWART, G. R., ed., *American Place Names, A Concise and Selective Dictionary* (New York, 1970).

STILLINGFLEET, EDWARD, *The Bishop of Worcester's Answer to Mr. Locke's Letter, Concerning Some Passages Relating to his Essay of Humane Understanding* (London, 1697).

—— *Origines Sacrae: or a Rational Account of the Grounds of Natural and Reveal'd Religion: Wherein the Foundations of Religion, and the Authority of the Scriptures are asserted and clear'd; with an Answer to the Modern Objections of Atheists and Deists* (Cambridge, 1701).

STUBBE, HENRY, *The Lord Bacon's Relation of the Sweating-sickness Examined, in a Reply to George Thomson, Pretender to Physick and Chymistry. Together with a Defence of Phlebotomy* (London, 1671).

STURMY, Captain SAMUELL, *The Mariners Magazine or Sturmys Mathematicall and Practical Arts* (London, 1669).

STRABO, *The Geography*, trans. H. L. Jones (Loeb edn., 8 vols.; 1917-32).

SUGGS, ROBERT C., *The Island Civilizations of Polynesia* (New York, 1960).

—— *The Hidden Worlds of Polynesia* (London, 1963).

—— *Marquesan Sexual Behaviour* (London, 1966).

Supplément au voyage de M. de Bougainville: ou journal d'un voyage autour du monde, fait par MM. Banks & Solander, . . . traduit de l'Anglois, par M. de Fréville (Paris, 1772).

SWEARINGEN, R. G., *The Prose Writings of Robert Louis Stevenson: A Guide* (London, 1980).

[SWIFT, JONATHAN], *A Tale of a Tub* (London, 1704).

—— *Travels into Several Remote Nations of the World. By Lemuel Gulliver* (2 vols.; London, 1726).

—— 'A Letter from Capt. Gulliver, to his Cousin Sympson', in *Travels into Several Remote Nations of the World*, in *The Works of J. S[wift]* (4 vols.; Dublin, 1735), iii.

—— 'A Project, For the universal benefit of Mankind', *Miscellaneous Works, Comical & Diverting: by T.R.D.J.S.D.O.P.I.I.* (London, 1720), 264–6.

—— *Journal to Stella*, ed. Harold Williams (2 vols.; Oxford, 1948).

—— *The Correspondence of Jonathan Swift*, ed. Harold Williams (5 vols.; Oxford, 1963–5).

SYMSON, WILLIAM, *A New Voyage to the East Indies* (London, 1715).

TAATAMATA, to Rupert Brooke, 2 May 1914, MS, Brooke Papers, King's College Library, Cambridge.

TABOULET, GEORGES, and DEMARIAUX, JEAN-CLAUDE, *La Vie dramatique de Gustave Viaud, frère de Pierre Loti* (Paris, 1961).

TAGART, EDWARD, *A Memoir of the late Captain Peter Heywood, R.N. with extracts from his Diaries and Correspondence* (London, 1832).

TAYLOR, A. C., 'Charles de Brosses, the Man behind Cook', in B. Greenhill (ed.), *The Opening of the Pacific—Image and Reality* (London, 1971).

TAYLOR, EDWARD, *The Poems of Edward Taylor*, ed. D. E. Stanford (New Haven, Conn., 1960).

TAILLEMITE, ÉTIENNE, 'Le séjour de Bougainville à Tahiti: Essai d'étude critique des témoignages', *Journal de la Société des Océanistes*, 24/24 (Dec. 1968), 3–10.

—— ed., *Bougainville et ses compagnons autour du monde 1766–1769: Journaux de navigation* (2 vols.; Paris, 1977).

TENNYSON, ALFRED, *Poems* (2 vols.; London, 1842).

TERRELL, JENNIFER, 'Joseph Kabris and his notes on the Marquesas', *Journal of Pacific History*, 17 (Jan. 1982), 102–12.

TERTULLIAN, *The Five Books of Quintus Sept. Flor. Tertullianus Against Marcion*, trans. Peter

Holmes, *Ante-Nicene Christian Library*, ed. A. Roberts and J. Donaldson, vii (Edinburgh, 1868).

THEOCRITUS, *Idylls*, trans. A. S. F. Gow (Cambridge, 1950).

THÉVENOT, M., ed., *Relations de divers voyages curieux* (Paris, 1663).

THOMAS, NICHOLAS, *Marquesan Societies: Inequality and Political Transformation in Eastern Polynesia* (Oxford, 1990).

THOMAS, RUSSELL, 'Yarn for Melville's *Typee*', *Philological Quarterly*, 15/1 (Jan. 1936), 16–29.

THOMSON, BASIL, ed., *Voyage of H.M.S. 'Pandora'* (London, 1915).

THOMSON, J. O., *History of Ancient Geography* (Cambridge, 1948).

THOMSON, ROBERT, 'Marquesas. Their Discovery, and Early History', MS, Council for World Mission archives, School of Oriental and African Studies, London, South Sea Journals, Box 9.

THOREAU, HENRY DAVID, *Walden*, ed. J. L. Shanley (Princeton, 1971).

THUCYDIDES, *History of the Peloponnesian War*, trans. C. F. Smith (Loeb edn., 4 vols., rev. 1928–35).

TINKER, R., 'Correspondence and Reports on the condition of the unevangelized', *Hawaiian Spectator*, 1/1 (Honolulu, Jan., 1838).

TODOROV, TZVETAN, *La Conquête de l'Amérique: la question de l'autre* (Paris, 1982).

TORQUEMADA, JUAN DE, 'Monarquia Indiana', trans. in *The Voyages of Pedro Fernández de Quirós, 1595 to 1606*, ed. C. Markham (2 vols.; London, 1904), ii.

TRYON, D. T., *Conversational Tahitian: An Introduction to the Tahitian Language of French Polynesia* (Berkeley, Calif., 1970).

TURNER, LOUIS, and ASH, JOHN, *The Golden Hordes: International Tourism and the Pleasure Periphery* (London, 1975).

[TYSSOT DE PATOT, SIMON], *Voyages et avantures de Jaques Massé* (Bordeaux, 1710).

[VAIRASSE D'ALAIS, DENIS], *Histoire des Sevarambes, peuples qui habitent une partie du troisième continent, communément appellé La Terre Australe. Contenant une relation du gouvernement, des moeurs, de la religion, & du langage de cette nation, inconnuë jusques à present aux peuples de l'Europe* (Amsterdam, [1680?]).

[——] 'A Voyage to Sevarambia, &c,', *Travels into Several Remote Nations of the World. By Capt. Lemuel Gulliver*, iii (London, 1727), pt. II.

VAN EEGHEN, I. H., 'The Voyages and Adventures of François Leguat', *Proceedings of the Huguenot Society of London*, 18/5 (1951).

VEDEL, EMILE, 'A propos de Pierre Loti à Tahiti', *Bulletin de la Société d'Etudes Océaniennes*, 5/50 (Mar. 1934), 288.

VESPUCCI, AMERIGO, *Mundus Novus* ('Letter to Lorenzo Pietro di Medici'), trans. G. T. Northrup (Princeton, 1916).

—— 'Letter from Seville, 1500', trans. F. J. Pohl, in *The European Reconnaissance*, ed. J. H. Parry, 174–85.

—— 'Letter from Lisbon, 1502', trans. F. J. Pohl, in *The European Reconnaissance*, ed. J. H. Parry, 185–90.

VIAUD, JULIEN, *see* Loti, Pierre.

VICKERS, BRIAN, ed., *Seventeenth-Century Prose* (London, 1969).

VILLEY, PIERRE, *Les Livres d'histoire moderne utilisés par Montaigne* (Paris, 1908).

—— *Les Essais de Montaigne* (Mayenne, 1972).

VIRGIL, *The Aeneid*, trans. H. R. Fairclough (2 vols.; Loeb edn., 1934–5).

VIVEZ, FRANÇOIS, 'Journal de Vivez' (Manuscrit de Versailles) in *Bougainville et ses compagnons* ed. Taillemite, ii.

—— 'Journal de Vivez' (Manuscrit de Rochefort), in *Bougainville et ses compagnons* ed. Taillemite, ii.

VOLTAIRE (FRANÇOIS-MARIE AROUET), *Dictionnaire philosophique* (London, 1764).

—— in G. R. Havens, *Voltaire's Marginalia on the Pages of Rousseau: A Comparative Study of Ideas* (Columbus, Ohio, 1933).

—— *Le Mondain*, in *Mélanges*, ed. Jacques van den Heuvel (Pléiade edn., 1961).

—— *Correspondence*, ed. Theodore Besterman (51 vols., Geneva, Banbury and Oxford, 1968–77).

—— *Candide ou l'optimisme*, in *Romans et contes*, ed. F. Deloffre and J. van den Heuvel (Pléiade edn., 1979).

—— *Les Oreilles du conte de Chesterfield et le chapelain Goudman*, in *Romans et contes*, ed. F. Deloffre and J. van den Heuvel (Pléiade edn., 1979).

A Voyage Round the World, in His Majesty's Ship the Dolphin . . . By an Officer on Board (London, 1767).

Voyages and Travels of Fletcher Christian, and a Narrative of the Mutiny, on board His Majesty's Ship Bounty, at Otaheite ([London], 1789).

WAFER, LIONEL, *A New Voyage and Description of the Isthmus of America* (London, 1699).

WAINWRIGHT, ALEXANDER D., *Robert Louis Stevenson: A Catalogue of the Henry E. Gerstley Stevenson Collection of Victorian Novelists, and Items from Other Collections of the Princeton University Library* (Princeton, NJ, 1971).

[WALDSEEMÜLLER, MARTIN], *Cosmographiae Introductio* (Saint Dié, Lorraine, 1507).

WALES, WILLIAM, *Remarks on Mr. Forster's Account of Captain Cook's last Voyage round the World, In the Years 1772, 1773, 1774, and 1775* (London, 1778).

—— 'Journal', in *Journals of Captain Cook*, ed. Beaglehole, ii. 776–869.

[WALPOLE, HORACE], *An Account of the Giants Lately Discovered* (London, 1766).

—— *Correspondence*, ed. W. S. Lewis (48 vols.; London, 1937–83).

WALLIS, HELEN, 'John Hawkesworth and the English Circumnavigators', *Commonwealth Journal*, 6 (1963), 167–71.

WALLIS, SAMUEL, 'His Majestys Ship Dolphin's Log Book', MS, Public Record Office, London, Adm. 55/35.

WARNER, OLIVER, ed., *An Account of the Discovery of Tahiti From the Journal of George Robertson* (London, 1955).

WATT, IAN, '*Robinson Crusoe* as a Myth', *Essays in Criticism*, 1 (1951), 95–119.

WATT, Sir JAMES, 'Medical Aspects and Consequences of Cook's Voyages', in R. Fisher and H. Johnston (eds.), *Captain James Cook and His Times* (Vancouver, 1979), 129–57.

WAUGH, ALEC, *The Coloured Countries* (London, 1930).

WECKMANN, LUIS, 'The Middle Ages in the Conquest of America', *Speculum*, 26 (1951), 130–41.

Weekly Journal; or, British Gazetteer (Sat., 1 Nov. 1718).

WEINREB, BEN, and HIBBERT, CHRISTOPHER, eds., *The London Encyclopaedia* (London, 1983).

WESLEY, JOHN, *The Journal of the Rev. John Wesley*, ed. Nehemiah Curnock (8 vols.; London, 1909–16).

WILKES, CHARLES, *Narrative of the United States Exploring Expedition, during the years 1838, 1839, 1840, 1841, 1842* (5 vols.; Philadelphia, 1844).

WILKINSON, C. S., *The Wake of the Bounty* (London, 1953).

WILLIAMS, DAVID, 'Peeping Tommo: *Typee* as Satire', *Canadian Review of American Studies*, 6/1 (Spring 1975), 36–49.

WILLIAMS, GLYNDWR, *The Expansion of Europe in the Eighteenth Century* (London, 1965).

WILLIAMSON, J. A., Introduction to William Dampier, *A Voyage to New Holland*, ed. J. A. Williamson (London, 1939).

—— *Cook and the Opening of the Pacific* (London, 1946).

[WILSON, WILLIAM, *et al.*], *A Missionary Voyage to the Southern Pacific Ocean, performed in the years 1796, 1797, 1798, in the Ship Duff, commanded by Captain James Wilson* (London, 1799).

WISE, Lieut. HENRY A., *Los Gringos: or an Inside View of Mexico and California, with Wanderings in Peru, Chili, and Polynesia* (London, 1849).

WITTKOWER, RUDOLF, 'Marvels of the East: A Study in the History of Monsters', in Rudolf Wittkower, *Allegory and the Migration of Symbols* (London, 1977).

WOOD, ANTHONY à, *Athenae Oxonienses, an Exact History of all the Writers and Bishops who have had their Education at the University of Oxford*, ed. Philip Bliss (4 vols.; London, 1813–1820).

WORDSWORTH, CHRISTOPHER, *Memoirs of William Wordsworth* (2 vols.; London, 1851).

WORDSWORTH, WILLIAM, to the *Weekly Entertainer*, 23 Oct. 1796, in the *Weekly Entertainer; or Agreeable and Instructive Repository*, 28 (7 Nov. 1796), 377.

Index